To Laura Kline, Pat Hollinger, and Bryan Walker

Preface

Philosophy: Contemporary Perspectives on Perennial Issues, fourth edition, is a collection of informative, interesting, and accessible readings that are designed to provide a solid introduction to traditional philosophical problems. Collectively, we have taught philosophy for over seven decades. As do many instructors, we have spent much time trying to find the best way to introduce our students to the subject. Consequently, in recent years, we have settled on a discussion approach to the course. With interesting topics and provocative readings, discussion and debate flourish, and class periods become more exciting. This book represents what we and many instructors who have used previous editions of the book have found to be most successful for enlivening classes in philosophy.

Features and Purpose of the Fourth Edition

The fourth edition of *Philosophy: Contemporary Perspectives on Perennial Issues* features several important revisions. One obvious change is in our subtitle: We hope to more strongly identify what the book is about and highlight the purpose we had in mind when selecting our readings. Our use of mainly twentieth-century writers allows us to present philosophy in a context that has some familiarity for students; it allows us to demonstrate that philosophical thinking is relevant to students in their own lives and time.

By providing contemporary writings on the traditional—or basic—issues of philosophy, we hope to provide students with vivid illustrations of the enduring nature and value of philosophy. We think we have done this in a way that answers our desire to provide an accessible, yet serious introduction to philosophy. Paradoxically, one critique made about the use of twentieth-century writings is that such material is often inaccessible to today's students because it can be more eclectic and jargon-laden than traditional or classic works, which were directed toward a literate, but nonprofessional, nonacademic audience. We have been mindful of this problem. By avoiding the most academic of twentieth-century writings, and by "class testing" the book through three editions, we believe that we have been faithful to the ambition for the book. We have developed a book that, while traditional in its scope of philosophical issues, is contemporary in its perspective—and we leave open to instructors the option to supplement our book with primary sources from classic philosophers.

An additional change with this new edition is through the introduction of headnotes at the beginning of the readings. The purpose of these is to provide students with some background information about the orientation that each writer brings to the essay. They are meant to provide context, but they are not meant to summarize the essays or limit the ability of students to develop their own interpretations of the essays.

We have made a number of changes in our choice of readings: Three new essays were commissioned specifically for this volume: In Part Six, K. D. Ellis discusses agnosticism and Joseph Kupfer presents a unique approach to the problem of religious belief; in Part Nine, E. Daniel Kaye provides a twentieth-century defense of utilitarianism. All three of these original essays received an enthusiastic response in trial runs with our students. Elsewhere in the book, we feature new readings that are drawn from previously published works: The new selection by Carl G. Hempel in Part One extends our discussion about the possibility and extent of genuine knowledge. It also provides a convenient bridge to Part Two on "Science, Common Sense, and the World." We have also included two new essays by women: Carol Gilligan discusses feminist ethics in Part Nine, and, in Part Eleven, Alison Jaggar presents the political philosophies that underlie the women's movement. Additionally, the essays by Habermas and Foucault which were in the third edition were replaced in Part Twelve by ones which are more accessible to beginning students. Finally, by popular demand, the appealing essay by R. M. MacIver has been restored to Part Nine.

These changes in selections have been made so we can adhere more closely to our stated aims of providing a book that is both provocative and comprehensible to beginning students. We dropped a few selections because the authors merely stated or explained a position without defending it. These were replaced by readings in which authors both advocate and defend their positions.

Without omitting essential material, we carefully edited and abridged selections which, although valuable, were too long. Many editorial footnotes have been added that, among other things, define a technical term, translate a foreign expression, explain a reference to a person or event, and clarify a fine point. We believe that these notes will be helpful to the beginning student.

We think the new headnotes are an important pedagogical feature. This revision of our text also retains a number of other useful features from previous editions: The general introduction discusses why philosophy is worthy of study, what it is all about, and how one should go about studying it. Each of the book's twelve parts begins with a preview that orients the student to the main problems to be discussed and clearly lays out the various solutions to them that philosophers have reached. Many of these have been revised for this volume. At the end of each part are study questions and an annotated list of readings.

The format of the book is suitable for a variety of teaching approaches and syllabi. The instructor may omit some parts entirely, skip over some of the selections within each part, or, as mentioned, supplement the contemporary readings with material of a more classic nature. It is also possible to rearrange readings from two or more parts to constitute a unit of study according to the instructor's choosing.

Acknowledgments

We would like to express our deep gratitude to all those people who helped us prepare this book. In addition we thank those who aided us with the first edition, including Paul Taylor, Ted Solomon, Richard Van Iten, Laura Kline, Rowena Wright, Annette Van Cleave, Robert Irelan, and Steven G. Isaacson. For the second edition, we thank John Elrod, Gary Comstock, Joseph Kupfer, William S. Robinson, Edna Wiser, Bernice Power, Barbara Larson, Ray Amsler, and, above all, David Hauser and Bryan Walker. For the third edition, Edna Wiser, Bernice Power, Ray Amsler, David Hauser, Kelly Frazier, Steve Worringham, John Walker, John Varley, and Steven Mumford. For this new edition, we are grateful to Edna Wiser, J. B. Silvers, Andrea Silvers, Margaret Langloss, William S. Robinson, and the many instructors who wrote us about the third edition. We are also indebted to Don Reisman and the entire staff of the College Division of St. Martin's Press for their encouragement and assistance. We are especially grateful to Frances Jones for her constant, kind help.

We would like to thank the following faculty who provided instructions to St. Martin's Press to aid us in our revision of *Philosophy: Contemporary Perspectives on Perennial Issues:* Keith R. David, William Jewell College; Sidney Gendin, Eastern Michigan University; Sallie B. King, James Madison University; Hugh S. Moorhead, Northeastern Illinois University; Elane O'Rourke, Moorpark College; Edward M. Sayles, The University of Michigan–Dearborn; Laura Shanner, Georgetown University; and Mary F. Stevenson, University of Colorado at Denver.

E. D. K.

A. D. K.

R. H.

Contents

Introduction: Philosophy and the Study of Philosophy

I. WHY STUDY PHILOSOPHY?

As you are reading these pages, the chances are that you have enrolled in a philosophy course or are thinking of taking one. Or perhaps you are just browsing out of curiosity. In either case you may be wondering, "What on earth is philosophy, anyway?" Unfortunately, this question is not an easy one to answer. Attempts to provide one-sentence answers are generally unilluminating and misleading. Our approach to answering the question will be as follows: We will talk about some of the chief aims or tasks of philosophy. In so doing, we hope not only to answer the question, Why study philosophy? but also the question, What is philosophy? The answer will be that philosophy is the enterprise which seeks to fulfill those aims or tasks.

A

Let us begin, then, by talking about some of the chief aims of philosophy. Among them let us consider five which are relevant to ordinary people as well as professional philosophers. These are (1) the critical scrutiny of our beliefs and convictions; (2) the bringing to light of our hidden assumptions or presuppositions; (3) the quest for a genuinely worthwhile life; (4) the effort to keep alive our sense of wonder about the world; and (5) the posing of certain questions which are not dealt with by other disciplines, and the attempt to answer them. We maintain that pursuing these aims constitutes a good reason both for philosophizing and for pursuing or studying philosophy. (These two activities are interconnected, for as you will see, you cannot adequately study philosophy without doing some philosophizing.)

1. Let us first consider some popular and widely held beliefs:

- Nice guys finish last. (So never give a sucker an even break. Or, don't be a fool.)
- If you can't see it, touch it, kick it, or walk around it, it isn't there. (Or at any rate it isn't worth bothering about.)
- Education is good for only one thing: getting a good job. If it doesn't do that (and maybe even if it does), it is a waste of time and money.
- The only or best measure of happiness is your socioeconomic status and your annual financial statement.

1

- Nonconformity is abnormal or immoral.
- Everything that happens is willed by God and thus is ultimately for the best.

There is no doubt that these are pervasive beliefs. Perhaps most or all of them are held by the proverbial man (or woman) on the street. Similarly, there are many other beliefs which could be added to the list. Generally, these are held in a rather naive and unquestioning manner. Indeed, many of their advocates are quite dogmatic in their adherence to such beliefs.

But the ordinary person isn't the only one who is dogmatic. There are people with some degree of sophistication and learning who hold just as tenaciously to certain other beliefs. Let us consider some of these:

- Human beings are nothing but complex physical and chemical systems, so their behavior is, in theory, explainable by the same laws that explain the behavior of billiard balls.
- Science and technology hold the keys to reality and to all human problems.
- All of our beliefs, values, and behaviors are products of our genes, our toilet training, our conditioning, our sexual fantasies, or all of the above.
- Capitalism is the best economic system ever invented and the one which is most in accord with human nature.
- Pure science is morally neutral; and since technology can be used for both good and ill, it is neither good nor bad in itself.
- Scientists are just after the truth; they cannot and should not take moral stands on issues except when they are wearing their "ordinary citizen" hats.

You may be wondering, "What does all this have to do with philosophy?" The answer is, "A great deal." For in reflecting on such claims as these, on what they mean, on whether they are true or false (or nonsensical), on what their implications are, on what life would be like if they were true (or if we believed them), we are already beginning to philosophize. Indeed, to a large extent this is what the activity of philosophizing consists of—the articulation, examination, and critical appraisal of our most cherished beliefs and convictions. Of course, there are some people who find such an enterprise threatening. This is one reason why philosophers have not always been popular. They engage in what the nineteenth-century German philosopher Nietzsche called untimely meditations. By this he meant reflections and thoughts which go against the cultural values and ideals of one's own time. To be sure, this may be unsettling. Nevertheless, such meditations can be healthy for both oneself and one's culture even if, in the end, one accepts one's culture's values and beliefs (as most of us do, at least to some extent). For as John Stuart Mill (a nineteenth-century British philosopher) said, believing what happens to be true, if you are dogmatic and closed minded about it, is worse than believing what happens to be false, as long as you are open minded and willing to discuss your beliefs and change them in the light of evidence, discussion, and criticism. Here, then, is one good reason for philosophizing.

2. We turn now to another. Philosophers have not only been concerned with the task of examining our naive beliefs and convictions. They have also tried to bring to light and make us aware of our assumptions or presuppositions. What does this mean? An assumption or presupposition is a belief which is taken for granted and, hence, of which we may not be conscious. Now, some of our assumptions are ordinary, commonsense beliefs—and, hence, beliefs which we hold consciously. For example:

- The sun will rise tomorrow.
- (In winter), spring will follow.
- If I drink a fifth of gin in a half-hour, I will get drunk. Etc.

But there are other assumptions which often lie behind these ordinary beliefs, assumptions to which we often appeal in order to justify these ordinary beliefs. These are the ones we refer to when we say that philosophers have tried to make us aware of our assumptions or presuppositions. For example, suppose you were to ask a friend to justify his or her belief that the sun will rise tomorrow. Your friend would probably do so by answering, "Because it's always been that way." Here we have reached a *basic* assumption, namely, that what has held in the past will continue to hold in the future. It is important to recognize that this is merely an assumption, not a proved fact. If you think otherwise, ask yourself, "How would I prove it?" By saying, "Well, it has always held in the past?" That would be merely repeating the assumption.

Consider some other assumptions which underlie various beliefs. There are some people who believe that criminals should be punished or even condemned. What is the assumption which underlies this belief? It is that human beings are free agents, that they are always capable of freely choosing to do or not do something, and hence that they are responsible for their actions. Or consider another case. There are some people who believe that the universe must have been created. What is the assumption which underlies this belief? It is that nothing can exist without a cause (and, hence, that the universe must have had a cause).

Part of what philosophers try to do, then, is to make us aware of our basic assumptions or presuppositions. Why is this important? Because as long as we are unaware of our assumptions we are not intellectually free. For if we are unaware of them, we are enslaved to them and to all of the consequences they entail. We are not free in our thinking because all that we think is confined to the limits which are set by our unrecognized assumptions. We must, then, first, become aware of them, and second, examine them critically. This is not to say that we must necessarily dismiss them. We undoubtedly will continue to hold many of them. But the manner in which they are held will be different. Here, then, is another good reason for philosophizing.

3. Let us turn to another. Consider the following claim: It is better to suffer an injustice than to do an injustice to another person, since acting unjustly corrupts one and makes one worse, whereas suffering an injustice does not. The man who said this was Socrates, a philosopher of ancient Greece, whose own "untimely meditations" were thought to be aimed at turning the world upside down and therefore cost him his life. For Socrates, the only worthwhile life for a human being is what he called the examined life. The unexamined life is not worth living, he said. This does not mean that if you are not a philosopher you should hang yourself. It means that a human being needs more than bed and bread in order not merely to survive but to live *well*. In short, what Socrates meant is this: A human being who has and acts on ideas, beliefs, and values, and has only a relatively short life span, would do well to think seriously about what to *be*; about what to do with his or her life; about what things are most important.

All this is especially true today, when so many of us are searching for values and purposes to guide our lives in the face of general dissatisfaction with events around us. It is also true in an age pervaded by a never-ending series of crises and dilemmas: abortion, starvation, economic setbacks, political strife, nuclear accidents, and so on. Having a well-developed sense of values and purpose is more important today than ever. This is especially true if we recall that we live in a society where manipulation of information and public opinion, and emphasis on the faddish and the superficial, are the rule rather than the exception. Being dissatisfied with the status quo is not enough. We must, each and every one of us, set our own priorities in order that our society, as well as our own lives, be straightened out.

The obvious place to begin such philosophizing is with the question, What do I want to be/do with my life? Too many of us get caught up in the "rat race" too early in life. We live in a society governed by certain assumptions and standards about human happiness and the good life which all too often are taken up unreflectively. We are taught that "success" and "happiness" can be measured in monetary terms, or in terms of socioeconomic status, or in terms of how many college degrees one has, and so on. Materialistic values come to be the measure of everything. We view our own well-being in comparison with that of others and take our bearings by reference to social standards that we often don't even think twice about.

Perhaps this is the wrong way to proceed. Perhaps we ought, each of us, to look inward, to find out what we want, what we value most, what kind of person we want to be, and what sort of life we aspire to. At the social level, too, it may be that our values and priorities need reordering. Do we really value electric gadgets so much that we are willing to risk nuclear disaster or increased risk of cancer to have more nuclear power plants? What, as a society, are our real values?

It may well be that underlying all of these individual and social values is the belief that happiness consists of the unlimited search for more and more material wealth. If so, it may also be true that such a view of happiness is an illusion: The more we have, the more we want and the less satisfied we are.

This is why Socrates believed that the best life comes from the realization that self-control, and not insatiable desires, is the source of happiness. Whether he was right or wrong, he was raising issues that are worth thinking about; for the answers we give them will bear on the way we live. Here, then, is another good reason for philosophizing.

4. But there is still another. Most of us, as human beings, are naturally curious. There are certain things which we encounter and various experiences which we have that make us wonder. Something may strike us as odd or strange or mysterious or difficult to comprehend, for example, the vastness of space. This sense of wonder and the desire to learn, to know, to contemplate the mysteries of life and the universe have given rise to philosophy, science, religion, art, and culture. Surely such activity makes us what we are—*human* beings, not mere animals. It does not matter if our wonder cannot always be satisfied. Indeed, it may be the case that our recognition of how little we know and how much there is to learn is precisely what makes life so interesting.

In our age of science and technology, with its continuous knowledge explosion (which makes the bits of information we learn by rote as outdated as last week's newspapers), it is important to keep this sense of wonder alive. We must appreciate how important it is to nurture our curiosity, not just to appreciate the significance of new breakthroughs in science but to help us recapture our sense of wonder about everyday life and experience. All too often we tend to leave it to experts to tell us what it all means. And all too often the experts are interested only in the practical dimensions of new discoveries in science, technology, medicine, and so on. But this is not enough. We want to keep in touch with these developments and connect them with our own search for meaning and understanding. We have to learn how to learn: how to adapt our beliefs and values in the presence of continuing changes in our understanding of things. It is only by doing this that we can avoid feeling alienated from developments in science and technology. And it is only by valuing the human need to ask basic questions about the cosmos and our place in it that we can preserve our sense of balance and our human qualities of curiosity and interest in the world around us.

Once again, it will be helpful to be a bit more specific. We live in an age governed by science and technology. The knowledge we receive from the sciences is often taken to be the highest or the only form of knowledge, capable in principle of answering all our questions and solving all our problems. Political decisions, our educational system, our personal outlooks, and our self-understanding all are governed by what has been called scientism, or the view that science is the measure of everything. Politically, this amounts to the idea that "experts" must make all decisions because only they have the knowledge to do so. Should we build a neutron bomb or more nuclear power plants? Should we engage in recombinant-DNA research and develop techniques for applying genetics to change society? What becomes of democracy in a technological age? And what about education? Is the only knowledge

worth having connected with the sciences? Is all learning just the memoriza-
tion of isolated and all too often useless bits of information? Does this view of
learning even help us understand science and the curiosity of scientists about
nature? In short, while human curiosity has given us science, do we now live
in a society in which the dominance of science actually stifles human curiosity
and creativity, and in which education is more like training than it is an
adventure in ideas?

Obviously, these are complex and difficult issues; and they only scratch
the surface in terms of the impact of science and technology on our society,
our educational system, our individual lives and outlooks, and the issues of
what knowledge and learning are and how best to nurture and satisfy our
natural curiosity. One can only hope that this curiosity will continue to flourish, even if this requires us to rethink our basic assumptions about knowledge, science, and learning. So here we have another good reason for philosophizing.

5. Philosophy has had yet another aim or task, namely, attempting to
provide answers to certain questions—questions which are very different
from most other kinds of questions. First, they differ from everyday questions, which can be answered by *simple* observation, such as "Is there beer in
the refrigerator?" Second, they differ from scientific questions, which can be
answered by experimental procedures, such as "What is the specific gravity of
lead?" Third, they differ from still other questions, which can be answered by
formal or linguistic determinations, such as "What is the square root of 9?"

What are some of the main features of philosophical questions? Isaiah
Berlin has called attention to some of them:[1] (1) They are often very general.
(2) They may have little practical utility (or if they do it is not always clear just
what it is). (3) They are such that there are no obvious and standard procedures or techniques for answering them.

It is perhaps the case that many philosophical questions possess all three
of these characteristics. For example, consider this question: Are there any
propositions which can be known to be true by thinking alone and which do
not require any appeal to experience in order to justify them? This question
possesses all three of the features just noted. However, there are other questions which are generally held to be philosophical but do not have all three
features, for example, Are there any circumstances in which abortion can be
justified? Certainly this question may at least have enormous practical consequences. Similarly, there are many moral questions which are quite specific
rather than general. Hence, there are at least some philosophical questions
which do not possess the first and/or second of the features mentioned by
Berlin.

However, the third feature does seem to be characteristic of almost all or
at least many philosophical questions. They are such that there is no obvious
or standard way to answer them. Indeed, this is why many people find that

[1]Isaiah Berlin, "Introduction" in *The Age of Enlightenment* (New York: Mentor Books, 1956).

there is, at first, something very peculiar about philosophical questions. And this is why some find that the study of philosophy is a very perplexing enterprise.

Let us turn to some examples which illustrate this point. Consider this question: Are walleyed pike found in Illinois? We know right off how to answer this question, namely, by observation, either our own or that of a naturalist. But now consider this question: Are there any entities in the universe which do not exist in either space or time? First, someone who has not had some exposure to philosophy may not understand just what is meant by this question. But second, even if the question is clarified, it remains the case that there seems to be no ordinary or standard procedure by which to attempt to answer it.

Similarly, consider this question: Did the campaigns of Alexander the Great occur in the fourth century B.C.? We cannot, of course, observe Alexander's military ventures ourselves. But we at least know how to look for the relevant evidence, pro or con, by which to provide an answer to the question. But now consider this question: Did the universe have a beginning in time? In this case not only do we not have the relevant evidence, whether from our own observation or from that of someone else, but it is not entirely clear how we would go about looking for what would constitute relevant evidence.

Let us take another example. If you were asked, "Are you quite certain that George Bush knows you?" you could answer the question easily. But suppose someone asked, "Can you be certain about what goes on in anyone else's mind?" Here the answer cannot be given so readily.

In the preceding examples we have contrasted some simple empirical or factual questions with philosophical ones. As we have seen, there are some standard procedures for finding answers to the former.

Let us now turn to some examples of a different sort. Consider this question: How many positive roots are there of the equation $x^2 = 4$? Anyone with a knowledge of elementary mathematics can answer this question. But now consider this question: Do numbers (not numerals) exist? This question is much more difficult to answer. Indeed, it is not clear just how one would attempt to answer it.

Similarly, consider these questions: What is the exact meaning of the word *oculist*? This can easily be answered. But contrast it with, What is the exact meaning of the word *person* (or *living*)? A precise and simple answer is not always available.

In these examples we again find that there is a generally agreed-upon procedure for answering the first question of each pair. To be sure, in these cases the procedure is a formal (or definitional or verbal) one rather than an empirical one. Nevertheless, it is a simple procedure. But this is not so for the second question of each pair.

To summarize: We have considered several pairs of questions. For the first member of each pair there is some well-attested, generally accepted, straightforward method of discovering the answer. The method differs, depending on whether the question involves primarily empirical or primarily formal procedures. But this is not so for the second member of each pair. Here we seem to run into an obstacle. Furthermore, the first question of each pair can be settled "once and for all," or at least with a high degree of probability. The second member of each pair cannot, or at least it is not immediately apparent how it could be.

Questions of the second sort are those with which philosophy is concerned. They include questions like these: Do minds exist as well as bodies? Are humans free agents? What is humanity's highest goal? What is the purpose of life? Does God exist? These questions are neither empirical nor formal. They cannot be answered solely by observing or running simple empirical tests. Nor can they be answered solely by formal procedures such as calculating—or by merely knowing the meanings of words.

In both Western and Eastern civilizations since a time many centuries B.C., it has been—and still is—the task of philosophy to deal with such questions. And they are still with us, for the reason given earlier. They have no simple answers. There are no purely empirical or formal means by which to answer them—or even attempt to answer them.

How, then, does one try to answer them? Through critical analysis and argument. One must first make the necessary distinctions in order to be sure we know precisely what we are asking. And then one must consider the arguments, pro and con, which have been given (or which we ourselves provide), weigh them, and critically evaluate them. There is no other way by which philosophical questions can be settled.

It should be apparent that the most important questions which we all face are philosophical questions. This is why the study of philosophy is of great value for everyone. And this is why as a member of the human race you have an obligation to wrestle with such questions.

The pursuit of these questions won't be easy. Nothing of value is. But we hope that you will be one of many who have found that pursuit to be exciting, provocative, and of enduring value.

We have shown that philosophical questions fall into a unique category in that: (1) They cannot be answered solely on the basis of simple, straightforward empirical procedures (such as opening the door and looking to see if there is beer in the refrigerator). (2) They cannot be answered solely on the basis of some formal procedure or by getting clear on the meaning of words (such as finding the sum of two numbers). It should be noted that it is not only philosophical questions that possess these two features. Many of the questions that are dealt with by the more advanced or theoretical sciences also have these features.

Consider for example questions which occur within the theory of evolution. One of them is the question of whether, over all of time, organisms *always* gradually change due to natural selection. Of course factual evidence gathered by paleontologists has some bearing on the answer. But it isn't clear what the evidence establishes. And in fact biologists differ in the answers they give to the question. Or consider questions in physics in the area of quantum mechanics. According to one interpretation what we call the world is subjective. It is not out there independently of us. It is tied intimately to observers in a subjective fashion. Its state of existence depends on how we perceive it. According to another interpretation, the world is objective. It is out there independently of us. It goes on even if we do not perceive it. Which answer is correct? Physicists disagree.

We have given two examples (and there are many more) of questions found in the sciences which are such that: (1) they cannot be answered solely by any simple empirical test; and (2) they cannot be answered solely by some formal or linguistic procedure. To that extent they are similar to philosophical questions. What difference, if any, is there, then, between philosophical and scientific questions? To the extent that scientific questions meet (1) and (2), they are indistinguishable from philosophical questions. And indeed many of the great philosophers were also scientists (e.g., Leibniz and Descartes, who lived in the seventeenth century), and many great scientists were also philosophers (e.g., Einstein). Of course, many other sorts of questions in the sciences do not meet those criteria and are more properly conceived as being strictly matters of science. Furthermore, many of the questions philosophy is concerned with have a sense of urgency about them and may have a bearing on our everyday lives in terms of what we think and do. That is generally not the case with the philosophical questions found in the sciences. Knowing which of the interpretations of quantum mechanics in physics is true probably would not have any impact on your life—your innermost convictions, your concerns, your goals, and your mode of living. On the other hand, knowing whether or not God exists, or whether we have free will, or whether there are any objective moral standards may have a crucial bearing on your life in thought and action. As someone once put it, in science, we ask questions; in philosophy, we find ourselves questioned.

B

Why study philosophy? We have tried to answer this question by discussing five of the main aims or tasks of philosophy: the critical scrutiny of our naive, cherished beliefs and convictions; the bringing to light of our assumptions or presuppositions; the quest for a worthwhile life (the examined life); the keeping alive of our sense of wonder about the world; and the attempt to answer certain vexing but important questions. We would maintain that the achievement of these aims provides us with an answer to the question, Why study philosophy? It also provides us with at least a partial answer to the question, What is philosophy?—namely, philosophy is that enterprise which seeks to fulfill those aims or tasks. And while this doesn't cover everything which comes under the heading of "philosophy," it does pertain to a good deal.

It is clear from what we have said so far that the pursuit of philosophy involves asking a lot of questions. This holds for all of the tasks of philosophy. Again, there are no easy answers to these questions; in some cases there may be none at all (or at least none which are obvious). But sometimes asking questions is more important than finding the answers to them. For we tend to think of answers as bits of information, and furthermore as useful information, as information that can solve a given problem in science, technology, or practical affairs. (For example: What is the most efficient way of getting X, whatever X is and regardless of the value or disvalue of X?) This view, too, is part of the legacy of our scientific culture and, hence, part of the belief system which requires philosophical investigation and scrutiny.

Objectively speaking, we are infinitesimally minute specks of a gigantic universe. This is no cause for despair. For we have certain capacities which make us qualitatively different from other specks: consciousness, thought, and appreciation. The more we ask questions, the more we extend and benefit from the capacities with which we are endowed. We need to step back from our immediate concerns in order to reflect on our personal and cultural beliefs and values, even though we have no guarantee as to the outcome. Perhaps, as John Maynard Keynes said, in the long run we'll all be dead. But then, *for us* it is the short run that counts. So why not make the most of it? It may be an exaggeration to say, with John Stuart Mill, that it is better to be a Socrates unsatisfied than a pig satisfied. But it is no exaggeration to say that the good life involves more than bread, beer, sex, and money. If you don't think so now, perhaps you will after you have read, digested, and discussed the readings in this book. And if after reading the book you still don't agree, you won't be any worse off for having given it a try.

And in order to give it a fair try you must be prepared to step back and reflect, to try to understand yourself and others, to examine your beliefs and values and those of others. You need to exercise your ability to be skeptical of those various beliefs and values, to ask for evidence or reasons for them, to dig out their assumptions and implications, and to look at them with a critical eye. (This does not mean that you must reject them.) We urge you to take seriously the idea that learning (and reading) are not the same as memorizing bits of information but involve posing difficult and fundamental questions about the meaning, truth, and implications of our most cherished and "obvious" beliefs and values. Again, this involves the ability to understand and take seriously beliefs which you don't agree with; it involves understanding and being true to yourself.

You may be thinking, "It sounds as if the pursuit of philosophy involves an awful lot of hard work." We will not deny that philosophy and the study of philosophy involve a good deal of effort. Is it worth it? We believe so. In the words of a contemporary philosopher, W. T. Jones, "Philosophy is the eternal search for truth, a search which inevitably fails and yet is never defeated; which continually eludes us, but which always guides us. This free, intellectual life of the mind is the noblest inheritance of the Western World; it is also the hope of our future."

You, the student, may also wonder just how to approach the study of philosophy once you have determined that it is important to gain more knowledge about this discipline. To help you in that quest we have provided some guides in the last section of this Introduction on how to study philosophy. These will aid you in organizing your study of philosophy and in communicating with others either through writing assignments or through discussion and argument. We feel that you will enjoy the study of philosophy much more if you learn to master both of these skills.

Before turning to those matters, let us first deal with the question: What is philosophy about? What sorts of problems is philosophy concerned with?

II. WHAT PHILOSOPHY IS ABOUT

Most of the main problems or questions with which philosophy is concerned may be thought of as falling into three main areas: problems pertaining to reality, problems pertaining to knowledge, and problems pertaining to value. We shall discuss each of these broad areas and note some of the main problems of each of them. The three areas are: metaphysics (or ontology), epistemology, and axiology.

A. Metaphysics: What Is Real?

Let us begin with a discussion of what is meant by the term 'reality' in the philosophical sense. In one very broad sense of the term, 'reality' may mean *whatever is*. But in this loose sense, of course, *anything is*—a ghost as well as a tree, an object of illusion as well as an object of veridical perception. In the philosophical sense of the term, 'reality' designates what is *real*, not necessarily or merely as opposed to what is unreal, but rather whatever is real in the sense of being *ultimately* real. It is difficult to explicate this meaning of the term 'reality' to anyone who has no familiarity with philosophical works. Its meaning can best be apprehended by examples, that is, by reading philosophical works in which philosophers distinguish, and give grounds for the distinction, between those kinds of things which merely have a surface reality from those which have a more fundamental or underlying reality. But as a start, one might say that in the philosophical sense, the term 'reality' refers to whatever is real rather than whatever is merely apparent. In fact, this problem of *appearance* versus *reality* has often been considered as one of the main problems of philosophy.

The area of philosophy which deals with the nature of reality is known as *metaphysics*. Let us consider some of the main *problems* (or questions) which fall under this division of philosophy.

1. The problem of the external world.
   Very briefly, this problem is constituted by such questions as:

Is there a world (or realm of objects) which exists external to our minds (for example, a world of matter)?

Or are there any good reasons for believing that such a world exists?

The beginning student might wonder: "Why on earth would anyone worry about questions like these? Of course such a world exists. We encounter it every day of our lives. How can we possibly doubt its reality?" In response we can only say: Some philosophers have found reasons for taking these questions seriously. And many have provided arguments which attempt to prove either that no such world exists or if it does, we have no conclusive evidence for thinking that it does. Others have attempted to support our commonsensical belief that such a world does exist.

2. The problem of the self (or mind, or soul).
   The main questions here are:

Does the self exist in any real, substantial way, as a unitary, continuous entity?
   If so, is it a special mental, non-material substance?
   Or is what I call my self identical with my body or some part of my body, for example, my brain?

Most of us think of our selves as having a substantial (although not material) reality. That is, each of us thinks of his/her self as a unitary entity, having a duration through time. Are there any good reasons for these beliefs?

3. The problem of freedom versus determinism.
   The main questions here are:

Are human beings genuinely free agents? That is, can they freely choose among alternatives?
   Or are their choices and actions determined?
   If the latter, what is meant here by 'determined'?
   What bearing do the answers to these questions have with regard to human responsibility?
   What bearing do they have on practical issues such as the punishment of criminals?

4. The problem of immortality or survival after death.
   The main questions here are:

Does the human self continue to exist after the death of the body?
   If so, does it continue to exist forever? (Is it immortal?)

5. The problem of a god (or gods).
   Here we are concerned with such questions as:

Is there any being whose existence transcends the natural universe—an eternal, divine being? (Or is there even more than one god?)
   If so, what is the nature of this being? (Is it infinite or finite, for example? Is it all-powerful? All-knowing? Supremely good?)

Many have held that such a being exists. Some philosophers have tried to prove that such a being must exist in order to explain such things as how the universe came into being. Others have examined these arguments and found them to be defective.

6. The problem of evil.

By many conceptions, God is held to be (among other things) omnipotent (all-powerful) and supremely good. But there is much evil in the world. This leads to a vexing problem:

> Is the existence of evil in the world compatible with the existence of an all-powerful *and* supremely benevolent God?
>
> If so, how?

The preceding problems fall into three main categories: problems pertaining to the natural world in general, problems pertaining to human beings, and problems pertaining to a being beyond the natural universe. Thus we may distinguish various sub-categories of metaphysics. There are many ways in which this might be done. A rough way of distinguishing them might be: general metaphysics (or ontology), philosophical anthropology, and philosophy of religion. Ontology is concerned with broad questions such as, "What kinds of things are real? Is there a real material world?" Philosophical anthropology deals with issues having to do with the nature of human selves. Philosophy of religion (or philosophical theology) has to do with problems about the existence and nature of a god or gods.

B. Epistemology: What Is Knowledge?

Let us turn now to a consideration of what is meant by the term 'knowledge' in the philosophical sense. The philosophical sense of the term has its roots in the ordinary sense of the term but is a refinement of it. We commonly contrast knowledge with ignorance. And we commonly think of knowledge as possessing some characteristics, whatever they may be, which are lacking in mere opinion or belief. Philosophers accept and insist upon these distinctions. However, with regard to the province of knowledge, as opposed to belief, they also ask further questions and make further distinctions. Some of these are: knowledge which is absolutely certain as opposed to probable knowledge; knowledge which is significant and informative as opposed to knowledge which is trivial (such as 'A is A').

The area of philosophy which pertains to the investigation of knowledge is known as *epistemology*. Let us consider some of the main epistemological problems.

1. The problem of the criterion of knowledge.

The main questions here are:

> What constitutes genuine knowledge—as opposed to opinion or belief?
> What is the criterion for knowledge?

2. The problem of the possibility of knowledge.

Once we have defined what genuine knowledge is, then the question arises:

Is any genuine knowledge attainable? Or is everything we claim to know merely an opinion or belief?

If so, what are the limits (if any) within which such knowledge is possible?

3. The problem of the sources of knowledge.

If we claim to have knowledge of reality (even within limits), then the question may be raised:

What are the sources or origins of such knowledge? (How does it arise? Where does it come from?)

4. The problem of the grounds of knowledge.

Let us suppose that we claim to have genuine knowledge and that we have indicated its sources, then an even more important question must be raised:

What are the *grounds* for our claims to have knowledge (as opposed to opinion)? That is, how can we *justify* our knowledge claims?

5. The problem of the right to believe.

It is an obvious fact that we all hold many beliefs, some of which may be items of knowledge. The main question which arises with regard to belief is:

When do we have a right to believe something?

In answer to the questions of epistemology—especially numbers 3 and 4—two main movements have arisen which hold competing and conflicting views. These are:

Empiricism: All of our knowledge of the world comes to us via sensory experience and must be justified by appealing to such experience. The only "knowledge" we have which requires no such empirical justification is purely verbal and hence trivial and uninformative, for example, 'Uncles are males'.

Rationalism: We can have some genuine knowledge of the world which can be justified without appealing to experience. Such knowledge can be justified by *thinking* as well as by our understanding of language. Such knowledge is not trivial or uninformative, but is significant.

Since much of our knowledge is found in the sciences, some or all of the preceding questions can be formulated with respect to science, along with many other related issues. These constitute the subject matter of a subdivision of epistemology known as philosophy of science.

Much of what we know or claim to know is based on inferences from other things which we know or claim to know. Thus another subdivision of epistemology is logic, which is concerned with criteria for making such inferences.

C. Axiology: What Is of Value?

The term 'value' in philosophy also has its roots in the ordinary sense of the term. However, philosophers often make further distinctions and refinements by asking such questions as: Are any values more ultimate than others (the latter being merely apparent or on-the-surface)? Are any values of greater importance to human life than others? If so, what are they?

The best way to approach the study of value is through a consideration of value judgments, or evaluative statements. Consider the following sets of statements:

A	B
1. Jones is six feet tall.	1. Jones is a good man.
2. The atomic bomb has killed many people.	2. The atomic bomb is a bad thing to have.
3. Most people keep promises.	3. Promise-keeping is right.
4. Murder is seldom committed.	4. Murder is wrong.

Consider the statements in group (A). Although they differ from each other, they all have something in common. They assert a *fact*, specific or general, without making any evaluations. They merely state that something is (or is the case). Let us call them *descriptive* statements.

But now consider those in group (B). All of these make some *evaluation*; they do not merely state that something is. They appraise certain things, specific or general. They state that something is good or bad, right or wrong. Let us call them *evaluative* statements.

When we reflect upon these two kinds of statements, certain questions arise. Some of these are:

Are the two kinds really different? Or might they be essentially the same (or at least very similar)? Granted that (A) statements assert facts about the natural world. What about (B) statements? Do they also assert some facts, or are they unique? That is, are (B) statements also descriptive?

Suppose one answered "No" to the latter question. Then another question arises: Why are (B) statements not descriptive? What makes them different from (A) statements? Or suppose that one answered "Yes" to that question and maintained that (B) statements are also descriptive. Then further questions arise: What do they describe? Do they describe objective facts, that is, facts which are the case apart from the person who utters such statements? Or do they merely describe or express certain subjective attitudes and feelings on the part of the person who utters them?

Some of the statements in group (B) are general in character, or at least they purport to be. For example, 'Murder is wrong.' Is the claim that, for example, murder is wrong something *absolute*? Or is it relative to historical eras, societies, individuals, or whatever? The same applies to other general (B) statements.

These sorts of questions and concerns give rise to two main problems concerning evaluative assertions. These are:

1. The problem of objectivism *versus* subjectivism.
   Are evaluative statements descriptive?
   If so, do they describe objective facts?
   Or do they merely describe or express our subjective attitudes, feelings, and tastes?
2. The problem of absolutism *versus* relativism.
   Are any evaluative statements applicable to all persons at all times and places?
   Or are they relative to cultures or eras?

The division of philosophy which deals with these sorts of questions is known as *axiology*, or theory of value, which has two main subdivisions: ethics and aesthetics. Axiology is concerned not only with the above questions, which pertain to the nature of value judgments, but also with certain questions which are specifically ethical in character, some which are specifically aesthetic in character, and some which apply to both.

Roughly, aesthetics is concerned with problems pertaining to the arts, and hence is often referred to as philosophy of art; ethics is concerned with issues pertaining to morality and conduct.

Among the chief problems of *ethics* are the following:

1. What is the good?
   Or what is the good life?
   That is, what is man's highest good?
2. Among our moral values, which of them are intrinsically good (good in themselves) as opposed to instrumentally good (good as means to ends)?
3. How, if at all, can we distinguish between right and wrong?
   Between what we ought to do and what we ought not to do?
   What is the correct standard of conduct?
4. Are the judgments we make about good, bad, etc., objective or subjective? Absolute or relative?

There are various other problems which pertain to ethics in a somewhat wider sense. These constitute what may be considered to be a third subdivision of axiology commonly known as social and political philosophy. We shall not attempt to list all of these problems. However, two of these are the subject of much contemporary interest. One is sometimes known as the problem of law *versus* liberty, or liberty *versus* autonomy. The law, or the state which imposes laws, is sometimes conceived as being a guardian of our liberties. On the other hand, by governing certain kinds of behavior or by imposing duties or requirements upon us, the law or state also restricts our liberties. A central question then arises: To what extent, if at all, and in what circumstances is the law or state justified in limiting or restricting our liberties? Another way of saying this is: We seem to have a conflict between authority and autonomy. How, if at all, can this conflict be resolved? The second is the problem of theories of society. Which form of society is best? For example, in the world at present there is tension between capitalism and communism and socialism. Is one of these more defensible? If so, on what grounds?

Finally, there is one problem which is both a question of reality and of value. This is the problem of *the meaning of life*.

The main questions of concern here are:

Does life have any objective purpose or meaning?

If so, what is it, and how can it be realized?

If not, does life have *any* meaning or purpose?

There are many problems with which philosophy is concerned. We have tried to indicate what some of the main ones are. Some of these are discussed in detail in this book. We have tried to focus on those which almost everyone is interested in. (See Previews to the Parts.) We hope that the readers will enjoy and profit from their study of these exciting and important problems.

But before we turn to some of the intriguing and important problems of philosophy, we have one more preliminary task. As you will see, reading philosophical works is very unlike reading most other types of works. To assist you in that regard we offer some comments on how to study philosophy.

III. HOW TO STUDY PHILOSOPHY

A. How to Read a Philosophical Work

Most works in philosophy are difficult to read. This is because philosophical problems are difficult to solve—or even attempt to solve. The editors of this book have chosen selections which have been understood by introductory students in the past. Nevertheless, reading these works will require more effort than reading a newspaper or even a history book.

It is recommended that you read each assignment *at least twice*. First read the entire assignment fairly rapidly in order to ascertain what issues are being discussed, where essential arguments occur, and so forth. Then, perhaps after a break, read the same assignment carefully and *take notes*. Such notes will, among other things, prove valuable when you are studying for exams.

Here are some general questions which you should ask and attempt to answer in writing during your second reading of every assignment:

1. What main thesis (or theses) is the author trying to establish or defend (or prove) in this selection?

2. What main thesis (or theses) is the author trying to oppose or refute, if any?

3. What are the author's arguments for the theses which he or she advocates or defends?

4. What are the author's arguments against the theses which he or she opposes, if any?

5. Has the author made a good case in behalf of the theses which he or she maintains or defends? For example, are the arguments good ones? If so, why? If not, why not?

6. Has the author made a good case against the theses which he or she denies or opposes? Is so, why? If not, why not?

7. What is *your* view on the main issue(s) discussed in this selection, and what are your reasons for holding it?

Note: An alternative way of dealing with question 1 is as follows:

1a. What question(s) is the author attempting to answer in this selection?
1b. How does he or she answer the question(s)?

A few comments should be made with regard to these questions.

1. Be sure to state the main theses in complete sentences. Don't just use a phrase or a partial sentence.

2. Be sure to formulate completely the arguments contained in the selections. Supply all the necessary premises and the conclusion. (See How to Structure and Appraise an Argument.)

3. Be sure to make your own critical appraisal of the author's arguments and views.

4. Be sure to defend whatever view you hold with the best reasons and arguments you can think of.

5. In some cases an author's discussion of what he or she defends is intimately connected with what he or she rejects. In such cases questions 1 and 2, and 3 and 4 may be answered conjointly.

6. Be sure to define or explain any technical and/or crucial terms in the selection.

7. Where relevant, identify the overall argument (or argumentative strategy) of the selection as well as the component arguments. (See How to Structure and Appraise an Argument.)

You will find that you cannot adequately understand a philosophical work just by reading it, or by reading and underlining. It is essential for you to try to convey the authors' main claims and arguments in writing. The above questions and suggestions will help you achieve a better understanding of the works you read. But of course, you must actually engage in the task of answering the study questions in writing. (Some instructors may provide specific study questions for the assigned readings.)

B. How to Structure and Appraise an Argument

The central method of philosophy consists of the presentation and critical evaluation of arguments. Hence, it is important to develop the ability to structure arguments and appraise them critically. The following remarks on this subject are not exhaustive, but they will illustrate some aspects of these activities.

1. Structuring an Argument
Consider this argument:

> If materialism is true, all our thoughts are produced by purely material antecedents. These are quite blind, and are just as likely to produce falsehoods as truths. We have thus no reason for believing any of our conclusions—including the truth of materialism, which is therefore a self-contradictory hypothesis.

First, identify the conclusion. If more than one inference is drawn, there may be two or more conclusions. Look for the one that is the final conclusion. Label it "C." Clearly, the final conclusion of the argument just given is as follows:

> C: Materialism is a self-contradictory hypothesis.

Second, identify the premise(s) from which the conclusion is drawn. The conclusion just stated is drawn from the previous statement:

> (If materialism is true) we have no reason for believing any of our conclusions.

That assertion is drawn from the previous statements and, hence, is a sub-conclusion for which the previous statements are premises.

We may now, *third*, structure the entire argument as follows (P = premise):

> P1. If materialism is true, all our thoughts are produced by purely material antecedents.

> P2. Purely material antecedents are blind and are just as likely to produce falsehoods as they are to produce truths.

> C1. Therefore, if materialism is true, we have no reason for believing any of our conclusions—including the truth of materialism.

> C2. Therefore, materialism is a self-contradictory hypothesis.

(For purposes of exams and the like, you do not have to include the P1, C1, etc. These are most useful when you first tackle an argument.)

2. Appraising an Argument
Next, criticize the argument. For example, *one* way of appraising an argument is to ask if all the premises are true or at least seem true. If one or more of the premises is false, then the conclusion cannot be known to be true on the basis of those premises, even if the logical structure of the argument is valid. A *second* way of attacking an argument is to ask whether the argument is logically valid. Even if the premises and conclusion are true, the argument itself may be faulty. So ask yourself, Does the conclusion really follow from the premises? That is, given the truth of the premises, are we entitled to infer

the conclusion? If not, why not? Of course, the best way to answer such questions is via the principles of logic. But there is an informal way by which one can often do this. And that consists in asking whether you can conceive of a counter instance. Can you think of a case in which, even though the premises are true, the conclusion need not be true?

A *third* way of appraising an argument is to ask whether or not the premises rest on any assumptions. If so, what are those assumptions? Do they seem acceptable? If so, why; if not, why not? If the argument employs an analogy, then, *fourth*, you should ask whether the analogy seems appropriate. If not, why not? A *fifth* way of criticizing an argument is to ask whether certain terms are *defined* in such a manner as to make the conclusion follow, but only through a process of circular reasoning.

There are, of course, many other ways of criticizing an argument. Among those which deserve mention are the following: *Sixth*, see if the argument commits the fallacy of equivocation (i.e., the use of a term or expression in two or more different senses within the context of the argument). If so, no valid conclusion can be drawn. *Seventh*, determine whether or not the argument involves an infinite regress. For example, if it is claimed that the only way to explain Y is because of X, then does X also require an explanation? If so, does *that*, in turn, also require one? And so forth.

3. *Arguments* versus *Descriptions*

Many students have great difficulty understanding the difference between (a) stating an argument and (b) describing an argument—or perhaps describing an author's approach to an argument. The difference is crucial, since we will be interested mainly in (a) and not in (b).

Suppose you were assigned an essay by A. B. Smith entitled "An Argument for God's Existence," and suppose you were asked to *state* (in writing) Smith's argument. If that were the case, you would be expected to explicitly formulate every premise which is needed for Smith or anyone else to be able to infer the conclusion, "Therefore God exists." That is, everything which is required in order to support that conclusion must be articulated, premise by premise, and nothing which is not required should be formulated as a premise.

Here is an example of what you should *not* do. You should not include among the premises assertions like "First Smith makes a distinction between . . . " or "Then Smith goes on to claim that . . . " Why is this wrong? First, because Smith's name probably does not occur anywhere in the article, except along with the title to indicate authorship. Second, if you included such assertions you would be implying that Smith wrote an article about herself rather than an article in which she attempted to prove or defend God's existence. But the subject matter of Smith's article is the existence of God, not the behavior of Smith.

Here is an example of what you *should* do. Consider the following passage from "A Critique of Ethics," by C. D. Jones.[2]

[2]Adapted from A. J. Ayer, *Language, Truth, and Logic* (New York: Dover, 1946), pp. 104–105.

There is a widely held ethical theory which has found great favor in our day and is commonly known as subjectivism. Subjectivism defines the rightness of actions and the goodness of ends in terms of the feelings of approval which a certain person, or group of people, has toward them. Thus, for the subjectivist, to say that something is good is to say that he, or people generally, approve of it or have a pro-feeling with regard to it. If this theory were correct, it would be very attractive, for it would mean that ethical assertions are not genuinely different from factual assertions.

Nevertheless I shall not adopt a subjectivist analysis of ethical terms or statements. I reject the subjectivist view that to call an action right or a thing good is to say that it is generally approved of for this reason: It is not self-contradictory to assert that some actions which are generally approved of are not right, or that some things which are generally approved of are not good. And I reject the alternative subjectivist view that a person who asserts that a certain action is right or that a certain thing is good, is saying that he himself approves of it, on the ground that: a person who confessed that he sometimes approved of what was bad or wrong would not be contradicting himself.

Suppose you are asked to state the argument contained in this passage. First ask yourself, Just what is Jones trying to prove or disprove by means of his argument? He says that he rejects a certain ethical theory, subjectivism. And it is clear that he rejects it because it is false or incorrect. So we have the following:

Conclusion: Subjectivism cannot be true (or correct).

Now, since he is concluding something about subjectivism, it would of course be helpful to define the term *subjectivism* or to characterize the theory of subjectivism. This could be done as a premise of the actual argument or via a definition or characterization which immediately precedes the actual (statement of the) argument. Let's use the former procedure here. Lay out every needed step in the argument. (Try to formulate the premises in such a manner that the structure of the argument becomes totally clear.) For example:

1. According to subjectivism, to say that "X is right (or good)" means either (a) "People generally approve of it" or (b) "I (the speaker) approve of it."

2. But it is not self-contradictory to say that (c) "X is generally approved of, but X is not right (or good)."

3. And it is not self-contradictory to say that (d) "I sometimes approve of X, but X is bad (or wrong)."

4. If subjectivism were true, it would be self-contradictory to say (c) and/or (d).

5. Therefore, subjectivism cannot be true.

Note that we have included only what is essential to the statement of the complete argument. All nonessential items have been omitted—including any reference to the author. But we have not omitted anything which is required to support the conclusion.

For every reading assignment you should look for all of the author's arguments (pro or con) with regard to his or her main theses, and state those arguments in writing. Don't despair if you find this a bit difficult at first. As with almost any skill, you will improve with practice.

You may be wondering, Why all this attention to arguments? Because philosophical questions cannot be answered on the basis of observation or experimentation. Nor can they be answered just by examining the meanings of words. They can be answered only through critical analysis and argumentation. Establishing a philosophical claim consists of proposing arguments which support it, and refuting a philosophical claim consists of either proposing other arguments against it or criticizing the arguments which have been put forth in its behalf. Thus, insofar as philosophy has a method, it consists of critical appraisal of arguments. But before you can appraise an argument you must know what the argument is.

4. *Overall Arguments and Component Arguments*

There is another distinction which we need to make before leaving the topic of arguments. It is important to distinguish between the component arguments and the overall argument of the work.

The component arguments, obviously, are those which make up or occur in the overall argument. These may be of two sorts. Sometimes an author presents arguments in behalf of the theses which he or she wishes to defend. In this case, of course, the arguments are intended to be good ones which constitute good grounds for the acceptance of some thesis or conclusion. But an author may also formulate arguments which others have put forth against the thesis he or she wishes to defend, or arguments which others have put forth in behalf of some alternative thesis. After stating such arguments, the author replies to them, trying to show that they are weak or fallacious, that they don't establish what they are taken to establish, and the like.

Now, in many philosophical (and other) works this process of presenting and replying to arguments occurs within the framework of a larger, overall argument. It is important to be clear as to what this overall argument is, because in some works an author's case for or against something finally rests on the overall argument and not merely on the component arguments. Or, perhaps more accurately, in many instances an author's case may gain strength by virtue of his or her overall argument.

What we have been calling the overall argument might also be thought of as the author's final argument. It is the logical pattern or structure of the case which he or she presents for or against something. In some cases the overall argument is easily identifiable. For example, an author may say that he wishes to defend the view that so-and-so is true and that he has, say, five arguments in behalf of so-and-so. Then he presents them—one, two, three, four, five. In other cases the overall argument may be somewhat more complex. For example, an author may intend to establish a certain thesis, T, by refuting its opposite, non-T. She then makes her case along the following lines: Here are the arguments which have been put forth in behalf of non-T. All of them are

invalid. Here are some arguments against non-T. All of them are valid. Therefore, T is true.

Or an author may proceed along these lines: The question I wish to
answer is Q. There are only three alternative answers—A, B, and C. A is
false, and here is why. B is false, and here is why. Therefore, C must be true.

In doing your assignments you should not merely write down or formulate the component arguments but also organize them into the overall argument of the essay or chapter.

5. *Theses and Arguments*

In reading any essay or chapter you should distinguish between the
author's theses and his or her arguments. Many students have difficulty in
grasping this distinction, but it is really a simple one. The main thesis is the
chief point which the author is trying to get across. Ask yourself, What is
the author trying to convince me of? The answer to that question constitutes
the main thesis. It is that which the author is trying to prove or at least defend,
or that which the author is trying to refute or attack.

Of course, an author may be trying both to defend one thesis and to attack
another. This is obvious in cases in which there is only one opposing point of
view. In such cases the author is attacking the thesis which is the logical
opposite of the one he or she is defending. However, there may be cases in
which the thesis being attacked is not merely the opposite of the one being
defended. Also, in some cases an author may be trying to defend more than
one main thesis, or to attack more than one.

Except in complex cases, a thesis is something which normally may be
stated in a single declarative sentence. It must be a complete sentence, not
just a word or phrase. Why must it be stated in a complete sentence? Because
a thesis is something which the author is either trying to establish as being
true or trying to establish as being false. Truth and falsity do not apply to
phrases. Only what a complete declarative sentence expresses has the capacity to be either true or false.

Let's take a simple example. Suppose you are reading an article in which
the author presents five arguments in behalf of God's existence. Then obviously the main thesis is "God exists" or "There is a God." The author's arguments then consist of both (a) the main thesis ("God exists"), which is the
conclusion of each of the arguments, and (b) all of the premises (other statements) from which that conclusion is supposed to follow.

In reading your assignments you should always state the main theses
and arguments in writing. This will help you with regard to both class discussion and examinations.

PART ONE

BELIEF AND KNOWLEDGE

PREVIEW

You, the reader, may be attending a college or university. One of the main reasons why colleges and universities were founded and continue to exist is to propagate knowledge. But this of course assumes that there really is any knowledge to be propagated! But is there anything that can rightfully be called genuine knowledge? Or might it be the case that what we—including the faculty and administration of colleges and universities—take to be knowledge is really just a bunch of beliefs or opinions? If so, can anyone ever really know anything?

Rene Descartes, who is the most influential figure in the theory of knowledge, was disgusted with the state of knowledge as he found it in the early seventeenth century. Much of what he had been taught was false. Disagreement on important issues, even among "authorities," was rampant. Descartes began thinking about the nature of knowledge in order to put it on a firm foundation.

> Several years have now passed since I first realized how many were the false opinions that in my youth I took to be true, and thus how doubtful were all the things I subsequently built upon these opinions. From the time I became aware of this, I realized that for once I had to raze everything in my life, down to the very bottom, so as to begin again from the first foundations, if I wanted to establish anything firm and lasting in the sciences.[1]

It is not difficult to get into Descartes' frame of mind. The government assures us that nuclear power stations are safe. The reactor at Three Mile Island suffers a catastrophic accident. Certain political leaders assure us that supply-side economics will reduce the government deficit. The deficit soars. One group of prestigious physicists tells us that violations of a nuclear test ban treaty would be verifiable. An equally qualified group asserts the opposite.

These quandaries make Descartes' project attractive. As in constructing a huge office building where one needs a strong foundation upon which to

---

[1]Rene Descartes, *Meditations on First Philosophy* (Indianapolis: Hackett, 1979), p. 13.

secure the upper floors, one needs a basic set of beliefs or propositions upon which to secure other beliefs. What sort of beliefs could serve as the foundation? Obviously, we must be very careful in selecting them since if they are faulty, that may infect what is built on them, hence undermining the project.

Descartes and many other philosophers, including contemporary ones, have thought that the foundation requires beliefs that are certain—beliefs about which one cannot be mistaken. The task then is to find such beliefs and begin constructing the knowledge edifice. Unfortunately, many philosophers have argued that it is enormously difficult to find even a single belief that is certain. Consider, for example, your belief that you are presently reading a philosophy book. Is that belief certain? Is it impossible that your belief is mistaken? Suppose that an hour ago a blood vessel in your brain burst. When discovered unconscious you were rushed to the emergency room of the nearest hospital. A team of doctors is presently doing exploratory surgery. A number of drugs were administered to you and you are now dreaming wildly. In fact, you are dreaming that you are reading a philosophy book about knowledge. Of course, your belief is mistaken, no one thought to bring your books with you to the hospital. Is this story possible? If it is, how can you be *certain* that you are now reading a philosophy book? If you cannot be certain of something so innocent, it looks very dim for our being certain of anything!

Main Questions

We started out trying to put knowledge on a firm foundation. We seemed to end up wondering if there is any knowledge. This constitutes the main question of this part:

1. Is genuine knowledge possible?

A closely related question concerns the nature or definition of knowledge. Notice that in the opening remarks the crucial move that led us to wonder if we have any knowledge was the assumption that if something is to count as knowledge it must be *certain*. Perhaps this condition needs examination. More generally, then, a second question central to this part is:

2. What is the definition of or criterion for knowledge?

But there is another question which is also closely related to (1) and (2). We often find ourselves in a position in which we *believe* something to be true (or false) but in which we would not claim to *know* it. Or we would not claim to know it with certainty. Further, as we shall see in our answer to (2), believing something is *one* of the conditions for knowing it. This leads to a third and very important question:

3. When do we have a right—a moral and intellectual right—to believe?

The issues here concern the concepts of evidence and belief. Is evidence required for belief, or is it justifiable at times to believe without having evidence for a belief?

Answers

With respect to question (1), there are two possible answers. The negative view is called skepticism; the affirmative, non-skepticism. In the strongest sense, these maintain:

Skepticism: the view that no one can *know* anything.
Non-skepticism: the view that knowledge is possible.

Perhaps few people have been skeptics in the sense just referred to. But some philosophers have been skeptical about whether we can have any knowledge about an *external world*. What is an external world? 'External world' is defined as: A world which is external to and independent of our minds and the contents of our minds, a world external to our consciousness. For example, a world of material objects: rocks, tables, nuclear reactors, bodies of humans and animals, and so forth. Generally, the problem of whether genuine knowledge is possible is discussed in these terms. This provides us with refined definitions of our two answers, namely:

1a. Skepticism: No one can know anything about an external world.

1b. Non-skepticism: Genuine knowledge about an external world is possible.

It is this sense of skepticism and its denial with which we are concerned.

To list the alternative answers to question (2) would be impractical. We will, via the readings, focus on the traditional answer to (2), known as the justified-true-belief account. (See selection 2, Section I.)

It is one thing to say that one's beliefs must be justified, if they are to be knowledge. It is a more difficult matter to say what the nature of the required justification is. A helpful approach might be to look at what passes as justification in science, rather than think abstractly about the nature of justification. After all, science is an extremely successful enterprise. Don't scientists, at least sometimes, have knowledge? (See selection 3.)

With regard to the question as to when we have a right to believe, there are two main views. Neither has a common name, hence we shall refer to them as the first view and the second view:

3a. First view: We have a right to believe something if and only if we have sufficient evidence for our belief. (Belief without evidence is *always* wrong.)

3b. Second view: Sometimes we have a right to believe something even if we don't have evidence for it, if certain conditions are met. (Belief without evidence is *sometimes* justifiable.)

Selections

The selections in Part One correspond to the issues raised in the Preview as follows:

Question	Answer	Selection
(1)	(1a) Skepticism	1
(1)	(1b) Non-skepticism	2, 3, 4
(2)		1, 2, 3, 4
(3)	(3a) First view	5
(3)	(3b) Second view	6

APPENDIX

In any discussion of knowledge it is important to distinguish between two kinds of knowledge and, correspondingly, two kinds of truths or propositions which may be known to be true or false. Consider the statements in the following lists.

A	*B*
1. Wolves are bred in zoos.	1. Uncles are males.
2. It is raining (at a certain place and time).	2. Either it is raining or it is not raining.
3. No objects of art have sold for more than $5 million.	3. No object can be in two places at once.

Clearly, there is a difference between these two kinds of statements. First, statements of type A, even if they are true, are at best contingently true. They could be false. But statements of type B are necessarily true and their negations are necessarily false.

Second, A-statements are dependent on experience, other than the experience of reading and understanding them, for their justification. In order to know whether it is raining outside your room, you have to look out, put your hand out the window, or whatever. But B-statements are not dependent on experience for their justification. In order to know that either it is raining or it isn't, you do not have to run any empirical "test."

Type A statements and our knowledge of them are said to be *a posteriori* (or contingent). Type B statements are said to be *a priori* (or necessary). We may now define these terms:

1. A statement is known *a posteriori* if you have to appeal to experience to find out whether the statement is true.

2. A statement is known *a priori* if you do not have to appeal to experience to find out whether the statement is true.

Someone may object: "But by the above definitions, *all* propositions are *a posteriori*, including the ones designated as *a priori*. These too *are* dependent upon experience. You cannot know that they are true, or even understand them, except through the experience of having come to know (and retain) the meanings of the words."

The reply to this is: any such understanding of the term 'experience' would indeed obliterate the distinction. But the fact is there are some propositions which one can know to be true merely by the "experience" of understanding the words. There are others in which more than that is required, namely experience of the actual facts in the world—not the "experience" of knowing meanings of words. It is this meaning of "experience" which the above definitions use. "Experience" here means experience of more than knowing meanings of words, experience which involves performing some empirical test, looking, feeling, hearing, etc.

Thus consider these propositions:

a. It is raining or it is not raining (here and now).
b. It is raining (here and now).

Statement (a) is *a priori* because you don't have to run any empirical test like looking. You don't need to turn to experiencing what the weather actually is like. But (b) is *a posteriori* because you cannot know it is true just by knowing what the words mean. You need to turn to the world and experience what the weather is like.

1 / A Defense of Skepticism

PETER UNGER

Peter Unger (1942–   ) is professor of philosophy at New York University. He studied at Oxford University. Unger's main work is in the theory of knowledge and the philosophy of mind. He has developed an extended series of arguments in defense of skepticism about knowledge, values, minds, and persons, and has tried to resituate these ideas in a more plausible framework. His arguments are highly original and provocative.

*I*n these pages, I try to argue compellingly for skepticism. . . . The type of skepticism for which I first argue is perhaps the most traditional one: skepticism about knowledge. This is the thesis that no one ever *knows* anything about anything. . . .*

I. A CLASSICAL FORM OF SKEPTICAL ARGUMENT

There are certain arguments for skepticism which conform to a familiar . . . pattern or form. These arguments rely, at least for their psychological power, on vivid descriptions of exotic *contrast cases*. The following is one such rough argument, this one in support of skepticism regarding any alleged *knowledge of an external world.*† The exotic contrast case here concerns an evil scientist, and is described to be in line with the most up-to-date developments of science, or science fiction. We begin by arbitrarily choosing something concerning an external world which might conceivably, we suppose, be *known*, in one way or another, e.g., that there are rocks or, as we will understand it, that there is at least one rock.

[*Argument*] Now, first, *if* someone, anyone *knows* that there are rocks, then the person *can know* the following quite exotic thing: There is *no* evil scientist deceiving him into *falsely* believing that there are rocks. This scientist uses electrodes to induce experiences and thus carries out his deceptions, concerning the existence of rocks or anything else. He first drills holes painlessly in the variously colored skulls, or shells, of his subjects and then implants his electrodes into the appropriate parts of their brains, or protoplasm, or systems. He sends patterns of electrical impulses into them through the electrodes, which are themselves connected by wires to a laboratory console

---

*[In this selection, Unger does not argue for this extreme thesis. Rather, he argues that: No one can know anything about an *external world*. See Section I, first paragraph.—Eds.]

†[The external world consists of objects which exist independently of being perceived, for example, chairs, rocks, etc. It is external to our minds.—Eds.]

on which he plays, punching various keys and buttons in accordance with his ideas of how the whole thing works and with his deceptive designs. The scientist's delight is intense, and it is caused not so much by his exercising his scientific and intellectual gifts as by the thought that he is deceiving various subjects about all sorts of things. Part of that delight is caused, on this supposition, by his thought that he is deceiving a certain person, perhaps yourself, into falsely believing that there are rocks. He is, then, an evil scientist, and he lives in a world which is entirely bereft of rocks.

[*Argument continued*] Now, as we have agreed, [1] *if you know* that there are rocks, then you *can know* that there is no such scientist doing this to you, [i.e., deceiving you to falsely believe that there are rocks.] But [2] no one *can* ever *know* that this exotic situation does *not obtain**; no one *can* ever *know* that there is *no* evil scientist who is, by means of electrodes, deceiving him into falsely believing there to be rocks. That is our second premiss, and it is also very difficult to deny. So, thirdly, as a consequence of these two premises, we have our skeptical conclusion: [3] You never *know* that there are rocks. But of course we have chosen our person, and the matter of there being rocks, quite arbitrarily, and this argument, it surely seems, may be generalized to cover any external matter at all. From this, we may conclude, finally, that [4] nobody ever *knows* anything about the external world.

[*Comments*] This argument is the same in form as the "evil demon" argument in Descartes' *Meditations*†; it is but a more modern, scientific counterpart, with its domain of application confined to matters concerning the external world.[1] Taking the *Meditations* as our source of the most compelling skeptical argument the philosophical literature has to offer, we may call any argument of this form *the classical argument* for skepticism. . . .

These arguments are exceedingly compelling. They tend to make skeptics of us all if only for a brief while. Anyone who would try to further skepticism, as I will try to do, will do well to link his own ideas to these arguments. For then, the very notable feelings and intuitions which they arouse may serve as support for the theses he would advance. . . .

II. ON TRYING TO REVERSE THIS ARGUMENT: EXOTIC CASES AND FEELINGS OF IRRATIONALITY

Our skeptical conclusion would not be welcome to many philosophers. Indeed, most philosophers would be inclined to try to reverse the argument, perhaps in the manner made popular by G. E. Moore.[2] They would not, I

---

*[Obtain: to occur or be prevalent in occurring.—Eds.]

†[Descartes was a seventeenth-century philosopher. Unger's argument is an up-to-date version of Descartes'.—Eds.]

[1]René Descartes, *Meditations on First Philosophy*, 2nd ed., 1642, in *The Philosophical Works of Descartes*, trans. E. S. Haldane and G. R. T. Ross (Cambridge, 1972), vol. 1, Meditation I, pp. 144–149. The crux of what I take to be the main argument occurs near the end of Meditation I.

[2]See several of Moore's most famous papers. But most especially, I suggest, see his "Four

think, wish to deny the first premiss, which in any case seems quite unobjectionable, at least in essential thrust. But even in its early formulation, they would be most happy to deny the second premiss, which is the more substantive one.*

[*Reverse Argument*] The Moorean attempt to reverse our argument will proceed like this: [1.] According to your argument, nobody ever *knows* that there are rocks. [2.] But I *do* know that there are rocks. This is something concerning the external world, and I do know it. Hence, [3.] somebody *does know* something about the external world. Mindful of our first premiss, the reversal continues: I can reason at least moderately well and thereby come to know things which I see to be entailed by things I already know. Before reflecting on classical arguments such as this, I may have never realized or even had the idea that from there being rocks it follows that there is *no evil* scientist who is deceiving me into *falsely* believing there to be rocks. But, having been presented with such arguments, I of course *now know* that this last *follows* from what I know. And so, while I might not have known *before* that there is no such scientist, at least [4.] I *now* do know that there is no evil scientist who is deceiving me into falsely believing that there are rocks. So far has the skeptical argument failed to challenge my knowledge successfully that it seems actually to have occasioned an increase in what I know about things.

[*Comments*] While the robust character of this reply has a definite appeal, it also seems quite daring. Indeed, the more one thinks on it, the more it seems to be somewhat foolhardy and even dogmatic. One cannot help but think that for all this philosopher really can *know*, he might have all his experience artificially induced by electrodes, these being operated by a terribly evil scientist who, having an idea of what his "protege" is saying to himself, chuckles accordingly. One thinks as well that for all *one can know oneself*, there really is no Moore or any other thinker with whose works one has actually had any contact. The belief that one has may, for all one really can *know*, be due to experiences induced by just such a chuckling operator. For all one can *know*, then, there may not really be any rocks. Positive assertions to the contrary, even on one's own part, seem quite out of place and even dogmatic.

[*Counter Argument*] Suppose that you yourself have just positively made an attempt to reverse; you try to be a Moore [and claim to know that there is no scientist who implanted electrodes and is deceiving you.] Now, [*case 1*] we may suppose that electrodes are removed, that your experiences are now brought about through your perception of actual surroundings, and you are, so to speak, forced to encounter your deceptive tormentor. Wouldn't you be

Forms of Scepticism" in his *Philosophical Papers* (New York, 1959), p. 226. [Moore was a twentieth-century philosopher in England who claimed to know with certainty that an external world exists.—Eds.]

*[Important! Before reading further, go back and reread the first and second premises of Unger's argument (Section I). They are the statements designated as (1) and (2).—Eds.]

made to feel quite *foolish,* even *embarrassed,* by your claims to *know?* Indeed, you would seem to be exposed quite clearly as having been, not only wrong, but rather irrational and even dogmatic. And [*case 2*] *if* there *aren't* ever any experiences of electrodes and so on, that happy fact can't mean that you are any *less* irrational and dogmatic in saying or thinking that you know. In thinking that you *know,* you will be equally and notably irrational and dogmatic. And, for at least *that* reason, in thinking yourself to *know* there is no such scientist, you will be *wrong* in *either* case. So it appears that one doesn't ever really *know* that there is no such scientist doing this thing.

[*Extension and Qualification*] Now, if you think or say to yourself that you are *certain* or *sure* that there is no scientist doing this, you may be doubly right, but even that does not seem to make matters much better for you. You may be right on *one* count because you may, I will suppose, *be* certain that there is no such scientist, and so be right *in what* you *think.* And in the second place, there may be no evil scientist deceiving you, so that you may be right *in that of which you are certain.* But, even if doubly right here, it seems just as dogmatic and irrational for you ever sincerely to profess this certainty. Thus it seems that, even if you *are* certain of the thing, and even if there *is no* scientist, you *shouldn't be certain* of it. It seems that you are *wrong,* then, and *not* right on a third count, namely, *in being certain* of the thing. It seems much better, perhaps perfectly all right, if you are instead only *confident* that there is no such scientist. It seems perfectly all right for you to *believe* there to be no evil scientist doing this. If you say not only that you believe it, but that you have some *reason* to believe this thing, what you say *may* seem somewhat suspect, at least on reasoned reflection, but it doesn't have any obvious tint of dogmatism or irrationality to it. Finally, you may simply *assert,* perhaps to yourself, *that there is no evil scientist who is deceiving me into falsely believing that there are rocks.* Perhaps strangely, this seems at least pretty nearly as foolhardy and dogmatic as asserting, or as thinking, *that you know the thing.* . . .

[*Comments*] This idea, that claims to *know* about external things are at least somewhat foolhardy and dogmatic, applies in all possible situations, even the most exotic cases. Suppose, for example, that you actually *do* have a sequence of experience which seems to indicate that an evil scientist was deceiving you into falsely believing that there are rocks. You seem to be confronting an exotic scientist who shows you electrodes, points out places of insertion on your skull or shell, and explains in detail how the whole thing works. And you seem to see no rocks outside the window of this scientist's laboratory. The scientist assures you that there really are no such things as rocks, that he only created an impression of such things by stimulating certain groups of cells in your brain. After enough of this sort of thing dominates your experiences, you *might* suppose that you *know* that there *is* an evil scientist who deceived you in the past, but he now does not. And you may also come to suppose that you *know* that there were *never any* rocks at all. But *should* you think you *know?* These latter experiences might *themselves* find no basis in reality, for all you really might *know.* For all you can *know,* it may be that all the time your experiences are induced by electrodes which are operated by *no* scientist, and it may be that there are no scientists at all, and plenty of rocks. Whether or not this is the case, you may always have new experience to the effect that it is. Is the new experience part of an encounter with *reality*, or is it *too* only part of an induced stream, or perhaps even a random sequence of experience? No matter how involved the going gets, it may always get still more involved. And each new turn may make any previously developed claim to *know* seem quite irrational and dogmatic, if not downright embarrassing. No matter what turns one's experience takes, the statement that one *knows* there to be no scientist *may* be wrong for the reason that there is a scientist. But it *will always* be wrong, it seems, for the reason of dogmatism and irrationality, however this last is to be explained. . . .

III. ORDINARY CASES

Largely because it is so exotic and bizarre, the case of a deceiving scientist lets one feel acutely the apparent irrationality in thinking oneself to *know*. But the exotic cases have no monopoly on generating feelings of irrationality.

[*Ordinary Cases*] [1.] If you are planning a philosophical book and trying to estimate the energy you will spend on each of the several chapters, you might think that you *know* that it will not take much to write the *third* chapter. For the argument *there* may seem *already* so *clearly* outlined in your head. But experience may later seem to show that this argument is far from clear. And much time and effort may become absorbed with no clear fruits to show for it. In that case, you will, I suggest, feel somewhat embarrassed and foolish, even if there is no other person to whom your idea that you *knew* was ever communicated. If you just *believed*, or even if you were quite *confident* that this chapter would not take much effort to write, then, I suggest, you would not feel nearly so foolish or embarrassed, oftentimes not at all.

[2.] Again, you may think you *know* that a certain city is the capital of a certain state, and you may feel quite content in this thought while watching another looking the matter up in the library. You will feel quite foolish, however, if the person announces the result to be *another* city, and if subsequent experience seems to show that announcement to be right. This will occur, I suggest, even if you are just an anonymous, disinterested bystander who happens to hear the question posed and the answer later announced. This is true even if the reference was a newspaper, *The Times*, and the capital was changed only yesterday. But these feelings will be very much less apparent, or will not occur at all, if you only feel very confident, at the outset, that the city is thus-and-such, which later is not announced. You might of course feel that you shouldn't be quite so confident of such things, or that you should watch out in the future. But you probably *wouldn't* feel, I suggest, that you were *irrational* to be confident of that thing at that time. Much less would you feel that you were *dogmatic* in so being.

[3.] Finally, if you *positively asserted* something to another in a conversation, as though reporting a *known fact*, later contrary experiences might well cause you to feel that you had overstepped the bounds of good sense and rationality. The feeling is that you have manifested a trait of a dogmatic personality. If you happen to be right, your extremely positive approach is not likely to be questioned. In case subsequent events seem to indicate you are wrong about the matter, then you come in for a severe judgement, whether or not this judgement is ever made out loud. This is a rather familiar social experience. (As I say this, even in trying to make my style a little less cautious, to be readable, I leave myself open to just such a judgement by putting the matter in such a positive, unqualified way.) I suggest that such feelings *ought* to be far *more* familiar, occurring even where you are *right* about the matter. They *should not* just occur where you are in fact wrong about things. Accordingly, we should avoid making these claims in *any* case, whether we be right or whether wrong in the matter, e.g., of which city is the capital of that state.

It is hard for us to think that there is any important similarity between such common cases as these and the case of someone thinking himself to *know* that *there are rocks*. Exotic contrast cases, like the case of the evil scientist, help one to appreciate that these cases are really essentially the same. By means of contrast cases, we encourage thinking of all sorts of new sequences of experience, sequences which people would never begin to imagine in the normal course of affairs. How would you react to such developments as *these*, no matter *how* exotic or unlikely? It appears that the proper reaction is to feel as irrational about claiming knowledge of rocks as you felt before, where, e.g., one was apparently caught in thought by the library reference to the state's capital. Who would have thought so, before thinking of contrast cases? Those cases help you see, I suggest, that in *either* case, no matter whether you are in fact right in the matter or whether wrong, thinking that you *know* manifests an attitude of dogmatism. Bizarre experiential sequences help show that there is no essential difference between any two external matters; the apparently most certain ones, like that of rocks, and the ones where thinking about *knowing* appears, even without the most exotic skeptical aids, *not* the way to think.

2 / A Critique of Skepticism

JOHN HOSPERS

John Hospers (1918–   ) taught at the University of Southern California and was for many years the director of the USC School of Philosophy. He is a wide-ranging philosopher and political theorist, who also works in aesthetics, ethics, and theory of knowledge. He is one of the founders of the modern Libertarian movement, as well as one of its most original philosophers.

I. REQUIREMENTS FOR KNOWING

*T*he word "know" is slippery. It is not always used in the same way. Here are some of its principal uses:

[*Senses of "know"*] 1. Sometimes when we talk about knowing, we are referring to *acquaintance* of some kind. For example, "Do you know Richard Smith?" means approximately the same as "Are you acquainted with Richard Smith? (have you met him? etc.) . . . "

2. Sometimes we speak of knowing *how*: Do you know how to ride a horse, do you know how to use a soldering iron? We even use a colloquial noun, "know-how," in talking about this. Knowing how is an *ability*—we know how to ride a horse if we have the ability to ride a horse, and the test of whether we have the ability is whether in the appropriate situation we can perform the activity in question. . . .

3. But by far the most frequent use of the word "know"—and the one with which we shall be primarily concerned—is the *propositional* sense: "I know that . . . " where the word "that" is followed by a proposition: "I know that I am now reading a book," "I know that I am an American citizen," and so on. There is some relation between this last sense of "know" and the earlier ones. We cannot be acquainted with Smith without knowing some things about him (without knowing *that* certain propositions about him are true), and it is difficult to see how one can know *how* to swim without knowing some true propositions about swimming, concerning what you must do with your arms and legs when in the water. (But the dog knows how to swim, though presumably he knows no propositions about swimming.) . . .

[*Conditions for knowing that*] Now, what is required for us to know in this third and most important sense? Taking the letter *p* to stand for any proposition, what requirements must be met in order for one to assert truly that he knows *p*? There are, after all, many people who claim to know something

36

when they don't; so how can one separate the rightful claims to know from the mistaken ones?

a. *p must be true.* The moment you have some reason to believe that a proposition is not true, this immediately negates a person's claim to know it: You can't know *p* if *p* isn't true. If I say, "I know *p*, but *p* is not true," my statement is self-contradictory,* for part of what is involved in knowing *p* is that *p* is true. Similarly, if I say, "He knows *p*, but *p* is not true," this too is self-contradictory. It may be that I *thought* I knew *p*; but if *p* is false, I didn't really know it. I only thought I did. If I nevertheless claim to know *p*, while admitting that *p* is false, my hearers may rightly conclude that I have not yet learned how to use the word "know." This is already implicit in our previous discussion, for what is it that you know about *p* when you know *p*? You know *that p is true*, of course; the very formulation gives away the case: Knowing *p* is knowing that *p* is true. . . .

But the truth-requirement, though necessary, is not sufficient. There are plenty of true propositions, for example in nuclear physics, that you and I do not know to be true unless we happen to be specialists in that area. But the fact that they are true does not imply that we know them to be true. . . .

b. *Not only must p be true: We must believe that p is true.* This may be called the "subjective requirement": We must have a certain attitude toward *p*—not merely that of wondering or speculating about *p*, but positively *believing* that *p* is true. "I know that *p* is true, but I don't believe that it is" would not only be a very peculiar thing to say, it would entitle our hearers to conclude that we had not learned in what circumstances to use the word "know." There may be numerous statements that you believe but do not know to be true, but there can be none which you know to be true but don't believe, since believing is a part (a defining characteristic) of knowing.

"I know *p*" implies "I believe *p*," and "He knows *p*" implies "He believes *p*," for believing is a defining characteristic of knowing. But believing *p* is *not* a defining characteristic of *p's being true*: *p* can be true even though neither he nor I nor anyone else believes it. (The earth was round even before anyone believed that it was.) There is no contradiction whatever in saying, "He believed *p* (that is, believed it to be true), but *p* is not true." Indeed, we say things of this kind all the time: "He believes that people are persecuting him, but of course it isn't true." . . .

We have now discussed two requirements for knowing, an "objective" one (*p* must be true) and a "subjective" one (one must believe *p*). Are these sufficient? Can you be said to know something if you believe it and if what you believe is true? If so, we can simply define knowledge as true belief, and that will be the end of the matter.

Unfortunately, however, the situation is not so simple. True belief is not yet knowledge. A proposition may be true, and you may believe it to be true, and yet you may not *know* it to be true. Suppose you believe that there are

---

*[A self-contradictory statement is one which both simultaneously affirms something and denies it. Broadly, it is of the form, "*p* and not-*p*."—Eds.]

sentient beings on Mars, and suppose that in the course of time, after space-travelers from the earth have landed there, your belief turns out to be true. The statement was true at the time you uttered it, and you also believed it at the time you uttered it—but did you *know* it to be true at the time you uttered it? Certainly not, we would be inclined to say; you were not in a position to know. It was a lucky guess. Even if you had *some* evidence that it was true, you didn't *know* that it was true at the time you said it. Some further condition, therefore, is required to prevent a lucky guess from passing as knowledge. . . .

c. *You must have evidence for p (reason to believe p).* When you guessed which tosses of the coin would be heads, you had no reason to believe that your guesses would be correct, so you did not *know*. But after you watched all the tosses and carefully observed which way the coin tossed each time, then you knew. You had the evidence of your senses—as well as of people around you, and photographs if you wished to take them—that this throw was heads, that one tails, and so on. Similarly, when you predict on the basis of tonight's red sunset that tomorrow's weather will be fair, you don't yet *know* that your prediction will be borne out by the facts; you have some reason (perhaps) to believe it, but you cannot be sure. But tomorrow when you go outdoors and see for yourself what the weather is like, you do know for sure; when tomorrow comes you have the full evidence before you, which you do not yet have tonight. Tomorrow the "evidence is in"; tonight, it is not knowledge but only an "educated guess."

[*Problem*] This, then is our third requirement—evidence. But at this point our troubles begin. How much evidence must there be? "Some evidence" won't suffice as an answer: there may be *some* evidence that tomorrow will be sunny, but you don't yet know it. How about "all the evidence that is available"? But this won't do either; all the evidence that is now available may not be enough. All the evidence that is now available is far from sufficient to enable us to know whether there are conscious beings on other planets. We just don't know, even after we have examined all the evidence at our disposal.

How about "enough evidence to give us *good reason* to believe it"? But how much evidence is this? I may have known someone for years and found him to be scrupulously honest during all that time; by virtually any criterion, this would constitute good evidence that he will be honest the next time—and yet he may not be; suppose that the next time he steals someone's wallet. I had good reason to believe that he would remain honest, but nevertheless I didn't *know* that he would remain honest, for it was not true. We are all familiar with cases in which someone had good reason to believe a proposition that nevertheless turned out to be false.

What then *is* sufficient? We are now tempted to say, "Complete evidence—all the evidence there could ever be—the works, everything." But if we say this, let us notice at once that there are very few propositions whose truth we can claim to know. Most of those propositions that in daily life we claim to know without the slightest hesitation we would *not* know according to this criterion. For example, we say, "I know that if I were to let go of this pencil, it would fall," and we don't have the slightest hesitation about it; but although we may have excellent evidence (pencils and other objects have always fallen when let go), we don't have *complete* evidence, for we have not yet observed the outcome of letting go of it *this* time. To take an even more obvious case, we say, "I know that there is a book before me now," but we have not engaged in every possible observation that would be relevant to determining the truth of this statement: We have not examined the object (the one we take to be a book) from *all* angles (and since there are an infinite number of angles, who could?), and even if we have looked at it steadily for half an hour, we have not done so for a hundred hours, or a million; and yet it would *seem* (though some have disputed this, as we shall see) that if one observation provides evidence, a thousand observations should provide more evidence—and when could the accumulation of evidence end? . . .

We might, nevertheless, stick to our definition and say that we really do *not* know most of the propositions that in daily life we claim to know. Perhaps I don't *know* that this is a book before me, that I am now indoors and not outdoors, that I am now reading sentences written in the English language, or that there are any other people in the world. But this is a rather astounding claim and needs to be justified. We are all convinced that we know these things: We act on them every day of our lives, and if we were asked outside a philosophy classroom whether we knew them, we would say "yes" without hesitation. Surely we cannot accept a definition of "know" that would practically define knowledge out of existence? But if not, what alternative have we?

"Perhaps we don't have to go so far as to say 'all the evidence,' 'complete evidence,' and so on. All we have to say is that we must have *adequate* evidence." But when is the evidence adequate? Is anything less than "all the evidence there could ever be" adequate? "Well, adequate for enabling us to know." But this little addition to our definition lands us in a circle. We are trying to define "know," and we cannot in doing so employ the convenient phrase "enough to enable us to know"—for the last word in this definition is the very one we are trying to define. But once we have dropped the phrase "to know," we are left with our problem once more: How much evidence is adequate evidence? Is it adequate when anything less than *all* the evidence is in? If not all the evidence is in, but only 99.99 percent of it, couldn't that .01 percent go contrary to the rest of it and require us to conclude that the proposition might not be true after all, and that therefore we didn't know it? Surely it has happened often enough that a statement that we thought we knew, perhaps even would have staked our lives on, turned out in the end to be false, or just doubtful. But in that case we didn't really *know* it after all: The evidence was good, even overwhelming, but yet not good enough, not really adequate, for it was not enough to guarantee the truth of the proposition. Can we know *p* with anything less than *all* the evidence there ever could be for *p*?

II. STRONG AND WEAK SENSES OF "KNOW"

[*Disputes About Knowing*] In daily life we say we know—not just believe or surmise, but *know*—that heavier-than-air objects fall, that snow is white, that we can read and write, and countless other things. If someone denies this, and no fact cited by the one disputant suffices to convince the other, we may well suspect that there is a verbal issue involved: in this case, that they are operating on two different meanings of "know," because they construe the third requirement—the evidence requirement—differently.

[*Case 1*] Suppose I say, "There is a bookcase in my office," and someone challenges this assertion. I reply, "I *know* that there is a bookcase in my office. I put it there myself, and I've seen it there for years. In fact, I saw it there just two minutes ago when I took a book out of it and left the office to go into the classroom." Now suppose we both go to my office, take a look, and there is the bookcase, exactly as before. "See, I *knew* it was here," I say. "Oh no," he replies, "you *believed with good reason* that it was still there, because you had seen it there often before and you didn't see or hear anyone removing it. But you didn't *know* it was there when you said it, for at that moment you were in the classroom and not in your office."

At this point, I may reply, "But I did know it was there, even when I said it. I knew it because *(1) I believed it, (2) I had good grounds on which to base the belief, and (3) the belief was true*. And I would call it knowledge whenever these three conditions are fulfilled. This is the way we use the word 'know' every day of our lives. One knows those true propositions that one believes with good reason. And when I said the bookcase was still in my office, I was uttering one of those propositions."

But now my opponent may reply, "But you still didn't know it. You had good reason to say it, I admit, for you had not seen or heard anyone removing it. You had good reason, but not *sufficient* reason. The evidence you gave was still compatible with your statement being false—and if it was false, you of course did not *know* that it was true. [*Case 2*] Suppose that you had made your claim to knowledge, and I had denied your claim, and we had both gone into your office, and to your great surprise (and mine too) the bookcase was no longer there. Could you *then* have claimed to know that it was still there?"

"Of course not. The falsity of a statement always invalidates the claim to know it. If the bookcase had not been there, I would not have been entitled to say that I knew it was there; my claim would have been mistaken."

"Right—it would have been mistaken. But now please note that the only difference between the two cases is that in the first case the bookcase was there and in the second case it wasn't. *The evidence in the two cases was exactly the same.* You had exactly the same reason for saying that the bookcase was still there in the *second* case (when we found it missing) that you did in the *first* case (when we found it still there). And since you—as you yourself admit—didn't know it in the second case, you couldn't have known it in the first case either. You believed it with good reason, but you didn't *know* it."

[*Solution*] Here my opponent may have scored an important point; he may have convinced me that since I admittedly didn't know in the second case I couldn't have known in the first case either. But here I may make an important point in return: "My belief was the same in the two cases; the evidence was the same in the two cases (I had seen the bookcase two minutes before, had heard or seen no one removing it). The only difference was that in the first case the bookcase was there and in the second case it wasn't (*p* was true in the first case, false in the second). But *this doesn't show that I didn't know* in the first case. What it does show is that *although I might have been mistaken, I wasn't mistaken*. Had the bookcase not been there, I couldn't have claimed to know that it was; but since the bookcase in fact *was* still there, I *did* know, although (on the basis of the evidence I had) I *might* have been mistaken."

"Yes, it turned out to be true—you were lucky. But as we both agree, a lucky guess isn't the same as knowledge."

"But this wasn't just a lucky guess. I had excellent reasons for believing that the bookcase was still there. So the evidence requirement was fulfilled."

"No, it wasn't. You had good reason, excellent reason, but not *sufficient* reason—both times—for believing that the bookcase was still there. But in the second case it wasn't there, so you didn't know; therefore, in the first case where your evidence was *exactly the same*, you didn't know either; you just believed it with good reason, but that wasn't enough: your reason wasn't sufficient, and so you didn't *know*."

Now the difference in the criterion of knowing between the two disputants begins to emerge. According to me, I did know *p* in the first case because my belief was based on excellent evidence and was also true. According to my opponent, I did not know *p* in the first case because my evidence was still less than complete—I wasn't in the room seeing or touching the bookcase when I made the statement. It seems, then, that I am operating with a less demanding definition of "know" than he is. I am using "know" in the *weak* sense, in which I know a proposition when I believe it, have good reason for believing it, and it is true. But he is using "know" in a more demanding sense: He is using it in the *strong* sense, which requires that in order to know a proposition, it must be true, I must believe it, and I must have absolutely *conclusive* evidence in favor of it.

[*Examples*] Let us contrast these two cases:

> Suppose that after a routine medical examination the excited doctor reports to me that the X-ray photographs show that I have no heart. I should tell him to get a new machine. I should be inclined to say that the fact that I have a heart is one of the few things that I can count on as absolutely certain. I can feel it beat. I know it's there. Furthermore, how could my blood circulate if I didn't have one? Suppose that later on I suffer a chest injury and undergo a surgical operation. Afterwards the astonished surgeons solemnly declare that they searched my chest cavity and found no heart, and that they made incisions and looked about in other likely places but found it not. They are convinced that I am without a heart. They are unable to understand how circulation can occur or what accounts for the thumping in my chest. But they are in agreement and obviously sincere, and they have

clear photographs of my interior spaces. What would be my attitude? Would it be to insist that they were all mistaken? I think not. I believe that I should eventually accept their testimony and the evidence of the photographs. I should consider to be false what I now regard as an absolute certainty. [When I say I know I have a heart, I know it in the weak sense.]

Suppose that as I write this paper someone in the next room were to call out to me, "I can't find an ink-bottle; is there one in the house?" I should reply, "Here is an ink-bottle." If he said in a doubtful tone, "Are you sure? I looked there before," I should reply, "Yes, I know there is; come and get it."

Now could it turn out to be false that there is an ink-bottle directly in front of me on this desk? Many philosophers have thought so. They would say that many things could happen of such a nature that if they did happen it would be proved that I am deceived. I agree that many extraordinary things could happen, in the sense that there is no logical absurdity in the supposition. It could happen that when I next reach for this ink-bottle my hand should seem to pass *through* it and I should not feel the contact of any object. It could happen that in the next moment the ink-bottle will suddenly vanish from sight; or that I should find myself under a tree in the garden with no ink-bottle about; or that one or more persons should enter this room and declare with apparent sincerity that they see no ink-bottle on this desk; or that a photograph taken now of the top of the desk should clearly show all of the objects on it except the ink-bottle. Having admitted that these things *could happen,* am I compelled to admit that if they did happen, then it would be proved that there is no ink-bottle here *now?* Not at all. I could say that when my hand seemed to pass through the ink-bottle I should *then* be suffering from hallucination; that if the ink-bottle suddenly vanished, it would have miraculously ceased to exist; that the other persons were conspiring to drive me mad, or were themselves victims of remarkable concurrent hallucinations; that the camera possessed some strange flaw or that there was trickery in developing the negative: . . . Not only do I not *have* to admit that those extraordinary occurrences would be evidence that there is no ink-bottle here; the fact is that I *do not* admit it. There is nothing whatever that could happen in the next moment or the next year that would by me be called *evidence* that there is not an ink-bottle here now. No future experience or investigation could prove to me that I am mistaken. Therefore, if I were to say, "I know that there is an ink-bottle here," I should be using "know" in the strong sense.[1]

It is in the weak sense that we use the word "know" in daily life, as when I say I know that I have a heart, that if I let go of this piece of chalk it will fall, that the sun will rise tomorrow, and so on. I have excellent reason (evidence) to believe all these things, evidence so strong that (so we say) it amounts to certainty. And yet there are events that could conceivably occur which, if they did occur, would cast doubt on the beliefs or even show them to be false. . . .

III. ARGUMENT AGAINST SKEPTICISM

[*Skepticism*] But the philosopher is apt to be more concerned with "know" in the strong sense. He wants to inquire whether there are any propositions that we can know without the shadow of a doubt will never be proved false, or

[1]Norman Malcolm, "Knowledge and Belief," in *Knowledge and Certainty,* pp. 66–68.

even rendered dubious to the smallest degree. "You can say," he will argue, "and I admit that it would be good English usage to say, that you know that you have a heart and that the sun is more than 90 million miles from the earth. But you don't know it until you have absolutely conclusive evidence, and you must admit that the evidence you have, while very strong, is not conclusive. So I shall say, using 'know' in the strong sense, that you do not know these propositions. I want then to ask what propositions can be known in the strong sense, the sense that puts the proposition forever past the possibility of doubt."

And on this point many philosophers have been quite skeptical; they have granted few if any propositions whose truth we could know in the strong sense. . . . Such a person is a *skeptic*. We claim (he says) to know many things about the world, but in fact none of these propositions can be known for certain. What are we to say of the skeptic's position?

[*Criticism*] Let us first note that in the phrase "know for certain" the "for certain" is redundant—how can we know except for certain? If it is less than certain, how can it be knowledge? We do, however, use the word "certain" ambiguously: (1) Sometimes we say "I am certain," which just means that I have a feeling of certainty about it—"I feel certain that I locked the door of the apartment"—and of course the feeling of certainty is no guarantee that the statement is true. People have very strong feelings of certainty about many propositions that they have no evidence for at all, particularly if they want to believe them or are consoled by believing them. The phrase "feeling certain," then, refers simply to a psychological state, whose existence in no way guarantees that what the person feels certain about is true. But (2) sometimes when we say "I am certain" we mean that it *is* certain—in other words, that we *do* know the proposition in question to be true. This, of course, is the sense of "certain" that is of interest to philosophers (the first sense is of more interest to psychiatrists in dealing with patients). Thus we could reformulate our question, "Is anything certain?" or "Are any propositions certain?"

"I can well understand," one might argue, "how you could question some statements, even most statements. But if you carry on this merry game until you have covered *all* statements, you are simply mistaken, and I think I can show you why. You may see someone in a fog or in a bad light and not know (not be certain) whether he has a right hand. But don't you know that *you* have a right hand? There it is! Suppose I now raise my hand and say, 'Here is a hand.' Now you say to me, 'I doubt that there's a hand.' But what evidence do you want? What does your doubt consist of? You don't believe your eyes, perhaps? Very well, then come up and touch the hand. You still aren't satisfied? Then keep on looking at it steadily and touching it, photograph it, call in other people for testimony if you like. If after all this you still say it isn't certain, what more do you want? Under what conditions would you admit that it *is* certain, that you *do* know it? I can understand your doubt when there is some condition left unfulfilled, some test left uncompleted. At the beginning, perhaps you doubted that *if* you tried to touch my hand you would find anything there to touch; but then you did touch, and so you resolved *that* doubt. You resolved further doubts by calling in other people and so on. You performed all the relevant tests, and they turned out favorably. So now, at the end of the process, what is it that you doubt? Oh, I know what you *say*: 'I still doubt that that's a hand.' But isn't this saying 'I doubt' now an empty formula? I can no longer attach any content to that so-called doubt, for there is nothing left to doubt; you yourself *cannot specify any further test that, if performed, would resolve your doubt.* 'Doubt' now becomes an empty word. You're not doubting now that *if* you raised your hand to touch mine, you would touch it, or that *if* Smith and others were brought in, they would also testify that this is a hand—we've already gone through all that. So what is it specifically that you doubt? What possible test is there the negative result of which you fear? I submit that there isn't any. You are confusing a situation in which doubt is understandable (*before* you made the tests) with the later situation in which it isn't, for it has all been dispelled. . . .

"But your so-called doubt becomes meaningless when there is nothing left to doubt—when the tests have been carried out and their results are all favorable. Suppose a physician examines a patient and says, 'It's probable that you have an inflamed appendix.' Here one can still doubt, for the signs may be misleading. So the physician operates on the patient, finds an inflamed appendix and removes it, and the patient recovers. *Now* what would be the sense of the physician's saying, 'It's *probable* that he had an inflamed appendix'? If seeing it and removing it made it only *probable*, what would make it certain? Or you are driving along and you hear a rapid regular thumping sound and you say, 'It's probable that I have a flat tire.' So far you're right; it's only probable—the thumping might be caused by something else. So you go out and have a look, and there is the tire, flat. You find a nail embedded in it, change the tire, and then resume your ride with no more thumping. Are you *now* going to say, 'It's merely *probable* that the car had a flat tire'? But if given all those conditions it would be merely probable, what in the world would make it certain? Can you describe to me the circumstances in which you would say it's certain? If you can't, then the phrase 'being certain' has no meaning as you are using it. You are simply using it in such a special way that it has no application at all, and there is no reason at all why anyone else should follow your usage. In daily life we have a very convenient and useful distinction between the application of the words 'probable' and 'certain'. We say appendicitis is probable *before* the operation, but when the physician has the patient's appendix visible before him on the operating table, now it's certain—that's just the kind of situation in which we apply the word 'certain', as opposed to 'probable'. Now you, for some reason, are so fond of the word 'probable' that you want to use it for everything—you use it to describe *both* the preoperative and postoperative situations, and the word 'certain' is left without any application at all. But this is nothing but a *verbal manipulation* on your part. You have changed nothing; you have only taken, as it were, two bottles with different contents, and instead of labeling them differently ('probable' and 'certain'), as the rest of us do, you put the same label ('probable') on both of them! What possible advantage is there in this? It's just verbal contrariness. And since you have pre-empted the word 'probable' to cover *both* the situations, we now have to devise a *different* pair of words to mark the perfectly obvious distinction between the situation *before* the surgery and the situation *during* the surgery—the same difference we previously marked by the words 'probable' and 'certain' until you used the word 'probable' to apply to both of them. What gain is there in this *verbal manipulation* of yours?" . . .

3 / *Justification in Science*

CARL G. HEMPEL

Carl Hempel (1905–   ) has for many years been one of the most influential philosophers in the philosophy of science. His works on the concepts of explanation and reduction have been seminal influences on generations of philosophers. His defense of the so-called covering law model of explanation, according to which explanations of events involve deductions from laws and initial conditions, is so influential it is often called "the Hempelian model." His book Aspects of Scientific Explanation *contains many of his important papers.*

I. A CASE HISTORY AS AN EXAMPLE

*A*s a simple illustration of some important aspects of scientific inquiry, let us consider Semmelweis' work on childbed fever. Ignaz Semmelweis, a physician of Hungarian birth, did this work during the years from 1844 to 1848 at the Vienna General Hospital. As a member of the medical staff of the First Maternity Division in the hospital, Semmelweis was distressed to find that a large proportion of the women who were delivered of their babies in that division contracted a serious and often fatal illness known as puerperal fever or childbed fever. In 1844, as many as 260 out of 3,157 mothers in the First Division, or 8.2 percent, died of the disease; for 1845, the death rate was 6.8 percent, and for 1846, it was 11.4 percent. These figures were all the more alarming because in the adjacent Second Maternity Division of the same hospital, which accommodated almost as many women as the First, the death toll from childbed fever was much lower: 2.3, 2.0, and 2.7 percent for the same years. In a book that he wrote later on the causation and the prevention of childbed fever, Semmelweis describes his efforts to resolve the dreadful puzzle.[1]

He began by considering various explanations that were current at the time; some of these he rejected out of hand as incompatible with well-established facts; others he subjected to specific tests.

One widely accepted view attributed the ravages of puerperal fever to "epidemic influences," which were vaguely described as "atmospheric-cosmic-telluric changes" spreading over whole districts and causing childbed fever in women in confinement. But how, Semmelweis reasons, could such influences have plagued the First Division for years and yet spared the Second? And how could this view be reconciled with the fact that while the fever was raging in the hospital, hardly a case occurred in the city of Vienna or in its surroundings? A genuine epidemic, such as cholera, would not be so selective. Finally, Semmelweis notes that some of the women admitted to the First Division, living far from the hospital, had been overcome by labor on their way and had given birth in the street; yet despite these adverse conditions, the death rate from childbed fever among these cases of "street birth" was lower than the average for the First Division.

On another view, overcrowding was a cause of mortality in the First Division. But Semmelweis points out that in fact the crowding was heavier in the Second Division, partly as a result of the desperate efforts of patients to avoid assignment to the notorious First Division. He also rejects two similar conjectures that were current by noting that there were no differences between the two Divisions in regard to diet or general care of the patients.

In 1846, a commission appointed to investigate the matter attributed the prevalence of illness in the First Division to injuries resulting from rough examination by the medical students, all of whom received their obstetrical training in the First Division. Semmelweis notes in refutation of this view that (a) the injuries resulting naturally from the process of birth are much more extensive than those that might be caused by rough examination; (b) the midwives who received their training in the Second Division examined their patients in much the same manner but without the same ill effects; (c) when, in response to the commission's report, the number of medical students was halved and their examinations of the women were reduced to a minimum, the mortality, after a brief decline, rose to higher levels than ever before.

Various psychological explanations were attempted. One of them noted that the First Division was so arranged that a priest bearing the last sacrament to a dying woman had to pass through five wards before reaching the sickroom beyond. The appearance of the priest, preceded by an attendant ringing

[1]The story of Semmelweis' work and of the difficulties he encountered forms a fascinating page in the history of medicine. A detailed account, which includes translations and paraphrases of large portions of Semmelweis' writings, is given in W. J. Sinclair, *Semmelweis: His Life and His Doctrine* (Manchester, England: Manchester University Press, 1909). Brief quoted phrases in this chapter are taken from this work. The highlights of Semmelweis' career are recounted in the first chapter of P. de Kruif, *Men Against Death* (New York: Harcourt, Brace & World, Inc., 1932).

a bell, was held to have a terrifying and debilitating effect upon the patients in the wards and thus to make them more likely victims of childbed fever. In the Second Division, this adverse factor was absent, since the priest had direct access to the sickroom. Semmelweis decided to test this conjecture. He persuaded the priest to come by a roundabout route and without ringing of the bell, in order to reach the sick chamber silently and unobserved. But the mortality in the First Division did not decrease.

A new idea was suggested to Semmelweis by the observation that in the First Division the women were delivered lying on their backs; in the Second Division, on their side. Though he thought it unlikely, he decided "like a drowning man clutching at a straw" to test whether this difference in procedure was significant. He introduced the use of the lateral position in the First Division, but again, the mortality remained unaffected.

At last, early in 1847, an accident gave Semmelweis the decisive clue for his solution of the problem. A colleague of his, Kolletschka, received a puncture wound in the finger, from the scalpel of a student with whom he was performing an autopsy, and died after an agonizing illness during which he displayed the same symptoms that Semmelweis had observed in the victims of childbed fever. Although the role of microorganisms in such infections had not yet been recognized at the time, Semmelweis realized that "cadaveric matter," which the student's scalpel had introduced into Kolletschka's bloodstream, had caused his colleague's fatal illness. And the similarities between the course of Kolletschka's disease and that of the women in his clinic led Semmelweis to the conclusion that his patients had died of the same kind of blood poisoning. He, his colleagues, and the medical students had been the carriers of the infectious material, for he and his associates used to come to the wards directly from performing dissections in the autopsy room and examine the women in labor after only superficially washing their hands, which often retained a characteristic foul odor.

Again, Semmelweis put his idea to a test. He reasoned that if he were right, then childbed fever could be prevented by chemically destroying the infectious material adhering to the hands. He therefore issued an order requiring all medical students to wash their hands in a solution of chlorinated lime before making an examination. The mortality from childbed fever promptly began to decrease, and for the year 1848 it fell to 1.27 percent in the First Division, compared to 1.33 in the Second.

In further support of his idea, or of his *hypothesis*, as we will also say, Semmelweis notes that it accounts for the fact that the mortality in the Second Division consistently was so much lower: the patients there were attended by midwives, whose training did not include anatomical instruction by dissection of cadavers.

The hypothesis also explained the lower mortality among "street births": women who arrived with babies in arms were rarely examined after admission and thus had a better chance of escaping infection.

Similarly, the hypothesis accounted for the fact that the victims of childbed fever among the newborn babies were all among those whose mothers had contracted the disease during labor; for then the infection could be transmitted to the baby before birth, through the common bloodstream of mother and child, whereas this was impossible when the mother remained healthy.

Further clinical experiences soon led Semmelweis to broaden his hypothesis. On one occasion, for example, he and his associates, having carefully disinfected their hands, examined first a woman in labor who was suffering from a festering cervical cancer; then they proceeded to examine twelve other women in the same room, after only routine washing without renewed disinfection. Eleven of the twelve patients died of puerperal fever. Semmelweis concluded that childbed fever can be caused not only by cadaveric material, but also by "putrid matter derived from living organisms."

II. BASIC STEPS IN TESTING A HYPOTHESIS

We have seen how, in his search for the cause of childbed fever, Semmelweis examined various hypotheses that had been suggested as possible answers. How such hypotheses are arrived at in the first place is an intriguing question which we will consider later. First, however, let us examine how a hypothesis, once proposed, is tested.

Sometimes, the procedure is quite direct. Consider the conjectures that differences in crowding, or in diet, or in general care account for the difference in mortality between the two divisions. As Semmelweis points out, these conflict with readily observable facts. There are no such differences between the divisions; the hypotheses are therefore rejected as false.

But usually the test will be less simple and straightforward. Take the hypothesis attributing the high mortality in the First Division to the dread evoked by the appearance of the priest with his attendant. The intensity of that dread, and especially its effect upon childbed fever, are not as directly ascertainable as are differences in crowding or in diet, and Semmelweis uses an indirect method of testing. He asks himself: Are there any readily observable effects that should occur if the hypothesis were true? And he reasons: *If the hypothesis were true, then* an appropriate change in the priest's procedure should be followed by a decline in fatalities. He checks this implication by a simple experiment and finds it false, and he therefore rejects the hypothesis.

Similarly, to test his conjecture about the position of the women during delivery, he reasons: *If this conjecture should be true, then* adoption of the lateral position in the First Division will reduce the mortality. Again, the implication is shown false by his experiment, and the conjecture is discarded.

In the last two cases, the test is based on an argument to the effect that *if* the contemplated hypothesis, say *H*, is true, *then* certain observable events (e.g., decline in mortality) should occur under specified circumstances (e.g., if the priest refrains from walking through the wards, or if the women are delivered in lateral position); or briefly, if *H* is true, then so is *I*, where *I* is a statement describing the observable occurrences to be expected. For convenience, let us say that *I* is inferred from, or implied by, *H*; and let us call *I* a *test implication of the hypothesis H.*

In our last two examples, experiments show the test implication to be false, and the hypothesis is accordingly rejected. The reasoning that leads to the rejection may be schematized as follows:

> If *H* is true, then so is *I*.
> 2a]   But (as the evidence shows) *I* is not true.
> _____
> *H* is not true.

Any argument of this form, called *modus tollens* in logic, is deductively valid; that is, if its premises (the sentences above the horizontal line) are true, then its conclusion (the sentence below the horizontal line) is unfailingly true as well. Hence, if the premises of (2a) are properly established, the hypothesis *H* that is being tested must indeed be rejected.

Next, let us consider the case where observation or experiment bears out the test implication *I*. From his hypothesis that childbed fever is blood poisoning produced by cadaveric matter, Semmelweis infers that suitable antiseptic measures will reduce fatalities from the disease. This time, experiment shows the test implication to be true. But this favorable outcome does not conclusively prove the hypothesis true, for the underlying argument would have the form

> If *H* is true, then so is *I*.
> 2b]   (As the evidence shows) *I* is true.
> _____
> *H* is true.

And this mode of reasoning, which is referred to as the *fallacy of affirming the consequent*, is deductively invalid, that is, its conclusion may be false even if its premises are true. This is in fact illustrated by Semmelweis' own experience. The initial version of his account of childbed fever as a form of blood poisoning presented infection with cadaveric matter essentially as the one and only source of the disease; and he was right in reasoning that if this hypothesis should be true, then destruction of cadaveric particles by antiseptic washing should reduce the mortality. Furthermore, his experiment did show the test implication to be true. Hence, in this case, the premises of (2b) were both true. Yet, his hypothesis was false, for as he later discovered, putrid material from living organisms, too, could produce childbed fever.

Thus, the favorable outcome of a test, i.e., the fact that a test implication inferred from a hypothesis is found to be true, does not prove the hypothesis to be true. Even if many implications of a hypothesis have been borne out by careful tests, the hypothesis may still be false. The following argument still commits the fallacy of affirming the consequent:

If H is true, then so are $I_1, I_2, \ldots, I_n$.

2c]   (As the evidence shows) $I_1, I_2, \ldots, I_n$ are all true.

H is true.

This too, can be illustrated by reference to Semmelweis' final hypothesis in its first version. As we noted earlier, his hypothesis also yields the test implications that among cases of street births admitted to the First Division, mortality from puerperal fever should be below the average for the Division and that infants of mothers who escape the illness do not contract childbed fever; and these implications, too, were borne out by the evidence—even though the first version of the final hypothesis was false.

But the observation that a favorable outcome of however many tests does not afford conclusive proof for a hypothesis should not lead us to think that if we have subjected a hypothesis to a number of tests and all of them have had a favorable outcome, we are no better off than if we had not tested the hypothesis at all. For each of our tests might conceivably have had an unfavorable outcome and might have led to the rejection of the hypothesis. A set of favorable results obtained by testing different test implications, $I_1, I_2, \ldots, I_n$, of a hypothesis, shows that as far as these particular implications are concerned, the hypothesis has been borne out; and while this result does not afford a complete proof of the hypothesis, it provides at least some support, some partial corroboration or confirmation for it. The extent of this support will depend on various aspects of the hypothesis and of the test data.

Let us now consider another example,[2] which will also bring to our attention some further aspects of scientific inquiry.

As was known at Galileo's time, and probably much earlier, a simple suction pump, which draws water from a well by means of a piston that can be raised in the pump barrel, will lift water no higher than about 34 feet above the surface of the well. Galileo was intrigued by this limitation and suggested an explanation for it, which was, however, unsound. After Galileo's death, his pupil Torricelli advanced a new answer. He argued that the earth is surrounded by a sea of air, which, by reason of its weight, exerts pressure upon the surface below and that this pressure upon the surface of the well forces water up the pump barrel when the piston is raised. The maximum length of 34 feet for the water column in the barrel thus reflects simply the total pressure of the atmosphere upon the surface of the well.

It is evidently impossible to determine by direct inspection or observation whether this account is correct, and Torricelli tested it indirectly. He reasoned that *if* his conjecture were true, *then* the pressure of the atmosphere

[2]The reader will find a fuller account of this example in Chap. 4 of J. B. Conant's fascinating book, *Science and Common Sense* (New Haven: Yale University Press, 1951). A letter by Torricelli setting forth his hypothesis and his test of it and an eyewitness report on the Puy-de-Dôme experiment are reprinted in W. F. Magie, *A Source Book in Physics* (Cambridge: Harvard University Press, 1963), pp. 70–75.

should also be capable of supporting a proportionately shorter column of mercury; indeed, since the specific gravity of mercury is about 14 times that of water, the length of the mercury column should be about 34/14 feet, or slightly less than 2½ feet. He checked this test implication by means of an ingeniously simple device, which was, in effect, the mercury barometer. The well of water is replaced by an open vessel containing mercury; the barrel of the suction pump is replaced by a glass tube sealed off at one end. The tube is completely filled with mercury and closed by placing the thumb tightly over the open end. It is then inverted, the open end is submerged in the mercury well, and the thumb is withdrawn, whereupon the mercury column in the tube drops until its length is about 30 inches—just as predicted by Torricelli's hypothesis.

A further test implication of that hypothesis was noted by Pascal, who reasoned that if the mercury in Torricelli's barometer is counterbalanced by the pressure of the air above the open mercury well, then its length should decrease with increasing altitude, since the weight of the air overhead becomes smaller. At Pascal's request, this implication was checked by his brother-in-law, Périer, who measured the length of the mercury column in the Torricelli barometer at the foot of the Puy-de-Dôme, a mountain some 4,800 feet high, and then carefully carried the apparatus to the top and repeated the measurement there while a control barometer was left at the bottom under the supervision of an assistant. Périer found the mercury column at the top of the mountain more than three inches shorter than at the bottom, whereas the length of the column in the control barometer had remained unchanged throughout the day.

III. THE ROLE OF INDUCTION IN SCIENTIFIC INQUIRY

We have considered some scientific investigations in which a problem was tackled by proposing tentative answers in the form of hypotheses that were then tested by deriving from them suitable test implications and checking these by observation or experiment.

But how are suitable hypotheses arrived at in the first place? It is sometimes held that they are inferred from antecedently collected data by means of a procedure called *inductive inference*, as contradistinguished from deductive inference, from which it differs in important respects.

In a deductively valid argument, the conclusion is related to the premisses in such a way that if the premisses are true, then the conclusion cannot fail to be true as well. This requirement is satisfied, for example, by any argument of the following general form:

If p, then q.
It is not the case that q.
_____

It is not the case that p.

Brief reflection shows that no matter what particular statements may stand at the places marked by the letters '*p*' and '*q*', the conclusion will certainly be true if the premisses are. In fact, our schema represents the argument form called *modus tollens*, to which we referred earlier.

Another type of deductively valid inference is illustrated by this example:

> Any sodium salt, when put into the flame of a Bunsen burner, turns the flame yellow.
> This piece of rock salt is a sodium salt.
>
> ---
>
> This piece of rock salt, when put into the flame of a Bunsen burner, will turn the flame yellow.

Arguments of the latter kind are often said to lead from the general (here, the premiss about all sodium salts) to the particular (a conclusion about the particular piece of rock salt). Inductive inferences, by contrast, are sometimes described as leading from premisses about particular cases to a conclusion that has the character of a general law or principle. For example, from premisses to the effect that each of the particular samples of various sodium salts that have so far been subjected to the Bunsen flame test did turn the flame yellow, inductive inference supposedly leads to the general conclusion that all sodium salts, when put into the flame of a Bunsen burner, turn the flame yellow. But in this case, the truth of the premisses obviously does *not* guarantee the truth of the conclusion; for even if it is the case that all samples of sodium salts examined so far did turn the Bunsen flame yellow, it remains quite possible that new kinds of sodium salt might yet be found that do not conform to this generalization. Indeed, even some kinds of sodium salt that have already been tested with positive result might conceivably fail to satisfy the generalization under special physical conditions (such as very strong magnetic fields or the like) in which they have not yet been examined. For this reason, the premisses of an inductive inference are often said to imply the conclusion only with more or less high probability, whereas the premisses of a deductive inference imply the conclusion with certainty.

The idea that in scientific inquiry, inductive inference from antecedently collected data leads to appropriate general principles is clearly embodied in the following account of how a scientist would ideally proceed:

> If we try to imagine how a mind of superhuman power and reach, but normal so far as the logical processes of its thought are concerned, . . . would use the scientific method, the process would be as follows: First, all facts would be observed and recorded, *without selection* or *a priori* guess as to their relative importance. Secondly, the observed and recorded facts would be analyzed, compared, and classified, *without hypothesis or postulates* other than those necessarily involved in the logic of thought. Third, from this analysis of the facts generalizations would be inductively drawn as to the relations, classificatory or causal, between them.

Fourth, further research would be deductive as well as inductive, employing inferences from previously established generalizations.[3]

This passage distinguishes four stages in an ideal scientific inquiry: (1) observation and recording of all facts, (2) analysis and classification of these facts, (3) inductive derivation of generalizations from them, and (4) further testing of the generalizations. The first two of these stages are specifically assumed not to make use of any guesses or hypotheses as to how the observed facts might be interconnected; this restriction seems to have been imposed in the belief that such preconceived ideas would introduce a bias and would jeopardize the scientific objectivity of the investigation.

But the view expressed in the quoted passage—I will call it *the narrow inductivist conception of scientific inquiry*—is untenable, for several reasons. A brief survey of these can serve to amplify and to supplement our earlier remarks on scientific procedure.

First, a scientific investigation as here envisaged could never get off the ground. Even its first phase could never be carried out, for a collection of *all* the facts would have to await the end of the world, so to speak; and even all the facts *up to now* cannot be collected, since there are an infinite number and variety of them. Are we to examine, for example, all the grains of sand in all the deserts and on all the beaches, and are we to record their shapes, their weights, their chemical composition, their distances from each other, their constantly changing temperature, and their equally changing distance from the center of the moon? Are we to record the floating thoughts that cross our minds in the tedious process? The shapes of the clouds overhead, the changing color of the sky? The construction and the trade name of our writing equipment? Our own life histories and those of our fellow investigators? All these, and untold other things, are, after all, among "all the facts up to now."

Perhaps, then, all that should be required in the first phase is that all the *relevant* facts be collected. But relevant to what? Though the author does not mention this, let us suppose that the inquiry is concerned with a specified *problem*. Should we not then begin by collecting all the facts—or better, all available data—relevant to that problem? This notion still makes no clear sense. Semmelweis sought to solve one specific problem, yet he collected quite different kinds of data at different stages of his inquiry. And rightly so; for what particular sorts of data it is reasonable to collect are not determined by the problem under study, but by a tentative answer to it that the investigator entertains in the form of a conjecture or hypothesis. Given the conjecture that mortality from childbed fever was increased by the terrifying appearance of the priest and his attendant with the death bell, it was relevant to collect data on the consequences of having the priest change his routine; but it would have been totally irrelevant to check what would happen if doctors and students disinfected their hands before examining their patients. With respect to

[3]A. B. Wolfe, "Functional Economics," in *The Trend of Economics*, ed. R. G. Tugwell (New York: Alfred A. Knopf, Inc., 1924), p. 450 (italics are quoted).

Semmelweis' eventual contamination hypothesis, data of the latter kind were clearly relevant, and those of the former kind totally irrelevant.

Empirical "facts" or findings, therefore, can be qualified as logically relevant or irrelevant only in reference to a given hypothesis, but not in reference to a given problem.

Suppose now that a hypothesis H has been advanced as a tentative answer to a research problem: What kinds of data would be relevant to H? Our earlier examples suggest an answer: A finding is relevant to H if either its occurrence or its nonoccurrence can be inferred from H. Take Torricelli's hypothesis, for example. As we saw, Pascal inferred from it that the mercury column in a barometer should grow shorter if the barometer were carried up a mountain. Therefore, any finding to the effect that this did indeed happen in a particular case is relevant to the hypotheses; but so would be the finding that the length of the mercury column had remained unchanged or that it had decreased and then increased during the ascent, for such findings would refute Pascal's test implication and would thus disconfirm Torricelli's hypothesis. Data of the former kind may be called positively, or favorably, relevant to the hypothesis; those of the latter kind negatively, or unfavorably, relevant.

In sum, the maxim that data should be gathered without guidance by antecedent hypotheses about the connections among the facts under study is self-defeating, and it is certainly not followed in scientific inquiry. On the contrary, tentative hypotheses are needed to give direction to a scientific investigation. Such hypotheses determine, among other things, what data should be collected at a given point in a scientific investigation.

It is of interest to note that social scientists trying to check a hypothesis by reference to the vast store of facts recorded by the U.S. Bureau of the Census, or by other data-gathering organizations, sometimes find to their disappointment that the values of some variable that plays a central role in the hypothesis have nowhere been systematically recorded. This remark is not, of course, intended as a criticism of data gathering. Those engaged in the process no doubt try to select facts that might prove relevant to future hypotheses. The observation is simply meant to illustrate the impossibility of collecting "all the relevant data" without knowledge of the hypotheses to which the data are to have relevance.

The second stage envisaged in our quoted passage is open to similar criticism. A set of empirical "facts" can be analyzed and classified in many different ways, most of which will be unilluminating for the purposes of a given inquiry. Semmelweis could have classified the women in the maternity wards according to criteria such as age, place of residence, marital status, dietary habits, and so forth; but information on these would have provided no clue to a patient's prospects of becoming a victim of childbed fever. What Semmelweis sought were criteria that would be significantly connected with those prospects; and for this purpose, as he eventually found, it was illuminating to single out those women who were attended by medical personnel with contaminated hands, for it was with this characteristic, or with the corresponding class of patients, that high mortality from childbed fever was associated.

Thus, if a particular way of analyzing and classifying empirical findings is to lead to an explanation of the phenomena concerned, then it must be based on hypotheses about how those phenomena are connected; without such hypotheses, analysis and classification are blind.

Our critical reflections on the first two stages of inquiry as envisaged in the quoted passage also undercut the notion that hypotheses are introduced only in the third stage, by inductive inference from antecedently collected data. But some further remarks on the subject should be added here.

Induction is sometimes conceived as a method that leads, by means of mechanically applicable rules, from observed facts to corresponding general principles. In this case, the rules of inductive inference would provide effective canons of scientific discovery; induction would be a mechanical procedure analogous to the familiar routine for the multiplication of integers, which leads, in a finite number of predetermined and mechanically performable steps, to the corresponding product. Actually, however, no such general and mechanical induction procedure is available at present; otherwise, the much-studied problem of the causation of cancer, for example, would hardly have remained unsolved to this day. Nor can the discovery of such a procedure ever be expected. For—to mention one reason—scientific hypotheses and theories are usually couched in terms that do not occur at all in the description of the empirical findings on which they rest and which they serve to explain. For example, theories about the atomic and subatomic structure of matter contain terms such as 'atom', 'electron', 'proton', 'neutron', 'psi-function', etc.; yet they are based on laboratory findings about the spectra of various gases, tracks in cloud and bubble chambers, quantitative aspects of chemical reactions, and so forth—all of which can be described without the use of those "theoretical terms." Induction rules of the kind here envisaged would therefore have to provide a mechanical routine for constructing, on the basis of the given data, a hypothesis or theory stated in terms of some quite novel concepts, which are nowhere used in the description of the data themselves. Surely, no general mechanical rule of procedure can be expected to achieve this. Could there be a general rule, for example, which, when applied to the data available to Galileo concerning the limited effectiveness of suction pumps, would, by a mechanical routine, produce a hypothesis based on the concept of a sea of air?

To be sure, mechanical procedures for inductively "inferring" a hypothesis on the basis of given data may be specifiable for situations of special, and relatively simple, kinds. For example, if the length of a copper rod has been measured at several different temperatures, the resulting pairs of associated values for temperature and length may be represented by points in a plane coordinate system, and a curve may be drawn through them in accordance with some particular rule of curve fitting. The curve then graphically represents a general quantitative hypothesis that expresses the length of the rod as a specific function of its temperature. But note that this hypothesis contains no novel terms; it is expressible in terms of the concepts of temperature and length, which are used also in describing the data. Moreover, the choice of "associated" values of temperature and length as data already presupposes a guiding hypothesis; namely, that with each value of the temperature, exactly one value of the length of the copper rod is associated, so that its length is indeed a function of its temperature alone. The mechanical curve-fitting routine then serves only to select a particular function as the appropriate one. This point is important; for suppose that instead of a copper rod, we examine a body of nitrogen gas enclosed in a cylindrical container with a movable piston as a lid and that we measure its volume at several different temperatures. If we were to use this procedure in an effort to obtain from our data a *general* hypothesis representing the volume of the gas as a function of its temperature, we would fail, because the volume of a gas is a function both of its temperature and of the pressure exerted upon it, so that at the same temperature, the given gas may assume different volumes.

Thus, even in these simple cases, the mechanical procedures for the construction of a hypothesis do only part of the job, for they presuppose an antecedent, less specific hypothesis (i.e., that a certain physical variable is a function of one single other variable), which is not obtainable by the same procedure.

There are, then, no generally applicable "rules of induction" by which hypotheses or theories can be mechanically derived or inferred from empirical data. The transition from data to theory requires creative imagination. Scientific hypotheses and theories are not *derived* from observed facts, but *invented* in order to account for them. They constitute guesses at the connections that might obtain between the phenomena under study, at uniformities and patterns that might underlie their occurrence. "Happy guesses"[4] of this kind require great ingenuity, especially if they involve a radical departure from current modes of scientific thinking, as did, for example, the theory of relativity and quantum theory. The inventive effort required in scientific research will benefit from a thorough familiarity with current knowledge in the field. A complete novice will hardly make an important scientific discovery, for the ideas that may occur to him are likely to duplicate what has been tried before or to run afoul of well-established facts or theories of which he is not aware.

Nevertheless, the ways in which fruitful scientific guesses are arrived at are very different from any process of systematic inference. The chemist

---

[4]This characterization was given already by William Whewell in his work *The Philosophy of the Inductive Sciences*, 2nd ed. (London: John W. Parker, 1847); II, 41. Whewell also speaks of "invention" as "part of induction" (p. 46). In the same vein, K. Popper refers to scientific hypotheses and theories as "conjectures"; see, for example, the essay "Science: Conjectures and Refutations" in his book *Conjectures and Refutations* (New York and London: Basic Books, 1962). Indeed, A. B. Wolfe, whose narrowly inductivist conception of ideal scientific procedure was quoted earlier, stresses that "the limited human mind" has to use "a greatly modified procedure," requiring scientific imagination and the selection of data on the basis of some "working hypothesis" (p. 450 of the essay cited in note 3).

Kekulé, for example, tells us that he had long been trying unsuccessfully to devise a structural formula for the benzene molecule when, one evening in 1865, he found a solution to his problem while he was dozing in front of his fireplace. Gazing into the flames, he seemed to see atoms dancing in snake-like arrays. Suddenly, one of the snakes formed a ring by seizing hold of its own tail and then whirled mockingly before him. Kekulé awoke in a flash. He had hit upon the now famous and familiar idea of representing the molecular structure of benzene by a hexagonal ring. He spent the rest of the night working out the consequences of this hypothesis.[5]

This last remark contains an important reminder concerning the objectivity of science. In his endeavor to find a solution to his problem, the scientist may give free rein to his imagination, and the course of his creative thinking may be influenced even by scientifically questionable notions. Kepler's study of planetary motion, for example, was inspired by his interest in a mystical doctrine about numbers and a passion to demonstrate the music of the spheres. Yet, scientific objectivity is safeguarded by the principle that while hypotheses and theories may be freely invented and *proposed* in science, they can be *accepted* into the body of scientific knowledge only if they pass critical scrutiny, which includes in particular the checking of suitable test implications by careful observation or experiment.

Interestingly, imagination and free invention play a similarly important role in those disciplines whose results are validated exclusively by deductive reasoning; for example, in mathematics. For the rules of deductive inference do not afford mechanical rules of discovery, either. As illustrated by our statement of *modus tollens* above, those rules are usually expressed in the form of general schemata, any instance of which is a deductively valid argument. If premises of the specified kind are given, such a schema does indeed specify a way of proceeding to a logical consequence. But for any set of premises that may be given, the rules of deductive inference specify an infinity of validly deducible conclusions. Take, for example, one simple rule represented by the following schema:

$$\frac{p}{p \text{ or } q}$$

It tells us, in effect, that from the proposition that p is the case, it follows that p or q is the case, where p and q may be any propositions whatever. The word 'or' is here understood in the "nonexclusive" sense, so that 'p or q' is tantamount to 'either p or q or both p and q'. Clearly, if the premiss of an argument of this type is true, then so must be the conclusion; hence, any argument of the specified form is valid. But this one rule alone entitles us to infer infinitely many different consequences from any one premiss. Thus, from 'the Moon

[5]Cf. the quotations from Kekulé's own report in A. Findlay, *A Hundred Years of Chemistry*, 2nd ed. (London: Gerald Duckworth & Co., 1948), p. 37; and W. I. B. Beveridge, *The Art of Scientific Investigation*, 3rd ed. (London: William Heinemann, Ltd., 1957), p. 56.

has no atmosphere', it authorizes us to infer any statement of the form 'the Moon has no atmosphere, or q', where for 'q' we may write any statement whatsoever, no matter whether it is true or false; for example, 'the Moon's atmosphere is very thin', 'the Moon is uninhabited', 'gold is denser than silver', 'silver is denser than gold', and so forth. (It is interesting and not difficult to prove that infinitely many different statements can be formed in English; each of these may be put in the place of the variable 'q'.) Other rules of deductive inference add, of course, to the variety of statements derivable from one premiss or set of premisses. Hence, if we are given a set of statements as premisses, the rules of deduction give no direction to our inferential procedures. They do not single out one statement as "the" conclusion to be derived from our premisses, nor do they tell us how to obtain interesting or systematically important conclusions; they provide no mechanical routine, for example, for deriving significant mathematical theorems from given postulates. The discovery of important, fruitful mathematical theorems, like the discovery of important, fruitful theories in empirical science, requires inventive ingenuity; it calls for imaginative, insightful guessing. But again, the interests of scientific objectivity are safeguarded by the demand for an *objective validation* of such conjectures. In mathematics, this means *proof* by deductive derivation from axioms. And when a mathematical proposition has been proposed as a conjecture, its proof or disproof still requires inventiveness and ingenuity, often of a very high caliber; for the rules of deductive inference do not even provide a general mechanical procedure for constructing proofs or disproofs. Their systematic role is rather the modest one of serving as *criteria of soundness for arguments* offered as proofs; an argument will constitute a valid mathematical proof if it proceeds from the axioms to the proposed theorem by a chain of inferential steps, each of which is valid according to one of the rules of deductive inference. And to check whether a given argument is a valid proof in this sense is indeed a purely mechanical task.

Scientific knowledge, as we have seen, is not arrived at by applying some inductive inference procedure to antecedently collected data, but rather by what is often called "the method of hypothesis," i.e., by inventing hypotheses as tentative answers to a problem under study and then subjecting these to empirical test. It will be part of such test to see whether the hypothesis is borne out by whatever relevant findings may have been gathered before its formulation; an acceptable hypothesis will have to fit the available relevant data. Another part of the test will consist in deriving new test implications from the hypothesis and checking these by suitable observations or experiments. As we noted earlier, even extensive testing with entirely favorable results does not establish a hypothesis conclusively, but provides only more or less strong support for it. Hence, while scientific inquiry is certainly not inductive in the narrow sense we have examined in some detail, it may be said to be *inductive in a wider sense*, inasmuch as it involves the acceptance of hypotheses on the basis of data that afford no deductively conclusive evidence for it, but lend it only more or less strong "inductive support," or confirmation. And any "rules of induction" will have to be conceived, in analogy to the rules of deduction, as canons of validation rather than of discovery. Far from generating a hypothesis that accounts for given empirical findings, such rules will presuppose that both the empirical data forming the "premisses" of the "inductive argument" and a tentative hypothesis forming its "conclusion" are *given*. The rules of induction would then state criteria for the soundness of the argument. According to some theories of induction, the rules would determine the strength of the support that the data lend to the hypothesis, and they might express such support in terms of probabilities.

4 / *The Fixation of Belief*

CHARLES SANDERS PEIRCE

Charles Sanders (C. S.) Peirce (1839–1914) was an American philosopher and mathematician who is generally regarded as the founder of American Pragmatism. His influence on logic, philosophy of science, scientific reasoning, semiotics, and linguistics is still evident today. He was one of the most original thinkers that the United States has produced.

*W*e generally know when we wish to ask a question and when we wish to pronounce a judgment, for there is a dissimilarity between the sensation of doubting and that of believing.

But this is not all which distinguishes doubt from belief. There is a practical difference. Our beliefs guide our desires and shape our actions. The Assassins, or followers of the Old Man of the Mountain,* used to rush into death at his least command, because they believed that obedience to him would insure everlasting felicity. Had they doubted this, they would not have acted as they did. So it is with every belief, according to its degree. The feeling of believing is a more or less sure indication of there being established in our nature some habit which will determine our actions. Doubt never has such an effect.

Nor must we overlook a third point of difference. Doubt is an uneasy and dissatisfied state from which we struggle to free ourselves and pass into the state of belief; while the latter is a calm and satisfactory state which we do not wish to avoid, or to change to a belief in anything else. On the contrary, we

*[Members of a cult.—Eds.]

cling tenaciously, not merely to believing, but to believing just what we do believe.

Thus, both doubt and belief have positive effects upon us, though very different ones. Belief does not make us act at once, but puts us into such a condition that we shall behave in a certain way, when the occasion arises. Doubt has not the least effect of this sort, but stimulates us to action until it is destroyed. This reminds us of the irritation of a nerve and the reflex action produced thereby; while for the analogue of belief, in the nervous system, we must look to what are called nervous associations—for example, to that habit of the nerves in consequence of which the smell of a peach will make the mouth water.

The irritation of doubt causes a struggle to attain a state of belief. I shall term this struggle *inquiry*, though it must be admitted that this is sometimes not a very apt designation.

The irritation of doubt is the only immediate motive for the struggle to attain belief. It is certainly best for us that our beliefs should be such as may truly guide our actions so as to satisfy our desires; and this reflection will make us reject any belief which does not seem to have been so formed as to insure this result. But it will only do so by creating a doubt in the place of that belief. With the doubt, therefore, the struggle begins, and with the cessation of doubt it ends. Hence, the sole object of inquiry is the settlement of opinion. We may fancy that this is not enough for us, and that we seek not merely an opinion, but a true opinion. But put this fancy to the test, and it proves groundless; for as soon as a firm belief is reached we are entirely satisfied, whether the belief be false or true. And it is clear that nothing out of the sphere of our knowledge can be our object, for nothing which does not affect the mind can be a motive for a mental effort. The most that can be maintained is that we seek for a belief that we shall *think* to be true. But we think each one of our beliefs to be true, and, indeed, it is mere tautology to say so.

That the settlement of opinion is the sole end of inquiry is a very important proposition. It sweeps away, at once, various vague and erroneous conceptions of proof. A few of these may be noticed here.

1. Some philosophers have imagined that to start an inquiry it was only necessary to utter a question or set it down on paper, and have even recommended us to begin our studies with questioning everything! But the mere putting of a proposition into the interrogative form does not stimulate the mind to any struggle after belief. There must be a real and living doubt, and without this all discussion is idle.

2. It is a very common idea that a demonstration must rest on some ultimate and absolutely indubitable propositions. These, according to one school, are first principles of a general nature; according to another, are first sensations. But in point of fact, an inquiry, to have that completely satisfactory result called demonstration, has only to start with propositions perfectly free from all actual doubt. If the premises are not in fact doubted at all, they cannot be more satisfactory than they are.

3. Some people seem to love to argue a point after all the world is fully convinced of it. But no further advance can be made. When doubt ceases, mental action on the subject comes to an end; and if it did go on, it would be without a purpose.

[1. The Method of Tenacity /] If the settlement of opinion is the sole object of inquiry, and if belief is of the nature of a habit, why should we not attain the desired end by taking any answer to a question which we may fancy and constantly reiterating it to ourselves, dwelling on all which may conduce to that belief and learning to turn with contempt and hatred from anything which might disturb it? This simple and direct method is really pursued by many men. I remember once being entreated not to read a certain newspaper lest it might change my opinion upon free trade. "Lest I might be entrapped by its fallacies and misstatements," was the form of expression. "You are not," my friend said, "a special student of political economy. You might, therefore, easily be deceived by fallacious arguments upon the subject. You might, then, if you read this paper, be led to believe in protection. But you admit that free trade is the true doctrine; and you do not wish to believe what is not true." I have often known this system to be deliberately adopted. Still oftener, the instinctive dislike of an undecided state of mind, exaggerated into a vague dread of doubt, makes men cling spasmodically to the views they have already taken. The man feels that, if he only holds to his belief without wavering, it will be entirely satisfactory. Nor can it be denied that a steady and immovable faith yields great peace of mind. It may, indeed, give rise to inconveniences, as if a man should resolutely continue to believe that fire would not burn him, or that he would be eternally damned if he received his *ingesta* otherwise than through a stomach pump. But then the man who adopts this method will not allow that its inconveniences are greater than its advantages. He will say, "I hold steadfastly to the truth and the truth is always wholesome." And in many cases it may very well be that the pleasure he derives from his calm faith overbalances any inconveniences resulting from its deceptive character. Thus, if it be true that death is annihilation, then the man who believes that he will certainly go straight to heaven when he dies, provided he has fulfilled certain simple observances in this life, has a cheap pleasure which will not be followed by the least disappointment. A similar consideration seems to have weight with many persons in religious topics, for we frequently hear it said, "Oh, I could not believe so-and-so, because I should be wretched if I did." When an ostrich buries its head in the sand as danger approaches, it very likely takes the happiest course. It hides the danger, and then calmly says there is no danger; and if it feels perfectly sure there is none, why should it raise its head to see? A man may go through life systematically keeping out of view all that might cause change in his opinions, and if he only succeeds—basing his method, as he does, on two fundamental psychological laws—I do not see what can be said against his doing so. It would be an egotistical impertinence to object that his procedure is irrational, for that only amounts to saying that his method of settling belief is not ours. He does not propose to himself to be rational, and indeed, will often talk with scorn of man's weak and illusive reason. So let him think as he pleases.

But this method of fixing belief, which may be called the method of tenacity, will be unable to hold its ground in practice. The social impulse is against it. The man who adopts it will find that other men think differently from him, and it will be apt to occur to him in some saner moment that their opinions are quite as good as his own, and this will shake his confidence in belief. This conception, that another man's thought or sentiment may be equivalent to one's own, is a distinctly new step, and a highly important one. It arises from an impulse too strong in man to be suppressed without danger of destroying the human species. Unless we make ourselves hermits, we shall necessarily influence each other's opinions; so that the problem becomes how to fix belief, not in the individual merely, but in the community.

[2. The Method of Authority /] Let the will of the state act, then, instead of that of the individual. Let an institution be created which shall have for its object to keep correct doctrines before the attention of the people, to reiterate them perpetually, and to teach them to the young; having at the same time power to prevent contrary doctrines from being taught, advocated, or expressed. Let all possible causes of a change of mind be removed from men's apprehensions. Let them be kept ignorant, lest they should learn of some reason to think otherwise than they do. Let their passions be enlisted, so that they may regard private and unusual opinions with hatred and horror. Then let all men who reject the established belief be terrified into silence. Let the people turn out and tar-and-feather such men, or let inquisitions be made into the manner of thinking of suspected persons, and when they are found guilty of forbidden beliefs, let them be subjected to some signal punishment. When complete agreement could not otherwise be reached, a general massacre of all who have not thought in a certain way has proved a very effective means of settling opinions in a country. If the power to do this be wanting, let a list of opinions be drawn up, to which no man of the least independence of thought can assent, and let the faithful be required to accept all these propositions, in order to segregate them as radically as possible from the influence of the rest of the world.

This method has, from the earliest times, been one of the chief means of upholding correct theological and political doctrines, and of preserving their universal or catholic character. In Rome, especially, it has been practiced from the days of Numa Pompilius to those of Pius Nonus. This is the most perfect example in history; but wherever there is a priesthood—and no religion has been without one—this method has been more or less made use of. Wherever there is aristocracy, or a guild, or any association of a class of men whose interests depend or are supposed to depend on certain propositions, there will inevitably be found some traces of this natural product of social feeling. Cruelties always accompany this system; and when it is consistently carried out, they become atrocities of the most horrible kind in the eyes of any rational man. Nor should this occasion surprise, for the officer of a society does not feel justified in surrendering the interests of that society for the sake of mercy, as he might his own private interests. It is natural, therefore, that sympathy and fellowship should thus produce a most ruthless power.

In judging this method of fixing belief, which may be called the method of authority, we must, in the first place, allow its immeasurable mental and moral superiority to the method of tenacity. Its success is proportionally greater; and in fact it has over and over again worked the most majestic results. The mere structures of stone which it has caused to be put together, in Siam, for example, in Egypt, and in Europe—have many of them a sublimity hardly more than rivaled by the greatest works of Nature. And, except the geological epochs, there are no periods of time so vast as those which are measured by some of these organized faiths. If we scrutinize the matter closely, we shall find that there has not been one of their creeds which has remained always the same; yet the change is so slow as to be imperceptible during one person's life, so that individual belief remains sensibly fixed. For the mass of mankind, then, there is perhaps no better method than this. If it is their highest impulse to be intellectual slaves, then slaves they ought to remain.

[3. The *A Priori* Method /] But no institution can undertake to regulate opinions upon every subject. Only the most important ones can be attended to, and on the rest men's minds must be left to the action of natural causes. This imperfection will be no source of weakness so long as men are in such a state of culture that one opinion does not influence another—that is, so long as they cannot put two and two together. But in the most priest-ridden states some individuals will be found who are raised above that condition. These men possess a wider sort of social feeling; they see that men in other countries and in other ages have held to very different doctrines from those which they themselves have been brought up to believe; and they cannot help seeing that it is the mere accident of their having been taught as they have, and of their having been surrounded with the manners and associations they have, that has caused them to believe as they do and not far differently. And their candor cannot resist the reflection that there is no reason to rate their own views at a higher value than those of other nations and other centuries; and this gives rise to doubts in their minds.

They will further perceive that such doubts as these must exist in their minds with reference to every belief which seems to be determined by the caprice either of themselves or of those who originated the popular opinions. The willful adherence to a belief, and the arbitrary forcing of it upon others, must, therefore, both be given up and a new method of settling opinions must be adopted, which shall not only produce an impulse to believe, but shall also decide what proposition it is which is to be believed. Let the action of natural preferences be unimpeded, then, and under their influence let men conversing together and regarding matters in different lights gradually develop beliefs in harmony with natural causes. This method resembles that by which conceptions of art have been brought to maturity. The most perfect example of it is to be found in the history of metaphysical philosophy. Systems of this sort have not usually rested upon observed facts, at least not in any great degree. They have been chiefly adopted because their fundamental propositions seemed "agreeable to reason." This is an apt expression; it does not mean that which agrees with experience, but that which we find ourselves inclined to believe. Plato, for example, finds it agreeable to reason that the distances of the celestial spheres from one another should be proportional to the different lengths of strings which produce harmonious chords. Many philosophers have been led to their main conclusions by considerations like this; but this is the lowest and least developed form which the method takes, for it is clear that another man might find Kepler's (earlier) theory, that the celestial spheres are proportional to the inscribed and circumscribed spheres of the different regular solids, more agreeable to *his* reason. But the shock of opinions will soon lead men to rest on preferences of a far more universal nature. Take, for example, the doctrine that man only acts selfishly—that is, from the consideration that acting in one way will afford him more pleasure than acting in another. This rests on no fact in the world, but it has had a wide acceptance as being the only reasonable theory.

This method is far more intellectual and respectable from the point of view of reason than either of the others which we have noticed. But its failure has been the most manifest. It makes of inquiry something similar to the development of taste; but taste, unfortunately, is always more or less a matter of fashion, and accordingly, metaphysicians have never come to any fixed agreement, but the pendulum has swung backward and forward between a more material and a more spiritual philosophy, from the earliest times to the latest. And so from this, which has been called the *a priori* method, we are driven, in Lord Bacon's phrase, to a true induction. We have examined into this *a priori* method as something which promised to deliver our opinions from their accidental and capricious element. But development, while it is a process which eliminated the effect of some casual circumstances, only magnifies that of others. This method, therefore, does not differ in a very essential way from that of authority. The government may not have lifted its finger to influence my convictions; I may have been left outwardly quite free to choose, we will say, between monogamy and polygamy, and appealing to my conscience only, I may have concluded that the latter practice is in itself licentious. But when I come to see that the chief obstacle to the spread of Christianity among a people of as high culture as the Hindoos has been a conviction of the immorality of our way of treating women, I cannot help seeing that, though governments do not interfere, sentiments in their development will be very greatly determined by accidental causes. Now, there are some people, among whom I must suppose that my reader is to be found, who, when they see that any belief of theirs is determined by any circumstance extraneous to the facts, will from that moment not merely admit in words that that belief is doubtful, but will experience a real doubt of it, so that it ceases to be a belief.

[4. The Method of Science. /] To satisfy our doubts, therefore, it is necessary that a method should be found by which our beliefs may be caused by nothing human, but by some external permanency—by something upon which our thinking has no effect. Some mystics imagine that they have such a method in a private inspiration from on high. But that is only a form of the method of tenacity, in which the conception of truth as something public is not yet developed. Our external permanency would not be external, in our sense, if it was restricted in its influence to one individual. It must be something which affects, or might affect, every man. And, though these affections are necessarily as various as are individual conditions, yet the method must be such that the ultimate conclusion of every man shall be the same. Such is the method of science. Its fundamental hypothesis, restated in more familiar language, is this: There are real things, whose characters are entirely independent of our opinions about them; those realities affect our senses according to regular laws, and, though our sensations are as different as our relations to the objects, yet, by taking advantage of the laws of perception, we can ascertain by reasoning how things really are, and any man, if he has sufficient experience and reason enough about it, will be led to the one true conclusion. The new conception here involved is that of reality. It may be asked how I know that there are any realities. If this hypothesis is the sole support of my method of inquiry, my method of inquiry must not be used to support my hypothesis. The reply is this: (1) If investigation cannot be regarded as proving that there are real things, it at least does not lead to a contrary conclusion; but the method and the conception on which it is based remain ever in harmony. No doubts of the method, therefore, necessarily arise from its practice, as is the case with all the others. (2) The feeling which gives rise to any method of fixing belief is a dissatisfaction at two repugnant propositions. But here already is a vague concession that there is some *one* thing to which a proposition should conform. Nobody, therefore, can really doubt that there are realities, or if he did, doubt would not be a source of dissatisfaction. The hypothesis, therefore, is one which every mind admits. So the social impulse does not cause me to doubt it. (3) Everybody uses the scientific method about a great many things, and only ceases to use it when he does not know how to apply it. (4) Experience of the method has not led me to doubt it, but, on the contrary, scientific investigation has had the most wonderful triumphs in the way of settling opinion. These afford the explanation of my not doubting the method or the hypothesis which it supposes; and not having any doubt, nor believing that anybody else whom I could influence has, it would be the merest babble for me to say more about it. If there be anybody with a living doubt upon the subject, let him consider it. . . .

At present I have only room to notice some points of contrast between the method of scientific investigation and other methods of fixing belief.

This is the only one of the four methods which presents any distinction of a right and a wrong way. If I adopt the method of tenacity and shut myself out from all influences, whatever I think necessary to doing this is necessary according to that method. So with the method of authority: The state may try to put down heresy by means which, from a scientific point of view, seem very ill-calculated to accomplish its purposes; but the only test *on that method* is what the state thinks, so that it cannot pursue the method wrongly. So with the *a priori* method. The very essence of it is to think as one is inclined to think. . . . But with the scientific method the case is different. I may start with known and observed facts to proceed to the unknown; and yet the rules which I follow in doing so may not be such as investigation would approve. The test of whether I am truly following the method is not an immediate appeal to my feelings and purposes, but, on the contrary, itself involves the application of the method. Hence it is that bad reasoning as well as good reasoning is possible; and this fact is the foundation of the practical side of logic. . . .

5 / *The Ethics of Belief*

W. K. CLIFFORD

W. K. Clifford (1845–1879) was an English mathematician and philosopher. He wrote many works in the area of scientific knowledge and several popular essays. The (abridged) essay that follows is his most famous.

A ship-owner was about to send to sea an emigrant-ship. He knew that she was old, and not over-well built at the first; that she had seen many seas and climes, and often had needed repairs. Doubts had been suggested to him that possibly she was not seaworthy. These doubts preyed upon his mind and made him unhappy; he thought that perhaps he ought to have her thoroughly overhauled and refitted, even though this should put him to great expense. Before the ship sailed, however, he succeeded in overcoming these melancholy reflections. He said to himself that she had gone safely through so many voyages and weathered so many storms that it was idle to suppose she would not come safely home from this trip also. He would put his trust in Providence, which could hardly fail to protect all these unhappy families that were leaving their father-land to seek for better times elsewhere. He would dismiss from his mind all ungenerous suspicions about the honesty of builders and contractors. In such ways he acquired a sincere and comfortable conviction that his vessel was thoroughly safe and seaworthy; he watched her departure with a light heart, and benevolent wishes for the success of the exiles in their strange new home that was to be; and he got his insurance money when she went down in mid-ocean and told no tales.

[1.] What shall we say of him? Surely this, that he was verily guilty of the death of those men. It is admitted that he did sincerely believe in the soundness of his ship; but the sincerity of his conviction can in no wise help him, because *he had no right to believe on such evidence as was before him.* He had acquired his belief not by honestly earning it in patient investigation, but by stifling his doubts. And although in the end he may have felt so sure about it that he could not think otherwise, yet inasmuch as he had knowingly and willingly worked himself into that frame of mind, he must be held responsible for it.

[2.] Let us alter the case a little, and suppose that the ship was not unsound after all; that she made her voyage safely, and many others after it. Will that diminish the guilt of her owner? Not one jot. When an action is once done, it is right or wrong forever; no accidental failure of its good or evil fruits can possibly alter that. The man would not have been innocent, he would only have been not found out. The question of right or wrong has to do with the origin of his belief, not the matter of it; not what it was, but how he got it; not whether it turned out to be true or false, but whether he had a right to believe on such evidence as was before him.

[1, 2 cont.] There was once an island in which some of the inhabitants professed a religion teaching neither the doctrine of original sin nor that of eternal punishment. A suspicion got abroad that the professors of this religion had made use of unfair means to get their doctrines taught to children. They were accused of wresting the laws of their country in such a way as to remove children from the care of their natural and legal guardians; and even of stealing them away and keeping them concealed from their friends and relations. A certain number of men formed themselves into a society for the purpose of agitating the public about this matter. They published grave accusations against individual citizens of the highest position and character, and did all in their power to injure those citizens in the exercise of their profession. So great was the noise they made, that a Commission was appointed to investigate the facts; but after the Commission had carefully inquired into all the evidence that could be got, it appeared that the accused were innocent. Not only had they been accused on insufficient evidence, but the evidence of their innocence was such as the agitators might easily have obtained, if they had attempted a fair inquiry. After these disclosures the inhabitants of that country looked upon the members of the agitating society, not only as persons whose judgment was to be distrusted, but also as no longer to be counted honorable men. For although they had sincerely and conscientiously believed in the charges they had made, *yet they had no right to believe on such evidence as was before them.* Their sincere convictions, instead of being honestly earned by patient inquiring, were stolen by listening to the voice of prejudice and passion.

Let us vary this case also, and suppose, other things remaining as before, that a still more accurate investigation proved the accused to have been really guilty. Would this make any difference in the guilt of the accusers? Clearly not; the question is not whether their belief was true or false, but whether they entertained it on wrong grounds. They would no doubt say, "Now you see that we were right after all; next time perhaps you will believe us." And they might be believed, but they would not thereby become honorable men. They would not be innocent, they would only be not found out. Every one of them, if he chose to examine himself *in foro conscientiae*,* would know that he had acquired and nourished a belief, when he had no right to believe on such evidence as was before him; and therein he would know that he had done a wrong thing.

It may be said, however, that in both of these supposed cases it is not the belief which is judged to be wrong, but the action following upon it. The ship-owner might say, "I am perfectly certain that my ship is sound, but still I feel it my duty to have her examined, before trusting the lives of so many people to her." And it might be said to the agitator, "However convinced you were of the justice of your cause and the truth of your convictions, you ought not to have made a public attack upon any man's character until you had examined the evidence on both sides with the utmost patience and care."

In the first place, let us admit that, so far as it goes, this view of the case is right and necessary; right, because even when a man's belief is so fixed that he cannot think otherwise, he still has a choice in regard to the action suggested by it, and so cannot escape the duty of investigating on the ground of the strength of his convictions; and necessary, because those who are not yet capable of controlling their feelings and thoughts must have a plain rule dealing with overt acts.

But this being premised as necessary, it becomes clear that it is not sufficient, and that our previous judgment is required to supplement it. For it is not possible so to sever the belief from the action it suggests as to condemn the one without condemning the other. No man holding a strong belief on one side of a question, or even wishing to hold a belief on one side, can investigate it with such fairness and completeness as if he were really in doubt and unbiased; so that the existence of a belief not founded on fair inquiry unfits a man for the performance of this necessary duty.

[3.] Nor is that truly a belief at all which has not some influence upon the actions of him who holds it. He who truly believes that which prompts him to an action has looked upon the action to lust after it, he has committed it already in his heart. If a belief is not realized immediately in open deeds, it is stored up for the guidance of the future. It goes to make a part of that aggregate of beliefs which is the link between sensation and action at every moment of all our lives, and which is so organized and compacted together that no part of it can be isolated from the rest, but every new addition modifies the structure of the whole. No real belief, however trifling and fragmentary it may seem, is ever truly insignificant; it prepares us to receive more of its like, confirms those which resembled it before, and weakens others; and so gradually it lays a stealthy train in our inmost thoughts, which may some day explode into overt action, and leave its stamp upon our character forever.

*[In the forum of his conscience.—Eds.]

[4.] And no one man's belief is in any case a private matter which concerns himself alone. Our lives are guided by that general conception of the course of things which has been created by society for social purposes. Our words, our phrases, our forms and processes and modes of thought are common property, fashioned and perfected from age to age; an heirloom which every succeeding generation inherits as a precious deposit and a sacred trust to be handed on to the next one, not unchanged but enlarged and purified, with some clear marks of its proper handiwork. Into this, for good or ill, is woven every belief of every man who has speech of his fellows. An awful privilege, and an awful responsibility, that we should help to create the world in which posterity will live.

In the two supposed cases which have been considered, it has been judged wrong to believe on insufficient evidence, or to nourish belief by suppressing doubts and avoiding investigation. The reason of this judgment is not far to seek: It is that in both these cases the belief held by one man was of great importance to other men. But for as much as no belief held by one man, however seemingly trivial the belief, and however obscure the believer, is ever actually insignificant or without its effect on the fate of mankind, we have no choice but to extend our judgment to all cases of belief whatever. Belief, that sacred faculty which prompts the decisions of our will, and knits into harmonious working all the compacted energies of our being, is ours not for ourselves, but for humanity. It is rightly used on truths which have been established by long experience and waiting toil, and which have stood in the fierce light of free and fearless questioning. Then it helps to bind men together, and to strengthen and direct their common action. It is desecrated when given to unproved and unquestioned statements, for the solace and private pleasure of the believer; to add a tinsel splendor to the plain straight road of our life and display a bright mirage beyond it; or even to drown the common sorrows of our kind by a self-deception which allows them not only to cast down but also to degrade us. Whoso would deserve well of his fellows in this matter will guard the purity of his belief with a very fanaticism of jealous care, lest at any time it should rest on an unworthy object and catch a stain which can never be wiped away.

It is not only the leader of men, statesman, philosopher, or poet, that owes this bounden duty to mankind. Every rustic who delivers in the village alehouse his slow, infrequent sentences may help to kill or keep alive the fatal superstitions which clog his race. Every hard-worked wife of an artisan may transmit to her children beliefs which shall knit society together, or rend it in pieces. No simplicity of mind, no obscurity of station can escape the duty of questioning all that we believe.

It is true that this duty is a hard one, and the doubt which comes out of it is often a very bitter thing. It leaves us bare and powerless where we thought that we were safe and strong. To know all about anything is to know how to deal with it under all circumstances. We feel much happier and more secure when we think we know precisely what to do, no matter what happens, than when we have lost our way and do not know where to turn. And if we have supposed ourselves to know all about anything, and to be capable of doing what is fit in regard to it, we naturally do not like to find that we are really ignorant and powerless, that we have to begin again at the beginning, and try to learn what the thing is and how it is to be dealt with—if indeed anything can be learned about it. It is the sense of power attached to a sense of knowledge that makes men desirous of believing, and afraid of doubting.

This sense of power is the highest and best of pleasures when the belief on which it is founded is a true belief, and has been fairly earned by investigation. For then we may justly feel that it is common property, and holds good for others as well as for ourselves. Then we may be glad, not that *I* have learned secrets by which I am safer and stronger, but that *we men* have got mastery over more of the world; and we shall be strong, not for ourselves, but in the name of Man and in his strength. But if the belief has been accepted on insufficient evidence, the pleasure is a stolen one. Not only does it deceive ourselves by giving us a sense of power which we do not really possess, but it is sinful, because it is stolen in defiance of our duty to mankind. That duty is to guard ourselves from such beliefs as from a pestilence, which may shortly master our own body and then spread to the rest of the town. What would be thought of one who, for the sake of a sweet fruit, should deliberately run the risk of bringing a plague upon his family and his neighbors?

[5.] And, as in other such cases, it is not the risk only which has to be considered; for a bad action is always bad at the time when it is done, no matter what happens afterwards. Every time we let ourselves believe for unworthy reasons, we weaken our powers of self-control, of doubting, of judicially and fairly weighing evidence. We all suffer severely enough from the maintenance and support of false beliefs and the fatally wrong actions which they lead to, and the evil born when one such belief is entertained is great and wide. But a greater and wider evil arises when the credulous character is maintained and supported, when a habit of believing for unworthy reasons is fostered and made permanent. If I steal money from any person, there may be no harm done by the mere transfer of possession; he may not feel the loss, or it may prevent him from using the money badly. But I cannot help doing this great wrong toward Man, that I make myself dishonest. What hurts society is not that it should lose its property, but that it should become a den of thieves; for then it must cease to be society. This is why we ought not to do evil that good may come; for at any rate this great evil has come, that we have done evil and are made wicked thereby. In like manner, if I let myself believe anything on insufficient evidence, there may be no great harm done by the mere belief; it may be true after all, or I may never have occasion to exhibit it in outward acts. But I cannot help doing this great wrong toward Man, that I make myself credulous. The danger to society is not merely that it should believe wrong things, though that is great enough, but that it should become credulous, and lose the habit of testing things and inquiring into them; for then it must sink back into savagery.

The harm which is done by credulity in a man is not confined to the fostering of a credulous character in others, and consequent support of false beliefs. Habitual want of care about what I believe leads to habitual want of care in others about the truth of what is told to me. Men speak the truth to one another when each reveres the truth in his own mind and in the other's mind; but how shall my friend revere the truth in my mind when I myself am careless about it, when I believe things because I want to believe them, and because they are comforting and pleasant? Will he not learn to cry "Peace" to me, when there is no peace? By such a course I shall surround myself with a thick atmosphere of falsehood and fraud, and in that I must live. It may matter little to me, in my cloud-castle of sweet illusions and darling lies; but it matters much to Man that I have made my neighbors ready to deceive. The credulous man is father to the liar and the cheat; he lives in the bosom of this his family, and it is no marvel if he should become even as they are. So closely are our duties knit together, that whoso shall keep the whole law, and yet offend in one point, he is guilty of all.

To sum up: It is wrong always, everywhere, and for any one to believe anything upon insufficient evidence. . . .

"But," says one, "I am a busy man; I have no time for the long course of study which would be necessary to make me in any degree a competent judge of certain questions, or even able to understand the nature of the arguments." Then he should have no time to believe.

---

6 / *The Will to Believe*

WILLIAM JAMES

William James (1842–1910) attended Harvard University Medical School and for a short time taught physiology at Harvard. His interests expanded first to psychology and later to philosophy. He was influential as one of the main developers of a movement in philosophy known as Pragmatism. The (abridged) essay that follows is a direct attack on the view of W. K. Clifford.

. . . *L*et us give the name of *hypothesis* to anything that may be proposed to our belief; and just as the electricians speak of live and dead wires, let us speak of any hypothesis as either *live* or *dead*. A live hypothesis is one which appeals as a real possibility to him to whom it is proposed. If I ask you to believe in the Mahdi,* the notion makes no electric connection with your nature—it refuses to scintillate with any credibility at all. As an hypothesis it is completely dead. To an Arab, however (even if he be not one of the Mahdi's followers), the hypothesis is among the mind's possibilities: It is alive. This shows that deadness and liveness in an hypothesis are not intrinsic properties, but relations to the individual thinker. They are measured by his willingness to act. The maximum of liveness in an hypothesis means willingness to act irrevocably. Practically, that means belief; but there is some believing tendency wherever there is willingness to act at all.

Next, let us call the decision between two hypotheses an *option*. Options may be of several kinds. They may be (1) *living* or *dead*, (2) *forced* or *avoidable*, (3) *momentous* or *trivial*; and for our purposes we may call an option a *genuine* option when it is of the forced, living, and momentous kind.

1. A living option is one in which both hypotheses are live ones. If I say to you, "Be a theosophist† or be a Mohammedan," it is probably a dead option, because for you neither hypothesis is likely to be alive. But if I say, "Be an agnostic or be a Christian," it is otherwise: Trained as you are, each hypothesis makes some appeal, however small, to your belief.

2. Next, if I say to you, "Choose between going out with your umbrella or without it," I do not offer you a genuine option, for it is not forced. You can easily avoid it by not going out at all. Similarly, if I say, "Either love me or hate me," "Either call my theory true or call it false," your option is avoidable. You may remain indifferent to me, neither loving nor hating, and you may decline to offer any judgment as to my theory. But if I say, "Either accept this truth or go without it," I put on you a forced option, for there is no standing place outside of the alternative. Every dilemma based on a complete logical disjunction, with no possibility of not choosing, is an option of this forced kind.

3. Finally, if I were Dr. Nansen‡ and proposed to you to join my North Pole expedition, your option would be momentous; for this would probably be your only similar opportunity, and your choice now would either exclude you from the North Pole sort of immortality altogether or put at least the chance of it into your hands. He who refuses to embrace a unique opportunity loses the prize as surely as if he tried and failed. *Per contra,*§ the option is trivial when the opportunity is not unique, when the stake is insignificant, or when the decision is reversible if it later prove unwise. Such trivial options abound in the scientific life. A chemist finds an hypothesis live enough to spend a year in its verification: He believes in it to that extent. But if his experiments prove inconclusive either way, he is quit for his loss of time, no vital harm being done.

---

*[In Mohammedanism, an expected spiritual and temporal ruler.—Eds.]
†[Practitioner of a system of religious belief based largely on certain Eastern traditions, such as Buddhism.—Eds.]
‡[An explorer, a contemporary of James.—Eds.]
§[By contrast.—Eds.]

It will facilitate our discussion if we keep all these distinctions well in mind. . . .

The thesis I defend is, briefly stated, this: *Our passional nature not only lawfully may, but must, decide an option between propositions, whenever it is a genuine option that cannot by its nature be decided on intellectual grounds; for to say, under such circumstances, "Do not decide, but leave the question open," is itself a passional decision—just like deciding yes or no—and is attended with the same risk of losing the truth. . . .*

Wherever the option between losing truth and gaining it is not momentous, we can throw the chance of *gaining truth* away, and at any rate save ourselves from any chance of *believing falsehood*, by not making up our minds at all till objective evidence has come. In scientific questions, this is almost always the case; and even in human affairs in general, the need of acting is seldom so urgent that a false belief to act on is better than no belief at all. Law courts, indeed, have to decide on the best evidence attainable for the moment, because a judge's duty is to make law as well as to ascertain it, and (as a learned judge once said to me) few cases are worth spending much time over: The great thing is to have them decided on *any* acceptable principle and gotten out of the way. But in our dealings with objective nature we obviously are recorders, not makers, of the truth; and decisions for the mere sake of deciding promptly and getting on to the next business would be wholly out of place. Throughout the breadth of physical nature facts are what they are quite independently of us, and seldom is there any such hurry about them that the risks of being duped by believing a premature theory need be faced. The questions here are always trivial options; the hypotheses are hardly living (at any rate not living for us spectators); the choice between believing truth or falsehood is seldom forced. The attitude of skeptical balance is therefore the absolutely wise one if we would escape mistakes. What difference, indeed, does it make to most of us whether we have or have not a theory of the Röntgen rays,* whether we believe or not in mind-stuff, or have a conviction about the causality of conscious states? It makes no difference. Such options are not forced on us. On every account it is better not to make them, but still keep weighing reasons *pro et contra*† with an indifferent hand.

I speak, of course, here of the purely judging mind. For purposes of discovery such indifference is to be less highly recommended, and science would be far less advanced than she is if the passionate desires of individuals to get their own faiths confirmed had been kept out of the game. . . . On the other hand, if you want an absolute duffer in an investigation, you must, after all, take the man who has no interest whatever in its results: He is the warranted incapable, the positive fool. The most useful investigator, because the most sensitive observer, is always he whose eager interest in one side of the question is balanced by an equally keen nervousness lest he become deceived. Science has organized this nervousness into a regular *technique*, her

*[X rays.—Eds.]
†[Pro and con.—Eds.]

so-called method of verification; and she has fallen so deeply in love with the method that one may even say she has ceased to care for truth by itself at all. It is only truth as technically verified that interests her. The truth of truths might come in merely affirmative form, and she would decline to touch it. Such truth as that, she might repeat with Clifford, would be stolen in defiance of her duty to mankind. Human passions, however, are stronger than technical rules. "Le coeur a ses raisons," as Pascal says, "que la raison ne connaît pas"*: and however indifferent to all but the bare rules of the game the umpire, the abstract intellect, may be, the concrete players who furnish him the materials to judge of are usually, each one of them, in love with some pet "live hypothesis" of his own. Let us agree, however, that wherever there is no forced option, the dispassionately judicial intellect with no pet hypothesis, saving us, as it does, from dupery at any rate, ought to be our ideal.

The question next arises, Are there not somewhere forced options in our speculative questions, and can we (as men who may be interested at least as much in positively gaining truth as in merely escaping dupery) always wait with impunity till the coercive evidence shall have arrived? It seems *a priori* improbable that the truth should be so nicely adjusted to our needs and powers as that. In the great boarding-house of nature, the cakes and the butter and the syrup seldom come out so even and leave the plates so clean. Indeed, we should view them with scientific suspicion if they did.

Moral questions immediately present themselves as questions whose solution cannot wait for sensible proof. A moral question is a question not of what sensibly exists, but of what is good, or would be good if it did exist. Science can tell us what exists; but to compare the *worths*, both of what exists and of what does not exist, we must consult, not science, but what Pascal calls our heart. Science herself consults her heart when she lays it down that the infinite ascertainment of fact and correction of false belief are the supreme goods for man. Challenge the statement, and science can only repeat it oracularly, or else prove it by showing that such ascertainment and correction bring man all sorts of other goods which man's heart in turn declares. The question of having moral beliefs at all or not having them is decided by our will. Are our moral preferences true or false, or are they only odd biological phenomena, making things good or bad for *us*, but in themselves indifferent? How can your pure intellect decide? If your heart does not *want* a world of moral reality, your head will assuredly never make you believe in one. . . .

Turn now from these wide questions of good to a certain class of questions of fact, questions concerning personal relations, states of mind between one man and another. *Do you like me or not?*—for example. Whether you do or not depends, in countless instances, on whether I meet you half-way, am willing to assume that you must like me, and show you trust and expectation. The previous faith on my part in your liking's existence is in such cases what makes your liking come. But if I stand aloof, and refuse to budge an inch until I have objective evidence, until you shall have done something apt, as the

---

*[The heart has its reasons that reason does not know.—Eds.]

absolutists say, *ad extorquendum assensum meum,** ten to one your liking never comes. How many women's hearts are vanquished by the mere sanguine insistence of some man that they *must* love him! He will not consent to the hypothesis that they cannot. The desire for a certain kind of truth here brings about that special truth's existence; and so it is in innumerable cases of other sorts. Who gains promotions, boons, appointments but the man in whose life they are seen to play the part of live hypotheses, who discounts them, sacrifices other things for their sake before they have come, and takes risks for them in advance? His faith acts on the powers above him as a claim, and creates its own verification.

A social organism of any sort whatever, large or small, is what it is because each member proceeds to his own duty with a trust that the other members will simultaneously do theirs. Wherever a desired result is achieved by the cooperation of many independent persons, its existence as a fact is a pure consequence of the precursive faith in one another of those immediately concerned. A government, an army, a commercial system, a ship, a college, an athletic team, all exist on this condition, without which not only is nothing achieved, but nothing is even attempted. A whole train of passengers (individually brave enough) will be looted by a few highwaymen, simply because the latter can count on one another, while each passenger fears that if he makes a movement of resistance, he will be shot before anyone else backs him up. If we believed that the whole car-full would rise at once with us, we should each severally rise, and train-robbing would never even be attempted. There are, then, cases where a fact cannot come at all unless a preliminary faith exists in its coming. *And where faith in a fact can help create the fact*, that would be an insane logic which should say that faith running ahead of scientific evidence is the "lowest kind of immorality" into which a thinking being can fall. Yet such is the logic by which our scientific absolutists pretend to regulate our lives!

In truths dependent on our personal action, then, faith based on desire is certainly a lawful and possibly an indispensable thing.

But now, it will be said, these are all childish human cases, and have nothing to do with great cosmic matters, like the question of religious faith. Let us then pass on to that. Religions differ so much in their accidents that in discussing the religious question we must make it very generic and broad. What then do we now mean by the religious hypothesis? Science says things are; morality says some things are better than other things; and religion says essentially two things.

First, she says that the best things are the more eternal things, the overlapping things, the things in the universe that throw the last stone, so to speak, and say the final word. . . .

The second affirmation of religion is that we are better off even now if we believe her first affirmation to be true.

Now, let us consider what the logical elements of this situation are *in case*

*[For forcing my agreement.—Eds.]

the religious hypothesis in both its branches be really true. . . . . So proceeding, we see, first, that religion offers itself as a *momentous* option. We are supposed to gain, even now, by our belief, and to lose by our nonbelief, a certain vital good. Secondly, religion is a *forced* option, so far as that good goes. We cannot escape the issue by remaining skeptical and waiting for more light, because, although we do avoid error in that way *if religion be untrue*, we lose the good, *if it be true*, just as certainly as if we positively chose to disbelieve. . . . Skepticism, then, is not avoidance of option; it is option of a certain particular kind of risk. *Better risk loss of truth than chance of error*—that is your faith-vetoer's exact position. He is actively playing his stake as much as the believer is; he is backing the field against the religious hypothesis, just as the believer is backing the religious hypothesis against the field. To preach skepticism to us as a duty until "sufficient evidence" for religion be found is tantamount therefore to telling us, when in presence of the religious hypothesis, that to yield to our fear of its being error is wiser and better than to yield to our hope that it may be true. It is not intellect against all passions, then; it is only intellect with one passion laying down its law. And by what, forsooth, is the supreme wisdom of this passion warranted? Dupery for dupery, what proof is there that dupery through hope is so much worse than dupery through fear? I, for one, can see no proof; and I simply refuse obedience to the scientist's command to imitate his kind of option, in a case where my own stake is important enough to give me the right to choose my own form of risk. If religion be true and the evidence for it be still insufficient, I do not wish, by putting your extinguisher upon my nature (which feels to me as if it had after all some business in this matter), to forfeit my sole chance in life of getting upon the winning side— that chance depending, of course, on my willingness to run the risk of acting as if my passional need of taking the world religiously might be prophetic and right.

All this is on the supposition that it really may be prophetic and right, and that, even to us who are discussing the matter, religion is a live hypothesis which may be true. Now, to most of us religion comes in a still further way that makes a veto on our active faith even more illogical. The more perfect and more eternal aspect of the universe is represented in our religions as having personal form. The universe is no longer a mere *It* to us, but a *Thou*, if we are religious; and any relation that may be possible from person to person might be possible here. For instance, although in one sense we are passive portions of the universe, in another we show a curious autonomy, as if we were small, active centres on our own account. We feel, too, as if the appeal of religion to us were made to our own active good-will, as if evidence might be forever withheld from us unless we met the hypothesis half-way. To take a trivial illustration: Just as a man who in a company of gentlemen made no advances, asked a warrant for every concession, and believed in no one's word without proof would cut himself off by such churlishness from all the social rewards that a more trusting spirit would earn, so here, one who should shut himself up in snarling logicality and try to make the gods extort his recognition willy-nilly, or not get it at all, might cut himself off forever from his only opportunity of making the gods' acquaintance. This feeling, forced on us we know not whence, that by obstinately believing that there are gods (although not to do so would be so easy both for our logic and our life) we are doing the universe the deepest service we can, seems part of the living essence of the religious hypothesis. If the hypothesis *were* true in all its parts, including this one, then pure intellectualism, with its veto on our making willing advances, would be an absurdity; and some participation of our sympathetic nature would be logically required. I, therefore , for one, cannot see my way to accepting the agnostic rules for truth-seeking, or wilfully agree to keep my willing nature out of the game. I cannot do so for this plain reason that *a rule of thinking which would absolutely prevent me from acknowledging certain kinds of truth if those kinds of truth were really there, would be an irrational rule.* That for me is the long and short of the formal logic of the situation, no matter what the kinds of truth might materially be. . . .

STUDY QUESTIONS

1. What condition must be met, according to Unger, if someone is to know something about the external world? Why is it plausible to insist on this condition? Can the condition be stated in a general way, that is, without reference to an evil scientist?

2. Can Unger argue, without contradicting himself, that no one ever knows anything about anything? about an external world?

3. What effect, if any, does the distinction between two kinds of knowledge made in the Preview to Part One have on Unger's version of skepticism?

4. State Hospers' argument against the skeptic. Do you think his argument is sufficient to refute skepticism? Why or why not?

5. What is there about Hospers' argument which makes it unique and very different from, say, the other arguments in Unger's essay?

6. Is "complete evidence" in Hospers' sense possible? Suppose it is. Would it satisfy Unger?

7. Explain why (according to Hempel) the scientific method does not result in hypotheses that have been proven or demonstrated as certain.

8. What are the problems with understanding scientific method in narrow inductivist terms?

9. Discuss the success of the Hospers/Hempel approach to knowledge in answering skepticism.

10. How would Peirce respond to Unger's skepticism? What attitude, belief, or doubt does Unger think we should have toward "There are rocks"?

11. How would Peirce evaluate Hospers' account of propositional knowledge? In particular, how would he construct the evidence condition?

12. Use Clifford's case to construct an adequate evidence condition. He thinks the origin of one's belief is relevant to whether one has the right to be sure or not. Which sorts of origins are acceptable and which are not?

13. Are beliefs actions? Why or why not?

14. Clifford holds that to believe when one does not have the right to believe is both intellectually and morally wrong. Why? Do you agree?

15. In his discussions of religious questions, James presents two arguments against what he calls the Skeptic (that is, anyone like Clifford). State the two arguments. Do they refute Clifford?

16. Supposedly, James would agree that Clifford's ship-owner did not have the right to believe. Exactly how, according to James, does the ship-owner case differ from cases in which one has the right to believe on no evidence?

17. What good does it do to worry about exactly how knowledge should be defined?

FURTHER READINGS

Ammerman, Robert A., and Marcus G. Singer, eds. *Belief, Knowledge and Truth.* New York: Scribner's, 1970. [A set of readings on the standard problems in the theory of knowledge.]

Ayer, A. J. *The Problem of Knowledge.* Baltimore: Penguin Books, 1956. [A theory of knowledge from an empiricist standpoint.]

Bowsma, O. K. "Descartes' Evil Genius." *Philosophical Review*, 58 (1949), 141–151. [A criticism of Descartes' skepticism; also relevant to Unger.]

Brody, Baruch A. *Beginning Philosophy.* Englewood Cliffs, N.J.: Prentice-Hall, 1977, pp. 211–233. [An elementary discussion of the nature of knowledge.]

Cohen, Morris R. "Religion and the Will to Believe." In Singer and Ammerman, pp. 231–234. [Relevant to the Clifford/James debate.]

Descartes, René. *Meditations on First Philosophy.* Indianapolis, Ind.: Hackett, 1979. [First published in 1641: the *locus classicus* for skepticism.]

Dretske, Fred. "Conclusive Reasons." *Australasian Journal of Philosophy*, 49 (1971), 1–22. [A very important response to Gettier and Goldman.]

Gettier, Edmund L. "Is Justified True Belief Knowledge?" *Analysis*, 23 (1963), 121–123. [A famous criticism of the justified-true-belief account of knowledge.]

Goldman, Alvin I. "A Causal Theory of Knowing." *Journal of Philosophy*, 64 (1967), 357–372. [A response to Gettier.]

Hamlyn, D. W. *The Theory of Knowledge.* Garden City. N.Y.: Anchor Books, 1970. [A comprehensive theory of knowledge from a Wittgensteinian point of view.]

Hume, David. *An Enquiry Concerning Human Understanding.* Indianapolis, Ind.: Hackett, 1977. [First published in 1748; a classic statement of an empiricist theory of knowledge.]

Moore, G. E. "A Defense of Common Sense." In *Philosophical Papers.* London: Allen and Unwin, 1959, pp. 32–59. [A critique of skepticism.]

Singer, Marcus G., and Robert A. Ammerman, eds. *Belief, Knowledge and Truth.* New York: Scribner's, 1970. [A set of readings on the standard problems in the theory of knowledge.]

PART TWO

SCIENCE,
COMMON SENSE,
AND THE WORLD

PREVIEW

*T*he following passage is from the famous physicist Galileo Galilei:

> Sounds . . . are produced in us and felt when . . . there is a rapid vibration of air, forming minutely small waves, which move certain cartilages of a certain drum which is in our ear. The various external ways in which this wave-motion of the air is produced are manifold, but can in large part be reduced to the vibrating of bodies which strike the air and form the waves which spread out with great velocity. . . . But I cannot believe that there exists in external bodies anything other than their size, shape, or motion . . . which could excite in us our tastes, sounds, and odors. And indeed I should judge that, if ears, tongues, and noses be taken away, the number, shape, and motion of bodies would remain, but not their tastes, sounds, and odors. The latter, external to the living creature, I believe to be nothing but mere names. . . .[1]

Though Galileo does not give his reasons, it is quite clear that he believes that ordinary objects do not have all the properties we normally attribute to them. For example, the rose outside our window is not really red and soft and sweet smelling. Those properties, as considered external to me, the observer, are mere names.

In other passages, Galileo suggests the rationale for his view. He holds that physics, which is the deepest and most general science, can fulfill its explanatory functions without ever appealing to color, texture, and odor. These kinds of qualities are not needed for a physical understanding of ordinary objects. The important qualities for a physical understanding of objects are, at least, shape, size, and motion.

---

[1] Galileo Galilei, *The Assayer*, selection reprinted in *Philosophy of Science*, ed. by Arthur Danto and Sidney Morgenbesser (Cleveland: World Publishing Co., 1960), p. 30.

Main Questions

Galileo's is only one of several possible lines of argument that challenge the commonsense understanding of ordinary objects. So, the first general issue in this part is the following:

1. Do ordinary objects have the qualities which we attribute to them on the basis of direct sense perception? (E.g., are stones hard? Are maple leaves green in the spring?)

Though common sense and the view held by Galileo differ radically, they share one central tenet. Both views maintain that physical objects have an existence independent of perceivers. On these views it makes perfect sense to speak of the possible existence of distant galaxies which no one has perceived or ever will perceive. Despite the "obviousness" of this tenet, you will discover in the readings interesting arguments that throw it into doubt. The second main question of the part is, then:

2. Do ordinary objects (desks, stones, cups, trees, etc.) exist even when they are not perceived?

Answers

There are many types of affirmative and negative answers to the first question. The readings provide two sharply contrasting viewpoints. Let us call the affirmative view represented in the text, commonsense realism, and the negative view, scientific realism.

1a. Commonsense realism: Ordinary objects have the qualities we attribute to them on the basis of sense perception.
1b. Scientific realism: Ordinary objects, as a proper understanding of science teaches us, do not have at least some of the qualities attributed to them on the basis of sense perception.

The shared realism label of the above two answers is meant to assert an affirmative answer to the second main question. Idealism is the view which asserts a negative answer.

2a. Realism: Ordinary objects exist even when not perceived.
2b. Idealism: Ordinary objects exist only when perceived.

Even if one is convinced of realism, it is important, and we shall add difficult, to construct the *argument* that entitles one to this "obvious" position.

Selections

The selections in Part Two correspond to the issues raised in the Preview as follows:

Question	Answer	Selection
(1)	(1b)	7
(1)	(1a)	8
(2)	(2b)	9
(2)	(2a)	10

.

7 / *Two Tables*

SIR ARTHUR EDDINGTON

Sir Arthur Eddington (1882–1944) taught physics and mathematics at Cambridge University in England. He was a very influential physicist and wrote a number of substantive books on the philosophy of physics, including The Nature of the Physical World *(1928) and* The Philosophy of Physical Science *(1939).*

I have settled down to the task of writing these lectures and have drawn up my chairs to my two tables. Two tables! Yes; there are duplicates of every object about me—two tables, two chairs, two pens.

This is not a very profound beginning to a course which ought to reach transcendent levels of scientific philosophy. But we cannot touch bedrock immediately; we must scratch a bit at the surface of things first. And whenever I begin to scratch, the first thing I strike is—my two tables.

One of them has been familiar to me from earliest years. It is a commonplace object of that environment which I call the world. How shall I describe it? It has extension; it is comparatively permanent; it is colored; above all it is *substantial*. By substantial I do not merely mean that it does not collapse when I lean up on it; I mean that it is constituted of "substance," and by that word I am trying to convey to you some conception of its intrinsic nature. It is a *thing*; not like space, which is a mere negation; nor like time, which is—Heaven knows what! But that will not help you to my meaning because it is the distinctive characteristic of a "thing" to have this substantiality, and I do not think substantiality can be described better than by saying that it is the kind of nature exemplified by an ordinary table. And so we go round in circles. After all if you are a plain commonsense man, not too much worried with scientific scruples, you will be confident that you understand the nature of an ordinary table. I have even heard of plain men who had the idea that they could better understand the mystery of their own nature if scientists would discover a way of explaining it in terms of the easily comprehensible nature of a table.

Table no. 2 is my scientific table. It is a more recent acquaintance and I do not feel so familiar with it. It does not belong to the world previously mentioned—that world which spontaneously appears around me when I open my eyes, though how much of it is objective and how much subjective I do not here consider. It is part of a world which in more devious ways has forced itself on my attention. My scientific table is mostly emptiness. Sparsely scattered in that emptiness are numerous electric charges rushing about with great speed; but their combined bulk amounts to less than a billionth of the bulk of the table itself. Notwithstanding its strange construction it turns out to be an entirely efficient table. It supports my writing paper as satisfactorily as table no. 1; for when I lay the paper on it the little electric particles with their headlong speed keep on hitting the underside, so that the paper is maintained in shuttlecock fashion at a nearly steady level. If I lean upon this table I shall not go through; or, to be strictly accurate, the chance of my scientific elbow going through my scientific table is so excessively small that it can be neglected in practical life. Reviewing their properties one by one, there seems to be nothing to choose between the two tables for ordinary purposes; but when abnormal circumstances befall, then my scientific table shows to advantage. If the house catches fire my scientific table will dissolve quite naturally into scientific smoke, whereas my familiar table undergoes a metamorphosis of its substantial nature which I can only regard as miraculous.

There is nothing *substantial* about my second table. It is nearly all empty space—space pervaded, it is true, by fields of force, but these are assigned to the category of "influences," not of "things." Even in the minute part which is not empty we must not transfer the old notion of substance. In dissecting matter into electric charges we have travelled far from that picture of it which first gave rise to the conception of substance, and the meaning of that conception—if it ever had any—has been lost by the way. The whole trend of modern scientific views is to break down the separate categories of "things," "influences," "forms," etc., and to substitute a common background of all experience. Whether we are studying a material object, a magnetic field, a geometrical figure, or a duration of time, our scientific information is summed up in measures; neither the apparatus of measurement nor the mode of using it suggests that there is anything essentially different in these problems. The measures themselves afford no ground for a classification by categories. We feel it necessary to concede some background to the measures—an external world; but the attributes of this world, except insofar as they are reflected in the measures, are outside scientific scrutiny. Science has at last revolted against attaching the exact knowledge contained in these measurements to a traditional picture-gallery of conceptions which convey no authentic information of the background and obtrude irrelevancies into the scheme of knowledge.

I will not here stress further the nonsubstantiality of electrons, since it is scarcely necessary to the present line of thought. Conceive them as substantially as you will, there is a vast difference between my scientific table with its substance (if any) thinly scattered in specks in a region mostly empty and the table of everyday conception which we regard as the type of solid reality—an incarnate protest against Berkeleian subjectivism.* It makes all the difference in the world whether the paper before me is poised as it were on a swarm of flies and sustained in shuttlecock fashion by a series of tiny blows from the swarm underneath, or whether it is supported because there is substance below it, it being the intrinsic nature of substance to occupy space to the

*[Bishop Berkeley thought that tables were sets of ideas.—Eds.]

exclusion of other substance; all the difference in conception at least, but no difference to my practical task of writing on the paper.

I need not tell you that modern physics has by delicate test and remorseless logic assured me that my second scientific table is the only one which is really there—wherever "there" may be. On the other hand I need not tell you that modern physics will never succeed in exorcising that first table—strange compound of external nature, mental imagery, and inherited prejudice—which lies visible to my eyes and tangible to my grasp. We must bid good-bye to it for the present, for we are about to turn from the familiar world to the scientific world revealed by physics. This is, or is intended to be, a wholly external world.

"You speak paradoxically of two worlds. Are they not really two aspects or two interpretations of one and the same world?"

Yes, no doubt they are ultimately to be identified after some fashion. But the process by which the external world of physics is transformed into a world of familiar acquaintance in human consciousness is outside the scope of physics. And so the world studied according to the methods of physics remains detached from the world familiar to consciousness, until after the physicist has finished his labors upon it. Provisionally, therefore, we regard the table which is the subject of physical research as altogether separate from the familiar table, without prejudging the question of their ultimate identification. It is true that the whole scientific inquiry starts from the familiar world and in the end it must return to the familiar world; but the part of the journey over which the physicist has charge is in foreign territory.

Until recently there was a much closer linkage; the physicist used to borrow the raw material of his world from the familiar world, but he does so no longer. His raw materials are ether, electrons, quanta, potentials, Hamiltonian functions, etc., and he is nowadays scrupulously careful to guard these from contamination by conceptions borrowed from the other world. There is a familiar table parallel to the scientific table, but there is no familiar electron, quantum, or potential parallel to the scientific electron, quantum, or potential. We do not even desire to manufacture a familiar counterpart to these things or, as we should commonly say, to "explain" the electron. After the physicist has quite finished his world-building a linkage or identification is allowed; but premature attempts at linkage have been found to be entirely mischievous.

8 / "Furniture of the Earth"

L. SUSAN STEBBING

L. Susan Stebbing (1885–1943) was a professor of philosophy at the University of London. She wrote several works in the areas of philosophical method and philosophy of science. The following excerpt is from her book Philosophy and the Physicists, *published in 1937.*

I enter my study and see the blue curtains fluttering in the breeze, for the windows are open. I notice a bowl of roses on the table; it was not there when I went out. Clumsily I stumble against the table, bruising my leg against its hard edge; it is a heavy table and scarcely moves under the impact of my weight. I take a rose from the bowl, press it to my face, feel the softness of the petals, and smell its characteristic scent. I rejoice in the beauty of the graded shading of the crimson petals. In short—I am in a familiar room, seeing, touching, smelling familiar things, thinking familiar thoughts, experiencing familiar emotions.

In some such way might any common reader describe his experiences in the familiar world that he inhabits. With his eyes shut he may recognize a rose from its perfume, stumble against a solid obstacle and recognize it to be a table, and feel the pain from its contact with his comparatively yielding flesh. You, who are reading this paper, may pause and look around you. Perhaps you are in your study, perhaps seated on the seashore, or in a cornfield, or on board ship. Wherever you may be, you will see objects distinguishable one from another, differing in color and in shape; probably you are hearing various sounds. You can see the printed marks on this page, and notice that they are black marks on a whitish background. That you are perceiving something colored and shaped you will not deny; that your body presses against something solid you are convinced; that, if you wish, you can stop reading this book, you know quite well. It may be assumed that you have some interest in philosophy; otherwise you would not be reading *this.* Perhaps you have allowed yourself to be persuaded that the page is not "really colored," that the seat upon which you are sitting is not "really solid"; that you hear only "illusory sounds." If so, it is for such as you that this chapter is written.

Imagine the following scene. You are handed a dish containing some apples—rosy-cheeked, green apples. You take the one nearest to you, and realize that you have been "had." The "apple" is too hard and not heavy enough to be really an apple; as you tap it with your finger-nail it gives out a sound such as never came from tapping a "real" apple. You admire the neatness of the imitation. To sight the illusion is perfect. It is quite sensible to

85

contrast this ingenious fake with a "real" apple, for a "real" apple is just an object that *really* is an apple, and not only *seems* to be one. This fake is an object that looks to your eyes to be an apple, but neither feels nor tastes as an apple does. As soon as you pick it up you know that it is not an apple; there is no need to taste it. We should be speaking in conformity with the rules of good English if we were to say that the dish contained real apples and imitation apples. But this mode of speaking does not lead us to suppose that there are two varieties of *apples*, namely real and imitation apples, as there are Bramley Seedlings and Blenheim pippins. Again, a shadow may be thrown on a wall, or an image may be thrown through a lantern onto a screen. We distinguish the shadow from the object of which it is the shadow, the image from that of which it is the image. Shadow and image are apprehensible only by sight; they really are visual, i.e., *seeable* entities. I can see a man, and I can see his shadow; but there is not both a *real* man and a *shadow* man; there is just the shadow of the man.

This point may seem to have been unduly labored. It is, however, of great importance. The words "real" and "really" are familiar words; they are variously used in everyday speech, and are not, as a rule, used ambiguously. The opposition between a *real* object and an *imitation* of a real object is clear. So, too, is the opposition between "really seeing a man" and having an illusion.[1] We can speak sensibly of the distinction between "the real size" and "the apparent size" of the moon, but we know that both these expressions are extremely elliptical. The significance of the words "real" and "really" can be determined only by reference to the context in which they are used. Nothing but confusion can result if, in one and the same sentence, we mix up language used appropriately for the furniture of earth and our daily dealings with it with language used for the purpose of philosophical and scientific discussion.

A peculiarly gross example of such a linguistic mixture is provided by one of Eddington's most picturesque passages:

> I am standing on a threshold about to enter a room. It is a complicated business. In the first place I must shove against an atmosphere pressing with a force of fourteen pounds on every square inch of my body. I must make sure of landing on a plank travelling at twenty miles a second round the sun—a fraction of a second too early or too late, the plank would be miles away. I must do this whilst hanging from a round planet head outward into space, and with a wind of ether blowing at no one knows how many miles a second through every interstice of my body. The plank has no solidity of substance. To step on it is like stepping on a swarm of flies. Shall I not slip through? No, if I make the venture one of the flies hits me and gives me a boost up again; I fall again and am knocked upwards by another fly; and so on. I may hope that the net result will be that I remain steady; but if unfortunately I should slip through the floor or be boosted too violently up to the ceiling the occurrence would be, not a violation of the laws of Nature, but a rare coincidence. (*N.Ph.W.* 342.)*

---

[1]Cf. "How easy is that bush supposed a bear!"
*[*N.Ph.W.* = *The Nature of the Physical World.*—Eds.]

Whatever we may think of Eddington's chances of slipping through the floor, we must regard his usage of language in this statement as gravely misleading to the common reader. I cannot doubt that it reveals serious confusion in Eddington's own thinking about "the nature of the physical world." Stepping on a plank is not the least like "stepping on a swarm of flies." This language is drawn from, and is appropriate to, our daily intercourse with the familiar furniture of earth. We understand well what it is like to step onto a solid plank; we can also imagine what it would be like to step onto a swarm of flies. We know that two such experiences would be quite different. The plank is solid. If it be securely fixed, it will support our weight. What, then, are we to make of the comparison of stepping onto a plank with stepping onto a swarm of flies? What can be meant by saying "the plank has no solidity of substance"?

Again, we are familiar with the experience of shoving against an obstacle, and with the experience of struggling against a strong head-wind. We know that we do not have "to shove against an atmosphere" as we cross the threshold of a room. We can imagine what it would be like to jump onto a moving plank. We may have seen in a circus an equestrian acrobat jump from the back of a swiftly moving horse onto the back of another horse moving with approximately the same speed. We know that no such acrobatic feat is required to cross the threshold of a room.

I may seem too heavy-handed in my treatment of a picturesque passage, and thus to fall under the condemnation of the man who cannot see a joke and needs to be "in contact with merry-minded companions"[2] in order that he may develop a sense of humor. But the picturesqueness is deceptive; the passage needs serious criticism since Eddington draws from it a conclusion that is important. "Verily," he says, "it is easier for a camel to pass through the eye of a needle than for a scientific man to pass through a door. And whether the door be barn door or church door it might be wiser that he should consent to be an ordinary man and walk in rather than wait until all the difficulties involved in a really scientific ingress are resolved." It is, then, suggested that an ordinary man has no difficulty in crossing the threshold of a room but that "a really scientific ingress" presents difficulties. The suggested contrast is as absurd as the use of the adjective "scientific" prefixed to "ingress," in this context, is perverse. Whatever difficulties a scientist, by reason of his scientific knowledge, may encounter in becoming a member of a spiritual church, these difficulties bear no comparison with the difficulties of the imagined acrobatic feat. Consequently, they are not solved by the consideration that Eddington, no less than the ordinary man, need not hesitate to cross the threshold of his room. The false emotionalism of the picture is reminiscent of Jeans's picture of human beings standing on "a microscopic fragment of a grain of sand." It is open to a similar criticism.[3]

---

[2]See *N.Ph.W.* 336.
[3]See above.

If Eddington had drawn this picture for purely expository purposes, it might be unobjectionable. The scientist who sets out to give a popular exposition of a difficult and highly technical subject must use what means he can devise to convey to his readers what it is all about. At the same time, if he wishes to avoid being misunderstood, he must surely warn his readers that, in the present stage of physics, very little can be conveyed to a reader who lacks the mathematical equipment required to understand the methods by which results are obtained and the language in which these results can alone find adequate expression. Eddington's picture seems to me to be open to the objection that the image of a swarm of flies used to explain the electronic structure of matter is more appropriate to the old-fashioned classical conceptions that found expression in a model than to the conceptions he is trying to explain. Consequently, the reader may be misled unless he is warned that nothing resembling the spatial relations of flies in a swarm can be found in the collection of electrons. No concepts drawn from the level of common-sense thinking are appropriate to subatomic, that is, microphysical, phenomena. Consequently, the language of common sense is not appropriate to the description of such phenomena. Since, however, the man in the street tends to think in pictures and may desire to know something about the latest developments of physics, it is no doubt useful to provide him with some rough picture. The danger arises when the scientist uses the picture for the purpose of making explicit denials, and expresses these denials in common-sense language used in such a way as to be devoid of sense. This, unfortunately, is exactly what Eddington has done in the passage we are considering, and indeed, in many other passages as well.

It is worthwhile to examine with some care what exactly it is that Eddington is denying when he asserts "that the plank has no solidity of substance." What are we to understand by "solidity"? Unless we do understand it we cannot understand what the denial of solidity to the plank amounts to. But we can understand "solidity" only if we can truly say the plank is solid. For "solid" just is the word we use to describe a certain respect in which a plank of wood resembles a block of marble, a piece of paper, and a cricket ball, and in which each of these differs from a sponge, from the interior of a soap-bubble, and from the holes in a net. We use the word "solid" sometimes as the opposite of "empty," sometimes as the opposite of "hollow," sometimes as the opposite of "porous." We may also, in a very slightly technical usage, contrast "solid" with "liquid" or with "gaseous." There is, no doubt, considerable variation in the precise significance of the word "solid" in various contexts. Further, as is the case with all words, "solid" may be misused, and may also be used figuratively. But there could not be a *misuse*, nor a *figurative* use, unless there were some correct and literal usages. The point is that the common usage of language enables us to attribute a meaning to the phrase "a solid plank"; but there is no common usage of language that provides a meaning for the word "solid" that would make sense if I were to say that the plank on which I stand is not *solid*. We oppose the solidity of the walls of a house to the emptiness of its unfurnished rooms; we oppose the solidity of a piece of pumice-stone to the porous loofah sponge. We do not deny that the pumice-stone is to some degree porous, that the bricks of the wall have chinks and crevices. But we do not know how to use a word that has no sensible opposite. If the plank is nonsolid, then what does "solid" *mean*? In the companion passage to the one quoted earlier, and to which reference was made in a preceding footnote, Eddington depicts the physicist, about to enter a room, as reflecting that "the plank is not what it appears to be—a continuous support for his weight." This remark is absurd. The plank appears to be capable of supporting his weight, and, as his subsequent entry into the room showed, it *was* capable of supporting his weight. If it be objected that the plank is "a support for his weight" but not "a *continuous* support," I would reply that the word "continuous" is here used without any assigned meaning. The plank appears *solid* in that sense of the word "solid" in which the plank is, in fact, solid. It is of the utmost importance to press the question: If the plank appears to be *solid*, but is really *nonsolid*, what does "solid" mean? If "solid" has no assignable meaning, then "nonsolid" is also without sense. If the plank is nonsolid, then where can we find an example to show us what "solid" means? The pairs of words, "solid"—"empty," "solid"—"hollow," "solid"— "porous," belong to the vocabulary of common-sense language; in the case of each pair, if one of the two is without sense, so is the other.

This nonsensical denial of solidity is very common in popular expositions of the physicist's conception of material objects. The author of a recently published book says: "A table, a piece of paper, no longer possess that solid reality which they appear to possess; they are both of them porous, and consist of very small electrically charged particles, which are arranged in a peculiar way."[4] How are we to understand the statement that the table *no longer* possesses "the solid reality" which it appears to possess? The context of the statement must be taken into account. The sentence quoted occurs in a summary of the view of the physical world according to classical physics. It immediately follows the statement: "This picture formed by the physicists has one great drawback as compared with the picture formed by the nonscientific man in the street. It is much more abstract." . . . Here we are concerned only with the suggestion that the nonscientific man forms one "picture" of the material world and the scientist another. There are, then, two pictures. Of what, we must ask, are they pictures? Where are we to find application for the words "solid reality," which we may not use with reference to the table? Again we must ask: If the table is nonsolid, what does "solid" mean?

No doubt the author had in mind the nineteenth-century view of the ultra-microscopic world as consisting of solid, absolutely hard, indivisible billiard-ball-like atoms, which were assumed to be solid and hard in a perfectly straightforward sense of the words "solid" and "hard." If so, it would be

---

[4]Ernst Zimmer, *The Revolution of Physics*, trans. H. Stafford Hatfield, 1936, p. 51. I have not been able to consult the German original, so I am unable to determine whether "solid reality" is a good rendering of Zimmer's meaning. Certainly the juxtaposition of the two words is unfortunate, but is evidently judged to be appropriate at least by his translator.

more appropriate to say that the modern physicist no longer believes that the table *consists* of solid atomic balls than to say that "the table no longer possesses solid reality." There is, indeed, a danger in talking about *the table* at all, for the physicist is not, in fact, concerned with tables. The recent habit of talking as though he were is responsible for much confusion of thought. It leads Eddington into the preposterous nonsense of the "two tables." This view will be familiar to everyone who is interested in the philosophy of the physicists. Nevertheless, it is desirable to quote a considerable part of Eddington's statement, since it is important to examine his view in some detail.

> I have settled down to the task of writing these lectures and have drawn up my chairs to my two tables. Two tables! Yes; there are duplicates of every object about me—two tables, two chairs, two pens. . . . One of them has been familiar to me from earliest years. It is a commonplace object of that environment which I call the world. How shall I describe it? It has extension; it is comparatively permanent; it is colored; above all, it is *substantial*. . . . Table no. 2 is my scientific table. It is a more recent acquaintance and I do not feel so familiar with it. . . . My scientific table is mostly emptiness. Sparsely scattered in that emptiness are numerous electric charges rushing about with great speed; but their combined bulk amounts to less than a billionth of the bulk of the table itself. Notwithstanding its strange construction it turns out to be an entirely efficient table. It supports my writing paper as satisfactorily as table no. 1; for when I lay the paper on it the little electric particles with their headlong speed keep on hitting the underside, so that the paper is maintained in shuttlecock fashion at a nearly steady level. If I lean upon this table I shall not go through; or, to be strictly accurate, the chance of my scientific elbow going through my scientific table is so excessively small that it can be neglected in practical life . . . There is nothing *substantial* about my second table. It is nearly all empty space—space pervaded it is true by fields of force, but these are assigned to the categories of "influences," not of "things."[5]

There is so much to criticize in this passage that it is difficult to know where to begin. Probably Eddington's defence against any criticism would be that this is one of the passages in which he was "leading the reader on"[6] (presumably—to put it vulgarly—"up the garden path"), and that consequently it must not be taken as giving "explicit statements" of his philosophical ideas. But he has nowhere expounded his philosophical ideas in nonpopular language. Moreover, the mistakes are so frequently repeated in his writings and seem to be so inextricably bound up with his philosophical conclusions that it is inevitable that these mistakes should be submitted to detailed criticism.

Perhaps the first comment that should be made is that Eddington takes quite seriously the view that there are *two tables*; one belongs to "the external world of physics," the other to "a world of familiar acquaintance in human consciousness." Eddington's philosophy may be regarded as the outcome of a sustained attempt to answer the question: How are the two tables related to

---

[5]*N.Ph.W.* xi, xii, xiii. I assume the reader's familiarity with the rest of the chapter in which this passage occurs.

[6]*N.P.Sc.* 291. [*N.P.Sc.* = *New Pathways in Science.*—Eds.]

one another? It never seems to occur to him that the form of the question is absurd. In answering the question he is hampered from the start by his initial assumption that the tables are *duplicates* of each other, that is, that it really isn't nonsensical to speak of two *tables*. I hazard the conjecture that Eddington is an inveterate visualizer,[7] and that once he has committed himself to the language of "two tables" he cannot avoid thinking of one as the shadow and of the other as the substance. (In this sentence, I have used the word "substance" simply as the correlative of "shadow." This usage has undoubtedly influenced Eddington's thinking on this topic.) It is evident that the scientific table is to be regarded as the shadow. There are statements that conflict with this interpretation, but Eddington does not leave us in doubt that, whenever he is using the language of *shadowing*, it is the scientific table that is a shadow of the familiar table. It is true that he says, "I need not tell you that modern physics has by delicate test and remorseless logic assured me that my second scientific table is the only one which is really there—wherever 'there' may be." Elsewhere he says, "Our conception of the familiar table was an illusion" (*N.Ph.W.* 323). These discrepancies result from the deep-seated confusions out of which his philosophy springs . . . At present we are concerned with the view—in conflict with the statements just quoted—that the scientific table is a shadow. "In the world of physics," he says, "we watch a shadowgraph performance of the drama of familiar life. The shadow of my elbow rests on the shadow table as the shadow ink flows over the shadow paper. It is all symbolic, and as a symbol the physicist leaves it" (xvi). Elsewhere he suggests that physicists would generally say that "the matter of this familiar table is *really* a curvature of space," but that is a view difficult to reconcile with either of the statements we are considering now.

Certainly there is much in the passage about the two tables that seems to conflict with the view of the scientific table as a shadow. It is said to be "mostly emptiness," but scattered in the emptiness are numerous electric charges whose "combined bulk" is compared in amount with "the bulk of the table itself." Is "the table itself" the familiar table? I think it must be. But the comparison of the *two* bulks is surely nonsensical. Moreover, a shadow can hardly be said to have *bulk*. Yet Eddington insists that the two tables are "parallel"—an odd synonym, no doubt, for a "shadow." He contrasts the scientific *table*, which has a familiar *table* parallel to it, with the scientific electron, quantum, or potential, which have no familiars that are parallel. Of the latter he says that the physicist is scrupulously careful to guard them "from contamination by conceptions borrowed from the other [i.e., the famil-

---

[7]The following passage is significant: "When I think of an electron there rises to my mind a hard, red, tiny ball; the proton similarly is neutral grey. Of course the color is absurd—perhaps not more absurd than the rest of the conception—but I am incorrigible" (*N.Ph.W.* xviii).

Cf. also, "I am liable to visualize a Test-match in Australia as being played upside down" (*N.P.Sc.* 314). Perhaps this habit is responsible for the queer statement (quoted above) that the feat of entering his study has to be accomplished whilst he is "hanging from a round planet head outward into space." Only, in that case, he has forgotten that his study would be hanging outward the same way. What is more important is that he has created a difficulty out of a mode of speech.

iar world." But if electrons, belonging to world no. 2, are to be scrupulously guarded from contamination by world no. 1, how can it make sense to say that they "keep on hitting the underside" of a sheet of paper that, indubitably, is part of the familiar furniture of earth? It is Eddington who reintroduces contamination when he talks in this fashion, and he does so because he supposes that there is a scientific table parallel to the familiar table. I venture to suggest that it is as absurd to say that there is a scientific table as to say that there is a familiar electron or a familiar quantum, or a familiar potential. Eddington insists upon the lack of familiar parallels in the latter cases; surely he is justified in doing so. What is puzzling is his view that there are parallel *tables*. It suggests a return to the days when physicists demanded a model; "the physicist," says Eddington, "used to borrow the raw material of his world from the familiar world, but he does so no longer" (xv). But if the "scientific table" is to be regarded as the product of the "raw material of the scientific world," how can it be regarded as parallel to the familiar table? Eddington seems unable to free himself from the conviction that the physicist is concerned with things of the same nature as the things of the familiar world; hence, *tables* are to be found in both world no. 1 and world no. 2. There is a statement in his exposition of "The Downfall of Classical Physics" that shows how deep-rooted this conviction is. "The atom," he says, "is as porous as the solar system. If we eliminated all the unfilled space in a man's body and collected his protons and electrons into one mass, the man would be reduced to a speck just visible with a magnifying glass" (*N.Ph.W.* 1–2). The comparison is useful enough; the absurdity comes from speaking of the speck as a *man*. If this statement stood alone, it might well be regarded as an expository device. But the constant cropping up of the parallel tables shows that Eddington does not regard it as absurd to think of the reduction as still leaving a *man*. When, later in the book, he is expounding the conception of space required by relativity theory, he points out that our difficulty in conceiving it is due to the fact that we are "using a conception of space which must have originated many millions of years ago and has become rather firmly embedded in human thought" (81). He adds: "But the space of physics ought not to be dominated by this creation of the dawning mind of an enterprising ape." It seems to me that in allowing himself to speak of the speck as a man, Eddington is allowing himself to be thus dominated. It is true that, in the statement just quoted, Eddington was speaking of relativity physics, but I do not think that "the creation of the dawning mind of an enterprising ape" is any more appropriate to the conception of space in atomic physics. . . . It must suffice at the moment to insist that a *man* is an object belonging to the familiar world, and has no duplicate in "the scientific world."

Perhaps we may be convinced of the absurdity of the notion that there are "duplicates of every object" in the familiar world if we return to the consideration of the description of a familiar scene with which this chapter opened. I spoke there of "blue curtains," of a crimson and scented rose, of a bruised leg. Neglecting at present the consideration of the bruised leg, which—judging by Eddington's account of the adventures of an elephant—is beneath the notice of a scientist, we may ask what duplicate of *blue* is to be found in the scientific world. The answer is that there is no duplicate. It is true that it has a "counterpart," but that is a very different matter. The counterpart of color is "its scientific equivalent electromagnetic wavelength" (88). "The wave," says Eddington, "is the reality—or the nearest we can get to a description of reality; the color is mere mind-spinning. The beautiful hues which flood our consciousness under stimulation of the waves have no relevance to the objective reality." It is obvious that here Eddington is regarding the scientific world as "the objective reality"; the familiar world is subjective. This does not square with the view that the scientific world is the shadow of the familiar world, but it is hopeless to attempt to extract from Eddington any consistent view of their relation. With this difficulty, however, we are not at the moment concerned. The point is that Eddington firmly extrudes *color* from the scientific world, and rightly so. But the *rose* is colored, the *table* is colored, the *curtains* are colored. How, then, can that which is not colored duplicate the rose, the curtains, the table? To say that an electromagnetic wave-length is colored would be as nonsensical as to say that symmetry is colored. Eddington does not say so. But he has failed to realize that a colored object could be *duplicated* only by something with regard to which it would not be meaningless to say that it was colored.

9 / *Science and the Physical World*

W. T. STACE

W. T. Stace (1886–1967) taught at Princeton University. He worked in ethics, the study of religion and culture, and was a significant figure in both the academic world and public culture.

*S*o far as I know scientists still talk about electrons, protons, neurons, and so on. We never directly perceive these; hence if we ask how we know of their existence the only possible answer seems to be that they are an inference from what we do directly perceive. What sort of an inference? Apparently a causal inference. The atomic entities in some way impinge upon the sense of the

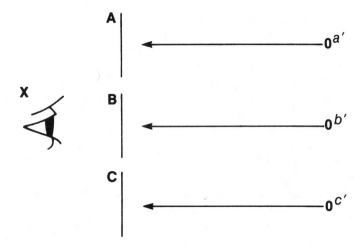

animal organism and cause that organism to perceive the familiar world of tables, chairs, and the rest.

But is it not clear that such a concept of causation, however interpreted, is invalid? The only reason we have for believing in the law of causation is that we *observe* certain regularities or sequences. We observe that, in certain conditions, A is always followed by B. We call A the cause, B the effect. And the sequence of A–B becomes a causal law. It follows that all *observed* causal sequences are between sensed objects in the familiar world of perception, and that all known causal laws apply solely to the world of sense and not to anything beyond or behind it. And this in turn means that we have not got, and never could have, one jot of evidence for believing that the law of causation can be applied *outside* the realm of perception, or that that realm can have any causes (such as the supposed physical objects) which are not themselves perceived.

Put the same thing in another way. Suppose there is an observed sequence A–B–C, represented by the vertical line in the diagram above. The observer X sees, and can see, nothing except things in the familiar world of perception. What *right* has he, and what *reason* has he, to assert a cause of A, B, and C, such as a', b', c', which he can never observe, behind the perceived world? He has no *right*, because the law of causation on which he is relying has never been observed to operate outside the series of perceptions and he can have, therefore, no evidence that it does so. And he has no *reason* because the phenomenon C is *sufficiently* accounted for by the cause B, B by A, and so on. It is unnecessary and superfluous to introduce a *second* cause b' for B, c' for C, and so forth. To give two causes for each phenomenon, one in one world and one in another, is unnecessary, and perhaps even self-contradictory.

Is it denied, then, it will be asked, that the star causes light waves, that the waves cause retinal changes, that these cause changes in the optic nerve, which in turn causes movements in the brain cells, and so on? No, it is not denied. But the observed causes and effects are all in the world of perception. And no sequence of sense-data can possibly justify going outside that world. If you admit that we never observe anything except sensed objects and their relations, regularities, and sequences, then it is obvious that we are completely shut in by our sensations and can never get outside them. Not only causal relations, but all other observed relations, upon which *any* kind of inferences might be founded, will lead only to further sensible objects and their relations. No inference, therefore, can pass from what is sensible to what is not sensible.

The fact is that atoms are not inferences from sensations. No one denies, of course, that a vast amount of perfectly valid inferential reasoning takes place in the physical theory of the atom. But it will not be found to be in any strict logical sense inference *from sense-data* to atoms*. An *hypothesis* is set up, and the inferential processes are concerned with the application of the hypothesis, that is, with the prediction by its aid of further possible sensations and with its own internal consistency.

That atoms are not inferences from sensations means, of course, that from the existence of sensations we cannot validly infer the existence of atoms. And this means that we cannot have any reason at all to believe that they exist. And that is why I propose to argue that they do not exist—or at any rate that one could not know if it they did, and that we have absolutely no evidence of their existence.

What status have they, then? Is it meant that they are false and worthless, merely untrue? Certainly not. No one supposes that the entries in the Nautical Almanac "exist" anywhere except on the pages of that book and in the brains of its compilers and readers. Yet they are "true," inasmuch as they enable us to predict certain sensations, namely, the positions and times of certain perceived objects which we call the stars. And so the formulae of the atomic theory are true in the same sense, and perform a similar function.

I suggest that they are nothing but shorthand formulae, ingeniously worked out by the human mind, to enable it to predict its experience, that is, to predict what sensations will be given to it. By "predict" here I do not mean to refer solely to the future. To calculate that there was an eclipse of the sun visible in Asia Minor in the year 585 B.C. is, in the sense in which I am using the term, to predict.

In order to see more clearly what is meant, let us apply the same idea to another case, that of gravitation. Newton formulated a law of gravitation in terms of "forces." It was supposed that this law—which was nothing but a mathematical formula—governed the operation of these existent forces. Nowadays it is no longer believed that these forces exist at all. And yet the law can be applied just as well without them to the prediction of astronomical phenomena. It is a matter of no importance to the scientific man whether the forces exist or not. That may be said to be a purely philosophical question.

---

*[Singular: sense-datum. A sense-datum is any object or quality which is immediately sensed, for example, a color, shape, sound, taste, etc. At times Stace calls these sensations.—Eds.]

And I think the philosopher should pronounce them fictions. But that would not make the law useless or untrue. If it could still be used to predict phenomena, it would be just as true as it was.

It is true that fault is now found with Newton's law, and that another law, that of Einstein, has been substituted for it. And it is sometimes supposed that the reason for this is that forces are no longer believed in. But this is not the case. Whether forces exist or not simply does not matter. What matters is the discovery that Newton's law does *not* enable us accurately to predict certain astronomical facts such as the exact position of the planet Mercury. Therefore another formula, that of Einstein, has been substituted for it which permits correct predictions. This new law, as it happens, is a formula in terms of geometry. It is pure mathematics and nothing else. It does not contain anything about forces. In its pure form it does not even contain, so I am informed, anything about "humps and hills in space-time." And it does not matter whether any such humps and hills exist. It is truer than Newton's law, not because it substitutes humps and hills for forces, but solely because it is a more accurate formula of prediction.

Not only may it be said that forces do not exist. It may with equal truth be said that "gravitation" does not exist. Gravitation is not a "thing," but a mathematical formula, which exists only in the heads of mathematicians. And as a mathematical formula cannot cause a body to fall, so gravitation cannot cause a body to fall. Ordinarily language misleads us here. We speak of the law "of" gravitation, and suppose that this law "applies to" the heavenly bodies. We are thereby misled into supposing that there are *two* things, namely, the gravitation and the heavenly bodies, and that one of these things, the gravitation, causes changes in the other. In reality nothing exists except the moving bodies. And neither Newton's law nor Einstein's law is, strictly speaking, a law of gravitation. They are both laws of moving bodies, that is to say, formulae which tell us how these bodies will move.

Now just as in the past "forces" were foisted into Newton's law (by himself, be it said), so now certain popularizers of relativity foisted "humps and hills in space-time" into Einstein's law. We hear that the reason why the planets move in curved courses is that they cannot go through these humps and hills, but have to go around them! The planets just get "shoved about," not by forces, but by the humps and hills! But these humps and hills are pure metaphors. And anyone who takes them for "existences" gets asked awkward questions as to what "curved space" is curved "in."

It is not irrelevant to our topic to consider *why* human beings invent these metaphysical monsters of forces and bumps in space-time. The reason is that they have never emancipated themselves from the absurd idea that science "explains" things. They were not content to have laws which merely told them *that* the planets will, as a matter of fact, move in such and such ways. They wanted to know "why" the planets move in those ways. So Newton replied, "Forces." "Oh," said humanity, "that explains it. We understand forces. We feel them every time someone pushes or pulls us." Thus the movements were supposed to be "explained" by entities familiar because analogous to the muscular sensations which human beings feel. The humps and hills were introduced for exactly the same reason. They seem so familiar. If there is a bump in the billiard table, the rolling billiard ball is diverted from a straight to a curved course. Just the same with the planets. "Oh, I see!" says humanity, "that's quite simple. That *explains* everything."

But scientific laws, properly formulated, never "explain" anything. They simply state, in an abbreviated and generalized form, *what happens*. No scientist, and in my opinion no philosopher, knows *why* anything happens, or can "explain" anything. Scientific laws do nothing except state the brute fact that "when *A* happens, *B* always happens too." And laws of this kind obviously enable us to predict. If certain scientists substituted humps and hills for forces, then they have just substituted one superstition for another. For my part I do not believe that *science* has done this, though some *scientists* may have. For scientists, after all, are human beings with the same craving for "explanations" as other people.

I think that atoms are in exactly the same position as forces and the bumps and hills of space-time. In reality the mathematical formulae, which are the scientific ways of stating the atomic theory, are simply formulae for calculating what sensations will appear in given conditions. But just as the weakness of the human mind demanded that there should correspond to the formula of gravitation a real "thing" which could be called "gravitation itself" or "force," so the same weakness demands that there should be a real thing corresponding to the atomic formulae, and this real thing is called the atom. In reality the atoms no more cause sensations than gravitation causes apples to fall. The only causes of sensations are other sensations. And the relation of atoms to sensations to be felt is not the relation of cause to effect, but the relation of a mathematical formula to the facts and happening which it enables the mathematician to calculate. . . .

It will not be out of place to give one more example to show how common fictitious existences are in science, and how little it matters whether they really exist or not. This example has no strange and annoying talk of "bent spaces" about it. One of the foundations of physics is, or used to be, the law of the conservation of energy. I do not know how far, if at all, this has been affected by the theory that matter sometimes turns into energy. But that does not affect the lesson it has for us. The law states, or used to state, that the amount of energy in the universe is always constant, that energy is never either created or destroyed. This was highly convenient, but it seemed to have obvious exceptions. If you throw a stone up into the air, you are told that it exerts in its fall the same amount of energy which it took to throw it up. But suppose it does not fall. Suppose it lodges on the roof of your house and stays there. What has happened to the energy which you can nowhere perceive as being exerted? It seems to have disappeared out of the universe. No, says the scientist, it still exists as *potential* energy. Now what does this blessed word "potential"—which is thus brought in to save the situation—mean as applied to energy? it means, of course, that the energy does not exist in any of its regular "forms," heat, light, electricity, etc. But this is merely negative. What positive meaning has the term? Strictly speaking, none whatever. Either the energy exists or it does not exist. There is no realm of the "potential" half-way between existence and nonexistence. And this existence of energy can only consist in its being exerted. If the energy is not being exerted, then it is not energy and does not exist. Energy can no more exist without energizing than heat can exist without being hot. The "potential" existence of the energy is, then, a fiction. The actual empirically verifiable facts are that if a certain quantity of energy *e* exists in the universe and then disappears out of the universe (as happens when the stone lodges on the roof), the same amount of energy *e* will always reappear, begin to exist again, in certain known conditions. That is the fact which the law of the conservation of energy actually expresses. And the fiction of potential energy is introduced simply because it is convenient and makes the equations easier to work. They could be worked quite well without it, but would be slightly more complicated. In either case the function of the law is the same. Its object is to apprise us that if in certain conditions we have certain perceptions (throwing up the stone), then in certain other conditions we shall get certain other perceptions (heat, light, stone hitting skull, or other such). But there will always be a temptation to hypostatize the potential energy as an "existence," and to believe that it is a "cause" which "explains" the phenomena.

If the views which I have been expressing are followed out, they will lead to the conclusion that, strictly speaking, *nothing exists exception sensations* (and the minds which perceive them). The rest is mental construction or fiction. But this does not mean that the conception of a star or the conception of an electron are worthless or untrue. Their truth and value consist in their capacity for helping us to organize our experience and predict our sensations.

10 / *Physical Objects as Not Reducible to Perceptions*

C. H. WHITELEY

C. H. Whiteley (1908–   ) has taught for many years at the University of Birmingham in England. His interests are in metaphysics and theory of knowledge. He writes on topics such as phenomenalism, which holds that physical objects are not directly perceived, but are rather "constructions" out of "sense-data" (perceptual items such as colors and shapes). On this view, which Whiteley rejects, the physical world, and thus science, rest upon the assumption that we do not directly perceive tables and trees.

*T*he problem I shall discuss is: What reason have we for believing that there are physical objects? My purpose is not either to raise or to dispel doubts as to the existence of physical objects; this doubt constitutes a medical rather than a philosophical problem. The point of asking the question is that, while there can be no reasonable difference of opinion as to whether there are physical objects, there can be and is reasonable difference of opinion as to how the notion of a physical object is to be analyzed; and if we are clear as to what grounds there are for believing in physical objects, we shall also be clearer as to what sort of physical objects we have grounds for believing in. Also, it is worthwhile to inquire which other beliefs are logically connected with, and which are logically independent of, the belief in physical objects.

I make one important assumption at the outset: namely, that by a physical object or process we mean something that exists or occurs apart from and independently of our perceptions, and of our experiences of other kinds. The distinction between the physical or "real" world and the "subjective" or "imaginary"—illusions, hallucinations, after-images, shadows, rainbows, mental pictures, what we merely suppose, imagine, or expect—is a distinction between things and events which exist or occur whether anybody is aware of them or not, and things and events which have their being only as and when somebody is aware of them. A belief in physical objects is a belief in things which are sometimes at least unobserved by the believer.

It is obvious that the existence of such things is not a question to be settled by sense-perception alone. That there is a material world cannot be established or even made plausible merely by looking, listening, touching; it is not *given* in the way in which the existence of something red and something round, of sounds, smells, aches, feelings of sadness, can be given. I do not mean that the something red or round cannot be a physical object; I mean that it cannot be known to be a physical object just by looking at it or otherwise perceiving it. For I cannot, simply by perceiving something, tell whether that something continues to exist when I cease to perceive it. This logical necessity is not evaded by naïve realism, which holds that the something red or round which appears to sight is (usually at least) identical with a physical object; for though this may be so, we cannot know it just by looking. Nor is it evaded by phenomenalism; for no phenomenalist does or plausibly could analyze statements about physical objects into statements asserting the *actual* occurrence of sense-data; he must add statements about what sense-data *would* be sensed if certain conditions were fulfilled; and this fact is not given by sense-perception, but reasons for it are required. That there are physical objects is not something we observe or perceive, but something we suppose or assume (to call it a "hypothesis" or "postulate" is to suggest something rather too deliberate and self-conscious). In old-fashioned language, it is a transcendent belief; it goes beyond the evidence.

Thus there is no logical absurdity in denying or refusing to admit the existence of a material world. To say that there are no physical objects, while doubtless very foolish, does not involve a man in any logical contradiction, nor does it force him to shut his eyes to any patent and indisputable facts. An intellectually indolent percipient, whose few wants were supplied independently of his own efforts, might well abstain from supposing that there was a physical world. There is some evidence that young babies, who are more or less in this situation, do not believe that there are any material things—do not believe, for instance, that the rattle just dropped from the hand and the visitor just departed from the room are now anywhere at all.

If somebody did behave like this, in what way would he be worse off, and what other beliefs would he be debarred from entertaining? I answer—and this is my principal point—that he would be unable to make valid generalizations, or reliable forecasts of his future experience. He would have to do without the belief in an order in nature, in regular sequences of events, in causal laws. For if I confine myself to what I myself observe or am aware of, I can make no valid generalizations concerning the concomitance or sequence of types of phenomena. I find only that phenomena of one type are quite often accompanied or followed by phenomena of another type, but sometimes not. There is no type of sense-datum A of which it is true that whenever it occurs another type of sense-datum B accompanies or follows or precedes it. And this is the case however complex you make your A and your B. This point has often been overlooked. People know quite well that lightning is always accompanied by thunder, barking by the presence of dogs, that green apples are always sour, and the ground always gets dark and sticky after a heavy fall of rain; and they talk about these as though they were *phenomenal* regularities—as though the seeing of lightning always went along with the hearing of thunder, and so forth. But this is of course not the case. If, as some people have said, it was the business of science to disclose the order or regularity in phenomena, meaning by phenomena what we see and hear and feel, science would be a very unrewarding pursuit. For phenomena are disorderly and irregular, and scientists cannot make them out any different.

Many philosophers have indeed thought that natural regularities could be conceived without the postulation of actual unobserved things and events, if instead we postulate that certain phenomena would occur or would have occurred, given certain unfulfilled conditions. Instead of saying that whenever I hear barking there exists an actual dog, perceived or unperceived, I am to say that whenever I hear barking, I should perceive a dog if certain conditions were fulfilled—if my eyes were open and my sight normal, if there was an adequate amount of light, if I looked in the right direction and there was no opaque obstacle in my line of vision, etc. Such an interpretation in terms of possible phenomena would relieve us of any need to postulate another order of physical events over and above perceptual events, and would in this way be more economical. There are, however, three ways in which phenomenal generalizations of this kind cannot take the place of physical generalizations.

1. A physical generalization associates one uniform property with another uniform property: I mean that when something is asserted to be universally true of dogs, or pieces of iron, or cases of pneumonia, or falling bodies of a weight of ten pounds, it is assumed that there is some physical property or

group of properties which is common to all dogs, pieces of iron, etc. Phenomenal generalizations, however, concern associations between sets of diverse phenomena. If we wish to correlate the auditory phenomenon of barking with visual phenomena we must specify a set of canine sense-data, or views of dogs, which are not all alike in any sensory property, but form one class only in virtue of a very complex set of relations.

2. A physical generalization applies to *all* cases of a given type, and the study of nature aims at reducing to laws all events and all features of events. But phenomenal generalizations can never apply to all cases of a given type, but only to some of them, namely to those cases in which the supplementary conditions for observation are fulfilled. The physical generalization "There's no smoke without fire" applies to all instances of smoke, whether or not either the smoke or the fire is observed. But the corresponding phenomenal generalization brings under a uniformity-rule only those cases in which both the smoke and the fire are observed. Observed smoke can be correlated with observed fire; when I observe the smoke but not the fire, the observed smoke is correlated with nothing, and is an instance of no natural law (except in the forced and trivial sense in which a white cat with brown eyes and quick hearing is an instance of the law that all white cats with blue eyes are deaf); it forms no part of the order of nature.

3. A phenomenal generalization must always include a reference to conditions of observation, whereas physical generalizations are independent of these. We can say without qualification "Whenever it thunders, it lightens." But we can say "Whenever thunder is heard, lightning is seen" only if we add "provided that there is an observer with adequate eyesight, facing in the appropriate direction, having his eyes open and his view not obscured by any opaque object, etc." This difference does not merely prevent the phenomenal generalization from adequately replacing the physical one. It also means that there can be no generalizations on the phenomenal level which are universally valid. For it is impossible to give in purely phenomenal terms an adequate statement of all the conditions required for perceiving lightning besides the occurrence of lightning. It is curious that the analysis of physical-objects statements in terms of sense-data and the analysis of causation in terms of regular sequence should have been so often advocated by the same philosophers. For if we restrict our attention to phenomena, we can find no instances for the regular-sequence concept of cause to apply to.

If therefore, I am to make reliable generalizations about the course of events, and reliable forecasts about my future experiences, I must suppose that there are unperceived as well as perceived events. Thus the connection between the category of substance and that of cause is, as Kant suggested, not fortuitous but necessary. We do not discover that there are (perfect) regularities in nature, that is, in the physical world, as we discover that there are (imperfect) regularities amongst phenomena. On the contrary, the regularity is essential to the concept of nature; the assumption that the physical world is orderly is inseparable from the assumption that the physical world exists. It is only to the extent that I assume it to be orderly that I have any grounds for believing that there is a physical world at all. This may help to account for our strong inclination to regard physical determinism as a necessary *a priori* truth.

What, then, is the sort of supposition which will make it possible to believe in regular sequences and concomitances in the world, and to regulate our expectations accordingly? A simple and comprehensive answer cannot be given to this question. The precise character of the suppositions we make about physical objects and processes is subject to variation for different kinds of cases, and to modification with the improvement of our knowledge. One can, however, indicate the general line which must be followed.

There are, amongst the events which we are aware of, certain associations of characteristics which, while not invariable, are very common: for example, the association between the sound of barking and the sight of dogs, between the visual appearance of oranges and their characteristic flavor, between the brightness of sunshine and felt warmth, between the kinesthetic sensations of speech and the sound of my own voice, between the visible immersion of a lump of sugar in a cup of tea and its gradual disappearance, between the various members of the visible sequence black-coal . . . flame . . . red-coal . . . ashes, between the patter of raindrops, the sight of rain falling, the feeling of dampness on exposed parts of the body, and the darkening of the soil or pavement. (These are, of course, examples of several different kinds of association.)

The supposition required has two parts:

1. that to these imperfect phenomenal regularities there corresponds in each case a perfect physical regularity; that is, in each case in which there is a frequent association between phenomenal characteristics there are some corresponding physical characteristics which are invariably associated. Whereas the sound of barking is often but not always accompanied by the sight of a dog, there is some type of event, physical barking, which is always accompanied by the presence of some one type of physical object, a dog. Whereas the visual brightness of sunshine is only sometimes accompanied by a feeling of warmth, there is a physical entity, sunlight, and a physical entity, heat, which always goes with it. Whereas a person may be seen setting off from A and arriving at B without being seen at intermediate places at intermediate times, physical passage from A to B involves the temporally continuous traversing of a spatially continuous path. In general, whenever there is an imperfect but frequent association between a phenomenal characteristic A and a phenomenal characteristic B, there is a thing or process having a characteristic corresponding to A which is invariably associated with a thing or process having a characteristic corresponding to B. Thus whenever I hear barking, there exists a physical dog, whether or not there also occurs the experience of my seeing him.

2. The existence of the corresponding physical thing, or the occurrence of the corresponding physical process, is a necessary but not a sufficient condition for the awareness of the phenomenal characteristic. There can be no

hearing of barks without their being (physical) barks; but there can be barks without the hearing of barks. The further conditions, other than the existence of the dog or the occurrence of the bark, which are required if I am to have the corresponding perception of the dog or the bark, may be called the observation-conditions. Some of these conditions are pretty easy to discover. For instance, if I am to see anything at all, there must be a certain amount of light (but not enough to dazzle), and my vision must not be blocked by any obstacle. Other observation-conditions can only be discovered by much experimental research: for instance, the need for air or some other transmitting medium in the case of hearing, the need for integrity of the optic nerves in the case of sight. The occurrence of the appropriate sense-experience is determined jointly by the corresponding physical process and the relevant observation-conditions. (These conditions, of course, concern the properties of other physical things and processes, so that we cannot say just what they are without knowing something about physical things other than the one to be perceived. Learning about the properties of dogs, and learning about the properties of light and the human sense-organs, go hand in hand.) Thus the assumption of a physical world involves two supposed sets of regularities: an association between one physical characteristic and another, and an association between physical processes together with observation-conditions on the one hand and sense-experiences on the other.

So far, the physical world has been presented as a set of processes which occur independently of perceptions, which are related by laws of sequence and concomitance to other processes, and which together with the relevant observation-conditions determine specific sense-experiences of ours. These are purely relational properties; and nothing has been said so far about any other properties that physical objects may possess. On the view here advocated, namely that the justification of a belief in a physical world is that it makes possible the formulation of laws of nature, the only positive reason for attributing a property to physical objects would be that by assuming physical objects to possess this property we can account for the character of our perceptions, and explain how we come to perceive this rather than that, now rather than then. One way of accounting for the character of our perceptions would be to suppose that the sensory qualities which are present in them (the particular colors, sounds, tastes, etc.) are properties of physical objects and persist unperceived just as they appear when perceived. This is naïve realism. A completely naïve-realist theory would hold that all sensory qualities are properties of physical objects, and exist independently of perception; other theories are naïvely realistic to the extent that they identify the properties of physical things with those properties which are present in sense-experience.

Now the investigation of the properties of physical things is the business of the science of physics. And contemporary physics is not naïvely realistic in any degree. The properties which it attributes to physical objects are not sensory properties, but hypothetical properties defined by their relations to one another and to certain kinds of perceptions. The reason for this is often misunderstood. Philosophical criticism of naïve realism is apt to concentrate on the "argument from illusion," that is, on the *deceptiveness* of sense-perception. This is the wrong sort of criticism. Our perceptions can sometimes mislead us (that is, lead us to form false expectations about other perceptions to come) only because they also, and more often, lead us to form true expectations; perception could not be systematically misleading. But the question whether our perceptions induce in us true or false expectations is quite independent of the question whether they show us the permanent characteristics of material things. The damaging criticisms of naïve realism rest on this principle: Given that the physical object corresponding to a given sense-datum is something which, in conjunction with the relevant observation-conditions, determines the characteristics of that sense-datum, then if a given characteristic can be shown to be determined by the observation-conditions, there can be no reason for attributing it to the corresponding physical object. The successive modifications in our concept of the physical world arise from our increasing knowledge of the dependence of sensory properties upon observation-conditions. The challenge to naïve realism with respect to colors comes from optics. The challenge to naïve realism with respect to space and time comes from relativity-theory. The challenge to naïve realism with respect to beauty and ugliness comes from our understanding of the dependence of esthetic delight and disgust upon the dispositions and past experiences of the subject.

In abandoning naïve realism, scientific theory only carries further a process which pre-scientific common sense has already begun. The common-sense view of the physical world is by no means a purely naïve-realist view. When I look at an object from different angles and in different lights successively, the sensory properties which appear to me are many and various. Common sense does not hold that all these various sensory properties belong to the physical object and exist apart from my perception. Were that so, there would have to be either a multitude of physical objects or a constantly changing object to possess all these different properties. Common sense holds, on the contrary, that there is but one object with one shape, size, color, etc., which is unchanging throughout my changing perceptions. This postulation of a single set of physical properties corresponding to a multiplicity of sensory properties is the first and fundamental step away from naïve realism. A Berkeleian analysis, which reverses this step, is a greater affront to common sense and provokes more resistance from it than a Lockean analysis which takes a step or two further in the same direction.*

It is a belief of common sense that at least some sensory properties are not properties of physical objects, but are due to conditions of observation (quantity and quality of light, distance, defects of vision, etc.). As to whether *any* sensory properties are also physical properties, I am not convinced that common sense has any clear and consistent view. Of course we say that grass is

---

*[Berkeley and Locke were eighteenth-century British philosophers.—Eds.]

green and roses are red. But does this mean more than that if we look at them under suitable conditions green and red are the colors we shall see? It is not clear to me that common sense is committed to the belief that objects have any colors when unperceived. (Examining the way we talk about the matter is of no help. Given that a certain piece of cloth looks bluish in artificial light and grayish in daylight, are we to presume that its color changes with changes in the light, and say "It *is* blue in artificial light and gray in daylight," or are we to presume that it has a color independently of the light, and say "It is really gray, but it looks blue in artificial light?" Ordinary idiom allows us to say either of these things indifferently.) By contrast, there are some properties which common sense does attribute to physical objects apart from perception—size and weight, for instance. When I conclude that this brick must have made that hole in the window, though nobody saw it do so, I credit the brick with having a size and weight at a time when it was not being perceived. But size and weight are not sensory properties. Blueness is a way things look; but heaviness is not a way things look or feel. A thing can, of course, look or feel heavy; but its *being* heavy is something different—it is heavy if it will hold down or make dents in other objects, if you can't lift it with one hand, and so on; and these causal characteristics are not ways of looking or feeling. Properties like size and weight, which common sense does attribute to unperceived objects, bear the same sort of relation to sense-experience as the concepts of modern physics. Thus it seems to me that one can abandon naïve realism in all its forms without abandoning any belief to which common sense is committed.

To sum up: That there are physical objects is a supposition, not a datum. The use of the supposition is to account for the regularities in sensory phenomena, to enable the course of events to be set in a framework of regular sequences and concomitances. It is confirmed by the success we achieve in ordering our experiences by its aid, in making our generalizations continually more extensive and more exact. Being a supposition, and not an inevitable and invariable category of thought, it is subject to modification as we learn more about the conditions under which perception takes place. Scientific concepts are related to sense-experience in a remoter and more complex fashion than common-sense concepts of physical objects. But they are not of an entirely different order. The common-sense concept of "table" is not, like "blue" or "bang" or "stench," a merely phenomenal concept; it is explanatory and theoretical.

STUDY QUESTIONS

1. What, in detail, are the two contrasting descriptions of a table that Eddington gives? Are they incompatible?

2. Physics, according to Eddington, teaches us that only the scientific table "is really there." What does (could) he mean by this? What reasons does he give for believing it?

3. How can Eddington's view, expressed in question 2, be reconciled with his claim that the two tables can perhaps be identified?

4. State and evaluate Stebbing's argument that Eddington cannot reasonably claim that planks and rocks are not solid.

5. Stebbing writes, "It is evident that the scientific table according to Eddington is to be regarded as the shadow." Is it evident?

6. Suppose that while driving you hear a thumping sound and quite naturally make a causal inference to the car's having a flat tire. Notice that the flat was not perceived directly but was inferred from something which was directly perceived. What is the difference between this example and the kind of inference which scientists supposedly make to electrons, protons, and so on? Surely your inference is innocent enough, but according to Stace the scientists' are not. Why?

7. How would Whiteley respond to Stace's view, expressed in question 8?

8. Why can phenomenal generalizations not replace physical generalizations?

FURTHER READINGS

Ayer, A. J. *The Problem of Knowledge.* Baltimore: Penguin Books, 1962, Chap. 3. [A discussion of phenomenalism.]

Berkeley, George. *Three Dialogues Between Hylas and Philonous.* Indianapolis, Ind.: Hackett, 1979. [First published in 1713; a clear, systematic version of idealism by an important figure in the history of philosophy.]

Galilei, Galileo. "Two Kinds of Properties." In A. Danto and S. Morgenbesser, eds., *Philosophy of Science.* Cleveland: Meridian Books, 1960, pp. 27–32. [A critique of common sense by the famous Renaissance scientist.]

Hospers, John. *An Introduction to Philosophical Analysis,* 2nd ed. Englewood Cliffs, N.J.: Prentice-Hall, 1967, pp. 493–565. [An overview of theories of perception.]

Moore, G. E. "Proof of an External World." In *Philosophical Papers.* London: Allen and Unwin, 1959, pp. 126–148. [A defense of certain commonsense views of perception.]

Mundle, C. W. K. *Perception: Facts and Theories.* London: Oxford University Press, 1971. [An excellent defense of a modified commonsense view.]

Nagel, Ernest. *The Structure of Science.* New York: Harcourt Brace Jovanovich, 1961, Chap. 6. [A discussion of the existence of theoretical entities.]

Russell, Bertrand. *Our Knowledge of the External World.* London: Allen and Unwin, 1929. [A systematic development of Russell's view at one point in his life.]

Ryle, Gilbert. "The World of Science and the Everyday World." In *Dilemmas.* Cambridge: Cambridge University Press, 1954, pp. 68–81. [Discusses certain supposed rivalries between science and common sense.]

Vesey, Godfrey. *Perception.* Garden City, N.Y.: Doubleday, 1971. [A criticism of causal theories of perception.]

PART THREE

FREEDOM, DETERMINISM, AND RESPONSIBILITY

PREVIEW

Almost all of us assume that we have free will, that we at least sometimes freely choose whether or not to perform a certain action. We think that neither the act which we performed nor any other was necessitated. And we think that even if I did act A, I could have done otherwise; I could have performed B, or C, etc.

All of these assumptions have come under attack in recent times—by psychologists, psychiatrists, physiologists, and others. Consider the following discussion from B. F. Skinner's novel, *Walden Two*:

> "Isn't it time we talked about freedom?" I said. "We parted a day or so ago on an agreement to let the question ring. It's time to answer, don't you think?"
>
> "My answer is simple enough," said Frazier. "I deny that freedom exists at all. I must deny it—or my program would be absurd. You can't have a science about a subject matter which hops capriciously about. Perhaps we can never *prove* that man isn't free; it's an assumption. But the increasing success of a science of behavior makes it more and more plausible."
>
> "On the contrary, a simple personal experience makes it untenable," said Castle. "The experience of freedom. I know that I'm free."
>
> "It must be quite consoling," said Frazier.[1]

In *Walden Two* Skinner sketches a modern utopia—one built on "appropriate" technology and a determined effort to utilize a science of behavioral engineering. In the dialog just quoted, the sarcastic Frazier is Skinner's spokesman. Castle, the philosopher, is the stubborn one. If you lack the dogmatic confidence of Frazier and Castle, and instead are pulled by each position, you have been teased by the philosophical problem of free will. Do we or do we not have free will? That is, do some of our actions result from free choice? That is the crux of the problem.

---

[1]B. F. Skinner, *Walden Two* (Toronto: Macmillan, 1948), p. 257.

The main problem of this part is often referred to as the problem of free will *versus* determinism or the free will/determinism controversy. We all have some sense of what free will is. What is meant by 'determinism'?

Determinism, in its broadest form, is the view that every event in the universe has a cause. One consequence of determinism is: Since human acts are events, they too *all* have causes. Another consequence is: Every event—including every action—is in principle predictable.

But precisely how is the broad claim, 'Every event (including every act) has a cause' to be interpreted? While there are various views on this, the interpretation accepted by most, including most writers on the free will/determinism controversy, and especially those who deny free will, is:

For every event E, there is a set of antecedent conditions, $C1 \ldots Cn$, which are sufficient to produce E to the exclusion of any other event. (Given $C1 \ldots Cn$, E and only E can occur.)

Again, this holds for all actions, too.

We have already referred to the characterization of determinism as the claim that 'Every event has a cause' as the broad sense of determinism—or of the word 'determinism'. Let us refer to the characterization just given as the strict sense. It will be important to bear this sense in mind since, again, it is this sense of determinism that is accepted by those who deny that we have free will.

The denial of determinism is called 'indeterminism'. Thus, indeterminism is the claim: Not every event has a cause. Some events have no cause. Thus, indeterminism is simply the negation of the broad sense of determinism.

The problem of free will would not grab us with such force were it not for the fact that the concept of freedom is intimately related to the concepts of responsibility and punishment. The following quotation is from a work by Clarence Darrow, the jurist best known for his defense of Thomas Scopes in the famous "monkey trial":

> Before any progress can be made in dealing with crime the world must fully realize that crime is only a part of conduct; that each act, criminal or otherwise, follows a cause; that given the same conditions the same result will follow forever and ever; that all punishment for the purpose of causing suffering, or growing out of hatred, is cruel and anti-social; that however much society may feel the need of confining the criminal, it must first of all understand that the act had an all-sufficient cause for which the individual was in no way responsible, and must find the cause of his conduct, and, so far as possible, remove the cause.[2]

This provocative passage deserves critical attention. But the present point is that it raises two very important issues which are intimately related to the free will problem. Thus, in addition to the previous question with which this part is concerned, we can add the following: Under what conditions, if

---

[2]Clarence Darrow, *Crime: Its Causes and Treatment* (New York: Thomas Y. Crowell, 1922), p. 36.

any, is a person responsible for his or her actions? Under what conditions, if any, is the punishment of a person justifiable? The readings in this part discuss not only the free will problem but also the consequences of that problem for questions concerning responsibility and punishment.

Main Questions

This leads us to the main questions of this part. The primary question is:

1. Does (genuine) free will exist? Are any of our actions, even if not all, freely chosen by us? Or is everything we do determined by antecedent causes which are sufficient to bring about the actions we do, to the exclusion of all others?

As noted, there are two additional important and related questions:

2. Are we morally responsible for (any of) our actions?
3. Should criminals be punished for their crimes? If so, what is the motive for such punishment?

Answers

The main answers to the first question have, in some cases, been given different labels. For simplicity we settle on these:

1a. Hard determinism
1b. Soft determinism
1c. Self-determinism

(1b. is also referred to as Compatibilism. 1c. is also referred to as the Agency Theory. It is a variant of what is known as Libertarianism.)

The answers which these labels designate are:

1a. Hard determinism: Since determinism (strict sense) is true, and since human actions are events, free will cannot exist.

Thus according to hard determinism: for any act A, there is a set of antecedent conditions sufficient to produce A to the exclusion of all other acts.

1b. Soft determinism: Determinism (strict sense) is true; nevertheless, some acts are free. Hence free will *does* exist. And it is compatible with determinism.

Which acts are free? According to soft determinism: Free acts are those for which the immediate cause is an internal, psychological state—a desire, willing, choosing, etc., within the agent. Hence unfree acts are those for which the immediate cause is external to the agent—and hence one in which the agent is compelled. Thus all events, including acts, are caused, but some acts are *also* free.

1c. Self-determinism: Determinism (strict sense) is false. For some events, *some human acts*, it does not hold. In those cases the acts result from our free choice. Hence free will *does* exist.

Thus, according to self-determinism: All events are caused. But for some events, *some human acts*, there is no set of antecedent conditions sufficient to produce a given act to the exclusion of all others. In such cases, I act out of free will.

Note: Such acts are caused, according to self-determinism. Hence indeterminism is false (in this view). But *I myself* am the cause. And hence determinism is false (in this view). Why?

Determinism claims that for every act A, there is a set of conditions $C1 \ldots Cn$, such that given their occurrence, A must occur to the exclusion of all else. That is, determinism claims that since all acts are events, they must be produced by other *events*, namely the conditions $C1 \ldots Cn$. But according to self-determinism that is false. Some acts, however few, are caused or initiated by *me, a person*, and not by a set of conditions or events. Thus, self-determinism is the denial of the *strict* interpretation of determinism.

We turn now to the related questions.

The answers to question (2) are obviously yes or no. Hence, with regard to the question of responsibility:

2a. Affirmative answer: Yes, we are responsible for at least many of our actions.

2b. Negative answer: No, we are not responsible for our actions, or at least, not for most or some of them.

With regard to question (3) of whether or not criminals should be punished, we again have:

3a. Affirmative answer: Yes.
3b. Negative answer: No.

Concerning the motive for such punishment, we find these main alternative answers:

Revenge or retribution: To get back at the criminal or give him his "just due."
Rehabilitation: To cure him of his sick behavior.
Deterrence: To prevent others from committing similar crimes.

Selections

In this part, the chief answers to our questions are represented as follows:

Question	Answer	Selection
(1)	(1a) Hard determinism	11, 14
(1)	(1b) Soft determinism	12

(1)	(1c) Self-determinism	13
(2)	(2b) Negative	11, 14
(2)	(2a) Affirmative	12, 13
(3)	(3b) Negative	15
(3)	(3a) Affirmative	16

(Selections 15 and 16 also deal with the proper motive for punishment.)

11 / The Delusion of Free Will

ROBERT BLATCHFORD

Robert Blatchford (1851–1943) was an English writer whose popular works were widely read and exerted great influence in England, the United States, and elsewhere. The following extract is from his book Not Guilty *(1913).*

[I. INTRODUCTION]

*T*he free will delusion has been a stumbling block in the way of human thought for thousands of years. Let us try whether common sense and common knowledge cannot remove it. . . .

The free will party* claims that man is responsible for his acts, because his will is free to choose between right and wrong. . . .

When a man says his will is free, he means that it is free of all control or interference: that it can overrule heredity and environment.

We reply that the will is ruled by heredity and environment.

The cause of all the confusion on this subject may be shown in a few words.

When the free will party says that man has a free will, they mean that he is free to act as he chooses to act.

There is no need to deny that. *But what causes him to choose?*

That is the pivot upon which the whole discussion turns.

The free will party seems to think of the will as something independent of the man, as something outside him. They seem to think that the will decides without the control of the man's reason.

If that were so, it would not prove the man responsible. "The will" would be responsible, and not the man. It would be as foolish to blame a man for the act of a "free" will as to blame a horse for the action of its rider.

But I am going to prove to my readers, by appeals to their common sense and common knowledge, that *the will is not free*; and that *it is ruled by heredity and environment.*

[II. REASONS GIVEN FOR FREE WILL AND CRITICISMS OF THEM]

1. To begin with, the average man will be against me. He [says he] knows that he chooses between two courses every hour, and often every minute, and he thinks his choice is free. But that is a delusion: His choice is not free. He can

---

*[The believers in genuine free will.—Eds.]

"choose," and does "choose." But he can only "choose" as his heredity and his environment cause him to choose. He never did choose and never will choose except as his heredity and his environment—his temperament and his training—cause him to choose. And his heredity and his environment have fixed his choice before he makes it.

2. The average man says, "I know that I can act as I wish to act." But [I ask:] what causes him to wish?

The free will party says, "We know that a man can and does choose between two acts." But [I ask:] what settles the choice?

There is a cause for every wish, a cause for every "choice"; and every cause of every wish and choice arises from heredity, or from environment.

For a man acts always from *temperament*, which is *heredity*, or from *training*, which is *environment*.

And in cases where a man hesitates in his choice between two acts, the hesitation is due to a conflict between his temperament and his training, or, as some would express it, "between his desire and his conscience."

[*Example.*] A man is practicing at a target with a gun, when a rabbit crosses his line of fire. The man has his eye and his sights on the rabbit, and his finger on the trigger. The man's will is "free." If he presses the trigger the rabbit will be killed.

Now, how does the man decide whether or not he shall fire? He decides by feeling, and by reason.

He would like to fire, just to make sure that he could hit the mark. He would like to fire, because he would like to have the rabbit for supper. He would like to fire, because there is in him the old, old hunting instinct, to kill.

But the rabbit does not belong to him. He is not sure that he will not get into trouble if he kills it. Perhaps—if he is a very uncommon kind of man—he feels that it would be cruel and cowardly to shoot a helpless rabbit.

Well. The man's will is "free." He can fire if he likes; he can let the rabbit go if he likes. How will he decide? On what does his decision depend?

His decision depends upon the relative strength of his desire to kill the rabbit, and of his scruples about cruelty, and the law.*

Not only that, but, if we knew the man fairly well, we could guess how his "free" will would act before it acted. The average sporting Briton would kill the rabbit. But we know that there are men who would on no account shoot any harmless wild creature.

Broadly put, we may say that the sportsman would will to fire, and that the humanitarian would not will to fire.

Now, as both their wills are "free," it must be something outside the wills that makes the difference.

Well. The sportsman will kill, because he is a sportsman; the humanitarian will not kill, because he is a humanitarian.

And what makes one man a sportsman and another a humanitarian? Heredity and environment; temperament and training.

---

*[Because he was hunting on someone else's private property.—Eds.]

One man is merciful, another cruel, by nature; or one is thoughtful and the other thoughtless, by nature. That is a difference of heredity.

One may have been taught all his life that to kill wild things is "sport"; the other may have been taught that it is inhuman and wrong: That is a difference of environment.

Now, the man by nature cruel or thoughtless, who has been trained to think of killing animals as sport, becomes what we call a sportsman, because heredity and environment have made him a sportsman.

The other man's heredity and environment have made him a humanitarian.

The sportsman kills the rabbit because he is a sportsman, and he is a sportsman because heredity and environment have made him one.

That is to say the "free will" is really controlled by heredity and environment. . . .

3. But, it may be asked, how do you account for a man doing the thing he does not wish to do?

No man ever did a thing he did not wish to do. When there are two wishes the stronger rules.

[*Example.*] Let us suppose a case. A young woman gets two letters by the same post; one is an invitation to go with her lover to a concert, the other is a request that she will visit a sick child in the slums. The girl is very fond of music, and is rather afraid of the slums. She wishes to go to the concert, and to be with her lover; she dreads the foul street and the dirty home, and shrinks from the risk of measles or fever. But she goes to the sick child, and she foregoes the concert. Why?

Because her sense of duty is stronger than her self-love.

Now, her sense of duty is partly due to her nature—that is, to her heredity—but it is chiefly due to environment. Like all of us, this girl was born without any kind of knowledge, and with only the rudiments of a conscience. But she has been well taught, and the teaching is part of her environment.

We may say that the girl is "free" to act as she "chooses," but she *does* act as she has been *taught* that she *ought* to act. This teaching, which is part of her environment, controls her will.

We may say that a man is "free" to act as he chooses. He is free to act as *he* "chooses," but *he* will "choose" as heredity and environment cause *him* to choose. For heredity and environment have made him that which he is.

A man is said to be free to decide between two courses. But really he is only "free" to decide in accordance with his temperament and training. . . .

How, then, can we believe that free will is outside and superior to heredity and environment? . . .

4. "What! Cannot a man be honest if he choose?" Yes, if he "choose." But that is only another way of saying that he can be honest if his nature and his training lead him to choose honesty.

"What! Cannot I please myself whether I drink or refrain from drinking?" Yes. But that is only to say you will not drink because it pleases *you* to be sober.

But it pleases another man to drink, because his desire for drink is strong, or because his self-respect is weak.

And you decide as you decide, and he decides as he decides, because you are *you* and he is *he*; and heredity and environment made you both that which you are.

And the sober man may fall upon evil days, and may lose his self-respect, or find the burden of his trouble greater than he can bear, and may fly to drink for comfort, or oblivion, and may become a drunkard. Has it not been often so?

And the drunkard may, by some shock, or some disaster, or some passion, or some persuasion, regain his self-respect, and may renounce drink, and lead a sober and useful life. Has it not been often so?

And in both cases the freedom of the will is untouched: It is the change in the environment that lifts the fallen up, and beats the upright down. . . .

The apostles of free will believe that all men's wills are free. But a man can only will that which he is able to will. And one man is able to will that which another man is unable to will. To deny this is to deny the commonest and most obvious facts of life. . . .

[III. ARGUMENTS AGAINST FREE WILL]

1. We all know that we can foretell the action of certain men in certain cases, because we know the men.

We know that under the same conditions Jack Sheppard* would steal, and Cardinal Manning† would not steal. We know that under the same conditions the sailor would flirt with the waitress, and the priest would not; that the drunkard would get drunk, and the abstainer would remain sober. We know that Wellington‡ would refuse a bribe, that Nelson‡ would not run away, that Buonaparte§ would grasp at power, that Abraham Lincoln would be loyal to his country, that Torquemada‖ would not spare a heretic. Why? If the will is free, how can we be sure, before a test arises, how the will must act?

Simply because we know that heredity and environment have so formed and molded men and women that under certain circumstances the action of their wills is certain.

Heredity and environment having made a man a thief, he will steal. Heredity and environment having made a man honest, he will not steal.

That is to say, heredity and environment have decided the action of the will, before the time has come for the will to act.

---

*[A famous criminal.—Eds.]
†[A cardinal of the Roman Catholic Church.—Eds.]
‡[British military men.—Eds.]
§[Napoleon.—Eds.]
‖[A fifteenth-century Spanish inquisitor.—Eds.]

This being so—and we all know that it is so—what becomes of the sovereignty of the will?

Let any man that believes that he can "do as he likes" ask himself *why* he *likes*, and he will see the error of the theory of free will, and will understand why the will is the servant and not the master of the man: For the man is the product of heredity and environment, and these control the will.

[*Examples*] As we want to get this subject as clear as we can, let us take one or two familiar examples of the action of the will.

Jones and Robinson meet and have a glass of whiskey. Jones asks Robinson to have another. Robinson says, "No thank you, one is enough." Jones says, "All right: Have another cigarette." Robinson takes the cigarette. Now, here we have a case where a man refuses a second drink but takes a second smoke. Is it because he would like another cigarette but would not like another glass of whiskey? No. It is because he knows that it is *safer* not to take another glass of whiskey.

How does he know that whiskey is dangerous? He has learned it—from his environment.

"But he *could* have taken another glass if he wished."

But he could not wish to take another, because there was something he wished more strongly—to be safe.

And why did he want to be safe? Because he had learned—from his environment—that it was unhealthy, unprofitable, and shameful to get drunk. Because he had learned—from his environment—that it is easier to avoid forming a bad habit than to break a bad habit when formed. Because he valued the good opinion of his neighbors, and also his position and prospects.

These feelings and this knowledge ruled his will, and caused him to refuse the second glass. . . .

Now suppose Smith asks Williams to have another glass. Williams takes it, takes several, finally goes home—as he often goes home. Why?

Largely because drinking is a habit with him. And not only does the mind instinctively repeat an action but, in the case of drink, a physical craving is set up and the brain is weakened. It is easier to refuse the first glass than the second; it is easier to refuse the second than the third; and it is very much harder for a man to keep sober who has frequently gotten drunk.

So when poor Williams has to make his choice, he has habit against him, he has a physical craving against him, and he has a weakened brain to think with.

"But Williams could have refused the first glass."

No. Because in his case the desire to drink, or to please a friend, was stronger than his fear of the danger. Or he may not have been so conscious of the danger as Robinson was. He may not have been so well taught, or he may not have been so sensible, or he may not have been so cautious. So that his heredity and environment, his temperament and training, led him to take the drink, as surely as Robinson's heredity and environment led him to refuse it.

And now it is my turn to ask a question. If the will is "free," if conscience is a sure guide, how is it that the free will and the conscience of Robinson caused him to keep sober, while the free will and conscience of Williams caused him to get drunk?

Robinson's will was curbed by certain feelings which failed to curb the will of Williams. Because in the case of Williams the feelings were stronger on the other side.

It was the nature and the training of Robinson which made him refuse the second glass, and it was the nature and the training of Williams which made him drink the second glass.

What had free will to do with it? . . .

2. Those who exalt the power of the will, and belittle the power of environment, belie their words by their deeds.

For they would not send their children among bad companions or allow them to read bad books. They would not say the children have free will and therefore have power to take the good and leave the bad.

They know very well that evil environment has power to pervert the will, and that good environment has power to direct it properly.

They know that children may be made good or bad by good or evil training, and that the will follows the training.

That being so, they must also admit that the children of other people may be good or bad by training.

And if a child gets bad training, how can free will save it? Or how can it be blamed for being bad? It never had a chance to be good. That they know this is proved by their carefulness in providing their own children with better environment.

As I have said before, every church, every school, every moral lesson is a proof that preachers and teachers trust to good environment, and not to free will, to make children good.

In this, as in so many other matters, actions speak louder than words.

That, I hope, disentangles the many knots into which thousands of learned men have tied the simple subject of free will; and disposes of the claim that man is responsible because his will is free.

12 / The Problem of Free Will

W. T. STACE

*W. T. Stace (1886–1967) taught at Princeton University. He worked in
ethics, the study of religion and culture, and was a significant figure in both
the academic world and public culture.*

[I. INTRODUCTION]

[A] great problem which the rise of scientific naturalism has created for the
modern mind concerns the foundations of morality. . . .

I shall first discuss the problem of free will, for it is certain that if there is
not free will there can be no morality. Morality is concerned with what men
ought and ought not to do. But if a man has not freedom to choose what he
will do, if whatever he does is done under compulsion, then it does not make
sense to tell him that he ought not to have done what he did and that he ought
to do something different. All moral precepts would in such case be meaningless. Also if he acts always under compulsion, how can he be held morally
responsible for his actions? How can he, for example, be punished for what he
could not help doing?

[II. THE PROBLEM OF FREE WILL]

It is to be observed that those learned professors of philosophy or psychology
who deny the existence of free will do so only in their professional moments
and in their studies and lecture rooms. For when it comes to doing anything
practical, even of the most trivial kind, they invariably behave as if they and
others were free. They inquire from you at dinner whether you will choose
this dish or that dish. They will ask a child why he told a lie, and will punish
him for not having chosen the way of truthfulness. All of which is inconsistent
with a disbelief in free will. This should cause us to suspect that the problem is
not a real one; and this, I believe, is the case. The dispute is merely verbal, and
is due to nothing but a confusion about the meanings of words. It is what is
now fashionably called a semantic problem.

How does a verbal dispute arise? Let us consider a case which, although it
is absurd in the sense that no one would ever make the mistake which is
involved in it, yet illustrates the principle which we shall have to use in the
solution of the problem. Suppose that someone believed that the word "man"
means a certain sort of five-legged animal; in short that "five-legged animal"

is the correct *definition* of man. He might then look around the world, and rightly observing that there are no five-legged animals in it, he might proceed to deny the existence of men. This preposterous conclusion would have been reached because he was using an incorrect definition of "man." All you would have to do to show him his mistake would be to give him the correct definition; or at least to show him that his definition was wrong. Both the problem and its solution would, of course, be entirely verbal. The problem of free will, and its solution, I shall maintain, is verbal in exactly the same way. The problem has been created by the fact that learned men, especially philosophers, have assumed an incorrect definition of free will, and then finding that there is nothing in the world which answers to their definition have denied its existence. As far as logic is concerned, their conclusion is just as absurd as that of the man who denies the existence of men. The only difference is that the mistake in the latter case is obvious and crude, while the mistake which deniers of free will have made is rather subtle and difficult to detect.

Throughout the modern period, until quite recently, it was assumed, both by the philosophers who denied free will and by those who defended it, that *determinism is inconsistent with free will*. If a man's actions were wholly determined by chains of causes stretching back into the remote past, so that they could be predicted beforehand by a mind which knew all the causes, it was assumed that they could not in that case be free. This implies that a certain definition of actions done from free will was assumed, namely that they are actions *not* wholly determined by causes or predictable beforehand. Let us shorten this by saying that free will was defined as meaning indeterminism. This is the incorrect definition which has led to the denial of free will. As soon as we see what the true definition is we shall find that the question whether the world is deterministic, as Newtonian science implied, or in a measure indeterministic, as current physics teaches, is wholly irrelevant to the problem.

[III. PROOF OF FREE WILL]

Of course there is a sense in which one can define a word arbitrarily in any way one pleases. But a definition may nevertheless be called correct or incorrect. It is correct if it accords with a *common usage* of the word defined. It is incorrect if it does not. And if you give an incorrect definition, absurd and untrue results are likely to follow. For instance, there is nothing to prevent you from arbitrarily defining a man as a five-legged animal, but this is incorrect in the sense that it does not accord with the ordinary meaning of the word. Also it has the absurd result of leading to a denial of the existence of men. This shows that *common usage is the criterion for deciding whether a definition is correct or not*. And this is the principle which I shall apply to free will. I shall show that indeterminism is not what is meant by the phrase "free will" *as it is commonly used*. And I shall attempt to discover the correct definition by inquiring how the phrase is used in ordinary conversation.

Here are a few samples of how the phrase might be used in ordinary conversation. It will be noticed that they include cases in which the question whether a man acted with free will is asked in order to determine whether he was morally and legally responsible for his acts.

> *Jones*   I once went without food for a week.
> *Smith*   Did you do that of your own free will?
> *Jones*   No. I did it because I was lost in a desert and could find no food.

But suppose that the man who had fasted was Mahatma Gandhi. The conversation might then have gone:

> *Gandhi*   I once fasted for a week.
> *Smith*   Did you do that of your own free will?
> *Gandhi*   Yes. I did it because I wanted to compel the British Government to give India its independence.

Take another case. Suppose that I had stolen some bread, but that I was as truthful as George Washington. Then, if I were charged with the crime in court, some exchange of the following sort might take place:

> *Judge*   Did you steal the bread of your own free will?
> *Stace*   Yes. I stole it because I was hungry.

Or in different circumstances the conversation might run:

> *Judge*   Did you steal of your own free will?
> *Stace*   No. I stole because my employer threatened to beat me if I did not.

At a recent murder trial in Trenton some of the accused had signed confessions, but afterwards asserted that they had done so under police duress. The following exchange might have occurred:

> *Judge*   Did you sign this confession of your own free will?
> *Prisoner*   No. I signed it because the police beat me up.

Now suppose that a philosopher had been a member of the jury. We could imagine this conversation taking place in the jury room:

> *Foreman of the Jury*   The prisoner says he signed the confession because he was beaten, and not of his own free will.
> *Philosopher*   This is quite irrelevant to the case. There is no such thing as free will.
> *Foreman*   Do you mean to say that it makes no difference whether he signed because his conscience made him want to tell the truth or because he was beaten?
> *Philosopher*   None at all. Whether he was caused to sign by a beating or by some desire of his own—the desire to tell the truth, for example—in either case

his signing was causally determined, and therefore in neither case did he act of his own free will. Since there is no such thing as free will, the question whether he signed of his own free will ought not to be discussed by us.

The foreman and the rest of the jury would rightly conclude that the philosopher must be making some mistake. What sort of a mistake could it be? There is only one possible answer. The philosopher must be using the phrase "free will" in some peculiar way of his own which is not the way in which men usually use it when they wish to determine a question of moral responsibility. That is, he must be using an incorrect definition of it as implying action not determined by causes.

Suppose a man left his office at noon, and was questioned about it. Then we might hear this:

> *Jones*　Did you go out of your own free will?
> *Smith*　Yes. I went out to get my lunch.

But we might hear:

> *Jones*　Did you leave your office of your own free will?
> *Smith*　No. I was forcibly removed by the police.

We have now collected a number of cases of actions which, in the ordinary usage of the English language, would be called cases in which people have acted of their own free will. We should also say in all these cases that they *chose* to act as they did. We should also say that they could have acted otherwise, if they had chosen. For instance, Mahatma Gandhi was not compelled to fast; he chose to do so. He could have eaten if he had wanted to. When Smith went out to get his lunch, he chose to do so. He could have stayed and done some more work, if he had wanted to. We have also collected a number of cases of the opposite kind. They are cases in which men were not able to exercise their free will. They had no choice. They were compelled to do as they did. The man in the desert did not fast of his own free will. He had no choice in the matter. He was compelled to fast because there was nothing for him to eat. And so with the other cases. It ought to be quite easy, by an inspection of these cases, to tell what we ordinarily mean when we say that a man did or did not exercise free will. We ought therefore to be able to extract from them the proper definition of the term. Let us put the cases in a table:

Free Acts	*Unfree Acts*
Gandhi fasting because he wanted to free India.	The man fasting in the desert because there was no food.
Stealing bread because one is hungry.	Stealing because one's employer threatened to beat one.
Signing a confession because one wanted to tell the truth.	Signing because the police beat one.

Free Acts	Unfree Acts
Leaving the office because one wanted one's lunch.	Leaving because forcibly removed.

It is obvious that to find the correct definition of free acts we must discover what characteristic is common to all the acts in the left-hand column, and is, at the same time, absent from all the acts in the right-hand column. This characteristic which all free acts have, and which no unfree acts have, will be the defining characteristic of free will.

Is being uncaused, or not being determined by causes, the characteristic of which we are in search? It cannot be, because although it is true that all the acts in the right-hand column have causes, such as the beating by the police or the absence of food in the desert, so also do the acts in the left-hand column. Mr. Gandhi's fasting was caused by his desire to free India, the man leaving his office by his hunger, and so on. Moreover there is no reason to doubt that these causes of the free acts were in turn caused by prior conditions, and that these were again the results of causes, and so on back indefinitely into the past. Any physiologist can tell us the causes of hunger. What caused Mr. Gandhi's tremendously powerful desire to free India is no doubt more difficult to discover. But it must have had causes. Some of them may have lain in peculiarities of his glands or brain, others in his past experiences, others in his heredity, others in his education. Defenders of free will have usually tended to deny such facts. But to do so is plainly a case of special pleading, which is unsupported by any scrap of evidence. The only reasonable view is that all human actions, both those which are freely done and those which are not, are either wholly determined by causes, or at least as much determined as other events in nature. It may be true, as the physicists tell us, that nature is not as deterministic as was once thought. But whatever degree of determinism prevails in the world, human actions appear to be as much determined as anything else. And if this is so, it cannot be the case that what distinguishes actions freely chosen from those which are not free is that the latter are determined by causes while the former are not. Therefore, being uncaused or being undetermined by causes must be an incorrect definition of free will.

What, then, is the difference between acts which are freely done and those which are not? What is the characteristic which is present to all the acts in the left-hand column and absent from all those in the right-hand column? Is it not obvious that, although both sets of actions have causes, the causes of those in the left-hand column are *of a different kind* from the causes of those in the right-hand column? The free acts are all caused by desires, or motives, or by some sort of internal psychological states of the agent's mind. The unfree acts, on the other hand, are all caused by physical forces or physical conditions outside the agent. Police arrest means physical force exerted from the outside; the absence of food in the desert is a physical condition of the outside world. We may therefore frame the following rough definitions. *Acts freely done are those whose immediate causes are psychological states in the agent. Acts not freely done are those whose immediate causes are states of affairs external to the agent.**

It is plain that if we define free will in this way, then free will certainly exists, and the philosopher's denial of its existence is seen to be what it is— nonsense. For it is obvious that all those actions of men which we should ordinarily attribute to the exercise of their free will, or of which we should say that they freely chose to do them, are in fact actions which have been caused by their own desires, wishes, thoughts, emotions, impulses, or other psychological states.

[IV. OBJECTIONS AND REPLIES]

In applying our definition we shall find that it usually works well, but that there are some puzzling cases which it does not seem exactly to fit. These puzzles can always be solved by paying careful attention to the ways in which words are used, and remembering that they are not always used consistently. I have space for only one example. Suppose that a thug threatens to shoot you unless you give him your wallet, and suppose that you do so. Do you, in giving him your wallet, do so of your own free will or not? If we apply our definition, we find that you acted freely, since the immediate cause of the action was not an actual outside force but the fear of death, which is a psychological cause. Most people, however, would say that you did not act of your own free will but under compulsion. Does this show that our definition is wrong? I do not think so. . . . In the case under discussion, though no actual force was used, the gun at your forehead so nearly approximated to actual force that we tend to say the case was one of compulsion. It is a borderline case.

Here is what may seem like another kind of puzzle. According to our view an action may be free though it could have been predicted beforehand with certainty. But suppose you told a lie, and it was certain beforehand that you would tell it. How could one then say, "You could have told the truth"? The answer is that it is perfectly true that you could have told the truth *if* you had wanted to. In fact you would have done so, for in that case the causes producing your action, namely your desires, would have been different, and would therefore have produced different effects. It is a delusion that predict-

**[Note that these "definitions" are criteria for distinguishing between *acts* freely done and acts not freely done. They are not definitions of what free or free will and their opposites *mean*. Stace has indicated what the definitions of free and unfree are in the paragraph following his examples of conversations and in the examples themselves. It is clear that Stace's actual definitions of free and unfree are:*

  free = uncompelled
  unfree = compelled

*What, then, is he providing in these italicized sentences? Criteria for distinguishing *which* acts are genuinely free and which are unfree —Eds.]*

ability and free will are incompatible. This agrees with common sense. For if, knowing your character, I predict that you will act honorably, no one would say when you do act honorably that this shows you did not do so of your own free will.

[V. THE COMPATIBILITY OF FREE WILL, DETERMINISM, AND RESPONSIBILITY]

Since free will is a condition of moral responsibility, we must be sure that our theory of free will gives a sufficient basis for it. To be held morally responsible for one's actions means that one may be justly punished or rewarded, blamed or praised, for them. But it is not just to punish a man for what he cannot help doing. How can it be just to punish him for an action which it was certain beforehand that he would do? We have not attempted to decide whether, as a matter of fact, all events, including human actions, are completely determined. For that question is irrelevant to the problem of free will. But if we assume for the purposes of argument that complete determinism is true, but that we are nevertheless free, it may then be asked whether such a deterministic free will is compatible with moral responsibility. For it may seem unjust to punish a man for an action which it could have been predicted with certainty beforehand that he would do.

But that determinism is incompatible with moral responsibility is as much a delusion as that it is incompatible with free will. You do not excuse a man for doing a wrong act because, knowing his character, you felt certain beforehand that he would do it. Nor do you deprive a man of a reward or prize because, knowing his goodness or his capabilities, you felt certain beforehand that he would win it.

Volumes have been written on the justification of punishment. But so far as it affects the question of free will, the essential principles involved are quite simple. The punishment of a man for doing a wrong act is justified either on the ground that it will correct his own character or on the ground that it will deter other people from doing similar acts. . . . The question, then, is how, if we assume determinism, punishment can correct character or deter people from evil actions.

Suppose that your child develops a habit of telling lies. You give him a mild beating. Why? Because you believe that his personality is such that the usual motives for telling the truth do not cause him to do so. You therefore supply the missing cause, or motive, in the shape of pain and the fear of future pain if he repeats his untruthful behavior. And you hope that a few treatments of this kind will condition him to the habit of truth-telling, so that he will come to tell the truth without the infliction of pain. You assume that his actions are determined by causes, but that the usual causes of truth-telling do not in him produce their usual effects. You therefore supply him with an artificially injected motive, pain and fear, which you think will in the future cause him to speak truthfully.

The principle is exactly the same where you hope, by punishing one man, to deter others from wrong actions. You believe that the fear of punishment will cause those who might otherwise do evil to do well. . . .

Thus we see that moral responsibility is not only consistent with determinism but requires it. The assumption on which punishment is based is that human behavior is causally determined. If pain could not be a cause of truth-telling there would be no justification at all for punishing lies. If human actions and volitions were uncaused, it would be useless either to punish or reward, or indeed to do anything else to correct people's bad behavior. For nothing that you could do would in any way influence them. Thus moral responsibility would entirely disappear. If there were no determinism of human beings at all, their actions would be completely unpredictable and capricious, and therefore irresponsible. And this is in itself a strong argument against the common view of philosophers that free will means being undetermined by causes.

13 / *Freedom and Determinism*

RICHARD TAYLOR

Richard Taylor (1919–   ) is a professor of philosophy who taught for many years at Union College in New York. He has written highly acclaimed and widely discussed books and articles on a variety of philosophical problems in the philosophy of religion, metaphysics, and the philosophy of mind.

I. FREEDOM

*T*o say that it is, in a given instance, up to me what I do, is to say that I am in that instance *free* with respect to what I then do. Thus, I am sometimes free to move my finger this way and that, but not, certainly, to bend it backward or into a knot. But what does this mean?

It means, first, that there is no *obstacle* or *impediment* to my activity. Thus, there is sometimes no obstacle to my moving my finger this way and that, though there are obvious obstacles to my moving it far backward or into a knot. Those things, accordingly, that pose obstacles to my motions limit my freedom. . . .

Further, to say that it is, in a given instance, up to me what I do means that nothing *constrains* or *forces* me to do one thing rather than another. Constraints are like obstacles, except that while the latter prevent, the former enforce. Thus, if my finger is being forcibly bent to the left—by a machine, for instance, or by another person, or by any force that I cannot overcome—then I am not free to move it this way and that. . . .

Obstacles and constraints, then, both obviously limit my freedom. To say I am free to perform some action thus means at least that there is no obstacle to my doing it, and that nothing constrains me to do otherwise.*

Now if we rest content with this observation, as many have, and construe free activity simply as activity that is unimpeded and unconstrained, there is evidently no inconsistency between affirming both the thesis of determinism and the claim that I am sometimes free. For to say that some action of mine is neither impeded nor constrained does not by itself imply that it is not causally determined. The absence of obstacles and constraints are mere negative conditions, and do not by themselves rule out the presence of positive causes. It might seem, then, that we can say of some of my actions that there are conditions antecedent to their performance so that no other actions were possible, and also that these actions were unobstructed and unconstrained. And to say that would logically entail that such actions were both causally determined and free.

II. SOFT DETERMINISM

It is this kind of consideration that has led many philosophers to embrace what is sometimes called soft determinism.[†] All versions of this theory have in common three claims, by means of which, it is naïvely supposed, a reconciliation is achieved between determinism and freedom. . . .

The three claims of soft determinism are (1) that the thesis of determinism is true, and that accordingly all human behavior, voluntary or other, like the behavior of all other things, arises from antecedent conditions, given which no other behavior is possible—in short, that all human behavior is caused and determined; (2) that voluntary behavior is nonetheless free to the extent that it is not externally constrained or impeded; and (3) that, in the absence of such obstacles and constraints, the causes of voluntary behavior are certain states, events, or conditions within the agent himself; namely, his own acts of will or volitions, choices, decisions, desires, and so on.

Thus, on this view, I am free, and therefore sometimes responsible for what I do, provided nothing prevents me from acting according to my own choice, desire, or volition, or constrains me to act otherwise.* There may, to be sure, be other conditions for my responsibility—such as, for example, an understanding of the probable consequences of my behavior, and that sort of

---

*[Note that this conception of 'free' coincides with Stace's, although it is expressed differently.—Eds.]

[†][Also known as compatibilism.—Eds.]

thing—but absence of constraint or impediment is, at least, one such condition. And, it is claimed, it is a condition that is compatible with the supposition that my behavior is caused—for it is, by hypothesis, caused by my own inner choices, desires, and volitions.*

III. THE REFUTATION OF THIS

The theory of soft determinism looks good at first . . .—but no great acumen is needed to discover that, far from solving any problem, it only camouflages it.

My free actions are those unimpeded and unconstrained motions that arise from my own inner desires, choices, and volitions; let us grant this provisionally. But now, whence arise those inner states that determine what my body shall do? Are they within my control or not? Having made my choice or decision and acted upon it, could I have chosen otherwise or not?

Here the determinist, hoping to surrender nothing and yet to avoid the problem implied in that question, bids us not to ask it; the question itself, he announces, is without meaning. . . .

But it is not nonsense to ask whether the causes of my actions—my own inner choices, decisions, and desires—are themselves caused. And of course they are, if determinism is true, for on that thesis everything is caused and determined. And if they are, then we cannot avoid concluding that, given the causal conditions of those inner states, I could not have decided, willed, chosen, or desired otherwise than I in fact did, for this is a logical consequence of the very definition of determinism. . . .

IV. EXAMPLES

Such is the dialectic of the problem. The easiest way to see the shadowy quality of soft determinism, however, is by means of examples.

Let us suppose that my body is moving in various ways, that these motions are not externally constrained or impeded, and that they are all exactly in accordance with my own desires, choices, or acts of will and whatnot. When I will that my arm should move in a certain way, I find it moving in that way, unobstructed and unconstrained. When I will to speak, my lips and tongue move, unobstructed and unconstrained, in a manner suitable to the formation of the words I choose to utter. Now given that this is a correct description of my behavior, namely, that it consists of the unconstrained and unimpeded motions of my body in response to my own volitions, then it follows that my behavior is free, on the soft determinist's definition of "free." It follows further that I am responsible for that behavior; or at least that if I am not, it is not from any lack of freedom on my part.

*[As Stace said, these acts are caused by my internal, psychological states.—Eds.]

But if the fulfillment of these conditions renders my behavior free—that is to say, if my behavior satisfies the conditions of free action set forth in the theory of soft determinism—then my behavior will be less free if we assume further conditions that are perfectly consistent with those already satisfied.

We suppose further, accordingly, that while my behavior is entirely in accordance with my own volitions, and thus "free" in terms of the conception of freedom we are examining, my volitions themselves are caused. To make this graphic, we can suppose that an ingenious physiologist can induce in me any volition he pleases, simply by pushing various buttons on an instrument to which, let us suppose, I am attached by numerous wires. All the volitions I have in that situation are, accordingly, precisely the ones he gives me. By pushing one button, he evokes in me the volition to raise my hand; and my hand, being unimpeded, rises in response to that volition. By pushing another, he induces the volition in me to kick, and my foot, being unimpeded, kicks in response to that volition. We can even suppose that the physiologist puts a rifle in my hands, aims it at some passer-by, and then, by pushing the proper button, evokes in me the volition to squeeze my finger against the trigger, whereupon the passer-by falls dead of a bullet wound.

This is the description of a man who is acting in accordance with his inner volitions, a man whose body is unimpeded and unconstrained in its motions, these motions being the effects of those inner states. It is hardly the description of a free and responsible agent. It is the perfect description of a puppet. To render a man your puppet, it is not necessary forcibly to constrain the motions of his limbs, after the fashion that real puppets are moved. A subtler but no less effective means of making a man your puppet would be to gain complete control of his inner states and ensure, as the theory of soft determinism does ensure, that his body will move in accordance with them.

The example is somewhat unusual, but it is no worse for that. It is perfectly intelligible, and it does appear to refute the soft determinist's conception of freedom. . . . The example can, moreover, be modified in perfectly realistic ways, so as to coincide with actual and familiar cases. One can, for instance, be given a compulsive desire for certain drugs, simply by having them administered to him over a course of time. Suppose, then, that I do, with neither my knowledge nor consent, thus become a victim of such a desire and act upon it. Do I act freely, merely by virtue of the fact that I am unimpeded in my quest for drugs? In a sense I do, surely, but I am hardly free with respect to whether or not I shall use drugs. I never chose to have the desire for them inflicted upon me.

Nor does it, of course, matter whether the inner states which allegedly prompt all my "free" activity are evoked in me by another agent or by perfectly impersonal forces. Whether a desire which causes my body to behave in a certain way is inflicted upon me by another person, for instance, or derived from hereditary factors, or indeed from anything at all, matters not the least. In any case, if it is in fact the cause of my bodily behavior, I cannot but act in accordance with it. Wherever it came from, whether from personal or impersonal origins, it was entirely caused or determined, and not within my control. Indeed, if determinism is true, as the theory of soft determinism holds it to be,* all those inner states which cause my body to behave in whatever ways it behaves must arise from circumstances that existed before I was born; for the chain of causes and effects is infinite, and none could have been the least different, given those that preceded.

V. SIMPLE INDETERMINISM

We might at first now seem warranted in simply denying determinism, and saying that, insofar as they are free, my actions are not caused; or that, if they are caused by my own inner states—my own desires, impulses, choices, volitions, and whatnot—then these, in any case, are not caused. . . .

Only the slightest consideration will show, however, that this simple denial of determinism has not the slightest plausibility. For let us suppose it is true, and that some of my bodily motions—namely, those that I regard as my free acts—are not caused at all or, if caused by my own inner states, that these are not caused. We shall thereby avoid picturing a puppet to be sure—but only by substituting something even less like a man; for the conception that now emerges is not that of a free man, but of an erratic and jerking phantom, without any rhyme or reason at all.

Suppose that my right arm is free, according to this conception; that is, that its motions are uncaused. It moves this way and that from time to time, but nothing causes these motions. Sometimes it moves forth vigorously, sometimes up, sometimes down; sometimes it just drifts vaguely about— these motions all being wholly free and uncaused. Manifestly I have nothing to do with them at all; they just happen, and neither I nor anyone can ever tell what this arm will be doing next. It might seize a club and lay it on the head of the nearest bystander, no less to my astonishment than to his. There will never be any point in asking why these motions occur, or in seeking any explanation of them, for under the conditions assumed there is no explanation. They just happen, from no causes at all.

This is no description of free, voluntary, or responsible behavior. Indeed, so far as the motions of my body or its parts are entirely uncaused, such motions cannot even be ascribed to me as my behavior in the first place, since I have nothing to do with them. The behavior of my arm is just the random motion of a foreign object. Behavior that is mine must be behavior that is within my control, but motions that occur from no causes are without the control of anyone. I can have no more to do with, and no more control over, the uncaused motions of my limbs than a gambler has over the motions of an honest roulette wheel. I can only, like him, idly wait to see what happens.

Nor does it improve things to suppose that my bodily motions are caused by my own inner states, so long as we suppose these to be wholly uncaused.

*[Recall that soft determinism accepts determinism, in the strict interpretation, as true.— Eds.]

The result will be the same as before. My arm, for example, will move this way and that, sometimes up and sometimes down, sometimes vigorously and sometimes just drifting about, always in response to certain inner states, to be sure. But since these are supposed to be wholly uncaused, it follows that I have no control over them and hence none over their effects. If my hand lays a club forcefully on the nearest bystander, we can indeed say that this motion resulted from an inner club-wielding desire of mine; but we must add that I had nothing to do with that desire, and that it arose, to be followed by its inevitable effect, no less to my astonishment than to his. Things like this do, alas, sometimes happen. We are all sometimes seized by compulsive impulses that arise we know not whither, and we do sometimes act upon these. But since they are far from being examples of free, voluntary, and responsible behavior, we need only to learn that behavior was of this sort to conclude that it was not free, voluntary, nor responsible. It was erratic, impulsive, and irresponsible.

VI. DETERMINISM* AND SIMPLE INDETERMINISM AS THEORIES

Both determinism and simple indeterminism are loaded with difficulties, and no one who has thought much on them can affirm either of them without some embarrassment. Simple indeterminism has nothing whatever to be said for it, except that it appears to remove the grossest difficulties of determinism, only, however, to imply perfect absurdities of its own. Determinism, on the other hand, is at least initially plausible. Men seem to have a natural inclination to believe in it; it is, indeed, almost required for the very exercise of practical intelligence. And beyond this, our experience appears always to confirm it, so long as we are dealing with everyday facts of common experience, as distinguished from the esoteric researches of theoretical physics. But determinism, as applied to human behavior, has implications which few men can casually accept, and they appear to be implications which no modification of the theory can efface.

Both theories, moreover, appear logically irreconcilable to the two items of data that we set forth at the outset; namely, (1) that my behavior is sometimes the outcome of my deliberation and (2) that in these and other cases it is sometimes up to me what I do. Since these were our data, it is important to see, as must already be quite clear, that these theories cannot be reconciled to them.†

*[In this section, Taylor presents criticisms of determinism and briefly, at the end, of indeterminism. It is important to understand that, by 'determinism' he means the strict interpretation. Note also that, since hard determinism bases its denial of free will on the acceptance of strict determinism, Taylor's criticism is also a criticism of hard determinism.—Eds.]

†[These items were originally mentioned in a section not reprinted in this selection. He there writes, "there are . . . two things about myself of which I feel quite certain . . . The first is that I deliberate, with the view of making a decision; a decision, namely, to do this thing or that. And the

[*Determinism*] I can deliberate only about my own future actions, and then only if I do not already know what I am going to do. If a certain nasal tickle warns me that I am about to sneeze, for instance, then I cannot deliberate whether to sneeze or not; I can only prepare for the impending convulsion. But if determinism is true, then there are always conditions existing anteced- ently to everything I do, sufficient for my doing just that, and such as to render it inevitable. If I can know what those conditions are and what behav- ior they are sufficient to produce, then I can in every such case know what I am going to do and cannot then deliberate about it.

By itself this only shows, of course, that I can deliberate only in ignorance of the causal conditions of my behavior; it does not show that such conditions cannot exist. It is odd, however, to suppose that deliberation should be a mere substitute for clear knowledge. Ignorance is a condition of speculation, infer- ence, and guesswork, which have nothing whatever to do with deliberation. A prisoner awaiting execution may not know when he is going to die, and he may even entertain the hope of reprieve, but he cannot deliberate about this. He can only speculate, guess—and wait.

Worse yet, however, it now becomes clear that I cannot deliberate about what I am going to do if it is even possible for me to find out in advance, whether I do in fact find out in advance or not. I can deliberate only with the view to deciding what to do, to making up my mind; and this is impossible if I believe that it could be inferred what I am going to do from conditions already existing, even though I have not made that inference myself. If I believe that what I am going to do has been rendered inevitable by conditions already existing, and could be inferred by anyone having the requisite sagacity, then I cannot try to decide whether to do it or not, for there is simply nothing left to decide. I can at best only guess or try to figure it out myself or, all prognostics failing, I can wait and see; but I cannot deliberate. I deliberate in order to *decide* what *to* do, not to *discover* what it is that I am *going* to do. But if determinism is true, then there are always antecedent conditions sufficient for everything that I do, and this can always be inferred by anyone having the requisite sagacity; that is, by anyone having a knowledge of what those conditions are and what behavior they are sufficient to produce.

This suggests what in fact seems quite clear, that determinism cannot be reconciled with our second datum either, to the effect that it is sometimes up to me what I am going to do. For if it is ever really up to me whether to do this thing or that, then, as we have seen, each alternative course of action must be such that I can do it; not that I can do it in some abstruse or hypothetical sense of "can"; nor that I could do it if only something were true that is not true; but in the sense that it is then and there within my power to do it. But this is never so, if determinism is true, for on the very formulation of that theory whatever happens at any time is the only thing that can then happen, given all that

---

second is that whether or not I deliberate about what to do, it is sometimes up to me what I do . . . We must . . . if we ever hope to be wiser, adjust our theories to our data and not try to adjust our data to our theories." (*Metaphysics*, New York: Prentice-Hall, 1963), p. 37.—Eds.]

precedes it. It is simply a logical consequence of this that whatever I do at any time is the only thing I can then do, given the conditions that precede my doing it. Nor does it help in the least to interpose, among the causal antecedents of my behavior, my own inner states, such as my desires, choices, acts of will, and so on. For even supposing these to be always involved in voluntary behavior—which is highly doubtful in itself—it is a consequence of determinism that these, whatever they are at any time, can never be other than what they then are. Every chain of causes and effects, if determinism is true, is infinite. This is why it is not now up to me whether I shall a moment hence be male or female. The conditions determining my sex have existed through my whole life, and even prior to my life. But if determinism is true, the same holds of anything that I ever am, ever become, or ever do. It matters not whether we are speaking of the most patent facts of my being, such as my sex; or the most subtle, such as my feelings, thoughts, desires, or choices. Nothing could be other than it is, given what was; and while we may indeed say, quite idly, that something—some inner state of mine, for instance—*could* have been different, had only something *else* been different, any consolation of this thought evaporates as soon as we add that whatever would have to have been different could not have been different.

[*Indeterminism*] It is even more obvious that our data cannot be reconciled to the theory of simple indeterminism. I can deliberate only about my own actions; this is obvious. But the random, uncaused motion of any body whatever, whether it be a part of my body or not, is no action of mine and nothing that is within my power. I might try to guess what these motions will be, just as I might try to guess how a roulette wheel will behave, but I cannot deliberate about them or try to decide what they shall be, simply because these things are not up to me. Whatever is not caused by anything is not caused by me, and nothing could be more plainly inconsistent with saying that it is nevertheless up to me what it shall be.

VII. THE THEORY OF AGENCY [SELF-DETERMINISM]

The only conception of action that accords with our data is one according to which men—and perhaps some other things too—are sometimes, but of course not always, self-determining beings; that is, beings which are sometimes the causes of their own behavior. In the case of an action that is free, it must be such that it is caused by the agent who performs it, but such that no antecedent conditions were sufficient for his performing just that action. In the case of an action that is both free and rational, it must be such that the agent who performed it did so for some reason, but this *reason* cannot have been the *cause* of it.

[*Virtue of the Theory*] Now this conception fits what men take themselves to be; namely, beings who act, or who are agents, rather than things that are merely acted upon, and whose behavior is simply the causal consequence of conditions which they have not wrought. When I believe that I have done something, I do believe that it was I who caused it to be done, I who made something happen, and not merely something within me, such as one of my own subjective states, which is not identical with myself. If I believe that something not identical with myself was the cause of my behavior—some event wholly external to myself, for instance, or even one internal to myself, such as a nerve impulse, volition, or whatnot—then I cannot regard that behavior as being an act of mine, unless I further believe that I was the cause of that external or internal event. My pulse, for example, is caused and regulated by certain conditions existing within me, and not by myself. I do not, accordingly, regard this activity of my body as my action, and would be no more tempted to do so if I became suddenly conscious within myself of those conditions or impulses that produce it. This is behavior with which *I* have nothing to do, behavior that is not within my immediate control, behavior that is not only not free activity, but not even the activity of an agent to begin with; it is nothing but a mechanical reflex. Had I never learned that my very life depends on this pulse beat, I would regard it with complete indifference, as something foreign to me, like the oscillations of a clock pendulum that I idly contemplate.

[*Drawbacks*] Now this conception of activity, and of an agent who is the cause of it, involves two rather strange metaphysical notions that are never applied elsewhere in nature. The first is that of a *self* or *person*—for example, a man—who is not merely a collection of things or events, but a substance and a self-moving being. For on this view it is a man himself, and not merely some part of him or something within him, that is the cause of his own activity. Now we certainly do not know that a man is anything more than an assemblage of physical things and processes, which act in accordance with those laws that describe the behavior of all other physical things and processes. Even though a man is a living being, of enormous complexity, there is nothing, apart from the requirements of this theory, to suggest that his behavior is so radically different in its origin from that of other physical objects, or that an understanding of it must be sought in some metaphysical realm wholly different from that appropriate to the understanding of nonliving things.

Second, this conception of activity involves an extraordinary conception of *causation*, according to which an agent, which is a substance and not an event, can nevertheless be the cause of an event. Indeed, if he is a free agent then he can, on this conception, cause an event to occur—namely, some act of his own—without anything else causing him to do so. This means that an agent is sometimes a cause, without being an antecedent sufficient condition; for if I affirm that I am the cause of some act of mine, then I am plainly not saying that my very existence is sufficient for its occurrence, which would be absurd. If I say that my hand causes my pencil to move, then I am saying that the motion of my hand is, under the other conditions then prevailing, sufficient for the motion of the pencil. But if I then say that I cause my hand to move, I am not saying anything remotely like this, and surely not that the motion of my self is sufficient for the motion of my arm and hand, since these are the only things about me that are moving.

This conception of the causation of events by beings or substances that are not events is, in fact, so different from the usual philosophical conception of a cause that it should not even bear the same name, for "being a cause" ordinarily just means "being an antecedent sufficient condition or set of conditions." Instead, then, of speaking of agents as *causing* their own acts, it would perhaps be better to use another word entirely, and say, for instance, that they *originate* them, *initiate* them, or simply that they *perform* them.

Now this is on the face of it a dubious conception of what a man is. Yet it is consistent with our data, reflecting the presuppositions of deliberation, and appears to be the only conception that is consistent with them, as determinism and simple indeterminism are not. The theory of agency avoids the absurdities of simple indeterminism by conceding that human behavior is caused, while at the same time avoiding the difficulties of determinism by denying that every chain of causes and effects is infinite. Some such causal chains, on this view, have beginnings, and they begin with agents themselves. Moreover, if we are to suppose that it is sometimes up to me what I do, and understand this in a sense which is not consistent with determinism, we must suppose that I am an agent or a being who initiates his own actions, sometimes under conditions which do not determine what action he shall perform. Deliberation becomes, on this view, something that is not only possible but quite rational, for it does make sense to deliberate about activity that is truly my own and that depends in its outcome upon me as its author, and not merely upon something more or less esoteric that is supposed to be intimately associated with me, such as my thoughts, volitions, choices, or whatnot.

One can hardly affirm such a theory of agency with complete comfort, however, and wholly without embarrassment, for the conception of men and their powers which is involved in it is strange indeed, if not positively mysterious. In fact, one can hardly be blamed here for simply denying our data outright, rather than embracing this theory to which they do most certainly point. Our data—to the effect that men do sometimes deliberate before acting, and that when they do, they presuppose among other things that it is up to them what they are going to do—rest upon nothing more than fairly common consent. These data might simply be illusions. It might in fact be that no man ever deliberates, but only imagines that he does, that from pure conceit he supposes himself to be the master of his behavior and the author of his acts. . . .

These are, then, dubitable conceptions, despite their being so well implanted in the common sense of mankind. . . . Perhaps here, as elsewhere in metaphysics, we should be content with discovering difficulties, with seeing what is and what is not consistent with such convictions as we happen to have, and then drawing such satisfaction as we can from the realization that, no matter where we begin, the world is mysterious and the men who try to understand it are even more so. This realization can, with some justification, make one feel wise, even in the full realization of his ignorance.

14 / Free-Will and Psychoanalysis

JOHN HOSPERS

John Hospers (1918–   ) taught at the University of Southern California and was for many years the director of the USC School of Philosophy. He is a wide-ranging philosopher and political theorist, who also works in aesthetics, ethics, and theory of knowledge. He is one of the founders of the modern Libertarian movement, as well as one of its most original philosophers.

[Note: In the opening paragraph, the author makes reference to Schlick (a philosopher). M. Schlick held the same position as that of W. T. Stace. He too tried to show that free will and determinism are compatible and co-exist. And he did it by arguments similar to Stace's. Hence whenever you find the name 'Schlick', you may substitute 'Stace'.]

I. [CRITICISM OF SOFT DETERMINISM]

Schlick's analysis is indeed clarifying and helpful to those who have fallen victim to the confusions he exposes—and this probably includes most persons in their philosophical growing-pains. But *is* this the end of the matter? Is it true that all acts, though caused, are free as long as they are not compelled in the sense which he specifies? May it not be that, while the identification of "free" with "uncompelled" is acceptable, the area of compelled acts is vastly greater than he or most other philosophers have ever suspected? . . . We remember statements about human beings being pawns of their early environment, victims of conditions beyond their control, the result of causal influences stemming from their parents, and the like, and we ponder and ask, "Still, are we really free?" Is there not something in what generations of sages have said about man being fettered? Is there not perhaps something too facile, too sleight-of-hand, in Schlick's cutting of the Gordian knot? For example, when a metropolitan newspaper headlines an article with the words "Boy Killer Is Doomed Long Before He Is Born,"[1] and then goes on to describe how a twelve-year-old boy has been sentenced to prison for the murder of a girl, and how his parental background includes records of drunkenness, divorce, social maladjustment, and paresis, are we still to say that his act, though

[1] *New York Post*, Tuesday, May 18, 1948, p. 4.

135

voluntary and assuredly *not* done at the point of a gun, is free? The boy has early displayed a tendency toward sadistic activity to hide an underlying masochism and "prove that he's a man"; being coddled by his mother only worsens this tendency until, spurned by a girl in his attempt on her, he kills her—not simply in a fit of anger, but calculatingly, deliberately. Is he free in respect of his criminal act, or for that matter in most of the acts of his life? Surely to ask this question is to answer it in the negative. Perhaps I have taken an extreme case; but it is only to show the superficiality of the Schlick analysis the more clearly. Though not everyone has criminotic tendencies, everyone has been molded by influences which in large measure at least determine his present behavior; he is literally the product of these influences, stemming from periods prior to his "years of discretion," giving him a host of character traits that he cannot change now even if he would. So obviously does what a man is depend upon how a man comes to be, that it is small wonder that philosophers and sages have considered man far indeed from being the master of his fate. It is not as if man's will were standing high and serene above the flux of events that have molded him; it is itself caught up in this flux, itself carried along on the current. An act is free when it is determined by the man's character, say moralists; but what if the most decisive aspects of his character were already irrevocably acquired before he could do anything to mold them? What if even the degree of will power available to him in shaping his habits and disciplining himself now to overcome the influence of his early environment is a factor over which he has no control? What are we to say of this kind of "freedom"? Is it not rather like the freedom of the machine to stamp labels on cans when it has been devised for just that purpose? Some machines can do so more efficiently than others, but only because they have been better constructed.

II. [THE EVIDENCE FROM PSYCHOANALYSIS]

It is not my purpose here to establish this thesis in general, but only in one specific respect which has received comparatively little attention, namely, the field referred to by psychiatrists as that of unconscious motivation. In what follows I shall restrict my attention to it because it illustrates as clearly as anything the points I wish to make.

Let me try to summarize very briefly the psychoanalytic doctrine on this point.[2] The conscious life of the human being, including the conscious decisions and volitions, is merely a mouthpiece for the unconscious—not directly

---

[2] I am aware that the theory presented below is not accepted by all practicing psychoanalysts. Many non-Freudians would disagree with the conclusions presented below. But I do not believe that this fact affects my argument, as long as the concept of unconscious motivation is accepted. I am aware, too, that much of the language employed in the following descriptions is animistic and metaphorical; but as long as I am presenting a view I would prefer to "go the whole hog" and present it in its most dramatic form. The theory can in any case be made clearest by the use of such language, just as atomic theory can often be made clearest to students with the use of models.

for the enactment of unconscious drives, but of the compromise between unconscious drives and unconscious reproaches. There is a Big Three behind the scenes which the automaton called the conscious personality carries out: The id, an "eternal gimme," presents its wish and demands its immediate satisfaction; the super-ego says no to the wish immediately upon presentation; and the unconscious ego, the mediator between the two, tries to keep peace by means of compromise.[3]

To go into examples of the functioning of these three "bosses" would be endless; psychoanalytic case books supply hundreds of them. The important point for us to see in the present context is that *it is the unconscious that determines what the conscious impulse and the conscious action shall be.* . . .

We have always been conscious of the fact that we are not masters of our fate in every respect—that there are many things which we cannot do, that nature is more powerful than we are, that we cannot disobey laws without danger of reprisals, etc. We have become "officially" conscious, too, though in our private lives we must long have been aware of it, that we are not free with respect to the emotions that we feel—whom we love or hate, what types we admire, and the like. More lately still we have been reminded that there are unconscious motivations for our basic attractions and repulsions, our compulsive actions or inabilities to act. But what is not welcome news is that our very acts of volition, and the entire train of deliberations leading up to them, are but facades for the expression of unconscious wishes, or rather, unconscious compromises and defenses.

[1.] A man is faced by a choice: Shall he kill another person or not? Moralists would say, "Here is a free choice—the result of deliberation, an action consciously entered into." And yet, though the agent himself does not know it, and has no awareness of the forces that are at work within him, his choice is already determined for him: His conscious will is only an instrument, a slave, in the hands of a deep unconscious motivation which determines his action. If he has a great deal of what the analyst calls "freefloating guilt," he will not; but if the guilt is such as to demand immediate absorption in the form of self-damaging behavior, this accumulated guilt will have to be discharged in some criminal action. The man himself does not know what the inner clockwork is; he is like the hands on the clock, thinking they move freely over the face of the clock.

[2.] A woman has married and divorced several husbands. Now she is faced with a choice for the next marriage: shall she marry Mr. A, or Mr. B, or nobody at all? She may take considerable time to "decide" this question and her decision may appear as a final triumph of her free will. Let us assume that A is a normal, well-adjusted, kind and generous man while B is a leech, an impostor, one who will become entangled constantly in quarrels with her. If she belongs to a certain classifiable psychological type, she will inevitably choose B, and she will do so even if her previous husbands have resembled B,

---

[3]This view is very clearly developed in Edmund Bergler, *Divorce Won't Help*, especially Chapter I.

so that one would think that she "had learned from experience." Consciously, she will of course "give the matter due consideration," etc., etc. To the psychoanalyst all this is irrelevant chaff in the wind—only a camouflage for the inner workings about which she knows nothing consciously. If she is of a certain kind of masochistic strain, as exhibited in her previous set of symptoms, she *must* choose B: Her superego, always out to maximize the torment in the situation, seeing what dazzling possibilities for self-damaging behavior are promised by the choice of B, compels her to make the choice she does, and even to conceal the real basis of the choice behind an elaborate facade of rationalization. . . .

[3.] A man has wash-compulsion. He must be constantly washing his hands—he uses up perhaps 400 towels a day. Asked why he does this, he says, "I need to, my hands are dirty"; and if it is pointed out to him that they are not really dirty, he says, "They feel dirty anyway, I feel better when I wash them." So once again he washes them. He "freely decides" every time; he feels that he must wash them, he deliberates for a moment perhaps, but he always ends by washing them. What he does not see, of course, are the invisible wires inside him pulling him inevitably to do the thing he does: The infantile id-wish concerns preoccupation with dirt, the super-ego charges him with this, and the terrified ego must respond, "No, I don't like dirt, see how clean I like to be, look how I wash my hands!"

Let us see what further "free acts" the same patient engages in (this is an actual case history): He is taken to a concentration camp and given the worst of treatment by the Nazi guards. In the camp he no longer chooses to be clean, does not even try to be—on the contrary, his choice is now to wallow in filth as much as he can. All he is aware of now is a disinclination to be clean, and every time he must choose he chooses not to be. Behind the scenes, however, another drama is being enacted: The super-ego, perceiving that enough torment is being administered from the outside, can afford to cease pressing its charges in this quarter—the outside world is doing the torturing now, so the super-ego is relieved of the responsibility. Thus, the ego is relieved of the agony of constantly making terrified replies in the form of washing to prove that the super-ego is wrong. The defense no longer being needed, the person slides back into what is his natural predilection anyway, for filth. This becomes too much even for the Nazi guards: They take hold of him one day, saying "We'll teach you how to be clean!" drag him into the snow, and pour bucket after bucket of icy water over him until he freezes to death. Such is the end-result of an original wish, caught in the machinations of a destroying super-ego.

[4.] Let us take, finally, a less colorful, more everyday example. A student at a university, possessing wealth, charm, and all that is usually considered essential to popularity, begins to develop the following personality-pattern: Although well taught in the graces of social conversation, he always makes a *faux pas* somewhere, and always in the worst possible situation; to his friends he makes cutting remarks which hurt deeply—and always apparently aimed in such a way as to hurt the most: A remark that would not hurt A but would hurt B he invariably makes to B rather than to A, and so on. None of this is conscious. Ordinarily he is considerate of people, but he contrives always (unconsciously) to impose on just those friends who would resent it most, and at just the times when he should know that he should not impose: At 3 o'clock in the morning, without forewarning, he phones a friend in a nearby city demanding to stay at his apartment for the weekend; naturally the friend is offended, but the person himself is not aware that he has provoked the grievance ("common sense" suffers a temporary eclipse when the neurotic pattern sets in, and one's intelligence, far from being of help in such a situation, is used in the interest of the neurosis), and when the friend is cool to him the next time they meet, he wonders why and feels unjustly treated. Aggressive behavior on his part invites resentment and aggression in turn, but all that he consciously sees is others' behavior toward him—and he considers himself the innocent victim of an unjustified "persecution."

Each of these acts is, from the moralist's point of view, free: He chose to phone his friend at 3 A.M.; he chose to make the cutting remark that he did, etc. What he does not know is that an ineradicable masochistic pattern has set in. His unconscious is far more shrewd and clever than is his conscious intellect; it sees with uncanny accuracy just what kind of behavior will damage him most, and unerringly forces him into that behavior. Consciously, the student "doesn't know why he did it"—he gives different "reasons" at different times, but they are all, once again, rationalizations cloaking the unconscious mechanism which propels him willy-nilly into actions which his "common sense" eschews.

The more of this sort of thing one observes, the more he can see what the psychoanalyst means when he talks about *the illusion of freedom.* And the more of a psychiatrist one becomes, the more he is overcome with a sense of what an illusion this free-will can be. In some kinds of cases most of us can see it already: It takes no psychiatrist to look at the epileptic and sigh with sadness at the thought that soon this person before you will be as one possessed, not the same thoughtful intelligent person you knew. But people are not aware of this in other contexts, for example when they express surprise at how a person whom they have been so good to could treat them so badly. Let us suppose that you help a person financially or morally or in some other way, so that he is in your debt; suppose further that he is one of the many neurotics who unconsciously identify kindness with weakness and aggression with strength. Then he will unconsciously take your kindness to him as weakness and use it as the occasion for enacting some aggression against you. He can't help it, he may regret it himself later; still, he will be driven to do it. If we gain a little knowledge of psychiatry, we can look at him with pity, that a person otherwise so worthy should be so unreliable—but we will exercise realism too, and be aware that there are some types of people that you cannot be good to in "free" acts of their conscious volition; they will use your own goodness against you. . . .

We talk about free-will, and we say, for example, the person is free to do so-and-so if he can do so *if* he wants to—and we forget that his wanting to is itself caught up in the stream of determinism, that unconscious forces drive him into the wanting or not wanting to do the thing in question. The analogy of the puppet whose motions are manipulated from behind by invisible wires, or better still, by springs inside, is a telling one at almost every point.

And the glaring fact is that it all started so early, before we knew what was happening. The personality-structure is inelastic after the age of five, and comparatively so in most cases after the age of three. Whether one acquires a neurosis or not is determined by that age—and just as involuntarily as if it had been a curse of God. If, for example, a masochistic pattern was set up, under pressure of hyper-narcissism combined with real or fancied infantile deprivation, then the masochistic snowball was on its course downhill long before we or anybody else knew what was happening, and long before anyone could do anything about it. To speak of human beings as "puppets" in such a context is no idle metaphor, but a stark rendering of a literal fact: Only the psychiatrist knows what puppets people really are; and it is no wonder that the protestations of philosophers that "the act which is the result of a volition, a deliberation, a conscious decision, is free" leave these persons, to speak mildly, somewhat cold.

But, one may object, all the states thus far described have been abnormal, neurotic ones. The well-adjusted (normal) person at least is free.

Leaving aside the question of how clearly and on what grounds one can distinguish the neurotic from the normal, let me use an illustration of a proclivity that everyone would call normal, namely, the decision of a man to support his wife and possibly a family, and consider briefly its genesis, according to psychoanalytic accounts.[4]

Every baby comes into the world with a full-fledged case of megalomania—interested only in himself, acting as if believing that he is the center of the universe and that others are present only to fulfill his wishes, and furious when his own wants are not satisfied immediately no matter for what reason. Gratitude, even for all the time and worry and care expended on him by the mother, is an emotion entirely foreign to the infant, and as he grows older it is inculcated in him only with the greatest difficulty; his natural tendency is to assume that everything that happens to him is due to himself, except for denials and frustrations, which are due to the "cruel, denying" outer world, in particular the mother; and that he owes nothing to anyone, is dependent on no one. This omnipotence-complex, or illusion of nondependence, has been called the "autarchic fiction." Such a conception of the world is actually fostered in the child by the conduct of adults, who automatically attempt to fulfill the infant's every wish concerning nourishment, sleep, and attention. The child misconceives causality and sees in these wish-fulfillments not the results of maternal kindness and love, but simply the result of his own omnipotence.

This fiction of omnipotence is gradually destroyed by experience, and its destruction is probably the deepest disappointment of the early years of life.

[4]E.g., Edmund Bergler, *The Battle of the Conscience*, Chapter I.

First of all, the infant discovers that he is the victim of organic urges and necessities: hunger, defecation, urination. More important, he discovers that the maternal breast, which he has not previously distinguished from his own body (he has not needed to, since it was available when he wanted it), is not a part of himself after all, but of another creature upon whom he is dependent. He is forced to recognize this, e.g., when he wants nourishment and it is at the moment not present; even a small delay is most damaging to the "autarchic fiction." Most painful of all is the experience of weaning, probably the greatest tragedy in every baby's life, when his dependence is most cruelly emphasized; it is a frustrating experience because what he wants is no longer there at all; and if he has been able to some extent to preserve the illusion of nondependence heretofore, he is not able to do so now—it is plain that the source of his nourishment is not dependent on him, but he on it. The shattering of the autarchic fiction is a great disillusionment to every child, a tremendous blow to his ego which he will, in one way or another, spend the rest of his life trying to repair. How does he do this?

First of all, his reaction to frustration is anger and fury; and he responds by kicking, biting, etc., the only way he knows. But he is motorically helpless, and these measures are ineffective, and only serve to emphasize his dependence the more. Moreover, against such responses of the child the parental reaction is one of prohibition, often involving deprivation of attention and affection. Generally the child soon learns that this form of rebellion is profitless, and brings him more harm than good. He wants to respond to frustration with violent aggression, and at the same time learns that he will be punished for such aggression, and that in any case the latter is ineffectual. What face-saving solution does he find? Since he must "face facts," since he must in any case "conform" if he is to have any peace at all, he tries to make it seem as if he himself is the source of the commands and prohibitions: The *external* prohibitive force is *internalized*—and here we have the origin of conscience. By making the prohibitive agency seem to come from within himself, the child can "save face"—as if saying, "The prohibition comes from within me, not from outside, so I'm not subservient to external rule, I'm only obeying rules I've set up myself," and thus to some extent saving the autarchic fiction, and at the same time avoiding unpleasant consequences directed against himself by complying with parental commands.

Moreover, the boy[5] has unconsciously never forgiven the mother for his dependence on her in early life, for nourishment and all other things. It has upset his illusion of nondependence. These feelings have been repressed and are not remembered; but they are acted out in later life in many ways—e.g., in the constant deprecation man has for woman's duties such as cooking and housework of all sorts ("All she does is stay home and get together a few meals, and she calls that work"), and especially in the man's identification

---

[5]The girl's development after this point is somewhat different. Society demands more aggressiveness of the adult male, and hence there are more super-ego strictures on tendencies toward passivity in the male; accordingly his defenses must be stronger.

with the mother in his sex experiences with women. By identifying with someone one cancels out in effect the person with whom he identifies— replacing that person, unconsciously denying his existence, and the man, identifying with his early mother, playing the active role in "giving" to his wife as his mother has "given" to him, is in effect the denial of his mother's existence, a fact which is narcissistically embarrassing to his ego because it is chiefly responsible for shattering his autarchic fiction. In supporting his wife, he can unconsciously deny that his mother gave to him, and that he was dependent on her giving. Why is it that the husband plays the provider, and wants his wife to be dependent on no one else, although twenty years before he was nothing but a parasitic baby? This is a face-saving device on his part: He can act out the reasoning, "See, I'm not the parasitic baby, on the contrary I'm the provider, the giver." His playing the provider is a constant face-saving device, to deny his early dependence which is so embarrassing to his ego. It is no wonder that men generally dislike to be reminded of their babyhood, when they were dependent on women.

Thus, we have here a perfectly normal adult reaction which is unconsciously motivated. The man "chooses" to support a family—and his choice is as unconsciously motivated as anything could be. (I have described here only the "normal" state of affairs, uncomplicated by the well-nigh infinite number of variations that occur in actual practice.)

III. [THE IMPLICATIONS FOR RESPONSIBILITY]

Now, what of the notion of responsibility? What happens to it on our analysis?

Let us begin with an example, not a fictitious one. A woman and her two-year-old baby are riding on a train to Montreal in mid-winter. The child is ill. The woman wants badly to get to her destination. She is, unknown to herself, the victim of a neurotic conflict whose nature is irrelevant here except for the fact that it forces her to behave aggressively toward the child, partly to spite her husband whom she despises and who loves the child, but chiefly to ward off super-ego charges of masochistic attachment. Consciously she loves the child, and when she says this she says it sincerely, but she must behave aggressively toward it nevertheless, just as many children love their mothers but are nasty to them most of the time in neurotic pseudo-aggression. The child becomes more ill as the train approaches Montreal; the heating system of the train is not working, and the conductor pleads with the woman to get off the train at the next town and get the child to a hospital at once. The woman refuses. Soon after, the child's condition worsens, and the mother does all she can to keep it alive, without, however, leaving the train, for she declares that it is absolutely necessary that she reach her destination. But before she gets there the child is dead. After that, of course, the mother grieves, blames herself, weeps hysterically, and joins the church to gain surcease from the guilt that constantly overwhelms her when she thinks of how her aggressive behavior has killed her child.

Was she responsible for her deed? In ordinary life, after making a mistake, we say, "Chalk it up to experience." Here we should say, "Chalk it up to the neurosis." *She* could not help it if her neurosis forced her to act this way— she didn't even know what was going on behind the scenes; her conscious self merely acted out its assigned part. This is far more true than is generally realized: Criminal actions in general are not actions for which their agents are responsible; the agents are passive, not active—they are victims of a neurotic conflict. Their very hyper-activity is unconsciously determined.

To say this is, of course, not to say that we should not punish criminals. Clearly, for our own protection, we must remove them from our midst so that they can no longer molest and endanger organized society. And of course, if we use the word "responsible" in such a way that justly to hold someone responsible for a deed is by definition identical with being justified in punishing him, then we can and do hold people responsible. But this is like the sense of "free" in which free acts are voluntary ones. It does not go deep enough. In a deeper sense we cannot hold the person responsible: We can hold his neurosis responsible, but *he is not responsible for his neurosis*, particularly since the age at which its onset was inevitable was an age before he could even speak.

The neurosis is responsible—but isn't the neurosis a part of *him*? We have been speaking all the time as if the person and his unconscious were two separate beings; but isn't he one personality, including conscious and unconscious departments together?

I do not wish to deny this. But it hardly helps us here; for what people want when they talk about freedom, and what they hold to when they champion it, is the idea that the *conscious* will is the master of their destiny. "I am the master of my fate, I am the captain of my soul"—and they surely mean their conscious self, the self that they can recognize and search and introspect. Between an unconscious which willy-nilly determines your actions, and an external force which pushes you, there is little if anything to choose. The unconscious is just *as if* it were an outside force; and indeed, psychiatrists will assert that the inner Hitler (your super-ego) can torment you far more than any external Hitler can. Thus, the kind of freedom that people want, the only kind they will settle for, is precisely the kind that psychiatry says that they cannot have.

Heretofore it was pretty generally thought that, while we could not rightly blame a person for the color of his eyes or the morality of his parents, or even for what he did at the age of three, or to a large extent what impulses he had and whom he fell in love with, one *could* do so for other of his adult activities, particularly the acts he performed voluntarily and with premeditation. Later this attitude was shaken. Many voluntary acts came to be recognized, at least in some circles, as compelled by the unconscious. . . . The usual examples, such as the kleptomaniac and the schizophrenic, apparently satisfy most philosophers, and with these exceptions removed, the rest of mankind is permitted to wander in the vast and alluring fields of freedom and responsibility. So far, the inroads upon freedom left the vast majority of humanity untouched; they began to hit home when psychiatrists began to realize, though philosophers did not, that the domination of the conscious by the unconscious extended not merely to a few exceptional individuals, but to all human beings, that the "big three behind the scenes" are not respecters of persons, and dominate us all, even including that *sanctum sanctorum* of freedom, our conscious will. To be sure, the domination by the unconscious in the case of "normal" individuals is somewhat more benevolent than the tyranny and despotism exercised in neurotic cases, and therefore the former have evoked less comment; but the principle remains in all cases the same: The unconscious is the master of every fate and the captain of every soul. . . .

IV. [DOES FREE-WILL EXIST?]

Assuming the main conclusions of this paper to be true, is there any room left for freedom?

This, of course, all depends on what we mean by "freedom." In the senses suggested at the beginning of this paper, there are countless free acts, and unfree ones as well. When "free" means "uncompelled," and only external compulsion is admitted, again there are countless free acts. But now we have extended the notion of compulsion to include determination by unconscious forces. With this sense in mind, our question is, "With the concept of compulsion thus extended, and in the light of present psychoanalytic knowledge, is there any freedom left in human behavior?"

If practicing psychoanalysts were asked this question, there is little doubt that their answer would be along the following lines: They would say that they were not accustomed to using the term "free" at all, but that if they had to suggest a criterion for distinguishing the free from the unfree, they would say that a person's freedom is present *in inverse proportion to his neuroticism*; in other words, the more his acts are determined by a *malevolent* unconscious, the less free he is. Thus, they would speak of *degrees* of freedom. They would say that as a person is cured of his neurosis, he becomes more free—free to realize capabilities that were blocked by the neurotic affliction. The psychologically well-adjusted individual is in this sense comparatively the most free. Indeed, those who are cured of mental disorders are sometimes said to have *regained their freedom*: They are freed from the tyranny of a malevolent unconscious which formerly exerted as much of a domination over them as if they had been the abject slaves of a cruel dictator.

But suppose one says that a person is free only to the extent that his acts are *not unconsciously determined at all*, be they unconsciously benevolent *or* malevolent? If this is the criterion, psychoanalysts would say, most human behavior cannot be called free at all: Our impulses and volitions having to do with our basic attitudes toward life, whether we are optimists or pessimists, tough-minded or tender-minded, whether our tempers are quick or slow, whether we are "naturally self-seeking" or "naturally benevolent" (and *all the acts consequent upon these things*), what things annoy us, whether we take to blondes or brunettes, old or young, whether we become philosophers or artists or businessmen—all this has its basis in the unconscious. If people generally call most acts free, it is not because they believe that compelled acts should be called free; it is rather through not knowing how large a proportion of our acts actually are compelled. Only the comparatively "vanilla-flavored" aspects of our lives—such as our behavior toward people who don't really matter to us—are exempted from this rule.

These, I think, are the two principal criteria for distinguishing freedom from the lack of it which we might set up on the basis of psychoanalytic knowledge. Conceivably we might set up others. In every case, of course, it remains trivially true that "it all depends on how we choose to use the word." The facts are what they are, regardless of what words we choose for labeling them. But if we choose to label them in a way which is not in accord with what human beings, however vaguely, have long had in mind in applying these labels, as we would be doing if we labeled as "free" many acts which we know as much about as we now do through modern psychoanalytic methods, then we shall only be manipulating words to mislead our fellow creatures.

---

15 / *The Crime of Punishment*

KARL MENNINGER

Karl Menninger (1893–   ) is a renowned psychiatrist and founder of the Menninger Clinic. He has written extensively on the treatment of criminals. His book The Crime of Punishment *(1968) develops views expressed in the following essay.*

[I]

*F*ew words in our language arrest our attention as do "crime," "violence," "revenge," and "injustice." We abhor crime; we adore justice; we boast that we live by the rule of law. Violence and vengefulness we repudiate as unworthy of our civilization, and we assume this sentiment to be unanimous among all human beings.

Yet crime continues to be a national disgrace and a world-wide problem. It is threatening, alarming, wasteful, expensive, abundant, and apparently increasing! In actuality it is decreasing in frequency of occurrence, but it is certainly increasing in visibility and the reactions of the public to it.

Our system for controlling crime is ineffective, unjust, expensive. Prisons seem to operate with revolving doors—the same people going in and out and in and out. *Who cares?*

Our city jails and inhuman reformatories and wretched prisons are jammed. They are known to be unhealthy, dangerous, immoral, indecent, crime-breeding dens of iniquity. Not everyone has smelled them, as some of us have. Not many have heard the groans and the curses. Not everyone has seen the hate and despair in a thousand blank, hollow faces. But, in a way, we all know how miserable prisons are. *We want them to be that way.* And they are. *Who cares?*

Professional and big-time criminals prosper as never before. Gambling syndicates flourish. White-collar crime may even exceed all others, but goes undetected in the majority of cases. We are all being robbed and we know who the robbers are. They live nearby. *Who cares?*

The public filches millions of dollars worth of food and clothing from stores, towels and sheets from hotels, jewelry and knick-knacks from shops. The public steals, and the same public pays it back in higher prices. *Who cares?*

Time and time again somebody shouts about this state of affairs, just as I am shouting now. The magazines shout. The newspapers shout. The television and radio commentators shout (or at least they "deplore"). Psychologists, sociologists, leading jurists, wardens, and intelligent police chiefs join the chorus. Governors and mayors and Congressmen are sometimes heard. They shout that the situation is bad, bad, bad, and getting worse. Some suggested that we immediately replace obsolete procedures with scientific methods. A few shout contrary sentiments. Do the clear indications derived from scientific discovery for appropriate changes continue to fall on deaf ears? Why is the public so long-suffering, so apathetic, and thereby so continuingly self-destructive? How many Presidents (and other citizens) do we have to lose before we do something?

The public behaves as a sick patient does when a dreaded treatment is proposed for his ailment. We all know how the aching tooth may suddenly quiet down in the dentist's office, or the abdominal pain disappear in the surgeon's examining room. Why should a sufferer seek relief and shun it? Is it merely the fear of the pain of the treatment? Is it the fear of unknown complications? Is it distrust of the doctor's ability? All of these, no doubt.

But, as Freud made so incontestably clear, the sufferer is always somewhat deterred by a kind of subversive, internal opposition to the work of cure. He suffers on the one hand from the pains of his affliction and yearns to get well. But he suffers at the same time from traitorous impulses that fight against the accomplishment of any change in himself, even recovery! Like Hamlet, he wonders whether it may be better after all to suffer the familiar pains and aches associated with the old method than to face the complications of a new and strange, even though possibly better, way of handling things.

The inescapable conclusion is that society *wants* crime, *needs* crime, and gains definite satisfactions from the present mishandling of it! We condemn crime; we punish offenders for it; but we need it. The crime and punishment ritual is a part of our lives. We need crimes to wonder at, to enjoy vicariously, to discuss and speculate about, and to publicly deplore. We need criminals to identify ourselves with, to envy secretly, and to punish stoutly. They do for us the forbidden, illegal things we *wish* to do, and, like scapegoats of old, they bear the burdens of our displaced guilt and punishment—"the iniquities of us all." . . .

Fifty years ago, Winston Churchill declared that the mood and temper of the public in regard to crime and criminals is one of the unfailing tests of the civilization of any country. Judged by this standard, how civilized are we?

The chairman of the President's National Crime Commission . . . declared recently that organized crime flourishes in America because enough of the public wants its services, and most citizens are apathetic about its impact. It will continue uncurbed as long as Americans accept it as inevitable and, in some instances, desirable.

[II]

Are there steps that we can take which will reduce the aggressive stabs and self-destructive lurches of our less well-managing fellow men? Are there ways to prevent and control the grosser violations, other than the clumsy traditional maneuvers which we have inherited? These depend basically upon intimidation and slow-motion torture. We call it punishment, and justify it with our "feeling." We know it doesn't work.

Yes, there *are* better ways. There are steps that could be taken; some *are* taken. But we move too slowly. Much better use, it seems to me, could be made of the members of my profession and other behavioral scientists than having them deliver courtroom pronunciamentos. The consistent use of a diagnostic clinic would enable trained workers to lay what they can learn about an offender before the judge who would know best how to implement the recommendation.

This would no doubt lead to a transformation of prisons, if not to their total disappearance in their present form and function. Temporary and permanent detention will perhaps always be necessary for a few, especially the professionals, but this could be more effectively and economically performed with new types of "facility" (that strange, awkward word for institution).

I assume it to be a matter of common and general agreement that our object in all this is to protect the community from a repetition of the offense by the most economical method consonant with our other purposes. Our "other purposes" include the desire to prevent these offenses from occurring, to reclaim offenders for social usefulness, if possible, and to detain them in protective custody, if reclamation is *not* possible. But how?

The treatment of human failure or dereliction by the infliction of pain is still used and believed in by many nonmedical people. "Spare the rod and spoil the child" is still considered wise counsel by many.

Whipping is still used by many secondary schoolmasters in England, I am informed, to stimulate study, attention, and the love of learning. Whipping was long a traditional treatment for the "crime" of disobedience on the part of children, pupils, servants, apprentices, employees. And slaves were treated for centuries by flogging for such offenses as weariness, confusion, stupidity, exhaustion, fear, grief, and even overcheerfulness. It was assumed and stoutly defended that these "treatments" cured conditions for which they were administered.

Meanwhile, scientific medicine was acquiring many new healing methods and devices. Doctors can now transplant organs and limbs; they can remove brain tumors and cure incipient cancers; they can halt pneumonia, meningitis, and other infections; they can correct deformities and repair breaks and tears and scars. But these wonderful achievements are accomplished on *willing* subjects, people who voluntarily ask for help by even heroic measures. And the reader will be wondering, no doubt, whether doctors can do anything with or for people who *do not want* to be treated at all, in any way! Can doctors cure willful aberrant behavior? Are we to believe that crime is a *disease* that can be reached by scientific measures? Isn't it merely "natural meanness" that makes all of us do wrong things at times even when we "know better"? And are not self-control, moral stamina, and will power the things needed? Surely there is no medical treatment for the lack of those!

[III]

Let me answer this carefully, for much misunderstanding accumulates here. I would say that according to the prevalent understanding of the words, crime is *not* a disease. Neither is it an illness, although I think it *should* be! It *should* be treated, and it could be; but it mostly isn't.

These enigmatic statements are simply explained. Diseases are undesired states of being which have been described and defined by doctors, usually given Greek or Latin appellations, and treated by long-established physical and pharmacological formulae. Illness, on the other hand, is best defined as a state of impaired functioning of such a nature that the public expects the sufferer to repair to the physician for help. The illness may prove to be a disease; more often it is only vague and nameless misery, but something which doctors, not lawyers, teachers, or preachers, are supposed to be able and willing to help.

When the community begins to look upon the expression of aggressive violence as the symptom of an illness or as indicative of illness, it will be because it believes doctors can do something to correct such a condition. At present, some better-informed individuals do believe and expect this. However angry at or sorry for the offender, they want him "treated" in an effective way so that he will cease to be a danger to them. And they know that traditional punishment, "treatment-punishment," will not effect this.

What *will?* What effective treatment is there for such violence? It will surely have to begin with motivating or stimulating or arousing in a cornered individual the wish and hope and intention to change his methods of dealing with the realities of life. Can this be done by education, medication, counseling, training? I would answer *yes*. It can be done successfully in a majority of cases, if undertaken in time.

The present penal system and the existing legal philosophy do not stimulate or even expect such a change to take place in the criminal. Yet change is what medical science always aims for. The prisoner, like the doctor's other patients, should emerge from his treatment experience a different person, differently equipped, differently functioning, and headed in a different direction than when he began the treatment.

It is natural for the public to doubt that this can be accomplished with criminals. But remember that the public *used* to doubt that change could be effected in the mentally ill. No one a hundred years ago believed mental illness to be curable. Today *all* people know (or should know) that *mental illness is curable* in the great majority of instances and that the prospects and rapidity of cure are directly related to the availability and intensity of proper treatment.

The forms and techniques of psychiatric treatment used today number in the hundreds. No one patient requires or receives all forms, but each patient is studied with respect to his particular needs, his basic assets, his interests, and his special difficulties. A therapeutic team may embrace a dozen workers—as in a hospital setting—or it may narrow down to the doctor and the spouse. Clergymen, teachers, relatives, friends, and even fellow patients often participate informally but helpfully in the process of readaptation.

All of the participants in this effort to bring about a favorable change in the patient—that is, in his vital balance and life program—are imbued with what we may call a *therapeutic attitude*. This is one in direct antithesis to attitudes of avoidance, ridicule, scorn, or punitiveness. Hostile feelings toward the subject, however justified by his unpleasant and even destructive behavior, are not in the curriculum of therapy or in the therapist. This does not mean that therapists approve of the offensive and obnoxious behavior of the patient; they distinctly disapprove of it. But they recognize it as symptomatic of continued imbalance and disorganization, which is what they are seeking to change. They distinguish between disapproval, penalty, price, and punishment.

Doctors charge fees; they impose certain "penalties" or prices, but they have long since put aside primitive attitudes of retaliation toward offensive patients. A patient may cough in the doctor's face or may vomit on the office rug; a patient may curse or scream or even struggle in the extremity of his pain. But these acts are not "punished." Doctors and nurses have no time or thought for inflicting unnecessary pain even upon patients who may be difficult, disagreeable, provocative, and even dangerous. It is their duty to care for them, to try to make them well, and to prevent them from doing themselves or others harm. This requires love, not hate. This is the deepest meaning of the therapeutic attitude. Every doctor knows this; every worker in a hospital or clinic knows it (or should).

There is another element in the therapeutic attitude. It is the quality of hopefulness. If no one believes that the patient can get well, if no one—not even the doctor—has any hope, there probably won't be any recovery. Hope is just as important as love in the therapeutic attitude.

"But you were talking about the mentally ill," readers may interject, "those poor, confused, bereft, frightened individuals who yearn for help from you doctors and nurses. Do you mean to imply that willfully perverse individuals, our criminals, can be similarly reached and rehabilitated? Do you really believe that effective treatment of the sort you visualize can be applied to people *who do not want any help,* who are so willfully vicious, so well aware of the wrongs they are doing, so lacking in penitence or even common decency that punishment seems to be the only thing left?"

Do I believe there is effective treatment for offenders, and that they *can* be changed? *Most certainly and definitely I do.* Not all cases, to be sure; there are also some physical afflictions which we cannot cure at the moment. Some provision has to be made for incurables—pending new knowledge—and these will include some offenders. But I believe the majority of them would prove to be curable. The willfulness and the viciousness of offenders are part of the thing for which they have to be treated. These must not thwart the therapeutic attitude.

It is simply not true that most of them are "fully aware" of what they are doing, nor is it true that they want no help from anyone, although some of them say so. Prisoners are individuals: Some want treatment, some do not. Some don't know what treatment is. Many are utterly despairing and hopeless. Where treatment is made available in institutions, many prisoners seek it even with the full knowledge that doing so will not lessen their sentences. In some prisons, seeking treatment by prisoners is frowned upon by the officials.

Various forms of treatment are even now being tried in some progressive courts and prisons over the country—educational, social, industrial, religious, recreational, and psychological treatments. Socially acceptable behavior, new work–play opportunities, new identity and companion patterns all help toward community reacceptance. Some parole officers and some wardens have been extremely ingenious in developing these modalities of rehabilitation and reconstruction—more than I could list here even if I knew them all. But some are trying. The secret of success in all programs, however, is the replacement of the punitive attitude with a therapeutic attitude.

Offenders with propensities for impulsive and predatory aggression should not be permitted to live among us unrestrained by some kind of social control. *But the great majority of offenders, even "criminals," should never become prisoners if we want to "cure" them.*

[IV]

There are now throughout the country many citizens' action groups and programs for the prevention and control of crime and delinquency. With such attitudes of inquiry and concern, the public could acquire information (and incentive) leading to a change of feeling about crime and criminals. It will discover how unjust is much so-called "justice," how baffled and frustrated many judges are by the ossified rigidity of old-fashioned, obsolete laws and state constitutions which effectively prevent the introduction of sensible procedures to replace useless, harmful ones.

I want to proclaim to the public that things are not what it wishes them to be, and will only become so if it will take an interest in the matter and assume some responsibility for its own self-protection.

Will the public listen?

If the public does become interested, it will realize that we must have more facts, more trial projects, more checked results. It will share the dismay of the President's Commission in finding that no one knows much about even the incidence of crime with any definiteness or statistical accuracy.

The average citizen finds it difficult to see how any research would in any way change his mind about a man who brutally murders his children. But just such inconceivably awful acts most dramatically point up the need for research. Why should—how can—a man become so dreadful as that in our culture? How is such a man made? Is it comprehensible that he can be born to become so depraved?

There are thousands of questions regarding crime and public protection which deserve scientific study. What makes some individuals maintain their interior equilibrium by one kind of disturbance of the social structure rather than by another kind, one that would have landed him in a hospital? Why do some individuals specialize in certain types of crime? Why do so many young people reared in areas of delinquency and poverty and bad example never become habitual delinquents? (Perhaps this is a more important question than why some of them do.)

The public has a fascination for violence, and clings tenaciously to its yen for vengeance, blind and deaf to the expense, futility, and dangerousness of the resulting penal system. But we are bound to hope that this will yield in time to the persistent, penetrating light of intelligence and accumulating scientific knowledge. The public will grow increasingly ashamed of its cry for retaliation, its persistent demand to punish. This is its crime, *our* crime against criminals—and, incidentally, our crime against ourselves. For before we can diminish our sufferings from the ill-controlled aggressive assaults of fellow citizens, we must renounce the philosophy of punishment, the obsolete, vengeful penal attitude. In its place we would seek a comprehensive constructive social attitude—therapeutic in some instances, restraining in some instances, but preventive in its total social impact.

In the last analysis this becomes a question of personal morals and values. No matter how glorified or how piously disguised, vengeance as a human motive must be personally repudiated by each and every one of us. This is the message of old religions and new psychiatries. Unless this message is heard, unless we, the people—the man on the street, the housewife in the home—can give up our delicious satisfactions in opportunities for vengeful retaliation on scapegoats, we cannot expect to preserve our peace, our public safety, or our mental health.

16 / *The Humanitarian Theory of Punishment*

C. S. LEWIS

C. S. Lewis (1898–1963) was a professor of medieval and renaissance English at Cambridge University for many years. However he is most famous for his numerous books and essays in which he defends various topics pertaining to Christian thought and practice. His works are in print and are widely read by those interested in religious belief.

[I. THE HUMANITARIAN THEORY]

*I*n England we have lately had a controversy about Capital Punishment. I do not know whether a murderer is more likely to repent and make a good end on the gallows a few weeks after his trial or in the prison infirmary thirty years later. I do not know whether the fear of death is an indispensable deterrent. I need not, for the purpose of this article, decide whether it is a morally permissible deterrent. Those are questions which I propose to leave untouched. My subject is not Capital Punishment in particular, but that theory of punishment in general which the controversy showed to be almost universal among my fellow-countrymen. It may be called the Humanitarian theory. Those who hold it think that it is mild and merciful. In this I believe that they are seriously mistaken. I believe that the 'Humanity' which it claims is a dangerous illusion and disguises the possibility of cruelty and injustice without end. I urge a return to the traditional or Retributive theory not solely, not even primarily, in the interests of society, but in the interests of the criminal.

According to the Humanitarian theory, to punish a man because he deserves it, and as much as he deserves, is mere revenge and, therefore, barbarous and immoral. It is maintained that the only legitimate motives for punishing are the desire to deter others by example or to mend the criminal. When this theory is combined, as frequently happens, with the belief that all crime is more or less pathological, the idea of mending tails off into that of healing or curing, and punishment becomes therapeutic. Thus it appears at first sight that we have passed from the harsh and self-righteous notion of giving the wicked their deserts to the charitable and enlightened one of tending the psychologically sick. What could be more amiable? One little point which is taken for granted in this theory needs, however, to be made explicit. The things done to the criminal, even if they are called cures, will be just as compulsory as they were in the old days when we called them punishments. If a tendency to steal can be cured by psychotherapy, the thief will no doubt be forced to undergo the treatment. Otherwise, society cannot continue.

My contention is that this doctrine, merciful though it appears, really means that each one of us, from the moment he breaks the law, is deprived of the rights of a human being.

[II. ARGUMENTS AGAINST THE THEORY]

The reason is this. The Humanitarian theory removes from Punishment the concept of Desert. But the concept of Desert is the only connecting link between punishment and justice. It is only as deserved or undeserved that a sentence can be just or unjust. I do not here contend that the question "Is it deserved?" is the only one we can reasonably ask about a punishment. We may very properly ask whether it is likely to deter others and to reform the criminal. But neither of these two last questions is a question about justice. There is no sense in talking about a "just deterrent" or a "just cure." We demand of a deterrent not whether it is just but whether it will deter. We demand of a cure not whether it is just but whether it succeeds. Thus when we cease to consider what the criminal deserves and consider only what will cure him or deter others, we have tacitly removed him from the sphere of justice altogether; instead of a person, a subject of rights, we now have a mere object, a patient, a "case."

The distinction will become clearer if we ask who will be qualified to determine sentences when sentences are no longer held to derive their propriety from the criminal's deservings. On the old view the problem of fixing the right sentence was a moral problem. Accordingly, the judge who did it was a person trained in jurisprudence; trained, that is, in a science which deals with rights and duties, and which, in origin at least, was consciously accepting guidance from the Law of Nature and from Scripture. We must admit that in the actual penal code of most countries at most times these high originals were so much modified by local custom, class interests, and utilitarian concessions as to be very imperfectly recognizable. But the code was never in principle, and not always in fact, beyond the control of the conscience of the society. And when (say, in eighteenth-century England) actual punishments conflicted too violently with the moral sense of the community, juries refused to convict and reform was finally brought about. This was possible because, so long as we are thinking in terms of Desert, the propriety of the penal code, being a moral question, is a question on which every man has the right to an opinion, not because he follows this or that profession, but because he is simply a man, a rational animal enjoying the Natural Light. But all this is changed when we drop the concept of Desert. The only two questions we may now ask about a punishment are whether it deters and whether it cures. But these are not questions on which anyone is entitled to have an opinion simply because he is a man. He is not entitled to an opinion even if, in addition to being a man, he should happen also to be a jurist, a Christian, and a moral theologian. For they are not questions about principle but about matter of fact; and for such *cuiquam in sua arte credendum*.* Only the expert "penologist" (let barbarous things have barbarous names), in the light of previous experiment, can tell us what is likely to deter: Only the psychotherapist can tell us what is likely to cure. It will be in vain for the rest of us, speaking simply as men, to say, "But this punishment is hideously unjust, hideously disproportionate to the criminal's deserts." The experts with perfect logic will reply, "But nobody was talking about deserts. No one was talking about *punishment* in your archaic, vindictive sense of the word. Here are the statistics proving that this treatment deters. Here are the statistics proving that this other treatment cures. What is your trouble?"

The Humanitarian theory, then, removes sentences from the hands of jurists whom the public conscience is entitled to criticize and places them in the hands of technical experts whose special sciences do not even employ such categories as rights or justice. It might be argued that since this transference results from an abandonment of the old idea of punishment, and, therefore, of all vindictive motives, it will be safe to leave our criminals in such hands. I will not pause to comment on the simple-minded view of fallen human nature which such a belief implies. Let us rather remember that the "cure" of criminals is to be compulsory; and let us then watch how the theory actually works in the mind of the Humanitarian. The immediate starting point of this article was a letter I read in one of our Leftist weeklies. The author was pleading that a certain sin, now treated by our laws as a crime, should henceforward be treated as a disease. And he complained that under the present system the offender, after a term in jail, was simply let out to return to his original environment, where he would probably relapse. What he complained of was not the shutting up but the letting out. On his remedial view of

*[We must believe the expert in his own field.—Eds.]

punishment the offender should, of course, be detained until he was cured. And of course the official straighteners are the only people who can say when that is. The first result of the Humanitarian theory is, therefore, to substitute for a definite sentence (reflecting to some extent the community's moral judgment on the degree of ill-desert involved) an indefinite sentence terminable only by the word of those experts—and they are not experts in moral theology nor even in the Law of Nature—who inflict it. Which of us, if he stood in the dock, would not prefer to be tried by the old system?

It may be said that by the continued use of the word "punishment" and the use of the verb "inflict" I am misrepresenting Humanitarians. They are not punishing, not inflicting, only healing. But do not let us be deceived by a name. To be taken without consent from my home and friends; to lose my liberty; to undergo all those assaults on my personality which modern psychotherapy knows how to deliver; to be re-made after some pattern of "normality" hatched in a Viennese laboratory to which I never professed allegiance; to know that this process will never end until either my captors have succeeded or I have grown wise enough to cheat them with apparent success—who cares whether this is called Punishment or not? That it includes most of the elements for which any punishment is feared—shame, exile, bondage, and years eaten by the locust—is obvious. Only enormous ill-desert could justify it; but ill-desert is the very conception which the Humanitarian theory has thrown overboard.

If we turn from the curative to the deterrent justification of punishment we shall find the new theory even more alarming. When you punish a man *in terrorem*,[1] making of him an "example" to others, you are admittedly using him as a means to an end; someone else's end. This, in itself, would be a very wicked thing to do. On the classical theory of Punishment it was of course justified on the ground that the man deserved it. That was assumed to be established before any question of "making him an example" arose. You then, as the saying is, killed two birds with one stone; in the process of giving him what he deserved you set an example to others. But take away desert and the whole morality of the punishment disappears. Why, in Heaven's name, am I to be sacrificed to the good of society in this way?—unless, of course, I deserve it.

But that is not the worst. If the justification of exemplary punishment is not to be based on desert but solely on its efficacy as a deterrent, it is not absolutely necessary that the man we punish should even have committed the crime. The deterrent effect demands that the public should draw the moral, "If we do such an act we shall suffer like that man." The punishment of a man actually guilty whom the public think innocent will not have the desired effect; the punishment of a man actually innocent will, provided the public think him guilty. But every modern State has powers which make it easy to fake a trial. When a victim is urgently needed for exemplary purposes and a guilty victim cannot be found, all the purposes of deterrence will be

---

[1]"To cause terror."

equally served by the punishment (call it "cure" if you prefer) of an innocent victim, provided that the public can be cheated into thinking him guilty. It is no use to ask me why I assume that our rulers will be so wicked. The punishment of an innocent, that is, an undeserving, man is wicked only if we grant the traditional view that righteous punishment means deserved punishment. Once we have abandoned that criterion, all punishments have to be justified, if at all, on other grounds that have nothing to do with desert. Where the punishment of the innocent can be justified on those grounds (and it could in some cases be justified as a deterrent) it will be no less moral than any other punishment. Any distaste for it on the part of a Humanitarian will be merely a hang-over from the Retributive theory.

[III. FURTHER CRITICISMS]

It is, indeed, important to notice that my argument so far supposes no evil intentions on the part of the Humanitarian and considers only what is involved in the logic of his position. My contention is that good men (not bad men) consistently acting upon that position would act as cruelly and unjustly as the greatest tyrants. They might in some respects act even worse. Of all tyrannies a tyranny sincerely exercised for the good of its victims may be the most oppressive. It may be better to live under robber barons than under omnipotent moral busybodies. The robber baron's cruelty may sometimes sleep, his cupidity may at some point be satiated; but those who torment us for our own good will torment us without end, for they do so with the approval of their own conscience. They may be more likely to go to Heaven yet at the same time likelier to make a Hell of earth. Their very kindness stings with intolerable insult. To be "cured" against one's will and cured of states which we may not regard as disease is to be put on a level with those who have not yet reached the age of reason or those who never will; to be classed with infants, imbeciles, and domestic animals. But to be punished, however severely, because we have deserved it, because we "ought to have known better," is to be treated as a human person made in God's image.

In reality, however, we must face the possibility of bad rulers armed with a Humanitarian theory of punishment. A great many popular blueprints for a Christian society are merely what the Elizabethans called "eggs in moonshine" because they assume that the whole society is Christian or that the Christians are in control. This is not so in most contemporary States. Even if it were, our rulers would still be fallen men and, therefore, neither very wise nor very good. As it is, they will usually be unbelievers. And since wisdom and virtue are not the only or the commonest qualifications for a place in the government, they will not often be even the best unbelievers.

The practical problem of Christian politics is not that of drawing up schemes for a Christian society, but that of living as innocently as we can with unbelieving fellow-subjects under unbelieving rulers who will never be perfectly wise and good and who will sometimes be very wicked and very foolish. And when they are wicked the Humanitarian theory of punishment will put in their hands a finer instrument of tyranny than wickedness ever had before. For if crime and disease are to be regarded as the same thing, it follows that any state of mind which our masters choose to call disease can be treated as crime and compulsorily cured. It will be vain to plead that states of mind which displease government need not always involve moral turpitude and do not therefore always deserve forfeiture of liberty. For our masters will not be using the concepts of Desert and Punishment but those of disease and cure. We know that one school of psychology already regards religion as a neurosis. When this particular neurosis becomes inconvenient to government, what is to hinder government from proceeding to "cure" it? Such "cure" will, of course, be compulsory; but under the Humanitarian theory it will not be called by the shocking name of Persecution. No one will blame us for being Christians, no one will hate us, no one will revile us. The new Nero will approach us with the silky manners of a doctor, and though all will be in fact as compulsory as the *tunica molesta** or Smithfield or Tyburn,† all will go on within the unemotional therapeutic sphere, where words like "right" and "wrong" or "freedom" and "slavery" are never heard. And thus when the command is given, every prominent Christian in the land may vanish overnight into Institutions for the Treatment of the Ideologically Unsound, and it will rest with the expert jailers to say when (if ever) they are to re-emerge. But it will not be persecution. Even if the treatment is painful, even if it is lifelong, even if it is fatal, that will be only a regrettable accident; the intention was purely therapeutic. In ordinary medicine there were painful operations and fatal operations; so in this. But because they are "treatment," not punishment, they can be criticized only by fellow-experts and on technical grounds, never by men as men and on grounds of justice.

This is why I think it essential to oppose the Humanitarian theory of punishment, root and branch, wherever we encounter it. It carries on its front a semblance of mercy which is wholly false. That is how it can deceive men of good will. The error began, perhaps, with Shelley's statement that the distinction between mercy and justice was invented in the courts of tyrants. It sounds noble, and was indeed the error of a noble mind. But the distinction is essential. The older view was that mercy "tempered" justice, or (on the highest level of all) that mercy and justice had met and kissed. The essential act of mercy was to pardon; and pardon in its very essence involves the recognition of guilt and ill-desert in the recipient. If crime is only a disease which needs cure, not a sin which deserves punishment, it cannot be pardoned. How can you pardon a man for having a gumboil or a club foot? But the Humanitarian theory wants simply to abolish Justice and substitute Mercy for it. This means that you start being "kind" to people before you have considered their rights, and then force upon them supposed kindnesses which no one but you will recognize as kindnesses and which the recipient will feel as abominable cruel-

*[An annoying tunic worn as a punishment.—Eds.]
†[Two places of execution.—Eds.]

ties. You have overshot the mark. Mercy, detached from Justice, grows unmerciful. That is the important paradox. As there are plants which will flourish only in mountain soil, so it appears that Mercy will flower only when it grows in the crannies of the rock of Justice: Transplanted to the marsh-lands of mere Humanitarianism, it becomes a man-eating weed, all the more dangerous because it is still called by the same name as the mountain variety. But we ought long ago to have learned our lesson. We should be too old now to be deceived by those humane pretensions which have served to usher in every cruelty of the revolutionary period in which we live. These are the "precious balms" which will "break our heads."[2] . . .

STUDY QUESTIONS

1. Blatchford begins by stating four reasons given by others to show that we have free will. What are they? How does he reply to each?

2. Toward the end of the selection, Blatchford gives two direct arguments against free will. State them. Are they good arguments? Why or why not?

3. How does Blatchford attempt to prove determinism? In your view has he succeeded? Why or why not?

4. Many philosophers have thought that if one's actions are not free, then one is not responsible for them. Is that Blatchford's view?

5. Exactly what is the semantic confusion, according to Stace, which gives rise to the problem of free will? Is a person who holds the hard determinist position semantically confused? What does an ordinary person in the street mean by 'free'?

6. Discuss Stace's "thug with a gun to your head" case. Why does it seem to present a special problem? Is Stace's solution adequate?

7. How does Stace connect the concepts of free will, moral responsibility, and punishment?

8. How does Taylor criticize soft determinism? Can you develop a new form of soft determinism that will answer Taylor's objection?

9. Taylor raises worries about what he calls "simple indeterminism." Does the agency theory avoid those worries?

10. What does Hospers' criticism of soft determinism add to Taylor's objections?

11. Can Stace's definition of 'free' withstand Hospers' essay?

12. Is Menninger really opposed to all punishment, or is he opposed to punishment understood in a particular way? What properties make something punishment?

[2]Psalm cxli. 6.

13. Which of Lewis' arguments against the humanitarian theory are "in principle" objections, and which depend on specific empirical conditions in a society?

14. Now that you have studied the issues in this part of the book, what are the practical consequences of that study for you?

FURTHER READINGS

Ayer, A. J. "Freedom and Necessity." In *Philosophical Essays*. London: Macmillan, 1954, pp. 271–284. [A defense of compatibilism.]

Brody, Baruch A. *Beginning Philosophy*. Englewood Cliffs, N.J.: Prentice-Hall, 1977, pp. 162–187. [An elementary discussion of the important positions on the free will problem.]

Campbell, C. A. "Is 'Free Will' a Pseudo-Problem?" *Mind*, 60 (1951), 441–465. [A defense of libertarianism.]

Hook, Sidney, ed. *Determinism and Freedom*. New York: Collier Books, 1961. [A good set of readings on the topics of this section.]

Hospers, John. *An Introduction to Philosophical Analysis*, 2nd ed. Englewood Cliffs, N.J.: Prentice-Hall, 1967, pp. 279–348. [A clear overview of the free will and responsibility topics.]

Hume, David. *An Enquiry Concerning Human Understanding*. Indianapolis, Ind.: Hackett, 1977, Sec. 8. [First published in 1748; a classic statement of compatibilism.]

MacKay, D. M. "On the Logical Indeterminacy of a Free Choice." *Mind*, 69 (1960), 31–40. [Poses a difficulty for the perfect prediction of human actions.]

Ree, Paul. "Determinism and the Illusion of Moral Responsibility." In P. Edwards and A. Pap, eds., *A Modern Introduction to Philosophy*, 3rd ed. New York: Free Press, 1973, pp. 10–27. [A powerful defense of the hard determinist position.]

Salmon, Wesley C. "Determinism and Indeterminism in Modern Science." In Joel Feinberg, ed. *Reason and Responsibility*, 4th ed. Encino, Calif.: Dickenson, 1978, pp. 331–346. [As the title indicates.]

Smart, J. J. C. "Free-Will, Praise and Blame." *Mind*, 70 (1961), 291–306. [On the nature of praise and blame within a compatibilist framework.]

PART FOUR

BODIES, MINDS,
AND PERSONS

PREVIEW

*H*uman beings find it quite easy to regard themselves as special. This attitude manifests itself in innumerable ways. For example, we take ourselves to be the masters of everything save other people, and for a long time we found it inconceivable that our home, the earth, was not the center of the universe.

It should not take much reflection to shake at least some of our parochialism. Many beasts are stronger than we are; viruses are more fertile, cockroaches more highly adapted, stones more durable, and so on. When we are pressed, our special feature turns out to be our minds. With respect to thinking and feeling, we are number one. For this reason we believe ourselves to be persons, not mere objects, who are different from other living things.

What is a person? In particular, what sort of things must we be in order to explain our amazing mental life? Are we just bodies? Or do we also have nonmaterial minds? Such questions constitute what is commonly known as the mind-body problem.

For some thinkers, there is no such problem. One of them, Richard Taylor, writes:

> There are vexing, unsolved problems of psychology . . . but there are no mind-body problems. The reason why . . . is because there are no such things as *minds* in the first place.[1]

But of course, not everyone would agree with the view expressed in this quotation. According to certain philosophers, we must be radically different from most, if not all, of the other entities in the universe.

Two passages which point toward our special nature from quite different directions follow. The first is from the writings of an eighteenth-century theologian, Johann Michael Schmidt; the second, from the textbook of a contemporary philosopher.

> Not many years ago it was reported from France that a man had made a statue that could play various pieces on the Fleuttraversier,* placed the flute to its lips and took it down again, rolled its eyes, etc. But no one has yet invented an image that

[1]R. Taylor, "How to Bury the Mind-Body Problem," *The American Philosophical Quarterly*, 1969.
*[Transverse flute.—Eds.]

thinks, or wills, or composes, or even does anything at all similar. Let anyone who wishes to be convinced look carefully at the last fugal work of . . . Bach . . . I am sure that he will soon need his soul if he wishes to observe all the beauties contained therein, let alone wishes to play it to himself or to form a judgment of the author. Everything that the champions of materialism put forward must fall to the ground in view of this single example.[2]

Take the case of vision. Light-waves impinge upon the retina of your eye, producing there an inverted image of the object seen. . . . The optic nerve is stimulated, a chemical-electrical impulse passes along it, and finally, in a very small fraction of a second, the occipital lobe of the brain is stimulated; then a visual sensation occurs. Up to the occurrence of the sensation, every step of the process can be located in space, somewhere inside your head. But supposing you are looking at a solid green wall, where is your sensation of green? Is it in your head, inside your brain somewhere? If so, where? Would someone opening your head or looking at it through a super-x-ray microscope find the green you were seeing? Would it make sense to say that the green was 4 inches behind your eyes?[3]

Both passages suggest that there are certain features of human beings that cannot be accounted for by materialism, the view that people are nothing but their bodies. Furthermore, whatever mental abilities or states people have can be accounted for by their bodies, in particular their brains and nervous systems.

Look again at the quotations. The first suggests that our ability to write and appreciate music is incompatible with materialism. It is claimed that such activities require a soul. The second passage takes a mundane happening, the experience of a green wall, and suggests that this ordinary event cannot be understood materialistically. One's experiences exist, but they are not parts of one's body.

Which view is correct? That represented in the first passage above (by Taylor) or that represented in the two succeeding quotations (by Schmidt and Hospers)?

Main Questions

This leads us to the main question of this part, which is:

What is a person?
Is a person solely a material body (including a brain, nerve system, etc.)?
Or is a person not only a body but also a non-material mind, or soul, or psyche, or personality, etc.?

---

[2]Quoted from Douglas R. Hofstadter, *Godel, Escher, Bach: An Eternal Golden Braid*, New York, 1980, p. 27. Schmidt does not make the point here, but another defect from his point of view is that the materialist position is incompatible with the thesis that human beings are immortal. See Part Five.

[3]John Hospers, *An Introduction to Philosophical Analysis* (Prentice-Hall: Englewood Cliffs, N.J.), 1967, pp. 379–380.

(It should be stressed that by 'mind' we are asking about something *non-material*. Hence, we cannot equate minds with, say, brains.)

It should be pointed out that there are some related questions, such as:

If we do have non-material minds, do they survive the death of our bodies?

Can machines perform the things that humans do—for example, think?

These issues will be taken up in Part Five.

Answers

Three main answers have been given to the chief question of this part. These can be characterized simply as answers to the metaphysical problem, "What kinds of things in the universe are ultimately real?" Hence they can be described without making direct reference to the mind-body problem or to the main problem of Part Four: What is a person? In these *broad* terms, the three positions may be defined as follows:

Dualism: The universe contains two unique and irreducible kinds of things: material things and non-material (mental) things.

Materialism: The universe contains only one kind of things: material things.

Idealism: The universe contains only one kind of things: mental things.

When these main positions are characterized *with reference to the mind-body problem*, the definitions must be expanded so as to bring out this reference. If so, we have the following:

(a) Dualism: The universe contains two kinds of things: material and non-material (mental) things. A person consists (or is made up) of both. A person's body is obviously material. But a person also is (or has) something non-material—a mind.

(b) Materialism: The universe contains one kind of things: material things. Hence, a person is solely a material thing. There is nothing non-material about a person.

(c) Idealism: The universe contains one kind of things: non-material (mental) things. Hence, a person exists solely as something non-material (or mental). (It is usually held that it is a mind and the contents of that mind.)

A problem for dualism has always been: If both minds and bodies exist, what is the relationship between them? Interactionism is the view that minds and bodies of human beings interact causally.

It should be pointed out that dualism has been held in two forms: the older *traditional* dualism and the newer *revised* dualism:

Traditional dualism: A person consists of two unique and distinct kinds of substances: a physical substance or body, and a mental (non-material) substance or mind. The material substance (body) has certain attributes, such as occupying space. The mental substance (mind) has other different attributes, such as thinking. (Interactionist dualism holds that mind and body can interact with one another.)

Revised dualism: A person is more of a unitary entity than traditional dualism conceives of him to be. On the other hand, a person is not completely material, as materialism conceives him to be. Rather, a person is a psychophysical organism. If you want to talk in the older terms of "substances," then a person consists of only one kind of substance, his material body. The body has certain states or attributes which are purely material, such as mass, occupying of space, and so forth. But a person is also able to *experience* certain states which are uniquely non-material or mental, such as thoughts, sensations, feelings, and so on. These cannot in any way be reduced to material states.

In short, the dualism of the traditional sort is a dualism of two kinds of *substances*, each with its own kind of states. The dualism of the revised sort is a dualism of two kinds of *states*, material and non-material.

Obviously, the dualism of the revised sort is much "weaker" than traditional dualism. The traditional dualist claims that, in addition to our having material bodies (one kind of substance), we also have non-material minds (another kind of substance). Theoretically, the one could exist without the other. Hence, for a traditional dualist, survival after death is at least possible. The revised dualist denies that there are such things as mental substances—minds, or souls, or psyches. Again, a person is an organism, a highly complex one. That material organism (body) exists in various states or has various (material) attributes. But a person (perhaps because of a highly developed brain or whatever) can also *experience* various states—thoughts, sensations, etc.—which are uniquely *non-material* or mental.

It should be mentioned that there are several types of materialism. At least three are prominent in philosophical discussions and deserve to be at least roughly characterized here. All materialists agree that everything that exists is material, but what about so-called "mental" phenomena (pains, sensations, beliefs)? They are of course material, yet this allows for the following interestingly different treatments of mental phenomena:

(d) Identity Theory: "Mental" phenomena are strictly identical with brain processes.

(e) Behaviorism: Mental phenomena are sets of acts of behavior. For example, having a pain *is* doing and saying certain things; it is nothing but behaving in certain ways.

(f) Functionalism: Mental phenomena are states of a device that are characterized in terms of their relations to the input, output, and other internal states of the device.

The final essay, "Where Am I?", raises the main questions of Part Four by provoking us to think about *personal identity*: Who am *I*? What am *I*? How might I change and still be the *same* self? The essay challenges common sense and a number of implicit philosophical accounts of personal identity.

Selections

The main answers to the questions of this part are represented as follows:

Answer	Selection
(a) Dualism (traditional)	17
(a) Dualism (revised)	18
(b) Materialism	19, 20, 21

17 / The Mind as Distinct from the Body

C. E. M. JOAD

C. E. M. Joad (1891–1953) was a well-known English writer who wrote many books and articles in philosophy. He was also widely acclaimed as a speaker. Hence his writings and speeches were read or heard by enormous numbers of students as well as the public at large.

I. THE RELATIONSHIP OF MIND AND BODY

*I*t is obvious that one of the most important things about the mind is its relationship to the body. Mind and body are continually interacting in an infinite number of different ways. Mind influences body and body mind at every moment of our waking life. If I am drunk I see two lamp-posts instead of one; if I fail to digest my supper I have a nightmare and see blue devils; if I smoke opium or inhale nitrous oxide gas I shall see rosy-colored visions and pass into a state of beatitude. These are instances of the influence of the body upon the mind. If I see a ghost my hair will stand on end; if I am moved to anger my face will become red; if I receive a sudden shock I shall go pale. These are instances of the influence of the mind upon the body.

The examples just quoted are only extreme and rather obvious cases of what is going on all the time. Many thinkers indeed assert that mind and body are so intimately associated that there can be no event in the one which does not produce some corresponding event in the other, although the corresponding event, which we may call the effect of the first event, may be too small to be noticed. The interaction between mind and body is, at any rate, a fact beyond dispute. Yet when we come to reflect upon the manner of this interaction, it is exceedingly difficult to see how it can occur. Mind,[1] it is clear, must be something which is immaterial; if it were material it would be part of the body. The contents of, or even the events which happen in the mind— that is to say, wishes, desires, thoughts, aspirations, hopes, and acts of will— are also immaterial. The body, on the other hand, is matter and possesses the usual qualities of matter, such as size, weight, density, inertia, occupancy of space, and so forth.

Now there is no difficulty in understanding how one material thing can be influenced by another. Each possesses the same attributes of size, shape,

[1]It is important to emphasize the fact that the word *mind* does not mean the same as the word *brain*; the brain *is* material.

and weight, in virtue of which each can, as it were, communicate with or "get at" the other. Thus a paving stone can crush an egg because the egg belongs to the same order of being as the stone. But how can the paving stone crush a wish, or be affected by a thought? Material force and mass have no power over ideas; ideas do not exert force, nor do they yield to mass. How, in short, can that which has neither size, weight, nor shape, which cannot be seen, heard, or touched, and which does not occupy space come into contact with that which has these properties? . . .

The issue between those who endeavor to interpret mind action in terms of body action, and those who contend for the unique, distinct, and in some sense independent status of mind is not capable of definite settlement. . . . The most that can be done is to suggest certain objections that can be and have been brought against the materialist position . . . and at the same time to indicate a number of independent considerations which seem to demand a different kind of approach to psychology, and a different interpretation of its problems. This interpretation, to put it briefly, insists that [1.] a living organism is something over and above the matter of which its body is composed; that it is, in short, an expression of a *principle of life*, and that life is a force, stream, entity, spirit, call it what you will, that cannot be described or accounted for in material terms; [2.] that in human beings this principle of life expresses itself at the level of what is called *mind*, that this mind is distinct from both body and brain, . . . and [3.] that *no* account of mind action which is given in terms of brain action, gland activity, or *bodily responses* to *external stimuli* can, therefore, be completely satisfactory. This is the view which in some form or other is held by those who find a materialist explanation of psychology unsatisfactory, and in this [essay] we shall be concerned with the reasons for it.

II. BIOLOGICAL CONSIDERATIONS

1. Purposiveness / Some of these reasons, and perhaps the most important, are derived in part from regions which lie outside the scope of psychology proper; they belong to biology, and are based on a consideration of the characteristics which all living beings are found to possess in common. With regard to one of these "alleged"[2] characteristics of living organisms it is necessary to say a few words, since it constitutes a starting point for the method of interpretation with which we shall be concerned in this [essay.] The characteristic in question is that to which we give the name of purposiveness, and because of this characteristic it is said that any attempt to interpret the behavior of living creatures in terms of material response to stimuli must inevitably break down. . . .

---

[2]I insert the word *alleged* in order to indicate the controversial character of the subject. There is no doubt that it would be thought unsafe by many biologists to assume the existence of the characteristic in question, although I myself do not wish to deny it.

What, therefore, is meant by saying that living creatures are purposive? Primarily, that in addition to those of their movements which may be interpreted as responses to existing situations, they also act in a way which seems to point to the existence of a spontaneous impulse or need to bring about some other situation which does not yet exist. This impulse or need is sometimes known as a conation; a good instance of the sort of thing that is meant is the impulse we feel to maintain the species by obtaining food or seeking a mate. The impulse is chiefly manifested in the efforts a living organism will make to overcome any obstacle which impedes the fulfillment of its instinctive need. It will try first one way of dealing with it and then another, as if it were impelled by some overmastering force which drove it forward to the accomplishment of a particular purpose. Thus the salmon, proceeding upstream, leaping over rocks and breasting the current in order to deposit her spawn in a particular place, is acting in a way which it is difficult to explain in terms of a response to external stimuli. An organism again will seek to preserve the trend of natural growth and development by which alone the purpose of existence will be fulfilled; in its endeavor to reach and to maintain what we may call its natural state or condition, it is capable, if need arises, of changing or modifying its bodily structure. If you take the hydroid plant Antennularia and remove it from the flat surface to which it is accustomed to adhere, it will begin to proliferate long wavy roots or fibers in the effort to find something solid to grip, while everybody has heard of the crab's habit of growing a new leg in place of one that has been knocked off.

Activity of this kind seems difficult to explain on materialist lines as the response to a stimulus; it appears rather to be due to the presence of a living, creative impulse to develop in the face of any obstacle in a certain way. . . .

2. Foresight and Expectation / When we apply this conclusion to human psychology, we are immediately struck by the fact that the individual not only exhibits in common with other organisms this characteristic of purposive behavior, but is in many cases conscious of the nature of the purpose which inspires his behavior. The man who studies in order to pass an examination is not only impelled by a push from behind; he is drawn forward by a pull from in front. This pull in front can only become operative if he can be credited with the capacity to conceive the desirability of a certain state of affairs—namely, the passing of the examination, which does not yet exist; he shows, in other words, foresight and expectation. It is activities of this kind which seem most insistently to involve the assumption of a mind to do the foreseeing and expecting. In other words, the capacity to be influenced by events which lie in the future seems inexplicable on the stimulus-response basis; the *thought* of what does not exist may be allowed to influence the mind, but it is difficult to see how the nonexistent can stimulate the body.

The explanation of our capacity for being influenced by the thought of events that do not yet exist raises much the same difficulty as our undoubted responsiveness to events that have existed but do so no longer, and it will be desirable to consider the problem first of all from this point of view. . . .

III. CONSIDERATIONS OF MEANING

[3. **The Apprehension of Meaning** /] An important fact about our mental life is that we are capable of appreciating meaning. A statement of fact written on a piece of paper is, so far as its material content is concerned, merely a number of black marks inscribed on a white background. Considered, then, as a collection of visual, physical stimuli, it is comparatively unimportant; what is important is the meaning which is attached to these marks. If they inform us, for example, that we have received a legacy of ten thousand pounds it is not the black marks on the white background but the meaning they convey that effects a disturbance in our emotional life sufficiently profound to keep us awake all night. Now the meaning of the marks is obviously not a physical stimulus; it is something immaterial. How, then, is its effect to be explained in terms of bodily responses to physical stimuli, which the mind merely registers? Let us take one or two further examples in order to present the difficulty in a concrete form.

Let us suppose that I am a geometrician and am thinking about the properties of a triangle. As I do not wish at this point to enter into the vexed question of whether *some* physical stimulus is or is not necessary to initiate every chain of reasoning, we will assume that in this case there was a physical stimulus—it may have been a chance remark about Euclid, or the appearance of a red, triangular road signpost, while I am driving a car—a stimulus which we will call X, which prompted me to embark upon the train of speculations about the triangle. My reasoning proceeds until I arrive at a conclusion, which takes the form of a geometrical proposition expressed in a formula. I carry this formula in my head for a number of days and presently write it down. In due course I write a book, setting forth my formula and giving an account of the reasoning which led me to it. The book is read and understood by A. Presently it is translated into French, and is read and understood by B. Later still I deliver a lecture on the subject which is heard and understood by C. As A, B, and C have each of them understood my formula and the reasoning upon which it is based, we may say that the reasoning process has had for them the same meaning throughout. If it had not, they would not all have reached the same conclusion and understood the same thing by it. Yet in each of the four cases the sensory stimulus was different; for myself it was X, for A it was a number of black marks on a white background, for B a number of different black marks on a white background, and for C a number of vibrations in the atmosphere impinging upon his eardrums. It seems incredible that all these different stimuli should have been able to produce a consciousness of the same meaning, if our respective reactions to them were confined to physical responses (which must in each case have been different) which were subsequently reflected in our minds by a process of mental registration of the different responses. The stimuli being different, the intervention of something possessed of the capacity to grasp the *common* element among these physically different entities alone seems able to account for the facts, but the common element is the meaning, which is immaterial and can be grasped, therefore, only by a mind.

4. Synthesizing Power of Mind / This conclusion is reinforced by what we may call the synthesizing power of mind. Synthesizing means putting together, and one of the most remarkable powers that we possess is that of taking a number of isolated sensations and forming them into a whole . . .

Let us consider for a moment the case of aesthetic appreciation. The notes of a symphony considered separately consist merely of vibrations in the atmosphere. Each note may, when sounded in isolation, produce a pleasant sensation, and as one note is struck after another we get a sequence of pleasant sensations. But although this is a sufficient description of the symphony considered as a collection of material events, and of our reactions to these events considered merely in terms of sensations, it is quite clear that we normally think of a symphony as being something more than this. We think of it in fact as a whole, and it is as a whole that it gives what is called aesthetic pleasure. Now in thinking of the symphony in this way our mind is going beyond the mere sequence of pleasant sensations which its individual notes produce, and putting them together into some sort of pattern. If the notes were arranged in a different order, although the actual vibrations which impinged upon our senses would be the same, the pleasurable aesthetic effect would be destroyed.

It seems to follow that our pleasure in a symphony cannot be wholly accounted for, although it may depend upon our physical responses to the stimuli of the individual notes; in order to obtain aesthetic pleasure we must somehow be able to perceive it as more than the sum total of the individual notes—that is, as a whole pattern or arrangement. The pleasure ceases when the *wholeness* of the object perceived is destroyed, as it is, for example, by the transposition of certain notes. We may compare the difference between the physical sensations which are our responses to the visual stimuli of the colours and canvas of which a picture is composed, with our synthesized perception of a picture as a work of art.

We must conclude, then, that we possess the power of realizing external objects not merely as collections of physical stimuli, which of course they are, but as wholes in which the actual sensory elements are combined to form a single object of a higher order. This faculty of combining or putting together seems to involve the existence not only of a mind, but of a mind of an active, creative type which is able to go out beyond the raw material afforded by our bodily sensations, and to apprehend ideal objects as wholes which are more than the collection of physical events which compose their constituent parts.

IV. CONCLUSION

The conclusion to which the arguments . . . appear to point is that, in addition to the body and brain, the composition of the living organism includes an immaterial element which we call mind; that this element, although it is in very close association with the brain, is more than a mere glow or halo surrounding the cerebral structure, the function of which is confined to reflecting the events occurring in that structure; that, on the contrary, it is in some sense independent of the brain, and in virtue of its independence is able in part to direct and control the material constituents of the body, using them to carry out its purposes in relation to the external world of objects, much as a driver will make use of the mechanism of his motorcar. Mind so conceived is an active, dynamic, synthesizing force; it goes out beyond the sensations provided by external stimuli and arranges them into patterns, and it seems to be capable on occasion of acting without the provocation of bodily stimuli to set it in motion. It is, in other words, creative; that is, it carries on activities which even the greatest conceivable extension of our physiological knowledge would not enable us to infer from observing the brain. . . .

18 / *Why I Am a Dualist*

W I L L I A M   S .   R O B I N S O N

William S. Robinson (1940–   ) has taught philosophy for several years at Iowa State University. His publications include two books and numerous articles—which have been widely acclaimed—mainly in the areas of philosophy of mind and philosophy of artificial intelligence. This essay was written expressly for this book and was revised for this edition.

I

I believe that people and other animals have sensations and that these are not purely material things. Since I also believe that some things—rocks and trees, for example—*are* purely material things, I believe that the world as a whole contains (at least) two different kinds of things. This explains why my view is called dualism. The controversial part of this view, however, is the claim that there are sensations which are not purely material things.

To understand this claim we need to understand what a *sensation* is, what a *purely material thing* is, and what argument can be given for the claim. Let us begin with the term *sensation*. It is a difficult and somewhat technical matter to give a satisfactory definition of this term. Fortunately, we do not really need to have one. I have claimed that the world contains at least two kinds of things and this would be true even if there were just one thing of each kind. So it would be enough if we had one example of a sensation for which we can make a clear case that it is not a purely material thing. I will in fact give a little more than enough; I will describe three kinds of sensations and the reader will then be able to provide more. The three are pains, afterimages, and ringing in the ears.

To make sure that our attention is focused on the right thing, it is very important to make sure that we distinguish these three kinds of things from their *causes*. This can be done by considering cases in which the causal situation is somewhat out of the ordinary. (In fact, as we shall see, the very terms *afterimage* and *ringing in the ears* involve the idea that there is a certain peculiarity about their causes.) The usual cause of a pain is damage to some part of the body. Typically, the pain is felt to be located in the part of the body which has been damaged. (The "damage" may, of course, be either from some external cause or from an internal one, as in disease or a congenital defect.) There are, however, cases called "phantom limb," in which amputees suffer pains in limbs they no longer possess. That is, they hurt and seek medical relief; when the doctor asks *where* they hurt, their only natural reply is, for example, "In my right elbow," even though they are all too well aware that they do not have a right arm.

The actual cause of such a pain lies in conditions of neural cells in the shoulder, spinal cord, or brain. It is at such locations that doctors may intervene to relieve the pain. So the case of phantom limb does not show that pains are not physically caused or that they do not depend on what goes on in a person's nervous system. It does not show that pains are not purely material things. What it does do is help get our attention focused on the pain itself as distinguished from the injury which may be its cause. Once we have understood this case, those of us who do have arms should be able to distinguish clearly between a hit on the elbow (or a cut, bruise, or chipped bone)—that is, an injury—and the pain we feel when we are thus injured. It is only the pain and not the injury which I am claiming is not purely material.

Afterimages are like things which we see in that (1) they come in different colors and (2) our knowledge of what color they are has something to do with our eyes. They are unlike things we see in that they are not "there" to be seen. That is, we may be having a yellow afterimage when there is nothing yellow reflecting light into our eyes (and no yellow light being reflected into them by white things either). In fact, we may have a yellow afterimage when our eyes are closed and, thus, when they are not receiving reflected light of any kind whatever. Afterimages are caused by relatively bright illuminations of our retinas; but they have the complementary color of that illumination and they occur only after that illumination has ceased. Thus, knowing the color of an afterimage is easily distinguishable from knowing something about the light which causes it. Once again, it is not *these* considerations which are supposed to support dualism. Their point is rather to prepare the way for the argument by getting our attention focused on the kind of colored thing which I am claiming to be not purely material.

The case is very similar with ringing in the ears; so similar, in fact, that it will be enough to merely relate the following actual incident. I once was leaning against a doorjamb while conversing with the occupant of an office. After a while I became aware of a thin, whistle-like sound. I wondered whether it was just a ringing in my ears or a very loud whistle very far away. I did not know which, and I turned my head and moved into and out of the office to find out. I was astonished to find that neither of my hypotheses was correct; the cause was a very small vibration very close, namely, a little air escaping from a valve in a thermostat on the wall about six inches from my ear. However, I have become aware of exactly similar sounds on other occasions when examination turned up no cause outside my head. These sounds are sensations, and so is the one I became aware of while talking to my colleague, even though it (like most pains in *my* right elbow) was caused in a manner which is typical for the kind of sensation it was.

Let us turn now to the notion of a purely material thing. Although I have mentioned rocks and trees as examples, it will not do to merely illustrate what is meant by "purely material things." This is because there are many examples of discovering quite new kinds of purely material things, and we have to know what counts as discovering a new *material* thing as opposed to discovering a new *non*material thing (or showing that something, whether new or old, is nonmaterial). Thus, for example, when electrons were added to the list of things which scientists talked about, they were regarded as newly discovered material things and not as some kind of nonmaterial thing. There is the further reason that as physics has developed, its basic concepts have changed—even those as basic as "particle," "space," and "matter." If we tie our understanding of "material" too closely to particular views in physics, we leave ourselves open to finding that the physicists of tomorrow are no longer talking about purely "material" things. We need some way of understanding "material" which will enable us to avoid such a consequence.

There is one way—and only one—of getting what we need here which is plausible, straightforward, and in accord with all the noncontroversial cases. This approach is to make use of two truths which are rather obvious and are so basic to our understanding of "material" that hardly anything would be left of the idea if they were denied. They are as follows: (A) What a material thing is made of is parts which are material; and (B) if a thing is made of (only) material things, it is material. These truths suggest the following approach: Start with anything whose materiality is uncontroversial, for example, any ordinary, visible, tangible inanimate thing. Enlarge your set of material things by the rule, Whatever a material thing is made of is material. This will give you, for example, molecules, atoms, and electrons as material things. Enlarge your set of material things further by the rule, Whatever is composed of only material things is material. This gives you very large material things, such as planets, solar systems, and galaxies. A material thing, then, is any member of the largest collection which can be generated by this procedure.

This gives us a workable understanding of "material thing," but we must say a few words about *purely* material things. Some musical instruments are highly decorated with ivory inlays, delicate carvings, and sometimes even paintings. Assuming that tonal quality has not been sacrificed, we may say that such an instrument lives in two quite distinct aesthetic modes, neither of which is reducible to or accountable for in terms of the other. Its visual excellence is not explainable or even describable by reference to its tonal qualities, and vice versa. Such a visually pleasing object *is* a musical instrument; but because of its visual dimension I think it is natural to say that it is not *purely* a musical instrument.

Contrast the case of a thing which is "both" an arrangement of transistors, wires, circuit chips, and buttons and "also" a calculator. *In a sense* such a thing lives in two modes. For we can talk about what the calculator does— adding, taking roots, storing information, and so forth—or we can talk about how it works. These two ways of talking about it reflect the different interests of the user and the manufacturer (or repairer), and tend to remain distinct. Nonetheless, I shall say that a calculator is *purely* an arrangement of transistors, wires, and so on, because what it does can be fully accounted for by reference to how the transistors and other parts work and how they are connected.

When I claim that sensations are not purely material things, I am not denying that it *may* turn out that pains are aspects of the same things that are also material things—just as in claiming that some object is not purely a musical instrument I would not be denying that a carving may be a thing that is also a musical instrument. A materialism which claimed *only* that everything is material without insisting that everything is *purely* material would be a very weak and uninteresting form of materialism. What I do deny, when I deny that sensations are purely material, is the interesting materialist claim that sensations can be fully accounted for by reference to the uncontroversially material aspect of material things.

II

Before proceeding to the argument for dualism, we must have a more concrete understanding of materialism. There is ample evidence that there is some kind of connection between sensations and brains. For example, in a famous series of experiments Wilder Penfield produced sensations in a number of patients by directly stimulating their brains with electrodes.[1] It is also

[1]Wilder Penfield, *The Excitable Cortex in Conscious Man* (Springfield, Ill.: C. C Thomas, 1958).

known that destroying some parts of the brain, or changing their operation by means of electrode stimulation or drugs, can prevent some pains from occurring. These facts lead to the view that *if* sensations are purely material things, they will be very intimately related to material things which are parts of brains. There are just three ways for a materialist to conceive of this relationship. First, it may be held that sensations are made of neurons, as engines are made of rods, pistons, valves, etc., or houses are made of bricks, shingles and beams. Second, it may be held that sensations are *states* of people rather than being *things*. A claim which parallels this one in form is: "Sound waves are *states* of air rather than *things*." The natural development of this view narrows what the state is *of* down to some collection of neurons in the brain. For the state of the rest of my body (i.e., besides my retina or elbow) does not have anything to do with the color of my afterimage or the throbbing of my elbow; and, as I remarked earlier, one does not even need an elbow in order to have pain "in" it. The only thing whose possession seems really required for a sensation to occur is a brain or some part of a brain. Thus, this second way of conceiving materialism must be formulated in this way: Sensations are states of collections of neurons (in the brain). (Compare: Sound waves are states of collections of air molecules—namely, states of being alternately more and less compressed.) Third, it may be held that while sensations are not themselves composed of anything, they are parts of brains. [This makes them material, by principle A. Therefore, if they had parts those parts would (by the same principle) be material; and then sensations would be material in the first way (i.e., by being made out of material things). Thus, if the third alternative is to be independent of the success of the first, we must include in it the supposition that sensations have no parts.]

Now, the key fact in the argument for dualism is that none of these three alternatives is *intelligible*. It is important to understand what this means, so let us consider some illustrations. The view that the earth is flat is false, and even obviously false, in the light of the evidence we have. It is, however, an *intelligible* view; it *could* have turned out that we live on an enormous plate (after all, asteroids are typically not even approximately spherical). We know what it would have been like to have had evidence that this was the case. When we hear that people used to think the earth is flat, we understand what they believed; we understand what they would have meant if they had said, "The earth is flat"; and we understand that with limited evidence this may have been a reasonable view to hold. Contrast this case with the claim that the universe is made of numbers. This is not an intelligible view. We have no idea what it would be like for this to be true; we have no idea what it would be like to have evidence supporting such a claim; we do not understand how, even granting severely limited evidence, people could have found it reasonable to believe this. When we read in a history of philosophy that Pythagoras is reputed to have made such a claim, we can only wonder what he meant; that is to say, we can only wonder what intelligible claim it was which he made, which is being reported to us in these words, which, as they stand, are unintelligible. (For example, perhaps he meant that the distances between planets stand to each other in exact integral ratios. *This* claim is intelligible even though it is quite unworthy of being believed.) We can see the unintelligibility clearly by trying to articulate a detailed explanation of the claim. Let us try to imagine how we are to start. "First, you take 1, and then another 1, and then you have 2, . . . and then you have a grain of sand." How could *numbers* give us a grain of sand? What could possibly *explain* where the hardness or the color come from, if all we had to work with was numbers? It is this kind of unintelligibility that I find in such claims as "Sensations are made of neurons," "Sensations are states of collections of neurons," and "Sensations are (in part) what brains are made of." . . . Again, consider the idea that you or your friend is really a character in someone else's dream. This is a sophisticated joke that sometimes occurs to students when their philosophy professors ask them to consider how they know they are not dreaming. But let us try to take it seriously; let us imagine reading in *The New York Times* one morning that scientists report having discovered yesterday that Sting, lead singer of The Police, is actually nothing but the dream character of the group's drummer, Stewart Copeland. Only the most unthinking could fail to recognize this as a hoax. The reason is not that finding out that a body is made of dream-stuff is a particularly difficult thing to do or that we haven't appropriated sufficient funds to do it correctly. The reason is that we have no idea what could count as finding out such a thing.

The first two formulations of materialism, stated above, require similar treatment and I will consider them together; then I will make some remarks about the third alternative. A particular example of the first alternative is, "This pain is made of neurons X, Y, and Z." An example of the second alternative is, "Jones's hurting is (or consists in) Jones's neurons X, Y, and Z firing in pattern P_1." (Patterns of neuron firings can be characterized by such properties as the order in which neurons involved in the pattern fire, the ratios of times between firings, the ratios of intensities of output of each neuron, the ratios of durations of firing, and the length of time between repetitions of a sequence of firings. For example, pattern P_1 might be repeated sequences—say, twenty repetitions per second—of firings of X, followed by Y, followed by Y again, followed by Z; where the ratio of firing intervals is 2:1:3 and the ratio of durations is 1:4:2:3.) Neither of these examples is intelligible. We do not understand what it would be like for them to be true; we do not understand what it would be like to find evidence pointing to their truth. We have no articulated account—not even an untested one—that shows us how to *explain* where pain (or color, or ringing) comes from, if all we have to work with is neural firing rates, ratios, and so on.

The following examples will help us focus attention on the point at which the unintelligibility of the cases just discussed occurs, by showing what intelligibility looks like in parallel cases in which it is present. A ladder is composed of parts—parts which are not ladders themselves, but rungs and sides. This composition is fully intelligible because when you understand what a rung is, what a side is, and how they are arranged, you thereby understand how a ladder can help you get onto a roof. Again, being properly aligned is a state of my car, and this state is (or consists in) some of the parts of my car being in a certain arrangement. This composition is fully intelligible because when you understand what rods, chassis, and so forth are and how they are arranged after the bolts have been properly tightened, you thereby understand why the wheels contact the road in a rectangle rather than a parallelogram. By contrast, you could know all you wished about neural firing sequences, intensities, and timing: You would not thereby understand that the person in whose brain they occur must be in pain.

We have to be careful at this point to distinguish between evidence that one thing *causes* another and evidence that one thing is *made of* (composed of, consists of or in) others. Some viruses cause warts, but warts are not made out of those viruses; my parents caused me but are not parts of me. My cells, by contrast, did not bring me into existence; they are what I am made of. The experiments by Penfield which I mentioned earlier are evidence that sensations are caused by neural firings. *This* claim is not only intelligible but so well supported that it is hard to imagine how a reasonable person could deny it. Now, if I knew which neural firings cause which sensations and I knew that a neural firing of a certain kind was about to occur, I would be able to predict that a certain kind of sensation was about to occur. In this sense one could say that if I knew everything about neurons I would know which sensations would be forthcoming. But all this does not give any intelligibility to the idea that a red afterimage may really be composed of neurons or that a C-sharp ringing in the ears is just some neurons firing in a certain pattern. When you think about the parts of a ladder in their arrangement, you can *see why* the whole thus composed does what it does. If you knew all about the innards of an Atari set, you would *understand why*, when you put it into a certain state by pushing the right buttons, it plays "Breakout." But you cannot in this way understand that there should be pain or a red afterimage through getting to know the details of a neural firing pattern. Why should a firing interval ratio of 2:1:3:2 go with hurting (for example) whereas one of 1:4:2:3 goes with itching? What has a duration ratio of 5:3:4:1:2 got to do with red in my afterimage, rather than blue or yellow? The problem with these questions is not that it would take a lot of research to answer them. The problem is that we have no idea what could count as a research program designed to answer them.

Let us turn to the third alternative, that is, the view that sensations are (in part) what brains are made of.[2] According to this view, a list of brain parts which includes only such items as carbon atoms, subatomic particles, neurons, and water molecules must be incomplete. A complete list would have to include, for example, pains and ringing in the ears. To imagine this is to imagine that a neural scientist might have reason to say, with a perfectly straight face, something like the following: "I have applied the laws of physics

---

[2]The discussion in this and the next two paragraphs is an extreme condensation of an argument that can be found in my "Sellarsian Materialism," *Philosophy of Science* 49 (1982), pp. 212–227.

and chemistry to neural cells in the brain and I have found a discrepancy. The firings of these cells cannot be adequately accounted for by physics and chemistry alone. Therefore, we must introduce some pains or ringings in the ears in order to find conditions that will adequately explain the observed neural firings." But this is not intelligible. We can imagine a discrepancy, of course, and we can imagine anybody *saying* anything. What we cannot imagine is that it could be reasonable for a neural scientist to account for a discrepancy by bringing in sensations as the overlooked parts.

There is, however, one approach which seems to hold promise of giving us a way of imagining just such a possibility. This approach suggests that we model the discovery that pains are brain parts on the discovery of subatomic particles. The pattern of such discoveries is, roughly, this. One takes some unquestionably material thing and subjects it to some unusual conditions, for example, bombardment in a cyclotron. One observes how it reacts, and then one attempts to explain the reaction. Particles are assumed to exist if they are required for such explanations. Particles introduced into physics in this way are, in accord with principle A, taken by everyone to be material. To extend this pattern to sensations is to suppose that pains, for example, might turn out to be needed to explain something that goes on in the brain which would otherwise be inexplicable.

This extension of the method of introducing particles, however, is not really intelligible. Of course, it could happen that when we try to explain in detail how brains work we will be surprised and will have to revise some current theories to account for new evidence. Such revision might even involve supposing that there are things in the brain which we have not yet recognized. What we do not understand, however, is how it could be reasonable to take the newly required things to be pains or afterimages. The reason behind this unintelligibility is as follows. When physicists introduce a new particle, they introduce it as having a force associated with it, so that how it affects other particles is built right into what it is. For example, electrons were not *discovered* to have a negative charge, and they could not have been discovered to have it—for the theory of electrons lays it down that the particles which it calls electrons are just the ones with a negative charge. Similarly, genes were *introduced* as trait carriers rather than being discovered to be so. Now, pains, afterimages, and so forth are not introduced as interacting in some way with neurons or carbon compounds. The pattern by which particles are introduced in physics does not explain how something that is not introduced as having a certain force can be discovered to have it. Thus, we really have no model for "discovering" that pains make neurons or chemical compounds operate in any particular way. We have no model for making intelligible a claim that "this neuron fires now because, in addition to the electrochemical forces on it (which by themselves are insufficient to make it fire), there is present a lime-green afterimage." Without such a model, however, the idea that pains might explain operations in brains remains a mere form of words with no intelligible interpretation; and so, therefore, does the idea that pains might be parts of brains.

If I were to believe that sensations are purely material things, I would have to believe either that they are composed of neurons or that they are states of collections of neurons or that they are parts of brains. I have argued that none of these consequences is intelligible. It is not reasonable to believe that claims are true when they are unintelligible to you. So I do not believe these consequences. Neither, therefore, do I believe what leads to them, that is, the claim that sensations are purely material. That is why I am a dualist.[3]

19 / *The Case for Materialism*

RICHARD TAYLOR

Richard Taylor (1919–   ) is a professor of philosophy who taught for many years at Union College in New York. He has written highly acclaimed and widely discussed books and articles on a variety of philosophical problems in the philosophy of religion, metaphysics, and the philosophy of mind.

I. INTRODUCTION

Sometimes the simplest and most obvious distinctions give rise to the profoundest intellectual difficulties, and things most commonplace in our daily experience drive home to us the depths of our ignorance. Men have fairly well fathomed the heavens, so that perhaps nothing counts as surer knowledge than astronomy, the science of the things most distant from us, and yet the grass at our feet presents impenetrable mysteries. In like manner, our knowledge of man, of human history, of cultures remote in time and distance, fills volumes, and yet each of us is bewildered by that one being that is closest to him, namely, himself, as soon as he asks the most elementary questions. And oddly, it seems that the simplest question one can ask about himself—the question namely, What am I?—is the very hardest to answer, and nonetheless the most important. One can ask of many other things, including some very complex ones—such as a tree, a drop of water, or a machine—just what they are, and be quite certain that his answers, though incomplete, are nonetheless not wholly wrong. But when one asks what he himself is, what he is in his

---

[3]The editors are grateful to Prof. Robinson for having written this essay for this volume.

innermost nature; when he asks what is that "I" with which he is so intimately concerned and which is for him the very center of the universe, then he is bewildered, and must fall back on philosophical speculations of the most difficult sort.

It is, moreover, this simple and basic question that has the greatest philosophical ramifications. All morals, religion, metaphysics, and law turn upon it. Law and morality, for example, presuppose the existence of moral agents who have responsibilities and are capable of incurring guilt. But obviously, certain kinds of things can have responsibilities, and certain others cannot; and if men are in fact beings of the latter kind, then morality and law, as traditionally conceived, are nonsense. Again, many religions presuppose that men are spiritual beings, capable of surviving the destruction of their bodies in death. If a man is in fact nothing of the sort, then those religions rest upon a misconception. It is thus imperative that we try to find some answer to this basic and simple question. . . .

II. THE REALITY OF THE SELF AND THE BODY

However unsure I may be of the nature of myself and of the relation of myself to my body, I can hardly doubt the reality of either. Whether I am identical with my body, or whether I am a spirit, or soul, or perhaps only a collection of thoughts and feelings—whatever I am, I cannot doubt my own being, cannot doubt that I am part of the world, even prior to any philosophical reflection on the matter. For surely if I know anything at all, as presumably I do, then I know that I exist. There seems to be nothing I could possibly know any better. And this is, of course, quite consistent with my great ignorance as to the nature of that self of whose existence I feel so assured.

I know, further, that I have a body. I may have learned this from experience, in the same way that I have learned of the existence of innumerable other things, or I may not have; it is, in any case, something I surely know. I may also have only the vaguest conception, or even a totally erroneous one, of the relationship between myself and my body; I can nevertheless no more doubt the reality of the one than the other. I may also be, as I surely am, quite ignorant of the nature and workings of my body and even of many of its parts, but no such ignorance raises the slightest doubt of its reality.

Now what is the connection between these, between myself and my body? Just what relationship am I affirming by "have," when I say with such confidence that I have a body? Abstractly, there seem to be just three general possibilities. In the first place, my having a body might consist simply in the *identity* of myself with my body, or of my *being* a body. Or second, it might amount to *possession*, such that my having a body consists essentially in this body's being among the various other things that I own or possess, it being at the same time, perhaps, in some way unique among these. Or finally, there may be some special, perhaps highly metaphysical relationship between the two, such as that I as a person am one thing, my body another quite different thing, the two being somehow connected to each other in a special way, appropriately expressed by the assertion that the one *has* the other.

Now there are great difficulties in all these suggestions, and, under the third, numerous special theories are possible, as we shall see. We had best, however, begin with the simplest view, to see then whether any of the others are any better.

III. MATERIALISM

I know that I have a body, and that this is a material thing, though a somewhat unusual and highly complicated one. There would, in fact, be no other reason for calling it my body, except to affirm that it is entirely material, for nothing that is not matter could possibly be a part of my body. Now if my having a body consists simply in the identity of myself with my body, then it follows that I *am* a body, and nothing more. Nor would the affirmation of the identity of myself with my body be at all inconsistent with saying that I have a body, for we often express the relationship of identity in just this way. Thus, one might correctly say of a table that it *has* four legs and a top, or of a bicycle that it *has* two wheels, a frame, a seat, and handle bars. In such cases, no one would suppose that the table or the bicycle is one thing, and its parts or "body" another, the two being somehow mysteriously connected. The table or the bicycle just *is* its parts, suitably related. So likewise, I might just *be* the totality of my bodily parts, suitably related and all functioning together in the manner expressed by saying that I am a living body, or a living, material animal organism.

This materialistic conception of a person has the great advantage of simplicity. We do know that there are bodies, that there are living animal bodies, and that some of these are in common speech denominated men. A person is, then, on the view, nothing mysterious or metaphysical, at least as regards the *kind* of thing he is.

A consequence of this simplicity is that we need not speculate upon the relationship between one's body and his mind, or ask how the two are connected, or how one can act upon the other, all such questions being rendered senseless within the framework of this view, which in the first place denies that we are dealing with two things. The death of the animal organism—which is, of course, an empirical fact and not subject to speculation—will, moreover, be equivalent to the destruction of the person, consisting simply in the cessation of those functions which together constitute being alive. Hence, the fate of a person is simply, on this view, the fate of his body, which is ultimately a return to the dust whence he sprang. This alleged identity of oneself with his body accounts, moreover, for the solicitude every man has for his body, and for its health and well-being. If a person is identical with his body then any threat to the latter is a threat to himself, and he must view the destruction of it as the destruction of himself. And such, in fact, does seem to be the attitude of all men, whatever may be their philosophical or religious opinions. Again, the distinction that every man draws between himself and other persons, or himself and other things, need be no more than the distinction between one body and others. When I declare that some foreign object— a doorknob, for instance, or a shoe—is no part of myself, I may be merely making the point that it is no part of my body. I would, surely, be more hesitant in declaring that my hand, or my brain and nervous system, which are physical objects, are no parts of me.

Such a conception has nevertheless always presented enormous difficulties, and these have seemed so grave to most philosophers that almost any theory, however absurd when examined closely, has at one time or another seemed to them preferable to materialism. Indeed, the difficulties of materialism are so grave that, for some persons, they need only to be mentioned to render the theory unworthy of discussion.

IV. THE MEANING OF "IDENTITY"

By "identity" the materialist must mean a strict and total identity of himself and his body, nothing less. Now to say of anything, X, and anything, Y, that X and Y are identical, or that they are really one and the same thing, one must be willing to assert of X anything whatever that he asserts of Y, and vice versa. This is simply a consequence of their identity, for if there is anything whatever that can be truly asserted of any object X, but cannot be truly asserted of some object Y, then it logically follows that X and Y are two different things, and not the same thing. In saying, for instance, that the British wartime prime minister and Winston Churchill are one and the same person, one commits himself to saying of either whatever he is willing to say of the other—such as, that he lived to a great age, smoked cigars, was a resolute leader, was born at Blenheim, and so on. If there were any statement whatever that was true of, say, Mr. Churchill, but not true of the wartime prime minister, then it would follow that Mr. Churchill was not the wartime prime minister, that we are here referring to two different men, and not one.

The question can now be asked, then, whether there is anything true of me that is not true of my body, and vice versa. [1.] There are, of course, ever so many things that can be asserted indifferently of both me and my body without absurdity. For instance, we can say that I was born at such and such place and time, and it is not the least odd to say this of my body as well. Or we can say that my body now weighs exactly so many pounds, and it would be just as correct to give this as my weight; and so on.

[2.] But now consider more problematical assertions. It might, for instance, be true of me at a certain time that I am morally blameworthy or praiseworthy. Can we then say that my body or some part of it, such as my brain, is in exactly the same sense blameworthy or praiseworthy? Can moral predicates be applied without gross incongruity to any physical object at all? Or suppose I have some profound wish or desire, or some thought—the desire, say, to be in some foreign land at a given moment, or thoughts of the

Homeric gods. It seems at least odd to assert that my body, or some part of it, wishes that it were elsewhere, or has thoughts of the gods. How, indeed, can any purely physical state of any purely physical object ever be a state that is *for* something, or of something, in the way that my desires and thoughts are such? And how, in particular, could a purely physical state be in this sense *for* or *of* something that is not real? Or again, suppose that I am religious, and can truly say that I love God and neighbor, for instance. Can I without absurdity say that my body or some part of it, such as my foot or brain, is religious, and loves God and neighbor? Or can one suppose that my being religious, or having such love, consists simply in my body's being in a certain state, or behaving in a certain way? If I claim the identity of myself with my body, I must say all these odd things; that is, I must be willing to assert of my body, or some part of it, everything I assert of myself. There is perhaps no logical absurdity or clear falsity in speaking thus of one's corporeal frame, but such assertions as these are at least strange, and it can be questioned whether, as applied to the body, they are even still meaningful.

[3.] The disparity between bodily and personal predicates becomes even more apparent, however, if we consider epistemological predicates, involved in statements about belief and knowledge. Thus, if I believe something— believe, for instance, that today is February 31—then I am in a certain state; the state, namely, of having a certain belief which is in this case necessarily a false one. Now how can a physical state of any physical object be identical with that? And how, in particular, can anything be a *false* physical state of an object? The physical states of things, it would seem, just *are*, and one cannot even think of anything that could ever distinguish one such state from another as being either true or false. A physiologist might give a complete physical description of a brain and nervous system at a particular time, but he could never distinguish some of those states as true and others as false, nor would he have any idea what to look for if he were asked to do this. At least, so it would certainly seem.

V. PLATONIC DUALISM

[A.] It is this sort of reflection that has always led metaphysicians and theologians to distinguish radically between the mind or soul of a man and his body, ascribing properties to the mind that are utterly different in kind from those exhibited by the body; properties which, it is supposed, could not be possessed by any body, just because of its nature as a physical object.

The simplest and most radical of such views *identifies* the person or self with a soul or mind, and declares its relationship to the body to be the almost accidental one of mere occupancy, possession, or use. Thus Plato,* and many mystical philosophers before and after him, thought of the body as a veritable prison of the soul, a gross thing of clay from which the soul one day gladly

---

*[A philosopher of ancient Greece.—Eds.]

escapes, to live its own independent and untrammeled existence, much as a bird flees its cage or a snake sheds its skin. A person, thus conceived, is a non-material substance—a *spirit*, in the strictest sense—related to an animal body as possessor to thing possessed, tenant to abode, or user to thing used. A person *has* a body only in the sense that he, perhaps temporarily, occupies, owns, or uses a body, being all the while something quite distinct from it and having, perhaps, a destiny quite different from the melancholy one that is known sooner or later to overtake the corporeal frame.

This dualism of mind and body has been, and always is, firmly received by millions of unthinking men, partly because it is congenial to the religious framework in which their everyday metaphysical opinions are formed, and partly, no doubt, because every man wishes to think of himself as something more than just one more item of matter in the world. Wise philosophers, too, speak easily of the attributes of the mind as distinct from those of the body, thereby sundering the two once and for all. Some form of dualism seems in fact indicated by the metaphysical, moral, and epistemological difficulties of materialism which are, it must be confessed, formidable indeed.

[B.] But whatever difficulties such simple dualism may resolve, it appears to raise others equally grave. For one thing, it is not nearly as simple as it seems. Whatever a partisan of such a view might say of the simplicity of the mind or soul, a *man* is nonetheless, on this view, *two* quite disparate things, a mind and a body, having almost nothing in common and only the flimsiest connection with each other. This difficulty, once it is acutely felt, is usually minimized by conceiving of a man, in his true self as nothing but a mind, and representing his body as something ancillary to this true self, something that is not really any part of him at all but only one among the many physical objects that he happens to possess, use, or what not, much as he possesses and uses various other things in life. His body does, to be sure, occupy a preeminent place among such things, for it is something without which he would be quite helpless; but this renders it no more a part or whole of his true self or person than any other of the world's physical things.

[1.] Possession, however, is essentially a social concept, and sometimes a strictly legal one. Something counts as one of my possessions by virtue of my title to it, and this is something conferred by men, in accordance with conventions and laws fabricated by men themselves. Thus does a field or a building count as one of my possessions. But a certain animal body, which I identify as mine, is not mine in any sense such as this. My dominion over my body arises from no human conventions or laws, and is not alterable by them. The body of a slave, though it may be owned by another man in the fullest sense of ownership that is reflected in the idea of possession, is nevertheless the slave's body in a metaphysical sense in which it could not possibly be the body of his master. One has, moreover, a solicitude for his body wholly incommensurate with his concern for any treasure, however dear. The loss of the latter is regarded as no more than a loss, though perhaps a grave one, while the abolition of one's body cannot be regarded as the mere loss of something clearly held, but is contemplated by any man as an appalling and total calamity.

[2.] The ideas of occupancy or use do not express the relation of mind and body any better. *Occupancy*, for instance, is a physical concept; one thing occupies another by being in or upon it. But the mind, on this view, is no physical thing, and no sense can be attached to its resting within or upon any body; the conception is simply ridiculous. Nor does one simply *use* his body the way he uses implements and tools. One does, to be sure, sometimes use his limbs and other parts, over which he has voluntary control, in somewhat the manner in which he uses tools; but many of one's bodily parts, including some that are vital, the very existence of which may be unknown to him, are not within his control at all. They are nonetheless parts of his body. Artificial devices, too, like hearing aids, spectacles, and the like, do not in the least become parts of one's body merely by being used, even in the case of a man who can barely do without them. They are merely things worn or used. Nor can one say that one's body is that physical being in the world upon which one absolutely depends for his continuing life, for there are many such things. One depends on the sun, for instance, and the air he breathes; without these he would perish as certainly as if deprived of his heart; yet no one regards the sun or the air around him as any part of his body.

A man does not, then, *have* a body in the way in which he has anything else at all, and any comparison of the body to a material possession or instrument is about as misleading as likening it to a chamber in which one is more or less temporarily closeted. The connection between oneself and his body is far more intimate and metaphysical than anything else we can think of. One's body is at least a part of himself, and is so regarded by every man. Yet it is not merely a part, as the arm is part of the body; and we are so far without any hint of how the mind and the body are connected. . . .

VI. MATERIALISM AGAIN

One thing should by now seem quite plain, however, and that is that the difficulties of simple materialism are not overcome by any form of dualism. There is, therefore, no point in recommending dualism as an improvement over materialism. To assert that a man is both body *and* mind—that is, that he is two things rather than one—not only does not remove any problem involved in saying that he is one thing only, namely, a body, but introduces all the problems of describing the connection between those two things. We are led to conclude, then, that a metaphysical understanding of human nature must be sought within the framework of materialism, according to which a man is entirely identical with his body.

All forms of dualism arise from the alleged disparity between persons and physical objects. Men, it is rightly noted, are capable of thinking, believing, feeling, wishing, and so on; but bodies, it is claimed, are capable of none of these things, and the conclusion is drawn that men are not bodies. Yet it cannot be denied that men *have* bodies; hence, it is decided that a man, or a person, is a nonphysical entity, somehow more or less intimately related to a body. But here it is rarely noted that whatever difficulties there may be in applying personal and psychological predicates and descriptions to bodies, precisely the same difficulties are involved in applying such predicates and descriptions to *anything whatever*, including spirits or souls. If, for example, a philosopher reasons that a body cannot think, and thereby affirms that, since a person thinks, a person is a soul or spirit or mind rather than a body, we are entitled to ask how a spirit can think. For surely, if a spirit or soul can think, we can affirm that a body can do so; and if we are then asked *how* a body can think, our reply can be that it thinks in precisely the manner in which the dualist supposes a soul thinks. The difficulty of imagining how a body thinks is not in the least lessened by asserting that something else, which is not a body, thinks. And so it is with every other personal predicate or description. Whenever faced with the dualist's challenge to explain how a body can have desires, wishes, how it can deliberate, choose, repent, how it can be intelligent or stupid, virtuous or wicked, and so on, our reply can always be: The body can do these things, and be these things, in whatever manner one imagines the soul can do these things and be these things. For to repeat, the difficulty here is in seeing how *anything at all* can deliberate, choose, repent, think, be virtuous or wicked, and so on, and *that* difficulty is not removed but simply glossed over by the invention of some new thing, henceforth to be called the "mind" or "soul."

It becomes quite obvious what is the source of dualistic metaphysics when the dualist or soul philosopher is pressed for some description of the mind or soul. The mind or soul, it turns out in such descriptions, is just whatever it is that thinks, reasons, deliberates, chooses, feels, and so on. But the fact with which we began was that *men* think, reason, deliberate, choose, feel, and so on. And we do in fact have some fairly clear notion of what we mean by a man, for we think of an individual man as a being existing in space and time, having a certain height and weight—as a being, in short, having many things in common with other objects in space and time, and particularly with those that are living, that is, with other animals. But the dualist, noting that a man is significantly different from other beings, insofar as he, unlike most of them, is capable of thinking, deliberating, choosing, and so on, suddenly asserts that it is not a man, as previously conceived, that does these things at all, but something else, namely, a mind or soul, or something that does not exist in space and time nor have any height and weight, nor have, in fact, any material properties at all. And then when we seek some understanding of what this mind or soul is, we find it simply described as a thing that thinks, deliberates, feels, and so on. But surely the proper inference should have been that men are like all other physical objects in some respects—e.g., in having size, mass, and location in space and time; that they are like some physical objects but unlike others in certain further respects—e.g., in being living, sentient, and so on; and like no other physical objects at all in still other respects—e.g., in being rational, deliberative, and so on. And of course none of this suggests that men are not physical objects, but rather that they are precisely physical objects, like other bodies in some ways, unlike many other bodies in other ways, and unlike any other bodies in still other respects.

The dualist or soul philosopher reasons that since men think, feel, desire, choose and so on, and since such things cannot be asserted of bodies, then men are not bodies. Reasoning in this fashion, we are forced to the conclusion that men are not bodies—though it is a stubborn fact that men nevertheless *have* bodies. So the great problem then is to connect men, now conceived as souls or minds, to their bodies. But philosophically, it is just exactly as good to reason that, since men think, feel, desire, choose, etc., and since men are bodies—i.e., are living, animal organisms having the essential material attributes of weight, size, and so on—then *some* bodies think, feel, desire, choose, etc. This argument is just as good as the dualist's argument and does not lead us into a morass of problems concerning the connection between soul and body.

VII. THE SOURCE OF DUALISTIC THEORIES

Why, then, does the dualist's argument have, and this one lack, such an initial plausibility? Why have so many philosophers been led into dualistic metaphysical views, on the basis of arguments apparently no stronger than other arguments having simpler conclusions but which are rarely even considered?

Part of the answer is perhaps that, when we form an idea of a *body* or a *physical object*, what is most likely to come to mind is not some man or animal but something much simpler, such as a stone or a marble. When we are then invited to consider whether a physical object might think, deliberate, choose, and the like, we are led to contemplate the evident absurdity of supposing things like *that* do such things, and thus we readily receive the claim that bodies cannot think, deliberate, choose, and the like, and the dualist extracts his conclusion. But suppose we began somewhat differently. Suppose we began with a consideration of two quite dissimilar physical objects—a living, animal body, of the kind commonly denominated "man," on the one hand, and a simple body, of the kind denominated "stone," on the other. Now let it be asked whether there is any absurdity in supposing that one of these things might be capable of thinking, deliberating, choosing, and the like. Here there is no absurdity at all in asserting that an object of the first kind might indeed have such capacities, but evidently not one of the second kind—from which we would conclude, not that men are not physical objects, but rather that they are physical objects which are significantly different from other physical objects, such as stones. And there is, of course, nothing the least astonishing in this.

But how, one may wonder, can a "mere physical object" have feelings? But here the answer should be: Why, if it is a physical object of a certain familiar kind, should it not have feelings? Suppose, for example, that it is a living body, like a frog or mouse, equipped with a complicated and living nervous system. Where is the absurdity in asserting that a "mere physical object" of this sort can feel? Evidently there is none. Hardly anyone would want to insist that beings of this sort—frogs and mice, for instance—must have souls to enable them to feel. It seems enough that they have complicated living nervous systems.

The same type of answer can be given if it is asked how a "mere physical object" can think. If we suppose that it is a physical object of a certain familiar kind, namely, a living body having the form and other visible attributes of a man, and possessed of an enormously complex living brain and nervous system—in short, that the object in question is a living human being—then there is no absurdity in supposing that this being thinks. Any argument purporting to show that such a being cannot think, and must therefore have a nonmaterial soul to do its thinking for it, would be just as good an argument to show that frogs and mice cannot feel, and must therefore have souls to do their feeling for them. The outcome of such philosophizing is just as good, and just as absurd, in the one case as it is in the other.

Now the materialist would, of course, like to maintain that psychological states, such as feeling, believing, desiring, and so on, are really nothing but perfectly *familiar kinds* of material states, that is, states of the body, particularly of the brain and nervous system; states that are either observable or testable by the usual methods of biology, physics, and chemistry. But this, as we have seen earlier, seems to be a vain hope, and will always be an obstacle to any simple materialism. There is always, it seems, something that can be asserted of certain psychological states which makes little if any sense when asserted of any ordinary or familiar state of matter. One can say of a belief, for instance, that it is true or false, but this can never be said, except metaphorically or derivatively, of any familiar state of matter, such as an arrangement of molecules; we could say of such a thing that it is true or false, only if we first assumed that it is identical with some belief that is such. Again, one can say of a desire that it is the desire *for* this or that—for instance, the desire for food; of a fear that it is a fear *of* something—for instance, a fear of heights; but of no familiar state of matter can it be said that it is, in the same sense, *for* or *of* anything. It just *is* the state of matter that it is. Suppose, for example, that the materialist should say that the feeling of hunger is simply *identical* with a certain familiar state of the body; not merely that it is prompted by that state but that it *is* that state, and is describable in terms of the concepts of physics and chemistry. Thus, let us suppose him to claim that hunger just *is* the state consisting of having an empty stomach, together with a deficiency of certain salts or other substances in the blood, and a certain physical disequilibrium of the nervous system consequent upon these conditions. Now there is, of course, no doubt an intimate connection between such states as these and the desire for food, but the assertion of their *identity* with that desire will always be plagued because, unlike the desire, those bodily states can be fully described without mentioning food at all, and without saying that they are in any sense states that are *for* food. Indeed, the notion of something being *for* or *of* something else, in the sense in which a desire may be a desire *for* food, or a fear may be a fear *of* heights, is not a concept of physics or chemistry at all. And yet it can surely be said of a certain desire that it is a desire for food, or of a certain fear that it is a fear of heights. The referential character of such states seems, indeed, essential to any proper description of them. Significantly, when those substances that are physiologically associated with such states are artificially administered to someone, in the effort to create within him those states themselves, the effort fails. It is fairly well known, for example, what physiological changes a man undergoes when he is in a state of fear; but when these changes are artificially evoked in him, he does not experience fear in the usual sense. He describes his state as being vaguely *like* fear, but finds that he is not afraid *of* anything.

But while psychological states are thus evidently not identical with any familiar bodily states, it does not follow that they are identical with no state of matter at all. They may, in fact, be unfamiliar states of matter, that is, states of the body that are not observable or testable by the ordinary methods of biology, physics, and chemistry. This suggestion is not as question-begging as it appears, for it is conceded by the most resolute soul philosophers and dualists that psychological states are strange ones in this respect at least, that they are not thus observable. From the fact that some state is unobservable by the usual methods of scientific observation, nothing whatever follows with respect to the truth or falsity of materialism. From the fact that a certain state is in some respect unusual it does not follow that it is a state of an unusual thing, of a soul rather than a body, but rather, that if it is a state of the body it is an unusual one, and if it is a state of the soul it is no less unusual. Nothing is made clearer, more comprehensible, or less strange by postulating some new substance as the subject of certain states not familiar to the natural sciences, and then baptizing that new substance "the mind" or "the soul." Nor does one avoid materialism at this point by saying that by the "mind" or "soul" we just *mean* that which is the subject of psychological states; for while that might indeed be true, it is nevertheless an open question whether what we thus mean by the "mind" or "soul" might not turn out, after all, to be what we ordinarily denominate "the body." The existence of nothing whatever can be derived from any definitions of terms. . . .

VIII. CONCLUSION

Of course we cannot, by these reflections, pretend to have solved the problems of mind and matter, nor to have proved any theory of materialism. Human nature is mysterious, and remains so, no matter what one's metaphysical theory is or how simple it is. It does nevertheless seem evident that no dualistic theory of man renders human nature any less mysterious, and that whatever questions are left unanswered by the materialist are left equally unanswered, though perhaps better concealed, by his opponents.

20 / Behaviorism

JOHN B. WATSON

John B. Watson (1878–1958) was an American psychologist and founder of the school known as behaviorism. His views were instrumental in the movement to conduct an empirical study of animal and human behaviors. The following excerpt is from his well-known book Behaviorism, *published in 1924.*

I. WHAT IS BEHAVIORISM?

*B*ehaviorism . . . holds that the subject matter of human psychology *is the behavior of the human being.* Behaviorism claims that consciousness is neither a definite nor a usable concept. The behaviorist, who has been trained always as an experimentalist, holds, further, that belief in the existence of consciousness goes back to the ancient days of superstition and magic. . . .

The extent to which most of us are shot through with a savage background is almost unbelievable. Few of us escape it. Not even a college education seems to correct it. If anything, it seems to strengthen it, since the colleges themselves are filled with instructors who have the same background. Some of our greatest biologists, physicists, and chemists, when outside of their laboratories, fall back upon folk lore which has become crystallized into religious concepts. These concepts—these heritages of a timid savage past— have made the emergence and growth of scientific psychology extremely difficult.

One example of such a religious concept is that every individual has a *soul* which is separate and distinct from the *body.* This soul is really a part of a supreme being. This ancient view led to the philosophical platform called "dualism." This dogma has been present in human psychology from earliest antiquity. No one has ever touched a soul, or seen one in a test tube, or has in any way come into relationship with it as he has with the other objects of his daily experience. . . .

With the development of the physical sciences which came with the Renaissance, a certain release from this stifling soul cloud was obtained. A man could think of astronomy, of the celestial bodies and their motions, of gravitation and the like, without involving soul. Although the early scientists were as a rule devout Christians, nevertheless they began to leave soul out of their test tubes.

Psychology and philosophy, however, in dealing as they thought with nonmaterial objects, found it difficult to escape the language of the church, and hence the concept of mind or soul as distinct from the body came down almost unchanged in essence to the latter part of the nineteenth century.

Wundt, the real father of experimental psychology, unquestionably wanted in 1879 a scientific psychology. He grew up in the midst of a dualistic philosophy of the most pronounced type. He could not see his way clear to a solution of the mind-body problem. His psychology, which has reigned supreme to the present day, is necessarily a compromise. He substituted the term *consciousness* for the term soul. Consciousness is not quite so unobservable as soul. We observe it by peeking in suddenly and catching it unawares as it were (*introspection*). . . .

All other introspectionists are equally illogical. In other words, they do not tell us what consciousness is, but merely begin to put things into it by assumption; and then when they come to analyze consciousness, naturally they find in it just what they put into it. Consequently, in the analyses of consciousness made by certain of the psychologists you find such elements as *sensations* and their ghosts, the *images*. . . . And so it goes. Literally hundreds of thousands of printed pages have been published on the minute analysis of this intangible something called "consciousness." And how do we begin work upon it? Not by analyzing it as we would a chemical compound, or the way a plant grows. No, those things are material things. This thing we call consciousness can be analyzed only by *introspection*—a looking in on what takes place inside of us.

As a result of this major assumption that there is such a thing as consciousness and that we can analyze it by introspection, we find as many analyses as there are individual psychologists. There is no way of experimentally attacking and solving psychological problems and standardizing methods.

II. THE ADVENT OF THE BEHAVIORISTS

In 1912 the objective psychologists or behaviorists reached the conclusion that they could no longer be content to work with Wundt's formulations. They felt that the 30-odd barren years since the establishment of Wundt's laboratory had proved conclusively that the so-called introspective psychology of Germany was founded upon wrong hypotheses—that no psychology which included the religious mind-body problem could ever arrive at verifiable conclusions. They decided either to give up psychology or else to make it a natural science. . . .

In his first efforts to get uniformity in subject matter and in methods the behaviorist began his own formulation of the problem of psychology by sweeping aside all mediaeval conceptions. He dropped from his scientific vocabulary all subjective terms such as sensation, perception, image, desire, purpose, and even thinking and emotion as they were subjectively defined.

The behaviorist asks: Why don't we make what we can *observe* the real field of psychology? Let us limit ourselves to things that can be observed, and formulate laws concerning only those things. Now what can we observe? We can observe *behavior—what the organism does or says*. And let us point out at once: that *saying* is doing—that is, *behaving*. Speaking overtly or to ourselves (thinking) is just as objective a type of behavior as baseball.

The rule, or measuring rod, which the behaviorist puts in front of him always is: Can I describe this bit of behavior I see in terms of "stimulus and response"? By stimulus we mean any object in the general environment or any change in the tissues themselves due to the physiological condition of the animal, such as the change we get when we keep an animal from sex activity, when we keep it from feeding, when we keep it from building a nest. By response we mean anything the animal does—such as turning toward or away from a light, jumping at a sound, and more highly organized activities such as building a skyscraper, drawing plans, having babies, writing books, and the like.

You will find, then, the behaviorist working like any other scientist. His sole object is to gather facts about behavior—verify his data—subject them both to logic and to mathematics (the tools of every scientist). He brings the new-born individual *into his experimental nursery* and begins to set problems: What is the baby doing now? What is the stimulus that makes him behave this way? He finds that the stimulus of tickling the cheek brings the response of turning the mouth to the side stimulated. The stimulus of the nipple brings out the sucking response. The stimulus of a rod placed on the palm of the hand brings closure of the hand and the suspension of the whole body by that hand and arm if the rod is raised. Stimulating the infant with a rapidly moving shadow across the eye will not produce blinking until the individual is sixty-five days of age. Stimulating the infant with an apple or stick of candy or any other object will not call out attempts at reaching until the baby is around 120 days of age. Stimulating a properly brought up infant at any age with snakes, fish, darkness, burning paper, birds, cats, dogs, monkeys, will not bring out that type of response which we call "fear" (which to be objective we might call reaction "X") which is a catching of the breath, a stiffening of the whole body, a turning away of the body from the source of stimulation, a running or crawling away from it. . . .

On the other hand, there are just two things which will call out a fear response, namely, a loud sound, and loss of support.

Now the behaviorist finds from observing children brought up *outside of his nursery* that hundreds of these objects will call out fear responses. Consequently, the scientific question arises: If at birth only two stimuli will call out fear, how do all these other things ever finally come to call it out? Please note that the question is not a speculative one. It can be answered by experiments, and the experiments can be reproduced and the same findings can be had in every other laboratory if the original observation is sound. Convince yourself of this by making a simple test.

If you will take a snake, mouse or dog and show it to a baby who has never seen these objects or been frightened in other ways, he begins to manipulate it, poking at this, that or the other part. Do this for ten days until you are logically certain that the child will always go toward the dog and never run away from it (positive reaction) and that it does not call out a fear response at any time. In contrast to this, pick up a steel bar and strike upon it loudly behind the infant's head. Immediately the fear response is called forth. Now try this: At the instant you show him the animal and just as he begins to reach for it, strike the steel bar behind his head. Repeat the experiment three or four times. A new and important change is apparent. The animal now calls out the same response as the steel bar, namely a fear response. We call this, in behavioristic psychology, the *conditioned emotional response*—a form of *conditioned reflex*.

Our studies of conditioned reflexes make it easy for us to account for the child's fear of the dog on a thoroughly natural science basis without lugging in consciousness or any other so-called mental process. A dog comes toward the child rapidly, jumps upon him, pushes him down and at the same time barks loudly. Oftentimes one such combined stimulation is all that is necessary to make the baby run away from the dog the moment it comes within his range of vision. . . .

III. DOES THIS BEHAVIORISTIC APPROACH LEAVE ANYTHING OUT OF PSYCHOLOGY?

After so brief a survey of the behavioristic approach to the problems of psychology, one is inclined to say: "Why, yes, it is worthwhile to study human behavior in this way, but the study of behavior is not the whole of psychology. It leaves out too much. Don't I have sensations, perceptions, conceptions? Do I not forget things and remember things, imagine things, have visual images and auditory images of things I once have seen and heard? Can I not see and hear things that I have never seen or heard in nature? Can I not be attentive or inattentive? Can I not will to do a thing or will not to do it, as the case may be? Do not certain things arouse pleasure in me, and others displeasure? Behaviorism is trying to rob us of everything we have believed in since earliest childhood."

Having been brought up on introspective psychology, as most of us have, you naturally ask these questions and you will find it hard to put away the old terminology and begin to formulate your psychological life in terms of behaviorism. Behaviorism is new wine and it will not go into old bottles. It is advisable for the time being to allay your natural antagonism and accept the behavioristic platform at least until you get more deeply into it. Later you will find that you have progressed so far with behaviorism that the questions you now raise will answer themselves in a perfectly satisfactory natural science way. Let me hasten to add that if the behaviorist were to ask you what you mean by the subjective terms you have been in the habit of using he could soon make you tongue-tied with contradictions. He could even convince you that you do not know what you mean by them. You have been using them uncritically as part of your social and literary tradition.

This is the fundamental starting point of behaviorism. You will soon find that instead of self-observation being the easiest and most natural way of studying psychology, it is an impossible one; you can observe in yourselves only the most elementary forms of response. You will find, on the other hand, that when you begin to study what your neighbor is doing, you will rapidly become proficient in giving a reason for his behavior and in setting situations (presenting stimuli) that will make him behave in a predictable manner. . . .

IV. WHAT IS A STIMULUS?

If I suddenly flash a strong light in your eye, your pupil will contract rapidly. If I were suddenly to shut off all light in the room in which you are sitting, the pupil would begin to widen. If a pistol shot were suddenly fired behind you, you would jump and possibly turn your head around. If hydrogen sulphide were suddenly released in your sitting room, you would begin to hold your nose and possibly even seek to leave the room. If I suddenly made the room very warm, you would begin to unbutton your coat and perspire. If I suddenly made it cold, another response would take place.

Again, on the inside of us we have an equally large realm in which stimuli can exert their effect. For example, just before dinner the muscles of your stomach begin to contract and expand rhythmically because of the absence of food. As soon as food is eaten those contractions cease. By swallowing a small balloon and attaching it to a recording instrument we can easily register the response of the stomach to lack of food and note the lack of response when food is present. In the male, at any rate, the pressure of certain fluids (semen) may lead to sex activity. In the case of the female possibly the presence of certain chemical bodies can lead in a similar way to overt sex behavior. The muscles of our arms and legs and trunk are not only subject to stimuli coming from the blood; they are also stimulated by their own responses—that is, the muscle is under constant tension; any increase in that tension, as when a movement is made, gives rise to a stimulus which leads to another response in that same muscle or in one in some distant part of the body; any decrease in that tension, as when the muscle is relaxed, similarly gives rise to a stimulus. . . .

The two commonsense classifications of response are "external" and "internal"—or possibly the terms "overt" (explicit) and "implicit" are better. By external or overt responses we mean the ordinary doings of the human being: he stoops to pick up a tennis ball, he writes a letter, he enters an automobile and starts driving, he digs a hole in the ground, he sits down to write a lecture, or dances, or flirts with a woman, or makes love to his wife. We do not need instruments to make these observations. On the other hand, responses may be wholly confined to the muscular and glandular systems inside the body. A child or hungry adult may be standing stock still in front of a window filled with pastry. Your first exclamation may be "He isn't doing anything" or "He is just looking at the pastry." An instrument would show that his salivary glands are pouring out secretions, that his stomach is rhythmically contracting and expanding, and that marked changes in blood pressure are taking place—that the endocrine glands are pouring substances into the blood. The internal or implicit responses are difficult to observe, not because they are inherently different from the external or overt responses, but merely because they are hidden from the eye. . . .

V. AN EXAMPLE: JEALOUSY

Ask any group of individuals what they mean by jealousy—what the stimulus is that produces it, what the pattern of the response is, and you get only the vaguest, most unserviceable kind of replies. Ask these same individuals what the unlearned (unconditioned) stimulus is that calls out the response; ask them what the unlearned (unconditioned) response pattern is. To both questions you get unscientific answers. Most individuals say, "Oh, jealousy is a pure instinct." If we diagram thus

$$S. . . . . R$$
$$? \qquad\qquad\qquad\qquad\qquad\qquad ?$$

we have to put a question mark under both stimulus and response.

And yet jealousy is one of the most powerful factors in the organization of present-day individuals. It is recognized by the courts as one of the strongest of "motives" leading to action. Robberies and murders are committed because of it; careers are both made and unmade because of it; marital quarrels, separations and divorces are probably more frequently to be traced to it than to any other single cause. Its almost universal permeation through the whole action stream of all individuals has led to the view that it is an inborn instinct. And yet the moment you begin to observe people and try to determine what kinds of situations call out jealous behavior and what the details of that behavior are, you see that the situations are highly complex (social) and that the reactions are all highly organized (learned). This in itself should make us doubt its hereditary origin. Let us watch people for awhile to see if their behavior will not throw light upon the situations and the responses.

In the first place, as we have said, the situation is always a social one—it involves people. What people? *Always the person who calls out our conditioned love responses.* This may be the mother, father, or brother, sister or sweetheart, wife or husband—the object of homosexual attachments also must be admitted to this group. The wife-husband situation is second only to the sweetheart one for calling out violent response. This brief examination helps us somewhat in our understanding of jealousy. The situation is always a substitutive one, that is, conditioned. It involves the person calling out conditioned love responses. This generalization, if true, takes it out of the class of inherited forms of behavior at once.

The responses in adults are legion. I have taken notes on a great many cases among both children and adults. To vary our procedure let us take the responses of an adult first. *Case A.* A is a "very jealous husband," married two years to a beautiful young woman only slightly younger. They go out frequently to parties. If his wife (1) dances a little close to her partner, (2) if she sits out a dance to talk to a man and talks in a low tone to him, (3) if in a moment of gaiety she kisses another man in the open light of the room before everyone, (4) if she goes out even with other women to lunch or tea or to shop, (5) if she invites her own group of friends for a party at home—then jealous behavior is exhibited. Such stimuli bring out the responses (1) refusal to talk or dance with his wife, (2) increased tension of all his muscles, mouth shuts tightly, eyes seem to grow smaller, jaw "hardens." He next withdraws himself from other people in the room. His face becomes flushed, then black. *This behavior may and usually does persist for days after the affair is started. He will talk to no one about the affair. Mediation is impossible.* The jealous state seems to have to run itself down or out. The wife herself by no amount of assurance of love, of innocence, by no system of apology or obeisance can do anything towards hastening recovery. Yet his wife is devoted to him and has never been even in the slightest measure unfaithful, as he himself admits verbally when not in the jealous state. In a person less well bred, less well schooled, it is easy to see that his behavior might become overt—he might blacken his wife's eye, or if there were a real male aggressor, might attack or murder him. . . .

So far our experiments on jealousy are merely preliminary. If any generalization at all can be made, it would seem to take the following form: Jealousy is a bit of behavior whose stimulus is a (conditioned) love stimulus the response to which is rage—but a pattern of rage containing possibly the original visceral components but in addition parts of many habit patterns (fighting, boxing, shooting, talking). We may use this diagram to hold our facts together:

$$(C)S. \ldots\ldots\ldots\ldots\ldots\ldots (U\&C)R$$

| Sight (or sound) of loved object being tampered or interfered with. | *Stiffening of whole body,* clenching of hands, reddening and then blackening of face—pronounced breathing, fighting, verbal recrimination, etc. |

Naturally this is reduced only to the barest schematism. The response may take many forms and the stimulus may consist of far more subtle factors than I have noted here, but I believe we are on the right track in trying to formulate jealousy in these terms. . . .

21 / The Mind-Body Problem

JERRY A. FODOR

Jerry A. Fodor (1935–   ) is professor of philosophy and psychology at the City University of New York. His works in linguistics, the philosophy of language, the philosophy of mind, and the philosophy of psychology have been tremendously influential. Fodor's goal is to provide a philosophy of mind that defends a classical rationalist view of knowledge and human behavior, according to which many of our cognitive capacities are innate, that is, hardwired into the brain.

. . . *M*odern philosophy of science has been devoted largely to the formal and systematic description of the successful practices of working scientists. The philosopher does not try to dictate how scientific inquiry and argument ought to be conducted. Instead he tries to enumerate the principles and practices that have contributed to good science. The philosopher has devoted the most attention to analyzing the methodological peculiarities of the physical sciences. The analysis has helped to clarify the nature of confirmation, the logical structure of scientific theories, the formal properties of statements that express laws and the question of whether theoretical entities actually exist.

It is only rather recently that philosophers have become seriously interested in the methodological tenets of psychology. Psychological explanations of behavior refer liberally to the mind and to states, operations and processes of the mind. The philosophical difficulty comes in stating in unambiguous language what such references imply.

Traditional philosophies of mind can be divided into two broad categories: dualist theories and materialist theories. In the dualist approach the mind is a nonphysical substance. In materialist theories the mental is not distinct from the physical; indeed, all mental states, properties, processes and operations are in principle identical with physical states, properties, processes and operations. Some materialists, known as behaviorists, maintain that all talk of mental causes can be eliminated from the language of psychology in favor of talk of environmental stimuli and behavioral responses. Other materialists, the identity theorists, contend that there are mental causes and that they are identical with neurophysiological events in the brain.*

In the past 15 years a philosophy of mind called functionalism that is neither dualist nor materialist has emerged from philosophical reflection on developments in artificial intelligence, computational theory, linguistics, cy-

---

*[Recall our discussion of behaviorism and identity theory in the Preview to this part.–Eds.]

bernetics and psychology. All these fields, which are collectively known as the cognitive sciences, have in common a certain level of abstraction and a concern with systems that process information. Functionalism, which seeks to provide a philosophical account of this level of abstraction, recognizes the possibility that systems as diverse as human beings, calculating machines and disembodied spirits could all have mental states. In the functionalist view the psychology of a system depends not on the stuff it is made of (living cells, mental or spiritual energy) but on how the stuff is put together. Functionalism is a difficult concept, and one way of coming to grips with it is to review the deficiencies of the dualist and materialist philosophies of mind it aims to displace.

The chief drawback of dualism is its failure to account adequately for mental causation. If the mind is nonphysical, it has no position in physical space. How, then, can a mental cause give rise to a behavioral effect that has a position in space? To put it another way, how can the nonphysical give rise to the physical without violating the laws of the conservation of mass, of energy and of momentum?

The dualist might respond that the problem of how an immaterial substance can cause physical events is not much obscurer than the problem of how one physical event can cause another. Yet there is an important difference: there are many clear cases of physical causation but not one clear case of nonphysical causation. Physical interaction is something philosophers, like all other people, have to live with. Nonphysical interaction, however, may be no more than an artifact of the immaterialist construal of the mental. Most philosophers now agree that no argument has successfully demonstrated why mind-body causation should not be regarded as a species of physical causation.

Dualism is also incompatible with the practices of working psychologists. The psychologist frequently applies the experimental methods of the physical sciences to the study of the mind. If mental processes were different in kind from physical processes, there would be no reason to expect these methods to work in the realm of the mental. In order to justify their experimental methods many psychologists urgently sought an alternative to dualism.

In the 1920's John B. Watson of Johns Hopkins University made the radical suggestion that behavior does not have mental causes. He regarded the behavior of an organism as its observable responses to stimuli, which he took to be the causes of its behavior. Over the next 30 years psychologists such as B. F. Skinner of Harvard University developed Watson's ideas into an elaborate world view in which the role of psychology was to catalogue the laws that determine causal relations between stimuli and responses. In this "radical behaviorist" view the problem of explaining the nature of the mind-body interaction vanishes; there is no such interaction.

Radical behaviorism has always worn an air of paradox. For better or worse, the idea of mental causation is deeply ingrained in our everyday language and in our ways of understanding our fellow men and ourselves.

For example, people commonly attribute behavior to beliefs, to knowledge and to expectations. Brown puts gas in his tank because he believes the car will not run without it. Jones writes not "acheive" but "achieve" because he knows the rule about putting *i* before *e*. Even when a behavioral response is closely tied to an environmental stimulus, mental processes often intervene. Smith carries an umbrella because the sky is cloudy, but the weather is only part of the story. There are apparently also mental links in the causal chain: observation and expectation. The clouds affect Smith's behavior only because he observes them and because they induce in him an expectation of rain.

The radical behaviorist is unmoved by appeals to such cases. He is prepared to dismiss references to mental causes, however plausible they may seem, as the residue of outworn creeds. The radical behaviorist predicts that as psychologists come to understand more about the relations between stimuli and responses they will find it increasingly possible to explain behavior without postulating mental causes.

The strongest argument against behaviorism is that psychology has not turned out this way; the opposite has happened. As psychology has matured, the framework of mental states and processes that is apparently needed to account for experimental observations has grown all the more elaborate. Particularly in the case of human behavior psychological theories satisfying the methodological tenets of radical behaviorism have proved largely sterile, as would be expected if the postulated mental processes are real and causally effective.

Nevertheless, many philosophers were initially drawn to radical behaviorism because, paradoxes and all, it seemed better than dualism. Since a psychology committed to immaterial substances was unacceptable, philosophers turned to radical behaviorism because it seemed to be the only alternative materialist philosophy of mind. The choice, as they saw it, was between radical behaviorism and ghosts.

By the early 1960's philosophers began to have doubts that dualism and radical behaviorism exhausted the possible approaches to the philosophy of mind. Since the two theories seemed unattractive, the right strategy might be to develop a materialist philosophy of mind that nonetheless allowed for mental causes. Two such philosophies emerged, one called logical behaviorism and the other called the central-state identity theory.

Logical behaviorism is a semantic theory about what mental terms mean. The basic idea is that attributing a mental state (say thirst) to an organism is the same as saying that the organism is disposed to behave in a particular way (for example to drink if there is water available). On this view every mental ascription is equivalent in meaning to an if-then statement (called a behavioral hypothetical) that expresses a behavioral disposition. For example, "Smith is thirsty" might be taken to be equivalent to the dispositional statement "If there were water available, then Smith would drink some." By definition a behavioral hypothetical includes no mental terms. The if-clause of the hypothetical speaks only of stimuli and the then-clause speaks only of behavioral responses. Since stimuli and responses are physical events, logical behaviorism is a species of materialism.

The strength of logical behaviorism is that by translating mental language into the language of stimuli and responses it provides an interpretation of psychological explanations in which behavioral effects are attributed to mental causes. Mental causation is simply the manifestation of a behavioral disposition. More precisely, mental causation is what happens when an organism has a behavioral disposition and the if-clause of the behavioral hypothetical expressing the disposition happens to be true. For example, the causal statement "Smith drank some water because he was thirsty" might be taken to mean "If there were water available, then Smith would drink some, and there was water available."

I have somewhat oversimplified logical behaviorism by assuming that each mental ascription can be translated by a unique behavioral hypothetical. Actually the logical behaviorist often maintains that it takes an open-ended set (perhaps an infinite set) of behavioral hypotheticals to spell out the behavioral disposition expressed by a mental term. The mental ascription "Smith is thirsty" might also be satisfied by the hypothetical "If there were orange juice available, then Smith would drink some" and by a host of other hypotheticals. In any event the logical behaviorist does not usually maintain he can actually enumerate all the hypotheticals that correspond to a behavioral disposition expressing a given mental term. He only insists that in principle the meaning of any mental term can be conveyed by behavioral hypotheticals.

The way the logical behaviorist has interpreted a mental term such as thirsty is modeled after the way many philosophers have interpreted a physical disposition such as fragility. The physical disposition "The glass is fragile" is often taken to mean something like "If the glass were struck, then it would break." By the same token the logical behaviorist's analysis of mental causation is similar to the received analysis of one kind of physical causation. The causal statement "The glass broke because it was fragile" is taken to mean something like "If the glass were struck, then it would break, and the glass was struck."

By equating mental terms with behavioral dispositions the logical behaviorist has put mental terms on a par with the nonbehavioral dispositions of the physical sciences. That is a promising move, because the analysis of nonbehavioral dispositions is on relatively solid philosophical ground. An explanation attributing the breaking of a glass to its fragility is surely something even the staunchest materialist can accept. By arguing that mental terms are synonymous with dispositional terms, the logical behaviorist has provided something the radical behaviorist could not: a materialist account of mental causation.

Nevertheless, the analogy between mental causation as construed by the logical behaviorist and physical causation goes only so far. The logical behaviorist treats the manifestation of a disposition as the sole form of mental causation, whereas the physical sciences recognize additional kinds of causation. There is the kind of causation where one physical event causes another, as when the breaking of a glass is attributed to its having been struck. In fact, explanations that involve event-event causation are presumably more basic than dispositional explanations, because the manifestation of a disposition (the breaking of a fragile glass) always involves event-event causation and not vice versa. In the realm of the mental many examples of event-event causation involve one mental state's causing another, and for this kind of causation logical behaviorism provides no analysis. As a result the logical behaviorist is committed to the tacit and implausible assumption that psychology requires a less robust notion of causation than the physical sciences require.

Event-event causation actually seems to be quite common in the realm of the mental. Mental causes typically give rise to behavioral effects by virtue of their interaction with other mental causes. For example, having a headache causes a disposition to take aspirin only if one also has the desire to get rid of the headache, the belief that aspirin exists, the belief that taking aspirin reduces headaches and so on. Since mental states interact in generating behavior, it will be necessary to find a construal of psychological explanations that posits mental processes: causal sequences of mental events. It is this construal that logical behaviorism fails to provide.

Such considerations bring out a fundamental way in which logical behaviorism is quite similar to radical behaviorism. It is true that the logical behaviorist, unlike the radical behaviorist, acknowledges the existence of mental states. Yet since the underlying tenet of logical behaviorism is that references to mental states can be translated out of psychological explanations by employing behavioral hypotheticals, all talk of mental states and processes is in a sense heuristic. The only facts to which the behaviorist is actually committed are facts about relations between stimuli and responses. In this respect logical behaviorism is just radical behaviorism in a semantic form. Although the former theory offers a construal of mental causation, the construal is Pickwickian.* What does not really exist cannot cause anything, and the logical behaviorist, like the radical behaviorist, believes deep down that mental causes do not exist.

An alternative materialist theory of the mind to logical behaviorism is the central-state identity theory. According to this theory, mental events, states and processes are identical with neurophysiological events in the brain, and the property of being in a certain mental state (such as having a headache or believing it will rain) is identical with the property of being in a certain neurophysiological state. On this basis it is easy to make sense of the idea that a behavioral effect might sometimes have a chain of mental causes; that will be the case whenever a behavioral effect is contingent on the appropriate sequence of neurophysiological events.

The central-state identity theory acknowledges that it is possible for men-

---

*[Special or esoteric.—Eds.]

tal causes to interact causally without ever giving rise to any behavioral effect, as when a person thinks for a while about what he ought to do and then decides to do nothing. If mental processes are neurophysiological, they must have the causal properties of neurophysiological processes. Since neurophysiological processes are presumably physical processes, the central-state identity theory ensures that the concept of mental causation is as rich as the concept of physical causation.

The central-state identity theory provides a satisfactory account of what the mental terms in psychological explanations refer to, and so it is favored by psychologists who are dissatisfied with behaviorism. The behaviorist maintains that mental terms refer to nothing or that they refer to the parameters of stimulus-response relations. Either way the existence of mental entities is only illusory. The identity theorist, on the other hand, argues that mental terms refer to neurophysiological states. Thus he can take seriously the project of explaining behavior by appealing to its mental causes.

The chief advantage of the identity theory is that it takes the explanatory constructs of psychology at face value, which is surely something a philosophy of mind ought to do if it can. The identity theory shows how the mentalistic explanations of psychology could be not mere heuristics but literal accounts of the causal history of behavior. Moreover, since the identity theory is not a semantic thesis, it is immune to many arguments that cast in doubt logical behaviorism. A drawback of logical behaviorism is that the observation "John has a headache" does not seem to mean the same thing as a statement of the form "John is disposed to behave in such and such a way." The identity theorist, however, can live with the fact that "John has a headache" and "John is in such and such a brain state" are not synonymous. The assertion of the identity theorist is not that these sentences mean the same thing but only that they are rendered true (or false) by the same neurophysiological phenomena.

The identity theory can be held either as a doctrine about mental particulars (John's current pain or Bill's fear of animals) or as a doctrine about mental universals, or properties (having a pain or being afraid of animals). The two doctrines, called respectively token physicalism and type physicalism, differ in strength and plausibility. Token physicalism maintains only that all the mental particulars that happen to exist are neurophysiological, whereas type physicalism makes the more sweeping assertion that all the mental particulars there could possibly be are neurophysiological. Token physicalism does not rule out the logical possibility of machines and disembodied spirits having mental properties. Type physicalism dismisses this possibility because neither machines nor disembodied spirits have neurons.

Type physicalism is not a plausible doctrine about mental properties even if token physicalism is right about mental particulars. The problem with type physicalism is that the psychological constitution of a system seems to depend not on its hardware, or physical composition, but on its software, or program. Why should the philosopher dismiss the possibility that silicon-based Martians have pains, assuming that the silicon is properly organized? And why should the philosopher rule out the possibility of machines having beliefs, assuming that the machines are correctly programmed? If it is logically possible that Martians and machines could have mental properties, then mental properties and neurophysiological processes cannot be identical, however much they may prove to be coextensive.

What it all comes down to is that there seems to be a level of abstraction at which the generalizations of psychology are most naturally pitched. This level of abstraction cuts across differences in the physical composition of the systems to which psychological generalizations apply. In the cognitive sciences, at least, the natural domain for psychological theorizing seems to be all systems that process information. The problem with type physicalism is that there are possible information-processing systems with the same psychological constitution as human beings but not the same physical organization. In principle all kinds of physically different things could have human software.

This situation calls for a relational account of mental properties that abstracts them from the physical structure of their bearers. In spite of the objections to logical behaviorism that I presented above, logical behaviorism was at least on the right track in offering a relational interpretation of mental properties: to have a headache is to be disposed to exhibit a certain pattern of relations between the stimuli one encounters and the responses one exhibits. If that is what having a headache is, however, there is no reason in principle why only heads that are physically similar to ours can ache. Indeed, according to logical behaviorism, it is a necessary truth that any system that has our stimulus-response contingencies also has our headaches.

All of this emerged 10 or 15 years ago as a nasty dilemma for the materialist program in the philosophy of mind. On the one hand the identity theorist (and not the logical behaviorist) had got right the causal character of the interactions of mind and body. On the other the logical behaviorist (and not the identity theorist) had got right the relational character of mental properties. Functionalism has apparently been able to resolve the dilemma. By stressing the distinction computer science draws between hardware and software the functionalist can make sense of both the causal and the relational character of the mental.

The institution underlying functionalism is that what determines the psychological type to which a mental particular belongs is the causal role of the particular in the mental life of the organism. Functional individuation is differentiation with respect to causal role. A headache, for example, is identified with the type of mental state that among other things causes a disposition for taking aspirin in people who believe aspirin relieves a headache, causes a desire to rid oneself of the pain one is feeling, often causes someone who speaks English to say such things as "I have a headache" and is brought on by overwork, eyestrain and tension. This list is presumably not complete. More will be known about the nature of a headache as psychological and physiological research discovers more about its causal role.

Functionalism construes the concept of causal role in such a way that a mental state can be defined by its causal relations to other mental states. In this respect functionalism is completely different from logical behaviorism. Another major difference is that functionalism is not a reductionist thesis. It does not foresee, even in principle, the elimination of mentalistic concepts from the explanatory apparatus of psychological theories.

The difference between functionalism and logical behaviorism is brought out by the fact that functionalism is fully compatible with token physicalism. The functionalist would not be disturbed if brain events turn out to be the only things with the functional properties that define mental states. Indeed, most functionalists fully expect it will turn out that way.

Since functionalism recognizes that mental particulars may be physical, it is compatible with the idea that mental causation is a species of physical causation. In other words, functionalism tolerates the materialist solution to the mind-body problem provided by the central-state identity theory. It is possible for the functionalist to assert both that mental properties are typically defined in terms of their relations and that interactions of mind and body are typically causal in however robust a notion of causality is required by psychological explanations. The logical behaviorist can endorse only the first assertion and the type physicalist only the second. As a result functionalism seems to capture the best features of the materialist alternatives to dualism. It is no wonder that functionalism has become increasingly popular.

Machines provide good examples of two concepts that are central to functionalism: the concept that mental states are interdefined and the concept that they can be realized by many systems. The illustration on page 205 contrasts a behavioristic Coke machine with a mentalistic one. Both machines dispense a Coke for 10 cents. (The price has not been affected by inflation.) The states of the machines are defined by reference to their causal roles, but only the machine on the left would satisfy the behaviorist. Its single state ($S0$) is completely specified in terms of stimuli and responses. $S0$ is the state a machine is in if, and only if, given a dime as the input, it dispenses a Coke as the output.

The machine on the right in the illustration has interdefined states ($S1$ and $S2$), which are characteristic of functionalism. $S1$ is the state a machine is in if, and only if, (1) given a nickel, it dispenses nothing and proceeds to $S2$, and (2) given a dime, it dispenses a Coke and stays in $S1$. $S2$ is the state a machine is in if, and only if, (1) given a nickel, it dispenses a Coke and proceeds to $S1$, and (2) given a dime, it dispenses a Coke and a nickel and proceeds to $S1$. What $S1$ and $S2$ jointly amount to is the machine's dispensing a Coke if it is given a dime, dispensing a Coke and a nickel if it is given a dime and a nickel and waiting to be given a second nickel if it has been given a first one.

Since $S1$ and $S2$ are each defined by hypothetical statements, they can be viewed as dispositions. Nevertheless, they are not behavioral dispositions because the consequences an input has for a machine in $S1$ or $S2$ are not

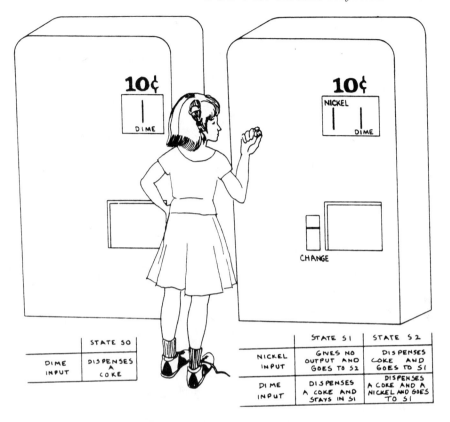

	STATE S0
DIME INPUT	DISPENSES A COKE

	STATE S1	STATE S2
NICKEL INPUT	GIVES NO OUTPUT AND GOES TO S2	DISPENSES COKE AND GOES TO S1
DIME INPUT	DISPENSES A COKE AND STAYS IN S1	DISPENSES A COKE AND A NICKEL AND GOES TO S1

TWO COKE MACHINES bring out the difference between behaviorism (the doctrine that there are no mental causes) and mentalism (the doctrine that there are mental causes). Both machines dispense a Coke for 10 cents and have states that are defined by reference to their causal role. The machine at the left is a behavioristic one: its single state (*S0*) is defined solely in terms of the input and the output. The machine at the right is a mentalistic one: its two states (*S1, S2*) must be defined not only in terms of the input and the output but also in terms of each other. To put it another way, the output of the Coke machine depends on the state the machine is in as well as on the input. The functionalist philosopher maintains that mental states are inter-defined, like the internal states of the mentalistic Coke machine.

specified solely in terms of the output of the machine. Rather, the consequences also involve the machine's internal states.

Nothing about the way I have described the behavioristic and mentalistic Coke machines puts constraints on what they could be made of. Any system whose states bore the proper relations to inputs, outputs and other states could be one of these machines. No doubt it is reasonable to expect such a system to be constructed out of such things as wheels, levers and diodes (token physicalism for Coke machines). Similarly, it is reasonable to expect that our minds may prove to be neurophysiological (token physicalism for human beings).

Nevertheless, the software description of a Coke machine does not logically require wheels, levers and diodes for its concrete realization. By the same token, the software description of the mind does not logically require neurons. As far as functionalism is concerned a Coke machine with states $S1$ and $S2$ could be made of ectoplasm, if there is such stuff and if its states have the right causal properties. Functionalism allows for the possibility of disembodied Coke machines in exactly the same way and to the same extent that it allows for the possibility of disembodied minds.

To say that $S1$ and $S2$ are interdefined and realizable by different kinds of hardware is not, of course, to say that a Coke machine has a mind. Although interdefinition and functional specification are typical features of mental states, they are clearly not sufficient for mentality. What more is required is a question to which I shall return below.

Some philosophers are suspicious of functionalism because it seems too easy. Since functionalism licenses the individuation of states by reference to their causal role, it appears to allow a trivial explanation of any observed event E, that is, it appears to postulate an E-causer. For example, what makes the valves in a machine open? Why, the operation of a valve opener. And what is a valve opener? Why, anything that has the functionally defined property of causing valves to open.

In psychology this kind of question-begging often takes the form of theories that in effect postulate homunculi* with the selfsame intellectual capacities the theorist set out to explain. Such is the case when visual perception is explained by simply postulating psychological mechanisms that process visual information. The behaviorist has often charged the mentalist, sometimes justifiably, of mongering this kind of question-begging pseudo explanation. The charge will have to be met if functionally defined mental states are to have a serious role in psychological theories.

The burden of the accusation is not untruth but triviality. There can be no doubt that it is a valve opener that opens valves, and it is likely that visual perception is mediated by the processing of visual information. The charge is that such putative functional explanations are mere platitudes. The functionalist can meet this objection by allowing functionally defined theoretical constructs only where mechanisms exist that can carry out the function and only where he has some notion of what such mechanisms might be like. One way of imposing this requirement is to identify the mental processes that psychology postulates with the operations of the restricted class of possible computers called Turing machines.

A Turing machine can be informally characterized as a mechanism with a finite number of program states. The inputs and outputs of the machine are written on a tape that is divided into squares each of which includes a symbol from a finite alphabet. The machine scans the tape one square at a time. It can erase the symbol on a scanned square and print a new one in its place. The

*[Internal little men.—Eds.]

machine can execute only the elementary mechanical operations of scanning, erasing, printing, moving the tape and changing state.

The program states of the Turing machine are defined solely in terms of the input symbols on the tape, the output symbols on the tape, the elementary operations and the other states of the program. Each program state is therefore functionally defined by the part it plays in the overall operation of the machine. Since the functional role of a state depends on the relation of the state to other states as well as to inputs and outputs, the relational character of the mental state is captured by the Turing-machine version of functionalism. Since the definition of a program state never refers to the physical structure of the system running the program, the Turing-machine version of functionalism also captures the idea that the character of a mental state is independent of its physical realization. A human being, a roomful of people, a computer and a disembodied spirit would all be a Turing machine if they operated according to a Turing-machine program.

The proposal is to restrict the functional definition of psychological states to those that can be expressed in terms of the program states of Turing machines. If this restriction can be enforced, it provides a guarantee that psychological theories will be compatible with the demands of mechanisms. Since Turing machines are very simple devices, they are in principle quite easy to build. Consequently by formulating a psychological explanation as a Turing-machine program the psychologist ensures that the explanation is mechanistic, even though the hardware realizing the mechanism is left open.

There are many kinds of computational mechanisms other than Turing machines, and so the formulation of a functionalist psychological theory in Turing-machine notation provides only a sufficient condition for the theory's being mechanically realizable. What makes the condition interesting, however, is that the simple Turing machine can perform many complex tasks. Although the elementary operations of the Turing machine are restricted, iterations of the operations enable the machine to carry out any well-defined computation on discrete symbols.

An important tendency in the cognitive sciences is to treat the mind chiefly as a device that manipulates symbols. If a mental process can be functionally defined as an operation on symbols, there is a Turing machine capable of carrying out the computation and a variety of mechanisms for realizing the Turing machine. Where the manipulation of symbols is important the Turing machine provides a connection between functional explanation and mechanistic explanation.

The reduction of a psychological theory to a program for a Turing machine is a way of exorcising the homunculi. The reduction ensures that no operations have been postulated except those that could be performed by a familiar mechanism. Of course, the working psychologist usually cannot specify the reduction for each functionally individuated process in every theory he is prepared to take seriously. In practice the argument usually goes in the opposite direction; if the postulation of a mental operation is essential to some cherished psychological explanation, the theorist tends to assume that there must be a program for a Turing machine that will carry out that operation.

The "black boxes" that are common in flow charts drawn by psychologists often serve to indicate postulated mental processes for which Turing reductions are wanting. Even so, the possibility in principle of such reductions serves as a methodological constraint on psychological theorizing by determining what functional definitions are to be allowed and what it would be like to know that everything has been explained that could possibly need explanation.

Such is the origin, the provenance and the promise of contemporary functionalism. How much has it actually paid off? This question is not easy to answer because much of what is now happening in the philosophy of mind and the cognitive sciences is directed at exploring the scope and limits of the functionalist explanations of behavior. I shall, however, give a brief overview.

An obvious objection to functionalism as a theory of the mind is that the functionalist definition is not limited to mental states and processes. Catalysts, Coke machines, valve openers, pencil sharpeners, mousetraps and ministers of finance are all in one way or another concepts that are functionally defined, but none is a mental concept such as pain, belief and desire. What, then, characterizes the mental? And can it be captured in a functionalist framework?

The traditional view in the philosophy of mind has it that mental states are distinguished by their having what are called either qualitative content or intentional content. I shall discuss qualitative content first.

It is not easy to say what qualitative content is; indeed, according to some theories, it is not even possible to say what it is because it can be known not by description but only by direct experience. I shall nonetheless attempt to describe it. Try to imagine looking at a blank wall through a red filter. Now change the filter to a green one and leave everything else exactly the way it was. Something about the character of your experience changes when the filter does, and it is this kind of thing that philosophers call qualitative content. I am not entirely comfortable about introducing qualitative content in this way, but it is a subject with which many philosophers are not comfortable.

The reason qualitative content is a problem for functionalism is straightforward. Functionalism is committed to defining mental states in terms of their causes and effects. It seems, however, as if two mental states could have all the same causal relations and yet could differ in their qualitative content. Let me illustrate this with the classic puzzle of the inverted spectrum.

It seems possible to imagine two observers who are alike in all relevant psychological respects except that experiences having the qualitative content of red for one observer would have the qualitative content of green for the other. Nothing about their behavior need reveal the difference because both of them see ripe tomatoes and flaming sunsets as being similar in color and both of them call that color "red." Moreover, the causal connection between their (qualitatively distinct) experiences and their other mental states could also be identical. Perhaps they both think of Little Red Riding Hood when they see ripe tomatoes, feel depressed when they see the color green and so on. It seems as if anything that could be packed into the notion of the causal role of their experiences could be shared by them, and yet the qualitative content of the experiences could be as different as you like. If this is possible, then the functionalist account does not work for mental states that have qualitative content. If one person is having a green experience while another person is having a red one, then surely they must be in different mental states.

The example of the inverted spectrum is more than a verbal puzzle. Having qualitative content is supposed to be a chief factor in what makes a mental state conscious. Many psychologists who are inclined to accept the functionalist framework are nonetheless worried about the failure of functionalism to reveal much about the nature of consciousness. Functionalists have made a few ingenious attempts to talk themselves and their colleagues out of this worry, but they have not, in my view, done so with much success. (For example, perhaps one is wrong in thinking one can imagine what an inverted spectrum would be like.) As matters stand, the problem of qualitative content poses a serious threat to the assertion that functionalism can provide a general theory of the mental.

Functionalism has fared much better with the intentional content of mental states. Indeed, it is here that the major achievements of recent cognitive science are found. To say that a mental state has intentional content is to say that it has certain semantic properties. For example, for Enrico to believe Galileo was Italian apparently involves a three-way relation between Enrico, a belief and a proposition that is the content of the belief (namely the proposition that Galileo was Italian). In particular it is an essential property of Enrico's belief that it is about Galileo (and not about, say, Newton) and that it is true if, and only if, Galileo was indeed Italian. Philosophers are divided on how these considerations fit together, but it is widely agreed that beliefs involve semantic properties such as expressing a proposition, being true or false and being about one thing rather than another.

It is important to understand the semantic properties of beliefs because theories in the cognitive sciences are largely about the beliefs organisms have. Theories of learning and perception, for example, are chiefly accounts of how the host of beliefs an organism has are determined by the character of its experiences and its genetic endowment. The functionalist account of mental states does not by itself provide the required insights. Mousetraps are functionally defined, yet mousetraps do not express propositions, and they are not true or false.

There is at least one kind of thing other than a mental state that has intentional content: a symbol. Like thoughts, symbols seem to be about things. If someone says "Galileo was Italian," his utterance, like Enrico's belief, expresses a proposition about Galileo that is true or false depending on

Galileo's homeland. This parallel between the symbolic and the mental underlies the traditional quest for a unified treatment of language and mind. Cognitive science is now trying to provide such a treatment.

The basic concept is simple but striking. Assume that there are such things as mental symbols (mental representations) and that mental symbols have semantic properties. On this view having a belief involves being related to a mental symbol, and the belief inherits its semantic properties from the mental symbol that figures in the relation. Mental processes (thinking, perceiving, learning and so on) involve causal interactions among relational states such as having a belief. The semantic properties of the words and sentences we utter are in turn inherited from the semantic properties of the mental states that language expresses.

Associating the semantic properties of mental states with those of mental symbols is fully compatible with the computer metaphor, because it is natural to think of the computer as a mechanism that manipulates symbols. A computation is a causal chain of computer states, and the links in the chain are operations on semantically interpreted formulas in a machine code. To think of a system (such as the nervous system) as a computer is to raise questions about the nature of the code in which it computes and the semantic properties of the symbols in the code. In fact, the analogy between minds and computers actually implies the postulation of mental symbols. There is no computation without representation.

The representational account of the mind, however, predates considerably the invention of the computing machine. It is a throwback to classical epistemology,* which is a tradition that includes philosophers as diverse as John Locke, David Hume, George Berkeley, René Descartes, Immanuel Kant, John Stuart Mill and William James.

Hume, for one, developed a representational theory of the mind that included five points. First, there exist "Ideas," which are a species of mental symbol. Second, having a belief involves entertaining an Idea. Third, mental processes are causal associations of Ideas. Fourth, Ideas are like pictures. And fifth, Ideas have their semantic properties by virtue of what they resemble: the Idea of John is about John because it looks like him.

Contemporary cognitive psychologists do not accept the details of Hume's theory, although they endorse much of its spirit. Theories of computation provide a far richer account of mental processes than the mere association of Ideas. And only a few psychologists still think that imagery is the chief vehicle of mental representation. Nevertheless, the most significant break with Hume's theory lies in the abandoning of resemblance as an explanation of the semantic properties of mental representations.

Many philosophers, starting with Berkeley, have argued that there is something seriously wrong with the suggestion that the semantic relation between a thought and what the thought is about could be one of resemblance. Consider the thought that John is tall. Clearly the thought is true only

*[The study of knowledge.—Eds.]

of the state of affairs consisting of John's being tall. A theory of the semantic properties of a thought should therefore explain how this particular thought is related to this particular state of affairs. According to the resemblance theory, entertaining the thought involves having a mental image that shows John to be tall. To put it another way, the relation between the thought that John is tall and his being tall is like the relation between a tall man and his portrait.

The difficulty with the resemblance theory is that any portrait showing John to be tall must also show him to be many other things: clothed or naked, lying, standing or sitting, having a head or not having one, and so on. A portrait of a tall man who is sitting down resembles a man's being seated as much as it resembles a man's being tall. On the resemblance theory it is not clear what distinguishes thoughts about John's height from thoughts about his posture.

The resemblance theory turns out to encounter paradoxes at every turn. The possibility of construing beliefs as involving relations to semantically interpreted mental representations clearly depends on having an acceptable account of where the semantic properties of the mental representations come from. If resemblance will not provide this account, what will?

The current idea is that the semantic properties of a mental representation are determined by aspects of its functional role. In other words, a sufficient condition for having semantic properties can be specified in causal terms. This is the connection between functionalism and the representational theory of the mind. Modern cognitive psychology rests largely on the hope that these two doctrines can be made to support each other.

No philosopher is now prepared to say exactly how the functional role of a mental representation determines its semantic properties. Nevertheless, the functionalist recognizes three types of causal relations among psychological states involving mental representations, and they might serve to fix the semantic properties of mental representations. The three types are causal relations among mental states and stimuli, mental states and responses and some mental states and other ones.

Consider the belief that John is tall. Presumably the following facts, which correspond respectively to the three types of causal relations, are relevant to determining the semantic properties of the mental representation involved in the belief. First, the belief is a normal effect of certain stimulations, such as seeing John in circumstances that reveal his height. Second, the belief is the normal cause of certain behavioral effects, such as uttering "John is tall." Third, the belief is a normal cause of certain other beliefs and a normal effect of certain other beliefs. For example, anyone who believes John is tall is very likely also to believe someone is tall. Having the first belief is normally causally sufficient for having the second belief. And anyone who believes everyone in the room is tall and also believes John is in the room will very likely believe John is tall. The third belief is a normal effect of the first two. In short, the functionalist maintains that the proposition expressed by a given mental representation depends on the causal properties of the mental states in which that mental representation figures.

The concept that the semantic properties of mental representations are determined by aspects of their functional role is at the center of current work in the cognitive sciences. Nevertheless, the concept may not be true. Many philosophers who are unsympathetic to the cognitive turn in modern psychology doubt its truth, and many psychologists would probably reject it in the bald and unelaborated way that I have sketched it. Yet even in its skeletal form, there is this much to be said in its favor: It legitimizes the notion of mental representation, which has become increasingly important to theorizing in every branch of the cognitive sciences. Recent advances in formulating and testing hypotheses about the character of mental representations in fields ranging from phonetics to computer vision suggest that the concept of mental representation is fundamental to empirical theories of the mind.

The behaviorist has rejected the appeal to mental representation because it runs counter to his view of the explanatory mechanisms that can figure in psychological theories. Nevertheless, the science of mental representation is now flourishing. The history of science reveals that when a successful theory comes into conflict with a methodological scruple, it is generally the scruple that gives way. Accordingly the functionalist has relaxed the behaviorist constraints on psychological explanations. There is probably no better way to decide what is methodologically permissible in science than by investigating what successful science requires.

STUDY QUESTIONS

1. Does having purposes, plans, expectations, and the like require that some future state of affairs have an effect on us? If it does, how would dualism help reduce the oddness of such a situation?

2. Can you think of any characteristics which humans have that cannot be adequately explained or accounted for except on the hypothesis that we have non-material minds? What are they? If you think there are none, why do you hold that view?

3. State Joad's four arguments on behalf of dualism. Critically evaluate each.

4. Joad holds that the four types of phenomena which he cites cannot be explained on the basis of the stimulus-response model of explanation (the view that all capacities of all organisms, including humans, are merely material responses to material stimuli). Do you agree? Why or why not?

5. Suppose one is trying to decide between two claims that have the following forms: (1) A is made of B and C; (2) A is caused by B and C. What sort of experiment would settle the issue? Suppose further that A is a sensation and B and C are neural structures. Are there any special problems for the experiment now?

6. The author of "Why I Am a Dualist" claims that the reader will be able to provide other examples of sensations besides those used in the paper. Can you do so? Also, try to give a general definition for "sensation." What difficulties do you encounter?

7. Jones plans to build a robot that says, "Ouch" if you hit it or cut its "skin." It is also supposed to say things like "Why did you do that?" and "Please don't do that again" on the appropriate occasions. It will also take aspirin when you hit it on the head and will be very hard to get into a dentist's chair unless you promise it novocaine. If Jones succeeds, do you think that would prove Robinson's main point to be wrong?

8. How does Taylor know he has a body? How does he know his body is a material thing?

9. What is a strict identity? What predicates present some difficulty for the claim that a person is identical to his/her body?

10. What difficulties convince Taylor that dualism is a mistaken theory? Do you agree?

11. What is introspective psychology? What theory of mind does Watson take it as being allied with? Why is introspective psychology a superstitious belief?

12. Try to sketch a behavioristic treatment of several psychological notions (e.g., being clever, being in pain, having a red afterimage). Do you notice any difficulties in such an approach?

13. Is the mind-body problem really a scientific issue and not a philosophical one? Justify your answer.

14. Evaluate Fodor's central argument against dualism.

15. Describe type physicalism and explain Fodor's worry about it.

16. Show that the issue of qualitative content is a serious problem for functionalism.

17. Fodor does not classify functionalism as a species of dualism or materialism. Why? Can you make a case for regarding functionalism as a species of materialism?

FURTHER READINGS

Blanchard, Brand, and B. F. Skinner. "The Problem of Consciousness—A Debate." *Philosophy and Phenomenological Research*, 27 (1967), 317–337. [Dualistic and behaviorist perspectives are represented in the debate.]

Broad, C. D. *The Mind and Its Place in Nature.* London: Routledge and Kegan Paul, 1925, Chapter 3. [A sensitive examination of dualism.]

Brody, Baruch A. *Beginning Philosophy.* Englewood Cliffs, N.J.: Prentice-Hall, 1977, pp. 139–161. [A clear, elementary treatment of dualism, behaviorism, and the identity theory.]

Chappell, V. C., ed. *The Philosophy of Mind.* Englewood Cliffs, N.J.: Prentice-Hall, 1962. [A fairly recent, comprehensive set of readings on the philosophy of mind.]

Dennett, Daniel C. "Why You Can't Make a Computer That Feels Pain." *Synthese,* 38 (1978), 415–456. [Argues that the traditional reasons for denying robot consciousness are mistaken.]

Descartes, René. *Meditations on First Philosophy.* Indianapolis, Ind.: Hackett, 1979. [First published in 1641; see especially Meditations I, II, and VI for the classical development of dualism.]

Hofstadter, Douglas R., and Daniel C. Dennett. *The Mind's I.* New York: Basic Books, 1981. [A collective of lively and provocative articles in the philosophy of mind.]

Hospers, John. *An Introduction to Philosophical Analysis,* 2nd ed. Englewood Cliffs, N.J.: Prentice-Hall, 1967, pp. 378–424. [An elementary overview of theories of mind.]

O'Conner, John, ed. *Modern Materialism: Readings on Mind-Body Identity.* New York: Harcourt Brace Jovanovich, 1969. [Exactly what the title indicates.]

Smart, J. J. C. "Sensations and Brain Processes." *Philosophical Review,* 68 (1959), 141–156. [A famous defense of the identity theory version of materialism.]

PART FIVE

PERSONS, MACHINES, AND IMMORTALITY

PREVIEW

As we saw, the main question of Part Four was: What is a person? Is a person solely a material body? Or is a person also something non-material: a self, psyche, soul, and so on? There are two important questions which are closely related to the above question(s). They are the subject matter of this part.

Consider the following transcript of a conversation between a psychotherapist and a female patient. (The lines in small letters are spoken by the patient. The ones in capitals are the therapist's responses.)

men are all alike.
IN WHAT WAY?

they're always bugging us about something or other.
CAN YOU THINK OF A SPECIFIC EXAMPLE?

well, my boyfriend made me come here.
YOUR BOYFRIEND MADE YOU COME HERE?

he noticed that i'm depressed much of the time.
I'M SORRY TO HEAR YOU ARE DEPRESSED.

he's right. i am unhappy.
DO YOU THINK COMING HERE WILL HELP YOU NOT TO BE UN-HAPPY?

i need some help, that much is clear.
WHAT WOULD IT MEAN TO YOU IF YOU GOT SOME HELP?

perhaps I could learn to get along with my mother.
TELL ME MORE ABOUT YOUR FAMILY.

my mother takes care of me.
WHO ELSE IN YOUR FAMILY TAKES CARE OF YOU?

my father.
YOUR FATHER?

you are like my father in some ways.
WHAT RESEMBLANCE DO YOU SEE?

you are not very aggressive, but i don't think you want me to notice that.
WHAT MAKES YOU THINK I AM NOT VERY AGGRESSIVE?

you don't argue with me.
WHY DO YOU THINK I DON'T ARGUE WITH YOU?

you are afraid of me.
DOES IT PLEASE YOU TO BELIEVE I AM AFRAID OF YOU?

it pleases my father to think i am afraid of him.
WHAT ELSE COMES TO MIND WHEN YOU THINK OF YOUR FATHER?

bullies.
DOES THAT HAVE ANYTHING TO DO WITH THE FACT THAT YOUR BOYFRIEND MADE YOU COME HERE?[1]

Who was the therapist? A computer (or computer program, LISA, at MIT). One is inclined to say that the computer is very perceptive!

In recent years, much research has gone on in the field commonly called artificial intelligence. While this research is prompted by varying motives and toward varying ends, it has led to the question of whether persons are but complicated machines, or conversely whether machines (robots, etc.) can have the characteristics usually ascribed to only human beings. A more modest form of this question is: Can machines think (in the normal, human sense of 'think')? If so, what bearing, if any, does this have on the issue of what persons are? This formulation of our question is the subject of two of the selections in this part.

Some years ago an obscure Arizona miner named James Kidd was concerned with the question of whether the soul survived the death of the body. In a handwritten will dated January 2, 1946, he wrote,

> this is my first and only will and is dated the second day of January 1946. I have no. heir's have not been married in my life, an after all my funeral expenses have been paid and $100. one hundred dollars to some preacher of the gospital to say fare well at my grave sell all my property which is all in cash and stocks with E F Hutton Co Phoenix some in safety box, and have this balance money to go into a research of some scientific proof of a soul of the human body which leaves at death I think in time there can be a Photograph of soul leaving the human at death.

> *James Kidd*

Kidd's will was taken seriously by a number of people. In 1967 it was probated in the Superior Court of the State of Arizona. Among the claimants to the money, which was valued at over $200,000, were philosophers, psychologists, religionists, and mediums. There were even some who claimed that they could fulfill the last request in Kidd's will.

The yearning for immortality seems to be a perennial one in the history of the human race. It has been held in many (though not all) cultures, dating

[1]Quoted in Carl Sagan, "In Praise of Robots." *Natural History Magazine*, Jan., 1975, p. 330.

back to ancient and perhaps even primitive times. But is there any basis for the belief? That is the question discussed in the other two selections in this part.

It is perhaps obvious that the belief in immortality is often closely linked with the belief in the existence of a divine being, a god. In religions like Christianity, both are central tenets of faith. However, these beliefs are logically distinct and independent of each other. Thus, even if there is no good reason to accept the belief in the existence of a god, it is quite possible that our selves are immortal or at least survive the death of the body. Since the questions are independent of each other, we will treat them separately in this volume. In this part we will be concerned with the problem of survival and immortality. In the next two parts we will turn to the problem of the existence of God.

Main Questions

The main questions, then, of this part are

1. Is there any essential difference between humans and certain machines, such as robots? Are persons merely machines?

Or alternatively: Can machines think? If so, what bearing does this have on what persons are?

2. Are we (or our minds, or selves, or souls, or personalities) immortal? Or do we in any way and for any time (even if not forever) survive the death of our bodies?

Answers

Unlike the questions in previous parts, the chief answers to these two questions have been given no commonly accepted labels. But in both cases, it is obvious that there are only two possible answers: Yes, or very likely; and no, or not very likely. So let us simply designate them the affirmative and the negative answers.

1a. The affirmative answer. Machines have all of the characteristics commonly thought to belong only to persons. (This implies that persons are or may be essentially machines.) Or:

1a. Yes, machines can think.

1b. The negative answer. Persons are unique and different from machines. No matter how much machines can do, they cannot have or be all that is involved in being a human person. Or:

1b. No, machines cannot think.

2a. The affirmative answer. A person is or has a non-material self, and that self (mind, soul, consciousness, etc.) is immortal, or at least survives the death of the body.

2b. The negative answer. Even if there is such an entity as the self (which is doubtful), it does not survive the death of the body, and hence cannot be immortal. Immortality is at best a myth.

Selections

The main answers to the questions in this section are represented as follows:

Question	Answer	Selection
(1)	(1a) The affirmative	22
(1)	(1b) The negative	23
(2)	(2b) The negative	24
(2)	(2a) The affirmative	25

22 / Can a Machine Think?

CHRISTOPHER EVANS

Christopher Evans (1931–1979) was an experimental psychologist and a computer scientist who personally knew and worked with earlier researchers in the field of artificial intelligence. He wrote several books and articles in various areas of psychology and in the area of artificial intelligence.

*I*n the early years of the Second World War when the British began, in ultra-secret, to put together their effort to crack German codes, they set out to recruit a team of the brightest minds available in mathematics and the then rather novel field of electronic engineering. Recruiting the electronic whizzes was easy, as many of them were to be found engrossed in the fascinating problem of radio location of aircraft—or radar as it later came to be called. Finding mathematicians with the right kind of obsessive brilliance to make a contribution in the strange field of cryptography was another matter. In the end they adopted the ingenious strategy of searching through lists of young mathematicians who were also top-flight chess players. As a result of a nation-wide trawl an amazing collection of characters were billeted together in the country-house surroundings of Bletchley Park, and three of the most remarkable were Irving John Good, Donald Michie, and Alan Turing. . . .

If contemporary accounts of what the workers at Bletchley were talking about in their few moments of spare time can be relied on, many of them were a bit over-optimistic if anything. Both Good and Michie believed that the use of electronic computers such as Colossus would result in major advances in mathematics in the immediate post-war era and Turing was of the same opinion. All three (and one or two of their colleagues) were also confident that it would not be long before machines were exhibiting intelligence, including problem-solving abilities, and that their role as simple number-crunchers was only one phase in their evolution. Although the exact substance of their conversations, carried long into the night when they were waiting for the test results of the first creaky Colossus prototypes, has softened with the passage of time, it is known the topic of machine intelligence loomed very large. They discussed, with a *frisson** of excitement and unease, the peculiar ramifications of the subject they were pioneering and about which the rest of the world knew (and still knows) so little. Could there ever be a machine which was able to solve problems that no human could solve? Could a computer ever beat a human at chess? Lastly, could a machine *think*?

*[Shudder.—Eds.]

219

Of all the questions that can be asked about computers none has such an eerie ring. Allow a machine intelligence perhaps, the ability to control other machines, repair itself, help us solve problems, compute numbers a million-fold quicker than any human; allow it to fly airplanes, drive cars, superintend our medical records and even, possibly, give advice to politicians. Somehow you can see how a machine might come to do all these things. But that it could be made to perform that apparently exclusively human operation known as *thinking* is something else, and something which is offensive, alien and threatening. Only in the most *outré** forms of science fiction, stretching back to Mary Shelley's masterpiece *Frankenstein*, is the topic touched on, and always with a sense of great uncertainty about the enigmatic nature of the problem area.

Good, Michie and their companions were content to work the ideas through in their spare moments. But Turing—older, a touch more serious and less cavalier—set out to consider things in depth. In particular, he addressed himself to the critical question: Can, or could, a machine think? The way he set out to do this three decades ago, and long before any other scientists had considered it so cogently, is of lasting interest. The main thesis was published in the philosophical journal *Mind* in 1952. Logically unassailable, when read impartially it serves to break down any barriers of uncertainty which surround this and parallel questions. Despite its classic status the work is seldom read outside the fields of computer science and philosophy, but now that events in computer science and in the field of artificial intelligence are beginning to move with the rapidity and momentum which the Bletchley scientists knew they ultimately would, the time has come for Turing's paper to achieve a wider public.

Soon after the war ended and the Colossus project folded, Turing joined the National Physical Laboratory in Teddington and began to work with a gifted team on the design of what was to become the world's most powerful computer, ACE. Later he moved to Manchester, where, spurred by the pioneers Kilburn, Hartree, Williams and Newman, a vigorous effort was being applied to develop another powerful electronic machine. It was a heady, hard-driving time, comparable to the state of events now prevailing in microprocessors, when anyone with special knowledge rushes along under immense pressure, ever conscious of the feeling that whoever is second in the race may as well not have entered it at all. As a result, Turing found less time than he would have hoped to follow up his private hobbies, particularly his ideas on computer game-playing—checkers, chess and the ancient game of Go—which he saw was an important sub-set of machine intelligence.

Games like chess are unarguably intellectual pursuits, and yet, unlike certain other intellectual exercises, such as writing poetry or discussing the inconsistent football of the hometown team, they have easily describable rules of operation. The task, therefore, would seem to be simply a matter of writing a computer program which "knew" these rules and which could

*[Excessive.—Eds.]

follow them when faced with moves offered by a human player. Turing made very little headway as it happens, and the first chess-playing programs which were scratched together in the late '40s and early '50s were quite awful—so much so that there was a strong feeling that this kind of project was not worth pursuing, since the game of chess as played by an "expert" involves some special intellectual skill which could never be specified in machine terms.

Turing found this ready dismissal of the computer's potential to be both interesting and suggestive. If people were unwilling to accept the idea of a machine which could play games, how would they feel about one which exhibited "intelligence," or one which could "think"? In the course of discussions with friends, Turing found that a good part of the problem was that people were universally unsure of their definitions. What exactly did one mean when one used the word "thought"? What processes were actually in action when "thinking" took place? If a machine was created which *could* think, how would one set about testing it? The last question, Turing surmised, was the key one, and with a wonderful surge of imagination spotted a way to answer it, proposing what has in computer circles come to be known as "The Turing Test for Thinking Machines." In the next section, we will examine the test, see how workable it is, and also try to assess how close computers have come, and will come, to passing it.

When Turing asked people whether they believed that a computer could think, he found almost universal rejection of the idea—just as I did when I carried out a similar survey almost thirty years later. The objections I received were similar to those that Turing documented in his paper "Computing Machinery and Intelligence," and I will summarize them here, adding my own comments and trying to meet the various objections as they occur.

I. THE OBJECTIONS

First there is the Theological Objection. This was more common in Turing's time than it is now, but it still crops up occasionally. It can be summed up as follows: "Man is a creation of God, and has been given a soul and the power of conscious thought. Machines are not spiritual beings, have no soul and thus must be incapable of thought." As Turing pointed out, this seems to place an unwarranted restriction on God. Why shouldn't he give machines souls and allow them to think if he wanted to? On one level I suppose it is irrefutable: if someone chooses to define thinking as something that *only* Man can do and that *only* God can bestow, then that is the end of the matter. Even then the force of the argument does seem to depend upon a confusion between "thought" and "spirituality," upon the old Cartesian dichotomy of the ghost in the machine.* The ghost presumably does the thinking while the machine is merely the vehicle which carries the ghost around.

---

*[Cartesian refers to Descartes, a seventeenth-century French philosopher who held that humans were "made up" of two substances, a material body and a non-material. This view was dubbed as the ghost in the machine by G. Ryle, a twentieth-century English philosopher.—Eds.]

Then there is the Shock/Horror Objection, which Turing called the "Heads in the Sand Objection." Both phrases will do though I prefer my own. When the subject of machine thought is first broached, a common reaction goes something like this: "What a horrible idea! How could any scientist work on such a monstrous development? I hope to goodness that the field of artificial intelligence doesn't advance a step further if its end-product is a thinking machine!" The attitude is not very logical—and it is not really an argument why it *could* not happen, but rather the expression of a heartfelt wish that it never will!

The Extra-sensory Perception Objection was the one that impressed Turing most, and impresses me least. *If* there were such a thing as extrasensory perception and *if* it were in some way a function of human brains, then it could well also be an important constituent of thought. By this token, in the absence of any evidence proving that computers are telepathic, we would have to assume that they could never be capable of thinking in its fullest sense. The same argument applies to any other "psychic" or spiritual component of human psychology. I cannot take this objection seriously because there seems to me to be no evidence which carries any scientific weight that extra-sensory perception does exist. The situation was different in Turing's time, when the world-renowned parapsychology laboratory at Duke University in North Carolina, under Dr. J. B. Rhine, was generating an enormous amount of material supposedly offering evidence for telepathy and precognition. This is not the place to go into the long, and by no means conclusive, arguments about the declining status of parapsychology, but it is certainly true that as far as most scientists are concerned, what once looked like a rather good case for the existence of telepathy, etc., now seems to be an extremely thin one. But even if ESP *is* shown to be a genuine phenomenon, it is, in my own view, something to do with the transmission of information from a source point to a receiver and ought therefore to be quite easy to reproduce in a machine. After all, machines can communicate by radio already, which is, effectively, ESP and is a far better method of long-distance communication than that possessed by any biological system.

The Personal Consciousness Objection is, superficially, a rather potent argument which comes up in various guises. Turing noticed it expressed particularly cogently in a report, in the *British Medical Journal* in 1949, on the Lister Oration for that year, which was entitled "The Mind of Mechanical Man." It was given by a distinguished medical scientist, Professor G. Jefferson. A short quote from the Oration will suffice:

> Not until a machine can write a sonnet or compose a concerto *because of thoughts and emotions felt*, and not by the chance fall of symbols, could we agree that machine equals brain—that is, not only write it but *know that it had written it*. No mechanism could feel (and not merely artificially signal, an easy contrivance) pleasure at its successes, grief when its valves fuse, be warmed by flattery, be made miserable by its mistakes, be charmed by sex, be angry or depressed when it cannot get what it wants.

The italics, which are mine, highlight what I believe to be the fundamental objection: the output of the machine is more or less irrelevant, no matter how impressive it is. Even if it wrote a sonnet—and a very good one—it would not mean much unless it had written it as the result of "thoughts and emotions felt," and it would also have to "know that it had written it." This could be a useful "final definition" of one aspect of human thought—but how would you establish whether or not the sonnet was written with "emotions"? Asking the computer would not help for, as Professor Jefferson realized, there would be no guarantee that it was not simply *declaring* that it had felt emotions. He is really propounding the extreme solipsist position* and should, therefore, apply the same rules to humans. Extreme solipsism is logically irrefutable ("I am the only real thing; all else is illusion") but it is so unhelpful a view of the universe that most people choose to ignore it and decide that when people say they are thinking or feeling they may as well believe them. In other words, Professor Jefferson's objection could be over-ridden if you *became* the computer and experienced its thoughts (if any)—only then could you really *know*. His objection is worth discussing in some depth because it is so commonly heard in one form or another, and because it sets us up in part for Turing's resolution of the machine-thought problem, which we will come to later.

The Unpredictability Objection argues that computers are created by humans according to sets of rules and operate according to carefully scripted programs which themselves are sets of rules. So if you wanted to, you could work out exactly what a computer was going to do at any particular time. It is, in principle, totally predictable. *If you have all the facts available you can predict a computer's behavior because it follows rules, whereas there is no way in which you could hope to do the same with a human because he is not behaving according to a set of immutable rules.* Thus there is an essential difference between computers and humans, so (the argument gets rather weak here) thinking, because it is unpredictable and does not blindly follow rules, must be an essentially human ability.

There are two comments: firstly, computers are becoming so complex that it is doubtful their behavior could be predicted even if everything was known about them—computer programmers and engineers have found that one of the striking characteristics of present-day systems is that they constantly spring surprises. The second point follows naturally: humans are *already* in that super-complex state and the reason that we cannot predict what they do is *not* because they have no ground rules but because (a) we don't know what the rules are, and (b) even if we did know them they would still be too complicated to handle. At best, the unpredictability argument is thin, but it is often raised. People frequently remark that there is always "the element of surprise" in a human. I have no doubt that this is just because *any* very

---

*[Solipsism: The view that all that exists is myself or mind and the contents of my mind. There is nothing external to me. —Eds.]

complex system is bound to be surprising. A variant of the argument is that humans are capable of error whereas the "perfect" computer is not. That may well be true, which suggests that machines are superior to humans, for there seems to be little point in having any information-processing system, biological or electronic, that makes errors in processing. It would be possible to build a random element into computers to make them unpredictable from time to time, but it would be a peculiarly pointless exercise.

The "See How Stupid They Are" Objection will not need much introduction. At one level it is expressed in jokes about computers that generate ridiculous bank statements or electricity bills; at another and subtler level, it is a fair appraisal of the computer's stupendous weaknesses in comparison with Man. "How could you possibly imagine that such backward, limited things could ever reach the point where they could be said to think?" The answer, as we have already pointed out, is that they may be dumb now but they have advanced at a pretty dramatic rate and show every sign of continuing to do so. Their present limitations may be valid when arguing whether they could be said to be capable of thinking *more* or in the *very* near future, but it has no relevance to whether they would be capable of thinking at some later date.

The "Ah But It Can't Do That" Objection is an eternally regressing argument which, for a quarter of a century, computer scientists have been listening to, partially refuting, and then having to listen to all over again. It runs: "Oh yes, you obviously make a computer do so and so—you have just demonstrated that, but of course you will never be able to make it do such and such." The such and such may be anything you name—once it was play a good game of chess, have a storage capacity greater than the human memory, read human hand-writing or understand human speech. Now that these "Ah buts" have (quite swiftly) been overcome, one is faced by a new range: beat the world human chess champion, operate on parallel as opposed to serial processing, perform medical diagnosis better than a doctor, translate satisfactorily from one language to another, help solve its own software problems, etc. When these challenges are met, no doubt it will have to design a complete city from scratch, invent a game more interesting than chess, admire a pretty girl/handsome man, work out the unified field theory, enjoy bacon and eggs, and so on. I cannot think of anything more silly than developing a computer which could enjoy bacon and eggs, but there is nothing to suggest that, provided enough time and money was invested, one could not pull off such a surrealistic venture. On the other hand, it might be *most* useful to have computers design safe, optimally cheap buildings. Even more ambitious (and perhaps comparable to the bacon and egg project but more worthwhile) would be to set a system to tackle the problem of the relationship between gravity and light, and my own guess is that before the conclusion of the long-term future (before the start of the twenty-first century), computers will be hard at work on these problems and will be having great success.

The "It Is Not Biological" Objection may seem like another version of the theological objection—only living things could have the capacity for thought, so non-biological systems could not possibly think. But there is a subtle edge that requires a bit more explanation. It is a characteristic of most modern computers that they are discrete state machines, which is to say that they are digital and operate in a series of discrete steps—on/off. Now the biological central nervous system may not be so obviously digital; though there is evidence that the neurone, the basic unit of communication, acts in an on/off, all or nothing way. But if it turned out that it were *not*, and operated on some more elaborate strategy, then it is conceivable that "thought" might only be manifest in things which had switching systems of this more elaborate kind. Put it another way: it might be possible to build digital computers which were immensely intelligent, but no matter how intelligent they became they would never be able to *think*. The argument cannot be refuted at the moment, but even so there is no shred of evidence to suppose that only non-digital systems can think. There may be other facets of living things that make them unique from the point of view of their capacity to generate thought, but none that we can identify, or even guess at. This objection therefore is not a valid one at present, though in the event of some new biological discovery, it may become so.

The Mathematical Objection is one of the most intriguing of the ten objections, and is the one most frequently encountered in discussions with academics. It is based on a fascinating exercise in mathematical logic propounded by the Hungarian, Kurt Gödel.* To put it rather superficially, Gödel's theorem shows that within any sufficiently powerful logical system (which could be a computer operating according to clearly defined rules), statements can be formulated which can neither be proved nor disproved *within the system*. In his famous 1936 paper, Alan Turing restructured Gödel's theorem so that it could apply specifically to machines. This effectively states that no matter how powerful a computer is, there are bound to be certain tasks that it cannot tackle on its own. In other words, you could not build a computer which could solve *every* problem no matter how well it is programmed; or, if you wanted to carry the thing to the realms of fancy, no computer (or any other digital system) could end up being God.

Gödel's theorem, and its later refinements by Alonzo Church, Bertrand Russell† and others, is interesting to mathematicians, not so much because it assumes an implicit limitation to mathematics itself, but the theorem has been used, incorrectly, by critics of machine intelligence to "prove" that computers could never reach the same intellectual level as Man. The weakness of the position is that it is based on the assumption that the human brain is not a formal logical system. But such evidence as we have suggests very strongly that it is and will, therefore, be bound by the same Gödel-limitations as are machines. There is also a tweak in the tail. While the theorem admittedly states that no system *on its own* can completely tackle its own problems— "understand itself"—it does *not* imply that the areas of mystery could not be tackled by some other system. No individual human brain could solve its own

---

*[A mathematician/logician.—Eds.]
†[Church and Russell: logician/philosophers.—Eds.]

problems or fully "know itself," but with the assistance of other brains these deficiencies might be corrected. Equally, and significantly, problem areas associated with complex computer systems could be solved totally and absolutely by other computer systems, provided that *they* were clever enough.

The last of the ten arguments against the concept of a thinking machine has become known as Lady Lovelace's Objection. . . . Lady Lovelace's Objection is, I suppose, the most commonly expressed criticism of the idea of computers with intellects paralleling, or exceeding, Man's. . . . In its modern form this comes up as, "A Computer cannot do anything that you have not programmed it to." The objection is so fundamental and so widely accepted that it needs detailed discussion.

In the most absolute and literal sense, this statement is perhaps perfectly correct and applies to any machine or computer that has been made or that could be made. According to the rules of the universe that we live in, nothing can take place without a prior cause; a computer will not spring into action without something powering it and guiding it on its way. In the case of the various tasks that a computer performs, the "cause"—to stretch the use of the word rather—is the program or sets of programs that control these tasks. Much the same applies to a brain: it, too, must come equipped with sets of programs which cause it to run through its repertoire of tasks. This might seem to support Lady Lovelace, at least to the extent that machines "need" a human to set them up, but it would also seem to invalidate the argument that this constitutes an essential difference between computers and people. But is there not still a crucial difference between brains and computers? No matter how sophisticated computers are, must there not always have been a human being to *write* its programs? Surely the same does not have to be said for humans?

To tackle this we need to remember that all brains, human included, are equipped at birth with a comprehensive collection of programs which are common to all members of a species and which are known as instincts. These control respiration, gastric absorption, cardiac activity, and, at a behavioral level, such reflexes as sucking, eyeblink, grasping and so on. There may also be programs which "cause" the young animal to explore its environment, exercise its muscles, play and so on. Where do these come from? Well, they are acquired over an immensely long-winded trial-and-error process through the course of evolution. We might call them permanent software ("firmware" is the phrase used sometimes by computer scientists) and they correspond to the suites of programs which every computer has when it leaves the factory, and which are to do with its basic running, maintenance, and so on.

In addition to this, all biological computers come equipped with a bank of what might best be described as raw programs. No one has the faintest idea whether they are neurological, biochemical, electrical or what—all we know is that they *must* exist. They start being laid down the moment the creature begins to interact with the world around it. In the course of time they build up into a colossal suite of software which ultimately enables us to talk, write, walk, read, enjoy bacon and eggs, appreciate music, think, feel, write books, or come up with mathematical ideas. These programs are useful only to the owner of that particular brain, vanish with his death and are quite separate from the "firmware."

If this seems too trivial a description of the magnificent field of human learning and achievement, it is only because anything appears trivial when you reduce it to its bare components: a fabulous sculpture to a quintillion highly similar electrons and protons, a microprocessor to a million impurities buried in a wafer of sand, the human brain into a collection of neurones, blood cells and chemical elements. What is not trivial is the endlessly devious, indescribably profound way in which these elements are structured to make up the whole. The real difference between the brain and most existing computers is that in the former, data acquisition and the initial writing and later modification of the program are done by a mechanism within the brain itself, while in the latter, the software is prepared outside and passed to the computer in its completed state. But I did use the word "most." In recent years increasing emphasis has been placed on the development of "adaptive" programs—software which can be modified and revised on the basis of the program's interaction with the environment. In simple terms these could be looked upon as "programs which learn for themselves," and they will, in due course, become an important feature of many powerful computer systems.

At this point the sceptic still has a few weapons in his armoury. The first is generally put in the form of the statement, "Ah, but even when computers *can* update their own software and acquire new programs for themselves, they will still only be doing this because of Man's ingenuity. Man may no longer actually write the programs, but had he not invented the idea of the self-adaptive program in the first place none of this could have happened." This is perfectly true but has little to do with whether or not computers could think, or perform any other intellectual exercise. It could place computers eternally in our debt, and we may be able to enjoy a smug sense of pride at having created them, but it offers no real restriction on their development.

The sceptic may also argue that no matter how clever or how intelligent you make computers, they will never be able to perform a creative task. Everything they do will inevitably spring from something they have been taught, have experienced or is the subject of some pre-existing program. There are two points being made here. One is that computers could never have an original or creative thought. The other is that the seeds of everything they do, no matter how intelligent, lie in their existing software. To take the second point first: again one is forced to say that the same comment applies to humans. Unless the argument is that some of Man's thoughts or ideas come from genuine inspiration—a message from God, angels, or the spirits of the departed—no one can dispute that all aspects of our intelligence evolve from preexisting programs and the background experiences of life. This evolution may be enormously complex and its progress might be impossible to track, but any intellectual flowerings arise from the seeds of experience planted in the fertile substrate of the brain.

There still remains the point about creativity, and it is one that is full of pitfalls. Before making any assumptions about creativity being an *exclusive* attribute of Man, the concept has to be defined. It is not enough to say "write a poem," "paint a picture," or "discuss philosophical ideas," because it is easy enough to program computers to do all these things. The fact that their poems, paintings and philosophical ramblings are pretty mediocre is beside the point: it would be just as unfair to ask them to write, say, a sonnet of Shakespearian calibre or a painting of da Vinci quality and fail them for lack of creativity as it would be to give the same task to the man in the street. Beware too of repeating the old saying, "Ah, but you have to program them to paint, play chess and so on," for the same is unquestionably true of people. Try handing a twelve-month-old baby a pot of paint or a chessboard if you have any doubts about the need for some measure of learning and experience.

Obviously a crisper definition of creativity is required, and here is one that is almost universally acceptable: If a person demonstrates a skill which has never been demonstrated before and which was not specifically taught to him by someone else, or in the intellectual domain provides an *entirely novel* solution to a problem—a solution which was not known to any other human being—then they can be said to have done something original or had an original or creative thought. There may be other forms of creativity of course, but this would undeniably be an example of it in action. There is plenty of evidence that humans are creative by this standard and the history of science is littered with "original" ideas which humans have generated. Clearly, until a computer also provides such evidence, Lady Lovelace's Objection still holds, at least in one of its forms.

But alas for the sceptics. This particular barrier has been overthrown by computers on a number of occasions in the past few years. A well-publicized one was the solution, by a computer, of the venerable "four-colour problem." This has some mathematical importance, and can best be expressed by thinking of a two-dimensional map featuring a large number of territories, say the counties of England or the states of the USA. Supposing you want to give each territory a colour, what is the minimum number of colours you need to employ to ensure that no two territories of the same colour adjoin each other?

After fiddling around with maps and crayons, you will find that the number seems to come out at four, and no one has ever been able to find a configuration where five colours are required, or where you can always get away with three. Empirically, therefore, four is the answer—hence the name of the problem. But if you attempt to demonstrate this mathematically and *prove* that four colours will do for any conceivable map, you will get nowhere. For decades mathematicians have wrestled with this elusive problem, and from time to time have come up with a "proof" which in the end turns out to be incomplete or fallacious. But the mathematical world was rocked when in 1977 the problem was handed over to a computer, which attacked it with stupendous frontal assault, sifting through huge combinations of possibilities and eventually demonstrating, to every mathematician's satisfaction, that four colours would do the trick. Actually, although this is spectacular testimony to the computer's creative powers, it is not really the most cogent example, for its technique was block-busting rather than heuristic (problem solving by testing hypotheses). It was like solving a chess problem by working out every possible combination of moves, rather than by concentrating on likely areas and experimenting with them. A better, and much earlier, demonstration of computer originality came from a program which was set to generate some totally new proofs in Euclidean geometry. The computer produced a completely novel proof of the well-known theorem which shows that the base angles of an isosceles triangle are equal, by flipping the triangles through 180 degrees and declaring them to be congruent. Quite apart from the fact that it had not before been known to Man, it showed such originality that one famous mathematician remarked, "If any of my students had done that, I would have marked him down as a budding genius."

And so Lady Lovelace's long-lasting objection can be overruled. We have shown that computers can be intelligent, and that they can even be creative— but we have not yet proved that they can, or ever could, *think*.

Now, what do we mean by the word "think"?

II. TOWARD THE ULTRA-INTELLIGENT MACHINE

The most common objections raised to the notion of thinking machines are based on misunderstandings of fairly simple issues, or on semantic confusions of one kind or another. We are still left with the problem of defining the verb "to think," and in this chapter we will attempt to deal with this, or at least to discuss one particular and very compelling way of dealing with it. From this position we shall find ourselves drifting inevitably into a consideration of the problem of creating thinking machines, and in particular to the eerie concept of the Ultra-Intelligent Machine.

Most people believe that they know what they mean when they talk about "thinking" and have no difficulty identifying it when it is going on in their own heads. We are prepared to believe other human beings think because we have experience of it ourselves and accept that it is a common property of the human race. But we cannot make the same assumption about machines, and would be skeptical if one of them told us, no matter how persuasively, that it too was thinking. But sooner or later a machine will make just such a declaration and the question then will be, how do we decide whether to believe it or not?

When Turing tackled the machine-thought issue, he proposed a characteristically brilliant solution which, while not entirely free from flaws, is nevertheless the best that has yet been put forward. The key to it all, he pointed out, is to ask what the signs and signals are that humans give out, from which we infer that *they* are thinking. It is clearly a matter of *what kind of conversation we can have with them*, and has nothing to do with what kind of face they have and what kind of clothes they wear. Unfortunately physical appearances automatically set up prejudices in our minds, and if we were having a spirited conversation with a microprocessor we might be very sceptical about its capacity for thought, simply because it did not look like any thinking thing we had seen in the past. But we *would* be interested in what it had to say and thus Turing invented his experiment or test.

Put a human—the judge or tester—in a room where there are two computer terminals, one connected to a computer, the other to a person. The judge, of course, does not know which terminal is connected to which, but can type into either terminal and receive typed messages back on them. Now the judge's job is to decide, by carrying out conversations with the entities on the end of the respective terminals, *which is which*. If the computer is very stupid, it will immediately be revealed as such and the human will have no difficulty identifying it. If it is bright, he may find that he can carry on quite a good conversation with it, though he may ultimately spot that it must be the computer. If it is exceptionally bright and has a wide range of knowledge, he may find it impossible to say whether it is the computer he is talking to or the person. In this case, Turing argues, the computer will have passed the test and could for all practical purposes be said to be a thinking machine.

The argument has a simple but compelling force; if the intellectual exchange we achieve with a machine is indistinguishable from that we have with a being we *know* to be thinking, then we are, to all intents and purposes, communicating with another thinking being. This, by the way, does not imply that the personal experience, state of consciousness, level of awareness or whatever, of the entity is going to be the same as that experienced by a human when he or she thinks, so the test is not for these particular qualities. They are not, in any case, the parameters which concern the observer.

At first the Turing Test may seem a surprising way of looking at the problem, but it is an extremely sensible way of approaching it. The question now arises; is any computer at present in existence capable of passing the test?—And if not, how long is it likely to be before one comes along? From time to time one laboratory or another claims that a computer has had at least a pretty good stab at it. Scientists using the big computer conferencing systems (each scientist has a terminal in his office and is connected to his colleagues via the computer, which acts as host and general message-sorter) often find it difficult to be sure, for a brief period of time at least, whether they are talking to the computer or to one of their colleagues. On one celebrated occasion at MIT, two scientists had been chatting via the network when one of them left the scene without telling the other, who carried on a cheery conversation with the computer under the assumption that he was talking to his friend. I have had the same spooky experience when chatting with computers which I have programmed myself, and often find their answers curiously perceptive and unpredictable.

To give another interesting example: in the remarkable match played in Toronto in August 1978 between the International Chess Master, David Levy, and the then computer chess champion of the world, Northwestern University's "Chess 4.7," the computer made a number of moves of an uncannily "human" nature. The effect was so powerful that Levy subsequently told me that he found it difficult to believe that he was not facing an outstanding human opponent. Few chess buffs who looked at the move-by-move transcripts of the match were, without prior knowledge, able to tell which had been made by the computer and which by the flesh-and-blood chess master. David Levy himself suggested that Chess 4.7 had effectively passed the Turing Test.

It would be nice to believe that I had been present on such an historic occasion, but this did not constitute a proper "pass." In the test as Turing formulated it, the judge is allowed to converse with either of his two mystery entities on any topic that he chooses, and he may use any conversational trick he wants. Furthermore he can continue the inquisition for as long as he wants, always seeking some clue that will force the computer to reveal itself. Both the computer and the human can lie if they want to in their attempts to fool the tester, so the answers to questions like "Are you the computer?" or "Do you watch much television?" will not give much away. Obviously any computer with a chance in hell of passing the test will have to have a pretty substantial bank of software at its disposal and not just be extremely bright in one area. Chess 4.7 for example might look as though it was thinking if it was questioned about chess, or, better still, invited to play the game, but switch the area of discourse to human anatomy, politics or good restaurants and it would be shown up as a dunderhead.

As things stand at present, computers have quite a way to go before they jump the hurdle so cleverly laid out for them by Turing. But this should not be taken as providing unmitigated comfort for those who resist the notion of advanced machine intelligence. It should now be clear the difference, in intellectual terms, between a human being and a computer is one of degree and not of kind.

Turing himself says in his *Mind* paper that he feels computers will have passed the test before the turn of the century, and there is little doubt that he would dearly have liked to live long enough to be around on the splendiferous occasion when "machine thinking" first occurred.

23 / What the Human Mind Can Do That the Computer Can't

MORTON HUNT

Morton Hunt (1920–   ) has written several books and articles in the area of social and political philosophy and on the topic of artificial intelligence.

Like creative acts, there are a number of important mental phenomena that have not yet been simulated by any computer program and, many cognitive scientists believe, probably never will be. Surprisingly, most of these are everyday aspects of our mental lives that we take for granted and that seem as natural and uncomplicated to us as eating and sleeping.

The first is that obvious, seemingly simple, but largely ineluctable phenomenon, consciousness. To philosophers through the centuries, and to psychologists of recent decades, this concept has proven as elusive as a drop of mercury under one's finger, but the only question we need ask ourselves here is: Can a machine be conscious? Let's say the current is on, the machine has a program stored in it, you address it from a terminal and, in response, it goes through various steps of solving a problem in very much the way a human being would. Now ask yourself: Was it conscious of its cognitive processes as you were of yours? The question answers itself: There is no reason to suppose so. Nothing built into any existing program that I have heard of is meant to, or does, as far as one can tell, yield a state corresponding to consciousness.

Much of our own thinking, to be sure, takes place outside of consciousness, but the results of these processes become conscious, and each of us *experiences* those conscious thoughts: we know them to be taking place in our own minds. We not only think, but perceive ourselves thinking. Artificial intelligence has no analog to this. As Donald Norman put it—and he was only one of many cognitive scientists who made similar remarks to me—"We don't have any programs today that are self-aware or that even begin to approach consciousness such as human beings have. I see this as a critical difference between human intelligence and artificial intelligence. The human mind is aware of itself as an identity, it can introspect, it can examine its own ideas and react to them—not just with thoughts about them but with emotions. We can't begin to simulate consciousness on a computer, and perhaps never will."

Not everyone would agree that consciousness may forever remain impossible to simulate, but what is clear is that it cannot be simulated at present—and for one very good reason: it remains the least understood and most puzzling of psychological phenomena. I am aware of my own thoughts, to be sure, but what is this "I"? How do I distinguish the "I" from the identity of other people or the rest of the world? Surely it is not a matter of the borders of my physical being, for in the dark, or blindfolded and bound, or even cut off by spinal anesthesia from all feeling, I would know myself: the borders are those of thought, not body. Actually, the question "What is this 'I'?" rarely concerns us, for we experience our own identity as a self-evident reality. But that ineluctable sense of I-ness does not exist in any computer; there is no evidence that any computer program has ever realized that it is itself, running in a particular machine, and not a similar program, running on another machine somewhere else.

Cognitive science does offer at least a rudimentary explanation of consciousness: it is thought to be the product of our internalizing the real world in our minds in symbolic form. We perceive not only the real world but also our own mental representation of it; the experience of the difference between the two results in self-awareness. We recognize that there is not only a real world but a simulacrum of it within us; therefore there must be an *us: cogito ergo sum,** yet again. The thought that we have thoughts is the crucial one that becomes consciousness; it is what Douglas Hofstadter, in *Gödel, Escher, Bach,* calls a "strange loop" of the mind, an interaction between different levels, a self-reinforcing resonance. "The self," he says, "comes into being at the moment it has the power to reflect itself." We contemplate our thoughts, but the awareness of doing so is itself a thought, and the foundation of consciousness.

Perhaps the key factor is that consciousness develops in us as a result of our cognitive history. . . . [T]he infant gradually becomes capable of thinking about external objects by means of mental images and symbols stored in memory. The newborn does not seem to be aware of the boundaries between itself and the rest of the world, but it perceives them more and more distinctly as its internal image of the world builds up. Consciousness emerges as a product of the child's mental development. The computer, in contrast, though it may acquire an ever-larger store of information, has no such sense or experience of its own history. Nor does it recognize that what is in its memory is a representation of something outside. To the computer, what is in its system is what *is*; it does not contemplate its thoughts as thoughts, but as the only reality. How could it, then, be aware of itself as an individual?

Some AI† enthusiasts do, however, argue that if a program examines its own problem-solving behavior and modifies it to improve it, as HACKER does, this is the equivalent of consciousness; so says Pamela McCorduck in *Machines Who Think.* John McCarthy of Stanford University, one of America's leading computer scientists, goes even further: he says it is possible to ascribe

---

*[I think, therefore I am (a crucial assertion in the work of seventeenth-century philosopher Descartes).—Eds.]

†[Artificial intelligence.—Eds.]

beliefs, free will, consciousness, and wants to a machine. In his view, even as simple a machine as a thermostat can be said to have beliefs (presumably the thermostat "believes" that the optimum temperature is the one it is set for). But such talk is either metaphorical or, more likely, anthropomorphic; it reads into the machine what the human observer feels, much as primitive people attribute rage to the volcano and prudence to the ant. There is no reason to suppose HACKER or a thermostat experience anything like awareness of the self; they merely respond to certain incoming stimuli with mechanical reactions. HACKER, to be sure, does register corrections in its program for future use, but so does a vine, growing around an obstruction. It seems most unlikely that anywhere within HACKER some small voice says, "I made an error, but I'm correcting it and I'll do better next time."

What difference does it make? If a machine can respond to its own errors and correct them, what does it matter that it isn't aware of doing so?

It matters a lot. Awareness of self is the essence of what being alive means to us. If, through some accident, you remained able to talk and reason but could not realize that you were doing so, would you not be as dead, from your own viewpoint, as if your brain had been destroyed?

More than that, with awareness of self we become conscious of the alternatives in our thoughts; we become conscious of our choices, and of our ability to will the things we choose to do. Choice and will are difficult to account for within a scientific psychology, since it views existence as a continuum in which no phenomenon occurs uncaused. If no event is, itself, a first cause, but is the product of antecedent forces, then the experience of choice and of will must be illusory; the acts of choosing and of willing, though they seem to be within our power, must be products of all that has happened to us in the past and is happening at the moment.

And yet when we are conscious of our own alternatives, that self-awareness is another level of causality—a set of influences in addition to those of the past and present. We are not automata, weighing all the pros and cons of any matter and inevitably acting in accord with our calculations. In mathematical decision theory, the totally rational human being does just that and always selects the most advantageous option; so does a well-designed computer program. But in reality we are aware of our own decision making, and that awareness in itself brings other forces to bear upon the decision— emotional responses to the situation, loyalties, moral values, a sense of our own identity—and these resonances, these loops of thought, affect the outcome.

A simple example: you are annoyed by something a friend has said or done, you fume about it, you imagine a conversation in which the two of you argue about it, you prepare your crushing remarks—and suddenly perceive all this as from a distance; in perspective, you see yourself as an outsider might see you, question your own thoughts and feelings, alter them, and, as a result, accept the friend's behavior and dismiss your anger, or, perhaps, call the friend and talk the matter over amicably.

Another example: like every writer I know, when I am writing a first draft

I rattle away at the typewriter, setting down words; but once I see them I think, That isn't quite right—that's not exactly what I mean, and tinker and revise and rewrite until the words are right. But it wasn't that the first words didn't say what I meant; rather, in seeing my thoughts, I had thoughts about them; the strange loop yielded something like freedom—the freedom to make a different choice among my thoughts. If the experiences of choice and will are not what they seem to be, they nonetheless reflect real processes that produce results different from those that would come about without them.

In any case, there is no doubt that we do not experience our thought processes as automatic but as within our control . . .

But what does "want" mean?* Can a machine want? In a sense; if its program calls for it to assign different weights to various subgoals and goals it will proceed to choose that option which its program reckons to have the greatest numerical value. All very neat and simple. Human beings are far less neat and far more complicated. We often desire things but lack the motivation to pursue them; conversely, we are sometimes so strongly motivated by beliefs, values, and emotions that we pursue a particular goal with a devotion far beyond what any realistic evaluation would warrant.

Of all the components in human motivation, the one least likely ever to be simulated by a computer is our capacity to find things interesting. It is a mystifying phenomenon. Why do we find any matter interesting? What makes us want to know about, or understand, something—especially something that has no practical value for us, such as the age of the universe or when human beings first appeared on earth? Why do we want to know if there is life elsewhere in the cosmos, if its replies to our messages could not arrive back here for centuries? Why did Pythagoras feel so powerfully impelled to prove his celebrated theorem?

This tendency in us, some cognitive scientists believe, is an intrinsic characteristic of our nervous system. We are driven to think certain thoughts, and to pursue certain goals, by an inherent neurological restlessness, a need to do something with the thoughts in our minds and with the world they represent. The computer, in contrast, is a passive system: its goals and the strength of its drive to reach them are those given it by its designer. Left to itself, it will sit inert, awaiting further orders. We will not; we look for new goals, and, to reach them, are forced to solve problems we did not have before; we do not let well enough alone.

Why don't we? Call it restlessness, call it curiosity, or perhaps, like the historian Huizinga, call it playfulness. Other animals play, but with us playfulness becomes cognitive: we play with our ideas, and afterward with the real-world counterparts of those ideas. How would you simulate that on a machine? Allen Newell and a few other AI researchers say there is no reason why a program could not be designed to be curious and to create new goals for itself, but they are a small minority; most cognitive scientists think other-

*[In the seventh paragraph the author brings up the issue of ascribing wants to a machine. —Eds.]

wise. Yet even if a machine could be programmed to cast about in some way for new goals and new problems, it would do so because it had been programmed to; it wouldn't do so because it wanted to. It wouldn't give a damn.

And that would be bound to affect the kinds of new problems it chose to tackle and the strength of its motivation to solve them. Maybe the biggest difference between artificial and human intelligence is just that simple: we care about the things we choose to do. Solving a new problem, discovering some new fact, visiting a new place, reading a new book, all make us feel good; that's why we do them. But how would one make a computer feel good? Some AI people have built rewards into their programs: if the machine makes right decisions, its program is automatically altered to strengthen that kind of response, and so it learns. Theoretically, a program could be rewarded if it did something new and different, so that its tendency would be not to maintain itself, unchanged, but to keep changing. But would it *want* to do so or *like* doing so? And lacking that, would there be any meaning to its changes? Perhaps computer-written music and poetry have been unimpressive because the computer itself was neither pleased nor displeased by its own product, as every creative artist is. Without that test, it wasn't able to tell whether it had created a work of genius or a piece of trash. And it didn't care.

We, on the other hand, care—and care most of all about those thoughts which express moral values. Each of us is not just an information processor but the product of a particular culture and its belief system. We perceive the world through the special focus of the values we have learned from parents, schools, books, and peers. Those values become a part of our decision-making processes; in making many of our choices, we weight the alternatives in accordance with our moral, religious, and political beliefs.

This aspect of human thinking can be, and has been, simulated on the machine, . . . in the form of the simulations of political decision making created by Jaime Carbonell and his colleagues. . . . POLITICS has simulated the reasoning of either a conservative or a liberal considering what the United States should do if, for instance, Russia were to build nuclear submarines. Both as conservative and as liberal, POLITICS flawlessly came to conclusions consonant with the assumptions it was programmed to draw upon. Carbonell's purpose was to test his theoretical model of the way in which ideology affects the decision-making process; he did not suggest that POLITICS could be developed into a machine that could do our political thinking for us. But his work does have two important implications for this discussion of what the human mind can do that the computer can't do.

First, even though POLITICS can simulate archetypal conservative or liberal political reasoning, it does so in a wholly predictable way; it produces decisions Carbonell could foresee because they are based entirely on the terms and conditions he had put into it. But that is not the way human beings think. Within any party or ideological group, there is a wide range of variations in how individuals interpret the tenets of that ideology. There are always mavericks, dissenters, and innovators, without whom every party, every church, and every culture would atrophy and die.

Second, within any given ideological group, some people have the emotional maturity, the richness of human experience, and the soundness of judgment to use its tenets wisely; others do not, and use them foolishly. This is not to say that wise persons will reach the same conclusions everywhere; I would not want the wisest judge in Russia, India, or Iran to hear a civil liberties case in which I was accused of slandering the state. But if it is true that within any culture, its ethical system has internal validity, some of its people will interpret those beliefs wisely, others foolishly, and the majority somewhere in between. Moral wisdom is not so much the product of a special method of reasoning as of an ability to harmonize moral beliefs with fundamental individual and societal needs. I do not see how artificial intelligence can simulate that.

Will artificial intelligence, then, ever outstrip human intelligence? Yes, astronomically—in certain ways; and clearly it is already doing so. But in other ways it does not now match our powers, much less exceed them, and seems unlikely to do so soon. And in still other ways it seems incapable of simulating human intellectual functioning at all.

For until it acquires perceptual systems as sophisticated as our own, it will not be able to learn directly from the environment. But the development of such systems is bound to prove more difficult, by many orders of magnitude, than the creation of a living cell—a feat not now imaginable—and lacking such perceptual systems, the machine will remain dependent on the human being for its information.

But that is the least of it. Until artificial intelligence can duplicate human mental development from birth onward; until it can absorb the intricacies and subtleties of cultural values; until it can acquire consciousness of self; until it becomes capable of playfulness and curiosity; until it can create new goals for itself, unplanned and uninstigated by any human programmer; until it is motivated not by goals alone but by some restless compulsion to be doing and exploring; until it can care about, and be pleased or annoyed by, its own thoughts; until it can make wise moral judgments—until all these conditions exist, the computer, it seems to me, will not match or even palely imitate the most valuable aspects of human thinking.

There is no doubt that the computer has already transformed our lives, and will continue to do so. But its chief influence will continue to be its utility as a tool. Supercalculators have radically changed, and will continue to change, all human institutions that require reckoning. Artificial intelligence will reconstruct many areas of problem solving—everything from the practice of medicine to literary and historical research and the investigation of the cosmos—and in so doing will change our ways of thinking as profoundly as did the invention of writing. Tools have powerful effects on the thinking as profoundly as did the invention of writing. Tools have powerful effects on the thinking of those who use them (the plow radically altered humankind's view of itself and of the world around it), but tools of the mind have the most powerful effects of all. Still, they are our tools, we their users.

But is it not possible that the computer will take over, outthink us, make our decisions for us, become our ruler? Not unless we assign it the power to make our decisions. Joseph Weizenbaum, in *Computer Power and Human Reason*, passionately argues that the computer represents a major danger to humanity not because it can forcibly take over but because we are heedlessly allowing it to make decisions for us in areas where we alone ought to make them. He sees the problem as a moral one rather than a struggle between human and machine: we ought not let the computer function as a psychotherapist, ought not rely on it to tell us whether to bomb civilian enemy targets or only military ones, ought not have it function as a judge in court.

Of course we ought not, but is there any real danger that we will? I hope not; I think not. The computer does not set its own goals: we do, and we human beings are jealous of our own powers. We have often delegated them to some leader—a human being, like ourselves, but one we took to be a greater person than we. Or we have asked some god (who often looks like us, enlarged) to make our decisions for us. But would we ever delegate our intellectual responsibilities to a machine that we ourselves created? I doubt it. Though human beings have often enough been fools, I find it hard to believe that we would ever be foolish enough to think our machines wiser than we; at least, not as long as we are aware of, and proud of, the human difference.

24 / The Myth of Immortality

CLARENCE DARROW

Clarence Darrow (1857–1938) was one of America's most famous criminal and trial lawyers, as well as a widely read author. Among his most famous cases were the Leopold and Loeb murder trial and the Scopes evolution trial. He was an agnostic and a vigorous opponent of traditional practices of punishment. This essay is a chapter from his autobiography.

[I. THE BELIEF IN IMMORTALITY]

*T*here is, perhaps, no more striking example of the credulity of man than the widespread belief in immortality. This idea includes not only the belief that death is not the end of what we call life, but that personal identity involving memory persists beyond the grave. So determined is the ordinary individual to hold fast to this belief that, as a rule, he refuses to read or to think upon the subject lest it cast doubt upon his cherished dream. Of those who may chance to look at this contribution, many will do so with the determination not to be convinced, and will refuse even to consider the manifold reasons that might weaken their faith. I know that this is true, for I know the reluctance with which I long approached the subject and my firm determination not to give up my hope. Thus the myth will stand in the way of a sensible adjustment to facts.

Even many of those who claim to believe in immorality still tell themselves and others that neither side of the question is susceptible of proof. Just what can these hopeful ones believe that the word "proof" involves? The evidence against the persistence of personal consciousness is as strong as the evidence for gravitation, and much more obvious. It is as convincing and unassailable as the proof of the destruction of wood or coal by fire. If it is not certain that death ends personal identity and memory, then almost nothing that man accepts as true is susceptible of proof.

The beliefs of the race and its individuals are relics of the past. Without careful examination, no one can begin to understand how many of man's cherished opinions have no foundation in fact. The common experience of all men should teach them how easy it is to believe what they wish to accept. Experienced psychologists know perfectly well that if they desire to convince a man of some idea, they must first make him *want* to believe it. There are so many hopes, so many strong yearnings and desires attached to the doctrine of immortality that it is practically impossible to create in any mind the wish to be mortal. Still, in spite of strong desires, millions of people are filled with doubts and fears that will not down. After all, is it not better to look the question squarely in the face and find out whether we are harboring a delusion?

It is customary to speak of a "belief in immortality." First, then, let us see what is meant by the word "belief." If I take a train in Chicago at noon, bound for New York, I believe I will reach that city the next morning. I believe it because I have been to New York. I have read about the city. I have known many other people who have been there, and their stories are not inconsistent with any known facts in my own experience. I have even examined the timetables, and I know just how I will go and how long the trip will take. In other words, when I board the train for New York I believe I will reach that city because I have *reason* to believe it.

But if I am told that next week I shall start on a trip to Goofville; that I shall not take my body with me; that I shall stay for all eternity: can I find a single fact connected with my journey—the way I shall go, the part of me that is to go, the time of the journey, the country I shall reach, its location in space, the way I shall live there—or anything that would lead to a rational belief that I shall really make the trip? Have I ever known anyone who has made the journey and returned? If I am really to believe, I must try to get some information about all these important facts.

But people hesitate to ask questions about life after death. They do not ask, for they know that only silence comes out of the eternal darkness of endless space. If people really believed in a beautiful, happy, glorious land waiting to receive them when they died; if they believed that their friends would be waiting to meet them; if they believed that all pain and suffering would be left behind: why should they live through weeks, months, and even years of pain and torture while a cancer eats its way to the vital parts of the body? Why should one fight off death? Because he does *not* believe in any real sense: He only hopes. Everyone knows that there is no real evidence of any such state of bliss; so we are told not to search for proof. We are to accept through faith alone. But every thinking person knows that faith can only come through belief. Belief implies a condition of mind that accepts a certain idea. This condition can be brought about only by evidence. True, the evidence may be simply the unsupported statement of your grandmother; it may be wholly insufficient for reasoning men; but, good or bad, it must be enough for the believer or he could not believe.

Upon what evidence, then, are we asked to believe in immortality? There is no evidence. One is told to rely on faith, and no doubt this serves the purpose so long as one can believe blindly whatever he is told. But if there is no evidence upon which to build a positive belief in immortality, let us examine the other side of the question. Perhaps evidence can be found to support a positive conviction that immortality is a delusion. . . .

[II. ARGUMENTS AGAINST IMMORTALITY]

The idea of continued life after death is very old. It doubtless had its roots back in the childhood of the race. In view of the limited knowledge of primitive man, it was not unreasonable. His dead friends and relatives visited him in dreams and visions and were present in his feeling and imagination until they were forgotten. Therefore the lifeless body did not raise the question of dissolution, but rather of duality. It was thought that man was a dual being possessing a body and a soul as separate entities, and that when a man died, his soul was released from his body to continue its life apart. Consequently, food and drink were placed upon the graves of the dead to be used in the long journey into the unknown. In modified forms, this belief in the duality of man persists to the present day.

But primitive man had no conception of life as having a beginning and an end. In this he was like the rest of the animals. Today everyone of ordinary intelligence knows how life begins, and to examine the beginnings of life leads to inevitable conclusions about the way life ends. If man has a soul, it must creep in somewhere during the period of gestation and growth.

All the higher forms of animal life grow from a single cell. Before the individual life can begin its development, it must be fertilized by union with another cell; then the cell divides and multiplies until it takes the form and pattern of its kind. At a certain regular time the being emerges into the world.

During its term of life millions of cells in its body are born, die, and are replaced until, through age, disease, or some catastrophe, the cells fall apart and the individual life is ended.

It is obvious that but for the fertilization of the cell under right conditions, the being would not have lived. It is idle to say that the initial cell has a soul. In one sense it has life; but even that is precarious and depends for its continued life upon union with another cell of the proper kind. The human mother is the bearer of probably ten thousand of one kind of cell, and the human father of countless billions of the other kind. Only a very small fraction of these result in human life. If the unfertilized cells of the female and the unused cells of the male are human beings possessed of souls, then the population of the world is infinitely greater than has ever been dreamed. Of course no such idea as belief in the immortality of the germ cells could satisfy the yearnings of the individual for a survival of life after death.

If that which is called a "soul" is a separate entity apart from the body, when, then, and where and how was this soul placed in the human structure? The individual began with the union of two cells, neither of which had a soul. How could these two soulless cells produce a soul? I must leave this search to the metaphysicians. When they have found the answer, I hope they will tell me, for I should really like to know.

We know that a baby may live and fully develop in its mother's womb and then, through some shock at birth, may be born without life. In the past these babies were promptly buried. But now we know that in many cases, where the bodily structure is complete, the machine may be set to work by artificial respiration or electricity. Then it will run like any other human body through its allotted term of years. We also know that in many cases of drowning, or when some mishap virtually destroys life without hopelessly impairing the body, artificial means may set it in motion once more, so that it will complete its term of existence until the final catastrophe comes. Are we to believe that somewhere around the stillborn child and somewhere in the vicinity of the drowned man there hovers a detached soul waiting to be summoned back into the body by a pulmotor? This, too, must be left to the metaphysicians.

The beginnings of life yield no evidence of the beginnings of a soul. It is idle to say that the something in the human being which we call "life" is the soul itself, for the soul is generally taken to distinguish human beings from other forms of life. There is life in all animals and plants, and at least potential life in inorganic matter. This potential life is simply unreleased force and matter—the great storehouse from which all forms of life emerge and are constantly replenished. It is impossible to draw the line between inorganic matter and the simpler forms of plant life, and equally impossible to draw the line between plant life and animal life, or between other forms of animal life and what we human beings are pleased to call the highest form. If the thing which we call "life" is itself the soul, then cows have souls; and, in the very nature of things, we must allow souls to all forms of life and to inorganic matter as well.

Life itself is something very real, as distinguished from the soul. Every man knows that his life had a beginning. Can one imagine an organism that has a beginning and no end? If I did not exist in the infinite past, why should I, or could I, exist in the infinite future? "But," say some, "your consciousness, your memory may exist even after you are dead. This is what we mean by the soul." Let us examine this point a little.

I have no remembrance of the months that I lay in my mother's womb. I cannot recall the day of my birth nor the time when I first opened my eyes to the light of the sun. I cannot remember when I was an infant, or when I began to creep on the floor, or when I was taught to walk, or anything before I was five or six years old. Still, all of these events were important, wonderful, and strange in a new life. What I call my "consciousness," for lack of a better word and a better understanding, developed with my growth and the crowding experiences I met at every turn. I have a hazy recollection of the burial of a boy soldier who was shot toward the end of the Civil War. He was buried near the schoolhouse when I was seven years old. But I have no remembrance of the assassination of Abraham Lincoln, although I must then have been eight years old. I must have known about it at the time, for my family and my community idolized Lincoln, and all America was in mourning at his death. Why do I remember the dead boy soldier who was buried a year before? Perhaps because I knew him well. Perhaps because his family was close to my childish life. Possibly because it came to me as my first knowledge of death. At all events, it made so deep an impression that I recall it now.

"Ah, yes," say the believers in the soul, "what you say confirms our own belief. You certainly existed when these early experiences took place. You were conscious of them at the time, even though you are not aware of it now. In the same way, may not your consciousness persist after you die, even though you are not now aware of the fact?"

On the contrary, my fading memory of the events that filled the early years of my life leads me to the opposite conclusion. So far as these incidents are concerned, the mind and consciousness of the boy are already dead. Even now, am I fully alive? I am seventy-one years old. I often fail to recollect the names of some of those I knew full well. Many events do not make the lasting impression that they once did. I know that it will be only a few years, even if my body still survives decay, when few important matters will even register in my mind. I know how it is with the old. I know that physical life can persist beyond the time when the mind can fully function. I know that if I live to an extreme old age, my mind will fail. I shall eat and drink and go to my bed in an automatic way. Memory—which is all that binds me to the past—will already be dead. All that will remain will be a vegetative existence; I shall sit and doze in the chimney corner, and my body will function in a measure even though the ego will already be practically dead. I am sure that if I die of what is called "old age," my consciousness will gradually slip away with my failing emotions; I shall no more be aware of the near approach of final dissolution than is the dying tree.

In primitive times, before men knew anything about the human body or the universe of which it is a part, it was not unreasonable to believe in spirits, ghosts, and the duality of man. For one thing, celestial geography was much simpler then. Just above the earth was a firmament in which the stars were set, and above the firmament was heaven. The place was easy of access, and in dreams the angels were seen going up and coming down on a ladder. But now we have a slightly more adequate conception of space and the infinite universe of which we are so small a part. Our great telescopes reveal countless worlds and planetary systems which make our own sink into utter insignificance in comparison. We have every reason to think that beyond our sight there is endless space filled with still more planets, so infinite in size and number that no brain has the smallest conception of their extent. Is there any reason to think that in this universe, with its myriads of worlds, there is no other life so important as our own? Is it possible that the inhabitants of the earth have been singled out for special favor and endowed with souls and immortal life? Is it at all reasonable to suppose that any special account is taken of the human atoms that forever come and go upon this planet? . . .

[III. OTHER MATTERS]

Some of those who profess to believe in the immortality of man—whether it be of his soul or his body—have drawn what comfort they could from the modern scientific doctrine of the indestructibility of matter and force. This doctrine, they say, only confirms in scientific language what they have always believed. This, however, is pure sophistry. It is probably true that no matter or force has ever been or ever can be destroyed. But it is likewise true that there is no connection whatever between the notion that personal consciousness and memory persist after death and the scientific theory that matter and force are indestructible. For the scientific theory carries with it a corollary, that the forms of matter and energy are constantly changing through an endless cycle of new combinations. Of what possible use would it be, then, to have a consciousness that was immortal, but which, from the moment of death, was dispersed into new combinations so that no two parts of the original identity could ever be reunited again?

These natural processes of change, which in the human being take the forms of growth, disease, senility, death, and decay, are essentially the same as the process by which a lump of coal is disintegrated in burning. One may watch the lump of coal burning in the grate until nothing but ashes remains. Part of the coal goes up the chimney in the form of smoke; part of it radiates through the house as heat; the residue lies in the ashes on the hearth. So it is with human life. In all forms of life nature is engaged in combining, breaking down, and recombining her store of energy and matter into new forms. The thing we call "life" is nothing other than a state of equilibrium which endures for a short span of years between the two opposing tendencies of nature—the one that builds up and the one that tears down. In old age, the tearing-down process has already gained the ascendancy, and when death intervenes, the equilibrium is finally upset by the complete stoppage of the building-up process, so that nothing remains but complete disintegration. The energy thus released may be converted into grass or trees or animal life; or it may lie dormant until caught up again in the crucible of nature's laboratory. But whatever happens, the man—the *You* and the *I*—like the lump of coal that has been burned, is gone, irrevocably dispersed. All the King's horses and all the King's men cannot restore it to its former unity.

The idea that man is a being set apart, distinct from all the rest of nature, is born of man's emotions, of his loves and hates, of his hopes and fears, and of the primitive conceptions of undeveloped minds. The *You* or the *I* which is known to our friends does not consist of an immaterial something called a "soul" which cannot be conceived. We know perfectly well what we mean when we talk about this *You* and this *Me*: and it is equally plain that the whole fabric that makes up our separate personalities is destroyed, dispersed, disintegrated beyond repair by what we call "death."

Those who refuse to give up the idea of immortality declare that nature never creates a desire without providing the means for its satisfaction. They likewise insist that all people, from the rudest to the most civilized, yearn for another life. As a matter of fact, nature creates many desires which she does not satisfy; most of the wishes of men meet no fruition. But nature does not create any emotion demanding a future life. The only yearning that the individual has is to keep on living—which is a very different thing. This urge is found in every animal, in every plant. It is simply the momentum of a living structure: or, as Schopenhauer* put it, "the will to live." What we long for is a continuation of our present state of existence, not an uncertain reincarnation in a mysterious world of which we know nothing.

All men recognize the hopelessness of finding any evidence that the individual will persist beyond the grave. As a last resort, we are told that it is better that the doctrine be believed even if it is not true. We are assured that without this faith, life is only desolation and despair. However that may be, it remains that many of the conclusions of logic are not pleasant to contemplate; still, so long as men think and feel, at least some of them will use their faculties as best they can. For if we are to believe things that are not true, who is to write our creed? Is it safe to leave it to any man or organization to pick out the errors that we must accept? The whole history of the world has answered this question in a way that cannot be mistaken.

And after all, is the belief in immortality necessary or even desirable for man? Millions of men and women have no such faith; they go on with their daily tasks and feel joy and sorrow without the lure of immortal life. The things that really affect the happiness of the individual are the matters of daily living. They are the companionship of friends, the games and contemplations. They are misunderstandings and cruel judgments, false friends and debts, poverty and disease. They are our joys in our living companions and our sorrows over those who die. Whatever our faith, we mainly live in the

---

*[A nineteenth-century German philosopher who held that all living things exhibit a "will to live."—Eds.]

present—in the here and now. Those who hold the view that man is mortal are never troubled by metaphysical problems. At the end of the day's labor we are glad to lose our consciousness in sleep; and intellectually, at least, we look forward to the long rest from the stresses and storms that are always incidental to existence.

When we fully understand the brevity of life, its fleeting joys and unavoidable pains; when we accept the fact that all men and women are approaching an inevitable doom: the consciousness of it should make us more kindly and considerate of each other. This feeling should make men and women use their best efforts to help their fellow travellers on the road, to make the path brighter and easier as we journey on. It should bring a closer kinship, a better understanding, and a deeper sympathy for the wayfarer who must live a common life and die a common death.

25 / *Is Life after Death Possible?*

C. J. DUCASSE

C. J. Ducasse (1881–1969) was born in France but taught in the United States. His interests and writings were in many areas—the philosophy of religion, metaphysics, theory of knowledge, and psychical research. He was a member of the board of trustees of the American Society for Psychical Research.

*T*he question whether human personality survives death is sometimes asserted to be one upon which reflection is futile. Only empirical evidence, it is said, can be relevant, since the question is purely one of fact.

But no question is purely one of fact until it is clearly understood; and this one is, on the contrary, ambiguous and replete with tacit assumptions. Until the ambiguities have been removed and the assumptions critically examined, we do not really know just what it is we want to know when we ask whether a life after death is possible. Nor, therefore, can we tell until then what bearing on this question various facts empirically known to us may have.

To clarify its meaning is chiefly what I now propose to attempt. I shall . . . state, as convincingly as I can in the space available, the arguments commonly advanced to prove that such a life is impossible. After that, I shall consider the logic of these arguments, and show that they quite fail to establish the impossibility. Next, the tacit but arbitrary assumption, which makes them nevertheless appear convincing, will be pointed out. . . .

Let us turn to the first of these tasks. . . .

I. THE ARGUMENTS AGAINST SURVIVAL

There are, first of all, a number of *facts* which definitely suggest that both the existence and the nature of consciousness wholly depend on the presence of a functioning nervous system. [F1.] It is pointed out, for example, that wherever consciousness is observed, it is found associated with a living and functioning body. [F2]. Further, when the body dies, or the head is struck a heavy blow, or some anesthetic is administered, the familiar outward evidences of consciousness terminate, permanently or temporarily. [F3]. Again, we know well that drugs of various kinds—alcohol, caffeine, opium, heroin, and many others—cause specific changes at the time in the nature of a person's mental states. . . . [F4.] Again, the contents of consciousness, the mental powers, or even the personality, are modified in characteristic ways when certain regions of the brain are destroyed by disease or injury or are disconnected from the rest by such an operation as prefrontal lobotomy. . . .

That continued existence of mind after death is impossible has been argued also on the basis of *theoretical considerations*. [T1.] It has been contended, for instance, . . . that "consciousness" is only the name we give to certain types of behavior, which differentiate the higher animals from all other things in nature. According to this view, to say, for example, that an animal is conscious of a difference between two stimuli means nothing more than that it responds to each by different behavior. That is, the difference of *behavior* is what consciousness of difference between the stimuli *consists in*; and is not, as is commonly assumed, only the behavioral sign of something mental and not public, called "consciousness that the stimuli are different."

[T2.] Or again, consciousness, of the typically human sort called thought, is identified with the typically human sort of behavior called speech; and this, again, not in the sense that speech *expresses* or *manifests* something different from itself, called "thought," but in the sense that speech—whether uttered or only whispered—*is* thought itself. And obviously, if thought, or any mental activity, is thus but some mode of behavior of the living body, the mind cannot possibly survive death. . . .

II. THE ARGUMENTS EXAMINED

Such, in brief, are the chief reasons commonly advanced for holding that survival is impossible. Scrutiny of them, however, will, I think, reveal that they are not as strong as they first seem and far from strong enough to show that there can be no life after death.

[T1 and T2.] Let us consider first the assertion that "thought," or "consciousness," is but another name for subvocal speech, or for some other form of behavior, or for molecular processes in the tissues of the brain. As Paulsen and others have pointed out,[1] no evidence ever is or can be offered to support that assertion, because it is in fact but a disguised proposal to make the words "thought," "feeling," "sensation," "desire," and so on, denote facts quite different from those which these words are commonly employed to denote. To say that those words are but other names for certain chemical or behavioral events is as grossly arbitrary as it would be to say that "wood" is but another name for glass, or "potato" but another name for cabbage. What thought, desire, sensation, and other mental states are like, each of us can observe directly by introspection; and what introspection reveals is that they do not in the least resemble muscular contraction, or glandular secretion, or any other known bodily events. No tampering with language can alter the observable fact that thinking is one thing and muttering quite another; that the feeling called anger has no resemblance to the bodily behavior which usually goes with it; or that an act of will is not in the least like anything we find when we open the skull and examine the brain. Certain mental events are doubtless connected in some way with certain bodily events, but they are not those bodily events themselves. The connection is not identity.

[F2, F3, and F4.] This being clear, let us next consider the arguments offered to show that mental processes, although not identical with bodily processes, nevertheless depend on them. We are told, for instance, that some head injuries, or anesthetics, totally extinguish consciousness for the time being. As already pointed out, however, the strict fact is only that the usual bodily signs of consciousness are then absent. But they are also absent when a person is asleep; and yet, at the same time, dreams, which are states of consciousness, may be occurring.

It is true that when the person concerned awakens, he often remembers his dreams, whereas the person that has been anesthetized or injured has usually no memories relating to the period of apparent blankness. But this could mean that his consciousness was, for the first time, dissociated from its ordinary channels of manifestation, as was reported of the co-conscious personalities of some of the patients of Dr. Morton Prince.[2] Moreover, it sometimes occurs that a person who has been in an accident reports lack of memories not only for the period during which his body was unresponsive but also for a period of several hours *before* the accident, during which he had given to his associates all the ordinary external signs of being conscious as usual.

But, more generally, if absence of memories relating to a given period proved unconsciousness for that period, this would force us to conclude that we were unconscious during the first few years of our lives, and indeed have

[1]F. Paulsen, "Introduction to Philosophy," 2nd ed., trans. F. Thilly. pp. 82–83.

[2]"My Life as a Dissociated Personality," ed. Morton Prince (Boston: Badger).

been so most of the time since; for the fact is that we have no memories whatever of most of our days. That we were alive and conscious on any long past specific date is, with only a few exceptions, not something we actually remember, but only something which we infer must be true.

III. EVIDENCE FROM PSYCHICAL RESEARCH

[F1 and F2] Another argument advanced against survival was, it will be re-membered, that death must extinguish the mind, since all manifestations of it then cease. But to assert that they invariably then cease is to ignore altogether the considerable amount of evidence to the contrary, gathered over many years and carefully checked by the Society for Psychical Research. This evidence, which is of a variety of kinds, has been reviewed by Professor Gardner Murphy in an article published in the Journal of the Society.[3] He mentions first the numerous well-authenticated cases of apparition of a dead person to others as yet unaware that he had died or even been ill or in danger. The more strongly evidential cases of apparition are those in which the apparition conveys to the person who sees it specific facts until then secret. An example would be that of the apparition of a girl to her brother nine years after her death, with a conspicuous scratch on her cheek. Their mother then revealed to him that she herself had made that scratch accidentally while preparing her daughter's body for burial, but that she had then at once covered it with powder and never mentioned it to anyone.

Another famous case is that of a father whose apparition some time after death revealed to one of his sons the existence and location of an unsuspected second will, benefiting him, which was then found as indicated. Still another case would be the report by General Barter, then a subaltern in the British Army in India, of the apparition to him of a lieutenant he had not seen for two or three years. The lieutenant's apparition was riding a brown pony with black mane and tail. He was much stouter than at their last meeting, and, whereas formerly clean-shaven, he now wore a peculiar beard in the form of a fringe encircling his face. On inquiry the next day from a person who had known the lieutenant at the time he died, it turned out that he had indeed become very bloated before his death; that he had grown just such a beard while on the sick list; and that he had some time before bought and eventually ridden to death a pony of that very description.

Other striking instances are those of an apparition seen simultaneously by several persons. It is on record that an apparition of a child was perceived first by a dog, that the animal's rushing at it, loudly barking, interrupted the conversation of the seven persons present in the room, thus drawing their

---

[3]"An Outline of Survival Evidence," *Journal of the American Society for Psychical Research*, January, 1945.

attention to the apparition, and that the latter then moved through the room for some fifteen seconds, followed by the barking dog.[4]

Another type of empirical evidence of survival consists of communications, purporting to come from the dead, made through the persons commonly called sensitives, mediums, or automatists. Some of the most remarkable of these communications were given by the celebrated American medium, Mrs. Piper, who for many years was studied by the Society for Psychical Research, London, with the most elaborate precautions against all possibility of fraud. Twice, particularly, the evidences of identity supplied by the dead persons who purportedly were thus communicating with the living were of the very kinds, and of the same precision and detail, which would ordinarily satisfy a living person of the identity of another living person with whom he was not able to communicate directly, but only through an intermediary, or by letter or telephone.[5]

Again, sometimes the same mark of identity of a dead person, or the same message from him, or complementary parts of one message are obtained independently from two mediums in different parts of the world.

Of course, when facts of these kinds are recounted, as I have just done, only in abstract summary, they make little if any impression upon us. And the very word "medium" at once brings to our minds the innumerable instances of demonstrated fraud perpetrated by charlatans to extract money from the credulous bereaved. But the modes of trickery and sources of error, which immediately suggest themselves to us as easy, natural explanations of the seemingly extraordinary facts, suggest themselves just as quickly to the members of the research committees of the Society for Psychical Research. Usually, these men have had a good deal more experience than the rest of us with the tricks of conjurers and fraudulent mediums, and take against them precautions far more strict and ingenious than would occur to the average skeptic.[6]

But when, instead of stopping at summaries, one takes the trouble to study the detailed, original reports, it then becomes evident that they cannot all be just laughed off; for to accept the hypothesis of fraud or malobservation would often require more credulity than to accept the facts reported.

---

[4]The documents obtained by the Society for Psychical Research concerning this case, that of the lieutenant's apparition, and that of the girl with the scratch are reproduced in Sir Ernest Bennett's "Apparitions and Haunted Houses" (London: Faber and Faber, 1945), pp. 334–337, 28–35, and 145–150 respectively.

[5]A summary of some of the most evidential facts may be found in the book by M. Sage, entitled "Mrs. Piper and the Society for Psychical Research" (New York: Scott-Thaw Co., 1904); others of them are related in some detail in Sir Oliver Lodge's "The Survival of Man," sec. 4 (New York: Moffat, Yard and Co., 1909), and in A. M. Robbins' "Both Sides of the Veil," part 2 (Boston: Sherman, French, and Co., 1909). The fullest account is in the *Proceedings of the Society for Psychical Research*.

[6]Cf. H. Carrington, "The Physical Phenomena of Spiritualism, Fraudulent and Genuine" (Boston: Small, Maynard & Co., 1908).

IV. THE INITIAL ASSUMPTION BEHIND THE ARGUMENTS AGAINST SURVIVAL

We have now scrutinized . . . the reasons mentioned earlier for rejecting the possibility of survival, and we have found them all logically weak . . . It will be useful for us to . . . inquire why so many of the persons who advance those reasons nevertheless think them convincing.

It is, I believe, because these persons approach the question of survival with a certain unconscious metaphysical bias. It derives from a particular initial assumption which they tacitly make. It is that *to be real is to be material.** And to be material, of course, is to be some process or part of the perceptually public world, that is, of the world we all perceive by means of our so-called five senses.

Now, the assumption that to be real is to be material is a useful and appropriate one for the purpose of investigating the material world and of operating upon it; and this purpose is a legitimate and frequent one. But those persons, and most of us, do not realize that the validity of that assumption is strictly relative to that specific purpose. Hence they, and most of us, continue making the assumption, and it continues to rule judgment, even when, as now, the purpose in view is a different one, for which the assumption is no longer useful or even congruous.

The point is all-important here and therefore worth stressing. Its essence is that the conception of the nature of reality that proposes to define the real as the material is not the expression of an observable fact to which everyone would have to bow, but is the expression only of a certain direction of interest on the part of the persons who so define reality—of interest, namely, which they have chosen to center wholly in the material, perceptually public world. This specialized interest is of course as legitimate as any other, but it automatically ignores all the facts, commonly called facts of mind, which only introspection reveals. And that specialized interest is what alone compels persons in its grip to employ the word "mind" to denote, instead of what it commonly does denote, something else altogether, namely, the public behavior of bodies that have minds.

Only so long as one's judgment is swayed unawares by that special interest do the logically weak arguments against the possibility of survival, which we have examined, seem strong.

It is possible, however, and just as legitimate, as well as more conducive to a fair view of our question, to center one's interest at the start on the facts of mind as introspectively observable, ranking them as most real in the sense that they are the facts the intrinsic nature of which we most directly experience, the facts which we most certainly know to exist; and moreover, that they are the facts without the experiencing of which we should not know any other facts whatever—such, for instance, as those of the material world.

The sort of perspective one gets from this point of view is what I propose

---

*[This is to be interpreted as an identity claim. Thus x is real=x is material.—Eds.]

now to sketch briefly. For one thing, the material world is then seen to be but one among other objects of our consciousness. Moreover, one becomes aware of the crucially important fact that it is an object postulated rather than strictly given. What this means may be made clearer by an example. Suppose that, perhaps in a restaurant we visit for the first time, an entire wall is occupied by a large mirror and we look into it without realizing that it is a mirror. We then perceive, in the part of space beyond it, various material objects, notwithstanding that in fact they have no existence there at all. A certain set of the vivid color images which we call visual sensations was all that was strictly given to us, and these we construed, automatically and instantaneously, but nonetheless erroneously, as signs or appearances of the existence of certain material objects at a certain place.

Again, and similarly, we perceive in our dreams various objects which at the time we take as physical but which eventually we come to believe were not so. And this eventual conclusion, let it be noted, is forced upon us not because we then detect that something, called "physical substance," was lacking in those objects, but only because we notice, as we did not at the time, that their behavior was erratic—incoherent with their ordinary one. That is, their appearance was a *mere* appearance, deceptive in the sense that it did not then predict truly, as ordinarily it does, their later appearances. This, it is important to notice, is the *only* way in which we ever discover that an object we perceive was not really physical, or was not the particular sort of physical object we judged it to be.

These two examples illustrate the fact that our perception of physical objects is sometimes erroneous. But the essential point is that, even when it is veridical instead of erroneous, *all* that is literally and directly given to our minds is still only *some set of sensations*. These, on a given occasion, may be only color sensations; but they often include also tactual sensations, sounds, odors, and so on. It is especially interesting, however, to remark here in passing that, with respect to almost all the many thousands of persons and other "physical" objects we have perceived in a lifetime, *vivid color images* were the only data our perceiving strictly had to go by; so that, if the truth should happen to have been that those objects, like ghosts or images in a mirror, were actually intangible—that is, were *only* color images—we should never have discovered that this was the fact. For all we *directly* know, it *may* have been the fact!

To perceive a physical object, then, instead of merely experiencing passively certain sensations (something which perhaps hardly ever occurs) is always to *interpret*, that is to *construe*, given sensations as signs of, and appearances to us of, a postulated something other than themselves, which we believe is causing them in us and is capable of causing in us others of specific kinds. We believe this because we believe that our sensations too must have some cause, and we find none for them among our other mental states.

Such a postulated extramental something we call a physical object. We say that we observe physical objects, and this is true. But it is important for the present purpose to be clear that we "observe" them never in any more direct or literal manner than is constituted by the process of interpretive postulation just described—never, for example, in the wholly direct and literal manner in which we are able to observe our sensations themselves and our other mental states.

STUDY QUESTIONS

1. How does Evans answer the question in the title of his essay? What are his arguments (reasons) on behalf of that answer?

2. Do you agree with Evans' stand on the questions of whether a machine can think? Why or why not?

3. In your view, what sorts of evidence or data would provide an affirmative answer to the question, "Can a machine think"?

4. What sorts of evidence would support a negative answer to the question?

5. According to Hunt, what can the human mind do that the computer cannot?

6. Do you agree with his answer? Why or why not?

7. What point is Darrow trying to make in his discussion of taking a trip to Goofville?

8. Darrow argues against the belief in immortality. State his main arguments. Are they good arguments? Why or why not?

9. Some think that rejection of the belief in immortality leads to pessimism. Why does Darrow disagree? What is your view?

10. State the arguments against survival to which Ducasse refers. Critically evaluate his examination of those arguments.

11. Ducasse cites some evidence from psychical research. Is this supposed evidence sufficient to make likely the fact of survival? Why or why not?

12. What is the "initial assumption" behind the arguments against survival (according to Ducasse)? Do you agree that this assumption lies behind those arguments? Why or why not?

13. Adopt the standpoint of Darrow and criticize Ducasse. How would Ducasse respond?

14. What bearing, if any, does the question of survival and immortality have on the aims of philosophy discussed in the introduction to this book (Section I)?

15. Many people believe that if we did not survive death, our life on earth would have no meaning or purpose, and hence would not be worth living. Do you agree? Why or why not?

16. In your judgment, is a solution to the mind-body problem a requisite for an answer to the question of whether we survive the death of our bodies? Why or why not?

FURTHER READINGS

A. Persons and Machines

Anderson, A. R., ed. *Minds and Machines*. Englewood Cliffs, N.J.: Prentice-Hall, 1964. [A collection of provocative essays for and against artificial intelligence.]

Boden, Margaret. *Artificial Intelligence and Natural Man*. New York: Basic Books, 1977. [Perhaps the best single book on almost every aspect of this subject.]

Dreyfus, Hubert. *What Computers Can't Do: A Critique of Artificial Reason*. New York: Harper and Row, 1972. [An argument against artificial intelligence.]

Gunderson, Keith. *Mentality and Machines*. Garden City, N.Y.: Anchor Books, 1971. [Discusses the possibility of machines thinking and/or feeling.]

Scriven, Michael. "Man Versus Machine." In *Primary Philosophy*. New York: McGraw-Hill, 1966. [Very sympathetic to the view that robots, etc., are virtually no different from humans.]

B. Survival after Death and Immortality

Broad, C. D. *Lectures on Psychical Research*. New York: Humanities Press, 1962. [Takes seriously the claim that psychical research provides evidence for survival.]

Flew, Antony. *A New Approach to Psychical Research*. London: Watts, 1953. [Questions whether the belief in survival can be confirmed or discomfirmed by any empirical data.]

Lamont, Corliss. *The Illusion of Immortality*. New York: Wisdom Library, 1959. [A very lively and readable attack by a leading humanist on the belief in immortality.]

Penelhum, T. *Survival and Disembodied Existence*. London: Routledge and Kegan Paul, 1970. [Argues that a doctrine of survival based on the notion of the persistence of disembodied persons through time runs into difficulties, but that a theory of "astral or ectoplasmic" bodies does not encounter such difficulties.]

Russell, Bertrand. *Why I Am Not a Christian*. New York: Simon & Schuster and London: G. Allen and Unwin, 1957. [A criticism of the belief in survival after death and other religious doctrines.]

Taylor, A. E. *The Christian Hope of Immortality*. London: Geoffrey Bles, 1938. [An account which articulates the religious perspective on the issue of immortality.]

PART SIX

THE EXISTENCE
OF GOD

PREVIEW

In Primary Philosophy Michael Scriven writes,

> What kind of God, if any, exists? This is the primary problem about God, and it is simply stated. Nothing else about the issue is simple. And the problem's complexity is matched by its profundity. No other problem has such important consequences for our lives and our thinking about other issues, and to no other problem does the answer at first seem so obvious. There must be a God, for how else could the Universe have come to exist, or life and morality have any point? So one feels.[1]

We agree with Scriven that the problem is a profound one and that it has important consequences for our lives and our thinking about other matters. We also agree with his view (articulated later in the book) that it cannot be settled on the basis of how one feels but must be settled on the basis of reason and arguments. Many of these arguments, and criticisms of them, will be found in the selections contained in this part of the book and the next.

A number of questions arise in connection with the problem of God (or the problems of the existence of a god). Among them are these:

1. Are there any good reasons (based on either empirical evidence or rational arguments) for the belief that a god exists? If so, what are they? On the contrary, are there any good reasons to reject the belief? If so, what are they?

2. If a god exists, what sort of god is it? What are the attributes of God?

3. By many conceptions God is held to be, among other things, all-powerful and supremely benevolent. Can the fact of evil in the world be reconciled with such a belief?

4. There are some who hold that, even though reason and arguments fail, when it comes to the existence and nature of God we nevertheless have a right to have faith that such a being exists. Is this a tenable view? If so, why? If not, why not?

---

[1]Michael Scriven, *Primary Philosophy* (New York: McGraw-Hill, 1966), p. 87.

5. Some maintain that without God—or at least faith in God—life would have no meaning or purpose, and hence would not be worth living. Is this true?

Questions 1 and 2 will be taken up in this part; 3 and 4 in Part Seven; and 5 in Part Eight.

Main Questions

Hence the main questions of this part are:

1. Does God exist? Or are there any good reasons to believe that a god exists?
2. If so, what is the nature of that being? What are the attributes of God?

Answers

1. With regard to the question of whether or not a god exists, traditionally there have been three main answers. In recent years, a fourth position has been held. The three traditional answers are:

Theism: the view which affirms the existence of a god.
Atheism: the view which denies the existence of God or accepts no belief in God.
Agnosticism: the view that since we do not have sufficient evidence to decide, we should neither accept nor reject the existence of a god but keep the issue open, and for now, suspend our judgment.

Hence, we may state the main claims of each as follows:

1a. Theism: God does exist.
1b. Atheism: God does not exist. Or more commonly: there is no good reason for anyone to believe that God exists.
1c. Agnosticism (or skepticism): We don't have sufficient evidence to decide whether or not God exists. We must suspend our judgment for now.

Note: "Atheism" literally means without theism, that is, without the belief that there is God. Thus to be classified as an atheist, one does not need to claim that there is no God. All that is needed is to hold that there is no good reason for anyone to believe that God exists.

The above views all consider the claim that God exists to be a meaningful and even important one, even if that belief is deemed to be false or questionable. In recent years some philosophers have raised questions as to whether the claim that God exists, or any other theological claim, can be meaningful. Hence, we have a fourth approach to our first main question which we shall call:

1d. Noncognitivism: The claim that God exists is not a genuine claim at all. It is meaningless. (The same holds for the denial of it.)

In this part of the book, we will take the theistic claim to be a meaningful one, however, even if it is false. (One selection briefly refers to but does not represent the meaningless approach.)

There are, of course, many varieties of theism. According to one conception, God is wholly transcendent to the universe. According to another, God is wholly immanent within the natural universe. According to still another, God is (somehow) both transcendent and immanent. The latter is the view advocated by some religions today. There are still other conceptions of theism which are much looser than those just mentioned. Thus, according to some conceptions, God is merely a force operating within the natural universe. According to others, God is the sum total of all moral value. There is even a conception according to which God is identical with the natural universe! We will not be concerned with these looser conceptions of God in this volume. In so doing, we believe that most traditional believers would be in agreement with us, since they would hardly find those conceptions adequate. Therefore, in our consideration of questions 1 and 2—via the selections contained in this part—we will be concerned with what we will refer to as the traditional conception of God.

However, it must be noted that some thinkers have given up the traditional conception of God and yet still consider themselves to be theists. Hence for the sake of completeness we have included one essay (the last in this part) which supports the view of nontraditional theism.

It should also be pointed out that atheism may be understood in two different senses. It may be taken to be the view which denies the existence of God. While the theist affirms, the atheist denies. But atheism may also be understood simply as the rejection of the belief in God, rather than the denial of God's existence. If the theist is one who has a belief in God, then the atheist (in this sense) is merely one who is without such a belief. Agnosticism is the belief that, since we do not have sufficient reasons either to affirm or to deny God's existence, we must (for now, at least) suspend our judgment.

2. We said that we will be here concerned with the traditional conception of God. But—and this brings us to question 2—what is that conception? According to the traditional conception, advocated by religions like Christianity, God is held to be omnipotent (all-powerful), omniscient (all-knowing), supremely good (or omnibenevolent), infinite, eternal, a being who possesses all perfections, transcendent to the natural universe (supernatural), the creator of the universe. (Many who hold this conception also maintain that God is a person—one who loves us, answers prayers, and so forth.) The readings contained in both this part and the next assume, with one exception, that it is such a god that is at issue in the questions and answers pertaining to the existence of a god, the problem of evil, and the like. As we have indicated, one selection in this part rejects that traditional conception of God. Hence we have a fifth approach to our first main question:

1e. Nontraditional theism: God exists but God is not to be defined as the god of traditional theism.

Finally, some have questioned whether argumentation is the right way by which to approach the matter of religious belief. Hence we have a sixth view on the subject matter of this part:

1f. The nonargumentative view: The way to deal with belief in God is one which relies on factors or approaches other than that of argumentation, for example through poetry and literature.

Selections

The selections in this part represent the various answers to our first and second main questions as follows:

Question	Answer	Selection
(1)	(1a) Theism	26
(1)	(1b) Atheism	27–28
(1)	(1c) Agnosticism	29
(1)	(1d) Noncognitivism	(27)
(1)	(1e) Nontraditional theism	30
(1)	(1f) Nonargumentative view	31
(2)	(2a) Traditional theism	26–29
(2)	(2b) Noncognitivism	(27)
(2)	(2c) Nontraditional theism	30

26 / A Defense of Theism

E. K. DANIEL

E. K. Daniel (1936–   ) is a philosopher who teaches at a university in the North Central states. Many of his writings on the philosophy of religion, his area of specialization, have been published, as well as a dozen books and numerous journal articles in other fields. Using the pseudonym E. K. Daniel, he has written the following article expressly for this book.

I. INTRODUCTION

*I*n this essay, I propose to give a philosophical defense of theism. More specifically, I propose to defend *traditional theism*. By traditional theism, I mean the view that there exists a being, God, who has all the following attributes: God is "omnipotent (all-powerful), omniscient (all-knowing), supremely good (or omnibenevolent), infinite, eternal, a being who possesses all perfections, transcendent to the natural universe, but the creator of the universe."[1]

My philosophical defense of traditional theism will proceed as follows. I will state, clarify, and then defend the classical *arguments* which have been put forth for the existence of a God as defined above. That is, in Section II, I shall simply state the classical arguments (sometimes in more than one version). In Section III, I shall comment on and clarify those traditional arguments. Then in Section IV, I shall offer a defense of some of those arguments. My defense will follow an earlier defense, which was put forth by Julian Hartt.[2]

I stated above that I proposed to offer a *philosophical* defense of theism. As many have noted, theism is a *metaphysical* theory. In the work referred to above, Hartt has characterized what metaphysical theories are by contrasting them with *matter of fact* claims. What is the difference between the two? Matter of fact claims are simple reports about states of affairs and can be directly verified by sensory observation. Examples of such claims are "The book is on the table" or "It is at this moment raining outside our door." Metaphysical theories, on the other hand, are not simple factual reports, but statements of an entirely different sort. They cannot be directly verified through observation. Hence they must be proved or supported by arguments. Examples of metaphysical theories are "Human beings have minds as well as bodies" or "None of our acts is done out of free will." Since metaphysical theories cannot

---

[1]See Preview to Part Six of this volume.

[2]Hartt's defense appears in J. A. C. F. Auer and J. Hartt, *Humanism vs. Theism* (Yellow Springs, Ohio: Antioch Press, 1951), Part 2, Chaper 3.

be directly verified but must be proved, I shall offer such a proof (as noted above) by way of the classical arguments.

Let us now turn to a consideration of the classical arguments. My formulations of them will follow those of their original proponents.

II. ARGUMENTS FOR THE EXISTENCE OF GOD

The following are the main classical arguments for God's existence:

1. The Ontological Argument (*A Priori* Argument)
2. The First-Cause Argument (Cosmological Argument)
3. The Argument from Contingency (A Variant of the Cosmological Argument)
4. The Design Argument (Teleological Argument)
5. The Moral Argument
6. The Argument from Religious Experience
7. The Natural Law Argument

1. The Ontological Argument (*A Priori* Argument)

We have an idea of an all-perfect being, and that is what we mean by God. God is "that than which nothing greater can be conceived." That is, God is a being which contains or possesses all conceivable perfections. (Among these are such qualities as being all-powerful, all-knowing, etc.). Now, if this being "existed" merely as an idea in our minds, if this being did not actually possess existence, it would not be all-perfect. It would not be as great as a being who also existed. But this would contradict our agreed-upon definition of God: a being who is all-perfect. Hence, God must exist.

2. The First-Cause Argument (Cosmological Argument)

First Version / Every event must have a cause, and that cause, in turn, must have a cause, and so on. If there were no end to this backward progression of causes and effects, then their succession would be infinite. But an infinite series of causes and events is *unintelligible*. Hence, there must be a first cause which is itself uncaused. Such a being we call God. Therefore, God exists.

Second Version / Every event must have a cause. If we trace the succession of causes and effects within the universe backward to infinity, we find that we have only two alternatives. Either there is no *ultimate* first cause or there is such a cause which is itself uncaused. But if there were no ultimate first cause, then although there would be a cause for each event within the infinite succession, there would be no cause for the entire succession as a whole. But there must be a cause for the whole succession. Therefore, there must exist a being which is the first or ultimate cause and is itself uncaused. Such a being we call God. Therefore, God exists.

3. The Argument from Contingency (A Variant of the Cosmological Argument)

Everything that exists has either contingent or necessary existence. To say that anything has contingent existence is to say that its existence is dependent on the existence of something else. It cannot be the ground of its own existence. To say that anything has necessary existence is to say that its existence is not dependent on the existence of something else. It is self-sufficient, the ground of its own existence. Since the existence of contingent beings is not self-sufficient, it is impossible that only contingent beings exist. Therefore, there must exist a necessary being. This being we call God. Therefore, God exists. (Again, most theists do not consider this to be a distinct argument.)

4. The Design Argument (Teleological Argument)

The universe exhibits orderliness and, more importantly, *purpose*. Many things or events occur in an orderly fashion, for example, the behavior of the planets in our solar system. Many other things are correlated with one another in a way which is *purposeful*. Among these there is an adaptation of means to ends, as in the intricate structure of the human eye. It is especially things of the *second* sort—the *purposive* features of living organisms, and life itself—which require an explanation. They could not have come about by accident or chance. They must be a result of some greater plan. Just as the existence of, say, a watch indicates that a designer/creator (an intelligent mind) must have planned it and brought it into being, so the existence of the universe and various phenomena within the universe indicate that an even greater designer/creator (an intelligent Mind) must have planned it and brought it into being. Such a being is what we mean by God. Therefore, God exists.

5. The Moral Argument

First Form / Many people have a sense of moral obligation. They feel this claim of obedience to a moral law as coming from outside of themselves. No naturalistic account of this sense of obligation in terms of human needs or behavior can explain it. It can be explained only by the existence of a moral lawgiver outside of the natural universe. Hence, such a lawgiver must exist. Such a being we call God. Therefore, God exists.

Second Form / In the effort to fulfill our obligation, our pursuit of the good sometimes gets frustrated. If this constantly occurred, the world wouldn't really be good. So the world in which this happens cannot be ultimately real.

There must be a real world of genuine moral value, under the control of a supreme mind. Therefore, such a mind, God, must exist.

Or alternately: we have a duty to fulfill the highest good. For the world to be just, there must be agreement between our acting in accordance with our duty and the achievement of happiness. But in this world, that does not always happen. Therefore, there must be a guarantor that the virtuous will receive their reward, in some other world. Therefore, such a guarantor, God, must exist.

6. The Argument from Religious Experience

Many people claim to have experiences in which they have immediate and direct knowledge of God. Therefore, God exists. (Strictly speaking, this is not an argument on behalf of God's existence; for the advocate of this claim maintains that because one has a direct experience of God, it is not necessary to infer the existence of God by drawing a conclusion from a set of premises.)

7. The Natural Law Argument

There are natural laws (laws of nature). Where there are laws, there must be a lawgiver. Therefore, such a lawgiver, God, exists.

III. REMARKS ON THE ARGUMENTS

Let us now turn to some remarks on, and clarifications of, the classical arguments. I shall start with the second (the first-cause argument) and then at the end return to the first (the ontological argument).

2. *The First-Cause Argument.* We have seen that there are two versions of the cosmological (or first-cause) argument. What is the difference between the two? The major difference is this. Let us suppose that we were to start at the present moment and list all the events occurring within the universe. And let us further suppose we could determine the entire configuration of events which caused the present configuration of events. And let us suppose further that we could continue to trace back the configuration of causes for those prior events, and then the configuration of causes for *those* events, and so on.

The *first* version of the first-cause argument claims that there must be an end to this backward progression of causes and effects; for if there were not an end, the succession of causes and effects would be infinite. But according to the first version, an infinite series of causes and events is unintelligible and hence impossible. Why is it said that an infinite series of causes and events is *unintelligible*? For this reason. According to the first form of the argument, what we are seeking is an explanation of something, namely, the existence of the universe. Now, if we say the cause of, and hence explanation for, the universe is X, and the cause of and explanation for X is X', and the cause of and explanation for X' is X", and so on, to infinity, then we never arrive at an adequate explanation. So we have not given any explanation at all. Hence an infinite series of causes and events is unintelligible in that *it explains nothing*. Hence such an infinite series must be impossible. It makes no sense. There must be a satisfactory end point for an explanation to make sense. According to the argument, this end point is found in God.

The *second* version of the argument allows that there *could be* an infinite succession of causes and events which make up the history of the entire universe. But according to the second version, we still must seek a first cause in the sense that there must be a cause for the whole succession. That is to say, even if the universe existed *infinitely in time*, there must nevertheless be something which explains why the universe exists *at all*. As someone put it, what this version seeks is an answer to the question, Why is there a universe at all, rather than nothing?

It is necessary to clarify what is meant by the expression 'first cause'. This expression may mean either: (a) temporally first cause or (b) ultimate (or metaphysically) first cause. What is the difference between the two conceptions? And which of them is being argued for in the first-cause argument? As I have noted above, a temporal first cause would be one which was simply the first in the succession of causes and events, or, the cause of the initial configuration of events making up the universe. But an ultimate first cause would be one which explains why the entire succession of causes and events exists. Such a first cause does not merely provide an answer to the question, "How did the universe come into being?" or "At what point did the universe come into being?" Rather, it attempts to provide an answer to the question, "Why does a universe exist at all?"

Which of these two notions is being argued for in the first-cause argument? It could be maintained that in the first version, God is held to be a temporal first cause. But someone might object, "If that were true, then God would be a thing or event within the universe. But God, by definition, is conceived as transcendent to the universe and the creator of the universe." Further, as noted above, the second form of the argument grants that the universe may be an infinite succession of causes and events. Hence, in answer to our question, we see that the first cause must be what we have called an ultimate (or metaphysical) first cause. Again, the question is, Why is there a universe at all, whether it be finite *or* infinite? What accounts for there being a universe at all, rather than nothing?

3. *The Argument from Contingency.* As I have noted above, the argument from contingency can be considered to be a variant of the first-cause (cosmological) argument. The difference between it and the two versions of the cosmological argument is primarily one of emphasis. The first-cause argument stresses the sheer existence of the natural universe. According to this argument, the mere fact of its existence requires a cause. The argument from

contingency stresses the contingency of the universe and of everything within the universe. According to it, everything within the universe is dependent for its existence upon the existence of something else. Nothing *within* the universe is self-sufficient; nothing within the universe is the ground of its own existence. Similarly, according to this argument, there is nothing about the universe as a *whole* to indicate that it could be the ground of its own existence. That is to say, there is nothing about the universe as a whole to indicate that it contains the reason for its existence within itself. Hence, the universe itself must also be contingent; that is, it must be dependent upon something else for its existence. This something is God.

4. *The Design Argument.* Let us now consider the design (teleological) argument. How does it differ from the first-cause or the contingency arguments? Once again, the first-cause argument proceeds from the sheer existence of the natural universe. According to it, since the universe is contingent, the mere fact that it exists means that it must be explained. Therefore, one might say that the data on which the cosmological and contingency arguments are based are constituted by the existence of the universe, apart from whatever specific features it might have. But the design argument proceeds from certain *characteristics* of the existent universe, namely the orderliness, design, and purposiveness of certain phenomena in the universe and of the universe itself. It is not merely the fact that the universe exists which requires an explanation. Rather, it is the fact that the universe is orderly, and (more important) *purposive*, and evidently the product of intelligent design, which requires an explanation.

In what sense is the universe not merely orderly but *purposive* and thus the product of intelligent design (and creation)? It is purposive in that throughout the universe we note an arrangement or *adaptation of means to ends*. Consider an analogy. Suppose you were walking on a proverbial desert island (perhaps after a shipwreck) and you came upon an unusual antique watch. You immediately infer that it didn't just happen accidentally, but rather that someone must have designed and created it. Why? Not just because it is put together in an orderly way but because the parts are so arranged as to constitute an adaptation of means to end. That is, this part meshes with that one, which in turn was designed to make yet another part move, and so on, until the whole arrangement is an admirable adaptation of various means to the end of telling the time. Similarly with regard to the universe. We note many features of things in the universe and of the universe itself, which show an adaption of means to ends, for example, the existence of two sexes for the purpose of procreation of the species or the intricate construction of our eyes for the end of seeing, and so on. Similarly, it is maintained that the universe as a whole is also not merely orderly, but intricate and purposive. Hence, it too must be the product of intelligent planning and design by a vastly greater intelligence than man, namely, God.

It should be noted that the design argument is an argument by (or from) analogy. It says: Take any object of human contrivance, for example, a house or a watch. Because it is purposive, we rightfully infer it must have come about as the result of intelligent and purposeful design, on the part of a designer. Similarly for the universe. Because the universe, and much within it, is purposive, we also must rightfully infer that it could have come about only as the result of an even greater intelligent and purposeful design by an even greater designer, God. In short:

watch : watch designer/maker :: universe : universe designer/maker (God)

5. *The Moral Argument.* The first-cause and the related contingency arguments and the design argument all fall into one category. The moral argument and the argument from religious experience both fall into another. What is the difference between the two categories? The first-cause, contingency, and design arguments—if valid—would apply to the universe even if humans did not exist. That is to say, their logical worth depends solely on the existence of and certain features of the natural universe. But the moral and religious experience arguments pertain to phenomena which, as far as we know, are uniquely human. Let us first consider the moral argument. As we have noted in the previous section, there are two forms of this argument.

According to the *first* form, it is the fact that people at times have a sense of unqualified moral obligation which is felt as coming from outside of themselves, which necessitates the existence of God. Why? Because no naturalistic account in terms of human needs and behavior can fully explain this sense of unqualified obligation, this feeling of being under a compelling moral law.

The *second* form of the moral argument continues from this point and makes a second, but related, one. According to the second form, as people seek to fulfill their unqualified obligation, their duty to do good, they sometimes find that in their pursuit of such good, justice gets negated. How so? In order for the world to be fully just, there must be some correlation or agreement between pursuing our duty and acting in accordance with it, on the one hand, and achieving happiness, on the other. Now, it is a regrettable fact that, in this world, that correlation does not always occur; there are some who maximize their pursuit of the good and yet suffer greatly. Therefore, according to this argument, there must be a way of guaranteeing that such persons will receive their due reward at some other time or place. Therefore, God must exist in order to guarantee that justice is done. It will be apparent to the reader why this second form of the moral argument is sometimes referred to as the argument for remedying of injustice.[3]

6. *The Religious Experience Argument.* Throughout history many persons have claimed to have had unusual experiences in which they claimed that they had a personal and immediate encounter with a divine being. Sometimes when these experiences are unusually intense, they have a quality about them which is ineffable; that is to say, these experiences cannot be

---

[3]See the essay by Bertrand Russell in Part Six of this volume.

described or put into words. Such experiences are commonly referred to as *mystical* experiences. It is said that such experiences provide those who have them with direct awareness of God. Hence, no arguments on behalf of God's existence are needed; all such arguments are superfluous. As noted in the previous section, strictly speaking, this is not an *argument* on behalf of God's existence. It is, rather, a *claim* that the experiences in question are experiences of an objective and divine being, God. However, this is obviously a striking claim that itself needs to be supported by arguments. In short, according to this argument, what we are entitled to conclude is not the statement that God exists—something that is supposed to need no proof—but the statement that religious experiences really do provide those who have them with a direct and immediate awareness of an objective God.

7. *The Natural Law Argument.* The above arguments constitute the major classical arguments for the existence of God. For the sake of completeness, I have included in the previous section one more argument—the natural law argument. Since this argument is so brief, no comments need be made with regard to it.

Earlier, I stated that I would defer my remarks on the first of the classical arguments. I now turn to that task.

1. *The Ontological Argument.* All the previous arguments started with some *data*, whether it was the universe itself, some aspect of the universe, some phenomena in the natural universe, or some phenomena pertaining to human beings. From these data, these various arguments conclude that God must exist. The reader may have noticed that the ontological argument is completely different from the others. How so? The ontological argument begins with nothing else than our *idea*, or *definition*, of God and then concludes from that alone that God must exist. In other words, according to this argument, you need not look out to the world or aspects of the world to draw the conclusion that God exists. Rather, all that you need to do is to have a clear idea, conception, or definition of God; and once you have it, you will from it be able to deduce, or perhaps see, that God must be existent.

As I have noted above, this argument is sometimes referred to as the *a priori* argument for the existence of God. Similarly, the other arguments for God have been referred to as *a posteriori* arguments. In what sense are the latter *a posteriori*, and in what sense is the ontological argument *a priori*?

The reader may be familiar with the notion of *a priori* and *a posteriori* *statements* (or propositions). These have been defined as follows [see the Appendix to the Preview to Part One of this volume]:

1. A statement is known *a posteriori* if you have to appeal to experience to find out whether that statement is true.

2. A statement is known *a priori* if you do *not* have to appeal to experience to find out whether that statement is true.

Thus, the notions of *a priori* and *a posteriori* statements are common and familiar. But the notion of *a priori* and *a posteriori arguments* is less familiar. Let us ask: In what sense is the ontological argument an *a priori* one and the remaining arguments *a posteriori* ones? The conclusions of the cosmological, design, etc., arguments are based on facts—certain features of the world which one can discover by turning to experience, for example, the experience that a universe exists, that it is purposive, and so on. The facts are described in the premises of those arguments. Thus, the claim is: We can know the conclusion—"God exists"—to be true because it follows from those facts which we experience. But according to the ontological argument, we can draw that conclusion—"God exists"—without turning to any facts. We do not have to consult experience. Merely from our understanding of words, from our idea or definition of God—and from that alone—we can know that God does and *must* exist.

IV. A DEFENSE OF THE ARGUMENTS

In Section I, I said that my defense of theism will proceed by way of defending the classical arguments for the existence of God. I also said that my defense of the arguments would follow an earlier defense of them by Julian Hartt. Hartt classifies the *main* arguments into three categories:

A. The *a posteriori* arguments (cosmological, teleological, and moral arguments)
B. The *a priori* argument (ontological argument)
C. The appeal to religious experience

Let us take these in order.

A. The *A Posteriori* Arguments

Hartt's defense of these three arguments is extremely interesting and worthy of careful study. He mentions that: (a) there are several all-pervasive, broad characteristics of the world (universe)—or features of the world—which we experience; (b) each of the three *a posteriori* arguments focuses on one (or more) of these features; and (c) in each case, the feature(s) can only be explained by, and thus necessitate(s) the existence of, a being who is transcendent to the universe: God.

What are these features? And which of the three arguments focuses on which feature? We may put this in the form of a table:

Argument	Feature (of universe)
1. First-Cause (Cosmological)	finitude; contingency
2. Design (Teleological)	purposiveness; purposeful adaptation and arrangement

Argument	Feature (of universe)
3. Moral	(real) moral values; unqualified obligation

Again, in Hartt's view, these are objective features of the world (universe) which we experience, and each necessitates the existence of a (transcendent and infinite) God.

1. *The First-Cause (Cosmological) Argument.* The first-cause argument calls attention to and begins with the feature of *finitude* and the related feature of *contingency*. The argument also makes use of and rests on the notion of a *first cause* in connection with those features. Thus we find three variations. These different themes can give rise to several forms of the first-cause argument, or all of them can be included in a single argument. I propose to defend the cosmological argument by reformulating it as follows:

Everything in the universe is finite.

Whatever is finite is limited.*

Hence, whatever is limited cannot be the cause of its own existence.

Everything in the universe is contingent.

Whatever is contingent is dependent on something else for its existence.

Hence, whatever is contingent cannot be the cause of its own existence.

The totality of things making up the universe is also finite and contingent.

Thus, the totality (universe) must also have a cause for its existence.

Since it cannot be the cause of its own existence, the cause must be something external to the universe.

That is, since the universe cannot contain the reason for its existence within itself, the reason for its existence must be something external to it.

Hence, there must exist an infinite and self-subsistent (non-contingent) being who is the cause of the universe.

Unlike that which is finite and contingent, such a being must exist necessarily.

Such a being is commonly called God.

Therefore, there exists an infinite, necessary, and uncaused cause—God.

Someone may object: But why does the universe as a totality need a cause or explanation? Why can it not have existed infinitely in time? I reply: let us suppose it did.[4] Then what the cosmological argument seeks is to provide answers to some questions: (1) Why does anything exist at all? (2) Why does it

---

*[Note that this characterization of 'finite' is one which has nothing to do with another use of 'finite' which makes reference to time.—Eds.]

[4]See Section II, First-Cause Argument, second version.

exist as it does rather than some other way? Or (1) Why is there a world at all? (2) Why is there this kind of universe rather than some other one? The answer is: Because of the purpose of an unlimited, infinite, and necessary being—an ultimate first cause which is itself uncaused—God.

In summary: Why does the fact that the universe is finite and contingent necessitate God's existence? The answer is that whatever is finite is limited. Hence, it cannot cause itself. And whatever is contingent is dependent on something else for its existence. Hence, it cannot be the cause of its own existence. The universe—as well as everything in it—is finite and contingent. There is nothing about it to indicate that it could be the cause of its own existence. Since it cannot be the cause of its own existence, it must have been caused by something else—a being external to the universe. Therefore, such a being must exist: an unlimited, necessary, and uncaused cause—God.

2. *The Design (Teleological) Argument.* The design argument calls attention to another feature of the universe, that of *purposiveness*, or purposeful adaptation of means to ends.

The word *teleological* comes from the Greek word *telos*, meaning purpose or goal. Theism is a teleological metaphysics through and through. Hence, it is understandable and natural for there to be arguments which focus on the notion of purpose. Among them is the teleological argument for the existence of God. This argument claims that the many features of design, purpose, and adaptation in the universe are indications of a Cosmic Intelligence or Mind—God—which designed, planned, and brought the universe into existence. I propose to defend the teleological argument by reformulating it as follows:

> Suppose that while walking along an ocean beach, or a barren field, we come upon an object, such as a watch.
>
> If we examine the watch, we find that it shows evidence of purpose and design.
>
> We detect orderliness and intricacy.
>
> We find an adaptation of means to ends (the parts are arranged to work together to enable the hands to move and to enable us to tell time).
>
> All of this is evidence of rationality and design.
>
> Hence, there exists a rational being who designed and brought the watch into being.

Similarly:

> Look out at the universe and the things within it.
>
> The universe also shows evidence of design and purpose.
>
> We detect orderliness and intricacy.
>
> More importantly, we find purposiveness: a marvelous adaptation of means to ends.
>
> An example of such purposeful adaptation is the existence of two sexes for the end of procreation or the structure of the eye for the end of seeing.

All this is also evidence of rationality and design.

Hence, there must exist a rational being who designed and brought the universe into existence.

That is, there must exist a Cosmic Designer—God.

It may be objected: But could not the universe have resulted from chance? I reply: Although there may be chance *in* the universe, the universe *itself* is not the product of chance but of *intelligent purpose*. The environment in which we find ourselves is not a fortuitously functioning mechanism; nor is it an organism. It is imbued with *purpose*. Everyone admits that humans show evidence of mind and purposive behavior—as in designing and making a house. But we cannot suppose that purposeful activity is limited to humans and that everything else in nature is blind or the result of sheer chance. Why not? Because *our* minds, our intelligent planning, have not made the universe. Therefore, there must exist a being who designed the universe and brought it into existence.

In summary: Why does the fact that the universe is purposeful necessitate God's existence? The reason is that whatever is purposeful shows signs of intelligence—mind. Hence, what is purposive cannot have come about accidentally, or from something non-purposive. Hence, the only way to explain the purposiveness in the universe is: It got here because of the thought, design, and activity of a Cosmic Intelligence—God.

3. *The Moral Argument.* The features of finitude and contingency gave rise to the first-cause arguments. The feature of purposiveness gave rise to the design argument. The feature of the universe which the moral argument calls attention to is that of *moral values*, or the recognition and pursuit of moral values. I propose to defend the moral argument by reformulating it as follows:

> Our moral experience reveals certain data such as the sense of *unqualified obligation*.
>
> That moral experience discloses a world deeper and richer than our natural world.
>
> At times we feel called upon to make an unqualified response to what is right and good—even if we have to forfeit happiness or life.
>
> The good person does his duty, no matter what befalls him.
>
> These data of our moral experiences make no sense unless a transcendent being exists as the "shaper and governor" of the moral environment which in turn shapes and molds us.
>
> Hence, such a being—God—exists.

A second form of the moral argument continues:

> As we saw, we sometimes feel called upon to respond to the good, even if we have to at times forfeit happiness, or, indeed, life.

Thus, sometimes the pursuit of such good by humans gets frustrated.

If the world constantly frustrated our pursuit of the good, then it would not be the good.

Therefore the world in which this seems to happen is not the ultimately real world.

That world is one in which moral worth is "honored all the way through."

It must be a real world of genuine moral value and under the control of a supreme mind for that to happen.

Therefore, such a supreme mind—God—exists.

Or alternately:

We find ourselves under a sense of unqualified obligation to do our duty, to fulfill the highest good.

In order for the world to be a truly just world, there must be an agreement between our acting in accordance with our duty and the happiness we experience.

In this world, such an agreement of virtue with commensurate happiness does not always occur.

Hence, there must be a guarantor to ensure that those who best fulfill their duty will receive a reward (happiness) commensurate with their virtue.

Therefore, such a guarantor—God—must exist.

It may be objected: "But cannot our sense of obligation and our moral values be explained naturalistically, as the result of parental teaching, conditioning, etc.?" I reply: The data from which the moral argument begins are not just a sense of obligation, but of *unqualified* obligation. At times we find ourselves in a situation in which we are forced to choose and act by the intensity and urgency of the obligation. We think: "I must do this, even though I'd rather not." Furthermore, many of the decisions which we make in such cases *go against* what we were taught or conditioned to do. Hence no naturalistic explanations will work.

In summary: Why does the fact that the human realm of the universe is imbued with moral values necessitate the existence of God? Because: (1) We have a sense of *unqualified obligation*. This would make no sense unless God existed as the shaper and governor of morality. (2) Our pursuit of the good sometimes gets frustrated. If this constantly occurred, then it would not really be the good. Hence, the world in which this seems to happen cannot be real. So there must be a real world of moral value under the control of a supreme mind. Therefore such a mind—God—exists.

And perhaps: In order for the world to be just, there must be happiness commensurate with virtue. That does not always happen in this world. Hence, there must be a guarantor who will remedy this injustice in another world. Hence, such a guarantor—God—exists.

B. The *A Priori* (Ontological) Argument

As we have seen, the three *a posteriori* arguments are based on some experienced features of the world or some all-pervasive characteristics of the universe. By contrast, the *a priori* (or ontological) argument is based merely on the definition or idea (or concept) of God. It proceeds directly from that definition to the conclusion that such a being, God, really exists. That is, from the very idea or correct definition of God we may infer, or perhaps directly see or intuit, that God must exist. What is that idea or definition? God is "that than which nothing greater can be conceived." Or more simply, God is the greatest conceivable being: a being who has all perfections. Hence, the argument is:

> God is that than which none greater can be conceived.
>
> (God is the greatest conceivable being.)
>
> If such a being were only an idea in our minds, or only a possibility, then a greater being could be conceived, namely, one that actually existed, in reality, and not merely as an idea.
>
> But by definition, no being can be greater than God.
>
> Therefore, God must necessarily exist, not just as an idea in our minds, but in reality.

This argument does not have many advocates—for good reason. Its significance does not lie in its logical force. Hence, it has been accepted, by some, because of its religious character. It embodies the religious sentiment that God is all-sufficient, a wholly perfect being; that God is the explanation of his own nature and existence. The argument then tries to set forth what is apprehended in the very idea of God.

C. The Religious Experience Argument

At various times throughout history some have rejected the traditional, rational arguments for God. In place of such arguments they have presented arguments based on religious experience. Such an argument claims:

> There are irreducibly religious data which are given in religious experiences.
>
> These must be accounted for by any comprehensive and acceptable philosophy.
>
> The only adequate way of accounting for these data is the reality of God.
>
> Therefore, God exists.

What are these irreducibly religious data? (1) The deeply ingrained impulsion to worship, derived from something in the universe that arouses awe and reverence. (2) The mystical (direct) awareness of God in intense experiences. (3) The practical results of the religious life as manifested in certain persons. These data can be adequately understood only if they are seen to be the effect in persons of an encounter with and relation to God.

The religious experience argument also does not have the logical force of the *a posteriori* arguments. But, like the *a priori* (ontological) argument, it too has religious value. The religious experience argument maintains that: If God exists it is possible that all persons should have a dim awareness of him. And it is possible that this awareness should at times be clarified or sharpened in mystical experiences. As Hartt said, "If God exists, then the prime concern of religious activity and ultimately of all our activity is to bring us into the most positive and productive relationships with Him in whom is fullness of life. If God exists, then the 'data' of religious experience are in the main veridical and reliable. And then the arguments from religious experience may test the data by the theistic affirmation and weigh the theistic affirmation by the light of religious experience."[5]

V. CONCLUSION

In this essay I have been concerned to give a philosophical defense of theism by way of stating, explaining, and supporting the classical arguments for the existence of God. For the support of these arguments I have relied heavily on the earlier defense of them by Julian Hartt.

Someone may object: "But you haven't really proved theism to be true." If the objector means an absolutely conclusive proof, then indeed I have not given such a proof. I doubt that such a proof is possible. What I have tried to do is to present a defense of theism which makes religious belief in God to be plausible. Such belief, I maintain, is not utterly irrational; nor is it a matter of blind faith. Whether the reader finds my defense to be acceptable is for him or her to decide.[6]

---

[5]J. Hartt, Theism and the Existence of God, section IV. In Auer and Hartt.

[6]I would like to express my deep appreciation to John Walker for his many comments on and criticisms of this essay. In many ways the final version is a collaborative effort because of the help he gave. I would also like to express my gratitude to Steve Worringham for his many suggestions and for his help. Finally I would like to express my abiding gratitude to Steven Mumford for his constant help.—E. K. D.

27 / The Case for Atheism

ERNEST NAGEL

Ernest Nagel (1901–1985) was a professor of philosophy at Columbia University. In his lifetime he wrote several books in the area of philosophy of science and many articles on various topics that appeared in philosophical journals. The following essay is one he wrote for an anthology on comparative religions.

I

I must begin by stating what sense I am attaching to the word "atheism," and how I am construing the theme of this essay. I shall understand by "atheism" a critique and a denial of the major claims of all varieties of theism. And by theism I shall mean the view which holds, as one writer has expressed it, "that the heavens and the earth and all that they contain owe their existence and continuance in existence to the wisdom and will of a supreme, self-consistent, omnipotent, omniscient, righteous, and benevolent being, who is distinct from, and independent of, what he has created." Several things immediately follow from these definitions.

In the first place, atheism is not necessarily an irreligious concept, for theism is just one among many views concerning the nature and origin of the world. The denial of theism is logically compatible with a religious outlook upon life, and is in fact characteristic of some of the great historical religions. For as readers of this volume will know, early Buddhism is a religion which does not subscribe to any doctrine about a god; and there are pantheistic religions and philosophies which, because they deny that God is a being separate from and independent of the world, are not theistic in the sense of the word explained above.

The second point to note is that atheism is not to be identified with sheer unbelief, or with disbelief in some particular creed of a religious group. Thus, a child who has received no religious instruction and has never heard about God is not an atheist—for he is not denying any theistic claims. Similarly, an adult who has withdrawn from the faith of his fathers without reflection or because of frank indifference to any theological issue is also not an atheist— for such an adult is not challenging theism and is not professing any views on the subject. . . .

One final word of preliminary explanation. I propose to examine some *philosophic* concepts of atheism, and I am not interested in the slightest in the many considerations atheists have advanced against the evidences for some particular religious and theological doctrine—for example, against the truth of the Christian story. What I mean by "philosophical" in the present context is that the views I shall consider are directed against any form of theism, and have their origin and basis in a logical analysis of the theistic position, and in a comprehensive account of the world believed to be wholly intelligible without the adoption of a theistic hypothesis. . . .

II

As I see it, atheistic philosophies fall into two major groups: (1) those which hold that the theistic doctrine is meaningful, but reject it either on the ground that (a) the positive evidence for it is insufficient or (b) the negative evidence is quite overwhelming; and (2) those who hold that the theistic thesis is not even meaningful, and reject it (a) as just nonsense or (b) as literally meaningless, but interpreting it as a symbolic rendering of human ideals, thus reading the theistic thesis in a sense that most believers in theism would disavow. It will not be possible in the limited space at my disposal to discuss the second category of atheistic critiques; and in any event, most of the traditional atheistic critiques of theism belong to the first group.

But before turning to the philosophical examination of the major classical arguments for theism, it is well to note that such philosophical critiques do not quite convey the passion with which atheists have often carried on their analyses of theistic views. For historically, atheism has been, and indeed continues to be, a form of social and political protest, directed as much against institutionalized religion as against theistic doctrine. Atheism has been, in effect, a moral revulsion against the undoubted abuses of the secular power exercised by religious leaders and religious institutions.

Religious authorities have opposed the correction of glaring injustices, and encouraged politically and socially reactionary policies. Religious institutions have been havens of obscurantist thought and centers for the dissemination of intolerance. Religious creeds have been used to set limits to free inquiry, to perpetuate inhumane treatment of the ill and the underprivileged, and to support moral doctrines insensitive to human suffering.

These indictments may not tell the whole story about the historical significance of religion; but they are at least an important part of the story. The refutation of theism has thus seemed to many an indispensable step not only toward liberating men's minds from superstition but also toward achieving a more equitable reordering of society. And no account of even the more philosophical aspects of atheistic thought is adequate which does not give proper recognition to the powerful social motives that actuate many atheistic arguments.

But however this may be, I want now to discuss three classical arguments for the existence of God, arguments which have constituted at least a partial basis for theistic commitments. As long as theism is defended simply as dogma, asserted as a matter of direct revelation or as the deliverance of authority, belief in the dogma is impregnable to rational argument. In fact, however, reasons are frequently advanced in support of the theistic creed, and these reasons have been the subject of acute philosophical critiques.

III

[1. The Cosmological Argument /] One of the oldest intellectual defenses of theism is the cosmological argument, also known as the argument from a first cause. Briefly put, the argument runs as follows. Every event must have a cause. Hence an event A must have as cause some event B, which in turn must have a cause C, and so on. But if there is no end to this backward progression of causes, the progression will be infinite; and in the opinion of those who use this argument, an infinite series of actual events is unintelligible and absurd. Hence there must be a first cause, and this first cause is God, the initiator of all change in the universe.

[*Criticism.*] The argument is an ancient one . . . and it has impressed many generations of exceptionally keen minds. The argument is nonetheless a weak reed on which to rest the theistic thesis. Let us waive any question concerning the validity of the principle that every event has a cause, for though the question is important its discussion would lead us far afield. [1.] However, if the principle is assumed, it is surely incongruous to postulate a first cause as a way of escaping from the coils of an infinite series. For if everything must have a cause, why does not God require one for His own existence? [2.] The standard answer is that He does not need any, because He is self-caused.* But if God can be self-caused, why cannot the world be self-caused? Why do we require a God transcending the world to bring the world into existence and to initiate changes in it? On the other hand, the supposed inconceivability and absurdity of an infinite series of regressive causes will be admitted by no one who has competent familiarity with the modern mathematical analysis of infinity. The cosmological argument does not stand up under scrutiny.

[2. The Ontological Argument /] The second "proof" of God's existence is usually called the ontological argument. It too has a long history going back to early Christian days, though it acquired great prominence only in medieval times. The argument can be stated in several ways, one of which is the following. Since God is conceived to be omnipotent, he is a perfect being. A perfect being is defined as one whose essence or nature lacks no attributes (or properties) whatsoever, one whose nature is complete in every respect. But it is evident that we have an idea of a perfect being, for we have just defined the idea; and since this is so, the argument continues, God who is the perfect

---

*[Nagel uses the wrong word here. In place of "self-caused," substitute "uncaused." The cosmological argument holds that God is uncaused, not self-caused. Also in this paragraph and elsewhere, by "world" Nagel means universe, not the earth.—Eds.]

being must exist. Why must he? Because his existence follows from his defined nature. For if God lacked the attribute of existence, he would be lacking at least one attribute, and would therefore not be perfect. To sum up, since we have an idea of God as a perfect being, God must exist.

[*Criticism.*] There are several ways of approaching this argument, but I shall consider only one. The argument was exploded by the 18th-century philosopher Immanuel Kant. The substance of Kant's criticism is that it is just a confusion to say that existence is an attribute, and that though the *word* "existence" may occur as the grammatical predicate in a sentence, no attribute is being predicated of a thing when we say that the thing exists or has existence. Thus, to use Kant's example, when we think of $100 we are thinking of the nature of this sum of money; but the nature of $100 remains the same whether we have $100 in our pockets or not. Accordingly, we are confounding grammar with logic if we suppose that some characteristic is being attributed to the nature of $100 when we say that a $100 bill exists in someone's pocket.

To make the point clearer, consider another example. When we say that a lion has a tawny color, we are predicating a certain attribute of the animal, and similarly when we say that the lion is fierce or is hungry. But when we say the lion exists, all that we are saying is that something is (or has the nature of) a lion; we are not specifying an attribute which belongs to the nature of anything that is a lion. In short, the word "existence" does not signify any attribute, and in consequence no attribute that belongs to the nature of anything. Accordingly, it does not follow from the assumption that we have an idea of a perfect being that such a being exists. For the idea of a perfect being does not involve the attribute of existence as a constituent of that idea, since there is no such attribute. The ontological argument thus has a serious leak, and it can hold no water.

IV

[3. The Teleological Argument /] The two arguments discussed thus far are purely dialectical, and attempt to establish God's existence without any appeal to empirical data. The next argument, called the argument from design, is different in character, for it is based on what purports to be empirical evidence. . . .

One variant of it calls attention to the remarkable way in which different things and processes in the world are integrated with each other, and concludes that this mutual "fitness" of things can be explained only by the assumption of a divine architect who planned the world and everything in it. For example, living organisms can maintain themselves in a variety of environments, and do so in virtue of their delicate mechanisms which adapt the organisms to all sorts of environmental changes. There is thus an intricate pattern of means and ends throughout the animate world. But the existence of this pattern is unintelligible, so the argument runs, except on the hypothesis that the pattern has been deliberately instituted by a Supreme Designer. If we find a watch in some deserted spot, we do not think it came into existence by chance, and we do not hesitate to conclude that an intelligent creature designed and made it. But the world and all its contents exhibit mechanisms and mutual adjustments that are far more complicated and subtle than are those of a watch. Must we not therefore conclude that these things too have a Creator?

[*Criticism.*] [1.] The conclusion of this argument is based on an inference from analogy: The watch and the world are alike in possessing a congruence of parts and an adjustment of means to ends; the watch has a watch-maker; hence the world has a world-maker. But is the analogy a good one? Let us once more waive some important issues, in particular the issue of whether the universe is the unified system such as the watch admittedly is. [2.] And let us concentrate on the question of what is the ground for our assurance that watches do not come into existence except through the operations of intelligent manufacturers. The answer is plain. We have never run across a watch which has not been deliberately made by someone. But the situation is nothing like this in the case of the innumerable animate and inanimate systems with which we are familiar. [3.] Even in the case of living organisms, though they are generated by their parent organisms, the parents do not "make" their progeny in the same sense in which watchmakers make watches. And once this point is clear, the inference from the existence of living organisms to the existence of a Supreme Designer no longer appears credible.

[4.] Moreover, the argument loses all its force if the facts which the hypothesis of a divine designer is supposed to explain can be understood on the basis of a better supported assumption. And indeed, such an alternative explanation is one of the achievements of Darwinian biology. For Darwin showed that one can account for the variety of biological species, as well as for their adaptations to their environments, without invoking a divine creator and acts of special creation. The Darwinian theory explains the diversity of biological species in terms of chance variations in the structure of organisms, and of a mechanism of selection which retains those variant forms that possess some advantages for survival. The evidence for these assumptions is considerable; and developments subsequent to Darwin have only strengthened the case for a thoroughly naturalistic explanation of the facts of biological adaptation. In any event, this version of the argument from design has nothing to recommend it. . . .

V

[4. The Moral Argument /] The inconclusiveness of the three classical arguments for the existence of God was already made evident by Kant, in a manner substantially not different from the above discussion. There are, however, other types of arguments for theism that have been influential in the history of thought, two of which I wish to consider, even if only briefly.

Indeed, though Kant destroyed the classical intellectual foundations for theism, he himself invented a fresh argument for it. Kant's attempted proof is not intended to be a purely theoretical demonstration, and is based on the supposed facts of our moral nature. It has exerted an enormous influence on subsequent theological speculation. In barest outline, the argument is as follows. According to Kant, we are subject not only to physical laws like the rest of nature, but also to moral ones. These moral laws are categorical imperatives, which we must heed not because of their utilitarian consequences but simply because as autonomous moral agents it is our duty to accept them as binding. However, Kant was keenly aware that though virtue may be its reward, the virtuous man (that is, the man who acts out of a sense of duty and in conformity with the moral law) does not always receive his just desserts in this world; nor did he shut his eyes to the fact that evil men frequently enjoy the best things this world has to offer. In short, virtue does not always reap happiness. Nevertheless, the highest human good is the realization of happiness commensurate with one's virtue; and Kant believed that it is a practical postulate of the moral life to promote this good. But what can guarantee that the highest good is realizable? Such a guarantee can be found only in God, who must therefore exist if the highest good is not to be a fatuous ideal. The existence of an omnipotent, omniscient, and omnibenevolent God is thus postulated as a necessary condition for the possibility of a moral life.

[*Criticism.*] Despite the prestige this argument has acquired, it is difficult to grant it any force. It is enough to postulate God's existence. But as Bertrand Russell observed in another connection, postulation has all the advantages of theft over honest toil. No postulation carries with it any assurance that what is postulated is actually the case. And though we may postulate God's existence as a means to guaranteeing the possibility of realizing happiness together with virtue, the postulation establishes neither the actual realizability of this ideal nor the fact of his existence. Moreover, the argument is not made more cogent when we recognize that it is based squarely on the highly dubious conception that considerations of utility and human happiness must not enter into the determination of what is morally obligatory. . . .

[5. The Argument from Religious Experience /] One further type of argument, pervasive in much Protestant theological literature, deserves brief mention. Arguments of this type take their point of departure from the psychology of religious and mystical experience. Those who have undergone such experiences often report that during the experience they feel themselves to be in the presence of the divine and holy, that they lose their sense of self-identity and become merged with some fundamental reality, or that they enjoy a feeling of total dependence upon some ultimate power. The overwhelming sense of transcending one's finitude, which characterizes such vivid periods of life, and of coalescing with some ultimate source of all existence, is then taken to be compelling evidence for the existence of a supreme being. In a variant form of this argument, other theologians have identified God as the object which satisfies the commonly experienced need for integrating one's scattered and conflicting impulses into a coherent unity, or as the subject which is of ultimate concern to us. In short, a proof of God's existence is found in the occurrence of certain distinctive experiences.

[*Criticism.*] It would be flying in the face of well-attested facts were one to deny that such experiences frequently occur. But do these facts constitute evidence for the conclusion based on them? Does the fact, for example, that an individual experiences a profound sense of direct contact with an alleged transcendent ground of all reality, constitute competent evidence for the claim that there is such a ground and that it is the immediate cause of the experience? If well-established canons for evaluating evidence are accepted, the answer is surely negative. No one will dispute that many men do have vivid experiences in which such things as ghosts or pink elephants appear before them; but only the hopelessly credulous will without further ado count such experiences as establishing the existence of ghosts and pink elephants. To establish the existence of such things, evidence is required that is obtained under controlled conditions and that can be confirmed by independent inquirers. Again, though a man's report that he is suffering pain may be taken at face value, one cannot take at face value the claim, were he to make it, that it is the food he ate which is the cause (or a contributory cause) of his felt pain— not even if the man were to report a vivid feeling of abdominal disturbance. And similarly, an overwhelming feeling of being in the presence of the Divine is evidence enough for admitting the genuineness of such feeling; it is no evidence for the claim that a supreme being with a substantial existence independent of the experience is the cause of the experience.

VI

Thus far the discussion has been concerned with *noting inadequacies in various arguments widely used to support theism.* However, much atheistic criticism is also directed toward *exposing incoherencies in the very thesis of theism.* I want therefore to consider this aspect of the atheistic critique, though I will restrict myself to the central difficulty in the theistic position, which arises from the simultaneous attribution of omnipotence, omniscience, and omnibenevolence to the Deity. The difficulty is that of reconciling these attributes with the occurrence of evil in the world. Accordingly, the question to which I now turn is whether, despite the existence of evil, it is possible to construct a theodicy which will justify the ways of an infinitely powerful and just God to man. . . .

I do not believe it is possible to reconcile the alleged omnipotence and omnibenevolence of God with the unvarnished facts of human existence. In point of fact, many theologians have concurred in this conclusion; for in order to escape from the difficulty which the traditional attributes of God present, they have assumed that God is not all-powerful, and that there are limits as to what He can do in his efforts to establish a righteous order in the universe. But whether such a modified theology is better off is doubtful; and in any event, the question still remains whether the facts of human life support the claim that an omnibenevolent Deity, though limited in power, is revealed in the ordering of human history. It is pertinent to note in this connection that though there have been many historians who have made the effort, no historian has yet succeeded in showing to the satisfaction of his professional colleagues that the hypothesis of a Divine Providence is capable of explaining anything which cannot be explained just as well without this hypothesis.

VII

This last remark naturally leads to the question whether, apart from their polemics against theism, philosophical atheists have not shared a common set of positive views, a common set of philosophical convictions which set them off from other groups of thinkers. In one very clear sense of this query the answer is indubitably negative. For there never has been what one might call a "school of atheism" in the way in which there has been a Platonic school or even a Kantian school. . . .

Nevertheless, despite the variety of philosophic positions to which atheists have subscribed at one time or another in the history of thought, it seems to me that atheism is not simply a negative standpoint. At any rate, there is a certain quality of intellectual temper that has characterized, and continues to characterize, many philosophical atheists. . . . I want therefore to conclude this discussion with a brief enumeration of some points of positive doctrine to which by and large philosophical atheists seem to me to subscribe. . . .

In the first place, philosophical atheists reject the assumption that there are disembodied spirits, or that incorporeal entities of any sort can exercise a causal agency. On the contrary, atheists are generally agreed that if we wish to achieve any understanding of what takes place in the universe, we must look to the operations of organized bodies. Accordingly, the various processes taking place in nature, whether animate or inanimate, are to be explained in terms of the properties and structures of identifiable and spatio-temporally located objects. Moreover, the present variety of systems and activities found in the universe is to be accounted for on the basis of the transformations things undergo when they enter into different relations with one another—transformations which often result in the emergence of novel kinds of objects. . . .

In the second place, atheists generally manifest a marked empirical temper, and often take as their ideal the intellectual methods employed in the contemporaneous empirical sciences. Philosophical atheists differ considerably on important points of detail in their account of how responsible claims to knowledge are to be established. But there is substantial agreement among them that controlled sensory observation is the court of final appeal in issues concerning matters of fact. It is indeed this commitment to the use of an empirical method which is the final basis of the atheistic critique of theism. For at bottom this critique seeks to show that we can understand whatever a theistic assumption is alleged to explain, through the use of the proved methods of the positive sciences and without the introduction of empirically un-supported *ad hoc* hypotheses* about a Deity. It is pertinent in this connection to recall a familiar legend about the French mathematical physicist Laplace. According to the story, Laplace made a personal presentation of a copy of his now famous book on celestial mechanics to Napoleon. Napoleon glanced through the volume, and finding no reference to the Deity asked Laplace whether God's existence played any role in the analysis. "Sire, I have no need for that hypothesis," Laplace is reported to have replied. The dismissal of sterile hypothesis characterizes not only the work of Laplace; it is the uniform rule in scientific inquiry. The sterility of the theistic assumption is one of the main burdens of the literature of atheism both ancient and modern.

And finally, atheistic thinkers have generally accepted a utilitarian basis for judging moral issues, and they have exhibited a libertarian attitude toward human needs and impulses. The conceptions of the human good they have advocated are conceptions which are commensurate with the actual capacities of mortal men, so that it is the satisfaction of the complex needs of the human creature which is the final standard for evaluating the validity of a moral ideal or moral prescription.

In consequence, the emphasis of atheistic moral reflection has been this-worldly rather than other-worldly, individualistic rather than authoritarian. The stress upon a good life that must be consummated in this world has made atheists vigorous opponents of moral codes which seek to repress human impulses in the name of some unrealizable other-worldly ideal. The individualism that is so pronounced a strain in many philosophical atheists has made them tolerant of human limitations and sensitive to the plurality of legitimate moral goals. On the other hand, this individualism has certainly not prevented many of them from recognizing the crucial role which institutional arrangements can play in achieving desirable patterns of human living. In consequence, atheists have made important contributions to the development of a climate of opinion favorable to pursuing the values of a liberal civilization, and they have played effective roles in attempts to rectify social injustices.

Atheists cannot build their moral outlook on foundations upon which so many men conduct their lives. In particular, atheism cannot offer the incentives to conduct and the consolations for misfortune which theistic religions supply to their adherents. It can offer no hope of personal immortality, no threats of Divine chastisement, no promise of eventual recompense for injustices suffered, no blueprints to sure salvation. For on its view of the place of man in nature, human excellence and human dignity must be achieved within a finite life-span, or not at all, so that the rewards of moral endeavor must come from the quality of civilized living, and not from some source of dis-bursement that dwells outside of time. Accordingly, atheistic moral relection

---

*[Any hypothesis created for the special purpose of trying to save some theory or proposition.—Eds.]

at its best does not culminate in a quiescent ideal of human perfection, but is a vigorous call to intelligent activity—activity for the sake of realizing human potentialities and for eliminating whatever stands in the way of such realization. . . .

28 / *Why I Am Not a Christian*

BERTRAND RUSSELL

Bertrand Russell (1872–1970) was one of the most famous and prolific philosophers of the twentieth century. He is the author of almost a hundred books on a wide range of philosophical, social, and religious topics. He was well known for his controversial stands on religion, ethics, marriage, and the banning of the nuclear bomb.

I. INTRODUCTION

*T*he subject [of this essay] is "Why I Am Not a Christian."* Perhaps it would be as well, first of all, to try to make out what one means by the word *Christian.* It is used these days in a very loose sense by a great many people. Some people mean no more by it than a person who attempts to live a good life. In that sense I suppose there would be Christians in all sects and creeds; but I do not think that that is the proper sense of the word, if only because it would imply that all the people who are not Christians—all the Buddhists, Confucians, Mohammedans, and so on—are not trying to live a good life. I do not mean by a Christian any person who tries to live decently according to his lights. I think that you must have a certain amount of definite belief before you have a right to call yourself a Christian. The word does not have quite such a full-blooded meaning now as it had in the times of St. Augustine and St. Thomas Aquinas.† In those days, if a man said that he was a Christian it was known what he meant. You accepted a whole collection of creeds which were set out with great precision, and every single syllable of those creeds you believed with the whole strength of your convictions.

*[This essay was first presented as a public lecture.—Eds.]
†[Medieval theologians.—Eds.]

What Is a Christian?

Nowadays it is not quite that. We have to be a little more vague in our meaning of Christianity. I think, however, that there are two different items which are quite essential to anybody calling himself a Christian. The first is one of a dogmatic nature—namely, that you must believe in God and immortality. If you do not believe in those two things, I do not think that you can properly call yourself a Christian. Then, further than that, as the name implies, you must have some kind of belief about Christ. The Mohammedans, for instance, also believe in God and in immortality, and yet they would not call themselves Christians. I think you must have at the very lowest the belief that Christ was, if not divine, at least the best and wisest of men. If you are not going to believe that much about Christ, I do not think you have any right to call yourself a Christian. Of course, there is another sense, which you find in *Whitaker's Almanack* and in geography books, where the population of the world is said to be divided into Christians, Mohammedans, Buddhists, fetish worshipers, and so on; and in that sense we are all Christians. The geography books count us all in, but that is a purely geographical sense, which I suppose we can ignore. Therefore I take it that when I tell you why I am not a Christian I have to tell you two different things: first, why I do not believe in God and in immortality*; and, secondly, why I do not think that Christ was the best and wisest of men, although I grant him a very high degree of moral goodness.

But for the successful efforts of unbelievers in the past, I could not take so elastic a definition of Christianity as that. As I said before, in olden days it had a much more full-blooded sense. For instance, it included the belief in hell. Belief in eternal hell-fire was an essential item of Christian belief until pretty recent times. In this country, as you know, it ceased to be an essential item because of a decision of the Privy Council,† and from that decision the Archbishop of Canterbury and the Archbishop of York dissented; but in this country our religion is settled by Act of Parliament, and therefore the Privy Council was able to override their Graces and hell was no longer necessary to a Christian. Consequently I shall not insist that a Christian must believe in hell.

II. THE EXISTENCE OF GOD

To come to this question of the existence of God: It is a large and serious question, and if I were to attempt to deal with it in any adequate manner I should have to keep you here until Kingdom Come, so that you will have to excuse me if I deal with it in a somewhat summary fashion. You know, of course, that the Catholic Church has laid it down as a dogma that the exis-

---

*[In this essay Russell does not take up the issue of immortality. He does so in a companion essay. Both of these essays were published in *Why I Am Not a Christian and Other Essays*.—Eds.]

†[In England, a body of advisors whose function it is to advise the sovereign in matters of state.—Eds.]

tence of God can be proved by the unaided reason. That is a somewhat curious dogma, but it is one of their dogmas. They had to introduce it because at one time the freethinkers adopted the habit of saying that there were such and such arguments which mere reason might urge against the existence of God, but of course they knew as a matter of faith that God did exist. The arguments and the reasons were set out at great length, and the Catholic Church felt that they must stop it. Therefore they laid it down that the existence of God can be proved by the unaided reason, and they have had to set up what they considered were arguments to prove it. There are, of course, a number of them, but I shall take only a few.

1. The First-Cause Argument / Perhaps the simplest and easiest to understand is the argument of the First Cause. It is maintained that everything we see in this world has a cause, and as you go back in the chain of causes further and further you must come to a First Cause, and to that First Cause you give the name of God. That argument, I suppose, does not carry very much weight nowadays, because, in the first place, cause is not quite what it used to be. The philosophers and the men of science have got going on cause, and it has not anything like the vitality it used to have; but, apart from that, you can see that the argument that there must be a First Cause is one that cannot have any validity. I may say that when I was a young man and was debating these questions very seriously in my mind, I for a long time accepted the argument of the First Cause, until one day, at the age of eighteen, I read John Stuart Mill's* autobiography, and I there found this sentence: "My father taught me that the question 'Who made me?' cannot be answered, since it immediately suggests the further question 'Who made God?' " That very simple sentence showed me, as I still think, the fallacy in the argument of the First Cause. If everything must have a cause, then God must have a cause. If there can be anything without a cause, it may just as well be the world as God, so that there cannot be any validity in that argument. It is exactly of the same nature as the Hindu's view that the world rested upon an elephant and the elephant rested upon a tortoise; and when they said, "How about the tortoise?" the Indian said, "Suppose we change the subject." The argument is really no better than that. There is no reason why the world could not have come into being without a cause; nor, on the other hand, is there any reason why it should not have always existed. There is no reason to suppose that the world had a beginning at all. The idea that things must have a beginning is really due to the poverty of our imagination. Therefore, perhaps, I need not waste any more time upon the argument about the First Cause.

2. The Natural-Law Argument / Then there is a very common argument from natural law. That was a favorite argument all through the eighteenth century, especially under the influence of Sir Isaac Newton and his cosmogony. People observed the planets going around the sun according to the

*[A nineteenth-century British philosopher.—Eds.]

law of gravitation, and they thought that God had given a behest to these planets to move in that particular fashion, and that was why they did so. That was, of course, a convenient and simple explanation that saved them the trouble of looking any further for explanations of the law of gravitation. Nowadays we explain the law of gravitation in a somewhat complicated fashion that Einstein has introduced. I do not propose to give you a lecture on the law of gravitation, as interpreted by Einstein, because that again would take some time; at any rate, you no longer have the sort of natural law that you had in the Newtonian system, where, for some reason that nobody could understand, nature behaved in a uniform fashion. We now find that a great many things we thought were natural laws are really human conventions. You know that even in the remotest depths of stellar space there are still three feet · to a yard. That is, no doubt, a very remarkable fact, but you would hardly call it a law of nature. And a great many things that have been regarded as laws of nature are of that kind. On the other hand, where you can get down to any knowledge of what atoms actually do, you will find they are much less subject to law than people thought, and that the laws at which you arrive are statistical averages of just the sort that would emerge from chance. There is, as we all know, a law that if you throw dice you will get double sixes only about once in thirty-six times, and we do not regard that as evidence that the fall of the dice is regulated by design; on the contrary, if the double sixes came every time we should think that there was design. The laws of nature are of that sort as regards a great many of them. They are statistical averages such as would emerge from the laws of chance; and that makes this whole business of natural law much less impressive than it formerly was.

Quite apart from that, which represents the momentary state of science that may change tomorrow, the whole idea that natural laws imply a lawgiver is due to a confusion between natural and human laws. Human laws are behests commanding you to behave a certain way, in which way you may choose to behave, or you may choose not to behave; but natural laws are a description of how things do in fact behave, and being a mere description of what they in fact do, you cannot argue that there must be somebody who told them to do that, because even supposing that there were, you are then faced with the question, "Why did God issue just those natural laws and no others?" If you say that he did it simply from his own good pleasure, and without any reason, you then find that there is something which is not subject to law, and so your train of natural law is interrupted. If you say, as more orthodox theologians do, that in all the laws which God issues he had a reason for giving those laws rather than others—the reason, of course, being to create the best universe, although you would never think it to look at it—if there were a reason for the laws which God gave, then God himself was subject to law, and therefore you do not get any advantage by introducing God as an intermediary. You have really a law outside and anterior to the divine edicts, and God does not serve your purpose, because he is not the ultimate lawgiver. In short, this whole argument about natural law no longer has anything like the strength that it used to have. I am traveling on in time in my review of the arguments. The arguments that are used for the existence of God change their character as time goes on. They were at first hard intellectual arguments embodying certain quite definite fallacies. As we come to modern times they become less respectable intellectually and more and more affected by a kind of moralizing vagueness.

3. The Argument from Design / The next step in this process brings us to the argument from design. You all know the argument from design: Everything in the world is made just so that we can manage to live in the world, and if the world was ever so little different, we could not manage to live in it. That is the argument from design. It sometimes takes a rather curious form; for instance, it is argued that rabbits have white tails in order to be easy to shoot. I do not know how rabbits would view that application. It is an easy argument to parody. You all know Voltaire's remark, that obviously the nose was designed to be such as to fit spectacles. That sort of parody has turned out to be not nearly so wide of the mark as it might have seemed in the eighteenth century, because since the time of Darwin we understand much better why living creatures are adapted to their environment. It is not that their environment was made to be suitable to them but that they grew to be suitable to it, and that is the basis of adaptation. There is no evidence of design about it.

When you come to look into this argument from design, it is a most astonishing thing that people can believe that this world, with all the things that are in it, with all its defects, should be the best that omnipotence and omniscience have been able to produce in millions of years. I really cannot believe it. Do you think that, if you were granted omnipotence and omniscience and millions of years in which to perfect your world, you could produce nothing better than the Ku Klux Klan or the Fascists? Moreover, if you accept the ordinary laws of science, you have to suppose that human life and life in general on this planet will die out in due course: It is a stage in the decay of the solar system; at a certain stage of decay you get the sort of conditions of temperature and so forth which are suitable to protoplasm, and there is life for a short time in the life of the whole solar system. You see in the moon the sort of thing to which the earth is tending—something dead, cold, and lifeless.

I am told that that sort of view is depressing, and people will sometimes tell you that if they believed that, they would not be able to go on living. Do not believe it; it is all nonsense. Nobody really worries much about what is going to happen millions of years hence. Even if they think they are worrying much about that, they are really deceiving themselves. They are worried about something much more mundane, or it may merely be a bad digestion; but nobody is really seriously rendered unhappy by the thought of something that is going to happen to this world millions and millions of years hence. Therefore, although it is of course a gloomy view to suppose that life will die out—at least I suppose we may say so, although sometimes when I contemplate the things that people do with their lives I think it is almost a consolation—it is not such as to render life miserable. It merely makes you turn your attention to other things.

4. The Moral Arguments for Deity / Now we reach one stage further in what I shall call the intellectual descent that the theists have made in their argumentations, and we come to what are called the moral arguments for the existence of God. You all know, of course, that there used to be in the old days three intellectual arguments for the existence of God, all of which were disposed of by Immanuel Kant* in the *Critique of Pure Reason*; but no sooner had he disposed of those arguments than he invented a new one, a moral argument, and that quite convinced him. He was like many people: In intellectual matters he was skeptical, but in moral matters he believed implicitly in the maxims that he had imbibed at his mother's knee. That illustrates what the psychoanalysts so much emphasize—the immensely stronger hold upon us that our very early associations have than those of later times.

Kant, as I say, invented a new moral argument for the existence of God, and that in varying forms was extremely popular during the nineteenth century. It has all sorts of forms. One form is to say that there would be no right or wrong unless God existed. I am not for the moment concerned with whether there is a difference between right and wrong, or whether there is not: That is another question. The point I am concerned with is that, if you are quite sure there is a difference between right and wrong, you are then in this situation: Is that difference due to God's fiat or is it not? If it is due to God's fiat, then for God himself there is no difference between right and wrong, and it is no longer a significant statement to say that God is good. If you are going to say, as theologians do, that God is good, you must then say that right and wrong have some meaning which is independent of God's fiat, because God's fiats are good and not bad independently of the mere fact that he made them. If you are going to say that, you will then have to say that it is not only through God that right and wrong came into being, but that they are in their essence logically anterior to God. You could, of course, if you liked, say that there was a superior deity who gave orders to the God who made this world, or could take up the line that some of the gnostics took up—a line which I often thought was a very plausible one—that as a matter of fact this world that we know was made by the devil at a moment when God was not looking. There is a good deal to be said for that, and I am not concerned to refute it.

5. The Argument for the Remedying of Injustice / Then there is another very curious form of moral argument, which is this: They say that the existence of God is required in order to bring justice into the world. In the part of this universe that we know there is great injustice, and often the good suffer, and often the wicked prosper, and one hardly knows which of those is the more annoying; but if you are going to have justice in the universe as a whole

*[An eighteenth-century philosopher.—Eds.]

you have to suppose a future life to redress the balance of life here on earth. So they say that there must be a God, and there must be heaven and hell in order that in the long run there may be justice. That is a very curious argument. If you looked at the matter from a scientific point of view, you would say, "After all, I know only this world. I do not know about the rest of the universe, but so far as one can argue at all on probabilities one would say that probably this world is a fair sample, and if there is injustice here the odds are that there is injustice elsewhere also." Supposing you got a crate of oranges that you opened, and you found all the top layer of oranges bad, you would not argue, "The underneath ones must be good, so as to redress the balance." You would say, "Probably the whole lot is a bad consignment"; and that is really what a scientific person would argue about the universe. He would say, "Here we find in this world a great deal of injustice, and so far as that goes that is a reason for supposing that justice does not rule in the world; and therefore so far as it goes it affords a moral argument against deity and not in favor of one." Of course I know that the sort of intellectual arguments that I have been talking to you about are not what really moves people. What really moves people to believe in God is not any intellectual argument at all. Most people believe in God because they have been taught from early infancy to do it, and that is the main reason.

Then I think that the next most powerful reason is the wish for safety, a sort of feeling that there is a big brother who will look after you. That plays a very profound part in influencing people's desire for a belief in God.

III. THE CHARACTER OF CHRIST

I now want to say a few words upon a topic which I often think is not quite sufficiently dealt with by rationalists, and that is the question whether Christ was the best and the wisest of men. It is generally taken for granted that we should all agree that that was so. I do not myself. I think that there are a good many points upon which I agree with Christ a great deal more than the professing Christians do. I do not know that I could go with Him all the way, but I could go with Him much further than most professing Christians can. You will remember that He said, "Resist not evil: but whosoever shall smite thee on thy right cheek, turn to him the other also." That is not a new precept or a new principle. It was used by Lao-tse and Buddha some 500 or 600 years before Christ, but it is not a principle which as a matter of fact Christians accept. I have no doubt that the present Prime Minister,[1] for instance, is a most sincere Christian, but I should not advise any of you to go and smite him on one cheek. I think you might find that he thought this text was intended in a figurative sense.

Then there is another point which I consider excellent. You will remember that Christ said, "Judge not lest ye be judged." That principle I do not

---

[1] Stanley Baldwin.

think you would find was popular in the law courts of Christian countries. I have known in my time quite a number of judges who were very earnest Christians, and none of them felt that they were acting contrary to Christian principles in what they did. Then Christ says, "Give to him that asketh of thee, and from him that would borrow of thee turn not thou away." That is a very good principle. . . . I cannot help observing that the last general election was fought on the question of how desirable it was to turn away from him that would borrow of thee, so that one must assume that the Liberals and Conservatives of this country are composed of people who do not agree with the teaching of Christ, because they certainly did very emphatically turn away on that occasion.

Then there is one other maxim of Christ which I think has a great deal in it, but I do not find that it is very popular among some of our Christian friends. He says, "If thou wilt be perfect, go and sell that which thou hast, and give to the poor." That is a very excellent maxim, but, as I say, it is not much practiced. All these, I think, are good maxims, although they are a little difficult to live up to. I do not profess to live up to them myself; but then, after all, it is not quite the same thing as for a Christian.

1. Defects in Christ's Teaching / Having granted the excellence of these maxims, I come to certain points in which I do not believe that one can grant either the superlative wisdom or the superlative goodness of Christ as depicted in the Gospels; and here I may say that one is not concerned with the historical question. Historically it is quite doubtful whether Christ ever existed at all, and if He did we do not know anything about Him, so that I am not concerned with the historical question, which is a very difficult one. I am concerned with Christ as He appears in the Gospels, taking the Gospel narrative as it stands, and there one does find some things that do not seem to be very wise. For one thing, He certainly thought that His second coming would occur in clouds of glory before the death of all the people who were living at that time. There are a great many texts that prove that. He says, for instance, "Ye shall not have gone over the cities of Israel till the Son of Man be come." Then He says, "There are some standing here which shall not taste death till the Son of Man comes into His kingdom"; and there are a lot of places where it is quite clear that He believed that His second coming would happen during the lifetime of many then living. That was the belief of His earlier followers, and it was the basis of a good deal of His moral teaching. When He said, "Take no thought for the morrow," and things of that sort, it was very largely because He thought that the second coming was going to be very soon, and that all ordinary mundane affairs did not count. I have, as a matter of fact, known some Christians who did believe that the second coming was imminent. I knew a parson who frightened his congregation terribly by telling them that the second coming was very imminent indeed, but they were much consoled when they found that he was planting trees in his garden. The early Christians did really believe it, and they did abstain from such things as planting trees in their gardens, because they did accept from Christ the belief that the second coming was imminent. In that respect, clearly He was not so wise as some other people have been, and He was certainly not superlatively wise.

2. The Moral Problem / Then you come to moral questions. There is one very serious defect, to my mind, in Christ's moral character, and that is that He believed in hell. I do not myself feel that any person who is really profoundly humane can believe in everlasting punishment. Christ certainly as depicted in the Gospels did believe in everlasting punishment, and one does find repeatedly a vindictive fury against those people who would not listen to His preaching—an attitude which is not uncommon with preachers, but which does somewhat detract from superlative excellence. You do not, for instance, find that attitude in Socrates. You find him quite bland and urbane toward the people who would not listen to him; and it is, to my mind, far more worthy of a sage to take that line than to take the line of indignation. You probably all remember the sort of things that Socrates was saying when he was dying, and the sort of things that he generally did say to people who did not agree with him.

You will find that in the Gospels Christ said, "Ye serpents, ye generation of vipers, how can ye escape the damnation of hell?" That was said to people who did not like His preaching. It is not really to my mind quite the best tone, and there are a great many of these things about hell. There is, of course, the familiar text about the sin against the Holy Ghost: "Whosoever speaketh against the Holy Ghost it shall not be forgiven him neither in this world nor in the world to come." That text has caused an unspeakable amount of misery in the world, for all sorts of people have imagined that they have committed the sin against the Holy Ghost, and thought that it would not be forgiven them either in this world or in the world to come. I really do not think that a person with a proper degree of kindliness in his nature would have put fears and terrors of that sort into the world.

Then Christ says, "The Son of Man shall send forth His angels, and they shall gather out of His kingdom all things that offend, and them which do iniquity, and shall cast them into a furnace of fire; there shall be wailing and gnashing of teeth"; and He goes on about the wailing and gnashing of teeth. It comes in one verse after another, and it is quite manifest to the reader that there is a certain pleasure in contemplating wailing and gnashing of teeth, or else it would not occur so often. Then you all, of course, remember about the sheep and the goats; how at the second coming He is going to divide the sheep from the goats, and He is going to say to the goats, "Depart from me, ye cursed, into everlasting fire." He continues, "And these shall go away into everlasting fire." Then He says again, "If thy hand offend thee, cut it off; it is better for thee to enter into life maimed, than having two hands to go into hell, into the fire that never shall be quenched; where the worm dieth not and the fire is not quenched." He repeats that again and again also. I must say that I think all this doctrine, that hell-fire is a punishment for sin, is a doctrine of cruelty. It is a doctrine that put cruelty into the world and gave the world generations of cruel torture; and the Christ of the Gospels, if you could take Him as His chroniclers represent Him, would certainly have to be considered partly responsible for that.

There are other things of less importance. There is the instance of the Gadarene swine, where it certainly was not very kind to the pigs to put the devils into them and make them rush down the hill to the sea. You must remember that He was omnipotent, and He could have made the devils simply go away; but He chose to send them into the pigs. Then there is the curious story of the fig tree, which always rather puzzled me. You remember what happened about the fig tree. "He was hungry; and seeing a fig tree afar off having leaves, He came if haply He might find anything thereon; and when He came to it He found nothing but leaves, for the time of figs was not yet. And Jesus answered and said unto it: 'No man eat fruit of thee hereafter for ever' . . . and Peter . . . saith unto Him: 'Master, behold the fig tree which thou cursedst is withered away.'" This is a very curious story, because it was not the right time of year for figs, and you really could not blame the tree. I cannot myself feel that either in the matter of wisdom or in the matter of virtue Christ stands quite as high as some other people known to history. I think I should put Buddha and Socrates above Him in those respects.

IV. THE EMOTIONAL FACTOR

As I said before, I do not think that the real reason why people accept religion has anything to do with argumentation. They accept religion on emotional grounds. One is often told that it is a very wrong thing to attack religion, because religion makes men virtuous. So I am told; I have not noticed it. You know, of course, the parody of that argument in Samuel Butler's book, *Erewhon Revisited*. You will remember that in *Erewhon* there is a certain Higgs who arrives in a remote country, and after spending some time he escapes from that country in a balloon. Twenty years later he comes back to that country and finds a new religion in which he is worshiped under the name of the "Sun Child," and it is said that he ascended into heaven. He finds that the Feast of the Ascension is about to be celebrated, and he hears Professors Hanky and Panky say to each other that they never set eyes on the man Higgs, and they hope they never will; but they are the high priests of the religion of the Sun Child. He is very indignant, and he comes up to them, and he says, "I am going to expose all this humbug and tell the people of Erewhon that it was only I, the man Higgs, and I went up in a balloon." He was told, "You must not do that, because all the morals of this country are bound round this myth, and if they once know that you did not ascend into heaven they will all become wicked"; and so he is persuaded of that and he goes quietly away.

That is the idea—that we should all be wicked if we did not hold to the Christian religion. It seems to me that the people who have held to it have been for the most part extremely wicked. You find this curious fact, that the more intense has been the religion of any period and the more profound has been the dogmatic belief, the greater has been the cruelty and the worse has been the state of affairs. In the so-called ages of faith, when men really did believe the Christian religion in all its completeness, there was the Inquisition, with its tortures; there were millions of unfortunate women burned as witches; and there was every kind of cruelty practiced upon all sorts of people in the name of religion.

You find as you look around the world that every single bit of progress in humane feeling, every improvement in the criminal law, every step toward the diminution of war, every step toward better treatment of the colored races, or every mitigation of slavery, every moral progress that there has been in the world, has been consistently opposed by the organized churches of the world. I say quite deliberately that the Christian religion, as organized in its churches, has been and still is the principal enemy of moral progress in the world.

How the Churches Have Retarded Progress

You may think that I am going too far when I say that that is still so. I do not think that I am. Take one fact. You will bear with me if I mention it. It is not a pleasant fact, but the churches compel one to mention facts that are not pleasant. Supposing that in this world that we live in today an inexperienced girl is married to a syphilitic man; in that case the Catholic Church says, "This is an indissoluble sacrament. You must endure celibacy or stay together. And if you stay together, you must not use birth control to prevent the birth of syphilitic children." Nobody whose natural sympathies have not been warped by dogma, or whose moral nature was not absolutely dead to all sense of suffering, could maintain that it is right and proper that that state of things should continue.

That is only an example. There are a great many ways in which, at the present moment, the church, by its insistence upon what it chooses to call morality, inflicts upon all sorts of people undeserved and unnecessary suffering. And of course, as we know, it is in its major part an opponent still of progress and of improvement in all the ways that diminish suffering in the world, because it has chosen to label as morality a certain narrow set of rules of conduct which have nothing to do with human happiness; and when you say that this or that ought to be done because it would make for human happiness, they think that has nothing to do with the matter at all. "What has human happiness to do with morals? The object of morals is not to make people happy."

Fear, the Foundation of Religion

Religion is based, I think, primarily and mainly upon fear. It is partly the terror of the unknown and partly, as I have said, the wish to feel that you have a kind of elder brother who will stand by you in all your troubles and disputes.

Fear is the basis of the whole thing—fear of the mysterious, fear of defeat, fear of death. Fear is the parent of cruelty, and therefore it is no wonder if cruelty and religion have gone hand in hand. It is because fear is at the basis of those two things. In this world we can now begin a little to understand things, and a little to master them by help of science, which has forced its way step by step against the Christian religion, against the churches, and against the opposition of all the old precepts. Science can help us to get over this craven fear in which mankind has lived for so many generations. Science can teach us, and I think our own hearts can teach us, no longer to look around for imaginary supports, no longer to invent allies in the sky, but rather to look to our own efforts here below to make this world a fit place to live in, instead of the sort of place that the churches in all these centuries have made it.

What We Must Do

We want to stand upon our own feet and look fair and square at the world— its good facts, its bad facts, its beauties, and its ugliness; see the world as it is and be not afraid of it. Conquer the world by intelligence and not merely by being slavishly subdued by the terror that comes from it. The whole conception of God is a conception derived from the ancient Oriental despotisms. It is a conception quite unworthy of free men. When you hear people in church debasing themselves and saying that they are miserable sinners, and all the rest of it, it seems contemptible and not worthy of self-respecting human beings. We ought to stand up and look the world frankly in the face. We ought to make the best we can of the world, and if it is not so good as we wish, after all it will still be better than what these others have made of it in all these ages. A good world needs knowledge, kindliness, and courage; it does not need a regretful hankering after the past or a fettering of the free intelligence by the words uttered long ago by ignorant men. It needs a fearless outlook and a free intelligence. It needs hope for the future, not looking back all the time toward a past that is dead, which we trust will be far surpassed by the future that our intelligence can create.

29 / Why I Am an Agnostic

K. D. ELLIS

K. D. Ellis (1936–   ) is a philosopher who teaches at a state university in the Midwest. Writing extensively in the area of the philosophy of religion as well as in many other areas of philosophy, he has published several books and many journal articles. This essay was written expressly for this book.

About the gods, I am not able to know whether they exist or do not exist, nor what they are like in form; for the factors preventing knowledge are many: the obscurity of the subject and the shortness of human life.

—Protagoras, *On The Gods*

I. INTRODUCTION: THEISM, ATHEISM, AND AGNOSTICISM

*I*n discussions of the existence of God and related theological issues, it is customary to distinguish three main views or approaches. These are designated as 'theism', 'atheism', and 'agnosticism'. All three of these terms are used in a variety of senses. It would be tedious and pointless to catalogue all of them here. Since this is a *philosophical* essay, I shall select the definitions which are in accord with philosophical inquiry. Further, I shall characterize the three views in terms of the main thesis held by each. These are as follows:

Theism: There are good reasons for the belief in the existence of a god. Or at least: There is *a* good reason for the belief.

Atheism: There is *no* good reason for the belief in the existence of a god.

Before I characterize 'agnosticism' there are two expressions in the above theses that need to be explained. These are 'good reason(s)' and 'belief'. By 'good reason' I mean either reliable empirical evidence or sound rational arguments. By 'belief' I do *not* mean faith or blind trust or a feeling; rather I mean the acceptance of a claim as an item of knowledge. Thus to say "I believe X" is to say "I hold X to be true," or "I have good grounds to hold X to be true," or "I have knowledge that X is the case." Hence we could reformulate the main theses of (philosophical) theism and atheism as follows:

Theism: The existence of God is a truth which is known to be true on the basis of evidence or rational arguments (or both).

Atheism: There is *no* evidence or rational arguments capable of making the existence of God a truth which can be known—an item of knowledge.

To which most atheists would add:

The lack of such evidence or arguments is sufficient to entitle us to reject the belief in the existence of God.

That is:

Because there is no evidence or arguments, the *non-existence* of God is a truth which can be known—an item of knowledge.

I now turn to the thesis of 'agnosticism'.

Agnosticism: There are good reasons for the belief in the existence of a god, but none of these are compelling reasons. Further, there are good reasons against the belief.

Or if we also reformulate this thesis in terms of knowledge or lack of it, then we have:

Agnosticism: It is impossible to know whether a god exists or whether a god does not exist. There may be a god; or there may not be one. *No one* is or can be in a position to know which is the case.

To which some agnostics would add:

Therefore we should suspend our judgment on this issue and neither accept nor reject the belief in the existence of a god.

Finally, there is one other term that needs to be explained, namely '(a) god'. By '(a) god' I mean: a being who is (deemed to be) omnipotent, omniscient, omnibenevolent, perfect, infinite, eternal, supernatural, and thus transcendent to the natural universe. In other words, by 'God' I mean the god of traditional theism.[1]

II. WHY I AM NOT A THEIST

Again, a (philosophical) theist holds that there are good reasons for the belief in God—that is, reasons which are sufficient to allow one to say that it is a fact that there exists a god and therefore that we are entitled to say that "God exists" expresses a truth which can be known. And, again, 'good reason(s)' here is taken to mean either reliable empirical evidence or sound rational arguments. Since traditional theism takes the term 'God' to refer to a spiritual being, a being who is not part of the natural universe, and hence a being who is transcendent and hence non-spatial and non-temporal, the good reasons in question could hardly fall into the category of direct empirical evidence. Unlike the question, "Is there beer in the refrigerator?" the question "Does God exist?" cannot be answered by opening the door and looking or by any similar direct sensory experience. Thus the only good reasons which are applicable to this question would be sound *rational* arguments.

Such arguments have been put forth. The reader no doubt knows of the

[1]See the Preview to Part Six.

main five: the cosmological, teleological, moral, and ontological arguments, and the argument based on religious experience. Classical formulations of these—by their framers—may be found in any philosophy of religion anthology. An up-to-date formulation of them appears in E. K. Daniel's recent essay, "A Defense of Theism."[2] Now many of these arguments are deemed to be good arguments by many people, including philosophical theists. But many others find that these arguments are not convincing. That is why there are (philosophical) atheists and agnostics. Thus the best that one can honestly say about these arguments is: They may offer some support for the plausibility of the belief in a god, but they are not sufficiently strong enough to compel our assent to the conclusion that a god exists.

And that is precisely why I am not a theist. There are grave flaws in all of the arguments. For an excellent critique of all of these arguments, I urge the reader to see Ernest Nagel's essay, "The Case for Atheism."[3] As Nagel incisively shows, there are fallacies in all of the arguments. Hence none of them is a sound argument. And since I know of no such sound arguments, I conclude: There is no good reason for the belief in the existence of a god. By the nature of the case there can be no direct empirical evidence. But all of the rational arguments are fallacious. From which it follows that, contrary to what the (philosophical) theist maintains, there are no *good* reasons for the belief in the existence of a god. Hence the assertion that a god exists cannot possibly be an item of knowledge.

And that is why I am not a theist.

III. WHY I AM NOT AN ATHEIST

As we have seen, the (philosophical) atheistic thesis is: There is no good reason (by way of evidence or rational arguments) capable of making the existence of God a truth which can be known—an item of knowledge. Now, since the (philosophical) theist claims that there is (are) good reason(s), and since I have (in Section II) rejected the theist's claim, it would seem that my position is or ought to be that of the atheist. But there is a difference between the atheist's view and mine. It is true that we both agree on this much: There is no good reason for anyone to believe in the existence of a god. But the atheist takes the following two claims to be equivalent. Or at least he takes the second to be a consequence of the first. The two claims are:

(1)   There is no good reason for anyone to believe that a god exists.

(2)   God does not exist.

Thus the (philosophical) atheist often argues: If you have an argument with a set of premises and the conclusion which follows from the premises is for example: "There is no good reason for anyone to believe that the tooth

---

[2]See the first essay in Part Six of this volume.
[3]See the second essay in Part Six of this volume.

fairy exists," then that argument is the same as (or equivalent to) an argument with the same premisses and the conclusion "The tooth fairy does not exist." The same holds if, for tooth fairy, you plug in Loch Ness monster, Abominable Snowman, etc. In short any argument of this form

Premisses: P1, P2 . . . .
Conclusion: There is no good reason to believe that X exists.

is the same as (or equivalent to) an argument of this form

Same premisses as above.
Conclusion: X does not exist.

In short, the (philosophical) atheist makes a move here which is unwarranted. He says that we normally take the conclusion "There is no good reason to believe that X exists" to be the same as the conclusion "X does not exist." Now I admit that in many contexts this may be the case. Thus since we have no good reason to believe that flying hippopotamuses who sing Bach arias exist, we do indeed deny the existence of such creatures.

But in such arguments, we are talking about entities which, if they *did* exist, would exist as finite creatures within the natural universe. And in such contexts, I have no problem with making the move from "There is no good reason to believe that X exists" to "X does not exist."

But God—if there be a god—is not deemed to be a finite creature, empirically ascertainable within the natural universe. Suppose that all of the zoologists, natural historians, etc., of the world who are specialists on hippopotamuses have run exhaustive tests, with sophisticated equipment, and after decades of searching conclude that "There is no good reason (for anyone) to believe that flying hippopotamuses who sing Bach arias exist." Then that surely *does* warrant us in concluding "There are no flying hippopotamuses who sing Bach arias" or "Flying hippopotamuses who sing Bach arias *do not* exist." But there are—and can be—no such agreed-upon procedures for determining whether there are good reasons for the belief that a transcendent god exists. Hence even if it is true that these two arguments are the same or equivalent when they deal with entities within the natural universe

Premisses: P1, P2. . . .
Conclusion: There is no good reason to believe that X exists.

Same premisses as above.
Conclusion: X does not exist.

they are *not* the same or equivalent if X designates a (purported) non-natural, transcendent entity. Thus the (philosophical) atheist's main reason for his view fails.

And that is why I am not an atheist.

IV. WHY I AM AN AGNOSTIC

I have explained why I am not a theist and why I am not an atheist. Having said all that, I hasten to add that both the (philosophical) theist and the atheist have a point. That is, each has stressed or at least articulated a valuable insight which makes the major claim of each at least plausible, if not totally convincing. What is the valid point that each has stressed?

The theist has realized that the existence of the universe and certain of its features cry out for an explanation. In other words, it is a fact that there exists a universe—a universe which has certain remarkable properties: intricacy, orderliness, purposiveness, etc. So this leads to two questions which all theists have stressed, namely: (1) Why is there a universe at all, rather than nothing? (2) Why is there this particular sort of universe, with the above-mentioned properties, rather than some other sort? The cosmological argument, in its many forms and variants, has been brought in to answer question (1). The various teleological arguments have been brought in to answer question (2).

Now I firmly believe that the two questions which the (philosophical) theist asks are valid ones and hence deserve our attention. Why, indeed, is there something (a universe) rather than nothing? And why is there this particular something rather than some other one? These are tormenting questions for the intellect. So the theist deserves our gratitude for having asked them. But the mistake of the theist is in assuming that we have satisfactorily answered the questions by inferring the existence of God (the god of traditional theism). But there is another possible view here regarding these questions, namely: They are unanswerable. We don't—and can't—know why anything exists, or why this sort of universe exists. It's not just that we don't know yet. Rather it seems that we can never *know*.

So much for the point stressed by the (philosophical) theist. I turn now to the one stressed by the (philosophical) atheist. The atheist has realized that the various reasons and arguments which theists have put forth may *seem* plausible, but in fact, all are gravely flawed. All of them are fallacious in many ways. I shall not rehash these fallacies here. I refer the reader to Nagel's essay. By his penetrating critique, the (philosophical) atheist has done us a service in showing that even if arguments may appear to be plausible or sound, in fact they are defective because of the fallacies they commit.

But the mistake of the atheist is in what he concludes from all this. His position essentially may be summed up as follows.

> Here are all the arguments that have ever been put forth to prove the existence of a god.
> All of them are fallacious—for such and such reasons.
> Therefore the conclusion—"God exists"—does not follow from the premises of the arguments.
> Therefore the conclusion is false.
> (That is, God does not exist.)

That is the atheist's main argument—whether he explicitly states it or not. But his final conclusion simply does not follow from his premisses. That is, let us suppose that it is true that every argument that has ever been put forth for the conclusion "God exists" is utterly fallacious. It does *not* follow that the conclusion ("God exists") is false. All that does follow is: The conclusion cannot be validly inferred to be true *on the basis of those arguments*. But the conclusion could still be true. Thus there may be some other argument, which no one has devised yet, which is not fallacious and from which the conclusion follows. Or even if there are *no* such arguments to be found, it still *could* be true that there is a god, but *no one* can ever know that there is one.

To sum up: The (philosophical) theist has had a valid insight but has used it to attempt to infer something that does not logically follow. The (philosophical) atheist has had a different valid insight and has used it to attempt to infer something else that does not logically follow. The two "somethings," of course, are (T) "God exists" and (A) "God does not exist." I have tried to show that neither (T) nor (A) follows from the arguments put forth on behalf of them.

What this entails then is this:

(1) (T) could be true and (A) false.

or

(2) (A) could be true and (T) false.

Now which is true—(1) or (2)? (They can't both be true.) I submit: *We don't know.* And further there does not seem to be any way by which we ever could know which is true—(1) or (2). In short, we are in the same position as that of Protagoras way back in Ancient Greece: About a god, we are not able to know whether one exists or whether none exists. We may have hopes that one exists, or even reasons which *seem* to be plausible. But these do *not* entitle us to *know* that a god exists. Similarly, we may find that all of the proofs for a god are fallacious. But these do *not* entitle us to *know* that no god exists. There may be a god. Or there may not be a god. Which is true? We don't know, and it seems certain that we can never *know* which is true.

And that is why I am an agnostic.

V. CONCLUSION

I have tried to show that the insights which both philosophical theists and atheists started from and which prompted their inquiries are both valid ones. But the conclusions which they draw from those insights and starting points simply do not logically follow from them. Hence the major arguments on behalf of their conflicting conclusions are fallacious.

Thus we have two contradictory claims (conclusions): "God exists"; "God does not exist." They cannot both be true—if the terms in them are used univocally. So which of the two is true? I have tried to show that we cannot know which is true. Either there is a god or there is not. But we cannot know whether there is a god or whether there is no god. And there is no way by which we can know this. Hence it seems to me that of the three traditional views—(philosophical) theism, atheism, and agnosticism—the only tenable position to take is agnosticism. And (again) that is why I am an agnostic.[4]

---

30 / A Philosophical Theism: God as Growth

DAVID HAUSER

David Hauser (1953–   ) teaches philosophy at the Des Moines Area Community College in Ankeny, Iowa. As a result of numerous conversations with one of the co-editors, he has written the following essay expressly for this book.

I. INTRODUCTION

A. I love God. And I am aware of no wiser suggestions than when Jesus encouraged us to love *God* and neighbor. But consistent with these beliefs, I wonder, what is God like?

In my church school classes as a child, God was pictorially represented for me as a wise, elderly, bearded King. But when I came to reflect as a young adult, I realized that this conception of God was not *literally* true. I realized, for example, that the traditional conception of God also suggests that God is a spirit. But spirits do not have bodies; they are usually conceived of as being incorporeal. Thus, my childhood conception of God as an *embodied* King had to give. And so I asked myself, and I continue to ask myself, what is God like? My objective in the following pages is to begin an answer to this question.

B. I will not be speaking about God as I learned in my church school classes as a child. My comments about God will be nontraditional in that I will *not* be talking about God as spoken of by the biblical prophets. Instead, I will speak

---

[4]The author wishes to thank the editors of this book for having invited him to contribute this essay to it.

of God as revealed through my own reflections and other philosophers' reflections about God. In other words, my comments will be about the so-called "God of the philosophers" rather than about the so-called "God of the prophets."

It is important to understand this distinction; it points to two different ways of trying to know about God. The God of the prophets refers to the God known through the biblical prophets' visions of God. This God is conceived of as a personal, loving, all-powerful Being. God is all-knowing and all-good, and He has created us in His image. Very bluntly, this God is a *super person*, for He is a person with none of our human imperfections.

The God of the philosophers refers to God as known through humans' trying to reflect on or philosophize about what God is like. This God is not revealed through the vision of the prophets but through your or my using our own reason to reflect about the nature of God.

As conceived of by the philosophers, God has tended to be a much more abstract, theoretical God than the super person God of the prophets. For example, one way in which this God has been traditionally conceived of is as a first cause. The line of reasoning which the philosophers have appealed to in conceiving of God as a first cause is called the cosmological argument. One version of this argument asks, What has caused our world? The answer is, Some earlier cause has caused our world. In turn, what causes this earlier cause? Well, some still earlier cause is the answer. And so we discover a regress of earlier and earlier causes. But this regress of causes cannot go back forever because an infinite regress of earlier causes is impossible. Therefore, there must have been a first cause. This first cause is God.

Notice that the conceptions of God appealed to by the prophets *versus* the philosophers are two radically different ideas. A "super person" is a profoundly richer and different idea from that of a mere "first cause." Still, the *traditional* believer in God who is open to philosophical reflection is apt to suggest that these two different ideas of God still refer to one and the same God. There is *one* God known in two different ways.[1]

Now, my account of God is *nontraditional* in that I will *not* be arguing for this identification of the God of the prophets with the God of the philosophers. My position will be much less in that I will only be trying to clarify and defend the God of the philosophers. Why?

If I consider the arguments both for and against believing in the existence of the personal, loving God of the prophets, I suspect that these arguments will better support that God as such does not exist.

If this suspicion were correct, am I reduced to the atheist stance that God does not exist? Not yet. Two options remain. First, even if reason cannot be appealed to in direct defense of the prophets' God, perhaps reason can be appealed to indirectly in support of faith in revelation as the direct means of knowing this God. Rather than using arguments in direct defense of God, we

[1]For this type of position, see Etienne Gilson's profoundly wise little book, *God and Philosophy* (New Haven, Ct.: Yale University Press, 1941).

use arguments to defend revelation and use revelation as the direct means to know God.

This line of thought warrants serious exploration. Still, what if reflection would show that this faith in biblical revelation is not a wise faith? Would I be reduced to the atheistic rejection of God? No.

A second option remains. I may still use reason to clarify and defend God as accessible to philosophical reflection. That is, even if reason offers neither direct nor indirect support for the God of the prophets, reason can still be appealed to in clarification and defense of God as revealed to reason. And thus I turn to speaking about God as revealed to reflection rather than as the super person spoken of by the prophets.

II. A PHILOSOPHICAL CONCEPTION OF GOD

A. My thinking about God borrows heavily from the Western philosophical tradition, from the ancient Greek philosophers Plato and Aristotle and from the medieval philosopher Aquinas. Following these philosophers, I suggest that God is highest being. By "highest being" I allude to a hierarchy of things, certain things on this hierarcy being of higher being or greater value than others. As a crude example, a person is a higher reality or of greater value than a stone. A person can do a great deal more than a stone. (Many of the medieval philosophers advocated a hierarchy in which the traditional God was the highest reality. Then angels were at the next lower level, then people, then animals, then plants, and at the lowest level were unliving things such as stones.)

God is the highest reality. Now, what is the highest reality? The answer to this question will reveal God.

Consider the universe around us. Notice the basic difference between nonliving and living things. For example, earth, air, fire, and water are nonliving things, whereas plants, animals, and people are living things. Now, living things seem to have a greater value in and of themselves than nonliving things. We recognize this in that if we crush a stone, this is not a reason for sadness. But if we crush a tree or a fish or a person, this is sad. It is sad because we have destroyed a living thing, an entity of value.

Living things are of intrinsic value. But further, it is also of value that living things fully actualize their potentials. For example, if a teenager is killed in a car accident, this is sad not only because a living being has been killed but also because this living being was not able to actualize all of his or her potentials, to live a complete good life.

This is my argument thus far: Look around you. What seems the highest reality? Living things are higher than nonliving things. And as regards living things, reality is highest if they are able fully to actualize their potentials, to do all the growing that they can do.

The traditional theist may agree with my survey thus far but encourage me not to stop at this point. A reality even higher than actualized living things is the traditional God (and perhaps angels). In reply, I understand the traditional theist as suggesting that the traditional God and angels are higher than actualized living things. But what if I or you do not uncover this God or angels in our survey? I suggest that there still remains a highest reality even if it is not the super person—the God of the prophets.

Aristotle used the term *final cause* to refer to the state of complete actualization. For example, the final cause of an acorn is that it become an oak tree; that of a baby is that it become a mature adult. Growing things tend toward final cause, or completed growth. My suggestion, following Aristotle, is that highest reality is that things attain final cause, or complete actualization.

God is highest reality. Highest reality is that growing things completely realize their potentials, or attain final cause. Therefore, God is the culmination of growth, or final cause.

God, however, is not solely final cause or complete maturation. The journey to this end, the *actualizing process*, is just as significant as completion of this journey. For example, concerning humans, childhood, adolescence, and early adulthood are of their own intrinsic value (as well as being important in leading to the next stage of development). Highest reality is the entire path of growth, the journey as well as the culmination of the journey. In a word, highest reality or God is growth, the growing process and its total completion.

In summary, I agree with the Western philosophical tradition that God is highest reality. I try then to uncover highest reality. Nothing seems as high as living things and that living things accomplish all the growing that they have the potential to. Therefore, I conclude that God is this, namely, growing and its culmination.

B. Several further points about God are worth making.
1. *God is a "one" rather than a "many."* Suppose that God is growth. Does this mean that God is the multitude or class of all growing things? Would God be every different individual that grows? I suggest not. Again, following the medieval philosopher Aquinas, perhaps God is a "one" rather than a "many." In other words, perhaps God is somehow a *single* entity rather than a collection of all the different growing things. But how can God be a "one"? Perhaps God is a single entity in virtue of being the form or essence of growth shared in by all growing things.

The ancient Greek philosopher Plato advocated a theory of forms. He thought that visible things in our world participated in eternal forms which are recognized through reflection. For example, all trees would share or participate in a form of "treeness"; all chairs share or participate in a common form of "chairness." In parallel fashion, consider the class of all growing things. These things will share in the form of "growthness" akin to trees sharing in the form of treeness. My suggestion is that highest reality or God is a "one" in being the *form* of the growth process. God is the form which all growing things share in through growing.

2. *God is both immanent and transcendent.* In discussing God, you or I may wonder to what extent God is present to, or *immanent* within, our world *versus* independent of, or *transcendent* to, our world. In answer, as the form of the growth process, God is both immanent in and transcendent to the world in at least two different ways. First, the extent to which a growing thing has grown is present to, or immanent within, that being. For example, there are ways in which you or I have actually grown, and in these ways growth or God is present or immanent within our lives. On the other hand, there are other ways in which we have not grown and yet may still grow. In these ways, growth or God is potential within our lives, but not yet actual. In this sense, God transcends our current situation.

The second sense of immanence and transcendence is more difficult to understand. Consider again the example of chairs and the form of chairness. The form of chairness is present to or immanent within all chairs to the extent that they share in this form. On the other hand, chairness transcends individual chairs insofar as it is distinct from the chairs. In parallel fashion, the form of growthness is both immanent within growing things insofar as they share in this form but also transcendent to or distinct from the different growing things.

3. *God is fundamentally creative.* The traditional God of the prophets is portrayed in *Genesis* as a Creator. God wished to create the natural universe, and He did so.

As a simple illustration of creation, suppose that you wish to create a cake. You have an idea of the finished product which you wish to create, and you know how to create this product. You gather the ingredients together, mix them in the appropriate fashion, bake the mixture, and thereby create the cake. Parallel to this example, the traditional account of God suggests that God had an idea of what He wished to create, and He brought this idea about. He created our universe.

Now, my nontraditional suggestion of God as growth does not include that God is a Creator in this traditional sense. God *as growth* does not stand aside, wish to create a product, and then do it. But God as growth is still *creative.* What is as positively creative as growth or actualization? All things are created (generated, actualized) through participation in the essence of growth, or God.

4. *Faith in God. Wise or foolish?* My basic suggestion thus far is that God is the form of the growth process. Insofar as things grow, they share in God. On this view, what would "faith in God" amount to? Faith is usually construed as either belief or trust. "Faith in God" becomes belief or trust in the growth process.

Is this wise or foolish faith? How are we to distinguish wise *versus* foolish faith? One way for faith to be wise is to substantiate it with evidence and/or reason. Much evidence can be appealed to in support of a faith or trust in growth. What of reason? Arguments and philosophical analysis will be helpful in clarifying and defending what actually counts as growth. To trust accurately in growth requires being able to distinguish actual growth from only purported growth. There is a great deal of disagreement over what actually counts as growth, and so clear thinking will be extremely important here.

5. *God and prayer.* Does it make sense to pray to God in my nontraditional account? Yes, but prayer has a different meaning here than it does in the traditional view. In the traditional view, prayer is an appeal to God as a loving, powerful Father to help the petitioner in whatever way is needed. Prayer in my nontraditional account is to make an appeal for growth. For example, if I pray that my friend be successful in his or her job interview, I wish my friend well. I hope that whatever is most growthful for my friend happens. Or if I pray that my life will be richer through establishing loving friendship, this means that I hope for and have faith that this growth will take place in my own life. I pray that I can participate in God, or growth.

6. *Jesus' suggestion that we love God and neighbor.* Things share in God through growing. We support God in supporting growth. Jesus suggested that we love God and neighbor. In my nontraditional conception of God, to love God becomes to support growth. To love my neighbor becomes to support his or her growth simply because this growth is of value in and of itself. Further, in supporting another's growth, I love or support God as the essence of all growing things. I love God through loving my neighbor.

7. *God and the meaning of life.* One sense of the question, "What is the meaning of life?" refers to asking, what is it important for us to do with our lives? If it is important for us to support growth, our own and others' whenever and wherever we can, then support or love of God is at least a part of the meaning of life.

8. *God and the moral point of view.* A basic aspect of the moral point of view is to realize that other persons' pursuing their own lives is morally just as important as your or my pursuing our own. Or your pursuing your objectives is just as important morally as my pursuing mine. Now, consider this aspect of the moral point of view in relationship to God. If we support the form of growth (God) through respecting other persons' growth, perhaps to love God in such fashion is to live this aspect of the moral point of view.

9. *God and the problem of evil.* The classic problem of evil claims that there is an inconsistency between the traditional Judeo-Christian God and evil. If God were strong enough, knowledgeable enough, and good enough, He would not allow evil. Yet evil exists. Therefore, God does not exist. In reply, the theist tries to show ways in which the traditional God and evil are compatible. My point is not to consider this important dispute *as such*, but instead to ask what the problem of evil becomes given my reflections about God.

First, God is growth. Evil is roughly defined as obstacle(s) to growth. Moral evil or sin refers to a person's choosing to obstruct or harm one or more instances of growth. For example, if you or I choose to murder someone else, obviously we obstruct our victim's growth. Natural evil is an impersonal obstacle to or harming of growth. For example, if an earthquake results in the loss of life or limb, either of these losses are obstacles to growth.

Given these conceptions of God and evil, can both be within our world?

Yes. Consider our world. Obviously, it has many instances of growth, as well as numerous obstacles to this growth. Evil may hinder God or even destroy participation in God, but evil is neither logically nor physically incompatible with God. The problem or challenge of evil is not that it rules out the existence of God but that we fight the evil. We must combat the poverty, war, cruelty, ignorance, indifference, and so on that block growth. Acknowledging evil does not force us to abandon belief in God but on the contrary encourages us to fight in support of God, or growth.

Jesus spoke about the problem of evil with his disciples.[2] His disciples saw a man who had been blind since birth. They asked Jesus, Why was this man blind? Was his blindness some kind of punishment either for the man's or his parents' sinning? Jesus answered no, the point of the blindness (evil, obstacle) was not as punishment for sin but that the works of God could be "made manifest in him." In other words, the point of the blindness (or any evil) is that we fight it and through fighting it make manifest or actual the works of God/growth wherever evil occurs.

III. OBJECTIONS AND REPLIES

Both the traditional theist and the naturalist may object to my suggestions about God as growth.

A. The theist may reject my account because I consider God as something other than as a super person. The theist may protest that God is *"our Father who art in heaven."* As our Father, God is a person. Fathers are persons. Further, it is as our Father that God loves us. He knows our situation. And He has the power to help us when we need it. This is the God which people love and need, and who is worthy of our love. God is *not* some abstract, impersonal entity, whether this be conceived of as some "first cause" or as the form of the growth process. I, the traditional believer, love God as *my Father*, not as my earthly biological father but as my transcendent heavenly Father.

In reply, on a psychological and religious level I appreciate the traditional theist's love for God as a Father. Further, I acknowledge that it seems odd or even confused to speak of *love* of a God conceived of not as a *person* but as the *form* which all growing things share in. But what if honest, caring reflection were to reveal difficulties in conceiving of God as a loving, heavenly Father? Oh no, the traditional theist responds! But again, what if? My reply is that there is still highest reality. It is growth. We can know it. It is worthy of our support or love. And I choose to call it "God."

B. A further objection. I may be accused of equivocation. Equivocation is an informal logical fallacy of misleadingly shifting between two different senses of a term. As a silly example, suppose that someone argues that because a pot

[2](John 9, 1–3.)

(a cooking utensil) is not harmful, then no one can be hurt by pot (marijuana). Now, the naturalist or the theist may object that I equivocate when I speak of "God" as the form of the growth process. I confuse this unusual sense of the term with the usual sense of "God" as referring to the traditional super person. Even more perniciously, I could begin by speaking of "God" (growth) as existing, and then slip over to concluding that "God" (super person) exists.

In response, obviously such equivocation is unacceptable. But I avoid it by clearly distinguishing the two different senses of the term. And I do not argue that a super person exists because growth exists.

C. Another objection. My argument has been to define God as highest being. Then, assuming that highest being exists, I ask, What is highest being? Whatever it is, I have discovered God. But one objects, you have *defined* God into existence. You define God as something that happens to exist. Whether or not God exists ceases to be a question of fact and becomes one of definition. Further, if one defines God as some nonexisting reality (for example, as some Olympian god), then one defines God right out of existence.

In reply, I confirm that this objection is correct. In defining God as an existing reality, I do define God into existence. A consequence of my overall argument is that *whether* God exists ceases to be the question; the question is, *what* is God?

D. A further objection. The original debate between traditional theism and naturalism is a debate between two world views. Traditional theism asserts that a transcendent God exists who has created the natural universe. The atheistic naturalist asserts that the natural universe exists but that there is no transcendent creating God. My addition to this debate has been to consider an alternative conception of God. I define God as highest reality and then consider highest reality as the form of the growth process. But the theist and naturalist object, if you insist on calling growth "God," is not growth part of nature? Sure. And, continues the objection, if growth is part of nature, then your suggestion of a nontraditional theism (in terms of advocating a nontraditional conception of God as growth) is really just a disguised naturalism. You take one part of nature, namely, growth, and call it God. This is no theism. It is just a misleading way to stress a theme within naturalism.

In reply, the gist of this objection strikes me as correct. Growth is a basic process within nature. God as growth is that which is highest *within* nature. But there are still two senses in which God has a *transcendent* character even within nature. First, growing things usually have further growth which they have the potential to actualize. This further growth (or God) transcends a growing thing's current situation. Second, God is a *one*, the common form of the growth process. This common form transcends, or is distinct from, the many different things which share in this form through growing.

IV. SUMMARY

A. I defend what I call a nontraditional conception of God. I suggest that God is growth rather than the traditional conception of God as our heavenly Father.

Now I turn around and point out that my position about the philosophical nature of God is not that different from the traditional philosophical accounts of God. The great Christian philosopher Aquinas suggested that the God of the philosophers, the God as revealed to philosophical reflection, is the pure act of existence. For Aquinas, God's philosophical nature is pure existence. Philosophical reflection does not tell us *what* God is, but only *that* He is.

Now, I have suggested that we conceive of God philosophically as final cause, as *to have grown*. Notice the parallel between *to have grown* and *to be*.

It is not crucial that you understand this comparison. But realize that my account is not that different from Aquinas' in terms of what philosophical reflection reveals about God.

Where my position does differ significantly from the traditional view of Aquinas and his 20th-century advocate Etienne Gilson is that my account of God stops with what I can defend with human reason. I have stopped with the God of the philosophers, or growth. Aquinas and Gilson recognize the importance of this initial philosophical step but encourage us to take a further *religious* step. This further step is to take up religious faith in the prophets' visions of God as our heavenly Father and recognize that the God of the philosophers and of the prophets, although different in conception, is still *one* and the same God.

Perhaps Aquinas and Gilson are right in suggesting that the true *complete* God is only revealed through *both* the philosophical and religious steps. And perhaps this religious step is one which we must affirm with our hearts even if reason cannot substantiate it. But I diverge from Aquinas and Gilson here to suggest that should reason bar this traditional religious step, I believe that the sparser God of the philosophers (growth) still warrants our philosophical respect and religious worship. It does mine.

B. I love God, and I advocate respect for Jesus when he stressed how important it is that we love God with our whole person. I am almost apologetic when I encourage us to think about God, for this reflection may lead us away from the wise, powerful, bearded King that was presented to some of us as children. But if we do engage in reflection, and this reflection were to lead from a bearded King to growth, this is still not a trivial God. To support or love God requires you or me to support growth whenever and wherever we can. We must fight evil, or the obstacles to growth whenever and wherever we can. If I see a homeless man or woman, I love God or support growth by providing this person shelter. If I see a sick child, I love God in giving this child medicine. If I see an illiterate adult in a grocery store not able to buy a generic can of vegetables because he or she cannot read the nonpictured label, I love God in teaching this person how to read. If I see a suffering animal with a broken leg on the side of the highway, I serve or love God or growth in setting the animal's leg. We serve God in fighting the political repression of the Black peoples' growth in South Africa. You and I love God whenever and wherever we support our neighbors' growth.[3]

31 / The Art of Religious Communication

JOSEPH KUPFER

Joseph Kupfer (1945–   ) is a philosopher who teaches at Iowa State University. His main areas of specialization are ethics and aesthetics. In classes and talks he has related his knowledge of literature, especially poetry, to his interest in religious belief. As a result, he was asked to write this essay expressly for this book.

> The world is charged with the grandeur of God
> It will flame out, like shining from shook foil
> —GERARD MANLEY HOPKINS (*God's Grandeur*)

I

*T*he next time someone asks you why you believe in God, don't try to give a reason or provide an argument. Instead, play a song, perform a dance, or read a poem. You may perplex your questioner, but you won't be trying to do what cannot be done—justify belief in God.

Religious belief and interpretation of experience are better expressed artistically than argued for rationally. The aesthetic mode of communication contrasts sharply with the rational or discursive mode of argument. Where the rational tries to argue by giving reasons or evidence, the artistic reorients us with a vision. It reorients by displacing us from our usual stance in the world, shifting the way we interpret and value things. Unlike the rational,

---

[3]The editors are grateful to Dr. Hauser for having written this essay for this volume.

which strings thoughts together, the artistic communicates a way of seeing the world. As a result, we can see ourselves in a new light, see our undefined dissatisfactions or longings as spiritual clues. I shall begin by showing why rational justifications for God's existence must fail, then explain how and why the particular art of poetry can succeed in religious communication.

If religion were a matter of belief in the straightforward sense in which ordinary or scientific beliefs are true or false, then religious conviction might best be produced through rational argument. But if the question of divinity and belief in God is of a different nature, then arguments to justify such belief are not simply weak but are out of place. They are inappropriate because God's existence is unlike the existence of anything else. God is unlike anything else. This is why all rational arguments or proofs, including those yet to be thought up, must fail to establish God's existence.

What follows is an argument for the impossibility of a rational proof for God's existence. This "meta"-argument is itself rational. Offering a rational argument for why no rational argument can succeed in proving God's existence may seem paradoxical. It makes sense, however, because one of reason's tasks is to discover and clarify its own limits. The meta-argument concerns the limits of rational argument.

The existence of things is different from other aspects of them. It is more fundamental. The shape, weight, or color of something presupposes that it exists. Existence is not just one more quality that an entity may possess. For a thing to possess shape, weight, or color, it must exist. Existence is the fundamental fact upon which all others depend. This is what Kant means when he claims that existence is not a "predicate" or attribute. About our new dog, we might say, "By the way, it's a black dog." But we wouldn't say, "By the way, it exists" (unless perhaps we were in the habit of talking about imaginary dogs). Any particular predicate or quality of a thing, such as its color, is but one fact among many. But the thing must exist, must be, for it to possess any quality whatsoever. Whether a dog is black or yellow, it still exists. And unless it exists, it cannot be black or yellow.

Just as the existence of something is more basic than any of its particular features, so the existence of God is more basic than the existence of anything else. God is the "ground" of everything else. By the "ground" of everything, I mean that which is responsible for their existence. The existence of all things is made possible by this ground—God. Everything is His creation. What is most fundamental to all things, their existence, depends on God. Therefore, God's existence is the most fundamental "fact" in the world. How could we prove this fundamental fact through reason?

The only way we could try would be from knowledge or experience of the existence of these particular things. This would be to try to prove that the most fundamental, God, exists on the evidence provided by the less fundamental—the existence of particular things. But we cannot get to the ground of the existence of particular things, what is responsible for their coming-to-be, from reasoning about their existence.

We cannot proceed from parts of creation to its foundation. The source of creation is both more than all the parts and different from them in nature. The standard arguments for the existence of God proceed from part to part in the hope of getting to the necessity or probability of God's existence. Thus, from effect to cause, until we arrive at God as the first cause; from the design of the world to God as creator of design; or, from the idea of God as perfect to God's perfect existence. Such linear movement can only get us to another part, God as another thing in the world. This is inadequate. As simply another thing in the world, God cannot be the ground of all particular things.

When we proceed rationally from part to part to God, we are forever confined to the parts and their *particularity*. Our understanding must remain partial. This won't do because God is the ground of the whole. God is more than all the particular things which depend upon Him for their existence. As responsible for their existence, God also must be different from particular things. God cannot be just another thing among those with which we are acquainted. Another particular thing could not call into existence all particular things—the whole world. Such a thing would be no more than another piece in the entire picture; it could not account for the existence of the whole picture.

To ground the existence of all particular things, God must transcend them. He must be greater than them, beyond them in scope. The ground of the existence of all particular things cannot be another thing. As another particular thing, God could not possess a unique attribute necessary for Him to account for the existence of everything else. He would be on the same level, possessing the same status as all other particular things.

Finding an analogy for this notion is difficult. Any example from everyday life will involve some particular thing whose existence will be due to some other particular thing. But perhaps the following example will roughly suggest the relation of a transcendent ground to what it makes possible. Civilization or culture might be thought of as the ground of any individual's thoughts or achievements. Culture makes such thought or achievement possible but transcends it. Culture is a different kind of thing than any individual's achievement and exists independent of it. The difference between culture and God as ground, however, is that without all the particular thoughts and achievements taken together, there is no culture. Yet without His creation, God abides.

Because God transcends all the particular things whose existence He grounds, He is beyond our understanding. Rational arguments or justifications for God's existence endeavor to take us from what we understand to God, which cannot be understood. This is like trying to understand living things from knowledge of inanimate objects. Rational proof for God's existence built on what we understand of the world must fail.

II

To say that God is transcendent means that He cannot be comprehended: literally, held together in mind by means of a concept or definition. We use concepts to organize our ideas and sense qualities. The concept of "triangle" organizes the ideas of angle, line, three, and plane figure. The concept of "apple" organizes the sense qualities of spherical, red, juicy, and sweet. But whatever ideas we associate with God cannot themselves be put under and held together by some more inclusive concept. However we describe or refer to God, our descriptions cannot organize his attributes to make His nature comprehendible.

Art is suited to religious communication because it partakes of the transcendent. It lends itself to awareness and expression of transcendence by presenting sense qualities as organized but without a concept. Usually when we organize sensuous experience—colors, shapes, sounds, odors—we bring the experience under concepts to yield the perception of such objects as apples, houses, and automobiles. The sense qualities which belong together are related to each other and separated from those which aren't relevant by means of these organizing concepts. Concepts or definitions group sensuous experiences together as objects.

In art, the sense qualities form a unity but without a concept to do the unifying work. True, we may have concepts to describe items within a painting or poem, such as an apple, a tree, an automobile. But no concept covers the whole, organizing all the elements of the painting or poem. Think of the difference between arranging several pieces of colored paper into an image of an object, such as a tree, and arranging them simply into a pleasing pattern or design. In the first case, we are organizing the colored shapes according to a concept, a working definition of a tree. In the second case, we are organizing the colored shapes according to our sense of beauty or harmony, with no concept to direct us.

In this way, art transcends our rational understanding. This is why art moves us, enchants us, even changes how we see the world, but cannot be captured in a definition. This is also why we cannot adequately translate a poem into a prose paraphrase or explain its full meaning in discursive language. We can use language to indicate features of the poem which make it good. For example, we can note how the rhymes or images work together, contributing to the poem's unity. But this isn't the same as providing a concept by which to organize the poem's parts.

When we call something beautiful, we indicate that we have grasped a collection of sense qualities as a unified whole, but not as this or that thing, not as a tree or car. Our role in this organizing process is crucial. We don't automatically see the unity of a painting or hear musical notes integrated into a whole. Unless the artwork is simple, our effort is needed. To grasp the sensible qualities as a unity usually takes energy and imagination. When successful, we experience our own power to form shapes or colors, sounds or meanings into a unified whole without the aid of an organizing concept. We experience ourselves as having a transcendent dimension.

This ability which art calls forth transcends our understanding of the objects which make up our ordinary lives. The sensible material of which ordinary objects are made is transformed into something beyond the circumference imposed by concepts. The experience of art, and ourselves in the forming activity necessary to appreciate it, transcends our everyday way of perceiving objects by means of concepts.

The experience of art shares this transcendent dimension with God. Aesthetic transcendence can be further associated with God by the content of the work of art. Poetry, such as "Pied Beauty" by Gerard Manley Hopkins, can portray God as underlying the transcendence we experience when appreciating art. The poetic image can unite our felt transcendence with God's by penetrating our imaginative activity. We locate the source of our imaginative power outside ourselves, in God. The glimpse of transcendence gained through our organizing activity is joined to God's transcendence by means of the poetic presentation of God's grounding power.

PIED BEAUTY

Glory be to God for dappled things—
  For skies of couple-colour as a brinded cow;
    For rose-moles all in stipple upon trout that swim;
Fresh-firecoal chestnut-falls; finches' wings;
  Landscape plotted and pieced—fold, fallow, and plough;
    And all trades, their gear and tackle and trim.

All things counter, original, spare, strange;
  Whatever is fickle, freckled (who know how?)
    With swift, slow; sweet, sour; adazzle, dim;
He fathers-forth whose beauty is past change;
          Praise him.[1]

In this poem, Hopkins seizes upon the sensuous beauty of spotted things, and more broadly, things studded by contrasts, such as brightness and dimness. He portrays this sensible beauty as saturated with and dependent on God. The poem reveals nature's beauty by means of its own aesthetic strength. Images are vivid: trout, farmland, sky. Alliteration, repeating sounds, is heaped upon alliteration—just as God's creation is so abundant its variations must multiply into opposites. The dappling Hopkins describes is echoed in the alteration between consonance, repetition of consonant sounds, and assonance, repetition of vowel sounds. The consonance of couple-colour cow; fickle, freckled; is punctuated by the assonance of stipple, swim; rose-moles.

Hopkins even uses consonance to unite opposites—swift, slow; sweet, sour; adazzle, dim. This exemplifies the divine which underlies and unifies the opposites of nature. All foreground requires background, swift depends on slow, brilliance on dimness. God is of it all, all reflecting His grandeur.

Two rhymes join the stanzas: cow, plough, how; and swim, trim, dim,

---

[1] All selections of Hopkins' poetry are from *Poems and Prose of Gerard Manley Hopkins*, ed. W. H. Gardner (Baltimore: Penguin, 1953).

him. These rhymes are broken up, and "spotted" by the different rhymes within each stanza—things and wings, strange and change. In addition, the speckling of which the poem sings is echoed in the choppiness of the sounds and their arrangement: fold, fallow, and plough; fresh-firecoal chestnut-falls. We feel and hear the pied beauty in the look and sound of the words reinforcing the images they evoke.

The result is poetic richness and intensity similar to God's generosity in creating nature. Hopkins lavishes his alliteration, rhymes, and imagery in intimation of the inexhaustibility of God's creative energy. As Hopkins says in another poem, for all its excessive display, "Nature is never spent; There lives the dearest freshness deep down things" (*God's Grandeur*). The aesthetic plenitude of the poem is wed to the endlessly mottled beauty of the world as an expression of God's ceaseless creating.

Where reason tries to convince us that the visible world depends upon God (as designer or cause, for instance), poems such as this portray the world as divine. Where argument would change our minds by cognitive connection, the beauty of poetry moves us sensuously, emotionally, imaginatively, and then cognitively. Hopkins suffuses our perception or imagined perception of the world with the presence of God. He does this by presenting the beauty of the world as divinely generated. This includes the beauty of his own poetic creation.

A logical reconstruction of how this poem could reorient the way we see and feel the world might go something like this. The beauty of this poem enlivens us to the beauty of the natural world. The beauty of the natural world is presented as wrought by God. The beauty of Hopkins' poetry is fused to a vision of the world as a beautiful manifestation of God. The conclusion of this aesthetic process is the reader seeing the beauty of the world as God's perceptible presence. The conclusion is not a statement.

Rational argument would seek to establish a statement such as: The beauty of the world is the work of God. An argument would try to show how such a conclusion followed logically from premises. The poem, however, tries to alter the reader's perception by means of aesthetic experience. Poetry has an advantage over rational argument in its ability to embody the beauty about which it speaks.

The reader's perception of the beauty of the world as the manifestation of God is reinforced and colored by the beauty of Hopkins' own poetic creation. The result is that the beauty of the poem's construction carries over into the subject of the poem. The reader is led to see God as the foundation for the beauty, grace, depth, and enrichment not only of the natural, created world, but of Hopkins' own poetic creation. In this way, the poem lends its poetic beauty to its subject—God and His physical expression. The consequence is that the poem itself comes to be seen as another beautiful manifestation of God's generative force. The poetic speaker is heard as an exhibition of divine grace. The poem is eventually seen as falling within the scope of its own subject matter. The aesthetic strength of the poem (just as dappled things, pied and stippled) is God's beauty made manifest.

III

Because we are also part of nature, poetic rendering of the created world as divine should include the human. In the next poem by Hopkins, he portrays human beings as part of the natural order but also different from it. Humans alone can appreciate nature as a reflection of God. We alone can praise God and write a poem that illustrates the duality of imminent sensibility and divine transcendence.

AS KINGFISHERS CATCH FIRE

As kingfishers catch fire, dragonflies draw flame;
As tumbled over rim in roundy wells
Stones ring; like each tucked string tells, each hung bell's
Bow swung finds tongue to fling out broad its name;
Each mortal thing does one thing and the same:
Deals out that being indoors each one dwells;
Selves—goes itself; myself it speaks and spells,
Crying What I do is me: for that I came.

I say more: the just man justices;
Keeps grace: that keeps all his goings graces;
Acts in God's eye what in God's eye he is—
Christ—for Christ plays in ten thousand places,
Lovely in limbs, and lovely in eyes not his
To the Father through the features of men's faces.

In the first of Hopkins' poems, God is shown imminent in the world's beauty. In this poem, Christ is presented in human guise. A humanizing shift occurs when God-made-flesh is portrayed as dwelling within all of us. We are like the rest of creation, asserting our mortal place and prerogative. But we are also more. We are capable of morality (justice), divine inspiration (grace), and worship. We can know our special relation to God, including His spirit within us. We can see Hopkins' own poetic creation as a form of divine play—a feature of the face he offers God. By including the human in his poem and suggesting his own role, Hopkins moves closer to personalizing his poetic voice. However, that voice does not quite speak to us as coming from someone's private experience. We don't feel a subjective response to our possible needs or quests.

An important difference between poetic and argumentative speech is the respective role of the speaker in each. The poetic speaker should not be confused with the author. The author is a real person who creates the poetic speaker. This speaker, or narrative persona, has an identity which is completely determined by the words the author gives him or her to speak. All we could ever know about the poetic speaker's life or personality can be determined only from what we read in the poem. In many poems, attention to the speaker implicit in the poem enhances its aesthetic impact. The sense we get of his or her life colors the poem's content. In most arguments, the reverse is true; little is gained by thinking of the arguer implicit in the argument. The goal is usually to eliminate personality and individuality from the argument. It is supposed to stand on its own—as "reason's" speech to anyone. The argument is from anyone or no one in particular and to anyone, abstracted from context and individual experience.

The speaker in the poem, however, can address us as an individual situated in the world in a particular way. Because the narrator's voice can be personal, it may not speak to everyone, or to everyone in the same way. We are invited to respond subjectively to the speaker's personality and voice. In the next poem, by Anne Sexton, the narrator's personal testimony seems intended to help us develop our relationship to God.

SMALL WIRE

My faith
is a great weight
hung on a small wire,
as doth the spider
hang her baby on a thin web,
as doth the vine,
twiggy and wooden,
hold up grapes
like eyeballs,
as many angels
dance on the head of a pin.
God does not need
too much wire to keep Him there,
just a thin vein,
with blood pushing back and forth in it,
and some love.
As it has been said:
Love and a cough
cannot be concealed.
Even a small cough.
Even a small love.
So if you have only a thin wire,
God does not mind.
He will enter your hands
as easily as ten cents used to
bring forth a Coke.[2]

[2]All selections of Sexton's poetry are from *The Awful Rowing Toward God* (Boston: Houghton Mifflin, 1975).

The poetic speaker's concern over her own fragile faith turns into friendly support when she directly addresses us as "you." Her confessed weakness is offered to give us strength. We are encouraged to take heart from our own small steps toward God. Faith doesn't have to be rock solid to connect us with God. The narrator's testimony is an impetus for us to introspect. The need and doubt and final reassurance come from an individual who shares her inward gaze. As with Hopkins, Sexton appeals to the delicate strength of nature, reminding us that faith is rooted in our sensible human nature. We shouldn't expect or demand too much from it, but it will do. We just need to trust our openness to God, however small; we just need to have faith in ourselves.

When we pray or speak to God, our relation to ourselves is mediated. The thought of God enables us to "divide" ourselves into speaker and listener as we raise questions about ourselves and our lives. But this process, in which God provides a perspective on ourselves, also enables us to bridge the division which the self-examining instigates. For with self-understanding the self becomes one again. Rather than simple, uncritical unity, however, it is a unity achieved through the mediating activity of prayer or dialogue.

Similarly, Sexton's poem itself can mediate our relation to ourselves by introducing a divine element into our everyday thinking. By showing us how the poetic speaker's self-reflection involves God, we are provided the occasion for calling ourselves into question. Sexton's poem suggests a particular way of calling ourselves into question. We are offered a mode of self-address by which to perceive ourselves as naturally weak but whole individuals.

The poem can be heard as a testament to a particular way of seeing the world, the traces of religious experience. We can read it as a religious celebration: a renewal of one's relation with and vision of the divine. When we read responsively, we participate in the creation of the poetic-divine image the poet has begun. The text then mediates between the poet's aesthetic-religious experience and our own. By co-creating that image with and through the poet, we complete the mediation the text provides.

In the conclusion of "The Wall," the poetic speaker urges the reader to make the effort to overcome the limitations of the body to reach God.

> For all you who are going.
> and there are many who are climbing their pain,
> many who will be painted out with a black ink
> suddenly and before it is time,
> for those many I say,
> awkwardly, clumsily,
> take off your life like trousers,
> your shoes, your underwear,
> then take off your flesh,
> unpick the lock of your bones.
> In other words

> *take off the wall*
> *that separates you from God.*

The poem is more than the expression of faith the previous one was. The poetic persona directly exhorts us to make the effort to reach God. She tells us that it will require detaching ourselves from the physical, sensible qualities with which we identify. With this poem, we come full circle: from appreciating the beauty of the sensible world as the expression of God, through our relationship to God as both natural and divine, to our physical natures as keeping us from God. Taking these together, the suggestion is that we must journey to God through the physical, sensible realm, until we experience pure transcendence. Union with God is ultimately spiritual. After appreciating the world and ourselves as physical manifestations of God, we must go beyond the sensible.

At the beginning of this discussion, I suggested that art, and poetry in particular, was suited to reorient us in the world. It can change how we see the world and ourselves in it. But the reorientation may not endure as the poetic spell fades. We can lapse into our former perspective, no longer seeing the world "charged with the grandeur of God." Even after an inspirational, transforming poem, even after we have entered into the poetic speaker's experience, effort is needed to sustain the re-vision. A commitment is required to make the effort to see ourselves in the world as related to God. The commitment, I think, is unending. We don't just have the reorientation—once and for all. Neither can we hold onto it with ease. Instead, we must renew our viewpoint which is renewing our faith. We never fully arrive.

We can think of this effort as maintaining ourselves in our journey to God. The thirteenth-century philosopher–monk St. Bonaventure spoke of the spirit's journey to God as faith seeking understanding—each depending on the other. Because we can never completely understand God by bringing Him under a concept, we must have faith. Because our faith is but a small wire, it needs the support of understanding what we can of God's presence in our lives. Neither our faith nor our understanding are secure possessions, which means that we can become disoriented and lose our way. Our struggle is without resolution in the sense of completion and rest. Resolution should instead be understood as the resolve to continue the journey, to maintain the hold on our re-vision of the world.

The conclusion of Anne Sexton's poem "Rowing" is about this journey. By illuminating our struggle, it adds the dimension of effort to our divine reorientation toward life. We experience the poetic speaker's labor to find God, which on my interpretation includes seeing His presence in the world and ourselves. Access to this poetically created effort can round out our reorientation in the world by adding the element of resolve. Faith is not some blind belief, but the commitment to work to maintain our vision. The poem sheds light on our struggle not to be disheartened by doubt or the difficulty of the task. It intimates that the effort to reach God fill us with awe, of God and of the strength we borrow from Him to keep rowing.

and now, in my middle age,
about nineteen in the head I'd say,
I am rowing, I am rowing
though the oarlocks stick and are rusty
and the sea blinks and rolls
like a worried eyeball,
but I am rowing, I am rowing,
though the wind pushes me back
and I know that that island will not be perfect,
it will have the flaws of life,
the absurdities of the dinner table,
but there will be a door
and I will open it
and I will get rid of the rat inside of me,
the gnawing pestilential rat.
God will take it with his two hands
and embrace it.

As the African says:
This is my tale which I have told,
If it be sweet, if it be not sweet,
take somewhere else and let some return to me.
This story ends with me still rowing.[3]

STUDY QUESTIONS

1. Daniel first states the classical arguments on behalf of God's existence. Be sure that you understand these and how they differ from one another.

2. Has Daniel given an adequate defense of theism? Why or why not?

3. According to Nagel, atheistic philosophies fall into two groups. Distinguish between those groups.

4. State Nagel's criticisms of the traditional arguments for the existence of God. Critically evaluate those criticisms.

5. Nagel maintains (in the latter part of his essay) that there are incoherencies in the very thesis of theism. What are they (or what is one)?

6. Nagel maintains that atheism is not merely a negative viewpoint. Do you think he has supported that claim? Why or why not?

---

[3]The editors are grateful to Prof. Kupfer for having written this essay for this volume and to the publishers of Hopkins' and Sexton's poems for granting permission to include them in this book.

7. Russell attempts to show that (some of) the main arguments in behalf of the existence of God are invalid. State his criticisms. Do you agree with him? Why or why not?

8. State Russell's criticisms of the character of Christ. Do these seem valid to you? Why or why not?

9. What is the basis of religious belief, according to Russell? Do you agree? Why or why not?

10. Why does Ellis hold that agnosticism is preferable to both theism and atheism? Do you agree? Why or why not?

11. Critically evaluate Hauser's defense of nontraditional theism. Some have held that he should not call himself a theist at all. Do you agree? Why or why not?

12. What is Kupfer "up to" in his essay? What do you take to be his main thesis? Has he supported it? Critically evaluate his position.

13. Which of the essays in this part has, in your view, presented the best case either for or against the thesis that God exists? Give reasons for your view.

14. Is there any possible situation in which science should allow supernatural causes for an event or series of events? If so, describe the situation and justify your view. If not, explain why not.

15. Do you think that there is any historical evidence which justifies, at least to some degree, the claim that God has revealed himself to humans? Justify your answer.

16. Evaluate the following argument: "If God did not exist, then there would be no objective moral law, for moral laws must be decreed by some being, a being who is supremely good."

17. In Section I of the Introduction to this book, it was maintained that one of the tasks or aims of philosophy is the bringing to light of our hidden assumptions. Which, if any, of the essays in this part rely on assumptions, and what are those assumptions?

FURTHER READINGS

Angeles, Peter, ed. *Critiques of God*. Buffalo, N.Y.: Prometheus Books, 1976. [An excellent collection of essays representing atheistic and skeptical viewpoints on various facets of the problem of God's existence.]

Flew, Antony, and Alasdair MacIntyre. *New Essays in Philosophical Theology*. New York: Macmillan, 1955. [Contains interesting articles, both pro and con, representing a contemporary approach to the problem and focusing on the issue of the significance of discourse about God.]

Hick, John, ed. *The Existence of God*. New York: Macmillan, 1964. [A collection of both classical and contemporary selections which present the main philosophical arguments for the existence of God.]

Hume, David. *Dialogues Concerning Natural Religion*. New York: Haffner, 1961. [A detailed criticism of some of the traditional arguments for the existence of God, including a lengthy discussion of the problem of evil.]

Matson, Wallace I. *The Existence of God*. Ithaca, N.Y.: Cornell University Press, 1965. [A thorough examination and criticism of all of the classical arguments for God's existence.]

Mitchell, Basil, ed. *Philosophy of Religion*. Oxford: Oxford University Press, 1971. [A collection of recent important essays on issues of faith in God, language about God, and related topics.]

Nielsen, Kai. "In Defense of Atheism." In *Perspectives in Education, Religion and the Arts*. Albany, N.Y.: State University of New York Press, 1970. [See next entry.]

————. "Religion and Commitment." In R. H. Ayers and W. T. Blackstone, eds., *Religious Language and Knowledge*. Athens: University of Georgia Press, 1972. [Vigorous and stimulating criticisms of religious belief, focusing on the issue of whether religious discourse is significant.]

Russell, Bertrand, and F. C. Coppleston. The Existence of God—A Debate." *Humanitas* (Manchester, England). [A lively debate between a Roman Catholic believer and a skeptic.]

Scriven, Michael. *Primary Philosophy*. New York: McGraw-Hill, 1966. Chap. 4, pp. 87–167. [Contains a detailed and vigorous criticism of virtually every area of argument on behalf of the existence of God.]

Wisdom, John. "Gods." In John Wisdom, ed., *Philosophy and Psychoanalysis*. Oxford: R. Blackwell, 1957, pp. 144–181. [A subtle but provocative contemporary approach to the problem.]

PART SEVEN

GOD, FAITH, AND EVIL

PREVIEW

One of the greatest difficulties which confronts the believer in a (traditional) god is the problem of evil. The problem was succinctly stated in ancient times by Epicurus (371–342 B.C.). With regard to God: "Is he willing to prevent evil, but not able? then is he impotent [rather than all-powerful]? Is he able, but not willing? then is he malevolent [rather than supremely benevolent]? Is he both able and willing? whence then is evil?"[1] It would seem, then, that the existence of a traditional god is not consistent with the fact of evil in the world.

More recently, J. L. Mackie has formulated the problem very clearly.[2] Consider these three propositions:

A. God is omnipotent (all-powerful).
B. God is wholly good (supremely benevolent).
C. Evil exists.

There seems to be a contradiction[3] in holding all three of these propositions. Thus at most any two of them could be true, but not all three. So one must be

---

[1]This formulation of the problem actually stems from the eighteenth-century philosopher David Hume. See his "Dialogues Concerning Natural Religion," in C. W. Hendel, Jr., ed., *Hume: Selections* (New York: Scribner's, 1937), p. 365.

[2]*Mind*, vol. LXIV, no. 254, 1955.

[3]In its most direct form, two propositions are the logical contradictories of each other if they have this feature: they cannot both be true, *and* they cannot both be false. Hence if one is true, the second must be false; and if the second is true, the first must be false. Thus any propositions of these forms are the contradictories of each other.

All Xs are Ys.
Some Xs are not Ys.

No Xs are Ys.
Some Xs are Ys.

This is an X.
This is not an X.

In all cases the two propositions cannot be simultaneously true. So if one is true, the other must be false; and v.v. If three propositions are involved, as in the assertions (A), (B) and (C), above, then if

false. Why is there a contradiction or tension in holding all three? If (A) were true, God could have created a world with no evil. If (B) were true, God would have wished a world with no evil. Hence one of the three propositions is false. But (C) is clearly true. There is much evil in the world, including pointless and unnecessary evil. Therefore must not either (A) or (B) be false? If you answer no, then another question arises. How can the existence of evil be reconciled (be consistent with) the existence of an omnipotent and wholly good God?

Hence, if one recognizes the reality of evil, then it appears that God cannot be both all-powerful and supremely good. If so, then the only alternatives are the following:

1. God exists, a god who is fully able to prevent evil but does not wish to do so. Hence, being somewhat sadistic, God is not supremely benevolent.

2. God exists, a god who wishes to prevent evil from occurring, but does not have the ability to do so. Hence, God is not all-powerful but is at best a finite, limited being. Or

3. No god exists at all.

However, there are some thinkers—including those within the Christian tradition—who refuse to accept the fact that (1), (2), and (3) are the only alternatives. According to them, the fact of evil can be reconciled with the existence of a traditional god. Thus, they maintain that (4) God exists, a god who is both all-powerful and supremely benevolent but allows evil to exist for some purpose. (Just what that purpose is varies from one thinker to another.) The first two selections in this part of the book present opposing views with regard to the question of whether or not the existence of God is compatible with the fact of evil.

It should be pointed out (as the writers make clear) that in considering this problem it is necessary to distinguish between two conceptions of evil: natural evil, such as suffering and death which are brought about by natural phenomena like earthquakes, tornadoes, floods, and certain diseases; and moral evil, such as pain and suffering which are brought about by the actions (or inaction) of people. Some writers maintain that only the fact of natural evil is inconsistent with the existence of a (traditional) god. Others maintain that both natural and moral evil are inconsistent with the existence of such a god. That is, they maintain that God is responsible not only for natural evil but for moral evil as well. The reasons for that view will be considered in the selections which follow.

It should be noted that (1) by natural evil we mean the pain, suffering, death, etc., which result from natural (physical) phenomena such as earthquakes, diseases, etc. 'Evil' here does not refer to those phenomena themselves, but to the suffering, etc., which such disasters, etc., cause—especially

---

they are such that affirming all three is a contradiction, then at least one of them must be false. At most any two could be true.

A contradiction, or more accurately, self-contradiction, then, consists of the simultaneous affirmation of two or more propositions which cannot be jointly true (or jointly false). It is logically impossible for them to be jointly true (or false).

to humans. (2) Similarly by moral evil we mean the pain, suffering, misery, death, etc., which result from certain human actions, such as killing, stealing, deception, etc. Of course, such actions, and the persons who commit them, would also be called evil (by most people). But that is a different sense of 'evil'.

As any good dictionary will show, the word 'evil' (and its equivalent in other languages) has two primary meanings. These are

(1) whatever is morally wrong, immoral, bad;
(2) whatever is harmful, injurious, is characterized or accompanied by suffering; anything involving or causing misery, harm, or severe pain.

So roughly:

In (1) evil = immorality.
In (2) evil = pain and harm involving suffering. For short, evil = suffering.

Examples: Most people would consider actions such as murder, torture, deception, betrayal, to be instances of (1). Most people would consider the harm, severe pain, suffering, and death which result from tornadoes, floods, certain diseases, etc., to be instances of (2).

In the problem of evil: The problem of physical (natural) evil focuses solely on (2). Why does such evil (suffering)—or so much of it—exist? The problem of moral evil pertains to (1), of course. But it also focuses mainly on (2). Why does that kind of evil (suffering) exist?

In summary, by the problem of evil all who have dealt with this subject agree that the term 'evil' refers to the pain, suffering, deformity, misery, anguish, death, etc., which are the result of either purely physical (natural) phenomena or the result of certain human actions. To avoid the ambiguity of the word 'evil' (its two senses), it might be best to refer to this as *the problem of suffering.* And again the problem is: Can the existence of suffering (or at least severe or needless forms of it) be reconciled with the existence of an omnipotent and omnibenevolent God?

It might also be mentioned that some hold that there are certain conditions which must be met by any proposed solution to the problem of evil. These are listed below. Any proposed solution to the problem of evil must meet all of these conditions:

1. Any purported solution must recognize that evil is real. (Evil is neither an illusion nor a disguised good.)
2. For a traditional theist, any purported solution must not give up either God's omnipotence or his benevolence. (If you give up either, you no longer have the god of traditional theism.)
3. Any purported solution must admit that God is responsible for the fact that evil exists in the world—since He is supposed to have created man and the universe. Thus God wanted evil to exist.
4. Any purported solution must admit that God, being omniscient, fore-

saw in advance that evil would occur—even severe evil—and allowed it anyway.

In the Preview to Part Six we listed five questions or problems which have to do with the problem of God. The selections in Part Six dealt with the first two questions. With the problem of evil, we come to the third. We need not say any more about this question here.

We turn now to a brief discussion of question (4). There are many believers in the existence of a god who admit that, in the customary sense of "good reasons," there are no good reasons for belief in the existence of a god; that is, there is no genuine empirical evidence (evidence which is intersubjectively testable, repeatable), and there are no logically valid arguments. Some even admit that the problem of evil is a genuine one and poses a hardship for religious belief. Nevertheless, they maintain that, for various reasons, one still has a right to have faith in the existence of God, and even faith in the existence of a traditional god. Is this a tenable view? Can it be supported in any way?

Main Questions

In summary, the main questions of this part are:

1. Can the fact of evil in the world be reconciled with the existence of an all-powerful and supremely benevolent god?

2. Is faith in God (without evidence and without reasons) justifiable?

Answers

Again, there are no common labels for these answers. We will again simply call them the affirmative and negative answers.

1a. Affirmative answer: Yes. Evil can be reconciled with the existence of an omnipotent and supremely good god.

1b. Negative answer: No. The fact of evil is incompatible with the existence of a supremely good and all-powerful god.

2a. Affirmative answer: Yes. Faith, even if unreasonable, is justifiable or necessary.

2b. Negative answer: No. Faith in God without good reasons is unjustifiable and deplorable.

Selections

In this part, the answers to these questions are represented as follows:

Question	Answer	Selection
(1)	(1b) Negative	32
(1)	(1a) Affirmative	33

Question	Answer	Selection
(2)	(2a) Affirmative	34
(2)	(2b) Negative	35

Note

The opening selection (32) by H. J. McCloskey is rather long. For those who would prefer to assign or read it in an abridged version, we suggest the following deletions:

Section I. All of Section I

Section II. The last 12 paragraphs. (Starting with the paragraph that begins "However, because this is one . . . " to end of Section II.)

Section III. The last 4 paragraphs

32 / *God and Evil*

H. J. McCLOSKEY

H. J. McCloskey (1925–   ) was for many years a professor of philosophy at
La Trobe University in Melbourne, Australia and is currently a professor
emeritus there. He has written many articles on a variety of philosophical
issues, for both scholarly journals and other publications. The essay which
follows is one that has been reprinted many times.

I. THE PROBLEM STATED

*E*vil is a problem for the theist in that a contradiction is involved in the fact of
evil on the one hand, and the belief in the omnipotence and perfection of God
on the other. God cannot be both all-powerful and perfectly good if evil is real.
This contradiction is well set out in its detail by Mackie in his discussion of the
problem.[1] In his discussion Mackie seeks to show that this contradiction
cannot be resolved in terms of man's free will. In arguing in this way Mackie
neglects a large number of important points, and concedes far too much to the
theist. He implicitly allows that while physical evil creates a problem, this
problem is reducible to the problem of moral evil, and that therefore the
satisfactoriness of solutions of the problem of evil turns on the compatibility of
free will and absolute goodness. In fact physical evils create a number of
distinct problems which are not reducible to the problem of moral evil. Further, the proposed solution of the problem of moral evil in terms of free will
renders the attempt to account for physical evil in terms of moral good, and
the attempt thereby to reduce the problem of evil to the problem of moral evil,
completely untenable. Moreover, the account of moral evil in terms of free
will breaks down on more obvious and less disputable grounds than those
indicated by Mackie. Moral evil can be shown to remain a problem whether or
not free will is compatible with absolute goodness. I therefore propose in this
paper to reopen the discussion of "the problem of evil" by approaching it from

---

[1]"Evil and Omnipotence," *Mind*, 1955. [In the opening paragraphs of his essay Mackie
writes, "The problem of evil, in the sense in which I shall be using the phrase, is a problem only for
someone who believes that there is a God who is both omnipotent and wholly good. . . . In its
simplest form the problem is this: (A) God is omnipotent; (B) God is wholly good; and yet (C) evil
exists. There seems to be some contradiction between these three propositions, so that if any two
of them were true, the third would be false. But at the same time all three are essential parts of most
theological positions: The theologian, it seems, at once *must* adhere and cannot consistently
adhere to all three."] [For the definition of 'contradiction', see Note 3 to the Preview to this Part.—
Eds.]

a more general standpoint, examining a wider variety of solutions than those considered by Mackie and his critics.

The fact of evil creates a problem for the theist; but there are a number of simple solutions available to a theist who is content seriously to modify his theism. He can either admit a limit to God's power, or he can deny God's moral perfection. He can assert either (1) that God is not powerful enough to make a world that does not contain evil, or (2) that God created only the good in the universe and that some other power created the evil, or (3) that God is all-powerful but morally imperfect, and chose to create an imperfect universe. Few Christians accept these solutions, and this is no doubt partly because such "solutions" ignore the real inspiration of religious beliefs, and partly because they introduce embarrassing complications for the theist in his attempts to deal with other serious problems. However, if any one of these "solutions" is accepted, then the problem of evil is avoided, and a weakened version of theism is made secure from attacks based upon the fact of the occurrence of evil.

For more orthodox theism, according to which God is both omnipotent and perfectly good, evil creates a real problem; and this problem is well stated by the Jesuit Father G. H. Joyce. Joyce writes:

> The existence of evil in the world must at all times be the greatest of all problems which the mind encounters when it reflects on God and His relation to the world. If He is, indeed, all-good and all-powerful, how has evil any place in the world which He has made? Whence came it? Why is it here? If He is all-good why did He allow it to arise? If all-powerful why does He not deliver us from the burden? Alike in the physical and moral order creation seems so grievously marred that we find it hard to understand how it can derive in its entirety from God.[2]

The facts which give rise to the problem are of two general kinds, and give rise to two distinct types of problem. These two general kinds of evil are usually referred to as "physical" and as "moral" evil. These terms are by no means apt—suffering for instance is not strictly physical evil—and they conceal significant differences. However, this terminology is too widely accepted and too convenient to be dispensed with here, the more especially as the various kinds of evil, while important as distinct kinds, need not for our purposes be designated by separate names.

Physical evil and moral evil then are the two general forms of evil which independently and jointly constitute conclusive grounds for denying the existence of God in the sense defined, namely as an all-powerful, perfect Being. The acuteness of these two general problems is evident when we consider the nature and extent of the evils of which account must be given. To take physical evils, let's look first at the less important of these.

(a) Physical Evils / Physical evils are involved in the very constitution of the earth and animal kingdom. There are deserts and icebound areas; there are

---

[2]Joyce: *Principles of Natural Theology*, chap. 17. All subsequent quotations from Joyce in this paper are from this chapter of this work.

dangerous animals of prey, as well as creatures such as scorpions and snakes. There are also pests such as flies and fleas and the hosts of other insect pests, as well as the multitude of lower parasites such as tapeworms, hookworms, and the like. Secondly, there are the various natural calamities and the immense human suffering that follows in their wake—fires, floods, tempests, tidal-waves, volcanoes, earthquakes, droughts, and famines. Thirdly, there are the vast numbers of diseases that torment and ravage man. Diseases such as leprosy, cancer, poliomyelitis appear *prima facie** not to be creations which are to be expected of a benevolent Creator. Fourthly, there are the evils with which so many are born—the various physical deformities and defects such as misshapen limbs, blindness, deafness, dumbness, mental deficiency, and insanity. Most of these evils contribute toward increasing human pain and suffering; but not all physical evils are reducible simply to pain. Many of these evils are evils whether or not they result in pain. This is important, for it means that, unless there is one solution to such diverse evils, it is both inaccurate and positively misleading to speak of the problem of physical evil. Shortly I shall be arguing that no one "solution" covers all these evils, so we shall have to conclude that physical evils create not one problem but a number of distinct problems for the theist.

The nature of the various difficulties referred to by the theist as the problem of physical evil is indicated by Joyce in a way not untypical among the more honest, philosophical theists, as follows:

> The actual amount of suffering which the human race endures is immense. Disease has store and to spare of torments for the body: and disease and death are the lot to which we must all look forward. At all times, too, great numbers of the race are pinched by want. Nor is the world ever free for very long from the terrible sufferings which follow in the track of war. If we concentrate our attention on human woes, to the exclusion of the joys of life, we gain an appalling picture of the ills to which the flesh is heir. So too if we fasten our attention on the sterner side of nature, on the pains which men endure from natural forces—on the storms which wreck their ships, the cold which freezes them to death, the fire which consumes them–if we contemplate this aspect of nature alone we may be led to wonder how God came to deal so harshly with His Creatures as to provide them with such a home.

Many such statements of the problem proceed by suggesting, if not by stating, that the problem arises at least in part by concentrating one's attention too exclusively on one aspect of the world. This is quite contrary to the facts. The problem is not one that results from looking at only one aspect of the universe. It may be the case that over-all pleasure predominates over pain, and that physical goods in general predominate over physical evils, but the opposite may equally well be the case. It is both practically impossible and logically impossible for this question to be resolved. However, it is not an unreasonable presumption, with the large bulk of mankind inadequately fed and housed and without adequate medical and health services, to suppose

*[On first appearance.—Eds.]

that physical evils at present predominate over physical goods. In the light of the facts at our disposal, this would seem to be a much more reasonable conclusion than the conclusion hinted at by Joyce and openly advanced by less cautious theists, namely that physical goods in fact outweigh physical evils in the world.

However, the question is not, Which predominates, physical good or physical evil? The problem of physical evil remains a problem whether the balance in the universe is on the side of physical good or not, because the problem is that of accounting for the fact that physical evil occurs at all.

(b) Moral Evil / Physical evils create one of the groups of problems referred to by the theist as "the problem of evil." Moral evil creates quite a distinct problem. Moral evil is simply immorality—evils such as selfishness, envy, greed, deceit, cruelty, callousness, cowardice, and the larger-scale evils such as wars and the atrocities they involve.

Moral evil is commonly regarded as constituting an even more serious problem than physical evil. Joyce so regards it, observing:

> The man who sins thereby offends God. . . . We are called on to explain how God came to create an order of things in which rebellion and even final rejection have such a place. Since a choice from among an infinite number of possible worlds lay open to God, how came He to choose one in which these occur? Is not such a choice in flagrant opposition to the Divine Goodness?

Some theists seek a solution by denying the reality of evil or by describing it as a "privation" or absence of good. They hope thereby to explain it away as not needing a solution. This, in the case of most of the evils which require explanation, seems to amount to little more than an attempt to sidestep the problem simply by changing the name of that which has to be explained. It can be exposed for what it is simply by describing some of the evils which have to be explained. That is why a survey of the data to be accounted for is a most important part of the discussion of the problem of evil.

In *The Brothers Karamazov*, Dostoyevski introduces a discussion of the problem of evil by reference to some then recently committed atrocities. Ivan states the problem:

> "By the way, a Bulgarian I met lately in Moscow," Ivan went on . . . "told me about the crimes committed by Turks in all parts of Bulgaria through fear of a general rising of the Slavs. They burn villages, murder, outrage women and children, and nail their prisoners by the ears to the fences, leave them till morning, and in the morning hang them—all sorts of things you can't imagine. People talk sometimes of bestial cruelty, but that's a great injustice and insult to the beasts; a beast can never be so cruel as a man, so artistically cruel. The tiger only tears and gnaws and that's all he can do. He would never think of nailing people by the ears, even if he were able to do it. These Turks took a pleasure in torturing children too; cutting the unborn child from the mother's womb, and tossing babies up in the air and catching them on the points of their bayonets before their mothers' eyes. Doing it before the mother's eyes was what gave zest to the amusement. Here is another scene that I thought very interesting. Imagine a trembling mother with

her baby in her arms, a circle of invading Turks around her. They've planned a diversion: They pet the baby to make it laugh. They succeed; the baby laughs. At that moment, a Turk points a pistol four inches from the baby's face. The baby laughs with glee, holds out its little hands to the pistol, and he pulls the trigger in the baby's face and blows out its brains. Artistic, wasn't it?"[3]

Ivan's statement of the problem was based on historical events. Such happenings did not cease in the nineteenth century. *The Scourge of the Swastika* by Lord Russell of Liverpool contains little else than descriptions of such atrocities; and it is simply one of a host of writings giving documented lists of instances of evils, both physical and moral.

Thus the problem of evil is both real and acute. There is a clear *prima facie* case that evil and God are incompatible—both cannot exist. Most theists admit this, and that the onus is on them to show that the conflict is not fatal to theism; but a consequence is that a host of proposed solutions are advanced.

The mere fact of such a multiplicity of proposed solutions, and the widespread repudiation of each other's solutions by theists, in itself suggests that the fact of evil is an insuperable obstacle to theism as defined here. It also makes it impossible to treat of all proposed solutions, and all that can be attempted here is an examination of those proposed solutions which are most commonly invoked and most generally thought to be important by theists.

Some theists admit the reality of the problem of evil, and then seek to sidestep it, declaring it to be a great mystery which we poor humans cannot hope to comprehend. Other theists adopt a rational approach and advance rational arguments to show that evil, properly understood, is compatible with, and even a consequence of, God's goodness. The arguments to be advanced in this paper are directed against the arguments of the latter theists; but insofar as these arguments are successful against the rational theists, to that extent they are also effective in showing that the nonrational approach in terms of great mysteries is positively irrational.

II. PROPOSED SOLUTIONS TO
THE PROBLEM OF PHYSICAL EVIL

Of the large variety of arguments advanced by theists as solutions to the problem of physical evil, five popularly used and philosophically significant solutions will be examined. They are, in brief: **(i)** Physical good (pleasure) requires physical evil (pain) to exist at all. **(ii)** Physical evil is God's punishment of sinners. **(iii)** Physical evil is God's warning and reminder to man. **(iv)** Physical evil is the result of the natural laws, the operations of which are on the whole good. **(v)** Physical evil increases the total good.

[3] P. 244, Garnett translation, Heinemann.

(i) Physical Good Is Impossible without Physical Evil / Pleasure is possible only by way of contrast with pain. Here the analogy of color is used. If everything were blue we should, it is argued, understand neither what color is nor what blue is. So with pleasure and pain.

The most obvious defect of such an argument is that it does not cover all physical goods and evils. It is an argument commonly invoked by those who think of physical evil as creating only one problem, namely the problem of human pain. However, the problems of physical evils are not reducible to the one problem, the problem of pain; hence the argument is simply irrelevant to much physical evil. Disease and insanity are evils, but health and sanity are possible in the total absence of disease and insanity. Further, if the argument were in any way valid even in respect of pain, it would imply the existence of only a speck of pain, and not the immense amount of pain in the universe. A speck of yellow is all that is needed for an appreciation of blueness and of color generally. The argument is therefore seen to be seriously defective on two counts even if its underlying principle is left unquestioned. If its underlying principle is questioned, the argument is seen to be essentially invalid. Can it seriously be maintained that if an individual were born crippled and deformed and never in his life experienced pleasure, that he could not experience pain, not even if he were severely injured? It is clear that pain is possible in the absence of pleasure. It is true that it might not be distinguished by a special name and called pain, but the state we now describe as a painful state would nonetheless be possible in the total absence of pleasure. So too the converse would seem to apply. Plato brings this out very clearly in Book 9 of the *Republic* in respect of the pleasures of taste and smell. These pleasures seem not to depend for their existence on any prior experience of pain. Thus the argument is unsound in respect of its main contention; and in being unsound in this respect, it is at the same time ascribing a serious limitation to God's power. It maintains that God cannot create pleasure without creating pain, although as we have seen, pleasure and pain are not correlatives.

(ii) Physical Evil Is God's Punishment for Sin / This kind of explanation was advanced to explain the terrible Lisbon earthquake in the 18th century, in which 40,000 people were killed. There are many replies to this argument, for instance Voltaire's. Voltaire asked: "Did God in this earthquake select the 40,000 least virtuous of the Portugese citizens?" The distribution of disease and pain is in no obvious way related to the virtue of the persons afflicted, and popular saying has it that the distribution is slanted in the opposite direction. The only way of meeting the fact that evils are not distributed proportionately to the evil of the sufferer is by suggesting that all human beings, including children, are such miserable sinners, that our offences are of such enormity, that God would be justified in punishing all of us as severely as it is possible for humans to be punished; but even then, God's apparent caprice in the selection of His victims requires explanation. In any case it is by no means clear that young children, who very often suffer severely, are guilty of sin of such an enormity as would be necessary to justify their sufferings as punishment.

Further, many physical evils are simultaneous with birth—insanity, mental defectiveness, blindness, deformities, as well as much disease. No crime or sin of *the child* can explain and justify these physical evils as punishment; and for a parent's sin to be punished in the child is injustice or evil of another kind.

Similarly, the sufferings of animals cannot be accounted for as punishment. For these various reasons, therefore, this argument must be rejected. In fact it has dropped out of favor in philosophical and theological circles, but it continues to be invoked at the popular level.

(iii) Physical Evil Is God's Warning to Men / It is argued, for instance of physical calamities, that "they serve a moral end which compensates the physical evil which they cause. The awful nature of these phenomena, the overwhelming power of the forces at work, and man's utter helplessness before them rouse him from the religious indifference to which he is so prone. They inspire a reverential awe of the Creator who made them, and controls them, and a salutary fear of violating the laws which He has imposed" (Joyce). This is where immortality is often alluded to as justifying evil.

This argument proceeds from a proposition that is plainly false; and that the proposition from which it proceeds is false is conceded implicitly by most theologians. Natural calamities do not necessarily turn people to God, but rather present the problem of evil in an acute form; and the problem of evil is said to account for more defections from religion than any other cause. Thus if God's object in bringing about natural calamities is to inspire reverence and awe, He is a bungler. There are many more reliable methods of achieving this end. Equally important, the use of physical evil to achieve this object is hardly the course one would expect a benevolent God to adopt when other, more effective, less evil methods are available to Him, for example, miracles, special revelation, etc.

(iv) Evils Are the Results of the Operation of Laws of Nature / This fourth argument relates to most physical evil, but it is more usually used to account for animal suffering and physical calamities. These evils are said to result from the operation of the natural laws which govern these objects, the relevant natural laws being the various causal laws, the law of pleasure-[b]pain as a law governing sentient beings, etc. The theist argues that the nonoccurrence of these evils would involve either the constant intervention by God in a miraculous way, and contrary to his own natural laws, or else the construction of a universe with different components subject to different laws of nature; for God, in creating a certain kind of being, must create it subject to its appropriate law: He cannot create it and subject it to any law of His own choosing. Hence He creates a world which has components and laws good in their total effect, although calamitous in some particular effects.

Against this argument three objections are to be urged. First, it does not cover all physical evil. Clearly not all disease can be accounted for along these lines. Secondly, it is not to give a reason against God's miraculous intervention simply to assert that it would be unreasonable for Him constantly to intervene in the operation of His own laws. Yet this is the only reason that theists seem to offer here. If, by intervening in respect to the operation of His laws, God could thereby eliminate an evil, it would seem to be unreasonable and evil of Him not to do so. Some theists seek a way out of this difficulty by denying that God has the power miraculously to intervene; but this is to ascribe a severe limitation to His power. It amounts to asserting that when His Creation has been effected, God can do nothing else except contemplate it. The third objection is related to this, and is to the effect that it is already to ascribe a serious limitation to God's omnipotence to suggest that He could not make sentient beings which did not experience pain, nor sentient beings without deformities and deficiencies, nor natural phenomena with different laws of nature governing them. There is no reason why better laws of nature governing the existing objects are not possible on the divine hypothesis. Surely, if God is all-powerful, He could have made a better universe in the first place, or one with better laws of nature governing it, so that the operation of its laws did not produce calamities and pain. To maintain this is not to suggest that an omnipotent God should be capable of achieving what is logically impossible. All that has been indicated here is logically possible, and therefore not beyond the powers of a being Who is really omnipotent.

This fourth argument seeks to exonerate God by explaining that He created a universe sound on the whole, but such that He had no direct control over the laws governing His creations, and had control only in His selection of His creations. The previous two arguments attribute the detailed results of the operations of these laws directly to God's will. Theists commonly use all three arguments. It is not without significance that they betray such uncertainty as to whether God is to be *commended* or *exonerated*.

(v) The Universe Is Better with Evil in It / This is the important argument. One version of it runs:

> Just as the human artist has in view the beauty of his composition as a whole, not making it his aim to give to each several part the highest degree of brilliancy, but that measure of adornment which most contributes to the combined effect, so it is with God [Joyce].

Another version of this general type of argument explains evil not so much as a *component* of a good whole, seen out of its context as a mere component, but rather as a *means* to a greater good. Different as these versions are, they may be treated here as one general type of argument, for the same criticisms are fatal to both versions.

This kind of argument if valid simply shows that some evil may enrich the universe; it tells us nothing about *how much* evil will enrich this particular universe, and how much will be too much. So, even if valid in principle—and shortly I shall argue that it is not valid—such an argument does not in itself provide a justification for the evil in the universe. It shows simply that the evil which occurs might have a justification. In view of the immense amount of evil the probabilities are against it.

This is the main point made by Wisdom in his discussion of this argument. Wisdom sums up his criticism as follows:

> It remains to add that, unless there are independent arguments in favor of this world's being the best logically possible world, it is probable that some of the evils in it are not logically necessary to a compensating good; it is probable because there are so many evils.[4]

Wisdom's reply brings out that the person who relies upon this argument as a conclusive and complete argument is seriously mistaken. The argument, if valid, justifies only some evil. A belief that it justifies all the evil that occurs in the world is mistaken, for a second argument, by way of a supplement to it, is needed. This supplementary argument would take the form of a proof that all the evil that occurs is *in fact* valuable and necessary as a means to greater good. Such a supplementary proof is in principle impossible; so, at best, this fifth argument can be taken to show only that some evil *may be* necessary for the production of good, and that the evil in the world may perhaps have a justification on this account. This is not to justify a physical evil, but simply to suggest that physical evil might nonetheless have a justification, although we may never come to know this justification.

Thus the argument even if it is valid as a general form of reasoning is unsatisfactory because inconclusive. It is, however, also unsatisfactory in that it follows on the principle of the argument that, just as it is possible that evil in the total context contributes to increasing the total ultimate good, so equally, it will hold that good in the total context may increase the ultimate evil. Thus if the principle of the argument were sound, we could never know whether evil is really evil, or good really good. (Esthetic analogies may be used to illustrate this point.) By implication it follows that it would be dangerous to eliminate evil because we may thereby introduce a discordant element into the divine symphony of the universe; and, conversely, it may be wrong to condemn the elimination of what is good, because the latter may result in the production of more, higher goods.

So it follows that, even if the general principle of the argument is not questioned, it is still seen to be a defective argument. On the one hand, it proves too little—it justifies only some evil and not necessarily all the evil in the universe; on the other hand, it proves too much because it creates doubts about the goodness of apparent goods. These criticisms in themselves are fatal to the argument as a solution to the problem of physical evil.

However, because this is one of the most popular and plausible accounts of physical evil, it is worthwhile considering whether it can properly be claimed to establish even the very weak conclusion indicated above.

Why, and in what way, is it supposed that physical evils such as pain and

---

[4]*Mind*, 1931.

misery, disease and deformity will heighten the total effect and add to the value of the moral whole? The answer given is that physical evil enriches the whole by giving rise to moral goodness. Disease, insanity, physical suffering, and the like are said to bring into being the noble moral virtues—courage, endurance, benevolence, sympathy, and the like. This is what the talk about the enriched whole comes to. W. D. Niven makes this explicit in his version of the argument:

> Physical evil has been the goad which has impelled men to most of those achievements which made the history of man so wonderful. Hardship is a stern but fecund parent of invention. Where life is easy because physical ills are at a minimum we find man degenerating in body, mind, and character.

And Niven concludes by asking:

> Which is preferable—a grim fight with the possibility of splendid triumph; or no battle at all?[5]

The argument is: Physical evil brings moral good into being, and in fact is an essential precondition for the existence of some moral goods. Further, it is sometimes argued in this context that those moral goods which are possible in the total absence of physical evils are more valuable in themselves if they are achieved as a result of a struggle. Hence physical evil is said to be justified on the grounds that moral good plus physical evil is better than the absence of physical evil.

A common reply, and an obvious one, is that urged by Mackie.[6] Mackie

---

[5]W. D. Niven, *Encyclopedia of Religion and Ethics.*
Joyce's corresponding argument runs:
Pain is the great stimulant to action. Man no less than animals is impelled to work by the sense of hunger. Experience shows that were it not for this motive the majority of men would be content to live in indolent ease. Man must earn his bread.
One reason plainly why God permits suffering is that man may rise to a height of heroism which would otherwise have been beyond his scope. Nor are these the only benefits which it confers. That sympathy for others which is one of the most precious parts of our experience, and one of the most fruitful sources of well-doing, has its origin in the fellow-feeling engendered by endurance of similar trials. Furthermore, were it not for these trials, man would think little enough of a future existence, and of the need of striving after his last end. He would be perfectly content with his existence, and would reck little of any higher good. These considerations here briefly advanced suffice at least to show how important is the office filled by pain in human life, and with what little reason it is asserted that the existence of so much suffering is irreconcilable with the wisdom of the Creator.
And:
It may be asked whether the Creator could not have brought man to perfection without the use of suffering. Most certainly He could have conferred upon him a similar degree of virtue without requiring any effort on his part. Yet it is easy to see that there is a special value attaching to a conquest of difficulties such as man's actual demands, and that in God's eyes this may well be an adequate reason for assigning this life to us in preference to another. . . . Pain has value in respect to the next life, but also in respect to this. The advance of scientific discovery, the gradual improvement of the organization of the community, the growth of material civilization are due in no small degree to the stimulus afforded by pain.
[6]Mackie, "Evil and Omnipotence," *Mind*, 1955.

argues that while it is true that moral good plus physical evil together are better than physical good alone, the issue is not as simple as that, for physical evil also gives rise to and makes possible many moral evils that would not or could not occur in the absence of physical evil. It is then urged that it is not clear that physical evils (for example, disease and pain) plus some moral goods (for example, courage) plus some moral evil (for example, brutality) are better than physical good and those moral goods which are possible and which would occur in the absence of physical evil.

This sort of reply, however, is not completely satisfactory. The objection it raises is a sound one, but it proceeds by conceding too much to the theist, and by overlooking two more basic defects of the argument. It allows implicitly that the problem of physical evil may be reduced to the problem of moral evil; and it neglects the two objections which show that the problem of physical evil cannot be so reduced.

The theist therefore happily accepts this kind of reply, and argues that if he can give a satisfactory account of moral evil he will then have accounted for both physical and moral evil. He then goes on to account for moral evil in terms of the value of free will and/or its goods. This general argument is deceptively plausible. It breaks down for the two reasons indicated here, but it breaks down at another point as well. If free will alone is used to justify moral evil, then even if no moral good occurred, moral evil would still be said to be justified; but physical evil would have no justification. Physical evil is not essential to free will; it is only justified if moral good actually occurs, and if the moral good which results from physical evils outweighs the moral evils. This means that the argument from free will cannot alone justify physical evil along these lines; and it means that the argument from free will and its goods does not justify physical evil, because such an argument is incomplete, and necessarily incomplete. It needs to be supplemented by factual evidence that it is logically and practically impossible to obtain.

The correct reply, therefore, is first that the argument is irrelevant to many instances of physical evil, and secondly that it is not true that physical evil plus the moral good it produces is better than physical good and its moral goods. Much pain and suffering, in fact much physical evil generally, for example in children who die in infancy, animals, and the insane passes unnoticed; it therefore has no morally uplifting effects upon others, and cannot by virtue of the examples chosen have such effects on the sufferers. Further, there are physical evils such as insanity and much disease to which the argument is inapplicable. So there is a large group of significant cases not covered by the argument. And where the argument is relevant, its premise is plainly false. It can be shown to be false by exposing its implications in the following way.

We either have obligations to lessen physical evil or we have not. If we have obligations to lessen physical evil, then we are thereby reducing the total good in the universe. If, on the other hand, our obligation is to increase the total good in the universe, it is our duty to prevent the reduction of physical evil and possibly even to increase the total amount of physical evil. Theists usually hold that we are obliged to reduce the physical evil in the universe; but in maintaining this, the theist is, in terms of this account of physical evil, maintaining that it is his duty to reduce the total amount of real good in the universe, and thereby to make the universe worse. Conversely, if by eliminating the physical evil he is not making the universe worse, then that amount of evil which he eliminates was unnecessary and in need of justification. It is relevant to notice here that evil is not always eliminated for morally praiseworthy reasons. Some discoveries have been due to positively unworthy motives, and many other discoveries which have resulted in a lessening of the sufferings of mankind have been due to no higher a motive than a scientist's desire to earn a reasonable living wage.

This reply to the theist's argument brings out its untenability. The theist's argument is seen to imply that war plus courage plus the many other moral virtues war brings into play are better than peace and its virtues; that famine and its moral virtues are better than plenty; that disease and its moral virtues are better than health. Some Christians in the past, in consistency with this mode of reasoning, opposed the use of anesthetics to leave scope for the virtues of endurance and courage, and they opposed state aid to the sick and needy to leave scope for the virtues of charity and sympathy. Some have even contended that war is a good in disguise, again in consistency with this argument. Similarly, the theist should, in terms of this fifth argument, in his heart if not aloud regret the discovery of the Salk polio vaccine because Dr. Salk has in one blow destroyed infinite possibilities of moral good.

There are three important points that need to be made concerning this kind of account of physical evil. (*a*) We are told, as by Niven, Joyce, and others, that pain is a goad to action and that part of its justification lies in this fact. This claim is empirically false as a generalization about all people and all pain. Much pain frustrates action and wrecks people and personalities. On the other hand, many men work and work well without being goaded by pain or discomfort. Further, to assert that men need goading is to ascribe another evil to God, for it is to claim that God made men naturally lazy. There is no reason why God should not have made men naturally industrious; the one is no more incompatible with free will than the other. Thus the argument from physical evil being a goad to man breaks down on three distinct counts. Pain often frustrates human endeavor, pain is not essential as a goad with many men, and where pain is a goad to higher endeavors, it is clear that less evil means to this same end are available to an omnipotent God. (*b*) The real fallacy in the argument is in the assumption that all or the highest moral excellence results from physical evil. As we have already seen, this assumption is completely false. Neither all moral goodness nor the highest moral goodness is triumph in the face of adversity or benevolence toward others in suffering. Christ Himself stressed this when He observed that the two great commandments were commandments to love. Love does not depend for its possibility on the existence and conquest of evil. (*c*) The "negative" moral virtues which are brought into play by the various evils—courage, endurance, charity, sympathy, and the like—besides not representing the highest forms of moral virtue, are in fact commonly supposed by the theist and atheist alike not to have the value this fifth argument ascribes to them. We—theists and atheists alike—reveal our comparative valuations of these virtues and of physical evil when we insist on state aid for the needy; when we strive for peace, for plenty, and for harmony within the state.

In brief, the good man, the morally admirable man, is he who loves what is good knowing that it is good and preferring it because it is good. He does not need to be torn by suffering or by the spectacle of another's sufferings to be morally admirable. Fortitude in his own sufferings and sympathetic kindness in others' may reveal to us his goodness; but his goodness is not necessarily increased by such things.

Five arguments concerning physical evil have now been examined. We have seen that the problem of physical evil is a problem in its own right, and one that cannot be reduced to the problem of moral evil; and further, we have seen that physical evil creates not one but a number of problems to which no one nor any combination of the arguments examined offers a solution.

III. PROPOSED SOLUTIONS TO THE PROBLEM OF MORAL EVIL

The problem of moral evil is commonly regarded as being the greater of the problems concerning evil. As we shall see, it does create what appears to be insuperable difficulties for the theist; but so too, apparently, do physical evils.

For the theist moral evil must be interpreted as a breach of God's law and as a rejection of God Himself. It may involve the eternal damnation of the sinner, and in many of its forms it involves the infliction of suffering on other persons. Thus it aggravates the problem of physical evil, but its own peculiar character consists in the fact of sin. How could a morally perfect, all-powerful God create a universe in which occur such moral evils as cruelty, cowardice, and hatred, the more especially as these evils constitute a rejection of God Himself by His creations, and as such involve them in eternal damnation?

The two main solutions advanced relate to free will and to the fact that moral evil is a consequence of free will. There is a third kind of solution, more often invoked implicitly than as an explicit and serious argument, which need not be examined here as its weaknesses are plainly evident. This third solution is to the effect that moral evils and even the most brutal atrocities have their justification in the moral goodness they make possible or bring into being.

(i) Free Will Alone Provides a Justification for Moral Evil / This is perhaps the more popular of the serious attempts to explain moral evil. The argument in brief runs: Men have free will; moral evil is a consequence of free will; a universe in which men exercise free will even with lapses into moral evil is better than a universe in which men become *automata* doing good always because predestined to do so. Thus on this argument it is the mere fact of the supreme value of free will itself that is taken to provide a justification for its corollary moral evil.

(ii) The Goods Made Possible by Free Will Provide a Basis for Accounting for Moral Evil / According to this second argument, it is not the mere fact of free will that is claimed to be of such value as to provide a justification of moral evil, but the fact that free will makes certain goods possible. Some indicate the various moral virtues as the goods that free will makes possible, while others point to beatitude, and others again to beatitude achieved by man's own efforts or the virtues achieved as a result of one's own efforts. What all these have in common is the claim that the good consequences of free will provide a justification of the bad consequences of free will, namely moral evil.

Each of these two proposed solutions encounters two specific criticisms, which are fatal to their claims to be real solutions.

(i) [Free Will Alone Provides a Justification for Moral Evil. /] To consider first the difficulties to which the former proposed solution is exposed. (*a*) A difficulty for the first argument—that it is free will alone that provides a justification for moral evil–lies in the fact that the theist who argues in this way has to allow that it is logically possible on the free will hypothesis that all men should always will what is evil, and that even so, a universe of completely evil men possessing free will is better than one in which men are predestined to virtuous living. It has to be contended that the value of free will itself is so immense that it more than outweighs the total moral evil, the eternal punishment of the wicked, and the sufferings inflicted on others by the sinners in their evilness. It is this paradox that leads to the formulation of the second argument; and it is to be noted that when the explanation of moral evil switches to the second argument or to a combination of the first and second arguments, immediately the theist refuses to face the logical possibility of complete wickedness, and insists instead that in fact men do not always choose what is evil.

(*b*) The second difficulty encountered by the first argument relates to the possibility that free will is compatible with less evil, and even with no evil, that is, with absolute goodness. If it could be shown that free will is compatible with absolute goodness, or even with less moral evil than actually occurs, then all or at least some evil will be left unexplained by free will alone.

Mackie, in his recent paper, and Joyce, in his discussion of this argument, both contend that free will is compatible with absolute goodness. Mackie argues that if it is not possible for God to confer free will on men and at the same time ensure that no moral evil is committed, He cannot really be omnipotent. Joyce directs his argument rather to fellow-theists, and it is more of an *ad hominem* argument* addressed to them. He writes:

> Free will need not (as is often assumed) involve the power to choose wrong. Our ability to misuse the gift is due to the conditions under which it is exercised

*[Literally, argument directed to the man.—Eds.]

here. In our present state we are able to reject what is truly good, and exercise our power of preference in favor of some baser attraction. Yet it is not necessary that it should be so. And all who accept Christian revelation admit that those who attain their final beatitude exercise freedom of will, and yet cannot choose aught but what is truly good. They possess the knowledge of Essential Goodness; and to it, not simply to good in general, they refer every choice. Moreover, even in our present condition it is open to omnipotence so to order our circumstances and to confer on the will such instinctive impulses that we should in every election adopt the right course and not the wrong one.

To this objection, that free will is compatible with absolute goodness and that therefore a benevolent, omnipotent God would have given man free will and ensured his absolute virtue, it is replied that God is being required to perform what is logically impossible. It is logically impossible, so it is argued, for free will and absolute goodness to be combined, and hence, if God lacks omnipotence only in this respect, He cannot be claimed to lack omnipotence in any sense in which serious theists have ascribed it to Him.

Quite clearly, if free will and absolute goodness are logically incompatible, then God, in not being able to confer both on man, does not lack omnipotence in any important sense of the term. However, it is not clear that free will and absolute goodness are logically opposed; and Joyce does point to considerations which suggest that they are not logical incompatibles. For my own part I am uncertain on this point; but my uncertainty is not a factual one but one concerning a point of usage. It is clear that an omnipotent God could create rational agents predestined always to make virtuous "decisions"; what is not clear is whether we should describe such agents as having free will. The considerations to which Joyce points have something of the status of test cases, and they would suggest that we should describe such agents as having free will. However, no matter how we resolve the linguistic point, the question remains—Which is more desirable, free will and moral evil and the physical evil to which free will gives rise, or this special free will or pseudo-free will which goes with absolute goodness? I suggest that the latter is clearly preferable. Later I shall endeavor to defend this conclusion; for the moment I am content to indicate the nature of the value judgment on which the question turns at this point.

The second objection to the proposed solution of the problem of moral evil in terms of free will alone is related to the contention that free will is compatible with less moral evil than occurs, and possibly with no moral evil. We have seen what is involved in the latter contention. We may now consider what is involved in the former. It may be argued that free will is compatible with less moral evil than in fact occurs on various grounds. (1) God, if He were all-powerful, could miraculously intervene to prevent some or perhaps all moral evil; and He is said to do so on occasions in answer to prayers (for example, to prevent wars) or of His own initiative (for instance, by producing calamities which serve as warnings, or by working miracles, etc.).

(2) God has made man with a certain nature. This nature is often interpreted by theologians as having a bias to evil. Clearly God could have created

man with a strong bias to good, while still leaving scope for a decision to act evilly. Such a bias to good would be compatible with freedom of the will. (3) An omnipotent God could so have ordered the world that it was less conducive to the practice of evil.

These are all considerations advanced by Joyce, and separately and jointly, they establish that God could have conferred free will upon us, and at least very considerably *reduced* the amount of moral evil that would have resulted from the exercise of free will. This is sufficient to show that *not all* the moral evil that exists can be justified by reference to free will alone. This conclusion is fatal to the account of moral evil in terms of free will alone. The more extreme conclusion that Mackie seeks to establish—that absolute goodness is compatible with free will—is not essential as a basis for refuting the free will argument. The difficulty is as fatal to the claims of theism whether all moral evil or only some moral evil is unaccountable. However, whether Mackie's contentions are sound is still a matter of logical interest, although not of any real moment in the context of the case against theism, once the fact that less moral evil is compatible with free will has been established.

(ii) [The Goods Made Possible by Free Will Provide a Basis for Accounting for Moral Evil. /] The second free will argument arises out of an attempt to circumvent these objections. It is not free will but the value of the goods achieved through free will that is said to be so great as to provide a justification for moral evil.

(*a*) This second argument meets a difficulty in that it is now necessary for it to be supplemented by a proof that the number of people who practice moral virtue or who attain beatitude and/or virtue after a struggle is sufficient to outweigh the evilness of moral evil, the evilness of their eternal damnation, and the physical evil they cause to others. This is a serious defect in the argument, because it means that the argument can at best show that moral evil *may have* a justification, and not that it has a justification. It is both logically and practically impossible to supplement and complete the argument. It is necessarily incomplete and inconclusive even if its general principle is sound.

(*b*) This second argument is designed also to avoid the other difficulty of the first argument—that free will may be compatible with no evil and certainly with less evil. It is argued that even if free will is compatible with absolute goodness it is still better that virtue and beatitude be attained after a genuine personal struggle; and this, it is said, would not occur if God in conferring free will nonetheless prevented moral evil or reduced the risk of it. Joyce argues in this way:

> To receive our final beatitude as the fruit of our labors, and as the recompense of a hard-won victory, is an incomparably higher destiny than to receive it without any effort on our part. And since God in His wisdom has seen fit to give us such a lot as this, it was inevitable that man should have the power to choose wrong. We could not be called to merit the reward due to victory without being exposed to the possibility of defeat.

There are various objections which may be urged here. First, this argument implies that the more intense the struggle, the greater is the triumph and resultant good, and the better the world; hence we should apparently, on this argument, court temptation and moral struggles to attain greater virtue and to be more worthy of our reward. Secondly, it may be urged that God is being said to be demanding too high a price for the goods produced. He is omniscient. He knows that many will sin and not attain the goods or the Good free will is said to make possible. He creates men with free will, with the natures men have, in the world as it is constituted, knowing that in His doing so He is committing many to moral evil and eternal damnation. He could avoid all this evil by creating men with rational wills predestined to virtue, or He could eliminate much of it by making men's natures and the conditions in the world more conducive to the practice of virtue. He is said not to choose to do this. Instead, at the cost of the sacrifice of the many, He is said to have ordered things so as to allow fewer men to attain this higher virtue and higher beatitude that result from the more intense struggle.

In attributing such behavior to God, and in attempting to account for moral evil along these lines, theists are, I suggest, attributing to God immoral behavior of a serious kind—of a kind we should all unhesitatingly condemn in a fellow human being.

We do not commend people for putting temptation in the way of others. On the contrary, anyone who today advocated, or even allowed where he could prevent it, the occurrence of evil and the sacrifice of the many—even as a result of their own freely chosen actions—for the sake of the higher virtue of the few would be condemned as an immoralist. To put severe temptation in the way of the many, knowing that many and perhaps even most will succumb to the temptation, for the sake of the higher virtue of the few would be blatant immorality; and it would be immoral whether or not those who yielded to the temptation possessed free will. This point can be brought out by considering how a conscientious moral agent would answer the question: Which should I choose for other people, a world in which there are intense moral struggles and the possibility of magnificent triumphs and the certainty of many defeats, or a world in which there are less intense struggles, less magnificent triumphs, but more triumphs and fewer defeats, or a world in which there are no struggles, no triumphs, and no defeats? We are constantly answering less easy questions than this in a way that conflicts with the theist's contentions. If by modifying our own behavior we can save someone else from an intense moral struggle and almost certain moral evil, for example if by refraining from gambling or excessive drinking ourselves we can help a weaker person not to become a confirmed gambler or an alcoholic, or if by locking our car and not leaving it unlocked and with the key in it we can prevent people yielding to the temptation to become car thieves, we feel obliged to act accordingly, even though the persons concerned would freely choose the evil course of conduct. How much clearer is the decision with which God is said to be faced—the choice between the higher virtue of some and the evil of others, or the higher but less high virtue of many more, and the evil of many fewer. Neither alternative denies free will to men.

These various difficulties dispose of each of the main arguments relating to moral evil. There are in addition to these difficulties two other objections that might be urged.

If it could be shown that man has not free will, both arguments collapse; and even if it could be shown that God's omniscience is incompatible with free will, they would still break down. The issues raised here are too great to be pursued in this paper; and they can simply be noted as possible additional grounds from which criticisms of the main proposed solutions of the problem of moral evil may be advanced.

The other general objection is by way of a follow-up to points made in objections (*b*) to both arguments (i) and (ii). It concerns the relative value of free will and its goods and evils, and the value of the best of the alternatives to free will and its goods. Are free will and its goods so much more valuable than the next best alternatives that their superior value can really justify the immense amount of evil that is introduced into the world by free will?

Theologians who discuss this issue ask: Which is better—men with free will striving to work out their own destinies, or automata-machine-like creatures, who never make mistakes because they never make decisions? When put in this form we naturally doubt whether free will plus moral evil plus the possibility of the eternal damnation of the many and the physical evil of untold billions are quite so unjustified after all; but the fact of the matter is that the question has not been fairly put. The real alternative is, on the one hand, rational agents with free wills making many bad and some good decisions on rational and nonrational grounds, and "rational" agents predestined always "to choose" the right things for the right reasons—that is, if the language of automata must be used, rational automata. Predestination does not imply the absence of rationality in all senses of that term. God, were He omnipotent, could preordain the decisions and the reasons upon which they were based; and such a mode of existence would seem to be in itself a worthy mode of existence, and one preferable to an existence with free will, irrationality, and evil.

IV. CONCLUSION

In this paper it has been maintained that God, were He all-powerful and perfectly good, would have created a world in which there was no unnecessary evil. It has not been argued that God ought to have created a perfect world, nor that He should have made one that is in any way logically impossible. It has simply been argued that a benevolent God could, and would, have created a world devoid of superfluous evil. It has been contended that there is evil in this world—unnecessary evil—and that the more popular and philosophically more significant of the many attempts to explain this evil are completely unsatisfactory. Hence we must conclude from the existence of evil that there cannot be an omnipotent, benevolent God.

33 / The Problem of Evil

·JOHN HICK

*John Hick (1922–   ) has for many years taught at both Birmingham
University in England and at Claremont Graduate School in California. He
is the author of numerous books and articles in the philosophy of religion,
including the problem of evil and the nature of religious faith.*

[I. CLARIFICATION OF THE PROBLEM]

[A. The Problem /] To many, the most powerful positive objection to belief
in God is the fact of evil. Probably for most agnostics it is the appalling depth
and extent of human suffering, more than anything else, that makes the idea
of a loving Creator seem so implausible and disposes them toward one or
another of the various naturalistic theories of religion.

As a challenge to theism, the problem of evil has traditionally been posed
in the form of a dilemma: If God is perfectly loving, he must wish to abolish
evil; and if he is all-powerful, he must be able to abolish evil. But evil exists;
therefore God cannot be both omnipotent and perfectly loving.

[B. Untenable "Solutions" /] Certain solutions, which at once suggest
themselves, have to be ruled out so far as the Judaic-Christian faith is concerned.

To say, for example (with contemporary Christian Science), that evil is an
illusion of the human mind, is impossible within a religion based upon the
stark realism of the Bible. Its pages faithfully reflect the characteristic mixture
of good and evil in human experience. They record every kind of sorrow and
suffering, every mode of man's inhumanity to man and of his painfully insecure existence in the world. There is no attempt to regard evil as anything but
dark, menacingly ugly, heart-rending, and crushing. In the Christian scrip-
tures, the climax of this history of evil is the crucifixion of Jesus, which is
presented not only as a case of utterly unjust suffering, but as the violent and
murderous rejection of God's Messiah. There can be no doubt, then, that for
biblical faith, evil is unambiguously evil, and stands in direct opposition to
God's will.

Again, to solve the problem of evil by means of the theory (sponsored, for
example, by the Boston "Personalist" School)[1] of a finite deity who does the

---

[1]Edgar Brightman's *A Philosophy of Religion* (Englewood Cliffs, N.J.: Prentice-Hall, Inc., 1940),
chaps. 8–10, is a classic exposition of one form of this view.

best he can with a material, intractable and co-eternal with himself, is to have abandoned the basic premise of Hebrew-Christian monotheism; for the theory amounts to rejecting belief in the infinity and sovereignty of God.

Indeed, any theory which would avoid the problem of the origin of evil by depicting it as an ultimate constituent of the universe, coordinate with good, has been repudiated in advance by the classic Christian teaching, first developed by Augustine, that evil represents the going wrong of something which in itself is good.[2] Augustine holds firmly to the Hebrew-Christian conviction that the universe is *good*—that is to say, it is the creation of a good God for a good purpose. He completely rejects the ancient prejudice, widespread in his day, that matter is evil. There are, according to Augustine, higher and lower, greater and lesser goods in immense abundance and variety; but everything which has being is good in its own way and degree, except in so far as it may have become spoiled or corrupted. Evil—whether it be an evil will, an instance of pain, or some disorder or decay in nature—has not been set there by God, but represents the distortion of something that is inherently valuable. Whatever exists is, as such, and in its proper place, good; evil is essentially parasitic upon good, being disorder and perversion in a fundamentally good creation. This understanding of evil as something negative means that it is not willed and created by God; but it does not mean (as some have supposed) that evil is unreal and can be disregarded. Clearly, the first effect of this doctrine is to accentuate even more the question of the origin of evil.

[II. SOLUTION TO THE PROBLEM]

Theodicy,[3] as many modern Christian thinkers see it, is a modest enterprise, negative rather than positive in its conclusions. It does not claim to explain, nor to explain away, every instance of evil in human experience, but only to point to certain considerations which prevent the fact of evil (largely incomprehensible though it remains) from constituting a final and insuperable bar to rational belief in God.

In indicating these considerations it will be useful to follow the traditional division of the subject. There is the problem of *moral evil* or wickedness: Why does an all-good and all-powerful God permit this? And there is the problem of the *nonmoral evil* of suffering or pain, both physical and mental: Why has an all-good and all-powerful God created a world in which this occurs?

[A. Moral Evil /] Christian thought has always considered moral evil in its relation to human freedom and responsibility. To be a person is to be a finite center of freedom, a (relatively) free and self-directing agent responsible for one's own decision. This involves being free to act wrongly as well as to act

---

[2]See Augustine's *Confessions*, Book VII, chap. 12; *City of God*, Book XII, chap. 3; *Enchiridion*, chap. 4.

[3]The word "theodicy," from the Greek *theos* (God) and *dike* (righteous), means the justification of God's goodness in face of the fact of evil.

rightly. The idea of a person who can be infallibly guaranteed always to act rightly is self-contradictory. There can be no guarantee in advance that a genuinely free moral agent will never choose amiss. Consequently, the possibility of wrongdoing or sin is logically inseparable from the creation of finite persons, and to say that God should not have created beings who might sin amounts to saying that he should not have created people.

This thesis has been challenged in some recent philosophical discussions of the problem of evil, in which it is claimed that no contradiction* is involved in saying that God might have made people who would be genuinely free and who could yet be guaranteed always to act rightly. A quotation from one of these discussions follows:

> If there is no logical impossibility† in a man's freely choosing the good on one, or on several occasions, there cannot be a logical impossibility in his freely choosing the good on every occasion. God was not, then, faced with a choice between making innocent automata and making beings who, in acting freely, would sometimes go wrong: There was open to him the obviously better possibility of making beings who would act freely but always go right. Clearly, his failure to avail himself of this possibility is inconsistent with his being both omnipotent and wholly good.[4]

A reply to this argument is suggested in another recent contribution to the discussion.[5] If by a free action we mean an action which is not externally compelled but which flows from the nature of the agent as he reacts to the circumstances in which he finds himself, there is, indeed, no contradiction between our being free and our actions being "caused" (by our own nature) and therefore being in principle predictable. There is a contradiction, however, in saying that God is the cause of our acting as we do but that we are free beings in relation to God. There is, in other words, a contradiction in saying that God has made us so that we shall of necessity act in a certain way, and that we are genuinely independent persons in relation to him. If all our thoughts and actions are divinely predestined, however free and morally responsible we may seem to be to ourselves, we cannot be free and morally responsible in the sight of God, but must instead be his helpless puppets. Such "freedom" is like that of a patient acting out a series of posthypnotic suggestions: He appears, even to himself, to be free, but his volitions have actually been predetermined by another will, that of the hypnotist, in relation to whom the patient is not a free agent.

A different objector might raise the question of whether or not we deny

---

*[For the definition of 'contradiction', see Note 3 to the Preview to this Part. Understanding this concept is essential to understanding the next several paragraphs.—Eds.]

†[I.e., contradiction.—Eds.]

[4] J. L. Mackie, "Evil and Omnipotence," *Mind* (April, 1955), p. 209. A similar point is made by Antony Flew in "Divine Omnipotence and Human Freedom," *New Essays in Philosophical Theology*. An important critical comment on these arguments is offered by Ninian Smart in "Omnipotence, Evil and Supermen," *Philosophy* (April, 1961), with replies by Flew (January, 1962) and Mackie (April, 1962).

[5] Flew, in *New Essays in Philosophical Theology*.

God's omnipotence if we admit that he is unable to create persons who are free from the risks inherent in personal freedom. The answer that has always been given is that to create such beings is logically impossible. It is no limitation upon God's power that he cannot accomplish the logically impossible, since there is nothing here to accomplish, but only a meaningless conjunction of words[6]—in this case "person who is not a person." God is able to create beings of any and every conceivable kind; but creatures who lack moral freedom, however superior they might be to human beings in other respects, would not be what we mean by persons. They would constitute a different form of life which God might have brought into existence instead of persons. When we ask why God did not create such beings in place of persons, the traditional answer is that only persons could, in any meaningful sense, become "children of God," capable of entering into a personal relationship with their Creator by a free and uncompelled response to his love.

When we turn from the possibility of moral evil as a correlate of man's personal freedom to its actuality, we face something which must remain inexplicable even when it can be seen to be possible. For we can never provide a complete causal explanation of a free act; if we could, it would not be a free act. The origin of moral evil lies forever concealed within the mystery of human freedom.

The necessary connection between moral freedom and the possibility, now actualized, of sin throws light upon a great deal of the suffering which afflicts mankind. For an enormous amount of human pain arises either from the inhumanity or the culpable incompetence of mankind. This includes such major scourges as poverty, oppression and persecution, war, and all the injustice, indignity, and inequity which occur even in the most advanced societies. These evils are manifestations of human sin. Even disease is fostered to an extent, the limits of which have not yet been determined by psychosomatic medicine, by moral and emotional factors seated both in the individual and in his social environment. To the extent that all of these evils stem from human failures and wrong decisions, their possibility is inherent in the creation of free persons inhabiting a world which presents them with real choices which are followed by real consequences.

[B. Physical Evil /] We may now turn more directly to the problem of suffering. Even though the major bulk of actual human pain is traceable to man's misused freedom as a sole or part cause, there remain other sources of pain which are entirely independent of the human will, for example, earthquake, hurricane, storm, flood, drought, and blight. In practice, it is often impossible to trace a boundary between the suffering which results from human wickedness and folly and that which falls upon mankind from without. Both kinds of suffering are inextricably mingled together in human experience. For our present purpose, however, it is important to note that the latter category does

---

[6]As Aquinas said, ". . . nothing that implies a contradiction falls under the scope of God's omnipotence." *Summa Theologica*, part 1, question 25, article 4.

exist and that it seems to be built into the very structure of our world. In response to it, theodicy, if it is wisely conducted, follows a negative path. It is not possible to show positively that each item of human pain serves the divine purpose of good; but, on the other hand, it does seem possible to show that the divine purpose as it is understood in Judaism and Christianity could not be forwarded in a world which was designed as a permanent hedonistic paradise.

An essential premise of this argument concerns the nature of the divine purpose in creating the world. The skeptic's assumption is that man is to be viewed as a completed creation and that God's purpose in making the world was to provide a suitable dwelling-place for this fully formed creature. Since God is good and loving, the environment which he has created for human life to inhabit is naturally as pleasant and comfortable as possible. The problem is essentially similar to that of a man who builds a cage for some pet animal. Since our world, in fact, contains sources of hardship, inconvenience, and danger of innumerable kinds, the conclusion follows that this world cannot have been created by a perfectly benevolent and all-powerful deity.[7]

Christianity, however, has never supposed that God's purpose in the creation of the world was to construct a paradise whose inhabitants would experience a maximum of pleasure and a minimum of pain. The world is seen, instead, as a place of "soul-making" in which free beings grappling with the tasks and challenges of their existence in a common environment may become "children of God" and "heirs of eternal life." A way of thinking theologically of God's continuing creative purpose for man was suggested by . . . Irenaeus.* Following hints from St. Paul, Irenaeus taught that man has been made as a person in the image of God but has not yet been brought as a free and responsible agent into the finite likeness of God, which is revealed in Christ.[8] Our world, with all its rough edges, is the sphere in which this second and harder stage of the creative process is taking place.

[III. RELATED ISSUES]

[A. Consequences If There Were No Evil /] This conception of the world (whether or not set in Irenaeus' theological framework) can be supported by the method of negative theodicy. Suppose, contrary to fact, that this world were a paradise from which all possibility of pain and suffering were excluded. The consequences would be very far-reaching. For example, no one could ever injure anyone else: The murderer's knife would turn to paper or his bullets to thin air; the bank safe, robbed of a million dollars, would miraculously become filled with another million dollars (without this device, on

---

[7]This is the nature of David Hume's argument in his discussion of the problem of evil in his *Dialogues*, part 11.

*[An early Christian theologian and church father.—Eds.]

[8]See Irenaeus' *Against Heresies*, book IV, chaps. 37 and 38.

however large a scale, proving inflationary); fraud, deceit, conspiracy, and treason would somehow always leave the fabric of society undamaged. Again, no one would ever be injured by accident: The mountain-climber, steeplejack, or playing child falling from a height would float unharmed to the ground; the reckless driver would never meet with disaster. There would be no need to work, since no harm could result from avoiding work; there would be no call to be concerned for others in time of need or danger, for in such a world there could be no real needs or dangers.

To make possible this continual series of individual adjustments, nature would have to work by "special providences" instead of running according to general laws which men must learn to respect on penalty of pain or death. The laws of nature would have to be extremely flexible: Sometimes gravity would operate, sometimes not; sometimes an object would be hard and solid, sometimes soft. There could be no sciences, for there would be no enduring world structure to investigate. In eliminating the problems and hardships of an objective environment, with its own laws, life would become like a dream in which, delightfully but aimlessly, we would float and drift at ease.

One can at least begin to imagine such a world. It is evident that our present ethical concepts would have no meaning in it. If, for example, the notion of harming someone is an essential element in the concept of a wrong action, in our hedonistic paradise there could be no wrong actions—nor any right actions in distinction from wrong. Courage and fortitude would have no point in an environment in which there is, by definition, no danger or difficulty. Generosity, kindness, love, prudence, unselfishness, and all other ethical notions which presuppose life in a stable environment could not even be formed. Consequently, such a world, however well it might promote pleasure, would be very ill adapted for the development of the moral qualities of human personality. In relation to this purpose it would be the worst of all possible worlds.

It would seem, then, that an environment intended to make possible the growth in free beings of the finest characteristics of personal life must have a good deal in common with our present world. It must operate according to general and dependable laws; and it must involve real dangers, difficulties, problems, obstacles, and possibilities of pain, failure, sorrow, frustration, and defeat. If it did not contain the particular trials and perils which—subtracting man's own very considerable contribution—our world contains, it would have to contain others instead.

To realize this is not, by any means, to be in possession of a detailed theodicy. It is to understand that this world, with all its "heartaches and the thousand natural shocks that flesh is heir to," an environment so manifestly not designed for the maximization of human pleasure and the minimization of human pain, may be rather well adapted to the quite different purpose of "soul-making."[9]

---

[9]This brief discussion has been confined to the problem of human suffering. The large and intractable problem of animal pain is not taken up here. For a discussion of it, see, for example,

These considerations are related to theism as such. Specifically, Christian theism goes further in the light of the death of Christ, which is seen paradoxically both (as the murder of the divine Son) as the worst thing that has ever happened and (as the occasion of man's salvation) as the best thing that has ever happened. As the supreme evil turned to supreme good, it provides the paradigm for the distinctively Christian reaction to evil. Viewed from the standpoint of Christian faith, evils do not cease to be evils; and certainly, in view of Christ's healing work, they cannot be said to have been sent by God. Yet it has been the persistent claim of those seriously and wholeheartedly committed to Christian discipleship that tragedy, though truly tragic, may nevertheless be turned, through a man's reaction to it, from a cause of despair and alienation from God to a stage in the fulfillment of God's loving purpose for that individual. As the greatest of all evils, the crucifixion of Christ, was made the occasion of man's redemption, so good can be won from other evils. As Jesus saw his execution by the Romans as an experience which God desired him to accept, an experience which was to be brought within the sphere of the divine purpose and made to serve the divine ends, so the Christian response to calamity is to accept the adversities, pains, and afflictions which life brings, in order that they can be turned to a positive spiritual use.[10]

[B. Life after Death /] At this point, theodicy points forward in two ways to the subject of life after death.

First, although there are many striking instances of good being triumphantly brought out of evil through a man's or a woman's reaction to it, there are many other cases in which the opposite has happened. Sometimes obstacles breed strength of character, dangers evoke courage and unselfishness, and calamities produce patience and moral steadfastness. But sometimes they lead, instead, to resentment, fear, grasping selfishness, and disintegration of character. Therefore, it would seem that any divine purpose of soul-making which is at work in earthly history must continue beyond this life if it is ever to achieve more than a very partial and fragmentary success.

Second, if we ask whether the business of soul-making is worth all the toil and sorrow of human life, the Christian answer must be in terms of a future good which is great enough to justify all that has happened on the way to it.

Nels Ferre, *Evil and the Christian Faith* (New York: Harper & Row, Publishers, Inc., 1947), chap. 7; and Austin Farrer, *Love Almighty and Ills Unlimited* (New York: Doubleday & Company, Inc., 1961), chap. 5.

[10]This conception of providence is stated more fully in John Hick, *Faith and Knowledge* (Ithaca: Cornell University Press, 1957), chap. 7, from which some sentences are incorporated in this paragraph.

34 / Faith

RICHARD TAYLOR

Richard Taylor (1919–   ) is a professor of philosophy who taught for many years at Union College in New York. He has written highly acclaimed and widely discussed books and articles on a variety of philosophical problems, including metaphysics, philosophy of mind, and the philosophy of religion.

"*O*ur most holy religion," David Hume* said, "is founded on *faith*, not on reason." (All quotations are from the last two paragraphs of Hume's essay "Of Miracles.") He did not then conclude that it ought, therefore, to be rejected by reasonable men. On the contrary, he suggests that rational evaluation has no proper place in this realm to begin with, that a religious man need not feel in the least compelled to put his religion "to such a trial as it is, by no means, fitted to endure," and he brands as "dangerous friends or disguised enemies" of religion those "who have undertaken to defend it by the principles of human reason."

I want to defend Hume's suggestion, and go a bit farther by eliciting some things that seem uniquely characteristic of *Christian* faith, in order to show what it has, and what it has not, in common with other things to which it is often compared. I limited myself to Christian faith because I know rather little of any other, and faith is, with love and hope, supposed to be a uniquely Christian virtue.

I. FAITH AND REASON

Faith is not reason, else religion would be, along with logic and metaphysics, a part of philosophy, which it assuredly is not. Nor is faith belief resting on scientific or historical inquiry, else religion would be part of the corpus of human knowledge, which it clearly is not. More than that, it seems evident that by the normal, common-sense criteria of what is reasonable, the content of Christian faith is *un*reasonable. This, I believe, should be the starting point, the *datum*, of any discussion of faith and reason. It is, for instance, an essential content of the Christian faith that, at a certain quite recent time, God became man, dwelt among us in the person of a humble servant, and then, for a sacred purpose, died, to live again. Now, apologetics usually addresses itself

---

*[An eighteenth-century British philosopher.—Eds.]

to the *details* of this story, to show that they are not inherently incredible, but this is to miss the point. It is indeed *possible* to believe it, and in the strict sense the story is credible. Millions of people do most deeply and firmly believe it. But even the barest statement of the content of that belief makes it manifest that it does not and, I think, could not, ever result from rational inquiry. "Mere reason," Hume said, "is insufficient to convince us of its veracity." The Christian begins the recital of his faith with the words, "I believe," and it would be an utter distortion to construe this as anything like "I have inquired, and found it reasonable to conclude." If there were a man who could say that in honesty, as I think there is not, then he would, in a clear and ordinary sense, believe, but he would have no religious faith whatsoever, and his beliefs themselves would be robbed of what would make them religious.

Now if this essential and (it seems to me) obvious unreasonableness of Christian belief could be recognized at the outset of any discussion of religion, involving rationalists on the one hand and believers on the other, we would be spared the tiresome attack and apologetics upon which nothing ultimately turns, the believer would be spared what is, in fact, an uncalled-for task of reducing his faith to reason or science, which can, as Hume noted, result only in "exposing" it as neither, and the rationalist would be granted his main point, not as a conclusion triumphantly extracted, but as a datum too obvious to labor.

II. FAITH AND CERTAINTY

Why, then, does a devout Christian embrace these beliefs? Now this very question, on the lips of a philosopher, is wrongly expressed, for he invariably intends it as a request for reasons, as a means of putting the beliefs to that unfair "trial" of which Hume spoke. Yet there is a clear and definite answer to this question, which has the merit of being true and evident to anyone who has known intimately those who dwell in the atmosphere of faith. The reason the Christian believes that story around which his whole life turns is, simply, that he cannot help it. If he is trapped into eliciting grounds for it, they are grounds given after the fact of conviction. Within "the circle of faith," the question whether on the evidence one *ought* to believe "does not arise." One neither seeks nor needs grounds for the acceptance of what he cannot help believing. "Whoever is moved by *faith* to assent," Hume wrote, "is conscious of a continued miracle in his own person, which subverts all the principles of his understanding, and gives him a determination to believe. . . ." It is this fact of faith which drives philosophers to such exasperation, in the face of which the believer is nonetheless so utterly unmoved.

The believer sees his life as a gift of God, the world as the creation of God, his own purposes, insofar as they are noble, as the purposes of God, and history as exhibiting a divine plan, made known to him through the Christian story. He sees things this way, just because they do seem so, and he cannot help it. This is why, for him, faith is so "easy," and secular arguments to the contrary so beside the point. No one seeks evidence for that of which he is entirely convinced, or regards as relevant what seems to others to cast doubt. The believer is like a child who recoils from danger, as exhibited, for instance, in what he for the first time sees as a fierce animal; the child has no difficulty *believing* he is in peril, just because he cannot help believing it, yet his belief results not at all from induction based on past experience with fierce animals, and no reassurances, garnered from our past experience, relieve his terror at all.

III. SOME CONFUSIONS

If this is what religious faith essentially is—if, as a believer might poetically but, I think, correctly describe it, faith is an involuntary conviction, often regarded as a "gift," on the part of one who has voluntarily opened his mind and heart to receive it—then certain common misunderstandings can be removed.

In the first place, faith should never be likened to an *assumption*, such as the scientist's assumption of the uniformity of nature, or whatnot. An assumption is an intellectual device for furthering inquiry. It need not be a conviction nor, indeed, even a belief. But a half-hearted faith is no religious faith. Faith thus has that much, at least, in common with knowledge, that it is a *conviction*, and its subjective state is *certainty*. One thus wholly distorts faith if he represents the believer as just "taking" certain things "on faith," and then reasons, like a philosopher, from these beginnings, as though what were thus "taken" could, like an assumption, be rejected at will.

Again, it is a misunderstanding to represent faith as "mere tenacity." Tenacity consists in stubbornly clinging to what one hopes, but of which one is not fully convinced. The child who is instantly convinced of danger in the presence of an animal is not being tenacious or stubborn, even in the face of verbal reassurances, and no more is the Christian whose acts are moved by faith. The believer does not so much *shun* evidence as something that might *shake* his faith, but rather regards it as not to the point. In this he may appear to philosophers to be mistaken, but only if one supposes, as he need not, that one should hold only such beliefs as are rational.

Again, it is misleading to refer to any set of propositions, such as those embodied in a creed, as being this or that person's "faith." Concerning that content of belief in which one is convinced by faith, it is logically (though I think not otherwise) possible that one might be convinced by evidence, in which case it would have no more to do with faith or religion than do the statements in a newspaper. This observation has this practical importance, that it is quite possible—in fact, common—for the faith of different believers to be one and the same, despite creedal differences.

And finally, both "faith" (or "fideism") and "reason" (or "rationalism") can be, and often are, used as pejorative terms and as terms of commendation. Which side one takes here is arbitrary, for there is no non-question-begging way of deciding. A rationalist can perhaps find reasons for being a rationalist, though this is doubtful; but in any case it would betray a basic misunderstanding to expect a fideist to do likewise. This is brought out quite clearly by the direction that discussions of religion usually take. A philosophical teacher will often, for instance, labor long to persuade his audience that the content of Christian faith is unreasonable, which is a shamefully easy task for him, unworthy of his learning. Then, suddenly, the underlying assumption comes to light that Christian beliefs ought, therefore, to be abandoned by rational people! A religious hearer of this discourse might well reply that, religion being unreasonable but nonetheless manifestly worthy of belief, we should conclude with Hume that reason, in this realm at least, ought to be rejected. Now one can decide that issue by any light that is granted him, but it is worth stressing that the believer's position on it is just exactly as good, and just as bad, as the rational skeptic's.

35 / *Religion, Reason, and Faith*

RICHARD ROBINSON

Richard Robinson (1902–   ) was a Fellow and very popular teacher at Oriel College at Oxford University in England. He has written several books and many articles on a variety of philosophical problems, but the ones in which he had a passionate interest are in the field of the philosophy of religion.

I. RELIGION AND REASON

*T*here is something commonly accepted as a great good which I reject, namely religion.

Religion has held a big place in the thoughts and feelings of most of the human beings who have yet lived; and, though some have found it an inescapable evil, most have found it a great good. The founder of the Gifford lectures* said that "religion is of all things the most excellent and precious. . . ."

*[A famous philosophy lecture series in England.—Eds.]

The religious man feels that his god is the supreme good, and the worship of him is the supreme good for man; and he obtains an immense satisfaction in worship and obedience. His creed gives him the feeling that the universe is important and that he has his own humble but important part in it. "God is working his purpose out, as year succeeds to year"; and in this august enterprise the believer has an assured place. When he says that "man cannot be at ease in the world unless he has a faith to sustain him," the faith he is thinking of is in part that there is something extremely important to do. Thus his religion lays that specter of futility and meaninglessness, which man's self-consciousness and thoughtfulness are always liable to raise. The convert says to himself, in the words at the end of Tolstoy's *Anna Karenina*: "My whole life, every moment of my life, will be, not meaningless as before, but full of deep meaning, which I shall have power to impress on every action." The great comfort of such a belief is obvious.

But this is still less than half of the comfort religion can give. For it is not yet an answer to man's greatest horror, the death of his loved ones and himself. If his religion also makes him believe that death is not the end of life, that on the contrary he and his loved ones will live forever in perfect justice and happiness, this more than doubles his feeling of comfort and security. This doctrine of the happy survival of death is the chief attraction of the Christian religion to most of its adherents; and their first profound religious belief comes to them as a reassurance after their first realization that they are going to die. It is an easy defensive reaction against this terrible discovery. . . .

Such is the enormous comfort that religion can give. Because of it a man who deprives the people of the comfort of believing "in the final proportions of eternal justice" is often regarded as a "cruel oppressor, the merciless enemy of the poor and wretched" (Edmund Burke, "Reflections on the French Revolution," *Works*, v. 432).

But is it a cruel oppression to preach atheism? There is a sinister suggestion in this idea, namely the suggestion that we ought to preach religion whether or not it is true, and that we ought not to estimate rationally whether it is true, which implies that truth is below comfort in value.

It seems to me that religion buys its benefits at too high a price, namely at the price of abandoning the ideal of truth and shackling and perverting man's reason. The religious man refuses to be guided by reason and evidence in a certain field, the theory of the gods, theology. He does not say: "I believe that there is a god, but I am willing to listen to argument that I am mistaken, and I shall be glad to learn better." He does not seek to find and adopt the more probable of the two contradictories, "There is a god" and "There is no god." On the contrary, he makes his choice between those two propositions once for all. He is determined never to revise his choice, but to believe that there is a god no matter what the evidence. The secretary of the Christian Evidence Society wrote to *The Times** (March 19, 1953) and said: "When demand is made

*[Of London.—Eds.]

upon devout Christians to produce evidence in justification of their intense faith in God they are apt to feel surprised, pained, and even disgusted that any such evidence should be considered necessary." That is true. Christians do not take the attitude of reasonable inquiry toward the proposition that there is a god. If they engage in discussion on the matter at all, they seek more often to intimidate their opponent by expressing shock or disgust at his opinion, or disapproval of his character. They take the view that to hold the negative one of these two contradictories is a moral crime. They make certain beliefs wicked as such, without reference to the question whether the man has reached them sincerely and responsibly. This view, that certain beliefs are as such wicked, is implied in these two sentences in John's gospel (xvi. 8–9 and xx. 29): "He will reprove the world of sin . . . because they believe not in me," and "Blessed are they that have not seen, and yet have believed." There is an extensive example of this attitude in Newman's* fifteenth sermon.

Along with the view that certain beliefs are as such wicked, there often goes, naturally, the view that it is wicked to try to persuade a person to hold certain beliefs. The believer's complaint, "You are undermining my faith," implies that it is wrong as such to try to convince a man that there is no god. It implies that whether one believes the proposition or not, and whether one has a good reason to believe it or not, are irrelevant, because it is just wrong in itself to recommend this proposition. This view is contrary to the search for truth and the reasonable attitude of listening to argument and guiding oneself thereby.

If theology were a part of reasonable inquiry, there would be no objection to an atheist's being a professor of theology. That a man's being an atheist is an absolute bar to his occupying a chair of theology proves that theology is not an open-minded and reasonable inquiry. Someone may object that a professor should be interested in his subject and an atheist cannot be interested in theology. But a man who maintains that there is no god must think it a sensible and interesting question to ask whether there is a god; and in fact we find that many atheists are interested in theology. Professor H. D. Lewis tells (*Philosophy*, 1952, p. 347) that an old lady asked him what philosophy is, and, when he had given an answer, she said: "O I see, theology." She was nearly right, for theology and philosophy have the same subject-matter. The difference is that in philosophy you are allowed to come out with whichever answer seems to you the more likely.

In most universities the title of theology includes a lot of perfectly good science which is not theory of god, and which I do not reject, I mean the scientific study of the history of the Jews and their languages and their religious books. All that can be reasonable study, and usually is so. But it is a hindrance to the progress of knowledge that we are largely organized for research in such a way that a man cannot be officially paid to engage in these branches of research unless he officially maintains that there is a god. It is as if

---

*[Newman was a nineteenth-century English writer and a Roman Catholic cardinal.—Eds.]

a man could not be a professor of Greek unless he believed in Zeus and Apollo.*

Religious persons often consider gambling to be a bad thing. It certainly causes a great deal of misery. But much of the badness of gambling consists in its refusal to face the probabilities and be guided by them; and in the matter of refusing to face the probabilities religion is a worse offender than gambling, and does more harm to the habits of reason. Religious belief is, in fact, a form of gambling, as Pascal saw. It does more harm to reason than ordinary gambling does, however, because it is more in earnest.

It has been said that the physicist has just as closed a mind about cause as the Christian has about god. The physicist assumes through thick and thin that everything happens according to causal laws. He presupposes cause, just as the Christian presupposes god.

But the physicist does not *assume* that there is a reign of law; he hopes that there is. He looks for laws; but whenever a possible law occurs to him, he conscientiously tries to disprove it by all reasonable tests. He asserts at any time only such laws as seem at that time to have passed all reasonable tests, and he remains always prepared to hear of new evidence throwing doubt on those laws. This is far from the Christian attitude about god. The Christian does not merely hope that there is a god and maintain only such gods as the best tests have shown to be more probable than improbable.

The main irrationality of religion is preferring comfort to truth; and it is this that makes religion a very harmful thing on balance, a sort of endemic disease that has so far prevented human life from reaching its full stature. For the sake of comfort and security religion is prepared to sophisticate thought and language to any degree. For the sake of comfort and security there pours out daily, from pulpit and press, a sort of propaganda which, if it were put out for a nonreligious purpose, would be seen by everyone to be cynical and immoral. We are perpetually being urged to adopt the Christian creed not because it is true but because it is beneficial, or to hold that it must be true just because belief in it is beneficial. "The Christian faith," we are assured, "is a necessity for a fully adjusted personality" (a psychiatrist in the *Radio Times* for March 20, 1953, p. 33). Hardly a week passes without someone recommending theism on the ground that if it were believed there would be much less crime; and this is a grossly immoral argument. Hardly a week passes without someone recommending theism on the ground that unless it is believed the free nations will succumb to the Communists; and that is the same grossly immoral argument. It is always wicked to recommend anybody to believe anything on the ground he or anybody else will feel better or be more moral or successful for doing so, or on any ground whatever except that the available considerations indicate that it is probably true. The pragmatic suggestion, that we had better teach the Christian religion whether it is true or not, because people will be much less criminal if they believe it, is disgusting and

*[Greek gods.—Eds.]

degrading; but it is being made to us all the time, and it is a natural consequence of the fundamental religious attitude that comfort and security must
always prevail over rational inquiry.

This pragmatic fallacy is not the only fallacy into which religion is frequently led by preferring comfortingness to truth, though it is the main one.
The religious impulse encourages all the fallacies. It encourages the argument
*ad hominem,** that is the argument that my adversary's view must be false
because he is a wicked man: The atheist is impious, therefore he is wicked,
therefore his view is false. Religion encourages also the argument from ignorance: Instead of rejecting a proposition if it is probably false, the religious
man thinks himself entitled to accept it because it is not certainly false. Biased
selection of the instances is also very common in religious language. Any case
of a man getting his wish after praying for it, or being struck by lightning after
doing something mean, is taken as good evidence that there is a god who
gives and punishes. Contrary cases are not looked for; and if they obtrude
themselves they are dealt with by the further hypothesis that "God's ways are
inscrutable." Religious arguments even exhibit, very often, what seems the
most fallacious possible fallacy, namely inferring a theory from something
that contradicts the theory. Thus we often find: "Since no explanation is final,
God is the final explanation"; and "Since everybody believes in God, you are
wrong not to believe in God."

I have been saying that religion is gravely infected with intellectual dishonesty. You may find this very unlikely for a general reason. You may think it
very unlikely that such widespread dishonesty would go unnoticed. I do not
think so. I think, on the contrary, that it is quite common for a moral defect to
pervade a certain sphere and yet escape notice in that sphere, although the
people concerned are wide awake to its presence in other places. I think there
are plenty of other cases of this. One of them is that the English, who are
greater haters of the bully and the might-is-right man, nevertheless bully and
intimidate each other when driving a car. They know that power does not
confer any right, but they assume that horse-power does. Life is full of such
inconsistencies, because we can never see all the implications and applica-
tions of our principles. In religion it is particularly easy for intellectual dishonesty to escape notice, because of the common assumption that all honesty
flows from religion and religion is necessarily honest whatever it does.

II. FAITH

According to Christianity one of the great virtues is faith. Paul gave faith a
commanding position in the Christian scheme of values, along with hope and
love, in the famous thirteenth chapter of his first letter to the Corinthians.
Thomas Aquinas† held that infidelity is a very great sin, that infidels should

---

*[To or against the man.—Eds.]
†[A medieval theologian.—Eds.]

be compelled to believe, that heretics should not be tolerated, and that here-tics who revert to the true doctrine and then relapse again should not be received into penitence, but killed (*Summa Theologica*, 2-2, 1–16).

According to me this is a terrible mistake, and faith is not a virtue but a positive vice. More precisely, there is, indeed, a virtue often called faith, but that is not the faith which the Christians make much of. The true virtue of faith is faith as opposed to faithlessness, that is, keeping faith and promises and being loyal. Christian faith, however, is not opposed to faithlessness but to unbelief. It is faith as some opposite of unbelief that I declare to be a vice.

When we investigate what Christians mean by their peculiar use of the word "faith," I think we come to the remarkable conclusion that all their accounts of it are either unintelligible or false. Their most famous account is that in Heb. xi. 1: "Faith is the substance of things hoped for, the evidence of things not seen." This is obviously unintelligible. In any case, it does not make faith a virtue, since neither a substance nor an evidence can be a virtue. A virtue is a praiseworthy habit of choice, and neither a substance nor an evidence can be a habit of choice. When a Christian gives an intelligible account of faith, I think you will find that it is false. I mean that it is not a true dictionary report of how he and other Christians actually use the word. For example, Augustine asked: "What is faith but believing what you do not see?" (*Joannis Evang. Tract.*, c. 40, § 8). But Christians do not use the word "faith" in the sense of believing what you do not see. You do not see thunder; but you cannot say in the Christian sense: "Have faith that it is thundering," or "I have faith that it has thundered in the past and will again in the future." You do not see mathematical truths; but you cannot say in the Christian sense: "Have faith that there is no greatest number." If we take Augustine's "see" to stand here for "know," still it is false that Christians use the word "faith" to mean believing what you do not know, for they would never call it faith if anyone believed that the sun converts hydrogen into helium, although he did not know it.

A good hint of what Christians really mean by their word "faith" can be got by considering the proposition: "Tom Paine had faith that there is no god." Is this a possible remark, in the Christian sense of the word "faith"? No, it is an impossible remark, because it is self-contradictory, because part of what Christians mean by "faith" is belief that there *is* a god.

There is more to it than this. Christian faith is not merely believing that there is a god. It is believing that there is a god no matter what the evidence on the question may be. "Have faith," in the Christian sense, means "Make yourself believe that there is a god without regard to evidence." Christian faith is a habit of flouting reason in forming and maintaining one's answer to the question whether there is a god. Its essence is the determination to believe that there is a god no matter what the evidence may be.

No wonder that there is no true and intelligible account of faith in Chris-tian literature. What they mean is too shocking to survive exposure. Faith is a great vice, an example of obstinately refusing to listen to reason, something irrational and undesirable, a form of self-hypnotism. Newman wrote that "if we but obey God strictly, in time (through his blessing) faith will become like sight" (*Sermon* 15). This is no better than if he had said: "Keep on telling yourself that there is a god until you believe it. Hypnotize yourself into this belief."

It follows that, far from its being wicked to undermine faith, it is a duty to do so. We ought to do what we can toward eradicating the evil habit of believing without regard to evidence.

The usual way of recommending faith is to point out that belief and trust are often rational or necessary attitudes. Here is an example of this from Newman: "To hear some men speak (I mean men who scoff at religion), it might be thought we never acted on Faith or Trust, except in religious matters; whereas we are acting on trust every hour of our lives. . . . We trust our *memory* . . . the general soundness of our reasoning powers. . . . Faith in (the) sense of *reliance on the words of another* as opposed to trust in one-self . . . is the common meaning of the word" (*Sermon* 15).

The value of this sort of argument is as follows. It is certainly true that belief and trust are often rational. But it is also certainly true that belief and trust are often irrational. We have to decide in each case by rational consider-ations whether to believe and trust or not. Sometimes we correctly decide not to trust our memory on some point, but to look the matter up in a book. Sometimes even we correctly decide not to trust our own reason, like poor Canning deciding he was mad because the Duke of Wellington told him he was. But Christian faith is essentially a case of irrational belief and trust and decision, because it consists in deciding to believe and trust the proposition that there is a god no matter what the evidence may be.

Another common way to defend Christian faith is to point out that we are often obliged to act on something less than knowledge and proof. For exam-ple, Newman writes: "Life is not long enough for a religion of inferences; we shall never have done beginning if we determine to begin with proof. Life is for action. If we insist on proof for everything, we shall never come to action; to act you must assume, and that assumption is faith" (*Assent*, p. 92).

The value of this argument is as follows. It is true that we are often unable to obtain knowledge and proof. But it does not follow that we must act on faith, for faith is belief reckless of evidence and probability. It follows only that we must act on some belief that does not amount to knowledge. This being so, we ought to assume, as our basis for action, those beliefs which are more probable than their contradictories in the light of the available evidence. We ought not to act on faith, for faith is assuming a certain belief without refer-ence to its probability.

There is an ambiguity in the phrase "have faith in" that helps to make faith look respectable. When a man says that he has faith in the president he is assuming that it is obvious and known to everybody that there is a president, that the president exists, and he is asserting his confidence that the president will do good work on the whole. But if a man says he has faith in telepathy, he does not mean that he is confident that telepathy will do good work on the whole, but that he believes that telepathy really occurs sometimes, that telepathy exists. Thus the phrase "to have faith in x" sometimes means to be confident that good work will be done by x, who is assumed or known to exist, but at other times means to believe that x exists. Which does it mean in the phrase "have faith in God"? It means ambiguously both; and the self-evidence of what it means in the one sense recommends what it means in the other sense. If there is a perfectly powerful and good god it is self-evidently reasonable to believe that he will do good. In this sense "Have faith in God" is a reasonable exhortation. But it insinuates the other sense, namely "Believe that there is a perfectly powerful and good god, no matter what the evidence." Thus the reasonableness of trusting God if he exists is used to make it seem also reasonable to believe that he exists.

It is well to remark here that a god who wished us to decide certain questions without regard to the evidence would definitely *not* be a perfectly good god.

Even when a person is aware that faith is belief without regard to evidence, he may be led to hold faith respectable by the consideration that we sometimes think it good for a man to believe in his friend's honesty in spite of strong evidence to the contrary, or for a woman to believe in her son's innocence in spite of strong evidence to the contrary. But while we admire and love the love that leads the friend or parent to this view, we do not adopt or admire his conclusion unless we believe that he has private evidence of his own, gained by his long and intimate association, to outweigh the public evidence on the other side. Usually we suppose that his love has led him into an error of judgment, which both love and hate are prone to do.

This does not imply that we should never act on a man's word if we think he is deceiving us. Sometimes we ought to act on a man's word although we privately think he is probably lying. For the act required may be unimportant, whereas accusing a man of lying is always important. But there is no argument from this to faith. We cannot say that sometimes we ought to believe a proposition although we think it is false!

So I conclude that faith is a vice and to be condemned. As Plato* said, "It is unholy to abandon the probably true" (*Rp.* 607 c). Out of Paul's† "faith, hope, and love" I emphatically accept love and reject faith. As to hope, it is more respectable than faith. While we ought not to believe against the probabilities, we are permitted to hope against them. But still the Christian overtones of hope are other-worldly and unrealistic. It is better to take a virtue that avoids that. Instead of faith, hope, and love, let us hymn reason, love, and joy.

What is the application of this to the common phrase "a faith to live by"? A faith to live by is not necessarily a set of beliefs or valuations maintained without regard to evidence in an irrational way. The phrase can well cover also a criticized and rational choice of values. To decide, for example, that the pursuit of love is better than the pursuit of power, in view of the probable

*[A philosopher of ancient Greece.—Eds.]
†[The apostle.—Eds.]

effects of each on human happiness and misery, and to guide one's actions accordingly, is a rational procedure, and is sometimes called and may well be called "a faith to live by." In this case a faith to live by is a choice of values, a decision as to great goods and evils. . . . On the other hand, many "faiths to live by" are irrational and bad. Some people will not count anything as a faith to live by unless it deliberately ignores rational considerations; so that what they will consent to call a faith to live by must always be something that is bad according to me. Other people refuse to count anything as a faith to live by unless it includes a belief that the big battalions are on their side, so that according to them a man who rationally concludes that he is not the darling of any god by definition has no faith to live by. . . .

STUDY QUESTIONS

1. According to McCloskey, why is the fact of evil a problem for the theist?

2. What are the two general kinds of evil? State the proposed solutions to each. State McCloskey's criticisms of those solutions.

3. What conclusion(s) does McCloskey defend? State his arguments in behalf of those conclusion(s), and critically evaluate them.

4. Why does Hick rule out certain solutions to the problem of evil? Do you agree that they should be ruled out? Why or why not?

5. In your view, who has dealt with the problem of evil most adequately, Hick or McCloskey? Why?

6. What is the main claim that Taylor defends? What are his reasons for it?

7. State Robinson's main theses in "Religion, Reason, and Faith." State his arguments in behalf of these theses. Critically evaluate his position.

8. Why does Robinson hold that faith is a vice? Do you agree? Why or why not?

9. In "The Will to Believe" (see Part One), does William James provide a justifiable answer to Robinson's criticisms? Why or why not?

10. Adopt Robinson's standpoint and reply to James.

11. Evaluate the following: "The problem of evil is no problem at all for Christianity because any amount of pain and misery on earth is nothing compared with the infinite and eternal happiness which Christianity promises."

12. St. Augustine maintained that, although we think there are natural evils, in fact there are none. We think this way because we are not able to comprehend things as they really are. If we could view an earthquake or tornado or plague through God's eyes, we would see that it was just the right thing to occur at that particular place and time. Critically evaluate this argument.

13. The French philosopher Pascal held that the way to decide whether or not to believe in the existence of God is to ask whether believing or disbelieving is better and then bet accordingly. He maintains:

> If we wager that God exists and he does, then we gain eternal bliss; if he does not, we have lost nothing. If we wager that God does not exist and he does, then eternal misery is our share; if he does not, we gain only a lucky true belief. The obvious wager is to bet God exists. With such a bet we have everything to gain and nothing to lose. This is far superior to a bet where we have little to gain and everything to lose.

This is known as "Pascal's Wager." Evaluate this attempt to justify belief in God.

14. Would someone who accepts the existence of God on faith be acting in a manner which is consistent with the aims of philosophy discussed in the introduction to this book? Why or why not?

FURTHER READINGS

A. The Problem of Evil

Hick, John. *Evil and the God of Love*. New York: Harper & Row, 1966. [An attempt by a religious believer to solve the problem of evil.]

Hume, David. *Dialogues Concerning Natural Religion*. New York: Haffner, 1961. Pts. 10 and 11. [A vigorous formulation and discussion of the problem, along with criticisms of some of the classical arguments for the existence of God.]

Mackie, J. L. "Evil and Omnipotence." *Mind*, 64 (1955), 200–212. [A more technical but forceful statement of the argument from evil against belief in God.]

Madden, Edward H. "The Many Faces of Evil." *Philosophy and Phenomenological Research*, 24 (1964), 481–492. [A thorough examination of the problem by a nonbeliever.]

Pike, Nelson, ed. *God and Evil*. Englewood Cliffs, N.J.: Prentice-Hall, 1964. [A collection of classical and recent discussions of the problem from various standpoints.]

B. Religious Faith

Hick, John. *Faith and Knowledge*, 2nd ed. Ithaca, N.Y.: Cornell University Press, 1960. [An eloquent defense of religious faith.]

Hick, John. "Faith as Experiencing—As." In G. N. A. Vesy, *Talk of God*. New York: Macmillan, 1959. [Provides a new interpretation of the nature of faith.]

Kaufman, Walter. *The Faith of a Heretic*. Garden City, N.Y.: Doubleday, 1961. [A vigorous and readable work presenting the view against religious faith.]

Martin, C. B. *Religious Belief*. Ithaca, N.Y.: Cornell University Press, 1959. [A contemporary criticism of religious belief.]

Mitchell, Basil, ed. *Faith and Logic*. London: Allen & Unwin, 1957. [A collection of essays on religious faith and related topics by several contemporary thinkers.]

PART EIGHT

MEANING AND EXISTENCE

PREVIEW

In the *Myth of Sisyphus* Camus writes,

> There is but one truly philosophical problem, and that is suicide. Judging whether life is or is not worth living amounts to answering the fundamental question of philosophy. All the rest—whether the world has three dimensions, whether the mind has nine or twelve categories—comes afterwards. These are games; one must first answer. . . .

> If I ask myself how to judge that this question is more urgent than that, I reply that one judges by the actions it entails. I have never seen anyone die for the ontological argument [for the existence of God]. Galileo, who held a scientific truth of great importance, abjured it with the greatest of ease as soon as it endangered his life. In a certain sense, he did right. That truth was not worth the stake. Whether the earth or the sun revolves around the other is a matter of profound indifference. . . . On the other hand, I see many people die because they judge that life is not worth living. I see others paradoxically getting killed for the ideas or illusions that give them a reason for living (what is called a reason for living is also an excellent reason for dying). I therefore conclude that the meaning of life is the most urgent of questions.[1]

Many people would agree with Camus—even if they would not agree with the somewhat exaggerated manner in which he expresses his view. And surely almost every reflective and sensitive person has asked at one time or another, What is the meaning of life? What is it all about? What is the point of it all? And one tends to feel that if life has no meaning or purpose, then it is not worth living. Hence, surely the question of the meaning of life is one of the most important of all philosophical and "existential" questions. It will, hence, be examined in this part.

Of course, some have maintained that there is only one basis for providing meaning to life: God, or at least faith in God. Without the existence of God, or faith in his existence, life would have no meaning or purpose and, hence, would not be worth living. Others have also held that the scientific

---

[1]A. Camus, *The Myth of Sisyphus* (New York: Knopf, 1955), p. 3.

view of the world has led to a rejection of belief in God and, hence, to the result that life is meaningless. These claims need to be examined—and will be. This leads us to the main question of this part.

Main Question

The main question dealt with in this part is:

Does (human) life have a meaning and/or purpose?
If so, how? And what sort of meaning is it? If not, why not?

Answers

In turning to possible answers to this question, we find three main approaches or stances. These positions have no commonly accepted labels. Hence, we shall designate them by descriptive phrases, as follows:

a. The theistic answer. The theist maintains that the meaning of life can be found only in the existence of God or through faith in God's existence. Without the existence of God, or faith in God, life has no meaning, no purpose, and, hence, is not worth living.

b. The non-theistic alternative. Many people have questioned the theistic answer. In their view even if life has no meaning or purpose on any grand, cosmic scale, this does not entail that it has no meaning or purpose at all. On the contrary, it is maintained that, by denying such objective meaning or purpose, humans are free to forge their own meaning and purpose, and to do so within the bounds of the natural universe. No appeal to something which transcends the natural universe is required in order to give life genuine meaning and purpose. Hence, the theist's conclusion does not follow. Since meaning and purpose can be found without faith in God, life can be genuinely worth living without such faith.

c. The approach which questions the meaningfulness of the question. Some have maintained that "What is the meaning of life?" is an odd question. It is one which stems from confusion or for which there is no possible means to find a significant answer. Hence, the question itself is meaningless.

In summary, we have these answers to our question:

a. The theistic answer: Without God or faith in God, life can have no meaning or purpose and, hence, would be not worth living.

b. The non-theistic alternative: Life can have meaning and purpose and, hence, be worthwhile even if we give up the belief in God. Meaning is independent of God.

c. The third approach: The whole question, "What is the meaning of life?" is itself meaningless.

Most writers support either the theistic or non-theistic answer to our question. Hence, we have not included an essay which represents the third approach. Further, among the four selections you will find two vivid accounts by Tolstoy and Sartre, writers who were not merely philosophers but who are known for their literary works.

Selections

The two main answers to the question of whether life has meaning are represented in this part as follows:

Answer	Selection
(a) Theistic answer	36, 38
(b) Non-theistic alternative	37, 39

36 / The Dignity of Human Life

DAVID F. SWENSON

David F. Swenson (1876–1940) was a professor of philosophy at the University of Minnesota and was acknowledged as a great teacher. He translated many works by the Danish thinker Sören Kierkegaard and wrote a book about him. The following essay was originally one of Prof. Swenson's many public lectures and was published in a collection of his articles and lectures.

[I. THE NEED FOR A VIEW OF LIFE]

*M*an lives forward, but he thinks backward. As an active being, his task is to press forward to the things that are before, toward the goal where is the prize of the high calling. But as a thinking, active being, his forward movement is conditioned by a retrospect. If there were no past for a man, there could be no future; and if there were no future and no past, but only such an immersion in the present as is characteristic of the brute which perisheth, then there would be nothing eternal in human life, and everything distinctively and essentially human would disappear from our existence.

As a preparation for an existence in the present, the youth of a nation are trained in various skills and along devious lines, according to their capacities and circumstances, for the parts they are to play in existence; their natural talents are developed, some by extended periods of intellectual training, others for participation in various forms of business or technical training; but whatever be the ultimate end of the training, its purpose is to develop those latent powers they possess which will eventually prove of benefit to themselves or to others. But, in addition to this, which we may call a preparation for the external life, a something else is urgently needed, a something so fundamentally important that in its absence every other form of preparation is revealed as imperfect and incomplete, even ineffective and futile.

This so particularly indispensable something is a *view of life*, and a view of life is not acquired as a direct and immediate result of a course of study, the reading of books, or a communication of results. It is wholly a product of the individual's own knowledge of himself as an individual, of his individual capabilities and aspirations. A view of life is a principle of living, a spirit and an attitude capable of maintaining its unity and identity with itself in all of life's complexities and varying vicissitudes; and yet also capable of being declined, to use the terminology of the grammatical sciences, in all the infinite variety of cases that the language of life affords. Without this preparation the individual life is like a ship without a rudder, a bit of wreckage floating with the current to an uncomprehended destiny. A view of life is not objective knowledge, but subjective conviction. It is a part of man's own self, the source whence the stream of his life issues. It is the dominant attitude of the spirit which gives to life its direction and its goal. This is why it cannot be directly communicated or conveyed, like an article of commerce, from one person to another. If a view of life were a body of knowledge about life, or a direct and immediate implication from such knowledge, it would be subject to objective communication and systematic instruction. But it is rather a personal expression of what a man essentially is in his own inmost self, and this cannot be learned by rote, or accepted at the hands of some external authority. Knowledge is the answer or answers that things give to the questions we ask of them; a view of life is the reply a person gives to the question that life asks of him. We begin life by scrutinizing our environment, ourselves playing the role of questioners and examiners and critics; but at a later moment, when the soul comes of age and is about to enter upon its majority, it learns that the tables have been turned and the roles reversed; from that moment it confronts a question, a searching and imperative question, in relation to which no evasion can avail, and to which no shifting of responsibility is possible.

In discussing the problem of *a view of life which can give it meaning and dignity and worth,* I am well aware that no one can acquire a view of life by listening to a speech.* Nevertheless, a speech may serve the more modest purpose of stimulating a search, perhaps a more earnest search; and may render more articulate possibly the convictions of those who have already won some such conception, having made it their own by a heartfelt and spontaneous choice.

[II. ONE APPROACH]

All men are endowed by nature with a desire for happiness—a principle so obvious as scarcely to need any explanation, and certainly no defense. A human life without happiness or hope of happiness is not a life, but rather a death in life. Happiness is life's vital fluid and the very breath of its nostrils. Happiness and life are so much one and the same thing that the more profoundly any life discovers happiness, the more significant and abundant is that life itself. . . .

But for a thinking human being—and God made every man a thinker, whatever may be our estimate of that which men make of themselves—for a thinking human being, happiness cannot consist in the satisfaction of momentary impulse, of blind feeling, of brute immediacy. A pleasant absorption in the present, oblivious of prospect or retrospect, careless of the wider rela-

---

*[This essay was originally presented as an address to an audience.—Eds.]

tions or the deeper truth of life, can be called happiness only on the basis of frivolity and thoughtlessness. Just as life is not life unless it is happy, so happiness is not happiness unless it can be justified. In order really to be happiness it requires to be interpenetrated with a sense of *meaning, reason,* and *worth.*

For the quest of happiness, like every other human quest, faces a danger. The danger that confronts it is the possibility of error: the error of permitting oneself to be lured into promising paths that lead to no goal, and the error of coming to rest in hollow satisfactions and empty joys. It is possible to believe oneself happy, to seem happy to oneself and to others, and yet in reality to be plunged in the deepest misery; just as, on the other hand, it is possible to stand possessed of the greatest treasure, and yet, in thoughtlessness, to imagine oneself destitute, and through that very thoughtlessness not only neglect and ignore but actually deprive oneself of what one already has. The basic problem of life, the question in response to which a view of life seeks to propound an answer, may therefore be formulated as follows: What is that happiness which is also a genuine and lasting good? In what does it consist, and how may it be attained?

There exists an ancient handbook, an *Art of Rhetoric,* compiled for the guidance and information of orators and other public speakers, written by one of the greatest of Greek philosophers. In this handbook the author formulates the commonly prevailing conceptions of happiness as among the things useful for public speakers to know. . . . Happiness is said to be commonly defined as independence of life, as prosperity with virtue, as comfortable circumstances with security, or as the enjoyment of many possessions, together with the power to keep and defend them. Its constituent elements are noble birth, wealth, many good and influential friends, bodily health and beauty, talents and capacities, good fortune, honors, and lastly virtue. We readily perceive how strange and old-fashioned these conceptions are, how foreign to all our modern and enlightened notions. I shall therefore subjoin a more up-to-date consideration of the same subject, derived from a very modern author writing in a journal of today. The author raises the question as to what circumstances and conditions have the power to make him feel really alive, tingling with vitality, instinct with the joy of living. He submits a long list including a variety of things, of which I shall quote the chief: the sense of health; successful creative work, like writing books; good food and drink; pleasant surroundings; praise, not spread on too thick; friends and their company; beautiful things, books, music; athletic exercises and sports; daydreaming; a good fight in a tolerably decent cause; the sense of bodily danger escaped; the consciousness of being a few steps ahead of the wolf of poverty. . . . So speaks our modern writer. And now that I have juxtaposed these two accounts, I have to confess to the strange feeling that, despite the interval of more than two thousand years between them, they sound unexpectedly alike. . . . How strange to find such a similarity! Can it be that after all that has been said and written about the revolutionary and radical changes introduced into life by modern science, modern invention, and modern industry, the influence of the steam engine and the printing press, the telegraph and the radio, the automobile and the airplane, together with the absolutely devastating discoveries of astronomers—can it be, in spite of all this, that the current conceptions of life and its meaning have remained essentially unchanged? . . .

[III. PROBLEMS WITH THAT APPROACH]

However that may be, I do not think that anyone will deny that such views as these are widely held, and constitute the view of life perhaps of the majority of men. . . . But there are serious difficulties in the way of constructing a view of life out of such considerations.

[1.] The constituents of happiness are in both cases a multiplicity of things. . . . But the self which sets its heart upon any such multiplicity of external goods, which lives in them and by them and for them, dependent upon them for the only happiness it knows—such a self is captive to the diverse world of its desires. It belongs to the world and does not own itself. It is not in the deepest sense a self, since it is not free and is not a unity. The manifold conditions of its happiness split the self asunder; no ruling passion dominates its life; no concentration gives unity to the personality and single-mindedness to the will. Its name is legion, and its nature is doublemindedness. . . .

[2.] Reflection discovers yet another difficulty in connection with such views of life. Whoever seeks his happiness in external conditions, of whatever sort, seeks it in that which is in its essential nature precarious. He presumes upon the realization of conditions which are not intrinsic to him, or within his control. This happiness is subject to the law of uncertainty, to the qualification of an unyielding, mysterious *perhaps*. Here lurks the possibility of despair. Give a man the full satisfaction of his wishes and ambitions, and he deems himself happy; withdraw from him the smile of fortune's favor, and disappoint his expectation and his hope, and he will be plunged into despair. The shift from happiness to unhappiness in such a life is every moment imminent. . . .

[3.] A third consideration. Wealth and power and the like, even bodily health and beauty of person, are not in the strictest sense intrinsic values, but rather representative and comparative, conditional and hypothetical. Money is good—if I have learned how to use it; and so with power and influence, health and strength. But in themselves these things are abstract and neutral, and no man can truthfully say whether the acquirement of them in any individual case will work more good than harm. . . .

[4.] Lastly, it must be pointed out that the conditions of happiness as conceived in all such views of life inevitably imply a privileged status for the happy individual. They rest upon differential capabilities and exceptionally fortunate circumstances. To choose them as the end and aim of life constitutes an injury to the mass of men who are not so privileged. This one thought alone is of so arresting a quality as to give the deepest concern to every man who has the least trace of human sympathy and human feeling. I hope I have a soul not entirely a stranger to happy admiration; I know I feel moved to bend low in respect before exceptional talent and performance, and that I am eager to honor greatness and genius wherever I have the gift to understand it. And I am not so unfeeling as to refuse a tribute of sympathetic joy to those who rejoice in fortune's favors and bask in the smiles of outward success. But as the fundamental source of inspiration of my life, I need something that is not exclusive and differential, but inclusive and universal. I require to drink from a spring at which all men may refresh themselves; I need an aim that reconciles me to high and low, rich and poor, cultured and uncultured, sophisticated and simple; to the countless generations of the past as well as to the men and women of the future. I need a spiritual bond that binds me to all human beings in a common understanding of that which is fundamental and essential to human life. To have my life and happiness in that which is inaccessible to the many or to the few seems to me an act of treason to humanity, a cowardly and pusillanimous attack upon the brotherhood of man; for without the inner spiritual tie of an essential aim which all can reach and all can understand, the concept of the human race as a spiritual unity is destroyed, and nothing is left of mankind but a biological species, only slightly better equipped than the other animals to cope with the present state of their physical environment.

The differences between man and man are indeed inseparable from this our imperfect temporal existence; but I cannot and will not believe that their development constitutes the perfection of life itself. Rather is this to be found in the discovery and expectation of *something underlying and absolute*, something that can be found by all who seek it in earnest, something to which our lives may give expression, subordinating to its unifying principle the infinite multitude of ends, reducing them to their own relative measure and proportion, and refusing to permit the unimportant to become important, the relative to become absolute. The possibility of making this discovery and of giving it expression is, so it seems to me, *the fundamental meaning of life, the source of its dignity and worth*. The happiness that is found with this discovery is not invidious and divisive, but unifying and reconciling; it does not abrogate the differences, but it destroys their power to wound and to harm, the fortunate through being puffed up in arrogance and pride, the unfortunate through being depressed in envy and disappointment. For this happiness is not denied to any man, no matter how insignificant and humble.

[IV. THE ETHICO-RELIGIOUS VIEW OF LIFE]

Our criticism has brought us to the threshold of an ethical view of life. That the essence of life and its happiness are to be sought in the moral consciousness alone is the conviction that animates this address, and gives it its reason for being. This view holds that *the individual human self has an infinite worth,* that *the personality has an external validity,* that *the bringing of this validity to expression in the manifold relations and complications of life is the true task of the self,* that *this task gives to the individual's historical development an infinite significance,* because it is a process through which the personality in its truth and depth comes to its own. "Find your self," says the moral consciousness; "reclaim it in its total and in so far unworthy submergence in relative ends; dare to think the nothingness, the hollowness, the relativity, the precariousness, the lack of intrinsic meaning of that which constitutes the entire realm of the external and the manifold; liberate yourself from slavery to finite ends; have the courage to substitute the one thing needful for the many things wished for, and perhaps desirable, making first things first, and all other things secondary—and you will find that these other things will be added unto you in the measure in which you require them and can use them as servants and ministers of your highest good."

So speaks the voice within us, a still small voice, a soft whisper easily overwhelmed by the noise and traffic of life, but a voice, nevertheless, which no one can permit to be silenced except at the cost of acquiring restlessness instead of peace, anxiety instead of trust and confidence, a distracted spirit instead of harmony with one's self. The moral spirit finds the meaning of life in choice. It finds it in that which proceeds from man and remains with him as his inner essence rather than in the accidents of circumstance and turns of external fortune. The individual has his end in himself. He is no mere instrument in the service of something external, nor is he the slave of some powerful master; nor of a class, a group, or party; nor of the state or nation; nor even of humanity itself, as an abstraction solely external to the individual. Essentially and absolutely he is an end; only accidentally and relatively is he a means. And this is true of the meanest wage slave, so called, in industry's impersonal machine—precisely as true of him as it is of the greatest genius or the most powerful ruler.

Is there anyone so little stout-hearted, so effeminately tender, so extravagantly in love with an illusory and arbitrary freedom, as to feel that the glorious promise of such a view of life is ruined, its majestic grandeur shriveled into cramped pettiness, because the task which it offers the individual is not only an invitation, but also an obligation as well? Shall we confess that we cannot endure this "Thou must" spoken to ourselves,[1] even when the voice proceeds from no external power but from our inmost self, there where the human strikes its roots into the *divine*? Truly, it is this "Thou must" that is the *eternal* guarantee of our calling, the savior of our hope, the inspirer of our energy, the preserver of our aim against the shiftings of feeling and the vicissitudes of circumstance. It steels the will and makes it fast; it gives courage to begin after failure; it is the triumph over despondency and despair. For *duty is the eternal in a man, or that by which he lays hold of the eternal; and only through the eternal can a man become a conqueror of the life of time.* It is in the moral consciousness that a man begins truly to sense *the presence of God;* and every religion that

---

[1]Suggested by Emerson's "So nigh is grandeur to our dust." *Voluntaries.*

has omitted the ethical is in so far a misunderstanding of religion, reducing it to myth and poetry, having significance only for the imagination, but not for the whole nature of man as concrete reality. The moral consciousness is a lamp, a wonderful lamp; but not like the famous lamp of Aladdin,[2] which when rubbed had the power to summon a spirit, a willing servant ready and able to fulfill every wish. But whenever a human being rubs the lamp of his moral consciousness with moral passion, a Spirit does appear. This Spirit is God, and the Spirit is master and lord, and man becomes his servant. But this service is man's true freedom, for a derivative spirit like man, who certainly has not made himself, or given himself his own powers, cannot in truth impose upon himself the law of his own being. It is in the "Thou must" of God and man's "I can" that the divine image of God in human life is contained, to which an ancient book refers when it asserts that God made man in his own image. That is the inner glory, the spiritual garb of man, which transcends the wonderful raiment with which the Author of the universe has clothed the lilies of the field, raiment which in its turn puts to shame the royal purple of Solomon. The lilies of the field[3] cannot hear the voice of duty or obey its call; hence they cannot bring their will into harmony with the divine will. In the capacity to do this lies man's unique distinction among all creatures; here is his self, his independence, his glory and his crown.

I know that all men do not share this conviction. Youth is often too sure of its future. The imagination paints the vision of success and fortune in the rosiest tints; the sufferings and disappointments of which one hears are for youth but the exception that proves the rule; the instinctive and blind faith of youth is in the relative happiness of some form of external success. Maturity, on the other hand, has often learned to be content with scraps and fragments, wretched crumbs saved out of the disasters on which its early hopes suffered shipwreck. Youth pursues an ideal that is illusory; age has learned, O wretched wisdom! to do without an ideal altogether. But the ideal is there, implanted in the heart and mind of man by his Maker, and no mirages of happiness or clouds of disappointment, not the stupor of habit or the frivolity of thoughtlessness, can entirely erase the sense of it from the depths of the soul. . . .

Let us but learn to perceive that no differential talent, no privileged status, no fortunate eventuality, can at bottom be worthwhile as a consummation; that all such things are quite incapable of dignifying life; and when the misunderstandings with respect to the nature of a moral consciousness have been cleared away, the road will be open to the discovery of man as man. A preoccupation with the secondary thoughts and interests of life is always exhausting and trivializing, and in the end bewildering. Our true refreshment and invigoration will come through going back to the first and simplest thoughts, the primary and indispensable interests. We have too long lost ourselves in anxious considerations of what it may mean to be a shoemaker or

---

[2]S. Kierkegaard, *Postscript*, p. 124.
[3]S. Kierkegaard, *The Gospel of Suffering*, pp. 174–177.

a philosopher, a poet or a millionaire; in order to find ourselves, it is needful that we concentrate our energies upon the infinitely significant problem of what it means simply to be a man, without any transiently qualifying adjectives. When Frederick the Great asked his Court preacher if he knew anything about the future life, the preacher answered, "Yes, Your Majesty, it is absolutely certain that in the future life Your Highness will not be king of Prussia." And so it is; we were men before we became whatever of relative value we became in life, and we shall doubtless be human beings long after what we thus became or acquired will have lost its significance for us. On the stage some actors have roles in which they are royal and important personages; others are simple folk, beggars, workingmen, and the like. But when the play is over and the curtain is rolled down, the actors cast aside their disguises, the differences vanish, and all are once more simply actors. So, when the play of life is over, and the curtain is rolled down upon the scene, the differences and relativities which have disguised the men and women who have taken part will vanish, and all will be simply human beings. But there is this difference between the actors of the stage and the actors of life. On the stage it is imperative that the illusion be maintained to the highest degree possible; an actor who plays the role of king as if he was an actor, or who too often reminds us that he is assuming a role, is precisely a poor actor. But on the stage of life, the reverse is the case. There it is the task, not to preserve, but to expose the illusion; to win free from it while still retaining one's disguise. The disguising garment ought to flutter loosely about us, so loosely that the least wind of human feeling that blows may reveal the royal purple of humanity beneath. This revelation is the moral task; the moral consciousness is the consciousness of the dignity that invests human life when the personality has discovered itself, and is happy in the will to be itself.

Such is the view of life to which the present speaker is committed. He has sought to make it seem inviting, but not for a moment has he wished to deny that it sets a difficult task for him who would express it in the daily intercourse of life. Perhaps it has long since captured our imaginations; for it is no new gospel worked out to satisfy the imaginary requirements of the most recent fashions in human desire and feeling; on the contrary, it is an old, old view. But it is not enough that the truth of the significance inherent in having such a view of life should be grasped by the imagination, or by the elevated mood of a solemn hour; only the heart's profound movement, the will's decisive commitment,[4] can make that which is truth in general also a truth for me.

---

[4]*Postscript*, p. 226.

37 / The Meaning of Life

KURT BAIER

Kurt Baier (1917–   ), a professor of philosophy at the University of Pittsburgh, is the author of a book on ethics, The Moral Point of View, *which has been ranked as one of the most significant works of our time. He had taught earlier at the Canberra University College in Australia. This essay is an abridged version of his Inaugural Lecture delivered in 1957.*

I. INTRODUCTION

*T*olstoy,* in his autobiographical work "A Confession," reports how, when he was fifty and at the height of his literary success, he came to be obsessed by the fear that life was meaningless.

"At first I experienced moments of perplexity and arrest of life, as though I did not know what to do or how to live; and I felt lost and became dejected. But this passed, and I went on living as before. Then these moments of perplexity began to recur oftener and oftener, and always in the same form. They were always expressed by the questions: What is it for? What does it lead to? At first it seemed to me that these were aimless and irrelevant questions. I thought that it was all well known, and that if I should ever wish to deal with the solution it would not cost me much effort; just at present I had no time for it, but when I wanted to, I should be able to find the answer. The questions however began to repeat themselves frequently, and to demand replies more and more insistently, and like drops of ink always falling on one place they ran together into one black blot."[1]

[1.] A Christian living in the Middle Ages would not have felt any serious doubts about Tolstoy's questions. To him it would have seemed quite certain that life had a meaning, and quite clear what it was. The medieval Christian world picture assigned to man a highly significant, indeed the central part in the grand scheme of things. The universe was made for the express purpose of providing a stage on which to enact a drama starring Man in the title role.

[According to this view,] . . . the world was created by God in the year 4004 B.C. Man was the last and the crown of this creation, made in the likeness of God, placed in the Garden of Eden on earth, the fixed center of the universe, around which revolved the nine heavens of the sun, the moon, the planets, and the fixed stars, producing as they revolved in their orbits the

---

*[A nineteenth-century Russian novelist and thinker.—Eds.]

[1]Count Leo Tolstoy, "A Confession," reprinted in *A Confession, The Gospel in Brief, and What I Believe*, no. 229, The World's Classics (London: Geoffrey Cumberledge, 1940).

heavenly harmony of the spheres. And this gigantic universe was created for the enjoyment of man, who was originally put in control of it. Pain and death were unknown in paradise. But this state of bliss was not to last. Adam and Eve ate of the forbidden tree of knowledge, and life on this earth turned into a death-march through a vale of tears. Then, with the birth of Jesus, new hope came into the world. After He had died on the cross, it became at least possible to wash away with the purifying water of baptism some of the effects of Original Sin and to achieve salvation. That is to say, on condition of obedience to the law of God, man could now enter heaven and regain the state of everlasting, deathless bliss from which he had been excluded because of the sin of Adam and Eve.

To the medieval Christian the meaning of human life was therefore perfectly clear. The stretch on earth is only a short interlude, a temporary incarceration of the soul in the prison of the body, a brief trial and test, fated to end in death, the release from pain and suffering. What really matters is the life after the death of the body. One's existence acquires meaning not by gaining what this life can offer but by saving one's immortal soul from death and eternal torture, by gaining eternal life and everlasting bliss.

[2.] The scientific world picture which has found ever more general acceptance from the beginning of the modern era onwards is in profound conflict with all this. At first, the Christian conception of the world was discovered to be erroneous in various important details. The Copernican theory showed up the earth as merely one of several planets revolving round the sun, and the sun itself was later seen to be merely one of many fixed stars, each of which is itself the nucleus of a solar system similar to our own. Man, instead of occupying the center of creation, proved to be merely the inhabitant of a celestial body no different from millions of others. Furthermore, geological investigations revealed that the universe was not created a few thousand years ago but was probably millions of years old.

Disagreements over details of the world picture, however, are only superficial aspects of a much deeper conflict. The appropriateness of the whole Christian outlook is at issue. For Christianity, the world must be regarded as the "creation" of a kind of Superman, a person possessing all the human excellences to an infinite degree, and none of the human weaknesses, Who has made man in His image, a feeble, mortal, foolish copy of Himself. In creating the universe, God acts as a sort of playwright-cum-legislator-cum-judge-cum-executioner. In the capacity of playwright, He creates the historical world process, including man. He erects the stage and writes, in outline, the plot. He creates the *dramatis personae** and watches over them with the eye partly of a father, partly of the law. While on stage, the actors are free to extemporize, but if they infringe the divine commandments, they are later dealt with by their creator in His capacity of judge and executioner.

Within such a framework, the Christian attitudes toward the world are natural and sound: It is natural and sound to think that all is arranged for the

*[Persons of a drama.—Eds.]

best even if appearances belie it; to resign oneself cheerfully to one's lot; to be filled with awe and veneration in regard to anything and everything that happens; to want to fall on one's knees and worship and praise the Lord. These are wholly fitting attitudes within the framework of the world view just outlined. And this world view must have seemed wholly sound and acceptable because it offered the best explanation which was then available of all the observed phenomena of nature.

As the natural sciences developed, however, more and more things in the universe came to be explained without the assumption of a supernatural creator. Science, moreover, could explain them better, that is, more accurately and more reliably. The Christian hypothesis of a supernatural maker, whatever other needs it was capable of satisfying, was at any rate no longer indispensable for the purpose of explaining the existence or occurrence of anything. In fact, scientific explanations do not seem to leave any room for this hypothesis. The scientific approach demands that we look for a natural explanation of anything and everything. The scientific way of looking at and explaining things has yielded an immensely greater measure of understanding of, and control over, the universe than any other way. And when one looks at the world in this scientific way, there seems to be no room for a personal relationship between human beings and a supernatural perfect being ruling and guiding men. Hence many scientists and educated men have come to feel that the Christian attitudes toward the world and human existence are inappropriate. They have become convinced that the universe and human existence in it are without a purpose and therefore devoid of meaning. . . .[2]

II. THE PURPOSE OF MAN'S EXISTENCE

. . . Complaints such as these do not mean quite the same to everybody, but one thing, I think, they mean to most people: Science shows life to be meaningless, because life is without purpose. The medieval world picture provided life with a purpose; hence medieval Christians could believe that life had a meaning. The scientific account of the world takes away life's purpose and with it its meaning.

There are, however, two quite different senses of "purpose." Which one is meant? Has science deprived life of purpose in both senses? And if not, is it a harmless sense in which human existence has been robbed of purpose? Could human existence still have meaning if it did not have a purpose in that sense?

What are the two senses? In the first and basic sense, purpose is normally attributed only to persons or their behavior, as in "Did you have a purpose in leaving the ignition on?" In the second sense, purpose is normally attributed only to things, as in "What is the purpose of that gadget you installed in the

---

[2]See e.g. Edwyn Bevan, *Christianity*, pp. 211–227. See also H. J. Paton, *The Modern Predicament* (London: George Allen and Unwin Ltd., 1955), pp. 103–116, 374.

workshop?" The two uses are intimately connected. We cannot attribute a purpose to a thing without implying that someone did something, in the doing of which he had some purpose, namely, to bring about the thing with the purpose. Of course, *his* purpose is not identical with *its* purpose. In hiring laborers and engineers and buying materials and a site for a factory and the like, the entrepreneur's purpose, let us say, is to manufacture cars, but the purpose of cars is to serve as a means of transportation.

There are many things that a man may do, such as buying and selling, hiring laborers, plowing, felling trees, and the like, which it is foolish, pointless, silly, perhaps crazy, to do if one has no purpose in doing them. A man who does these things without a purpose is engaging in inane, futile pursuits. Lives crammed full with such activities devoid of purpose are pointless, futile, worthless. Such lives may indeed be dismissed as meaningless. But it should also be perfectly clear that acceptance of the scientific world picture does not force us to regard our lives as being without a purpose in this sense. Science has not only not robbed us of any purpose which we had before, but it has furnished us with enormously greater power to achieve these purposes. Instead of praying for rain or a good harvest or offspring, we now use ice pellets, artificial manure, or artificial insemination.

By contrast, having or not having a purpose, in the other sense, is value neutral. We do not think more or less highly of a thing for having or not having a purpose. "Having a purpose," in this sense, confers no kudos, "being purposeless" carries no stigma. A row of trees growing near a farm may or may not have a purpose: It may or may not be a windbreak, may or may not have been planted or deliberately left standing there in order to prevent the wind from sweeping across the fields. We do not in any way disparage the trees if we say they have no purpose, but have just grown that way. They are as beautiful, made of as good wood, as valuable, as if they had a purpose. And, of course, they break the wind just as well. The same is true of living creatures. We do not disparage a dog when we say that it has no purpose, is not a sheep dog or a watch dog or a rabbiting dog, but just a dog that hangs around the house and is fed by us.

Man is in a different category, however. To attribute to a human being a purpose in that sense is not neutral, let alone complimentary: It is offensive. It is degrading for a man to be regarded as merely serving a purpose. . . .

The Christian and the scientific world pictures do indeed differ fundamentally on this point. The latter robs man of a purpose in this sense. It sees him as a being with no purpose allotted to him by anyone but himself. It robs him of any goal, purpose, or destiny appointed for him by any outside agency. The Christian world picture, on the other hand, sees man as a creature, a divine artifact, something halfway between a robot (manufactured) and an animal (alive), a homunculus, or perhaps Frankenstein, made in God's laboratory, with a purpose or task assigned him by his Maker.

However, lack of purpose in this sense does not in any way detract from the meaningfulness of life. I suspect that many who reject the scientific outlook because it involves the loss of purpose of life, and therefore meaning, are guilty of a confusion between the two senses of "purpose" just distinguished. They confusedly think that if the scientific world picture is true, then their lives must be futile because that picture implies that man has no purpose given him from without. But this is muddled thinking, for, as has already been shown, pointlessness is implied only by purposelessness in the other sense, which is not at all implied by the scientific picture of the world. These people mistakenly conclude that there can be no purpose *in* life because there is no purpose *of* life; that *men* cannot themselves adopt and achieve purposes because *man*, unlike a robot or a watchdog, is not a creature with a purpose.[3]

However, not all people taking this view are guilty of the above confusion. Some really hanker after a purpose of life in this sense. To some people the greatest attraction of the medieval world picture is the belief in an omnipotent, omniscient, and all-good Father, the view of themselves as His children who worship Him, of their proper attitude to what befalls them as submission, humility, resignation in His will, and what is often described as the "creaturely feeling."[4] All these are attitudes and feelings appropriate to a being that stands to another in the same sort of relation, though of course on a higher plane, in which a helpless child stands to his progenitor. Many regard the scientific picture of the world as cold, unsympathetic, unhomely, frightening, because it does not provide for any appropriate object of this creaturely attitude. There is nothing and no one in the world, as science depicts it, in which we can have faith or trust, on whose guidance we can rely, to whom we can turn for consolation, whom we can worship or submit to—except other human beings. This may be felt as a keen disappointment, because it shows that the meaning of life cannot lie in submission to His will, in acceptance of whatever may come, and in worship. But it does not imply that life can have *no* meaning. It merely implies that it must have a different meaning from that which it was thought to have. Just as it is a great shock for a child to find that he must stand on his own feet, that his father and mother no longer provide for him, so a person who has lost his faith in God must reconcile himself to the idea that he has to stand on his own feet, alone in the world except for whatever friends he may succeed in making.

But is not this to miss the point of the Christian teaching? Surely, Christianity can tell us the meaning of life because it tells us the grand and noble end for which God has created the universe and man. No human life, however pointless it may seem, is meaningless because, in being part of God's plan, every life is assured of significance.

This point is well taken. It brings to light a distinction of some importance: We call a person's life meaningful not only if it is worthwhile but also if he has helped in the realization of some plan or purpose transcending his

---

[3]See e.g. "Is Life Worth Living?" B.B.C. Talk by the Rev. John Sutherland Bonnell, in *Asking Them Questions*, Third Series, ed. R. S. Wright (London: Geoffrey Cumberledge, 1950).

[4]See e.g. Rudolf Otto, *The Idea of the Holy*, pp. 9–11. See also C. A. Campbell, *On Selfhood and Godhood* (London: George Allen & Unwin Ltd., 1957), p. 246, and H. J. Paton, *The Modern Predicament*, pp. 69–71.

own concerns. A person who knows he must soon die a painful death can give significance to the remainder of his doomed life by, say, allowing certain experiments to be performed on him which will be useful in the fight against cancer. In a similar way, only on a much more elevated plane, every man, however humble or plagued by suffering, is guaranteed significance by the knowledge that he is participating in God's purpose.

What, then, on the Christian view, is the grand and noble end for which God has created the world and man in it? . . .

If we turn to those who are willing to state God's purpose in so many words, we encounter two insuperable difficulties. The first is to find a purpose grand and noble enough to explain and justify the great amount of undeserved suffering in this world. . . . Could a God be called omniscient, omnipotent, *and* all-good who, for the sake of satisfying his desire to be loved and served, imposes (or has to impose) on his creatures the amount of undeserved suffering we find in the world?

There is, however, a much more serious difficulty still: God's purpose in making the universe must be stated in terms of a dramatic story, many of whose key incidents symbolize religious conceptions and practices which we no longer find acceptable: the imposition of a taboo on the fruits of a certain tree; the sin and guilt incurred by Adam and Eve by violating the taboo; the wrath of God;[5] the curse of Adam and Eve and all their progeny; the expulsion from paradise; the Atonement by Christ's bloody sacrifice on the cross, which makes available by way of the sacraments God's Grace, by which alone men can be saved (thereby, incidentally, establishing the valuable power of priests to forgive sins and thus alone make possible a man's entry to heaven[6]); Judgment Day, on which the sheep are separated from the goats and the latter condemned to eternal torment in hell-fire.

Obviously it is much more difficult to formulate a purpose for creating the universe and man that will justify the enormous amount of undeserved suffering which we find around us, if that story has to be fitted in as well. For now we have to explain not only why an omnipotent, omniscient, and all-good God should create such a universe and such a man, but also why, foreseeing every move of the feeble, weak-willed, ignorant, and covetous creature to be created, He should nevertheless have created him and, having done so, should be incensed and outraged by man's sin, and why He should deem it necessary to sacrifice His own son on the cross to atone for this sin, which was, after all, only a disobedience of one of his commands, and why this atonement and consequent redemption could not have been followed by

---

[5]It is difficult to feel the magnitude of this first sin unless one takes seriously the words "Behold, the man has eaten of the fruit of the tree of knowledge of good and evil, and is become as one of us; and now, may he not put forth his hand, and take also of the tree of life, and eat, and live for ever?" Genesis iii, 22.

[6]See in this connection the pastoral letter of February 2, 1905, by Johannes Katschtaler, Prince Bishop of Salzburg, on the honor due to priests, contained in *Quellen zur Geschichte des Papsttums*, by Mirbt, pp. 497–499, translated and reprinted in *The Protestant Tradition*, by J. S. Whale (Cambridge: University Press, 1955), pp. 259–262.

man's return to paradise—particularly of those innocent children who had not yet sinned—and why, on Judgment Day, this merciful God should condemn some to eternal torment.[7] It is not surprising that in the face of these and other difficulties, we find, again and again, a return to the first view: that God's purpose cannot meaningfully be stated. . . .

There remains one fundamental hurdle which no form of Christianity can overcome: the fact that it demands of man a morally repugnant attitude toward the universe. It is now very widely held[8] that the basic element of the Christian religion is an attitude of worship toward a being supremely worthy of being worshipped and that it is religious feelings and experiences which apprise their owner of such a being and which inspire in him the knowledge or the feeling of complete dependence, awe, worship, mystery, and self-abasement. . . . Christianity thus demands of men an attitude inconsistent with one of the presuppositions of morality: that man is not wholly dependent on something else, that man has free will, that man is in principle capable of responsibility. . . .

III. THE MEANING OF LIFE

Perhaps some of you will have felt that I have been shirking the real problem. To many people the crux of the matter seems as follows. How can there be any meaning in our life if it ends in death? What meaning can there be in it that our inevitable death does not destroy? How can our existence be meaningful if there is no after-life in which perfect justice is meted out? How can life have any meaning if all it holds out to us are a few miserable earthly pleasures and even these to be enjoyed only rarely and for such a piteously short time?

I believe this is the point which exercises most people most deeply. . . .

What, then, is it that inclines us to think that if life is to have a meaning, there would have to be an after-life? It is this. The Christian world view contains the following propositions. The first is that since the Fall, God's curse of Adam and Eve, and the expulsion from paradise, life on earth for mankind has not been worthwhile, but a vale of tears, one long chain of misery, suffering, unhappiness, and injustice. The second is that a perfect after-life is awaiting us after the death of the body, and that we can enter this perfect life only on certain conditions, among which is also the condition of enduring our earthly existence to its bitter end. In this way, our earthly existence, which, in itself, would not (at least for many people if not all) be worth living, acquires meaning and significance: Only if we endure it can we gain admission to the realm of the blessed. . . .

---

[7]How impossible it is to make sense of this story has been demonstrated beyond any doubt by Tolstoy in his famous "Conclusion of a Criticism of Dogmatic Theology," reprinted in *A Confession, The Gospel in Brief, and What I Believe.*

[8]See e.g. the two series of Gifford Lectures most recently published: *The Modern Predicament*, by H. J. Paton (London: George Allen & Unwin Ltd., 1955), pp. 69 ff., and *On Selfhood and Godhood*, by C. A. Campbell (London: George Allen & Unwin Ltd. 1957), pp. 231–250.

It is not surprising, then, that when the implications of the scientific world picture begin to sink in, when we come to have doubts about the existence of God and another life, we are bitterly disappointed. For if there is no after-life, then all we are left is our earthly life, which we have come to regard as a necessary evil, the painful fee of admission to the land of eternal bliss. But if there is no eternal bliss to come and if this hell on earth is all, why hang on till the horrible end?

Our disappointment therefore arises out of these two propositions, that the earthly life is not worth living, and that there is another perfect life of eternal happiness and joy which we may enter upon if we satisfy certain conditions. We can regard our lives as meaningful if we believe both. We cannot regard them as meaningful if we believe merely the first and not the second. It seems to me inevitable that people who are taught something of the history of science will have serious doubts about the second. If they cannot overcome these, as many will be unable to do, then they must either accept the sad view that their life is meaningless or they must abandon the first proposition: that this earthly life is not worth living. They must find the meaning of their life in this earthly existence. But is this possible?

A moment's examination will show us that the Christian evaluation of our earthly life as worthless, which we accept in our moments of pessimism and dissatisfaction, is not one that we normally accept. Consider only the question of murder and suicide. On the Christian view, other things being equal, the most kindly thing to do would be for every one of us to kill as many of our friends and dear ones as still have the misfortune to be alive, and then to commit suicide without delay, for every moment spent in this life is wasted. On the Christian view, God has not made it that easy for us. He has forbidden us to hasten others or ourselves into the next life. Our bodies are his private property and must be allowed to wear themselves out in the way decided by Him, however painful and horrible that may be. . . .

On this view, murder is a less serious wrong than suicide. For murder can always be confessed and repented and therefore forgiven, suicide cannot— unless we allow the ingenious way out chosen by the heroine of Graham Greene's play, *The Living Room*, who swallows a slow but deadly poison and, while awaiting its taking effect, repents having taken it. Murder, on the other hand, is not so serious because, in the first place, it need not rob the victim of anything but the last lap of his march in the vale of tears, and, in the second place, it can always be forgiven. . . .

These views strike us as odd, to say the least. They are the logical consequence of the official medieval evaluation of this our earthly existence. If this life is not worth living, then taking it is not robbing the person concerned of much. The only thing wrong with it is the damage to God's property, which is the same both in the case of murder and suicide. We do not take this view at all. Our view, on the contrary, is that murder is the most serious wrong because it consists in taking away from some one else against his will his most precious possession, his life. For this reason, when a person suffering from an incurable disease asks to be killed, the mercy killing of such a person is regarded as a much less serious crime than murder because, in such a case, the killer is not robbing the other of a good against his will. Suicide is not regarded as a real crime at all, for we take the view that a person can do with his own possessions what he likes.

However, from the fact that these are our normal opinions, we can infer nothing about their truth. After all, we could easily be mistaken. Whether life is or is not worthwhile is a value judgment. Perhaps all this is merely a matter of opinion or taste. Perhaps no objective answer can be given. Fortunately, we need not enter deeply into these difficult and controversial questions. It is quite easy to show that the medieval evaluation of earthly life is based on a misguided procedure.

Let us remind ourselves briefly of how we arrive at our value judgments. When we determine the merits of students, meals, tennis players, bulls, bathing belles, we do so on the basis of some criteria and some standard or norm. Criteria and standards notoriously vary from field to field and even from case to case. But that does not mean that we have *no* idea about what are the appropriate criteria or standards to use. It would not be fitting to apply the criteria for judging bulls to the judgment of students or bathing belles. They score on quite different points. And even where the same criteria are appropriate, as in the judgment of students enrolled in different schools and universities, the standards will vary from one institution to another. Pupils who would only just pass in one would perhaps obtain honors in another. The higher the standard applied, the lower the marks, that is, the merit conceded to the candidate.

The same procedure is applicable also in the evaluation of a life. We examine it on the basis of certain criteria and standards. The medieval Christian view uses the criteria of the ordinary man: A life is judged by what the person concerned can get out of it: the balance of happiness over unhappiness, pleasure over pain, bliss over suffering. Our earthly life is judged not worthwhile because it contains much unhappiness, pain, and suffering, little happiness, pleasure, and bliss. The next life is judged worthwhile because it provides eternal bliss and no suffering.

Armed with these criteria, we can compare the life of this man and that, and judge which is more worthwhile, which has a greater balance of bliss over suffering. But criteria alone enable us merely to make comparative judgments of value, not absolute ones. We can say which is more and which is less worthwhile, but we cannot say which is worthwhile and which is not. In order to determine the latter, we must introduce a standard. But what standard ought we to choose?

Ordinarily, the standard we employ is the average of the kind. We call a man and a tree tall if they are well above the average of their kind. We do not say that Jones is a short man because he is shorter than a tree. We do not judge a boy a bad student because his answer to a question in the Leaving Examination is much worse than that given in reply to the same question by a young man sitting for his finals for the Bachelor's degree.

The same principles must apply to judging lives. When we ask whether a given life was or was not worthwhile, then we must take into consideration the range of worthwhileness which ordinary lives normally cover. Our end poles of the scale must be the best possible and the worst possible life that one finds. A good and worthwhile life is one that is well above average. A bad one is one well below.

The Christian evaluation of earthly lives is misguided because it adopts a quite unjustifiably high standard. Christianity singles out the major short-comings of our earthly existence: There is not enough happiness; there is too much suffering; the good and bad points are quite unequally and unfairly distributed; the underprivileged and underendowed do not get adequate compensation; it lasts only a short time. It then quite accurately depicts the perfect or ideal life as that which does not have any of these shortcomings. Its next step is to promise the believer that he will be able to enjoy this perfect life later on. And then it adopts as its standard of judgment the perfect life, dismissing as inadequate anything that falls short of it. Having dismissed earthly life as miserable, it further damns it by characterizing most of the pleasures of which earthly existence allows as bestial, gross, vile, and sinful, or alternatively as not really pleasurable.

This procedure is as illegitimate as if I were to refuse to call anything tall unless it is infinitely tall, or anything beautiful unless it is perfectly flawless, or any one strong unless he is omnipotent. Even if it were true that there is available to us an after-life which is flawless and perfect, it would still not be legitimate to judge earthly lives by this standard. We do not fail every candi-date who is not an Einstein. And if we do not believe in an after-life, we must of course use ordinary earthly standards.

I have so far only spoken of the worthwhileness, only of what a person can get out of a life. There are other kinds of appraisal. Clearly, we evaluate people's lives not merely from the point of view of what they yield to the persons that lead them, but also from that of other men on whom these lives have impinged. We judge a life more significant if the person has contributed to the happiness of others, whether directly by what he did for others, or by the plans, discoveries, inventions, and work he performed. Many lives that hold little in the way of pleasure or happiness for its owner are highly signifi-cant and valuable, deserve admiration and respect on account of the contribu-tions made.

It is now quite clear that death is simply irrelevant. If life can be worth-while at all, then it can be so even though it be short. And if it is not worth-while at all, then an eternity of it is simply a nightmare. It may be sad that we have to leave this beautiful world, but it is so only if and because it is beautiful. And it is no less beautiful for coming to an end. I rather suspect that an eternity of it might make us less appreciative, and in the end it would be tedious.

It will perhaps be objected now that I have not really demonstrated that life has a meaning, but merely that it can be worthwhile or have value. It must be admitted that there is a perfectly natural interpretation of the question, "What is the meaning of life?" on which my view actually proves that life has no meaning. I mean the interpretation discussed in section II of this [essay], where I attempted to show that, if we accept the explanations of natural science, we cannot believe that living organisms have appeared on earth in accordance with the deliberate plan of some intelligent being. Hence, on this view, life cannot be said to have a purpose, in the sense in which man-made things have a purpose. Hence it cannot be said to have a meaning or significance in that sense.

However, this conclusion is innocuous. People are disconcerted by the thought that life as such has no meaning in that sense only because they very naturally think it entails that no individual life can have meaning either. They naturally assume that *this* life or *that* can have meaning only if *life as such* has meaning. But it should by now be clear that your life and mine may or may not have meaning (in one sense) even if life as such has none (in the other). Of course, it follows from this that your life may have meaning while mine has not. The Christian view guarantees a meaning (in one sense) to every life, the scientific view does not (in any sense). By relating the question of the meaningfulness of life to the particular circumstances of an individual's existence, the scientific view leaves it an open question whether an individual's life has meaning or not. It is, however, clear that the latter is the important sense of "having a meaning." . . .

"But here lies the rub," it will be said. "Surely, it makes all the difference whether there is an after-life. This is where morality comes in." It would be a mistake to believe that. Morality is not the meting out of punishment and reward. To be moral is to refrain from doing to others what, if they followed reason, they would not do to themselves, and to do for others what, if they followed reason, they would want to have done. It is, roughly speaking, to recognize that others, too, have a right to a worthwhile life. Being moral does not make one's own life worthwhile, it helps others to make theirs so. . . .

IV. CONCLUSION

. . . My main conclusion is that acceptance of the scientific world picture provides no reason for saying that life is meaningless, but on the contrary every reason for saying that there are many lives which are meaningful and significant. My subsidiary conclusion is that one of the reasons frequently offered for retaining the Christian world picture, namely, that its acceptance gives us a guarantee of a meaning for human existence, is unsound. We can see that our lives can have a meaning even if we abandon it and adopt the scientific world picture instead. . . .

38 / My Confession

LEO TOLSTOY

Leo Tolstoy (1828–1920) was the author of many famous novels, especially his monumental War and Peace. *In his later years he underwent a crisis in his life which he gave an account of in a book. This essay is an extract from that volume.*

Although I regarded authorship as a waste of time, I continued to write during those fifteen years. I had tasted of the seduction of authorship, of the seduction of enormous monetary remunerations and applauses for my insignificant labour, and so I submitted to it, as being a means for improving my material condition and for stifling in my soul all questions about the meaning of my life and life in general.

In my writings I advocated, what to me was the only truth, that it was necessary to live in such a way as to derive the greatest comfort for oneself and one's family.

Thus I proceeded to live, but five years ago something very strange began to happen with me: I was overcome by minutes at first of perplexity and then of an arrest of life, as though I did not know how to live or what to do, and I lost myself and was dejected. But that passed, and I continued to live as before. Then those minutes of perplexity were repeated oftener and oftener, and always in one and the same form. These arrests of life found their expression in ever the same questions: "Why? Well, and then?"

At first I thought that those were simply aimless, inappropriate questions. It seemed to me that that was all well known and that if I ever wanted to busy myself with their solution, it would not cost me much labour,—that now I had no time to attend to them, but that if I wanted to I should find the proper answers. But the questions began to repeat themselves oftener and oftener, answers were demanded more and more persistently, and, like dots that fall on the same spot, these questions, without any answers, thickened into one black blotch.

There happened what happens with any person who falls ill with a mortal internal disease. At first there appear insignificant symptoms of indisposition, to which the patient pays no attention; then these symptoms are repeated more and more frequently and blend into one temporally indivisible suffering. The suffering keeps growing, and before the patient has had time to look around, he becomes conscious that what he took for an indisposition is the most significant thing in the world to him,—his death.

The same happened with me. I understood that it was not a passing indisposition, but something very important, and that, if the questions were going to repeat themselves, it would be necessary to find an answer for them. And I tried to answer them. The questions seemed to be so foolish, simple, and childish. But the moment I touched them and tried to solve them, I became convinced, in the first place, that they were not childish and foolish, but very important and profound questions in life, and, in the second, that, no matter how much I might try, I should not be able to answer them. Before attending to my Samára estate, to my son's education, or to the writing of a book, I ought to know why I should do that. So long as I did not know why, I could not do anything. I could not live. Amidst my thoughts of farming, which interested me very much during that time, there would suddenly pass through my head a question like this: "All right, you are going to have six thousand desyatínas* of land in the Government of Samára, and three hundred horses,—and then?" And I completely lost my senses and did not know what to think farther. Or, when I thought of the education of my children, I said to myself: "Why?" Or, reflecting on the manner in which the masses might obtain their welfare, I suddenly said to myself: "What is that to me?" Or, thinking of the fame which my works would get me, I said to myself: "All right, you will be more famous than Gógol, Púshkin, Shakespeare, Molière, and all the writers in the world,—what of it?" And I was absolutely unable to make any reply. The questions were not waiting, and I had to answer them at once; if I did not answer them, I could not live.

I felt that what I was standing on had given way, that I had no foundation to stand on, that that which I lived by no longer existed, and that I had nothing to live by. . . .

All that happened with me when I was on every side surrounded by what is considered to be complete happiness. I had a good, loving, and beloved wife, good children, and a large estate, which grew and increased without any labour on my part. I was respected by my neighbours and friends, more than ever before, was praised by strangers, and, without any self-deception, could consider my name famous. With all that, I was not deranged or mentally unsound,—on the contrary, I was in full command of my mental and physical powers, such as I had rarely met with in people of my age: physically I could work in a field, mowing, without falling behind a peasant; mentally I could work from eight to ten hours in succession, without experiencing any consequences from the strain. And while in such condition I arrived at the conclusion that I could not live, and, fearing death, I had to use cunning against myself, in order that I might not take my life.

This mental condition expressed itself to me in this form: my life is a stupid, mean trick played on me by somebody. Although I did not recognize that "somebody" as having created me, the form of the conception that some one had played a mean, stupid trick on me by bringing me into the world was the most natural one that presented itself to me.

Involuntarily I imagined that there, somewhere, there was somebody

---

*[A unit of land measurement comparable to our acre.—Eds.]

who was now having fun as he looked down upon me and saw me, who had lived for thirty or forty years, learning, developing, growing in body and mind, now that I had become strengthened in mind and had reached that summit of life from which it lay all before me, standing as a complete fool on that summit and seeing clearly that there was nothing in life and never would be. And that was fun to him—

But whether there was or was not that somebody who made fun of me, did not make it easier for me. I could not ascribe any sensible meaning to a single act, or to my whole life. I was only surprised that I had not understood that from the start. All that had long ago been known to everybody. Sooner or later there would come diseases and death (they had come already) to my dear ones and to me, and there would be nothing left but stench and worms. All my affairs, no matter what they might be, would sooner or later be forgotten, and I myself should not exist. So why should I worry about all these things? How could a man fail to see that and live,—that was surprising! A person could live only so long as he was drunk; but the moment he sobered up, he could not help seeing that all that was only a deception, and a stupid deception at that! Really, there was nothing funny and ingenious about it, but only something cruel and stupid.

Long ago has been told the Eastern story about the traveller who in the steppe is overtaken by an infuriated beast. Trying to save himself from the animal, the traveller jumps into a waterless well, but at its bottom he sees a dragon who opens his jaws in order to swallow him. And the unfortunate man does not dare climb out, lest he perish from the infuriated beast, and does not dare jump down to the bottom of the well, lest he be devoured by the dragon, and so clutches the twig of a wild bush growing in a cleft of the well and holds on to it. His hands grow weak and he feels that soon he shall have to surrender to the peril which awaits him at either side; but he still holds on and sees two mice, one white, the other black, in even measure making a circle around the main trunk of the bush to which he is clinging, and nibbling at it on all sides. Now, at any moment, the bush will break and tear off, and he will fall into the dragon's jaws. The traveller sees that and knows that he will inevitably perish; but while he is still clinging, he sees some drops of honey hanging on the leaves of the bush, and so reaches out for them with his tongue and licks the leaves. Just so I hold on to the branch of life, knowing that the dragon of death is waiting inevitably for me, ready to tear me to pieces, and I cannot understand why I have fallen on such suffering. And I try to lick that honey which used to give me pleasure; but now it no longer gives me joy, and the white and the black mouse day and night nibble at the branch to which I am holding on. I clearly see the dragon, and the honey is no longer sweet to me. I see only the inevitable dragon and the mice, and am unable to turn my glance away from them. That is not a fable, but a veritable, indisputable, comprehensible truth.

The former deception of the pleasures of life, which stifled the terror of the dragon, no longer deceives me. No matter how much one should say to me, "You cannot understand the meaning of life, do not think, live!" I am unable to do so, because I have been doing it too long before. Now I cannot help seeing day and night, which run and lead me up to death. I see that alone, because that alone is the truth. Everything else is a lie.

The two drops of honey that have longest turned my eyes away from the cruel truth, the love of family and of authorship, which I have called an art, are no longer sweet to me.

"My family" I said to myself, "but my family, my wife and children, they are also human beings. They are in precisely the same condition that I am in: they must either live in the lie or see the terrible truth. Why should they live? Why should I love them, why guard, raise, and watch them? Is it for the same despair which is in me, or for dulness of perception? Since I love them, I cannot conceal the truth from them,–every step in cognition leads them up to this truth. And the truth is death."

"Art, poetry?" For a long time, under the influence of the success of human praise, I tried to persuade myself that this was a thing which could be done, even though death should come and destroy everything, my deeds, as well as my memory of them; but soon I came to see that that, too, was a deception. It was clear to me that art was an adornment of life, a decoy of life. But life lost all its attractiveness for me. How, then, could I entrap others? So long as I did not live my own life, and a strange life bore me on its waves; so long as I believed that life had some sense, although I was not able to express it,—the reflections of life of every description in poetry and in the arts afforded me pleasure, and I was delighted to look at life through this little mirror of art; but when I began to look for the meaning of life, when I experienced the necessity of living myself, that little mirror became either useless, superfluous, and ridiculous, or painful to me. I could no longer console myself with what I saw in the mirror, namely, that my situation was stupid and desperate. It was all right for me to rejoice so long as I believed in the depth of my soul that life had some sense. At that time the play of lights—of the comical, the tragical, the touching, the beautiful, the terrible in life— afforded me amusement. But when I knew that life was meaningless and terrible, the play in the little mirror could no longer amuse me. No sweetness of honey could be sweet to me, when I saw the dragon and the mice that were nibbling down my support. . . .

In my search after the question of life I experienced the same feeling which a man who has lost his way in the forest may experience.

He comes to a clearing, climbs a tree, and clearly sees an unlimited space before him; at the same time he sees that there are no houses there, and that there can be none; he goes back to the forest, into the darkness, and he sees darkness, and again there are no houses.

Thus I blundered in this forest of human knowledge, between the clearings of the mathematical and experimental sciences, which disclosed to me clear horizons, but such in the direction of which there could be no house, and between the darkness of the speculative sciences, where I sunk into a deeper darkness, the farther I proceeded, and I convinced myself at last that there was no way out and could not be.

By abandoning myself to the bright side of knowledge I saw that I only turned my eyes away from the question. No matter how enticing and clear the horizons were that were disclosed to me, no matter how enticing it was to bury myself in the infinitude of this knowledge, I comprehended that these sciences were the more clear, the less I needed them, the less they answered my question.

"Well, I know," I said to myself, "all which science wants so persistently to know, but there is no answer to the question about the meaning of my life." But in the speculative sphere I saw that, in spite of the fact that the aim of the knowledge was directed straight to the answer of my question, or because of that fact, there could be no other answer than what I was giving to myself: "What is the meaning of my life?"—"None." Or, "What will come of my life?"—"Nothing." Or, "Why does everything which exists exist, and why do I exist?"—"Because it exists."

Putting the question to the one side of human knowledge, I received an endless quantity of exact answers about what I did not ask: about the chemical composition of the stars, about the movement of the sun toward the constellation of Hercules, about the origin of species and of man, about the forms of infinitely small, imponderable particles of ether; but the answer in this sphere of knowledge to my question what the meaning of my life was, was always: "You are what you call your life; you are a temporal, accidental conglomeration of particles. The interrelation, the change of these particles, produces in you that which you call life. This congeries will last for some time; then the interaction of these particles will cease, and that which you call life and all your questions will come to an end. You are an accidentally cohering globule of something. The globule is fermenting. This fermentation the globule calls its life. The globule falls to pieces, and all fermentation and all questions will come to an end." Thus the clear side of knowledge answers, and it cannot say anything else, if only it strictly follows its principles.

With such an answer it appears that the answer is not a reply to the question. I want to know the meaning of my life, but the fact that it is a particle of the infinite not only gives it no meaning, but even destroys every possible meaning.

Those obscure transactions, which this side of the experimental, exact science has with speculation, when it says that the meaning of life consists in evolution and the coöperation with this evolution, because of their obscurity and inexactness cannot be regarded as answers.

The other side of knowledge, the speculative, so long as it sticks strictly to its fundamental principles in giving a direct answer to the question, every-where and at all times has answered one and the same: "The world is something infinite and incomprehensible. Human life is an incomprehensible part of this incomprehensible *all*. . . ."

I lived for a long time in this madness, which, not in words, but in deeds, is particularly characteristic of us, the most liberal and learned of men. But, thanks either to my strange, physical love for the real working class, which made me understand it and see that it is not so stupid as we suppose, or to the sincerity of my conviction, which was that I could know nothing and that the best that I could do was to hang myself,–I felt that if I wanted to live and understand the meaning of life, I ought naturally to look for it, not among those who had lost the meaning of life and wanted to kill themselves, but among those billions departed and living men who had been carrying their own lives and ours upon their shoulders. And I looked around at the enormous masses of deceased and living men,—not learned and wealthy, but simple men,—and I saw something quite different. I saw that all these billions of men that lived or had lived, all, with rare exceptions, did not fit into my subdivisions,* and that I could not recognize them as not understanding the question, because they themselves put it and answered it with surprising clearness. Nor could I recognize them as Epicureans,† because their lives were composed rather of privations and suffering than of enjoyment. Still less could I recognize them as senselessly living out their meaningless lives, because every act of theirs and death itself was explained by them. They regarded it as the greatest evil to kill themselves. It appeared, then, that all humanity was in possession of a knowledge of the meaning of life, which I did not recognize and which I condemned. It turned out that rational knowledge did not give any meaning to life, excluded life, while the meaning which by billions of people, by all humanity, was ascribed to life was based on some despised, false knowledge.

The rational knowledge in the person of the learned and the wise denied the meaning of life, but the enormous masses of men, all humanity, recognized this meaning in an irrational knowledge. This irrational knowledge was faith, the same that I could not help but reject. That was God as one and three, the creation in six days, devils and angels, and all that which I could not accept so long as I had not lost my senses.

My situation was a terrible one. I knew that I should not find anything on the path of rational knowledge but the negation of life, and there, in faith, nothing but the negation of reason, which was still more impossible than the negation of life. From the rational knowledge it followed that life was an evil and men knew it,—it depended on men whether they should cease living, and yet they lived and continued to live, and I myself lived, though I had known long ago that life was meaningless and an evil. From faith it followed that, in order to understand life, I must renounce reason, for which alone a meaning was needed.

---

*[In a passage omitted here, Tolstoy characterizes four attitudes which people have toward life: living in ignorance of the problem of the meaning of life; ignoring it and trying to attain as much pleasure as possible; admitting that life is meaningless and committing suicide; and admitting that life is meaningless but continuing to live aimlessly.—Eds.]

†[A follower of Epicurius. Now: a sensualist in food, drink, etc.—Eds.]

There resulted a contradiction, from which there were two ways out: either what I called rational was not so rational as I had thought; or that which to me appeared irrational was not so irrational as I had thought. And I began to verify the train of thoughts of my rational knowledge.

In verifying the train of thoughts of my rational knowledge, I found that it was quite correct. The deduction that life was nothing was inevitable; but I saw a mistake. The mistake was that I had not reasoned in conformity with the question put by me. The question was, "Why should I live?" that is, "What real, indestructible essence will come from my phantasmal, destructible life? What meaning has my finite existence in this infinite world?" And in order to answer this question, I studied life.

The solutions of all possible questions of life apparently could not satisfy me, because my question, no matter how simple it appeared in the beginning, included the necessity of explaining the finite through the infinite, and vice versa.

I asked, "What is the extra-temporal, extra-causal, extra-spatial meaning of life?" But I gave an answer to the question, "What is the temporal, causal, spatial meaning of my life?" The result was that after a long labour of mind I answered, "None."

In my reflections I constantly equated, nor could I do otherwise, the finite with the finite, the infinite with the infinite, and so from that resulted precisely what had to result: force was force, matter was matter, will was will, infinity was infinity, nothing was nothing,—and nothing else could come from it.

There happened something like what at times takes place in mathematics: you think you are solving an equation, when you have only an identity. The reasoning is correct, but you receive as a result the answer: $a = a$, or $x = x$, or $0 = 0$. The same happened with my reflection in respect to the question about the meaning of my life. The answers given by all science to that question are only identities.

Indeed, the strictly scientific knowledge, that knowledge which, as Descartes did, begins with a full doubt in everything, rejects all knowledge which has been taken on trust, and builds everything anew on the laws of reason and experience, cannot give any other answer to the question of life than what I received,—an indefinite answer. It only seemed to me at first that science gave me a positive answer,—Schopenhauer's answer: "Life has no meaning, it is an evil." But when I analyzed the matter, I saw that the answer was not a positive one, but that it was only my feeling which expressed it as such. The answer, strictly expressed, as it is expressed by the Brahmins, by Solomon, and by Schopenhauer,* is only an indefinite answer, or an identity, $0 = 0$, life is nothing. Thus the philosophical knowledge does not negate

*[Brahmin: member of the highest caste in India. More generally, a highly cultured person. Solomon: a wise king of Old Testament times. Schopenhauer: a nineteenth-century German philosopher who was a pessimist.—Eds.]

anything, but only answers that the question cannot be solved by it, that for philosophy the solution remains insoluble.

When I saw that, I understood that it was not right for me to look for an answer to my question in rational knowledge, and that the answer given by rational knowledge was only an indication that the answer might be got if the question were differently put, but only when into the discussion of the question should be introduced the question of the relation of the finite to the infinite. I also understood that, no matter how irrational and monstrous the answers might be that faith gave, they had this advantage that they introduced into each answer the relation of the finite to the infinite, without which there could be no answer.

No matter how I may put the question, "How must I live?" the answer is, "According to God's law." "What real result will there be from my life?"— "Eternal torment or eternal bliss." "What is the meaning which is not destroyed by death?"—"The union with infinite God, paradise."

Thus, outside the rational knowledge, which had to me appeared as the only one, I was inevitably led to recognize that all living humanity had a certain other irrational knowledge, faith, which made it possible to live.

All the irrationality of faith remained the same for me, but I could not help recognizing that it alone gave to humanity answers to the questions of life, and, in consequence of them, the possibility of living.

The rational knowledge brought me to the recognition that life was meaningless,—my life stopped, and I wanted to destroy myself. When I looked around at people, at all humanity, I saw that people lived and asserted that they knew the meaning of life. I looked back at myself: I lived so long as I knew the meaning of life. As to other people, so even to me, did faith give the meaning of life and the possibility of living.

Looking again at the people of other countries, contemporaries of mine and those passed away, I saw again the same. Where life had been, there faith, ever since humanity had existed, had given the possibility of living, and the chief features of faith were everywhere one and the same.

No matter what answers faith may give, its every answer gives to the finite existence of man the sense of the infinite,—a sense which is not destroyed by suffering, privation, and death. Consequently in faith alone could we find the meaning and possibility of life. What, then, was faith? I understood that faith was not merely an evidence of things not seen, and so forth, not revelation (that is only the description of one of the symptoms of faith), not the relation of man to man (faith has to be defined, and then God, and not first God, and faith through him), not merely an agreement with what a man was told, as faith was generally understood,—that faith was the knowledge of the meaning of human life, in consequence of which man did not destroy himself, but lived. Faith is the power of life. If a man lives he believes in something. If he did not believe that he ought to live for some purpose, he would not live. If he does not see and understand the phantasm of the finite, he believes in that finite; if he understands the phantasm of the finite, he must believe in the infinite. Without faith one cannot live. . . .

In order that all humanity may be able to live, in order that they may continue living, giving a meaning to life, they, those billions, must have another, a real knowledge of faith, for not the fact that I, with Solomon and Schopenhauer, did not kill myself convinced me of the existence of faith, but that these billions had lived and had borne us, me and Solomon, on the waves of life.

Then I began to cultivate the acquaintance of the believers from among the poor, the simple and unlettered folk, of pilgrims, monks, dissenters, peasants. The doctrine of these people from among the masses was also the Christian doctrine that the quasi-believers of our circle professed. With the Christian truths were also mixed in very many superstitions, but there was this difference: the superstitions of our circle were quite unnecessary to them, had no connection with their lives, were only a kind of an Epicurean amusement, while the superstitions of the believers from among the labouring classes were to such an extent blended with their life that it would have been impossible to imagine it without these superstitions,—it was a necessary condition of that life. I began to examine closely the lives and beliefs of these people, and the more I examined them, the more did I become convinced that they had the real faith, that their faith was necessary for them, and that it alone gave them a meaning and possibility of life. In contradistinction to what I saw in our circle, where life without faith was possible, and where hardly one in a thousand professed to be a believer, among them there was hardly one in a thousand who was not a believer. In contradistinction to what I saw in our circle, where all life passed in idleness, amusements, and tedium of life, I saw that the whole life of these people was passed in hard work, and that they were satisfied with life. In contradistinction to the people of our circle, who struggled and murmured against fate because of their privations and their suffering, these people accepted diseases and sorrows without any perplexity or opposition, but with the calm and firm conviction that it was all for good. In contradistinction to the fact that the more intelligent we are, the less do we understand the meaning of life and the more do we see a kind of a bad joke in our suffering and death, these people live, suffer, and approach death, and suffer in peace and more often in joy. In contradistinction to the fact that a calm death, a death without terror or despair, is the greatest exception in our circle, a restless, insubmissive, joyless death is one of the greatest exceptions among the masses. And of such people, who are deprived of everything which for Solomon and for me constitutes the only good of life, and who withal experience the greatest happiness, there is an enormous number. I cast a broader glance about me. I examined the life of past and present vast masses of men, and I saw people who in like manner had understood the meaning of life, who had known how to live and die, not two, not three, not ten, but hundreds, thousands, millions. All of them, infinitely diversified as to habits, intellect, culture, situation, all equally and quite contrary to my ignorance knew the meaning of life and of death, worked calmly, bore privations and suffering, lived and died, seeing in that not vanity, but good.

I began to love those people. The more I penetrated into their life, the life of the men now living, and the life of men departed, of whom I had read and heard, the more did I love them, and the easier it became for me to live. Thus I lived for about two years, and within me took place a transformation, which had long been working within me, and the germ of which had always been in me. What happened with me was that the life of our circle,—of the rich and the learned,—not only disgusted me, but even lost all its meaning. All our acts, reflections, sciences, arts,—all that appeared to me in a new light. I saw that all that was mere pampering of the appetites, and that no meaning could be found in it; but the life of all the working masses, of all humanity, which created life, presented itself to me in its real significance. I saw that that was life itself and that the meaning given to this life was truth, and I accepted it.

---

39 / *Existentialism*

JEAN-PAUL SARTRE

Jean-Paul Sartre (1905–1980) was one of the most well-known and leading exponents of atheistic existentialism. He achieved fame not only for his philosophical works but also for his many novels, plays, and essays.

What is meant by the term *existentialism*? . . .

What complicates matters is that there are two kinds of existentialist; first, those who are Christian, among whom I would include Jaspers and Gabriel Marcel, both Catholic; and on the other hand the atheistic existentialists, among whom I class Heidegger*; then the French existentialists and myself. What they have in common is that they think that existence precedes essence, or, if you prefer, that subjectivity must be the starting point.

Just what does that mean? Let us consider some object that is manufactured, for example, a book or a paper-cutter: here is an object which has been made by an artisan whose inspiration came from a concept. He referred to the concept of what a paper-cutter is and likewise to a known method of production, which is part of the concept, something which is, by and large, a routine. Thus, the paper-cutter is at once an object produced in a certain way and, on the other hand, one having a specific use; and one can not postulate a man

---

*[Jaspers: twentieth-century German existentialist philosopher. Marcel: twentieth-century French philosopher. Heidegger: twentieth-century German philosopher.—Eds.]

who produces a paper-cutter but does not know what it is used for. Therefore, let us say that, for the paper-cutter, essence—that is, the ensemble of both the production routines and the properties which enable it to be both produced and defined—precedes existence. Thus, the presence of the paper-cutter or book in front of me is determined. Therefore, we have here a technical view of the world whereby it can be said that production precedes existence.

When we conceive God as the Creator, He is generally thought of as a superior sort of artisan. Whatever doctrine we may be considering, whether one like that of Descartes or that of Leibnitz, we always grant that will more or less follows understanding or, at the very least, accompanies it, and that when God creates He knows exactly what He is creating. Thus, the concept of man in the mind of God is comparable to the concept of paper-cutter in the mind of the manufacturer, and, following certain techniques and a conception, God produces man, just as the artisan, following a definition and a technique, makes a paper-cutter. Thus, the individual man is the realization of a certain concept in the divine intelligence.

In the eighteenth century, the atheism of the *philosophes* discarded the idea of God, but not so much for the notion that essence precedes existence. To a certain extent, this idea is found everywhere; we find it in Diderot, in Voltaire, and even in Kant. Man has a human nature; this human nature, which is the concept of the human, is found in all men, which means that each man is a particular example of a universal concept, man. In Kant, the result of this universality is that the wild-man, the natural man, as well as the bourgeois, are circumscribed by the same definition and have the same basic qualities. Thus, here too the essence of man precedes the historical existence that we find in nature.

Atheistic existentialism, which I represent, is more coherent. It states that if God does not exist, there is at least one being in whom existence precedes essence, a being who exists before he can be defined by any concept, and that this being is man, or, as Heidegger says, human reality. What is meant here by saying that existence precedes essence? It means that, first of all, man exists, turns up, appears on the scene, and, only afterwards, defines himself. If man, as the existentialist conceives him, is indefinable, it is because at first he is nothing. Only afterward will he be something, and he himself will have made what he will be. Thus, there is no human nature, since there is no God to conceive it. Not only is man what he conceives himself to be, but he is also only what he wills himself to be after this thrust toward existence.

Man is nothing else but what he makes of himself. Such is the first principle of existentialism. It is also what is called subjectivity, the name we are labeled with when charges are brought against us. But what do we mean by this, if not that man has a greater dignity than a stone or table? For we mean that man first exists, that is, that man first of all is the being who hurls himself toward a future and who is conscious of imagining himself as being in the future. Man is at the start a plan which is aware of itself, rather than a patch of moss, a piece of garbage, or a cauliflower; nothing exists prior to this plan; there is nothing in heaven; man will be what he will have planned to be. Not what he will want to be. Because by the word "will" we generally mean a conscious decision, which is subsequent to what we have already made of ourselves. I may want to belong to a political party, write a book, get married; but all that is only a manifestation of an earlier, more spontaneous choice that is called "will." But if existence really does precede essence, man is responsible for what he is. Thus, existentialism's first move is to make every man aware of what he is and to make the full responsibility of his existence rest on him. And when we say that a man is responsible for himself, we do not only mean that he is responsible for his own individuality, but that he is responsible for all men.

The word subjectivism has two meanings, and our opponents play on the two. Subjectivism means, on the one hand, that an individual chooses and makes himself; and, on the other, that it is impossible for man to transcend human subjectivity. The second of these is the essential meaning of existentialism. When we say that man chooses his own self, we mean that every one of us does likewise; but we also mean by that that in making this choice he also chooses all men. In fact, in creating the man that we want to be, there is not a single one of our acts which does not at the same time create an image of man as we think he ought to be. To choose to be this or that is to affirm at the same time the value of what we choose, because we can never choose evil. We always choose the good, and nothing can be good for us without being good for all.

If on the other hand, existence precedes essence, and if we grant that we exist and fashion our image at one and the same time, the image is valid for everybody and for our whole age. Thus, our responsibility is much greater than we might have supposed, because it involves all mankind. If I am a workingman and choose to join a Christian trade-union rather than be a communist, and if by being a member I want to show that the best thing for man is resignation, that the kingdom of man is not of this world, I am not only involving my own case—I want to be resigned for everyone. As a result, my action has involved all humanity. To take a more individual matter, if I want to marry, to have children; even if this marriage depends solely on my own circumstances or passion or wish, I am involving all humanity in monogamy and not merely myself. Therefore, I am responsible for myself and for everyone else. I am creating a certain image of man of my own choosing. In choosing myself, I choose man.

This helps us understand what the actual content is of such rather grandiloquent words as anguish, forlornness, despair. As you will see, it's all quite simple.

First, what is meant by anguish? The existentialists say at once that man is anguish. What that means is this: the man who involves himself and who realizes that he is not only the person he chooses to be, but also a lawmaker who is, at the same time, choosing all mankind as well as himself, can not help escape the feeling of his total and deep responsibility. Of course, there are many people who are not anxious; but we claim that they are hiding their anxiety, that they are fleeing from it. Certainly, many people believe that when they do something, they themselves are the only ones involved, and when someone says to them, "What if everyone acted that way?" they shrug their shoulders and answer, "Everyone doesn't act that way." But really, one should always ask himself, "What would happen if everybody looked at things that way?" There is no escaping this disturbing thought except by a kind of double-dealing. A man who lies and makes excuses for himself by saying "not everybody does that," is someone with an uneasy conscience, because the act of lying implies that a universal value is conferred upon the lie. . . .

There is no question here of the kind of anguish which would lead to quietism, to inaction. It is a matter of a simple sort of anguish that anybody who has had responsibilities is familiar with. For example, when a military officer takes the responsibility for an attack and sends a certain number of men to death, he chooses to do so, and in the main he alone makes the choice. Doubtless, orders come from above, but they are too broad; he interprets them, and on this interpretation depend the lives of ten or fourteen or twenty men. In making a decision he can not help having a certain anguish. All leaders know this anguish. That doesn't keep them from acting; on the contrary, it is the very condition of their action. For it implies that they envisage a number of possibilities, and when they choose one, they realize that it has value only because it is chosen. We shall see that this kind of anguish, which is the kind that existentialism describes, is explained, in addition, by a direct responsibility to the other men whom it involves. It is not a curtain separating us from action, but is part of action itself.

When we speak of forlornness, a term Heidegger was fond of, we mean only that God does not exist and that we have to face all the consequences of this. The existentialist is strongly opposed to a certain kind of secular ethics which would like to abolish God with the least possible expense. About 1880, some French teachers tried to set up a secular ethics which went something like this: God is a useless and costly hypothesis; we are discarding it; but meanwhile, in order for there to be an ethics, a society, a civilization, it is essential that certain values be taken seriously and that they be considered as having an *a priori* existence. It must be obligatory, *a priori*, to be honest, not to lie, not to beat your wife, to have children, etc., etc. So we're going to try a little device which will make it possible to show that values exist all the same, inscribed in a heaven of ideas, though otherwise God does not exist. In other words—and this, I believe, is the tendency of everything called reformism in France—nothing will be changed if God does not exist. We shall find ourselves with the same norms of honesty, progress, and humanism, and we shall have made of God an outdated hypothesis which will peacefully die off by itself.

The existentialist, on the contrary, thinks it very distressing that God does not exist, because all possibility of finding values in a heaven of ideas disappears along with Him; there can no longer be an *a priori* Good, since there is no infinite and perfect consciousness to think it. Nowhere is it written that the Good exists, that we must be honest, that we must not lie; because the fact is we are on a plane where there are only men. Dostoievsky said, "If God didn't exist, everything would be possible." That is the very starting point of existentialism. Indeed, everything is permissible if God does not exist, and as a result man is forlorn, because neither within him nor without does he find anything to cling to. He can't start making excuses for himself.

If existence really does precede essence, there is no explaining things away by reference to a fixed and given human nature. In other words, there is no determinism, man is free, man is freedom. On the other hand, if God does not exist, we find no values or commands to turn to which legitimize our conduct. So, in the bright realm of values, we have no excuse behind us, nor justification before us. We are alone, with no excuses.

That is the idea I shall try to convey when I say that man is condemned to be free. Condemned, because he did not create himself, yet, in other respects is free; because, once thrown into the world, he is responsible for everything he does. The existentialist does not believe in the power of passion. He will never agree that a sweeping passion is a ravaging torrent which fatally leads a man to certain acts and is therefore an excuse. He thinks that man is responsible for his passion.

The existentialist does not think that man is going to help himself by finding in the world some omen by which to orient himself. Because he thinks that man will interpret the omen to suit himself. Therefore, he thinks that man, with no support and no aid, is condemned every moment to invent man. Ponge,* in a very fine article, has said, "Man is the future of man." That's exactly it. But if it is taken to mean that this future is recorded in heaven, that God sees it, then it is false, because it would really no longer be a future. If it is taken to mean that, whatever a man may be, there is a future to be forged, a virgin future before him, then his remark is sound. But then we are forlorn.

To give you an example which will enable you to understand forlornness better, I shall cite the case of one of my students who came to see me under the following circumstances: his father was on bad terms with his mother, and, moreover, was inclined to be a collaborationist; his older brother had been killed in the German offensive of 1940, and the young man, with somewhat immature but generous feelings, wanted to avenge him. His mother lived alone with him, very much upset by the half-treason of her husband and the death of her older son; the boy was her only consolation.

The boy was faced with the choice of leaving for England and joining the Free French Forces—that is, leaving his mother behind—or remaining with his mother and helping her to carry on. He was fully aware that the woman lived only for him and that his going-off—and perhaps his death—would plunge her into despair. He was also aware that every act that he did for his mother's sake was a sure thing, in the sense that it was helping her to carry on, whereas every effort he made toward going off and fighting was an uncertain move which might run aground and prove completely useless; for example, on his way to England he might, while passing through Spain, be

---

*[Ponge: writer who was a contemporary of Sartre.—Eds.]

detained indefinitely in a Spanish camp; he might reach England or Algiers and be stuck in an office at a desk job. As a result, he was faced with two very different kinds of action: one, concrete, immediate, but concerning only one individual; the other concerned an incomparably vaster group, a national collectivity, but for that very reason was dubious, and might be interrupted en route. And, at the same time, he was wavering between two kinds of ethics. On the one hand, an ethics of sympathy, of personal devotion; on the other, a broader ethics, but one whose efficacy was more dubious. He had to choose between the two.

Who could help him choose? Christian doctrine? No. Christian doctrine says, "Be charitable, love your neighbor, take the more rugged path, etc., etc." But which is the more rugged path? Whom should he love as a brother? The fighting man or his mother? Which does the greater good, the vague act of fighting in a group, or the concrete one of helping a particular human being to go on living? Who can decide *a priori*? Nobody. No book of ethics can tell him. The Kantian* ethics says, "Never treat any person as a means, but as an end." Very well, if I stay with my mother, I'll treat her as an end and not as a means; but by virtue of this very fact, I'm running the risk of treating the people around me who are fighting, as means; and, conversely, if I go to join those who are fighting, I'll be treating them as an end, and, by doing that, I run the risk of treating my mother as a means.

If values are vague, and if they are always too broad for the concrete and specific case that we are considering, the only thing left for us is to trust our instincts. That's what this young man tried to do; and when I saw him, he said, "In the end, feeling is what counts. I ought to choose whichever pushes me in one direction. If I feel that I love my mother enough to sacrifice everything else for her—my desire for vengeance, for action, for adventure—then I'll stay with her. If, on the contrary, I feel that my love for my mother isn't enough, I'll leave." . . .

As for despair, the term has a very simple meaning. It means that we shall confine ourselves to reckoning only with what depends upon our will, or on the ensemble of probabilities which make our action possible. When we want something, we always have to reckon with probabilities. I may be counting on the arrival of a friend. The friend is coming by rail or street-car; this supposes that the train will arrive on schedule, or that the street-car will not jump the track. I am left in the realm of possibility; but possibilities are to be reckoned with only to the point where my action comports with the ensemble of these possibilities, and no further. The moment the possibilities I am considering are not rigorously involved by my action, I ought to disengage myself from them, because no God, no scheme, can adapt the world and its possibilities to my will. When Descartes said, "Conquer yourself rather than the world," he meant essentially the same thing. . . .

Actually, things will be as man will have decided they are to be. Does that

---

*[Kant was an eighteenth-century German philosopher who stressed acting from duty in his ethics.—Eds.]

mean that I should abandon myself to quietism? No. First, I should involve myself; then, act on the old saw, "Nothing ventured, nothing gained." Nor does it mean that I shouldn't belong to a party, but rather that I shall have no illusions and shall do what I can. For example, suppose I ask myself, "Will socialization, as such, ever come about?" I know nothing about it. All I know is that I'm going to do everything in my power to bring it about. Beyond that, I can't count on anything. Quietism is the attitude of people who say, "Let others do what I can't do." The doctrine I am presenting is the very opposite of quietism, since it declares, "There is no reality except in action." Moreover, it goes further, since it adds, "Man is nothing else than his plan; he exists only to the extent that he fulfills himself; he is therefore nothing else than the ensemble of his acts, nothing else than his life."

According to this, we can understand why our doctrine horrifies certain people. Because often the only way they can bear their wretchedness is to think, "Circumstances have been against me. What I've been and done doesn't show my true worth. To be sure, I've had no great love, no great friendship, but that's because I haven't met a man or woman who was worthy. The books I've written haven't been very good because I haven't had the proper leisure. I haven't had children to devote myself to because I didn't find a man with whom I could have spent my life. So there remains within me, unused and quite viable, a host of propensities, inclinations, possibilities, that one wouldn't guess from the mere series of things I've done."

Now, for the existentialist there is really no love other than one which manifests itself in a person's being in love. There is no genius other than one which is expressed in works of art; the genius of Proust is the sum of Proust's works; the genius of Racine is his series of tragedies. Outside of that, there is nothing. Why say that Racine could have written another tragedy, when he didn't write it? A man is involved in life, leaves his impress on it, and outside of that there is nothing. To be sure, this may seem a harsh thought to someone whose life hasn't been a success. But, on the other hand, it prompts people to understand that reality alone is what counts, that dreams, expectations, and hopes warrant no more than to define a man as a disappointed dream, as miscarried hopes, as vain expectations. In other words, to define him negatively and not positively. However, when we say, "You are nothing else than your life," that does not imply that the artist will be judged solely on the basis of his works of art; a thousand other things will contribute toward summing him up. What we mean is that a man is nothing else than a series of undertakings, that he is the sum, the organization, the ensemble of the relationships which make up these undertakings. . . .

At heart, what existentialism shows is the connection between the absolute character of free involvement, by virtue of which every man realizes himself in realizing a type of mankind, an involvement always comprehensible in any age whatsoever and by any person whosoever, and the relativeness of the cultural ensemble which may result from such a choice; . . .

This does not entirely settle the objection to subjectivism. In fact, the objection still takes several forms. First, there is the following: we are told, "So you're able to do anything, no matter what!" This is expressed in various ways. First we are accused of anarchy; then they say, "You're unable to pass judgment on others, because there's no reason to prefer one configuration to another"; finally they tell us, "Everything is arbitrary in this choosing of yours. You take something from one pocket and pretend you're putting it into the other."

These three objections aren't very serious. Take the first objection. "You're able to do anything, no matter what" is not to the point. In one sense choice is possible, but what is not possible is not to choose. I can always choose, but I ought to know that if I do not choose, I am still choosing. Though this may seem purely formal, it is highly important for keeping fantasy and caprice within bounds. If it is true that in facing a situation, for example, one in which, as a person capable of having sexual relations, of having children, I am obliged to choose an attitude, and if I in any way assume responsibility for a choice which, in involving myself, also involves all mankind, this has nothing to do with caprice, even if no *a priori* value determines my choice.

If anybody thinks that he recognizes here Gide's* theory of the arbitrary act, he fails to see the enormous difference between this doctrine and Gide's. Gide does not know what a situation is. He acts out of pure caprice. For us, on the contrary, man is in an organized situation in which he himself is involved. Through his choice, he involves all mankind, and he can not avoid making a choice: either he will remain chaste, or he will marry without having children, or he will marry and have children; anyhow, whatever he may do, it is impossible for him not to take full responsibility for the way he handles this problem. Doubtless, he chooses without referring to preestablished values, but it is unfair to accuse him of caprice. Instead, let us say that moral choice is to be compared to the making of a work of art. And before going any further, let it be said at once that we are not dealing here with an aesthetic ethics, because our opponents are so dishonest that they even accuse us of that. The example I've chosen is a comparison only.

Having said that, may I ask whether anyone has ever accused an artist who has painted a picture of not having drawn his inspiration from rules set up *a priori*? Has anyone ever asked, "What painting ought he to make?" It is clearly understood that there is no definite painting to be made, that the artist is engaged in the making of his painting, and that the painting to be made is precisely the painting he will have made. It is clearly understood that there are no *a priori* aesthetic values, but that there are values which appear subsequently in the coherence of the painting, in the correspondence between what the artist intended and the result. Nobody can tell what the painting of tomorrow will be like. Painting can be judged only after it has once been made. What connection does that have with ethics? We are in the same creative situation. We never say that a work of art is arbitrary. When we speak of

*[Famous twentieth-century French novelist.—Eds.]

a canvas of Picasso, we never say that it is arbitrary; we understand quite well that he was making himself what he is at the very time he was painting, that the ensemble of his work is embodied in his life.

The same holds on the ethical plane. What art and ethics have in common is that we have creation and invention in both cases. We can not decide *a priori* what there is to be done. I think that I pointed that out quite sufficiently when I mentioned the case of the student who came to see me, and who might have applied to all the ethical systems, Kantian or otherwise, without getting any sort of guidance. He was obliged to devise his law himself. Never let it be said by us that this man—who, taking affection, individual action, and kind-heartedness toward a specific person as his ethical first principle, chooses to remain with his mother, or who, preferring to make a sacrifice, chooses to go to England—has made an arbitrary choice. Man makes himself. He isn't ready made at the start. In choosing his ethics, he makes himself, and force of circumstances is such that he can not abstain from choosing one. We define man only in relationship to involvement. It is therefore absurd to charge us with arbitrariness of choice.

In the second place, it is said that we are unable to pass judgment on others. In a way this is true, and in another way, false. it is true in this sense, that, whenever a man sanely and sincerely involves himself and chooses his configuration, it is impossible for him to prefer another configuration, regardless of what his own may be in other respects. It is true in this sense, that we do not believe in progress. Progress is betterment. Man is always the same. The situation confronting him varies. Choice always remains a choice in a situation. . . .

But, nevertheless, one can still pass judgment, for, as I have said, one makes a choice in relationship to others. First, one can judge (and this is perhaps not a judgment of value, but a logical judgment) that certain choices are based on error and others on truth. If we have defined man's situation as a free choice, with no excuses and no recourse, every man who takes refuge behind the excuse of his passions, every man who sets up a determinism, is a dishonest man.

The objection may be raised, "But why mayn't he choose himself dishonesty?" I reply that I am not obliged to pass moral judgment on him, but that do define his dishonesty as an error. One can not help considering the truth of the matter. Dishonesty is obviously a falsehood because it belies the complete freedom of involvement. On the same grounds, I maintain that there is also dishonesty if I choose to state that certain values exist prior to me; it is self-contradictory for me to want them and at the same state that they are imposed on me. Suppose someone says to me, "What if I want to be dishonest?" I'll answer, "There's no reason for you not to be, but I'm saying that that's what you are, and that the strictly coherent attitude is that of honesty."

Besides, I can bring moral judgment to bear. When I declare that freedom in every concrete circumstance can have no other aim than to want itself, if man has once become aware that in his forlornness he imposes values, he can no longer want but one thing, and that is freedom, as the basis of all values. That doesn't mean that he wants it in the abstract. It means simply that the ultimate meaning of the acts of honest men is the quest for freedom as such. A man who belongs to a communist or revolutionary union wants concrete goals; these goals imply an abstract desire for freedom; but this freedom is wanted in something concrete. We want freedom for freedom's sake and in every particular circumstance. And in wanting freedom we discover that it depends entirely on the freedom of others, and that the freedom of others depends on ours. Of course, freedom as the definition of man does not depend on others, but as soon as there is involvement, I am obliged to want others to have freedom at the same time that I want my own freedom. I can take freedom as my goal only if I take that of others as a goal as well. Consequently, when, in all honesty, I've recognized that man is a being in whom existence precedes essence, that he is a free being who, in various circumstances, can want only his freedom, I have at the same time recognized that I can want only the freedom of others.

Therefore, in the name of this will for freedom, which freedom itself implies, I may pass judgment on those who seek to hide from themselves the complete arbitrariness and the complete freedom of their existence. Those who hide their complete freedom from themselves out of a spirit of seriousness or by means of deterministic excuses, I shall call cowards; those who try to show that their existence was necessary, when it is the very contingency of man's appearance on earth, I shall call stinkers. But cowards or stinkers can be judged only from a strictly unbiased point of view.

Therefore though the content of ethics is variable, a certain form of it is universal. Kant says that freedom desires both itself and the freedom of others. Granted. But he believes that the formal and the universal are enough to constitute an ethics. We, on the other hand, think that principles which are too abstract run aground in trying to decide action. Once again, take the case of the student. In the name of what, in the name of what great moral maxim do you think he could have decided, in perfect peace of mind, to abandon his mother or to stay with her? There is no way of judging. The content is always concrete and thereby unforeseeable; there is always the element of invention. The one thing that counts is knowing whether the inventing that has been done, has been done in the name of freedom. . . .

The third objection is the following: "You take something from one pocket and put it into the other. That is, fundamentally, values aren't serious, since you choose them." My answer to this is that I'm quite vexed that that's the way it is; but if I've discarded God the Father, there has to be someone to invent values. You've got to take things as they are. Moreover, to say that we invent values means nothing else but this: life has no meaning *a priori*. Before you come alive, life is nothing; it's up to you to give it a meaning, and value is nothing else but the meaning that you choose. In that way, you see, there is a possibility of creating a human community.

I've been reproached for asking whether existentialism is humanistic. It's been said, "But you said in *Nausea** that the humanists were all wrong. You made fun of a certain kind of humanist. Why come back to it now?" Actually, the word humanism has two very different meanings. By humanism one can mean a theory which takes man as an end and as a higher value. . . .

[Man] is constantly outside of himself; in projecting himself, in losing himself outside of himself, he makes for man's existing; and, on the other hand, it is by pursuing transcendent goals that he is able to exist; man, being this state of passing-beyond, and seizing upon things only as they bear upon this passing-beyond, is at the heart, at the center of this passing-beyond. There is no universe other than a human universe, the universe of human subjectivity. This connection between transcendency, as a constituent element of man—not in the sense that God is transcendent, but in the sense of passing beyond—and subjectivity, in the sense that man is not closed in on himself but is always present in a human universe, is what we call existentialism/humanism. Humanism, because we remind man that there is no lawmaker other than himself, and that in his forlornness he will decide by himself; because we point out that man will fulfill himself as man, not in turning toward himself, but in seeking outside of himself a goal which is just this liberation, just this particular fulfillment.

From these few reflections it is evident that nothing is more unjust than the objections that have been raised against us. Existentialism is nothing else than an attempt to draw all the consequences of a coherent atheistic position. It isn't trying to plunge man into despair at all. But if one calls every attitude of unbelief despair, like the Christians, then the word is not being used in its original sense. Existentialism isn't so atheistic that it wears itself out showing that God doesn't exist. Rather, it declares that even if God did exist, that would change nothing. There you've got our point of view. Not that we believe that God exists, but we think that the problem of His existence is not the issue. In this sense existentialism is optimistic, a doctrine of action, and it is plain dishonesty for Christians to make no distinction between their own despair and ours and then to call us despairing.

STUDY QUESTIONS

1. In the passage quoted in the Preview to this part, Camus maintains that the question of the meaning of life is the most urgent of all questions. Do you agree? Why or why not?

2. In your judgment, does Swenson also agree that the problem is as urgent as Camus maintains? If so, why? If not, why not?

3. State what you take to be Swenson's chief arguments on behalf of the theistic position. Critically evaluate those arguments.

*[A novel by Sartre.—Eds.]

4. In the General Introduction to this text (Section I), it was said that one of the tasks of philosophy is to examine our (often hidden) assumptions or presuppositions. What presuppositions do you find Swenson to be relying on?

5. Baier contrasts two opposing views (pictures) of the world, and their respective standpoints on the question of whether or not life is meaningful. State the chief theses of the two world views. State what each is said to imply regarding the issue of whether or not life has any meaning.

6. What does Baier conclude in his discussion? What are his reasons for reaching that conclusion? Do you agree? Why or why not?

7. How does Baier respond to the claim that the scientific account of the world takes away life's purpose and meaning? Do you agree? Why or why not?

8. How does Baier answer the question, "How can there be any meaning in our life if it ends in death?" Critically evaluate the answer.

9. Do you find Tolstoy's account, in terms of his personal life, to add to an understanding of our main question? Why or why not?

10. Critically evaluate Sartre's main views and his reasons on behalf of those views.

11. In your view, which of the authors represented in this part of the book has presented the best answer to the question of the meaning of life? Why do you consider his answer the best?

12. To what extent, if any, do the authors agree about the meaning of life? On what points do they differ?

13. Examine again Camus' claim (quoted in the Preview) that the meaning of life is the most urgent of questions. Having read the selections in this part, do you now agree or disagree? Why?

14. It has been maintained by some that without God, or faith in God, life would be without meaning or purpose and, hence, would not be worth living. Therefore, even if there is *no* god, it is better for one to *believe* that there is. Do you agree? Why or why not?

FURTHER READINGS

Britton, Karl. *Philosophy and the Meaning of Life.* Cambridge: Cambridge University Press, 1969. [Examines the bearing of philosophy on the question of the meaning of life.]

Frankl, Victor. *Man's Search for Meaning.* New York: Beacon, 1963. [A partially autobiographical account from the perspective of a psychologist.]

Klemke, E. D., ed. *The Meaning of Life.* New York: Oxford University Press, 1981. [Presents three approaches to the issue: the theistic perspective, the non-theistic alternative, and the approach which questions the question. Contains many of the most important essays on the topic.]

Lamont, Corliss. *The Philosophy of Humanism*. New York: Frederick Ungar, 1949, 1957, 1965. [Defends a humanistic approach to the issue in a very readable manner.]

May, Rollo. *Man's Search for Meaning*. New York: W. W. Norton, 1953. [Another treatment of the issue by a psychologist, but one well versed in philosophy.]

Munitz, Milton K. *The Mystery of Existence*. New York: New York University Press, 1965. [Not directly on the subject, but on an issue closely related to it.]

Nielsen, Kai. *Ethics Without God*. Buffalo, N.Y.: Prometheus Books, 1973. [Contains treatment of the subject within the broader context of ethics.]

Sanders, Steven, and David R. Cheney, eds. *The Meaning of Life*. Englewood Cliffs, N.J.: Prentice-Hall, 1980. [Another collection of essays; overlaps in part with Klemke.]

PART NINE

MORAL VALUES: GROUNDS AND NORMS

PREVIEW

*E*ach one of us is called upon to make moral choices and decisions, and we often evaluate the moral choices and actions of others, sometimes engaging in moral arguments or debates and taking stands on controversial moral questions surrounding issues such as abortion, the death penalty, etc. How should we go about making moral choices and decisions, justify our moral choices to ourselves and to others, evaluate those moral choices that others make, settle moral disagreements, and so on?

In this part we will consider some of the more influential attempts to answer these questions.

Suppose you are in a situation in which you must decide whether or not to tell a lie. Let us imagine that you have discovered that your roommate's steady date is secretly going out with somebody else. Your roommate has heard rumors to this effect and suspects that you know the truth. If asked, should you lie or tell the truth? How are you to decide; that is, on the basis of what sort of standards, values, and norms should you make and, if need be, justify or defend your decision?

1. You might base your decision regarding whether to lie to your roommate or not on selfish considerations, that is, on whether you would benefit from lying. You might decide, for example, that lying would make your roommate feel better and that this would make you feel better. Your decision is based on the impact the lie would have on you, rather than its potential effect on your roommate. If so, then for you the main or only ground for making moral decisions is the question, "What's in it for me?"

2. A second approach to moral decision making would be to decide what to do by estimating the consequences of our actions. If the consequences are, on the whole, good—or at least "better" than the available alternatives—we can and, indeed, ought to do the action which promotes those good conse-

411

quences. So if it turns out that lying to your roommate would promote better consequences than not lying, you ought to lie. But now the obvious question becomes, "What are 'good' consequences?" One possible answer would be: Whatever brings about the most happiness (or least unhappiness) for all those concerned—not just for yourself.

3. Suppose you subscribe to certain moral principles or laws, such as the "golden rule." Perhaps this rule or set of moral principles prohibits lying in all situations. That is, the principle says, "Never lie, no matter what." In this case your decision not to lie to your roommate will not be based on such factors as, for example, the desire to protect him/her. It will be based exclusively on the desire to follow the moral principle which you accept.

4. A fourth approach involves an appeal to divine laws or commandments. Such theories bid us discover, as best we can, what the divine laws prescribe or prohibit in any situation. Sources for making such a discovery include the Bible or other religious texts, the clergy, some religiously sanctioned moral code (e.g., the Ten Commandments), or some other religious authority. If you hold to this theory, you probably won't lie at all.

5. A fifth approach involves asking the question, "What kind of person am I or do I want to be?" That is, what kind of moral character traits and habits do I have or want to cultivate? Do I want to be an honest person? A "yes" person? And how will my character traits, my moral virtues, play a role in determining what I ought or ought not to do in any given situation?

6. You might want to consider whether your feelings of compassion, of care for your friends, as opposed to rules, commandments, the bottom line or selfishness is the most important element in your decision whether to lie to your roommate or tell her/him the truth.

Main Question

With this example and the approaches to it, we may now state the main question in this part. It is:

How do we arrive at and defend moral decisions about what to do or what not to do? That is, what is the correct moral standard or standards of conduct by which we decide what is right or wrong and by which we make moral assessments of right or wrong?

Answers

Our example and the discussion of it provides us with the main answers to the central question. These are:

a. Egoism: The proper standard of conduct is the enhancement of your own long-term self-interest or happiness.

b. Utilitarianism: The proper standard of conduct is the maximization of the greatest amount of happiness, or least amount of unhappiness, for *all* concerned, not just one's self.

c. Formalism: The proper standard of conduct is a rule which expresses the form, way, or procedure for conduct, but not the content of particular actions.

d. Divine command theory: The proper standard of conduct is whatever is commanded or forbidden by God.

e. Virtue ethics: The focus of morality is on moral character and virtue, on what kind of person one is, one's habits, etc. It is often assumed that a virtuous individual will do the morally right thing; indeed, sometimes the "morally right act" is defined as whatever the virtuous person would do in the circumstances. Sometimes moral virtue is connected with social practices and their proper fulfillment. Moral virtue then involves playing certain roles that are defined by practices, e.g., being a good citizen, etc.

f. Ethic of care: Morality focuses not on rules, appeals to consequences, selfishness, commands or practices, but on compassion, care, specific situations, cooperation. This ethic of care is what Carol Gilligan calls "a different voice," to indicate the claim that much of our ethical tradition, including a–e above, incorporates a male bias and ignores those aspects of morality—often exemplified more by females—that she calls the ethics of care. Morality must embody this dimension along with attention to rules and principles.

It may be helpful to add a comment or two concerning utilitarianism. The utilitarian believes that what is right or wrong is determined by how much good or value is brought into the world, or how much bad is prevented from coming into the world, as the result of any action. Good and bad values are defined in terms of things such as pleasure and pain, knowledge and ignorance, and so on. Many utilitarians take pleasure to be the highest value and pain the lowest, so that right is bringing about the greatest amount of pleasure one can, and wrong is increasing the amount of misery. Utilitarianism thus may require complex estimations of what the actual consequences of any action will be as part of the decision as to what is right or wrong in any given situation (especially since many actions bring both pleasure and pain in their wake).

Finally, there exists a distinction between "act" and "rule" utilitarianism that should be noted here. In the readings below, Kaye defends, and Ewing criticizes, act utilitarianism, which says that the Principle of Utility should be applied to every particular action directly. Rule utilitarianism was developed to deal with an objection to act utilitarianism: What if lying on a given occasion maximizes utility? According to rule utilitarianism, the Principle of Utility is applied to general practices, such as truth telling or lying. What would the consequences of everyone's lying be? What would the result of certain general practices be? It is assumed that it might be permissible to lie in a particular situation but that it would not maximize utility if everyone lied, or if lying were allowed as a general policy. So the rule utilitarian tells us to judge practices and policies by the Principle of Utility. Particular actions, such as lying on a particular occasion, are not (contrary to act utilitarianism) directly tied to the Principle of Utility. One is supposed to follow the rule against lying, which is directly justified by that principle. (The reader might consider MacIver's essay here.)

Selections

We present an essay which defends each of these six approaches to standards of conduct and which draws out some implications of each; then we include a criticism of some, so that the reader can develop her or his own philosophical thoughts on these important issues. It is hoped that this collection of essays on approaches to moral thinking and decision making will have some bearing on the reader's future conduct.

Answers	Defense	Criticism
(a) Egoism	40	41
(b) Utilitarianism	42	43
(c) Formalism	44	45
(d) Divine command theory	48	47
(e) Virtue ethics	46	
(f) Ethic of care	45	

40 / The Morality Trap

HARRY BROWNE

Harry Browne (1933–   ) is an investment banker living in Vancouver, British Columbia. He is the author of How I Found Freedom in an Unfree World, You Can Profit from a Monetary Crisis, *and* You Can Profit from the Coming Devaluation. *He espouses a libertarian philosophy.*

I. THE MORALITY TRAP

*T*he Morality Trap is the belief that you must obey a moral code created by someone else. . . .

Morality is a powerful word. Perhaps even more powerful is the word *immoral*. In an attempt to avoid being labeled *immoral*, many people allow themselves to be manipulated by others. . . .

It seems to me that there are three different kinds of morality. I call them *personal, universal,* and *absolute*. By looking at each of them, I think we can get a clearer idea of what morality is and how it can be useful in helping you to achieve your freedom.

A. Personal Morality

You act in ways that you hope will bring the best consequences to you. And the "best consequences" are those that bring you happiness.

You always have to consider the consequences of your actions; they're the point of anything you do. However, any given act will undoubtedly cause *many* consequences. You may see that a particular action will produce a consequence you want, but you might also be aware that it could produce other consequences that you don't want. . . .

Since you're always seeking numerous different goals, you try to foresee the ways in which something immediately desirable might get in the way of other things that are ultimately more desirable. You try to consider more than just what's immediately in front of you. You're placing things in a broader context.

Obviously, you can't expect to foresee *all* the consequences of a given act, but you can try to see all the significant ones. In some cases . . . there are obvious consequences that immediately rule out a proposed course of action. . . .

Because you can't foresee all the specific consequences of what you do, there's a need to have some generalized rules available that can help keep you out of situations that could be troublesome. Those rules can be valuable if they do two things: (1) steer you away from potential disasters; and (2) remind you of the things you must do to satisfy your most important *long-term* desires.

The basic question is: "How can I get something I want without hurting my chances for other things that are more important to me?"

It is this generalized, *long-term* attitude that underlies an individual's basic code of conduct. And when we speak of morality, I can't think of any other sensible reason to be concerned about the subject. Its purpose is to keep you aimed in the direction you most want to go.

Personal morality is an attempt to consider all the relevant consequences of your actions.

"Relevant" means those consequences that will affect *you*. How your actions affect others is only important insofar as that, in turn, affects you.

A personal morality is basic to your overall view of how you'll find happiness. . . .

And it's important that you form it yourself. No one else (including me) is qualified to tell you how to live. A realistic morality has to consider many personal factors: your emotional nature, abilities, strengths, weaknesses, and, most important, your goals.

Your code of conduct has to be consistent with your goals so that you don't do anything that would make those goals unattainable. A code devised by someone else will necessarily be based upon the goals *he* believes possible and desirable.

To be useful, a morality shouldn't include rules for every possible situation. It shouldn't be concerned with minor questions involving only immediate consequences. It's devised to prevent big problems for you and to keep you aimed toward the ultimate goals that mean the most to you. Moral questions are concerned only with matters that involve large consequences.

There's a difference, for instance, between investing three dollars in a movie that might prove to be a dud and investing your life savings in a risky business venture. There's also a difference between tasting a different food that's commonly eaten (such as snails) and sampling toadstools in the forest. The first might cause a stomachache; the second could poison you.

A useful morality will prevent you from doing things that might take years to correct, while keeping you aimed in the direction of the things that are most important to you.

And since such matters are an outgrowth of your own personal values, it's obvious that no one else can create your morality for you.

A *personal morality* is the attempt to consider all the relevant consequences of your actions. This is only one of three common types of moralities, however.

B. Universal Morality

The second type is a morality that is meant to apply to everyone in the world. A *universal morality* is one that's supposed to bring happiness to anyone who uses it.

When you're exposed to the ideas of someone who has apparently done well with his own life, it's easy to conclude that he has all the final answers. His reasoning makes sense to you; he has results to show for his ideas. What further proof could you need to demonstrate that he knows how to live?

He probably does know how to live—*his* life. It would be foolish not to consider the ideas such a person offers. But it would also be foolish to expect that, as intelligent as he may be, he could have answers that apply to every life in the world.

His ideas have worked for him because he's been wise enough to develop ideas that are consistent with his own nature. He hasn't tried to live by the standards created by others; he's found his own. And that's vitally important.

You must do the same thing, too—if you want your code of conduct to work that well for you. Your rules have to consider everything that's unique about you—your emotions, your aptitudes, your weak points, your hopes and fears. . . .

A universal morality is a code of conduct that is presumed to bring happiness to anyone who uses it. I don't believe there can be such a thing. The differences between individuals are far too great to allow for anything but the most general kinds of rules.

C. Absolute Morality

There's a third kind of morality. The first two are attempts to help you achieve happiness—one self-directed and the other coming from someone else. The third type is the opposite of this. An *absolute morality* is a set of rules to which an individual is expected to *surrender* his own happiness.

There are two main characteristics of an absolute morality:

1. It presumably comes from *an authority outside of the individual*. It comes from someone or somewhere more important than the individual himself.

2. It proposes that the individual should be "moral" *regardless of the consequences to himself*. In other words, doing what is "right" is more important than one's own happiness.

These two characteristics intertwine, so we'll consider them together.

[1.] Absolute morality is the most common type of morality, and it can be pretty intimidating. You can be made to appear "selfish," "whim-worshiping," "egotistic," "hedonistic," or "ruthless" if you merely assert that your own happiness is the most important thing in your life.

But what could be more important than your happiness? It's said that an authoritarian moral code is necessary to protect society. But who is society? Isn't it just a large group of people, each of whom has differing ideas concerning how one should live?

And if an individual is required to give up his own happiness, of what value is society to him?

It's also suggested that God commanded that we live by certain rules. But who can be sure he knows exactly when and how and what God said and what he meant? And even if that could be established once and for all, what would be the consequences to the individual if he acted otherwise? How do we know?

And if the code did come from God, it still had to be handled by human beings on its way to you. Whatever the absolute morality may be, you're relying upon someone else to vouch for its authority.

Suppose you use a holy book as your guide. I haven't yet seen one that doesn't have some apparent contradictions regarding conduct in it. Those contradictions may disappear with the proper interpretation; but who provides the interpretation? You'll do it yourself or you'll select someone to provide it for you. In either case, *you* have become the authority by making the choice.

There's no way someone else can become your authority; ultimately the decision will be yours in choosing the morality you'll live by—even if you choose to cite someone else (you've chosen) as the authority for your acts.

[2.] And there's no way you can ignore the consequences to yourself; a human being naturally acts in terms of consequences.

What happens, however, is that other people introduce consequences that they hope will influence you. They say that your "immoral" acts will: "prevent you from going to heaven" or "cause other people to disapprove of you" or "destroy society and cause chaos, and it will all be your fault."

Once again, however, it will be *you* deciding for yourself whether any of these consequences will result and whether any of them are important to you.

The absolute morality fails on its two important characteristics. Even if you choose to believe there's a higher authority, you are the authority who chooses what it is and what it is telling you to do. And since you'll always be considering consequences, even if you try to fix it so that you aren't, it's important to deliberately recognize the consequences and decide which ones are important to you. . . .

D. Your Morality

You are responsible for what happens to you (even if someone else offers to accept that responsibility), because you're the one who'll experience the consequences of your acts.

You are the one who decides what is right and what is wrong—no matter what meaning others may attach to those words. You don't have to obey blindly the dictates that you grew up with or that you hear around you now. Everything can be challenged, *should* be challenged, examined to determine its relevance to you and what you want.

As you examine the teachings of others, you may find that some of it is very appropriate to you, but much of it may be meaningless or even harmful. The important thing is to carefully reappraise any moral precept that has been guiding your actions.

As you examine each of the rules you've been living by, ask yourself:

- Is this rule something that *others* have devised on behalf of "society" to restrain individuals? Or have *I* devised it in order to make my life better for myself?
- Am I acting by an old, just-happens-to-be-there morality? Or is it something I've personally determined from the knowledge of who I am and what I want?
- Are the rewards and punishments attached to the rules vague and intangible? Or do the rules point to specific happiness I can achieve or unhappiness I can avoid?
- Is it a morality I've accepted because "someone undoubtedly knows the reason for it"? Or is it one I've created because *I* know the reason for it?
- Is it a morality that's currently "in style" and accepted by all those around me? Or is it a morality specifically tailored to *my* style?
- Is it a morality that's aimed *at* me and *against* my self-interest? Or is it a morality that's *for* me and comes *from me*?

All the answers must come from you—not from a book or a lecture or a sermon. . . .

No matter how you approach the matter, *you* are the sovereign authority who makes the final decisions. The more you realize that, the more your decisions will fit realistically with your own life. . . .

II. THE UNSELFISHNESS TRAP

The Unselfishness Trap is the belief that you must put the happiness of others ahead of your own.

Unselfishness is a very popular ideal, one that's been honored throughout recorded history. Wherever you turn, you find encouragement to put the happiness of others ahead of your own—to do what's best for the world, not for yourself.

If the ideal is sound, there must be something unworthy in seeking to live your life as you want to live.

So perhaps we should look more closely at the subject—to see if the ideal is sound. For if you attempt to be free, we can assume that someone's going to consider that to be selfish. . . .

Each person always acts in ways he believes will make him feel good or will remove discomfort from his life. Because everyone is different from everyone else, each individual goes about it in his own way.

One man devotes his life to helping the poor. Another one lies and steals. Still another person tries to create better products and services for which he hopes to be paid handsomely. One woman devotes herself to her husband and children. Another one seeks a career as a singer.

In every case, the ultimate motivation has been the same. Each person is doing what *he* believes will assure his happiness. What varies between them is the *means* each has chosen to gain his happiness.

We could divide them into two groups labeled "selfish" and "unselfish," but I don't think that would prove anything. For the thief and the humanitarian each has the same motive—to do what he believes will make him feel good.

In fact, we can't avoid a very significant conclusion: *Everyone is selfish.* Selfishness isn't really an issue, because everyone selfishly seeks his own happiness. . . .

A. A Better World?

Let's look first at the ideal of living for the benefit of others. It's often said that it would be a better world if everyone were unselfish. But would it be?

If it were somehow possible for everyone to give up his own happiness, what would be the result? Let's carry it to its logical conclusion and see what we find.

To visualize it, let's imagine that happiness is symbolized by a big red rubber ball. I have the ball in my hands—meaning that I hold the ability to be happy. But since I'm not going to be selfish, I quickly pass the ball to you. I've given up my happiness for you.

What will you do? Since you're not selfish either, you won't keep the ball; you'll quickly pass it on to your next-door neighbor. But he doesn't want to be selfish either, so he passes it to his wife, who likewise gives it to her children.

The children have been taught the virtue of unselfishness, so they pass it to playmates, who pass it to parents, who pass it to neighbors, and on and on and on.

I think we can stop the analogy at this point and ask what's been accomplished by all this effort. Who's better off for these demonstrations of pure unselfishness?

How would it be a better world if everyone acted that way? Whom would we be unselfish for? There would have to be a selfish person who would receive, accept, and enjoy the benefits of our unselfishness for there to be any purpose to it. But that selfish person (the object of our generosity) would be living by lower standards than we do.

For a more practical example, what is achieved by the parent who "sacrifices" himself for his children, who in turn are expected to sacrifice themselves for *their* children, etc.? The unselfishness concept is a merry-go-round that has no ultimate purpose. No one's self-interest is enhanced by the continual relaying of gifts from one person to another to another.

Perhaps most people have never carried the concept of unselfishness to this logical conclusion. If they did, they might reconsider their pleas for an unselfish world.

B. Negative Choices

But, unfortunately, the pleas continue, and they're a very real part of your life. In seeking your own freedom and happiness, you have to deal with those who tell you that you shouldn't put yourself first. That creates a situation in which you're pressured to act negatively—to put aside your plans and desires in order to avoid the condemnation of others.

One of the characteristics of a free man is that he's usually choosing positively—deciding which of several alternatives would make him the happiest; while the average person, most of the time, is choosing which of two or three alternatives will cause him the least discomfort.

When the reason for your actions is to avoid being called "selfish," you're making a negative decision and thereby restricting the possibilities for your own happiness.

You're in the Unselfishness Trap if you regretfully pay for your aunt's surgery with the money you'd saved for a new car, or if you sadly give up the vacation you'd looked forward to in order to help a sick neighbor.

You're in the trap if you feel you're *required* to give part of your income to the poor, or if you think that your country, community, or family has first claim on your time, energy, or money.

You're in the Unselfishness Trap any time you make negative choices that are designed to avoid being called "selfish."

It isn't that no one else is important. You might have a self-interest in someone's well-being, and giving a gift can be a gratifying expression of the affection you feel for him. But you're in the trap if you do such things in order to appear unselfish.

C. Helping Others

There *is* an understandable urge to give to those who are important and close to you. However, that leads many people to think that indiscriminate giving is the key to one's own happiness. They say that the way to be happy is to make others happy; get your glow by basking in the glow you've created for someone else.

It's important to identify that as a personal opinion. If someone says that giving is the key to happiness, isn't he saying that's the key to *his* happiness?

I think we can carry the question further, however, and determine how efficient such a policy might be. The suggestion to be a giver presupposes that you're able to judge what will make someone else happy. And experience has taught me to be a bit humble about assuming what makes others happy.

My landlady once brought me a piece of her freshly baked cake because she wanted to do me a favor. Unfortunately, it happened to be a kind of cake that was distasteful to me. I won't try to describe the various ways I tried to get the cake plate back to her without being confronted with a request for my judgment of her cake. It's sufficient to say that her well-intentioned favor interfered with my own plans.

And now, whenever I'm sure I know what someone else "needs," I remember that incident and back off a little. There's no way that one person can read the mind of another to know all his plans, goals, and tastes.

You may know a great deal about the desires of your intimate friends. But *indiscriminate* gift-giving and favor-doing is usually a waste of resources—or, worse, it can upset the well-laid plans of the receiver.

When you give to someone else, you might provide something he values—but probably not the thing he considers most important. If you expend those resources for *yourself*, you automatically devote them to what you consider to be most important. The time or money you've spent will most likely create more happiness that way.

If your purpose is to make someone happy, you're more apt to succeed if you make yourself the object. You'll never know another person more than a fraction as well as you can know yourself. . . .

D. Alternatives

As I indicated earlier . . . , it's too often assumed that there are only two alternatives: (1) Sacrifice your interests for the benefit of others; or (2) Make others sacrifice their interests for you. If nothing else were possible, it would indeed be a grim world.

Fortunately, there's more to the world than that. Because desires vary from person to person, it's possible to create exchanges between individuals in which both parties benefit.

For example, if you buy a house, you do so because you'd rather have the house than the money involved. But the seller's desire is different—he'd rather have the money than the house. When the sale is completed, each of you has received something of greater value than what you gave up— otherwise you wouldn't have entered the exchange. Who, then, has had to sacrifice for the other?

In the same way, your daily life is made up of dozens of such exchanges— small and large transactions in which each party gets something he values more than what he gives up. The exchange doesn't have to involve money; you may be spending time, attention, or effort in exchange for something you value.

Mutually beneficial relationships are possible when desires are compatible. Sometimes the desires are the same—like going to a movie together. Sometimes the desires are different—like trading your money for someone's house. In either case, it's the *compatibility* of the desires that makes the exchange possible.

No sacrifice is necessary when desires are compatible. So it makes sense to seek out people with whom you can have mutually beneficial relationships. . . .

An efficiently selfish person *is* sensitive to the needs and desires of others. But he doesn't consider those desires to be demands upon him. Rather, he sees them as *opportunities*—potential exchanges that might be beneficial to him. He identifies desires in others so that he can decide if exchanges with them will help him get what he wants.

He doesn't sacrifice himself for others, nor does he expect others to be sacrificed for him. He takes the third alternative—he finds relationships that are mutually beneficial so that no sacrifice is required.

E. Please Yourself

Everyone is selfish; everyone is doing what he believes will make himself happier. The recognition of that can take most of the sting out of accusations that you're being "selfish." Why should you feel guilty for seeking your own happiness when that's what everyone else is doing, too?

The demand that you be unselfish can be motivated by any number of reasons: that you'd help create a better world, that you have a moral obligation to be unselfish, that you give up your happiness to the selfishness of someone else, or that the person demanding it has just never thought it out.

Whatever the reason, you're not likely to convince such a person to stop his demands. But it will create much less pressure on you if you realize that it's *his* selfish reason. And you can eliminate the problem entirely by looking for more compatible companions.

To find constant, profound happiness requires that you be free to seek the gratification of your own desires. It means making positive choices.

If you slip into the Unselfishness Trap, you'll spend a good part of your time making negative choices—trying to avoid the censure of those who tell you not to think of yourself. . . .

If someone finds happiness by doing "good works" for others, let him. That doesn't mean that's the best way for you to find happiness.

And when someone accuses you of being selfish, just remember that he's only upset because you aren't doing what *he* selfishly wants you to do.

41 / *Egoism and Moral Scepticism*

J A M E S   R A C H E L S

James Rachels (1941–   ) teaches at the University of Alabama. Writing on ethics, he has had an important impact on ethical theory and has published several widely acclaimed works in this area.

1. Our ordinary thinking about morality is full of assumptions that we almost never question. We assume, for example, that we have an obligation to consider the welfare of other people when we decide what actions to perform or what rules to obey; we think that we must refrain from acting in ways harmful to others, and that we must respect their rights and interests as well as our own. We also assume that people are in fact capable of being motivated by such considerations, that is, that people are not wholly selfish and that they do sometimes act in the interests of others.

Both of these assumptions have come under attack by moral sceptics, as long ago as by Glaucon in Book II of Plato's *Republic*. Glaucon recalls the legend of Gyges, a shepherd who was said to have found a magic ring in a fissure opened by an earthquake. The ring would make its wearer invisible and thus would enable him to go anywhere and do anything undetected. Gyges used the power of the ring to gain entry to the Royal Palace where he seduced the Queen, murdered the King, and subsequently seized the throne. Now Glaucon asks us to determine that there are two such rings, one given to a man of virtue and one given to a rogue. The rogue, of course, will use his ring unscrupulously and do anything necessary to increase his own wealth and power. He will recognize no moral constraints on his conduct, and, since the cloak of invisibility will protect him from discovery, he can do anything he pleases without fear of reprisal. So, there will be no end to the mischief he will do. But how will the so-called virtuous man behave? Glaucon suggests that he will behave no better than the rogue: "No one, it is commonly believed, would have such iron strength of mind as to stand fast in doing right or keep his hands off other men's goods, when he could go to the marketplace and fearlessly help himself to anything he wanted, enter houses and sleep with any woman he chose, set prisoners free and kill men at his pleasure, and in a word go about among men with the powers of a god. He would behave no better than the other; both would take the same course."[1] Moreover, why shouldn't he? Once he is freed from the fear of reprisal, why shouldn't a man simply do what he pleases, or what he thinks is best for himself? What reason is there for him to continue being "moral" when it is clearly not to his own advantage to do so?

These sceptical views suggested by Glaucon have come to be known as *psychological egoism* and *ethical egoism* respectively. Psychological egoism is the view that all men are selfish in everything that they do, that is, that the only motive from which anyone ever acts is self-interest. In this view, even when men are acting in ways apparently calculated to benefit others, they are actually motivated by the belief that acting in this way is to their own advantage, and if they did not believe this, they would not be doing that action. Ethical egoism is, by contrast, a normative view about how men *ought* to act. It is the view that, regardless of how men do in fact behave, they have no obligation to do anything except what is in their own interests. According to the ethical egoist, a person is always justified in doing whatever is in his own interests, regardless of the effect on others.

Clearly, if either of these views is correct, then "the moral institution of

---

[1] *The Republic of Plato*, translated by F. M. Cornford (Oxford, 1941), p. 45.

life" [to use Butler's well-turned phrase] is very different than what we normally think. The majority of mankind is grossly deceived about what is, or ought to be, the case, where morals are concerned.

2. Psychological egoism seems to fly in the face of the facts. We are tempted to say: "Of course people act unselfishly all the time. For example, Smith gives up a trip to the country, which he would have enjoyed very much, in order to stay behind and help a friend with his studies, which is a miserable way to pass the time. This is a perfectly clear case of unselfish behavior, and if the psychological egoist thinks that such cases do not occur, then he is just mistaken." Given such obvious instances of "unselfish behavior," what reply can the egoist make? There are two general arguments by which he might try to show that all actions, including those such as the one just outlined, are in fact motivated by self-interest. Let us examine these in turn:

A. The first argument goes as follows. If we describe one person's action as selfish, and another person's action as unselfish, we are overlooking the crucial fact that in both cases, assuming that the action is done voluntarily, *the agent is merely doing what he most wants to do.* If Smith stays behind to help his friend, that only shows that he wanted to help his friend more than he wanted to go to the country. And why should he be praised for his "unselfishness" when he is only doing what he most wants to do? So, since Smith is only doing what he wants to do, he cannot be said to be acting unselfishly.

This argument is so bad that it would not deserve to be taken seriously except for the fact that so many otherwise intelligent people have been taken in by it. First, the argument rests on the premise that people never voluntarily do anything except what they want to do. But this is patently false; there are at least two classes of actions that are exceptions to this generalization. One is the set of actions which we may not want to do, but which we do anyway as a means to an end which we want to achieve; for example, going to the dentist in order to stop a toothache, or going to work every day in order to be able to draw our pay at the end of the month. These cases may be regarded as consistent with the spirit of the egoist argument, however, since the ends mentioned are wanted by the agent. But the other set of actions are those which we do, not because we want to, nor even because there is an end which we want to achieve, but because we feel ourselves *under an obligation* to do them. For example, someone may do something because he has promised to do it, and thus feels obligated, even though he does not want to do it. It is sometimes suggested that in such cases we do the action because, after all, we want to keep our promises; so, even here, we are doing what we want. However, this dodge will not work: if I have promised to do something, and if I do not want to do it, then it is simply false to say that I want to keep my promise. In such cases we feel a conflict precisely because we do *not* want to do what we feel obligated to do. It is reasonable to think that Smith's action falls roughly into this second category; he might stay behind, not because he wants to, but because he feels that his friend needs help.

But suppose we were to concede, for the sake of the argument, that all voluntary action is motivated by the agent's wants, or at least that Smith is so motivated. Even if this were granted, it would not follow that Smith is acting selfishly or from self-interest. For if Smith wants to do something that will help his friend, even when it means forgoing his own enjoyments, that is precisely what makes him *unselfish*. What else could unselfishness be, if not wanting to help others? Another way to put the same point is to say that it is the *object* of a want that determines whether it is selfish or not. The mere fact that I am acting on *my* wants does not mean that I am acting selfishly; that depends on *what it is* that I want. If I want only my own good, and care nothing for others, then I am selfish; but if I also want other people to be well-off and happy, and if I act on *that* desire, then my action is not selfish. So much for this argument.

B. The second argument for psychological egoism is this. Since so-called unselfish actions always produce a sense of self-satisfaction in the agent,[2] and since this sense of satisfaction is a pleasant state of consciousness, it follows that the point of the action is really to achieve a pleasant state of conscious-ness, rather than to bring about any good for others. Therefore, the action is "unselfish" only at a superficial level of analysis. Smith will feel much better with himself for having stayed to help his friend—if he had gone to the country, he would have felt terrible about it—and that is the real point of the action. According to a well-known story, this argument was once expressed by Abraham Lincoln:

> Mr. Lincoln once remarked to a fellow-passenger on an old-time mud-coach that all men were prompted by selfishness in doing good. His fellow-passenger was antagonizing this position when they were passing over a corduroy bridge that spanned a slough. As they crossed this bridge they espied an old razor-backed sow on the bank making a terrible noise because her pigs had got into the slough and were in danger of drowning. As the old coach began to climb the hill, Mr. Lincoln called out, "Driver, can't you stop just a moment?" Then Mr. Lincoln jumped out, ran back, and lifted the little pigs out of the mud and water and placed them on the bank. When he returned, his companion remarked: "Now, Abe, where does selfishness come in on this little episode?" "Why, bless your soul, Ed, that was the very essence of selfishness. I should have had no peace of mind all day had I gone on and left that suffering old sow worrying over those pigs. I did it to get peace of mind, don't you see?"[3]

This argument suffers from defects similar to the previous one. Why should we think that merely because someone derives satisfaction from help-ing others this makes him selfish? Isn't the unselfish man precisely the one who *does* derive satisfaction from helping others, while the selfish man does not? If Lincoln "got peace of mind" from rescuing the piglets, does this show him to be selfish, or, on the contrary, doesn't it show him to be compassionate

---

[2]Or, as it is sometimes said, "It gives him a clear conscience," or "He couldn't sleep at night if he had done otherwise," or "He would have been ashamed of himself for not doing it," and so on.

[3]Frank C. Sharp, *Ethics* (New York, 1928), pp. 75–76. Quoted from the Springfield (Ill.) *Monitor* in the *Outlook*, vol. 56, p. 1059.

and good-hearted? (If a man were truly selfish, why should it bother his conscience that *others* suffer—much less pigs?) Similarly, it is nothing more than shabby sophistry to say, because Smith takes satisfaction in helping his friend, that he is behaving selfishly. If we say this rapidly, while thinking about something else, perhaps it will sound all right; but if we speak slowly, and pay attention to what we are saying, it sounds plain silly.

Moreover, suppose we ask *why* Smith derives satisfaction from helping his friend. The answer will be, it is because Smith cares for him and wants him to succeed. If Smith did not have these concerns, then he would take no pleasure in assisting him; and these concerns, as we have already seen, are the marks of unselfishness, not selfishness. To put the point more generally: if we have a positive attitude toward the attainment of some goal, then we may derive satisfaction from attaining that goal. But the *object* of our attitude is *the attainment of that goal;* and we must want to attain the goal *before* we can find any satisfaction in it. We do not, in other words, desire some sort of pleasurable consciousness" and then try to figure out how to achieve it; rather, we desire all sorts of different things—money, a new fishing-boat, to be a better chess-player, to get a promotion in our work, etc.—and because we desire these things, we derive satisfaction from attaining them. And so, if someone desires the welfare and happiness of another person, he will derive satisfaction from that; but this does not mean that this satisfaction is the object of his desire, or that he is in any way selfish on account of it.

It is a measure of the weakness of psychological egoism that these insupportable arguments are the ones most often advanced in its favor. Why, then, should anyone ever have thought it a true view? Perhaps because of a desire for theoretical simplicity: In thinking about human conduct, it would be nice if there were some simple formula that would unite the diverse phenomena of human behavior under a single explanatory principle, just as simple formulae in physics bring together a great many apparently different phenomena. And since it is obvious that self-regard is an overwhelmingly important factor in motivation, it is only natural to wonder whether all motivation might not be explained in these terms. But the answer is clearly No; while a great many human actions are motivated entirely or in part by self-interest, only by a deliberate distortion of the facts can we say that all conduct is so motivated. This will be clear, I think, if we correct three confusions which are commonplace. The exposure of these confusions will remove the last traces of plausibility from the psychological egoist thesis.

The first is the confusion of selfishness with self-interest. The two are clearly not the same. If I see a physician when I am feeling poorly, I am acting in my own interest but no one would think of calling me "selfish" on account of it. Similarly, brushing my teeth, working hard at my job, and obeying the law are all in my self-interest but none of these are examples of selfish conduct. This is because selfish behavior is behavior that ignores the interests of others, in circumstances in which their interests ought not to be ignored. This concept has a definite evaluative flavor; to call someone "selfish" is not just to describe his action but to condemn it. Thus, you would not call me selfish for eating a normal meal in normal circumstances (although it may surely be in my self-interest); but you would call me selfish for hoarding food while others about are starving.

The second confusion is the assumption that every action is done *either* from self-interest or from the other-regarding motives. Thus, the egoist concludes that if there is no such thing as genuine altruism then all actions must be done from self-interest. But this is certainly a false dichotomy. The man who continues to smoke cigarettes, even after learning about the connection between smoking and cancer, is surely not acting from self-interest, not even by his own standards—self-interest would dictate that he quit smoking at once—and he is not acting altruistically either. He *is*, no doubt, smoking for the pleasure of it, but all that this shows is that undisciplined pleasure-seeking and acting from self-interest are very different. This is what led Butler to remark that "The thing to be lamented is, not that men have so great regard to their own good or interest in the present world, for they have not enough."[4]

The last two paragraphs show (*a*) that it is false that all actions are selfish, and (*b*) that it is false that all actions are done out of self-interest. And it should be noted that these two points can be made, and were, without any appeal to putative examples of altruism.

The third confusion is the common but false assumption that a concern for one's own welfare is incompatible with any genuine concern for the welfare of others. Thus, since it is obvious that everyone (or very nearly everyone) does desire his own well-being, it might be thought that no one can really be concerned with others. But again, this is false. There is no inconsistency in desiring that everyone, including oneself *and* others, be well-off and happy. To be sure, it may happen on occasion that our own interests conflict with the interests of others, and in these cases we will have to make hard choices. But even in these cases we might sometimes opt for the interests of others, especially when the others involved are our family or friends. But more importantly, not all cases are like this: sometimes we are able to promote the welfare of others when our own interests are not involved at all. In these cases not even the strongest self-regard need prevent us from acting considerately toward others.

Once these confusions are cleared away, it seems to me obvious enough that there is no reason whatever to accept psychological egoism. On the contrary, if we simply observe people's behavior with an open mind, we may find that a great deal of it is motivated by self-regard, but by no means all of it; and that there is no reason to deny that "the moral institution of life" can include a place for the virtue of beneficence.[5]

---

[4]*The Works of Joseph Butler*, edited by W. E. Gladstone (Oxford, 1896), vol. II, p. 26. It should be noted that most of the points I am making against psychological egoism were first made by Butler. Butler made all the important points; all that is left for us is to remember them (Butler: 1692–1752, British bishop and philosopher).

[5]The capacity for altruistic behavior is not unique to human beings. Some interesting experiments with rhesus monkeys have shown that these animals will refrain from operating a device for

3. The ethical egoist would say at this point, "Of course it is possible for people to act altruistically, and perhaps many people do act that way—but there is no reason why they *should* do so. A person is under no obligation to do anything except what is in his own interests."[6] This is really quite a radical doctrine. Suppose I have an urge to set fire to some public building (say, a department store) just for the fascination of watching the spectacular blaze; according to this view, the fact that several people might be burned to death provides no reason whatever why I should not do it. After all, this only concerns *their* welfare, not my own, and according to the ethical egoist the only person I need think of is myself.

Some might deny that ethical egoism has any such monstrous consequences. They would point out that it is really to my own advantage not to set the fire—for, if I do that, I may be caught and put into prison (unlike Gyges, I have no magic ring for protection). Moreover, even if I could avoid being caught it is still to my advantage to respect the rights and interests of others, for it is to my advantage to live in a society in which people's rights and interests are respected. Only in such a society can I live a happy and secure life; so, in acting kindly toward others, I would merely be doing my part to create and maintain the sort of society which it is to my advantage to have.[7] Therefore, it is said, the egoist would not be such a bad man; he would be as kindly and considerate as anyone else, because he would see that it is to his own advantage to be kindly and considerate.

This is a seductive line of thought, but it seems to me mistaken. Certainly it is to everyone's advantage (including the egoist's) to preserve a stable society where people's interests are generally protected. But there is no reason for the egoist to think that merely because *he* will not honor the rules of the social game, decent society will collapse. For the vast majority of people are not egoists, and there is no reason to think that they will be converted by his example—especially if he is discreet and does not unduly flaunt his style of life. What this line of reasoning shows is not that the egoist himself must act benevolently, but that he must encourage *others* to do so. He must take care to conceal from public view his own self-centered method of decision-making, and urge others to act on precepts very different from those on which he is willing to act.

The rational egoist, then, cannot advocate that egoism be universally adopted by everyone. For he wants a world in which his own interests are maximized; and if other people adopted the egoistic policy of pursuing their own interests to the exclusion of his interests, as he pursues his interests to the exclusion of theirs, then such a world would be impossible. So he himself will be an egoist, but he will want others to be altruists.

This brings us to what is perhaps the most popular "refutation" of ethical

---

securing food if this causes other animals to suffer pain. See Masserman, Wechkin, and Terris, "'Altruistic' Behavior in Rhesus Monkeys," *The American Journal of Psychiatry*, vol. 121 (1964), 584–585.

[6] I take this to be the view of Ayn Rand, in so far as I understand her confusing doctrine.

[7] Cf. Thomas Hobbes, *Leviathan* (London, 1651), chap. 17.

egoism current among philosophical writers—the argument that ethical ego-ism is at bottom inconsistent because it cannot be universalized.[8] The argu-ment goes like this:

To say that any action or policy of action is *right* (or that it *ought* to be adopted) entails that it is right for *anyone* in the same sort of circumstances. I cannot, for example, say that it is right for me to lie to you, and yet object when you lie to me (provided, of course, that the circumstances are the same). I cannot hold that it is all right for me to drink your beer and then complain when you drink mine. This is just the requirement that we be consistent in our evaluations; it is a requirement of logic. Now it is said that ethical egoism cannot meet this requirement because, as we have already seen, the egoist would not want others to act in the same way that he acts. Moreover, suppose he *did* advocate the universal adoption of egoistic policies: he would be saying to Peter, "You ought to pursue your own interests even if it means destroying Paul"; and he would be saying to Paul, "You ought to pursue your own interests even if it means destroying Peter." The attitudes expressed in these two recommendations seem clearly inconsistent—he is urging the advance-ment of Peter's interests at one moment, and countenancing their defeat at the next. Therefore, the argument goes, there is no way to maintain the doctrine of ethical egoism as a consistent view about how we ought to act. We will fall into inconsistency whenever we try.

What are we to make of this argument? Are we to conclude that ethical egoism has been refuted? Such a conclusion, I think, would be unwarranted; for I think that we can show, contrary to this argument, how ethical egoism can be maintained consistently. We need only to interpret the egoist's position in a sympathetic way: we should say that he has in mind a certain kind of world which he would prefer over all others; it would be a world in which his own interests were maximized, regardless of the effects on other people. The egoist's primary policy of action, then, would be to act in such a way as to bring about, as nearly as possible, this sort of world. Regardless of however morally reprehensible we might find it, there is nothing *inconsistent* in some-one's adopting this as his ideal and acting in a way calculated to bring it about. And if someone did adopt this as his ideal, then he would not advocate universal egoism; as we have already seen, he would want other people to be altruists. So, if he advocates any principles of conduct for the general public, they will be altruistic principles. This would not be inconsistent; on the con-trary, it would be perfectly consistent with his goal of creating a world in which his own interests are maximized. To be sure, he would have to be deceitful; in order to secure the good will of others, and a favorable hearing for his exhortations to altruism, he would have to pretend that he was himself prepared to accept altruistic principles. But again, that would be all right; from the egoist's point of view, this would merely be a matter of adopting the

---

[8]See, for example, Brian Medlin, "Ultimate Principles and Ethical Egoism," *Australasian Journal of Philosophy*, vol. 35 (1957), 111–118; and D. H. Monro, *Empiricism and Ethics* (Cambridge, 1967), chap. 16.

necessary means to the achievement of his goal—and while we might not approve of this, there is nothing inconsistent about it. Again, it might be said: "He advocates one thing, but does another. Surely, *that's* inconsistent." But it is not; for what he advocates and what he does are both calculated as means to an end (the *same* end, we might note); and as such, he is doing what is rationally required in each case. Therefore, contrary to the previous argument, there is nothing inconsistent in the ethical egoist's view. He cannot be refuted by the claim that he contradicts himself.

Is there, then, no way to refute the ethical egoist? If by "refute" we mean show that he has made some *logical* error, the answer is that there is not. However, there is something more that can be said. The egoist challenge to our ordinary moral convictions amounts to a demand for an explanation of why we should adopt certain policies of action, namely policies in which the good of others is given importance. We can give an answer to this demand, albeit an indirect one. The reason one ought not to do actions that would hurt other people is: other people would be hurt. The reason one ought to do actions that would benefit other people is: other people would be benefited. This may at first seem like a piece of philosophical sleight-of-hand, but it is not. The point is that the welfare of human beings is something that most of us value *for its own sake*, and not merely for the sake of something else. Therefore, when *further* reasons are demanded for valuing the welfare of human beings, we cannot point to anything further to satisfy this demand. It is not that we have no reason for pursuing these policies, but that our reason *is* that these policies are for the good of human beings.

So: if we are asked, "Why shouldn't I set fire to this department store?" one answer would be "Because if you do, people may be burned to death." This is a complete, sufficient reason which does not require qualification or supplementation of any sort. If someone seriously wants to know why this action shouldn't be done, that's the reason. If we are pressed further and asked the sceptical question "But why shouldn't I do actions that will harm others?" we may not know what to say—but this is because the questioner has included in his question the very answer we would like to give: "Why shouldn't you do actions that will harm others? Because, doing those actions would harm others."

The egoist, no doubt, will not be happy with this. He will protest that *we* may accept this as a reason, but *he* does not. And here the argument stops: there are limits to what can be accomplished by argument, and if the egoist really doesn't care about other people—if he honestly doesn't care whether they are helped or hurt by his actions—then we have reached those limits. If we want to persuade him to act decently toward his fellow humans, we will have to make our appeal to such other attitudes as he does possess, by threats, bribes, or other cajolery. That is all that we can do.

Though some may find this situation distressing (we would like to be able to show that the egoist is just *wrong*), it holds no embarrassment for common morality. What we have come up against is simply a fundamental requirement of rational action, namely, that the existence of reasons for action always depends on the prior existence of certain attitudes in the agent. For example, the fact that a certain course of action would make the agent a lot of money is a reason for doing it only if the agent wants to make money; the fact that practicing at chess makes one a better player is a reason for practicing only if one wants to be a better player; and so on. Similarly, the fact that a certain action would help the agent is a reason for doing the action only if the agent cares about his own welfare, and the fact that an action would help others is a reason for doing it only if the agent cares about others. In this respect ethical egoism and what we might call ethical altruism are in exactly the same fix; both require that the agent *care* about himself, or about other people, before they can get started.

So a nonegoist will accept "It would harm another person" as a reason not to do an action simply because he cares about what happens to that other person. When the egoist says that he does *not* accept that as a reason, he is saying something quite extraordinary. He is saying that he has no affection for friends or family, that he never feels pity or compassion, that he is the sort of person who can look on scenes of human misery with complete indifference, so long as he is not the one suffering. Genuine egoists, people who really don't care at all about anyone other than themselves, are rare. It is important to keep this in mind when thinking about ethical egoism; it is easy to forget just how fundamental to human psychological makeup the feeling of sympathy is. Indeed, a man without any sympathy at all would scarcely be recognizable as a man; and that is what makes ethical egoism such a disturbing doctrine in the first place. . . .

42 / A Defense of Utilitarianism

E. DANIEL KAYE

E. Daniel Kaye (1936–   ) is a philosopher who has written many books and articles in various areas of philosophy, including ethics. He currently teaches philosophy at a state university in the upper Midwest. He occasionally uses the pseudonym above.

I. EXPLANATORY REMARKS

*T*he term "utilitarianism" can be and has been defined in various ways. For the purpose of this essay, utilitarianism will be understood broadly as the view that: the proper standard of conduct for anyone is the maximization of the greatest amount of happiness, or least amount of unhappiness, for *all* concerned, not just one's self. By proper standard of conduct is meant a standard or criterion or rule which enables one to make moral decisions and enables one to make general assessments of behavior in terms of right and wrong. Thus utilitarianism claims that a right act is the one that tends toward the production of the greatest amount of happiness, or least amount of unhappiness, for *anyone* who may be affected by the performance of that action. Similarly, a wrong action is one that tends toward the greatest amount of unhappiness, or least amount of happiness, for anyone who may be affected by the performance of that action.

I turn now to a defense of utilitarianism, or more accurately to a case for Jeremy Bentham's defense of utilitarianism.[1] Thus a more accurate title for this essay would be: "A Defense of Bentham's Defense of Utilitarianism." Or to be still more accurate, I want to defend a highly qualified, amended, and extended version of Bentham's position. Hence an even more accurate title for the present essay is: "A Defense of a Qualified, Amended, and Extended Version of Bentham's Defense of Utilitarianism." Bentham's formulation and defense of utilitarianism occur primarily in three sections of his major work, *An Introduction to the Principles of the Morals and Legislation.* My exposition and defense will follow, at least to begin with, Bentham's discussion in those sections.

II. BENTHAM'S PRINCIPLE OF UTILITY

In his discussion Bentham takes up three "principles," one of which he supports, two of which he opposes. The one he defends is referred to as the Principle of Utility. Before stating the principle, Bentham begins with a brief discussion of concepts which play an important role in his theory. He writes:

> Nature has placed mankind under the governance of two sovereign masters, *pain* and *pleasure.* It is for them alone to point out what we ought to do, as well as to determine what we shall do. On the one hand the standard of right and wrong, on the other the chain of causes and effects, are fastened to their throne. They govern us in all we do, in all we say, in all we think: every effort we can make to throw off our subjection, will serve but to demonstrate and confirm it. In words a man may pretend to abjure their empire: but in reality he will remain subject to it all the while. The *Principle of Utility* recognizes this subjection. . . .

The reader may very well question whether Bentham was right in placing such an emphasis on pleasure and pain. Is it really the case that all of humankind is under the "governance" of these two "sovereign masters"? I shall return to a consideration of these questions later in this essay.

---

[1]Jeremy Bentham (1748–1832) was an English philosopher and political theorist who developed the utilitarian theory as a basis for political reform.

I turn now to Bentham's formulation of the standard of conduct which he defends, the principle of utility.

> By the principle of utility is meant that principle which approves or disapproves of every action whatsoever, according to the tendency which it appears to have to augment or diminish the happiness of the party whose interest is in question: or, what is the same thing in other words, to promote or to oppose that happiness.

Bentham's formulation is confusing. A principle cannot literally approve or disapprove of anything. It is obviously we who do the approving or disapproving. Hence we may reformulate the principle more accurately:

> By the principle of utility is meant the principle that every action is to be approved of or disapproved of according to the tendency which it appears to have to augment or diminish the happiness of anyone whose interest is in question. . . .

Thus: (1) An action is to be approved of if it tends to increase the happiness of anyone affected by it; and (2) an action is to be disapproved of if it tends to decrease the happiness of anyone affected by it. Bentham maintains that this holds not only in cases where the party whose interest is in question is an individual, but also in those cases where it is the community.

The reader may wonder: "What's this got to do with right and wrong, or with standards of conduct?" Here again Bentham is confusing. He says that any action that is conformable to the principle of utility is a right action (or at least not wrong). But as this is formulated every action could in principle be right in the sense that every action could be approved of *or* disapproved of. But apart from that, this formulation does not separate clearly right acts from wrong ones. Hence I take it that what Bentham really means is: A right action is one which deserves to be approved of on the grounds that it produces the greatest happiness for anyone affected by it. A wrong action is one which deserves to be disapproved of on the grounds that it diminishes the happiness of anyone affected by it. In short, the proper standard of conduct as reformulated is the principle of utility.

Bentham then turns to an objection. Someone might ask, "Where is your proof of the principle of utility?" Bentham replies:

> Is [the principle of utility] susceptible of any direct proof? It should seem not; for that which is used to prove everything else, cannot itself be proved: a chain of proofs must have their commencement somewhere. To give such a proof is as impossible as it is needless.

He adds that: Besides there has never been "a human creature breathing, however stupid or perverse, who has not on many perhaps on most occasions of his life deferred to it."

Is this an acceptable reply? Is it really true that "that which is used to prove everything else, cannot itself be proved" and that the effort to give such a proof is "as impossible as it is needless"? Or, on the contrary, do we have a right to ask for a proof of the principle of utility since it plays such an important role in Bentham's ethical theory? I would like now to argue that Bentham's reply is correct and justifiable.

Let me take a principle from another area—or actually a set of principles—which plays a role comparable to the role that the principle of utility plays in Bentham's theory. As a philosopher, I spend much of my time constructing arguments to support philosophical claims which I hold or to get answers to philosophical questions. Similarly, in dealing with opposing views or answers, I devote much time to appraising the arguments that others have put forth to support their views and answers. Now in constructing and appraising my own arguments and in criticizing the arguments of others, I have to appeal to certain principles, or laws, or rules of logic. There are many such principles, but for convenience let us designate them by L. Now suppose that I am appraising, say, four arguments, whether my own or those of others, and I say that arguments 1 and 4 are correct or valid arguments, whereas arguments 2 and 3 are incorrect or invalid. I arrive at those conclusions by appealing to L (or some subset of L). Another way of saying this is: I prove the conclusions of arguments 1 and 4 by showing that they are deduced validly from the premises on behalf of conclusions. Similarly, I disprove—or at least do not accept—the conclusions of arguments 2 and 3 by showing that the conclusions are not validly deducible from the premises put forth for those conclusions.

Now suppose someone said to me: "Well, you've proved the conclusions of 1 and 4 by appealing to L. And you've rejected the conclusions of 2 and 3 by also appealing to L. Now, where is your proof of L?" I would have to reply: But this is not a plausible question or acceptable request. We prove other propositions by L, the laws of logic. But we cannot prove the laws of logic by other propositions, because all of the other ones presuppose L. Nor can we prove the laws of logic by means of themselves, for this would be begging the question. But even if we could prove L, it would not help. Suppose that we could prove or deduce the principle of logic, L, from some other set of statements, K. Then how would we prove K? By something else, J, presumably. But then how can we prove J? "The question here is indefinitely self-repeating: we are caught in an *infinite regress*. Besides, how could we prove anything except by means of the principles of logic? These are themselves . . . the very principles of proof."[2]

Let us now return to Bentham and his claim about the principle of utility. Let us call it U. Bentham says that U is used to prove everything else (in ethics) and hence cannot itself be proved. I submit that in ethical deliberations, in arriving at moral decisions, in making moral appraisals in terms of right and wrong actions, U stands in exactly the same relation to all such matters as L does regarding the proofs of other things and the appraisal of arguments. To show that an action is (or would be) morally right, I appeal to U. To establish that certain actions are wrong, I must appeal to U. In short, U is used to prove

[2]John Hospers, *An Introduction to Philosophical Analysis*, 2nd edition (Englewood Cliffs: Prentice-Hall, 1967), p. 213.

everything else, and therefore it cannot itself be proved—and for the very same reason that L cannot be proved. And just as it is improper and self-defeating to attempt—or to ask for—a proof of L, in exactly the same manner it is improper and self-defeating to attempt—or to ask for—a proof of U. Hence Bentham is right with regard to the status of the principle of utility.

However, having said all this, it turns out that Bentham does implicitly offer a proof of (or argument for) the principle of utility. In the next section of his work, he turns to two other possible candidates for moral principles which he rejects. These are called the Principle of Asceticism and the Principle of Sympathy and Antipathy. Bentham provides reasons for holding that both of these are false, or unacceptable as moral standards. Hence Bentham's (unstated) argument on behalf of the principle of utility is:

1. There are three candidates for the position of being the proper standard of conduct: the principle of utility, the principle of asceticism, and the principle of sympathy and antipathy.
2. The principle of asceticism is false (or fails).
3. The principle of sympathy and antipathy is false (or fails).
4. Therefore the principle of utility is true and hence the only proper standard of conduct.

Whether or not this is a good (sound) argument, I shall discuss later. Meanwhile, let us turn now to the two principles—and hence proposed standards of conduct—which Bentham opposes and to his reasons for rejecting them.

III. THE TWO OPPOSING PRINCIPLES

Again, Bentham refers to the two views which he opposes as the Principle of Asceticism and the Principle of Sympathy and Antipathy. Both are adverse to the principle of utility.

Bentham formulates the principle of asceticism as follows:

> By the principle of asceticism I mean that principle, which like the principle of utility, approves or disapproves of any action, according to the tendency which it appears to have to augment or diminish the happiness of the party whose interest is in question; but in an inverse manner: approving of actions in as far as they tend to diminish his happiness; disapproving of them in as far as they tend to augment it.

Again, Bentham's formulation is confusing. What he means is:

> By the principle of asceticism I mean the principle that every action is to be approved of or disapproved of according to the tendency which it appears to have to augment or diminish the unhappiness of anyone whose interest is in question. . . .

Bentham's major criticism of this principle is: Unlike the principle of utility, it cannot be consistently pursued by anyone. "Let but one tenth of the inhabitants of this earth [try to] pursue it consistently, and in a day's time they will have turned it into a hell." This seems to me to be undeniably true.

Now I turn to Bentham's formulation of the principle of sympathy and antipathy.

> By the principle of sympathy and antipathy, I mean that principle which approves or disapproves of certain actions, not on account of their tending to augment the happiness, nor yet on account of their tending to diminish the happiness of the party whose interest is in question, but merely because a man finds himself disposed to approve or disapprove of them: holding up that approbation [approval] or disapprobation as a sufficient reason for itself, and disclaiming the necessity of looking out for any extrinsic ground.

Once again, this is confusing. What he means is:

> By the principle of sympathy and antipathy, I mean the principle that every action is to be approved of or disapproved of according to whether one finds oneself disposed of to approve or disapprove of it [on the basis of one's feelings or sentiments].

Bentham makes three criticisms of this principle. First:

> This is rather a principle in name than in reality: it is not a positive principle of itself, so much as a term employed to signify the negation of all principles. What one expects to find in a principle is something that points out some external consideration, as a means of warranting and guiding the internal sentiments of approbation [approval] and disapprobation: this expectation is but ill fulfilled by a proposition, which does neither more nor less than hold up each of these sentiments as a ground and standard for itself.

He continues:

> In looking over the catalogue of human actions (says a partisan of this principle) in order to determine which of them are to be marked with the seal of [say] disapprobation, you need but to take counsel of your own feelings: whatever you find in yourself a propensity to condemn, is wrong for that very reason.

Similarly whatever you find in yourself as a feeling of approval and a propensity to praise or support is right for that "reason" alone.

Surely, Bentham is correct. This "principle" is not a genuine principle or rule or standard of conduct (by which to make judgments of right and wrong) but the negation of one. It says: Rather than looking for *reasons* for distinguishing right from wrong actions, or asking about the likely consequences of our actions, just look inward and consult your *feelings*. Whatever you *feel* is right *is* right, and whatever you *feel* is wrong *is* wrong! This cannot be correct. A *moral* principle or standard of conduct requires more than an internal expression of our *feelings*. It requires something external—something which can guide our diverse and scattered internal feelings. For an action to be meaningfully assessed as right or wrong, it must be assessed as right or wrong on some *grounds* or reasons. Similarly for an action to *be* right or wrong there must be something external to our inner feelings which accounts for its rightness or wrongness.

Bentham's second criticism of the "principle" of sympathy and antipathy has to do with its application to our views and consequent behavior regarding punishment. According to this principle:

> If you hate much, punish much: if you hate little, punish little: punish as you hate.

Bentham offers this criticism:

> The principle of sympathy and antipathy is most apt to err on the side of severity. It is for applying punishment in many cases which deserve none: in many cases which deserve some, it is for applying more than they deserve. There is no incident imaginable, be it ever so trivial, and so remote from mischief, from which this principle may not extract a ground of punishment. Any difference in taste: any difference in opinion: upon one subject as well as upon another. No disagreement so trifling which perseverance and altercation will not render serious. Each becomes in the other's eyes an enemy, and, if laws permit, a criminal. This is one of the circumstances by which the human race is distinguished (not much indeed to its advantage) from the brute creation . . .

This seems to be a very apt description of our present theories and practice of penal justice—or more likely, injustice. Feelings of disapproval and hatred have throughout history led to countless acts of cruelty and injustice, but supposedly in the name of justice.

I turn now to Bentham's third criticism of the principle of sympathy and antipathy. The principle (and/or) the adherents of it conflate two things that must be distinguished. Bentham writes:

> There are two things which are very apt to be confounded but which it imports us carefully to distinguish: the motive or cause, which by operating on the mind of an individual, is productive of any act: and the ground or reason which warrants a legislator, or other bystander, in regarding that act with an eye of approbation [approval].

Take the case where I feel antipathy with regard to performing a certain action and consequently perform another action which results in very good effects. Then clearly:

> Antipathy . . . in such a case is a cause of the action which is attended with good effects: but this does not make it a right ground of [the] action. . . The only right ground of [an] action . . . is . . . the consideration of utility. . . Other principles . . . , other motives may be the reasons why such an act *has* been done: that is, the reasons or causes of its being done: but it is the [utility] alone that can be the reason why it might or ought to have been done.

Finally:

> Antipathy . . . requires always to be regulated, to prevent its doing mischief: to be regulated by what? always by the principle of utility. The principle of utility neither requires nor admits of any other regulator than itself.

Bentham is surely right. Our feelings of sympathy or antipathy may be—indeed are—*motives* or *causes* of many of the actions we do. But they do *not* constitute *grounds* for those actions. I may refrain from doing X simply because I feel antipathetic toward doing it. But this does not guarantee that I was morally right in refraining from doing X. Perhaps it was the action I *ought* to have done.

For the above three reasons, the principle of sympathy and antipathy fails as a candidate for being an acceptable moral standard of conduct. And since the principle of asceticism also fails, this supports the claim that the only proper and correct standard of conduct is the principle of utility (as defined in Section II, above).

IV. THE APPLICATION OF THE MORAL STANDARD

To all the above, one might respond: "Very well, you have presented the moral standard which you defend and argued against two opposing ones. But two questions remain. (1) What do you mean by happiness and unhappiness? (2) When you are, say, faced with a moral dilemma, how do you make a decision? How do you know or even assess which action will have (or is likely to have) the best consequences?"

For Bentham, the answer to (1) is quite simple. As we saw earlier, Bentham takes happiness to be essentially pleasure and unhappiness to be pain. Hence the moral standard he holds may be restated:

> A right action is one which is (or will be) productive of the greatest amount of pleasure, for all those concerned; or in some cases, the least amount of pain.
> A wrong action is one which is or will be productive of the greatest amount of pain, for all concerned; or in some cases, the least amount of pleasure.

But one might ask: "What is meant by pleasure here? Just physical pleasure—or what?" Bentham is not clear on this issue, but one must assume that he meant the term "pleasure" to denote psychological/mental pleasure as well as physical pleasure. But even if we interpret the term in this sense, is it plausible to identify happiness with pleasure in this extended sense? Is it plausible to base an ethical theory on pleasure/happiness and pain/unhappiness? Once again, I shall have to turn to these considerations after I have finished discussing Bentham's views.

I turn now to question (2). Even if we accept pleasures and the avoidance of pain as the ends we wish to pursue, how can we decide which actions will be the most pleasure-producing or the least pain-producing? Bentham's answer is: By a sort of "calculus." We can at least estimate the amounts of pleasure and/or pain that actions are likely to result in by using several criteria. Bentham writes:

> To a person considered by himself, the value of a pleasure or pain considered by itself, will be greater or less, according to the four following circumstances:
>
> 1. Its intensity.
> 2. Its duration.

3. Its certainty or uncertainty.
4. Its propinquity [nearness] or remoteness.

These are the circumstances which are to be considered in estimating a pleasure or a pain considered each of them by itself. But when the value of any pleasure or pain is considered for the purpose of estimating the tendency of any act by which it is produced, there are two other circumstances to be taken into account: these are,

5. Its fecundity [fruitfulness, productivity], or the chance it has of being followed by sensations of the same kind: that is, pleasure, if it be a pleasure: pains, if it be a pain.
6. Its purity, or the chance it has of not being followed by sensations of the opposite kind: that is, pains, if it be a pleasure: pleasures, if it be a pain. These two last, however, are in strictness scarcely to be deemed properties of the pleasure or the pain itself; they are not, therefore, in strictness to be taken into the account of the value of that pleasure or that pain. They are in strictness to be deemed properties only of the act, or other event, by which such pleasure or pain has been produced; and accordingly are only to be taken into the account of the tendency of such act or such event.

But what if one is not merely considering himself, but others as well, and especially when an act may concern several persons? Bentham continues:

To a number of persons, with reference to each of whom the value of a pleasure or a pain is considered, it will be greater or less, according to seven circumstances: to wit, the six preceding ones, viz.

1. Its intensity.
2. Its duration.
3. Its certainty or uncertainty.
4. Its propinquity or remoteness.
5. Its fecundity.
6. Its purity.

And one other; to wit:

7. Its extent; that is, the number of persons to whom it extends; or (in other words) who are affected by it.

Now, suppose that you are faced with a decision: Shall I do A or B? And suppose that the consequences of doing either are very likely to affect mainly or solely you. Then ask, "How great would be the intensity of pleasure if I did A? If I did B?" And suppose that, from past experience, you know that the units of pleasure derived from doing A would be the maximum, whereas the units of pleasure derived from doing B would be far less. Let us say you calculate that doing A will result in 10 Benthams of pleasure, whereas doing B would result in only 5 Benthams. Now ask the same question with regard to the likely duration of the pleasure that results as a consequence of A and B. And let us say that you calculate that doing A would result in long-lasting pleasure, whereas the pleasure from doing B would be very short in duration. So perhaps you assign 10 Benthams for A, and only 2 for B. Now ask the same question about the certainty or uncertainty of the pleasure resulting in each case. You decide that it is very close to certain that you would derive much pleasure if you did A, whereas there are risks with regard to B which make the outcome quite uncertain. So you assign, say, 9 Benthams for doing A and 3 for doing B. And so on with regard to the remaining criteria. And let us suppose your calculation results in the following assignments of pleasure units or Benthams:

	A	B
Intensity	10	5
Duration	10	2
Certainty or uncertainty	9	3
Propinquity or remoteness	5	5
Fecundity	8	2
Purity	6	4

Obviously, doing A would produce many more Benthams of pleasure than doing B. Hence A is what you ought to do.

Now, let us suppose that the decision you are faced with will have consequences not just for yourself, or primarily yourself, but for other people, perhaps a large number of people as well. Then we have to bring in the seventh condition and ask about the extent of doing A and doing B, that is, the number of persons who will be affected by doing A as opposed to the number who will be affected by doing B; and let us suppose that we can readily estimate that the number of persons affected by doing A will be very large, whereas the number affected by doing B would be negligible. Then, if with this new consideration, the intensity, duration, etc., of pleasure for all of those in the large number would be great, then A would still be the act you ought to perform. But, on the other hand, suppose that with this additional consideration, the intensity, duration, etc., of pleasure would be greatly reduced for that large number by doing A, and perhaps even severe pain would result to those persons as a result of doing A, then this could very well entail that doing B would be the right thing to do. For doing B would produce the overall greatest amount of pleasure—or perhaps least amount of pain—for all of the persons affected by your doing B.

Someone may object: "But look, no one can assign such numerical values to the amount of pleasure versus pain that would result in terms of the seven factors in Bentham's calculus. No one could do this even if we talked in terms of the amount of pleasure/pain *likely* to occur, let alone the amount that definitely will occur." Bentham seems to recognize this. But he still thinks that some assessment can be done given our knowledge of what most people find pleasurable or painful. So a rough calculation is possible. But even if this is doubtful, then I think Bentham would say that we can at least assign a rank ordering in terms of, say, positive (+), negative (−), and uncertain (?). So perhaps instead of a table like the one above, we could come up with something along these lines:

	A	B
Intensity	+	−
Duration	+	+
Certainty or uncertainty	+	?
Propinquity or remoteness	+	+
Fecundity	+	−
Purity—and perhaps	?	?
Extent	+	−

Then with such a "calculation," we could have greater chances of succeeding in our estimates of the consequences in terms of pleasure and pain. And in the above case, it would seem that we *ought* to do A.

V. OBJECTIONS AND REPLIES

I turn now to some objections which someone might raise at this point, including the ones I referred to in previous sections.

(1) Recall that Bentham bases his ethical theory partly on the claim that "Nature has placed mankind under the governance of two sovereign masters, pain and pleasure." Hence when Bentham claims that

> A right action is one that produces the greatest amount of happiness for anyone affected by it; and a wrong action is one that diminishes the amount of happiness for anyone affected by it.

it would seem that Bentham equates happiness with pleasure and unhappiness with pain. Hence one objection that someone might raise and to which I referred at the beginning of Section II is: "Was Bentham correct or justified in placing such an emphasis on pleasure and pain and then building an ethical theory on it? Doesn't this seem terribly hedonistic—and in the grossest sense?"

I reply: What else can we appeal to other than pleasure and pain? If I am questioned about a certain action I do (or have done or will do), I may be able to provide a reason which justifies my action. And if questioned again, I may (in some circumstances) be able to provide another reason. But ultimately this chain of reasons must stop when I provide an answer in terms of pursuit of pleasure and avoidance of pain; for if pressed as to why I prefer the first and avoid the second, I can no longer justify or give any reason for my answer.

David Hume[3] has demonstrated this nicely. Suppose you run across

---

[3]Hume was an eighteenth-century British philosopher. The passage quoted is from Appendix I to his book, *An Enquiry Concerning the Principles of Morals.*

someone, Mortimer, who is exercising vigorously and you wonder why he spends so much time and effort on it. Hume writes:

> Ask a man *why he uses exercise*; he will answer, *because he desires to keep his health*. If you enquire *why he desires health*, he will readily reply, *because sickness is painful*. If you push your enquiries farther, and desire a reason *why he hates pain*, it is impossible he can ever give any. This is an ultimate end, and is never referred to any other object.

Surely, Hume is right. If you were questioned in a similar manner—whether about exercising or whatever—and the questioning by someone got down to, "But why do you hate and avoid pain and prefer pleasure?" What could you possibly answer except, "I just do!" Hence it is impossible for you to justify your preference of pleasure over pain. We have here, indeed, reached an ultimate end such that no further justification can possibly be given.

Someone may object further: "But this only shows that when we try to justify our actions in terms of what *as a matter of fact* we do or don't do, we finally reach the preference for pleasure and dislike of pain—which cannot themselves be justified. But this does not mean that, when we have reached this 'ultimate end', the actions in question are *morally right*. It only shows that the actions which produce pleasure are the ones we prefer and that we as a matter of fact pursue those. But this doesn't prove that those are the actions we *ought* to do, the ones that are *right*." It seems to me that this does indeed prove that such actions are morally right. Suppose you are faced with a moral decision: Shall I do A or B? And suppose that doing A would result in severe pain to several other persons (or to even one); whereas doing B would not result in any pain to them and might even bring a modest amount of pleasure. Is there any doubt that you *ought* to do B, that you are *morally obligated* to do B? If anyone seriously insisted that A is the morally right action, you would think him deranged. I cannot see how anyone could arrive at any other conclusion— if he is a person of goodwill who seeks to be moral.

Hence Bentham was completely correct in saying:

> It is for [pleasure and pain] alone to point out what we ought to do. . . The standard of right and wrong . . . are fastened to their throne. They govern us in all we do, all we say, all we think: every effort we can make to throw off our subjection [to them], will serve but to demonstrate and confirm it.

As to the charge that the appeal to pleasure and pain represent gross hedonism, I reply: If pleasure and pain are limited solely to physical pleasure and physical pain, then such a charge would be justified. And if Bentham did so equate them, then this is a severe limitation to and justifiable criticism of his theory. But recall that at the beginning (Section I) I said that my defense of utilitarianism would be a qualified, amended, and extended defense of Bentham's theory. So whatever Bentham may have held, *I* at least do *not* make this identification. In assessing the amount of pleasure or pain which an action is likely to produce, I do not limit pleasure to physical pleasure or pain to physical pain. We must also include in our assessment psychological and even intellectual and perhaps spiritual pleasures as well as physical ones. And often these will deserve to be ranked highest when making our assessments. Hence the charge of gross hedonism is unfounded.

(2) The second objection to which I referred above pertained to Bentham's (implicit) argument on behalf of the principle of utility. Recall that he maintained that there are three (only three?) candidates for being the proper standard of conduct: the principle of utility (U), the principle of asceticism (A), and the principle of sympathy and antipathy (S). Hence his argument (which he did not himself formulate) is:

1. There are three possible standards of conduct: U, A, and S.
2. A is false (or fails).
3. S is false (or fails).
4. Therefore U is true and the only proper standard of conduct.

The objection raised (at the end of Section II) was: "Is this a sound argument? That is, is it an argument whose premises are all true and hence one from which the conclusion logically follows and thus is also true?"

It seems to me that, for reasons given above (Section III), premisses 2 and 3 are clearly true. But it is by no means obvious that premiss 1 is true. In fact many would say it is clearly false, for there are other viable candidates for the correct standard of conduct besides U, A, and S. Thus it seems that premiss 1 is false. Therefore the conclusion of the argument cannot be inferred to be true. The argument does *not* prove that the principle of utility is the correct standard of conduct.

I accept this as a valid criticism. However it seems to me that the collapse of this argument is irrelevant. For recall that Bentham himself actually claimed that the principle of utility cannot be proved by any argument, "for that which is used to prove everything else, cannot itself be proved." In my answer to the first objection, above, I showed that and why Bentham is right in my discussion of the passage from Hume. And I did so without any reliance on this (implicit) argument or proposed proof. Hence this second objection has no force. The collapse of Bentham's (implicit) argument does nothing to "dethrone" the principle of utility from its position of being the only correct and proper standard of conduct. I shall not rehash my reasons for maintaining this. I refer the reader to my response to the first objection.

(3) I turn now to a third possible objection. Someone might say: "But the utilitarian theory is a purely consequentialist one. It judges the rightness or wrongness of actions solely in terms of the consequences—the amount of pleasure or pain which results (or is likely to result) from the performance or non-performance of those actions."

I reply: What else can you meaningfully base your assessments and judgments of right and wrong on besides the consequences of actions? On their *intrinsic* "rightness" or "wrongness"? What does that mean? And if you attempted to base moral distinctions of right and wrong actions on such supposed intrinsic rightness or wrongness, with no concern for the consequences of such actions, wouldn't your assessments and judgments be utterly vacuous, devoid of content? All moral assessments would be pure speculations, divorced from the real world, or a matter of conflicting intuitions of "intrinsic" rightness or wrongness. One of the many virtues of the utilitarian standard of conduct is that it does make ethical deliberations meaningful and genuine by linking them concretely to the real world, the world in which people suffer and seek alleviation from pain. The only way to do this that is philosophically sound and true to fact is to appeal to the consequences of our actions.

(4) One final possible objection: "Isn't the utilitarian theory simply another form of ethical egoism—the view that, for each individual, right actions are those which enhance and further the self-interest of that individual?"

I reply: No. If there are any utilitarians who have placed their theories on an egoistic basis, then I reject all such. But most utilitarians—perhaps all—have made *this* a cardinal rule and foundation of their theory and standard of conduct: In calculating the amount of happiness and/or unhappiness (pleasure or pain) which is likely to result from one's actions, no one's happiness is to be counted as more important or as having any more weight than anyone else's. When you are faced with a decision—shall I do A or B?—the utilitarian theory says: In making your decision you must be sure that you do not weigh the balance in your favor. The theory is thereby highly democratic and impartial. It also allows for acts of genuine altruism. Hence utilitarianism is utterly opposed to ethical egoism.

VI. CONCLUSION

In this essay: First, I clarified the notions of utilitarianism and proper standard of conduct, and I explained what my defense would consist of (Section I). Next, I presented and partially defended a modified version of Bentham's principle of utility (Section II). I then defended his rejection of the two opposing principles (Section III). Then I showed how the utilitarian standard of conduct can be applied, in terms of a revised version of Bentham's "calculus" (Section IV). Finally, I replied to some possible objections and thereby furthered my defense of a qualified, modified, and extended version of Bentham's theory (Section V). I submit that I have demonstrated that, even if Bentham's theory fails, the theory articulated and argued for in this essay succeeds. Hence I conclude that the utilitarian standard of conduct which I have explained and defended is the only correct and proper standard of conduct for any human being.[4]

[4] I would like to express my appreciation to the co-editors of this anthology for having invited me to write an original essay for it, and for their encouragement and support. I would also like to express my gratitude to those who, with great patience and kindness, suffered through numerous revisions, etc., in the preparation of the manuscript. Among these are, as always, Edna Wiser and Marge Langloss.

43 / A Critique of Utilitarianism

ARTHUR C. EWING

A. C. Ewing (1899–1974) was an important philosopher who taught at the University of St. Andrews in Scotland and wrote on ethics, political philosophy, and the eighteenth-century philosopher Kant. He was a major defender of "ethical intuitionism," the view that what is right or wrong, good or bad, can be directly known or intuited.

*I*f pleasure or happiness is the only thing good-in-itself—and it is certainly the only thing about the *intrinsic* goodness of which there is anything like universal agreement—it seems irrational to hold that it makes any difference to its goodness who enjoys the happiness. And it seems reasonable to hold that it is our duty to produce as much good as possible and that it is wrong to neglect any opportunities to do so. From these assumptions we get a form of hedonism which differs from the egoistic form and seems to approach much more closely to what we ordinarily believe about ethical matters. The theory is most commonly known by the name of *Utilitarianism*. It is also sometimes called *Universalistic Hedonism*, "universalistic" because it considers everybody's good, and "hedonism" because it holds pleasure to be the only good. It maintains that our sole duty is to produce as much pleasure as possible, counting for this purpose a diminution of pain as equivalent to an increase in pleasure, and holds that in doing so we should count every man's pleasure as of equal worth to that of any other man. (It makes no distinction, any more than does egoistic hedonism, between happiness and pleasure, happiness being regarded as prolonged pleasure.) It thus agrees with egoistic hedonism as to what is good, but not as to what are the ultimate principles of ethical action. Both theories hold that pleasure is the only good, but while egoistic hedonism thinks we are under no obligation to further the happiness of anybody else except as a means to our own, the theory I am now going to discuss maintains that we are under a direct obligation to pursue happiness as such, to whomever the happiness belongs. The theory is now held by very few moral philosophers, but it was extremely important in the nineteenth and in a less fully thought-out form in the eighteenth century, and is no doubt approximately the working theory of vast numbers of people to-day in so far as they can be said to have an ethical theory at all. Its most important exponents in this country were John Stuart Mill[1] and Sidgwick.[2]

Now it is quite obvious that the amount of happiness or pain produced by our actions should be at least one of the chief criteria for deciding which actions we ought to perform. There are vast numbers of actions which are wrong for no other reason than that they tend to produce pain or unhappiness in other people, and if it can be shown that an act will lead to suffering, this is, usually at least, quite a sufficient reason why we ought not to perform it. Further, a utilitarian can deal with most of the relatively rare cases where it is right to inflict pain by contending that the infliction of pain now is necessary to avoid greater pain in the future or as a means to gain in happiness which is worth the cost. We must remember, as with egoistic hedonism, that under "pleasure" are meant to be comprised all satisfactions and joys and not only the relatively "lower" ones to which the term pleasure is most commonly applied in ordinary speech. We must further realize that the utilitarian is not bound to suppose that in practice we ought always to settle what we are to do by a direct calculation of the amount of pleasure likely to be produced. He usually insists on the contrary that there are certain rules of behaviour such as those against lying and stealing whose violation human experience has adequately shown to be productive of unhappiness, and that in consequence we do not need to calculate afresh each time the amount of happiness or unhappiness likely to be produced before deciding to obey one of these laws. The ultimate ground for their validity lies in the general happiness, but we need not go back to this ultimate ground each time, any more than we need before applying an established mathematical law go back each time to the axioms on which it is based. Nor can utilitarianism possibly be dismissed as selfish, for it bids us treat the happiness or pain of any other man as no less important than our own. And utilitarianism has the great attraction of being a relatively simple theory and one in close relation to verifiable empirical facts. For an Ethics which admits only one good will obviously be simpler to apply than one which admits several that may on occasion conflict, and pleasure and pain are after all feelings the occurrence of which we can easily verify in a straightforward empirical way. All this does not however prove it to be the true theory.

As compared to common-sense morality a consistent utilitarianism would be in some respects stricter and in others less strict. Ordinarily we consider that we are much more under an obligation to some people than to others. We admit indeed that we are under some obligation to help anyone in need, but we feel a very much stronger obligation to promote the happiness of our own family, as is shown by the general attitude to appeals for charity. It is clear that the money spent by a man in order to provide his son with a university education could save the lives of many people who were perishing

[1]*Utilitarianism* (1863). [1806–1873.—Eds.]
[2]*The Methods of Ethics* (1874). (1838–1900).—Eds.]

of hunger in a famine, yet most people would rather blame than praise a man who should deprive his son of a university education on this account. Further, while the obligation to contribute something to charity if one can afford it is generally recognized, only a very small minority of people have felt it their duty to curtail their comforts and luxuries very seriously on that account, and still less the comforts and luxuries of those dependent on them. Yet there can hardly be any doubt that, even if we allow for any indirect evil effects which might accrue, in most cases money given to any even tolerably well managed charity will do much more good by relieving the suffering of those in distress than would be done by using the same money to increase the pleasure of a person who is at all tolerably comfortable by enabling him to have a more pleasant house, better furniture, more tobacco, more holiday travel, etc. This does not, however, straightway prove the utilitarian wrong. He may reply that all but the very poor ought to give much more money to charity than on the average they do, and in view of the very small proportion of the national income that is spent on this and the vast amount of suffering in the world which calls for help, it seems to me plain that he is so far right. But, even if we grant this, it still seems plain to me, and I am sure would seem so to almost everybody else that, if a man were to deprive his wife and children against their will of all comforts and purchasable pleasures, leaving them only bare necessaries, on the ground that he could use the money thus saved to preserve several families from a greater pain or loss of happiness than he inflicted on his own by giving it to a charitable organization he would be acting wrongly not rightly. Again, suppose he obtained the money to give to the charity by stealing it from a man very much richer than himself. He might argue that the victim of his theft would lose little in happiness by being a few pounds worse off, while the people to whom he gave the money would be saved from great misery. Even if he kept the money himself, he might indeed argue that, being much poorer,[3] he would gain more in happiness from it than the other man lost. These reflections seem to disclose a sharp conflict between utilitarianism and even enlightened common-sense morality. According to the former there is an equal obligation to further the happiness of everybody, according to the latter we have special obligations to some people much stronger than those we have to others; according to the former what produces most happiness is always right, according to the latter it is wrong to produce happiness by stealing and lying.

The utilitarian however will contend that the conflict is not a real but only an apparent one. He will argue that, if we take a more far-sighted view, we can see that greater happiness is produced by recognizing and insisting on special obligations. Family life is a great source of happiness, and family life as we know it would be impossible if we did not look on ourselves as having much stronger obligations to members of our family than to perfect strangers. And,

---

[3]Note that I am referring to theft by a man who is comparatively poor, not by one who is starving, still less one whose family is starving. I am not prepared to say that it is wrong for such people to steal in a community where there are no other means such as poor relief available to save them from their desperate condition.

if we admitted the principle that the poor were ethically entitled to steal from the rich, the result would be a social confusion which would be far worse than the present system. But it seems to me that what the utilitarian has done here is to point out that a whole class of acts or system of recognized obligations produces good results in the way of happiness, not that each particular act does so. We may admit that it would be a bad thing if the poorer generally and indiscriminately tried to steal from the richer, but does it necessarily follow from this that to do so in any one instance is wrong? A poor man who is prepared to cheat a richer may say—It would be a bad thing if everybody acted like me, but why should not I do so, when it is certain that my action will not result in everybody acting like me? It seems only possible to answer such a question adequately if we say that it is *unfair* to profit by the rules governing society and yet refuse yourself to obey them. But if we appeal to fairness, we are introducing another consideration besides happiness. It may therefore be doubted whether we can give an adequate account of our obligations without abandoning utilitarianism and admitting that there are other obligations which we should not ignore even in order to produce greater happiness and that it is bad to acquire happiness by unfair means whether for ourselves or others. It is indeed difficult to maintain that it cannot under any circumstances be right to lie, etc., on utilitarian grounds, e.g., to save life, but it seems to me pretty clear that utilitarian principles, logically carried out, would result in far more cheating, lying and unfair action than any good man would tolerate. This is not of course the same thing as saying that utilitarians are more likely to cheat and lie than other people, but only that if they carried out their theory consistently they would be so.

We may add that utilitarianism is far from being so simple a theory to apply as has been claimed by its advocates. How are we going to measure against each other quite different kinds of pleasure and say how many times more pleasure seeing *Hamlet* will give a particular man than will a good dinner? And it becomes still more complicated when we introduce different agents who cannot be expected all to take the same amount of enjoyment in the same pleasures. Yet such calculations are necessary if we are to apply the utilitarian criterion consistently to all practical questions. Similar difficulties will no doubt arise with any ethical theory that takes account of consequences, as we surely must, but at least this shows that utilitarianism has less cause than might be thought to pride itself on its simplicity. It is about as difficult to estimate the relative pleasantness of different pleasures as it would be on a non-hedonistic view to estimate their relative goodness.

It is however very hard to give any conclusive disproof of utilitarianism by considering the kind of actions to which it would logically lead. For suppose I argue that utilitarianism is a mistaken theory because, if carried out consistently, it would require me in a given situation to do something which is wrong. Now in any actual instance of a kind that could provide a ground for dispute the effects will be very complicated and uncertain, so that will always leave a loophole for the utilitarian to argue that I am wrong in my views as to their bearing on general happiness and that the act which seems right to common sense is really after all on a long view that most productive of happiness. And even if there are some instances where this is very unplausible (as indeed I think there are), he may reply by amending common-sense ethics here and saying that the act we ordinarily think right in this case is not really so. We are not bound to and indeed cannot accept the common-sense view (where there is one) about every action. The utilitarian view could only be shaken by a very considerable series of such instances. As I have suggested already, I think that it can be shaken by citing a series of instances of cheating and lying where what a good man could not help regarding as a "dirty trick" seemed to add to the general happiness, but it is easier to attack utilitarianism by considering its bearing not on the question what we ought to do but rather on the question what is good in itself.

Now the answer of utilitarianism to this question is very simple. The only thing good in itself, it maintains, is pleasure. But there are all kinds of pleasures, and it is very difficult to regard them as all of equal value. To take an instance given by G. E. Moore,[4] a man who is watching a Shakesperian tragedy with full understanding and aesthetic appreciation at its highest pitch may be enjoying no more pleasure quantitatively than a drunkard who is amusing himself by smashing crockery, yet it is surely obvious that the former's pleasure is worth more than the latter's. But, if it is, there must be other factors besides pleasure on which the goodness of an experience depends, since the pleasure is *ex hypothesi** not greater in the former case than it is in the latter but only qualitatively better. Mill[5] tried indeed to reconcile his utilitarianism with the admission that a lesser pleasure might rationally be preferred to a greater on the ground of the superior quality of the former, but it is generally, and I think rightly, agreed among philosophers that he failed to escape inconsistency. To say that pleasure is the only good and yet admit that a lesser pleasure may be preferable to a greater is like saying that money is the only thing which counts and then adding that money earned by public work is better than the same amount of money earned by business. If pleasure is the only good, the more pleasure always the better.

In order to decide whether one pleasure can be qualitatively better than another let us consider the following instances. Let us suppose that you were offered 50 more years, each equal in quantity of pleasure to the most pleasant year you have ever spent, but that the pleasure was to be derived entirely from eating, drinking, playing childish games and lying in the sun. Imagine this proposed life shorn of every element of intelligence above that of an imbecile, of all aesthetic experience, of all love of other men. Now suppose that you were offered as an alternative 49 years of equal pleasure, but that in this case the pleasure was no longer to be derived exclusively from these sources but also from the exercise of intelligence, of love, and of a developed capacity to appreciate the best in art and literature, and suppose also that the

---

[4]*Ethics,* p. 147. [(1873–1958).—Eds.]
[5]*Utilitarianism,* Chap. II.
*[Ex hypothesi = by hypothesis.—Eds.]

effect of the two alternative lives on the general happiness would be equal, the superior advantages for other men that one would expect to accrue from the second life being neutralized and only just neutralized by some evil influence that would intervene if you chose the second and not if you chose the first. Can we doubt that it would be better to choose the second? Yet, if utilitarianism were true, it would certainly be better to choose the first since you would thereby obtain a year's more pleasure. The utilitarian may reply that you would soon get bored by the first life and not enjoy it, but suppose some drug or conditioning process were invented that would prevent you getting bored so that you really got the pleasure promised? It is not inconceivable that a drug might be invented which had these properties. To take a slightly less fanciful illustration, I think Huxley's* *Brave New World* is a good refutation of hedonism because it shows us an imaginary state of society which is hedonistically most satisfactory and yet ethically revolting.

Suppose again two communities in which an equal amount of pleasure was enjoyed and an equal amount of pain suffered. But suppose that in one community the citizens were selfish, unjust and capable only of pleasures which did not involve considerable intelligence, aesthetic appreciation, goodness or love, and that in the other community they derived their pleasures chiefly from those source which I have just excluded from the first. Surely it is plain that the state of the second community would be much better than the state of the first. Yet, if utilitarianism were true, the two states should be equal in value. Two objections may be made against this example. First, it may be objected that the qualities possessed by the members of the second community would of their inherent nature necessarily lead to a greater happiness than any possessed by the first. But we can meet this by supposing the second community to be much less advantageously situated than the first as regards wealth, health and external circumstances. These factors might quite conceivably counteract the advantages in respect of happiness which would otherwise accrue to them from their superior character. Secondly, it may be objected that we cannot measure happiness as exactly as these examples presuppose. To this we may reply by substituting "approximately equal" or "equal as far as we can tell" for "exactly equal." If we are not able to compare experiences in respect of pleasure, utilitarianism cannot be applied at all; and if we can compare them, there is a good sense in saying that two lives or two communities are "equal in happiness as far as we can tell," meaning that we have no reason to think either happier than the other. That is all that is needed for my illustrations, and this negative condition certainly may be fulfilled.

Thirdly, let us suppose a man revelling in the infliction of tortures on his enemy. Of course this will be very painful for his victim and may have other less direct detrimental consequences in the future for the general welfare, but we are not now asking whether this state of affairs is conducive to the general good, we are asking about its value or disvalue in itself. Let us just consider the state of mind of the man inflicting the suffering. He is enjoying himself,

*[Aldous Huxley (1894–1963), famous British writer.—Eds.]

yet can we say that his state of mind is good in itself? Surely it is on the contrary very bad indeed, and the more so the greater the pleasure. As a matter of fact his state of mind would still be very bad if he were not really inflicting the pain but only thought he was, like a witch-doctor who believed he could make his enemy suffer by roasting his effigy over a slow fire, yet in this case his victim would suffer no pain at all. But, if utilitarianism were true, the state should be good in itself because pleasurable, however deplorable its effects. Still less could it be the case on the utilitarian view that the state was made worse, not better, by increasing the pleasure.

Let us now take other instances which show up the defects of the utilitarian theory. Suppose a shipwreck in which two men are left clinging to a raft unable to support more than one. Let us call them A and B. Now suppose A to be a person whose life is of much less value to society or other individuals than that of B. Under these circumstances we should hold it a very meritorious act of A to surrender his place to B, but we should hold it the reverse of meritorious on the part of B to push off A. Yet the effect of the two acts would be almost the same; by either the life of A is sacrificed and that of B preserved. The only important difference in the effects seems to be that in the second case B will, if he is fundamentally good, be troubled by remorse, and if he is not so troubled, will probably deteriorate in character still further as the result of his action. But this cannot possibly be cited as a reason for the different estimate of the two actions, since unless it is already admitted that the second act is wrong there is no point in the remorse. Of course the utilitarian may argue that we are mistaken in thinking the second act wrong, if B is entitled to be certain that his life is really more important, and that the only reason why we think it wrong is because it would be a dangerous principle in general to allow a man to be judge whether his life was or was not more useful than that of another man. But the very most the utilitarian could maintain with the least show of plausibility would be that the action of B was excusable or not blameworthy; he could not possibly maintain that it was positively admirable, yet we should all admit that the action of A which had practically the same effects was not just excusable but positively admirable. Utilitarianism cannot account for this difference. The latter cannot be explained by effects on happiness but only by something intrinsically good in the nature of the one action. It is not a matter of pleasurable feelings—A probably did not enjoy drowning—but of something quite different from pleasure.

Finally, utilitarianism may be condemned as irreconcilable with the dictates of justice. The principle of utilitarianism tells us only to produce as much happiness as possible, thus implying that the way in which it is distributed does not matter. But justice requires that of two distributions which produce equal happiness we ought to prefer the fairer to the less fair, and that we ought to do this even if slightly less happiness is yielded by the former than by the latter. To take an extreme instance, suppose we could slightly increase the collective happiness of ten men by taking away all happiness from one of them, would it be right to do so? It is perhaps arguable that it would if the difference in happiness of the nine was very large, but not if it was very slight.

And if the happiness of the nine were purchased by the actual torture of the one, the injustice of it would seem to poison the happiness and render it worse than valueless even if they were callous enough to enjoy it. Yet on the utilitarian view any distribution of good, however unfair, ought to be preferred to any other, however just, if it would yield *the slightest* additional happiness. Again, ought an innocent man to be punished, if it would on the balance cause less pain with an equal deterrent effect to punish him than it would to punish the guilty? In view of these difficulties it is not surprising that to-day very few philosophers could be found to accept utilitarianism.

What modifications must be made in utilitarianism in order to deal with these examples satisfactorily? In the first place we must admit that not only the quantity but the quality of a pleasure is relevant, so that a lesser pleasure of a higher kind may rightly be preferred to a greater pleasure of a kind which is lower. But what makes one pleasure higher than another? It is not a difference in the nature of the pleasurable feeling as such. It is rather a difference in the activity of the mind with which it is connected or in its object. Some pleasures are regarded as higher than others, because they are connected with thinking, aesthetic experiences, love, moral action, and we regard these activities as higher than eating and drinking and as having an intrinsic value which must be added to any intrinsic value possessed by the pleasures they give as pleasure. Now, if we classify pleasures and activities according to their object, we value specially those concerned with the pursuit of truth, beauty and goodness. As regards the last, my example of the shipwreck has brought out the point that certain morally good acts of self-sacrifice have an intrinsic value not dependent on any pleasant feelings they produce, and my example of the man torturing his enemy has brought out the point that moral badness and not only pain is intrinsically evil. Most people who have thought about the subject have attributed an ultimate value to these three—truth, beauty and goodness (or rather the search for and attainment of them), as well as to love between human beings and (with the religious) to what they call contemplation of or communion with God.

Finally, the point that of two distributions of the same amount of happiness the fairer should be preferred to the unfair seems to show that not only the amount of good distributed but the way in which it is distributed can be intrinsically good (or evil). It is not possible indeed to *prove* that any of these things are good-in-themselves, but neither is it possible to prove that this is so with pleasure. As I have said, the utilitarian has to admit that he can know without proof that pleasure is good-in-itself. Cannot we equally see that these other things are so? Pleasure is only the good of one side of our nature, the feeling side; but we are not only feeling, we are also thinking and acting beings. If so, why should the good of our feeling side be the only one that is of value as an end in itself and not merely as a means to something else?

The utilitarian is indeed right in holding that whatever is good is pleasant. Even painful acts of self-sacrifice done because they are right or out of love give a certain amount of satisfaction to the person who does them, though this may easily be quite outweighed for him at the time by the suffering involved. But the utilitarian is still wrong in holding that what is good is so only because it is pleasurable. Although all good things are pleasant, their goodness is not in proportion to their pleasantness, and more often something is pleasant because it is good than good because it is pleasant. Yet a very large proportion of the ethical questions with which we are confronted can legitimately be answered by applying the utilitarian criterion. And this for two reasons. In the first place there are many cases of action where there simply are no relevant considerations but the pleasure or pain produced, since other values do not come in question in these particular cases. A sick man's virtue may be more important than his freedom from pain, but since he may just as well be virtuous if he is healthy, a doctor may usually freely prescribe for the latter without considering the former. A vast number of wrong actions are pronounced wrong simply because they give pain, and probably a large majority of actions pronounced good are so because they give pleasure or alleviate pain and are done on that account. Secondly, it is plain that actions which promote the other values, knowledge, beauty, love, virtue, justice, will also on the whole make for happiness. This explains why the utilitarian criterion is not so wildly off the mark that it is impossible for intelligent men to be deceived into accepting it as the only ultimate criterion in ethics.

It is of interest that utilitarianism made its mark especially in the field of political and large scale social reform. In these matters I think utilitarianism comes very much nearer to providing a completely satisfactory criterion than in the sphere of individual ethics. For here we are concerned rather with the removal of causes of unhappiness than with the direct promotion of positive good. You cannot produce high morality or fine art or science by law or make people love each other, and you had much better not try, but you can ameliorate their physical state and remove many causes of avoidable suffering. We must not regard it as an argument for utilitarianism that, if it were universally adopted and consistently carried out by everybody, we should be secure from war and soon end acute poverty throughout the world, for the same would be true of any at all plausible ethical theory, of which there are a great variety. But I wish for more straightforward utilitarian argument in politics, not less. I should like to emphasize this point strongly because, whatever is the ultimate truth about utilitarianism, it is plain at least that we have no right to increase greatly human unhappiness or subtract greatly from human happiness, unless this grave disadvantage be outweighed by a very important gain in respect of other goods, or could only be avoided by action that for some other reason was immoral (contingencies which do not seem to me at all likely). Now I shall not go into this point at length because I am not writing a book on Politics, but I am convinced that a careful survey of either Communism, Fascism, Nazism or Laissez-faire* Individualism would show that they have

*[Free-market capitalism.—Eds.]

made enormous sacrifices of human happiness which were not necessary to further any good that could rationally be approved by a sane man or to avoid action that could be called immoral. Hence they must be condemned even apart from the fact that they are of the greatest detriment also to goods other than happiness.

44 / The Deep Beauty of the Golden Rule

R. M. MacIVER

R. M. MacIver (1882–1970) was an influential sociologist and political scientist who taught for many years at Columbia University. His writings, in the functionalist tradition, were in the areas of government, culture, and society. He was a major theorist in the thirties and forties.

I

*T*he subject that learned men call ethics is a wasteland on the philosophical map. Thousands of books have been written on this matter, learned books and popular books, books that argue and books that exhort. Most of them are empty and nearly all are vain. Some claim that pleasure is *the* good; some prefer the elusive and more enticing name of happiness; others reject such principles and speak of equally elusive goals such as self-fulfillment. Others claim that *the* good is to be found in looking away from the self in devotion to the whole—which whole? in the service of God—whose God?—even in the service of the State—who prescribes the service? Here indeed, if anywhere, after listening to the many words of many apostles, one goes out by the same door as one went in.

The reason is simple. You say: "This is the way you should behave." But I say: "No, that is not the way." You say: "This is right." But I say: "No, that is wrong, and this is right." You appeal to experience. I appeal to experience against you. You appeal to authority: it is not mine. What is left? If you are strong, you can punish me for behaving my way. But does that prove anything except that you are stronger than I? Does it prove the absurd dogma that might makes right? Is the slavemaster right because he owns the whip, or Torquemada* because he can send his heretics to the flames?

From this impasse no system of ethical rules has been able to deliver itself. How can ethics lay down final principles of behavior that are not your values against mine, your group's values against my group's?

Which, by the way, does not mean that your rules are any less valid for you because they are not valid for me. Only a person of shallow nature and autocratic learnings would draw that conclusion. For the sake of your integrity you must hold to your own values, no matter how much others reject them. Without *your* values you are nothing. True, you should search them and test them and learn by *your* experience and gain wisdom where you can. Your values are your guides through life but you need to use your own eyes. If I have different guides I shall go another way. So far as we diverge, values are relative as between you and me. But your values cannot be relative for you or mine for me.

That is not here the issue. It is that the relativity of values between you and me, between your group and my group, your sect and my sect, makes futile nearly all learned disquisitions about the first principles of ethics.

By ethics I mean the philosophy of how men should behave in their relations to one another. I am talking about philosophy, not about religion. When you have a creed, you can derive from it principles of ethics. Philosophy cannot begin with a creed, but only with reasoning about the nature of things. It cannot therefore presume that the values of other men are less to be regarded than the values of the proponent. If it does, it is not philosophy but dogma, dogma that is the enemy of philosophy, the kind of dogma that has been the source of endless tyranny and repression.

Can it be a philosophy worth the name that makes a universal of your values and thus rules mine out of existence, where they differ from yours?

How can reasoning decide between my values and yours? Values do not claim truth in any scientific sense; instead they claim validity, rightness. They do not declare what is so but what *should* be so. I cling to my values, you to yours. Your values, some of them, do not hold for me; some of them may be repulsive to me; some of them may threaten me. What then? To what court of reason shall we appeal? To what court that you and I both accept is there any appeal?

The lack of any court is the final *fact* about final values. It is a fundamental fact. It is a terrifying fact. It is also a strangely challenging fact. It gives man his lonely autonomy, his true responsibility. If he has anything that partakes of the quality of a God it comes from this fact. Man has more than the choice to obey or disobey. If he accepts authority he also chooses the authority he accepts. He is responsible not only to others but, more deeply, to himself.

*[The notorious fifteenth-century Spanish churchman who was the main leader of the Inquisition.—Eds.]

II

Does all this mean that a universal ethical principle, applicable alike to me and you, even where our values diverge, is impossible? That there is no rule to go by, based on reason itself, in this world of irreconcilable valuations?

There is no rule that can prescribe both my values and yours or decide between them. There is one universal rule, and one only, that can be laid down, on ethical grounds—that is, apart from the creeds of particular religions and apart from the ways of the tribe that falsely and arrogantly universalize themselves.

Do to others as you would have others do to you. This is the only rule that stands by itself in the light of its own reason, the only rule that can stand by itself in the naked, warring universe, in the face of the contending values of men and groups.

What makes it so? Let us first observe that the universal herein laid down is one of procedure. It prescribes a mode of behaving, not a goal of action. On the level of goals, of *final* values, there is irreconcilable conflict. One rule prescribes humility, another pride; one prescribes abstinence, another commends the flesh-pots; and so forth through endless variations. All of us wish that *our* principle could be universal; most of us believe that it *should* be, that our *ought* ought to be all men's *ought*, but since we differ there can be on this level, no possible agreement.

When we want to make our ethical principle prevail we try to persuade others, to "convert" them. Some may freely respond, if their deeper values are near enough to ours. Others will certainly resist and some will seek to persuade us in turn—why shouldn't they? Then we can go no further except by resort to force and fraud. We can, if we are strong, dominate some and we can bribe others. We compromise our own values in doing so and we do not in the end succeed; even if we were masters of the whole world we could never succeed in making our principle universal. We could only make it falsely tyrannous.

So if we look for a principle in the name of which we can appeal to all men, one to which their reason can respond in spite of their differences, we must follow another road. When we try to make our values prevail over those cherished by others, we attack their values, their dynamic of behavior, their living will. If we go far enough we assault their very being. For the will is simply valuation in action. Now the deep beauty of the golden rule is that instead of attacking the will that is in other men, it offers their will a new dimension. "Do as you *would* have others . . . " As *you* would will others to do. It bids you expand your vision, see yourself in new relationships. It bids you transcend your insulation, see yourself in the place of others, see others in your place. It bids you test your values or at least your way of pursuing them. If you would disapprove that another should treat you as you treat him, the situations being reversed is not that a sign that, by the standard of your own values, you are mistreating him?

This principle obviously makes for a vastly greater harmony in the social scheme. At the same time it is the only universal of ethics that does not take sides with or contend with contending values. It contains no dogma. It bids everyone follow his own rule, as it would apply *apart* from the accident of his particular fortunes. It bids him enlarge his own rule, as it would apply whether he is up or whether he is down. It is an accident that you are up and I am down. In another situation you would be down and I would be up. That accident has nothing to do with my *final* values or with yours. You have numbers and force on your side. In another situation I would have the numbers and the force. All situations of power are temporary and precarious. Imagine then the situations reversed and that you had a more wonderful power than is at the command of the most powerful, the power to make the more powerful act toward you as you would want him to act. If power is your dream, then dream of a yet greater power—and act out the spirit of your dream.

But the conclusive argument is not in the terms of power. It goes far deeper, down to the great truth that power so often ignores and that so often in the end destroys it, the truth that when you maltreat others you detach yourself from them, from the understanding of them, from the understanding of yourself. You insulate yourself, you narrow your own values, you cut yourself off from that which you and they have in common. And this commonness is more enduring and more satisfying than what you possess in insulation. You separate yourself, and for all your power you weaken yourself. Which is why power and fear are such close companions.

This is the reason why the evil you do to another, you do also, in the end, to yourself. While if you and he refrain from doing evil, one to another—not to speak of the yet happier consequences of doing positive good—this reciprocity of restraint from evil will redound to the good of both.

That makes a much longer story and we shall not here enter upon it. Our sole concern is to show that the golden rule is the *only* ethical principle, as already defined, that can have clear right of way everywhere in the kind of world we have inherited. It is the only principle that allows every man to follow his own intrinsic values while nevertheless it transforms the chaos of warring codes into a reasonably well-ordered universe.

Let us explain the last statement. What are a man's intrinsic values? Beyond his mere self-seeking every human being needs, and must find, some attachment to a larger purpose. These attachments, in themselves and apart from the way he pursues them, are his intrinsic values. For some men they are centered in the family, the clan, the "class," the community, the nation, the "race." It is the warfare of their group-attachments that creates the deadliest disturbances of modern society. For some men the focus of attachment is found in the greater "cause," the faith, the creed, the way of life. The conflict of these attachments also unlooses many evils on society and at some historical stages has brought about great devastation.

The greatest evils inflicted by man on man over the face of the earth are wrought not by the self-seekers, the pleasure lovers, or the merely amoral, but by the fervent devotees of ethical principles, those who are bound body and soul to some larger purpose, the nation, the "race," the "masses," the "brethren" whoever they may be. The faith they invoke, whatever it may be, is not large enough when it sets a frontier between the members and the non-members, the believers and the non-believers. In the heat of devotion to that larger but exclusive purpose there is bred the fanaticism that corrodes and finally destroys all that links man to the common humanity. In the name of the cause, they will torture and starve and trample under foot millions on millions of their fellowmen. In its name they will cultivate the blackest treachery. And if their methods fail, as fail in the end they must, they will be ready, as was Hitler, to destroy their own cause or their own people, the chosen ones, rather than accept the reality their blinded purpose denied.

III

How then can we say that the golden rule does not disqualify the intrinsic values of such people—even of people like Hitler or, say, Torquemada? In the name of his values Torquemada burned at the stake many persons who differed from their fellows mainly by being more courageous, honest, and faithful to their faith. What then were Torquemada's values? He was a servant of the Church and the Church was presumptively a servant of Jesus Christ. It was not the intrinsic values of his creed that moved him and his masters to reject the Christian golden rule. Let us concede they had some kind of devotion to religion. It was the distorted, fanatical way in which they pursued the dimmed values they cherished, it was not the values themselves, to which their inhumanity can be charged.

Let us take the case of Hitler. Apart from his passion for Germany, or the German "folk," he would have been of no account, for evil or for good. That passion of itself, that in his view intrinsic value, might have inspired great constructive service instead of destruction. It was the method he used, and not the values he sought to promote thereby, that led to ruin, his blind trust in the efficacy of ruthless might. Belonging to a "folk" that had been reduced in defeat from strength to humiliation, fed on false notions of history and responsive to grotesque fallacies about a "master race," he conceived the resurgence of Germany in the distorted light of his vindictive imagination. Had Hitler been a member of some small "folk," no more numerous, say, than the population of his native Austria, he might have cherished the same values with no less passion, but his aspirations would have taken a different form and would never have expressed themselves in horror and tragedy.

The golden rule says nothing against Hitler's mystic adoration of the German "race," against any man's intrinsic values. By "intrinsic values" we signify the goals, beyond mere self-seeking, that animate a human being. If your group, your nation, your "race," your church, is for you a primary attachment, continue to cherish it—give it all you have, if you are so minded. But do not use means that are repugnant to the standards according to which you would have others conduct themselves to you and your values. If your nation were a small one, would you not seethe with indignation if some large neighbor destroyed its independence? Where, then, is your personal integrity if, belonging instead to the large nation, you act to destroy the independence of a small one? You falsify your own values, in the longer run you do them injury, when you pursue them in ways that cannot abide the test of the golden rule.

It follows that while this first principle attacks no intrinsic values, no primary attachments of men to goods that reach beyond themselves, it nevertheless purifies every attachment, every creed, of its accidents, its irrelevancies, its excesses, its false reliance on power. It saves every human value from the corruption that comes from the arrogance of detachment and exclusiveness, from the shell of the kind of absolutism that imprisons its vitality.

At this point a word of caution is in order. The golden rule does not solve for us our ethical problems but offers only a way of approach. It does not prescribe our treatment of others but only the spirit in which we should treat them. It has no simple mechanical application and often enough is hard to apply—what general principle is not? It certainly does not bid us treat others as others *want* us to treat them—that would be an absurdity. The convicted criminal wants the judge to set him free. If the judge acts in the spirit of the golden rule, within the limits of the discretion permitted him as judge, he might instead reason somewhat as follows: "How would I feel the judge ought to treat *me* were I in this man's place? What could I—the man I am and yet somehow standing where this criminal stands—properly ask the judge to do for me, to me? In this spirit I shall assess his guilt and his punishment. In this spirit I shall give full consideration to the conditions under which he acted. I shall try to understand *him*, to do what I properly can for him, while at the same time I fulfill my judicial duty in protecting society against the dangers that arise if criminals such as he go free."

IV

"Do to others as you would have others do to you." The disease to which all values are subject is the growth of a hard insulation. "I am right: I have the truth. If you differ from me, you are a heretic, you are in error. *Therefore* while you must allow me every liberty when you are in power I need not, in truth I ought not to, show any similar consideration for you." The barb of falsehood has already begun to vitiate the cherished value. While *you* are in power I advocate the equal rights of all creeds: when *I* am in power, I reject any such claim as ridiculous. This is the position taken by various brands of totalitarianism, and the communists in particular have made it a favorite technique in the process of gaining power, clamoring for rights they will use to destroy the rights of those who grant them. Religious groups have followed the same line. Roman Catholics, Calvinists, Lutherans, Presbyterians, and others have on occasion vociferously advocated religious liberty where they were in the minority, often to curb it where in turn they became dominant.

This gross inconsistency on the part of religious groups was flagrantly displayed in earlier centuries, but examples are still not infrequent. Here is one. *La Civilita Catholicâ*, a Jesuit organ published in Rome, has come out as follows:

> The Roman Catholic Church, convinced, through its divine prerogatives, of being the only true church, must demand the right to freedom for herself alone, because such a right can only be possessed by truth, never by error. As to other religions, the church will certainly never draw the sword, but she will require that by legitimate means they shall not be allowed to propagate false doctrine. Consequently, in a state where the majority of the people are Catholic, the Church will require that legal existence be denied to error. . . . In some countries, Catholics will be obliged to ask full religious freedom for all, resigned at being forced to cohabitate where they alone should rightly be allowed to live. . . . The Church cannot blush for her own want of tolerance, as she asserts it in principle and applies it in practice.[1]

Since this statement has the merit of honesty it well illustrates the fundamental lack of rationality that lies behind all such violations of the golden rule. The argument runs: "Roman Catholics know they possess the truth; *therefore* they should not permit others to propagate error." By parity of reasoning why should not Protestants say—and indeed they have often said it—"We know we possess the truth; therefore we should not tolerate the errors of Roman Catholics." Why then should not atheists say: "We know we possess the truth; therefore we should not tolerate the errors of dogmatic religion."

No matter what we believe, we are equally convinced that *we* are right. We have to be. That is what belief means, and we must all believe something. The Roman Catholic Church is entitled to declare that all other religious groups are sunk in error. But what follows? That other groups have not the right to believe they are right? That you have the right to repress them while they have no right to repress you? That they should concede to you what you should not concede to them? Such reasoning is mere childishness. Beyond it lies the greater foolishness that truth is advanced by the forceful suppression of those who believe differently from you. Beyond that lies the pernicious distortion of meanings which claims that liberty is only "the liberty to do right"—the "liberty" for me to what *you* think is right. This perversion of the meaning of liberty has been the delight of all totalitarians. And it might be well to reflect that it was the radical Rousseau* who first introduced the doctrine that men could be "forced to be free."

How much do they have truth who think they must guard it within the fortress of their own might? How little that guarding has availed in the past! How often it has kept truth outside while superstition grew moldy within!

---

[1]Quoted in the *Christian Century* (June 1948).
*[The eighteenth-century French philosopher and political theorist.—Eds.]

How often has the false alliance of belief and force led to civil dissension and the futile ruin of war! But if history means nothing to those who call themselves "Christian" and still claim exclusive civil rights for their particular faith, at least they might blush before this word of one they call their Master: "All things therefore whatsoever ye would that men should do unto you, even so do ye also unto them; for this is the law and the prophets."

45 / A Different Voice

CAROL GILLIGAN

Carol Gilligan (1936–   ) teaches at the Harvard Graduate School of Education, Laboratory of Human Relations. She writes on moral psychology and development, feminism, and the social sciences, and has been a major figure in the many areas of feminist studies.

[Carol Gilligan is criticizing a form of golden rule ethics in her essay. Lawrence Kohlberg (1927–1987), an influential developmental psychologist, developed an argument in moral psychology to show that the ethics of the golden rule, the ability to apply universal principles fairly, is the highest stage of moral development, that is, psychological maturity. On Kohlberg's scale of moral development, ethical egoism and obedience to authority (such as religion) are the least developed levels of moral development. Utilitarianism is higher, but not as advanced as golden rule morality. Gilligan challenges Kohlberg's theory because it embodies a gender-biased approach to the moral life, since males take abstract principles and rules more seriously than females, who take care, personal feelings, and concrete details more seriously. This "different voice" needs to supplement the appeal to rules and principles to round out the moral life, according to Gilligan.—Eds.]

Kohlberg's work delineates in its purest form a rational morality of justice and rights. While the power of this ethic lies in the respect accorded to the individual, its limitation lies in its failure to see a world of relationship, compassion, and care. Focusing on the individual as primary in his construction of the moral domain, Kohlberg derives the connections between people first from the constraint of authority and subsequently through deals of even exchange, stereotypic norms of relationship, societal systems of roles and rules, fair and equal contracts, and finally rational agreement. The aim of moral development is to free individuals from societal constraint, to make them "independent of civil society"[1] by protecting their rights and limiting their duties to the granting of reciprocal respect. In this sense, if Piaget's* perspective reflects the position of children caught in a situation of inequality and through cooperation overcoming its constraint, Kohlberg's† reflects the concern of adolescents struggling to free initiative from guilt, justifying by reason their separation from those to whom formerly they were bound. The educational lesson inherent in the development that Piaget and Kohlberg trace lies in its demonstration that although the experiences of equality and of freedom disrupt a social order based on constraint, they generate the more stable and adaptive social order of cooperation and mutual respect.

Yet, given that justice is deliberately blinded to ensure the impartial weighing of claims; given that equality is achieved by judging behind a "veil of ignorance"[2] that obscures the inequities of life; and given that rational decision is reached by a solitary game of "moral musical chairs,"[3] in which one assumes one is taking the other's position by putting oneself in his place—all this is an ethic whose limitation lies precisely in what is not seen. Thus, the shift from a morality of justice and rights to an ethic of responsibility and care is marked by a striking change in imagery from that of blindness to that of sight. Suddenly, the other appears reembodied in personal and social history, as different from the self but connected by living in a common social world. In the Didion‡ story, morality is premised on the ability to see the connection between self and stranger by understanding the narrative through which it extends. Thus, in the move from rights to responsibilities, the fundamental premise of moral judgment shifts from balancing separate individuals in a social system equilibrated by the logic of equality and reciprocity to seeing individuals as interdependent in a network of social relationship. As the mother sees her life-giving connection to her child as life-sustaining for her as well, so the little girl sees the fracture of relationship as the moral problem in Kohlberg's dilemma. Whereas justice emphasizes the autonomy of the person, care underlies the primacy of relationship. Thus,

---

[1]Lawrence Kohlberg, "From Is to Ought: How to Commit the Naturalistic Fallacy and Get Away with It in the Study of Moral Development," in Theodore Mischel, ed., *Cognitive Development and Epistemology* (New York: Academic Press, 1971).

*[Jean Piaget (1896–1980) was an eminent Swiss developmental child psychologist who argued that all ('normal') human beings go through several stages of cognitive growth, which reflect innate biological properties. The environment can either trigger or frustrate this development.—Eds.]

†[Lawrence Kohlberg (1927–1987) was an American psychologist who drew upon Piaget's work to develop a theory of moral development, with golden rule morality as the highest stage of moral maturity. (The ability to act on general moral principles mirrors the highest stage of cognitive development in Piaget's theory: abstraction and the ability to understand abstract rules and principles.)—Eds.]

‡[The reference is to Joan Didion's *Slouching toward Bethlehem*, which Gilligan mentions in an earlier essay not reproduced here.—Eds.]

[2]John Rawls, *A Theory of Justice* (Cambridge: Harvard University Press, 1971).

[3]Lawrence Kohlberg, "Moral Stages and Moralization: The Cognitive-Developmental Approach," in T. Lickona, ed., *Moral Development and Behavior: Theory, Research, and Social Issues* (New York: Holt, Rinehart and Winston, 1976).

justice gives rise to an ethic of rights, and care engenders an ethic of responsibility.

The implications for social science theory and research of the dualistic conception of morality that I propose emanate from the suggestion that moral development proceeds along two different but intersecting paths that run through different modes of experience and give rise to different forms of thought. Whereas the analytic logic of justice is consonant with rational social and ethical theories and can be traced through the resolution of hypothetical dilemmas, the ethic of care depends on the contextual understanding of relationship. Since the experiential basis for this understanding and the forms of thought through which it develops have never been systematically traced in psychological research, its manifestations have been described as personality traits or situational effects rather than seen as part of a developmental process.

To trace the interaction of thought and experience through which the understanding of care and responsibility develops requires a different moral theory and a different strategy of research. The analytic logic of justice is manifest in the deductive resolution of hypothetical dilemmas and informs the understanding of rules. In contrast, the ethic of care relies on the understanding of relationships and is manifest most clearly in the consideration of actual dilemmas of moral conflicts and choice. A language of responsibility and care that cannot be assimilated to the logic of justice was discovered empirically through a study of pregnant women who were considering abortion decisions.[4] Although abortion can be construed as a dilemma of rights, in which case the moral problem turns on whether or not the fetus is thought to have rights, the women who participated in the abortion study did not construe the problem this way. Rather, they tended to place the dilemma of abortion in the context of the relationships in which it arises, to see the decision poised at the juncture between two connections—of man and woman and of parent and child. Seen in this context, the pregnancy posed a problem of responsibility, and the women's different understandings of responsibility suggested a sequence in the development of care. This sequence appeared in the texts of in-depth clinical interviews with twenty-nine women of diverse age, race, and class who were facing in common the actual choice of whether to continue or abort a pregnancy. I will describe three modes in the understanding of responsibility and the two transitional phases between them, which indicate the development of the understanding of relationships and chart the growth of an ethic of care.

The language of responsibility begins by delineating connection to others

---

[4]Carol Gilligan, "In a Different Voice: Women's Conceptions of Self and Morality," *Harvard Educational Review* (November 1977), 47:481–517. I have benefited from David Shawver's discussion of this work in his essay, "Alternative Principles: There's More Than Justice as Fairness." For further description of the abortion decision study, see Carol Gilligan and Mary Belenky, "A Naturalistic Study of Abortion Decisions," in Robert Selman and Regina Yando, eds., *Clinical-Developmental Psychology* (San Francisco: Jossey-Bass Inc., 1980); and Carol Gilligan, *In a Different Voice: Psychological Theory and Women's Development* (Cambridge: Harvard University Press, 1982).

as a way of ensuring survival by providing access to the things one is power-less to get for oneself. In children this understanding of relationship is mani-fest in the contrast between people they like and people they don't like or people who do and do not meet their needs, and this contrast in turn guides the decision about whom they should care. The moral problem of inclusion, which lies at the center of the ethic of care, is played out through the consider-ation of who is and who is not my friend. In the context of the abortion dilemma, the choice at this level centers on whether the woman sees the baby as a potential friend, as in the wish to have a baby in order not "to feel lonely and stuff." Similarly, having a baby may provide a way to leave home or, conversely, may interfere with a wish to continue in school. Thus, relation-ships are seen either as a source of personal gratification or as an impediment to gratification, in which case they are experienced as threatening or disap-pointing.

In the first transition, the concern with self, which was initially egocentric and thus unreflective, comes to be reconstructed as "selfish" as the experi-ence of relationship extends the understanding of responsibility. A pregnan-cy can initiate this transition by demonstrating on a physical level the connec-tion between self and other and by indicating how through that connection the actions of self affect the other and the other affects the self. Given the incipient awareness of responsibility for conceiving a child and of the respon-sibility entailed in raising a child, the exercise of responsibility with respect to the abortion decision can be seen as a way of entering the world of adult relationships. The transitional nature of this understanding is evident, how-ever, as the concept of responsibility repeatedly turns back toward the self, although now with a focus on assessing the self's capacity to care for another.

When the concern with responsibility shifts to consideration of the needs of the other, the second mode is achieved. Now the self is seen as more powerful, since the capacity to give to others provides a means of establishing and maintaining relationships of mutual dependence and care. Relationships become an anchor of personal security by signifying membership in a social world where inclusion is premised on the ability to care and promises care and protection in return. Concern now shifts from the direct satisfaction of needs to maintaining interpersonal connection, and this shift is manifest in a change in perspective toward others from liking and not liking to hurting and not hurting. As the wish to sustain relationships develops, the injunction not to hurt others is seen as the way to ensure continuing connection with others by avoiding conflict with them. The avoidance of hurt to others, however, depends on understanding their feelings and discerning their needs, and the contextual nature of this psychological understanding differs from the logic of justice viewed as fairness. The concept of equity, which Piaget illustrates through the response of an eleven-year-old girl to the dilemma of whether or not to give a second roll to a younger child who had carelessly dropped his first in the water, indicates how a more differentiated interpersonal under-standing underlies an ethic of care. Focusing on the issue of care, the girl says that "the little boy ought to have taken care, but then he was a little boy, so they might give him a little more," explaining that older children should understand "that when you are little you don't understand what you are doing."[5]

In the abortion decision, concern for others is expressed at the second mode as a wish not to hurt them. This concern with not hurting may extend to the fetus, the woman's family, her lover, or even to people to whom her lover is connected, such as his wife and children. Decision making in a world that extends along connecting lines of interrelationship differs from the balancing of separate individual claims, since the logic of choice changes from that of rights to a consideration of responsibility in relationships. This distinction was evident in the responses of two lawyers to the dilemma of whether or not to tell the opposing counsel about a document that would support the "meritorious claim" of the other's client.[6] A female lawyer approached the dilemma by considering in turn her responsibility and relationship to everyone involved, whereas a male attorney saw the adversary system of justice as ensuring equal protection for everyone's rights. For the woman, respect for others entailed trying to see the situation through their eyes; for the man, it was manifest in the assumption that the others were capable of protecting their rights.

In the second mode of understanding of responsibility, the needs of others are fused with those of the self, and the focus on the position of the other is so strong that the other's views are experienced as one's own beliefs. Desiring above all not to be selfish and thus in danger of losing a relationship, a woman may confuse self with other, holding herself responsible for the actions of others and considering others responsible for the choices she makes. Since responsibility is directed toward others, choice itself is construed as response to them, and submission to others is considered to be a manifestation of care and concern.

If the egocentrism of the first mode leads to disappointing and unstable relationships, which ultimately do not meet individual needs, the construction of responsibility in the second mode creates in relationships problems of a sort manifest when the attempt to avoid hurt does not succeed in sustaining connection. The focus on not hurting others as the substance of a morality of care then gives way gradually to the realization that basing decisions on the wishes of others and holding them accountable for one's own choice constitutes an evasion of responsibility that erodes the fabric of relationship. Thus, in the second transition, concern for self reemerges to guide a new understanding of relationship as a dynamic process of interaction rather than a bond of mutual dependence. This reassessment centers on a new and more active understanding of care that includes both self and other in the realiza-

[5]Piaget, Moral Judgment, pp. 272–73.

[6]Sharry Langdale and Carol Gilligan, "The Contribution of Women's Thought to Developmental Theory: The Elimination of Sex Bias in Moral Development Research and Education," interim report submitted to the National Institute of Education, 1980; see also Carol Gilligan, Sharry Langdale, Nona Lyons, and J. Michael Murphy, Final Report to the National Institute of Education, 1982.

tion of their interdependence. Certainly the decision to have an abortion spurs this kind of reconsideration, since the clear and irrevocable choice brings into focus the issue of responsibility at the same time as the pregnancy highlights the reality of interconnection.

Thus, the discovery through experience of the greater complexity of psychological and social reality, of the ambivalence of feelings, and of the constraints of choice spurs a process of self-reflection and a reexamination of relationships. The transitional features of this process are apparent when the turning back of responsibility toward the other leads the woman to deem as selfish her consideration of herself. This consideration, however, centers on a new understanding of her participation in choice. Through this reexamination, the woman comes to see how decisions made in a context of relationship not only affect both self and other but change the dynamic of their interaction. Thus, the understanding of relationship changes from a static balance maintained by not hurting to a dynamic interaction that arises and is sustained through the activity of care.

Whereas in the second mode care is defined as not hurting others who are the focus of concern, in the third mode care is tied to seeing the connections between everyone involved and thus to a new understanding of what is going on. This expansion of vision widens the conception of responsibility, including both self and other in the world of relationships that care protects, which is affected by what happens to everyone involved. As the injunction against hurting comes to be elevated to an ideal of nonviolence in human relationships, the focus of care shifts from the other to the relationship itself. Given that conflicts will inevitably arise, since the experiences and perspectives of people diverge, modes of dealing with conflict are sought that strengthen rather than sever connection. The moral problem of inclusion that hinges on the capacity to assume responsibility for care is now seen within an expanded network of relationship and with a broader understanding of what responsibility entails.

With this expansion of vision and the commitment to see the network of interrelationship comes a heightened sense of responsibility, tempered, however, by the realization that in dilemmas of responsibility conflict will always remain. A woman working as a counselor in an abortion clinic described the inner turmoil that led her to decide that she "really had to face what was going on." Witnessing a late abortion, she saw the fetus clearly as a developing human life, yet at the same time she realized that the development of that life was contingent on responsible care. Realizing that rights could be universally extended, while the capacity for care was bound by personal and social constraints, she concluded that abortion could be the lesser of two evils in a situation which admitted no absolute good. Morality, then, was contingent on sustaining the connections that revealed the consequences of action, minimizing the occurrence of violence by generating an awareness of responsibility for hurt.

Thus, the ethic of care is dependent on sight, or the ability to discern what is going on, widening the lens on social reality to reveal the connections obscured by the justice approach. The commitment to seeing the other entails a responsiveness to the other's point of view, not as mirroring of one's own but as refracting a different psychological and social reality. Beginning with the assumption that relationship is the fundamental condition of social reality, the ethic of care is contextual in its insistence on seeing connections. Moral judgment thus cannot be abstracted from the context of individual and social history, and decision making relies on a process of communication to discover the other's position and to discern the chain of connections through which the consequences of action extend. Thus, dialogue replaces logical deduction as the mode of moral discovery, and the activity of moral understanding returns to the social domain.

By tracing the ethic of care through a sequence of three modes and delineating the transitions between them, I have indicated how this ethic develops through the changing experience and understanding of relationship. As the understanding of relationship is reflected in the conception of responsibility, the language of responsibility guides the decision about whom to include in the compass of care. The moral problem of inclusion then comes to be reconstructed as the universe of care expands through an elaboration of the network of relationship and the increasing awareness of interdependence.

Since the development of an ethic of care depends on the experience and understanding of relationship, it is not bound by the same cognitive constraints that apply to the understanding of justice and rights. No longer would only moral philosophers or analytic thinkers reach moral maturity but also people who have come through the experience of relationship to understand the dynamics of interdependence. Thus, the ethic of care restores the concept of love to the moral domain, uniting cognition and affect by tying reflection to the experience of relationship.

If the concept of morality contains a fundamental tension between the ethics of justice and of care, then the delineation of moral development requires a more complex rendering of social experience. The development of the idea of justice, as traced through the work of Piaget and Kohlberg, depends on the experience of equality and autonomy that generates and in turn is sustained by the logic of fairness and rights. In the life cycle, adolescence brings issues of equality to the fore, and the development of formal thought at that time can extend the understanding of fairness from a logic of rules to a principled conception of rights, which then provides a justification for freedom, individual respect, and separation from others. Thus, we would expect, as Kohlberg found, that the logic of justice flourishes during adolescence, especially in times of social change, when the sense of possibility expands. The flourishing of justice would be fostered by the development of analytic modes of thought and by the experience of equal participation in democratic social institutions.

In contrast, the ethic of care develops through relationships that give rise to an understanding of interdependence and is sustained by the ability to discern connection. The experiences that foster its growth are connections that extend through time, revealing the changing dynamic of interaction and making it possible to see the consequences of choice. Whereas the experience of relationship that underlies the capacity for care begins early in life, the experience of responsibility reaches its fullest extension only in the adult years. Since care depends on understanding the narrative through which human experience extends, its development is supported by the growth of contextual modes of understanding and by involvement in a world of coherent and continuing relationship.

From this description, it is easy to see how the development of the social sciences toward increasingly formal and analytic modes of thought, reflected in the separation of subject and object in the design of experimental research and manifest in the claim of value neutrality and objective truth, would foster the understanding of an ethic of justice and the elaboration of systems of rules at the expense of an ethic of care and an understanding of the narrative of social relationship. Thus, psychologists trace the development in children of the capacity to perform the reversible operations of equality and reciprocity and to understand the logic of justice that underlies citizenship in a democratic state but ignore their ability to discern the inequities manifest in human society or to respond with care to the inequalities inherent in the cycle of life. Piaget observes that perhaps it is in the relationship of parent and child that "one realizes most keenly how immoral it can be to believe too much in morality and how much more precious is a little humanity than all the rules in the world."[7] And yet his equation of morality with respect for rules sustains the division of cognition and affect and provides little basis for tracing the understanding that reflects and informs the growth of the capacity for care.

Although I have suggested that moral development proceeds along two different paths and have indicated the tension between two different modes of ethical thought, I do not mean to imply that these ethics remain separate or that their development is unconnected. Instead, through the tension between the universality of rights and the particularity of responsibility, between the abstract concept of justice as fairness and the more contextual understanding of care in relationships, these ethics keep one another alive and inform each other at critical points. In this sense, the concept of morality sustains a dialectical tension between justice and care, aspiring always toward the ideal of a world more caring and more just. Conceived of in this way, the dialectic of moral development can be seen to emerge from the cycle of human life, to be embedded in human experience, and thus to be present in both of the sexes. Its tension is manifest in people's responses to actual dilemmas of moral conflict and choice as well as in the current debate about the theory and practice of psychological research.

The age-old dialogue between justice and love, reason and compassion, fairness and forgiveness, reflects not just two opposing or complementary conceptions of the moral domain but the fundamental tension in human psychology between the experience of separation and the experience of connection. As the experiences of attachment and separation run through the

---

[7]Piaget, *Moral Judgment*, p. 191.

cycle of human life, they give rise to the paradoxical truths that describe our social experience: that we know ourselves as individual and separate only insofar as we live in connection with others, and that we experience relationship only insofar as we differentiate other from self. Despite their underlying interconnection, however, the experiences of self and relationship are discrete, and these discrete experiences in turn give rise to two different moral languages: the language of rights that justifies separation and thus fosters and protects autonomy, and the language of responsibilities that sustains relationships and informs the activity of care.

Although these languages are manifest in different vocabularies (rights in the more analytic concepts of fairness, equality, balance, equilibrium, reciprocity, truth, and deceit; responsibility in the more contextual concepts of harmony, relationship, care, love, hurt, friendship, and betrayal) and although the ethics they reflect address different problems (rights, the conflict of self vs. other; responsibilities, the relationship between self and other), they remain in tension with one another. A move toward separation and rights leaves a problem of relationship and care, whereas a move toward connection and responsibility leaves a problem of personal integrity and choice. In the texts of interviews with people about their experiences of actual moral conflict and choice, the intersection of these two languages is marked by references to "terrible ambiguity" or by the awareness of a fundamental contradiction that then leads to confusion and difficulty with choice. This confusion is apparent when problems of relationship are cast in the language of rights, as when a problem of deceit in sexual triangles is formulated as a conflict between one person's "right to truth" and another's "right to sanity," a formulation which defies resolution by logical deduction. Then the apparent impasse of judgment tends to spur the conclusion either that moral judgment itself is relative or that problems of human relationships do not belong in the moral domain. Conversely, when conflicts of rights are construed in the language of responsibility so that opposing claims are formulated as a "balance of selfishnesses," then no resolution can be seen as moral, and integrity of autonomous choice appears uncaring and selfish, a manifestation of indifference.

Through their dialogue, however, these languages address the moral problem of how we can live at once as separate individuals and in continuing relationship with one another. This dialectic of separation and attachment informs an understanding of moral maturity that encompasses both relationships of equality, sustained by the logic of justice, and relationships of interdependence, relying on an ethic of care. The ability to see and respond to differences without abandoning moral judgment to relativism underlies the capacity to understand and protect another person's integrity and vulnerability. Since we know that violence breeds violence in the cycle of human relationships and that differences are embedded in the cycle of life, the moral balance of equality requires as its complement an ethic of care. Seeing the potential for violence to eventuate in the catastrophic destruction of nuclear war, Erikson warned that "in our time, man must decide whether he can afford to continue the exploitation of childhood as an arsenal of irrational fears or whether the relationship between adult and child, like other inequalities, can be raised to a position of partnership in a more reasonable order of things."[8]

The absence of care in the social sciences is evident not only in the conception of morality as solely a problem of justice but also in the relationship between experimenter and subject in social science research. The use of deceit in experimentation, although considered one of the rules of the game, affects the experimenter as well as the victim and colors the results that are thereby obtained. As social scientists have begun to question the separation of experimenter and subject and to pay more attention to the context of research, they have begun to generate a series of findings that point to the contextual nature of psychological truth. The studies by Rosenthal and Jacobson on the effects of teachers' expectations on children's intelligence indicate that the dynamic of relationship operates in ways that challenge basic assumptions about individual behavior.[9] Recent evidence on adaptation to life[10] as well as on survival in old age[11] demonstrates the life-sustaining power of relationships and the importance throughout life of continuing connection.

The moral problem in psychology is reflected as well in the language of its discourse, wherein people are referred to as research "subjects" and love "objects" rather than seen as partners in a shared interaction or pursuit. This language maintains a distance, mistaken for objectivity, which obscures the dynamic of interrelationship and the socially constructed and provisional nature of truth. Then a moral problem arises to compromise the integrity of psychological treatment and research, and the absence of care opens the way to manipulation, exploitation, and the rationalization of hurt. If the ethical potential of the social sciences lies in their ability to discover the social processes that sustain life, then the realization of this potential may depend on a shift not only in the locus of power and truth but also in the substance of concern. As an ethic of individual integrity comes to be seen as necessarily joined to an ethic of nonviolence, social understanding may expand its current focus on self and society to illuminate more fully the network of relationship that reveals the interdependence of life.

[8]Erik Erikson, *Childhood and Society* (1950; rpt. New York: W. W. Norton, 1963).

[9]Robert Rosenthal and Leonore Jacobson, *Pygmalion in the Classroom* (New York: Holt, Rinehart and Winston, 1968).

[10]George Vaillant, *Adaptation to Life* (Boston: Little, Brown, 1977).

[11]Ellen Langer, "Old Age: An Artifact?" in James McGaugh and Sara Keisler, eds., *Aging: Biology and Behavior* (New York: Academic Press, 1980).

46 / Virtue Ethics

ALASDAIR MacINTYRE

Alasdair MacIntyre (1929–   ) currently teaches philosophy at the University of Notre Dame. He is a major contemporary philosopher who writes on ethics, political philosophy, philosophy of the social sciences, and culture. His writings on virtue ethics and related issues have been a major influence in the recent revival of these theories.

I

When Aristotle speaks of excellence in human activity, he sometimes though not always, refers to some well-defined type of human practice: flute-playing, or war, or geometry. I am going to suggest that this notion of a particular type of practice as providing the arena in which the virtues are exhibited and in terms of which they are to receive their primary, if incomplete, definition is crucial to the whole enterprise of identifying a core concept of the virtues. . . .

By a 'practice' I am going to mean any coherent and complex form of socially established cooperative human activity through which goods internal to that form of activity are realised in the course of trying to achieve those standards of excellence which are appropriate to, and partially definitive of, that form of activity, with the result that human powers to achieve excellence, and human conceptions of the ends and goods involved, are systematically extended. Tic-tac-toe is not an example of a practice in this sense, nor is throwing a football with skill; but the game of football is, and so is chess. Bricklaying is not a practice; architecture is. Planting turnips is not a practice; farming is. So are the enquiries of physics, chemistry and biology, and so is the work of the historian, and so are painting and music. In the ancient and medieval worlds the creation and sustaining of human communities—of households, cities, nations—is generally taken to be a practice in the sense in which I have defined it. Thus the range of practices is wide: arts, sciences, games, politics in the Aristotelian sense, the making and sustaining of family life, all fall under the concept. But the question of the precise range of practices is not at this stage of the first importance. Instead let me explain some of the key terms involved in my definition, beginning with the notion of goods internal to a practice.

Consider the example of a highly intelligent seven-year-old child whom I wish to teach to play chess, although the child has no particular desire to learn the game. The child does however have a very strong desire for candy and little chance of obtaining it. I therefore tell the child that if the child will play chess with me once a week I will give the child 50¢ worth of candy; moreover I tell the child that I will always play in such a way that it will be difficult, but not impossible, for the child to win and that, if the child wins, the child will receive an extra 50¢ worth of candy. Thus motivated the child plays and plays to win. Notice however that, so long as it is the candy alone which provides the child with a good reason for playing chess, the child has no reason not to cheat and every reason to cheat, provided he or she can do so successfully. But, so we may hope, there will come a time when the child will find in those goods specific to chess, in the achievement of a certain highly particular kind of analytical skill, strategic imagination and competitive intensity, a new set of reasons, reasons now not just for winning on a particular occasion, but for trying to excel in whatever way the game of chess demands. Now if the child cheats, he or she will be defeating not me, but himself or herself.

There are thus two kinds of good possibly to be gained by playing chess. On the one hand there are those goods externally and contingently attached to chess-playing and to other practices by the accidents of social circumstance— in the case of the imaginary child candy, in the case of real adults such goods as prestige, status and money. There are always alternative ways for achieving such goods, and their achievement is never to be had *only* by engaging in some particular kind of practice. On the other hand there are the goods internal to the practice of chess which cannot be had in any way but by playing chess or some other game of that specific kind. We call them internal for two reasons: first, as I have already suggested, because we can only specify them in terms of chess or some other game of that specific kind and by means of examples from such games (otherwise the meagerness of our vocabulary for speaking of such goods forces us into such devices as my own resort to writing of 'a certain highly particular kind of'); and secondly because they can only be identified and recognised by the experience of participating in the practice in question. Those who lack the relevant experience are incompetent thereby as judges of internal goods. . . .

A practice involves standards of excellence and obedience to rules as well as the achievement of goods. To enter into a practice is to accept the authority of those standards and the inadequacy of my own performance as judged by them. It is to subject my own attitudes, choices, preferences and tastes to the standards which currently and partially define the practice. Practices of course . . . have a history; games, sciences and arts all have histories. Thus the standards are not themselves immune from criticism, but none the less we cannot be initiated into a practice without accepting the authority of the best standards realised so far. If, on starting to listen to music, I do not accept my own incapacity to judge correctly, I will never learn to hear, let alone to appreciate, Bartok's last quartets. If, on starting to play baseball, I do not accept that others know better than I when to throw a fast ball and when not, I will never learn to appreciate good pitching let alone to pitch. In the realm of practices the authority of both goods and standards operates in such a way as to rule out all subjectivist and emotivist analyses of judgment. De gustibus *est* disputandum.*

We are now in a position to notice an important difference between what I have called internal and what I have called external goods. It is characteristic of what I have called external goods that when achieved they are always some individual's property and possession. Moreover characteristically they are such that the more someone has of them, the less there is for other people. This is sometimes necessarily the case, as with power and fame, and sometimes the case by reason of contingent circumstance as with money. External goods are therefore characteristically objects of competition in which there must be losers as well as winners. Internal goods are indeed the outcome of competition to excel, but it is characteristic of them that their achievement is a good for the whole community who participate in the practice. So when Turner transformed the seascape in painting or W. G. Grace advanced the art of batting in cricket in a quite new way their achievement enriched the whole relevant community.

But what does all or any of this have to do with the concept of the virtues? It turns out that we are now in a position to formulate a first, even if partial and tentative definition of a virtue: *A virtue is an acquired human quality the possession and exercise of which tends to enable us to achieve those goods which are internal to practices and the lack of which effectively prevents us from achieving any such goods.* Later this definition will need amplification and amendment. But as a first approximation to an adequate definition it already illuminates the place of the virtues in human life. For it is not difficult to show for a whole range of key virtues that without them the goods internal to practices are barred to us, but not just barred to us generally, barred in a very particular way.

It belongs to the concept of a practice as I have outlined it—and as we are all familiar with it already in our actual lives, whether we are painters or physicists or quarterbacks or indeed just lovers of good painting or first-rate experiments or a well-thrown pass—that its goods can only be achieved by subordinating ourselves to the best standard so far achieved, and that entails subordinating ourselves within the practice in our relationship to other practitioners. We have to learn to recognise what is due to whom; we have to be prepared to take whatever self-endangering risks are demanded along the way; and we have to listen carefully to what we are told about our own inadequacies and to reply with the same carefulness for the facts. In other words we have to accept as necessary components of any practice with internal goods and standards of excellence the virtues of justice, courage and honesty. For not to accept these, to be willing to cheat as our imagined child was willing to cheat in his or her early days at chess, so far bars us from achieving the standards of excellence or the goods internal to the practice that it renders the practice pointless except as a device for achieving eternal goods.

*[De gustibus *est* disputandum = matters of taste *are* disputable.—Eds.]

We can put the same point in another way. Every practice requires a certain kind of relationship between those who participate in it. Now the virtues are those goods by reference to which, whether we like it or not, we define our relationships to those other people with whom we share the kind of purposes and standards which inform practices. Consider an example of how reference to the virtues has to be made in certain kinds of human relationship. . . .

Just as, so long as we share the standards and purposes characteristic of practices, we define our relationships to each other, whether we acknowledge it or not, by reference to standards of truthfulness and trust, so we define them too by reference to standards of justice and of courage. If A, a professor, gives B and C the grades that their papers deserve, but grades D because he is attracted by D's blue eyes or is repelled by D's dandruff, he has defined his relationship to D differently from his relationship to the other members of the class, whether he wishes it or not. Justice requires that we treat others in respect of merit or desert according to uniform and impersonal standards; to depart from the standards of justice in some particular instance defines our relationship with the relevant person as in some way special or distinctive.

The case with courage is a little different. We hold courage to be a virtue because the care and concern for individuals, communities and causes which is so crucial to so much in practices requires the existence of such a virtue. If someone says that he cares for some individual, community or cause, but is unwilling to risk harm or danger on his, her or its own behalf, he puts in question the genuineness of his care and concern. Courage, the capacity to risk harm or danger to oneself, has its role in human life because of this connection with care and concern. This is not to say that a man cannot genuinely care and also be a coward. It is in part to say that a man who genuinely cares and has not the capacity for risking harm or danger has to define himself, both to himself and to others, as a coward.

I take it then that from the standpoint of those types of relationship without which practices cannot be sustained truthfulness, justice and courage—and perhaps some others—are genuine excellences, are virtues in the light of which we have to characterise ourselves and others, whatever our private moral standpoint or our society's particular codes may be. For this recognition that we cannot escape the definition of our relationships in terms of such goods is perfectly compatible with the acknowledgment that different societies have and have had different codes of truthfulness, justice and courage. Lutheran pietists brought up their children to believe that one ought to tell the truth to everybody at all times, whatever the circumstances or consequences, and Kant was one of their children. Traditional Bantu parents brought up their children not to tell the truth to unknown strangers, since they believed that this could render the family vulnerable to witchcraft. In our culture many of us have been brought up not to tell the truth to elderly great-aunts who invite us to admire their new hats. But each of these codes embodies an acknowledgment of the virtue of truthfulness. So it is also with varying codes of justice and of courage. . . .

To situate the virtues any further within practices it is necessary now to clarify a little further the nature of a practice by drawing two important contrasts. The discussion so far I hope makes it clear that a practice, in the sense intended, is never just a set of technical skills, even when directed towards some unified purpose and even if the exercise of those skills can on occasion be valued or enjoyed for their own sake. What is distinctive of a practice is in part the way in which conceptions of the relevant goods and ends which the technical skills serve—and every practice does require the exercise of technical skills—are transformed and enriched by these extensions of human powers and by that regard for its own internal goods which are partially definitive of each particular practice or type of practice. Practices never have a goal or goals fixed for all time—painting has no such goal nor has physics—but the goals themselves are transmuted by the history of the activity. It therefore turns out not to be accidental that every practice has its own history and a history which is more and other than that of the improvement of the relevant technical skills. This historical dimension is crucial in relation to the virtues.

To enter into a practice is to enter into a relationship not only with its contemporary practitioners, but also with those who have preceded us in the practice, particularly those whose achievements extended the reach of the practice to its present point. It is thus the achievement, and *a fortiori** the authority, of a tradition which I then confront and from which I have to learn. And for this learning and the relationship to the past which it embodies the virtues of justice, courage and truthfulness are prerequisite in precisely the same way and for precisely the same reasons as they are in sustaining present relationships within practices.

It is not only of course with sets of technical skills that practices ought to be contrasted. Practices must not be confused with institutions. Chess, physics and medicine are practices; chess clubs, laboratories, universities and hospitals are institutions. Institutions are characteristically and necessarily concerned with what I have called external goods. They are involved in acquiring money and other material goods; they are structured in terms of power and status, and they distribute money, power and status as rewards. Nor could they do otherwise if they are to sustain not only themselves, but also the practices of which they are the bearers. For no practices can survive for any length of time unsustained by institutions. Indeed so intimate is the relationship of practices to institutions—and consequently of the goods external to the goods internal to the practices in question—that institutions and practices characteristically form a single causal order in which the ideals and the creativity of the practice are always vulnerable to the acquisitiveness of the institution, in which the cooperative care for common goods of the practice is always vulnerable to the competitiveness of the institution. In this context the essential function of the virtues is clear. Without them, without justice, courage and truthfulness, practices could not resist the corrupting power of institutions.

*[With even stronger reason.—Eds.]

Yet if institutions do have corrupting power, the making and sustaining of forms of human community—and therefore of institutions—itself has all the characteristics of a practice, and moreover of a practice which stands in a peculiarly close relationship to the exercise of the virtues in two important ways. The exercise of the virtues is itself apt to require a highly determinate attitude to social and political issues; and it is always within some particular community with its own specific institutional forms that we learn or fail to learn to exercise the virtues. There is of course a crucial difference between the way in which the relationship between moral character and political community is envisaged from the standpoint of liberal individualist modernity and the way in which that relationship was envisaged from the standpoint of the type of ancient and medieval tradition of the virtues. . . . For liberal individualism a community is simply an arena in which individuals each pursue their own self-chosen conception of the good life, and political institutions exist to provide that degree of order which makes such self-determined activity possible. Government and law are, or ought to be, neutral between rival conceptions of the good life for man, and hence, although it is the task of government to promote law-abidingness, it is on the liberal view no part of the legitimate function of government to inculcate any one moral outlook.

By contrast, on the particular ancient and medieval view . . . political community not only requires the exercise of the virtues for its own sustenance, but it is one of the tasks of government to make its citizens virtuous, just as it is one of the tasks of parental authority to make children grow up so as to be virtuous adults. The classical statement of this analogy is by Socrates in the *Crito*.* It does not of course follow from an acceptance of the Socratic view of political community and political authority that we ought to assign to the modern state the moral function which Socrates assigned to the city and its laws. Indeed the power of the liberal individualist standpoint partly derives from the evident fact that the modern state is indeed totally unfitted to act as moral educator of any community. But the history of how the modern state emerged is of course itself a moral history. If my account of the complex relationship of virtues to practices and to institutions is correct, it follows that we shall be unable to write a true history of practices and institutions unless that history is also one of the virtues and vices. For the ability of a practice to retain its integrity will depend on the way in which the virtues can be and are exercised in sustaining the institutional forms which are the social bearers of the practice. The integrity of a practice causally requires the exercise of the virtues by at least some of the individuals who embody it in their activities; and conversely the corruption of institutions is always in part at least an effect of the vices. . . .

---

*[Socrates (470 400 b.c.), Greek philosopher, whose most famous student, Plato (428–348 b.c.) expressed some of Socrates' teachings in his dialogues. The *Crito* is a dialogue about civil disobedience.—Eds.]

II

I have defined the virtues partly in terms of their place in practices. But surely, it may be suggested, some practices—that is, some coherent human activities which answer to the description of what I have called a practice—are evil. So in discussions by some moral philosophers of this type of account of the virtues it has been suggested that torture and sado-masochistic sexual activities might be examples of practices. But how can a disposition be a virtue if it is the kind of disposition which sustains practices and some practices issue in evil? My answer to this objection falls into two parts.

First I want to allow that there *may* be practices—in the sense in which I understand the concept—which simply *are* evil. I am far from convinced that there are, and I do not in fact believe that either torture or sado-masochistic sexuality answer to the description of a practice which my account of the virtues employs. But I do not want to rest my case on this lack of conviction, especially since it is plain that as a matter of contingent fact many types of practice may on particular occasions be productive of evil. For the range of practices includes the arts, the sciences and certain types of intellectual and athletic game[s]. And it is at once obvious that any of these may under certain conditions be a source of evil: the desire to excel and to win can corrupt, a man may be so engrossed by his painting that he neglects his family, what was initially an honourable resort to war can issue in savage cruelty. But what follows from this? . . .

That the virtues need initially to be defined and explained with reference to the notion of a practice . . . in no way entails approval of all practices in all circumstances. That the virtues—as the objection itself presupposed—*are* defined not in terms of good and right practices, but of practices, does not entail or imply that practices as actually carried through at particular times and places do not stand in need of moral criticism. And the resources for such criticism are not lacking. There is in the first place no inconsistency in appealing to the requirements of a virtue to criticise a practice. Justice may be initially defined as a disposition which in its particular way is necessary to sustain practices; it does not follow that in pursuing the requirements of a practice violations of justice are not to be condemned. Moreover . . . a morality of virtues requires as its counterpart a conception of moral law. Its requirements too have to be met by practices. . . .

47 / God and the Good

KAI NIELSEN

Kai Nielsen (1926–   teaches at the University of Calgary. He writes on ethics, social and political philosophy, and Marxism and has made important contributions to Marxist social theory, political philosophy, ethics, and philosophy of religion.

I. [INTRODUCTION]

*I*t is the claim of many influential Christian and Jewish theologians (Brunner, Buber, Barth, Niebuhr, and Bultmann—to take outstanding examples) that the *only* genuine basis for morality is in religion. And any old religion is not good enough. The only truly adequate foundation for moral belief is a religion that acknowledges the absolute sovereignty of the Lord found in the prophetic religions.

These theologians will readily grant what is plainly true, namely, that as matter of fact many nonreligious people behave morally, but they contend that without a belief in God and his Law there is no *ground* or *reason* for being moral. The sense of moral relativism, skepticism, and nihilism rampant in our age is due in large measure to the general weakening of religious belief in an age of science. Without God there can be no objective foundation for our moral beliefs. As Brunner puts it, "The believer *alone* clearly perceives that the Good, as it is recognized in faith, is the sole Good, and all that is otherwise called good cannot lay claim to this title, at least in the ultimate sense of the word." "The Good consists in always doing what God wills at any particular moment." This "Good" can only "take place in unconditional obedience" to God, the ground of our being. Without God life would have no point and morality would have no basis. Without religious belief, without the Living God, there could be no adequate answer to the persistently gnawing questions: What ought we to do? How ought I to live?

Is this frequently repeated claim justified? Are our moral beliefs and conceptions based on or grounded in a belief in the God of Judaism, Christianity, and Islam? More specifically still, we need to ask ourselves three very fundamental questions: (1) Is being willed by God the or even a *fundamental* criterion for that which is so willed being morally good or for its being something that ought to be done? (2) Is being willed by God the *only* criterion for that which is so willed being morally good or for its being something that ought to be done? (3) Is being willed by God the only *adequate* criterion for that which is so willed being morally good or being something that ought to be done? I shall argue that the fact that God wills something—if indeed that is a fact—cannot be a fundamental criterion for its being morally good or obligatory and thus it cannot be the only criterion or the only adequate criterion for moral goodness or obligation.

II. [PRELIMINARY MATTERS]

By way of preliminaries we first need to get clear what is meant by a "fundamental criterion." When we speak of the criterion for the goodness of an action or attitude we speak of some *measure* or *test* by virtue of which we may decide which actions or attitudes are good or desirable, or, at least, are the least undesirable of the alternative actions or attitudes open to us. A moral criterion is the measure we use for determining the value or worth of an action or attitude. We have such a measure or test when we have some generally relevant considerations by which we may decide whether something is whatever it is said to be. A fundamental moral criterion is (a) a test or measure used to judge the legitimacy of moral rules and/or acts or attitudes, and (b) a measure that one would give up last if one were reasoning morally. (In reality, there probably is no *single* fundamental criterion, although there are fundamental criteria.)

There is a further preliminary matter we need to consider. In asking about the basis or authority for our moral beliefs we are not asking about how we came to have them. If you ask someone where he got his moral beliefs, he should answer that he got them from his parents, parent surrogates, teachers, etc.[1] They are beliefs which he has simply been conditioned to accept. But the validity or soundness of a belief is independent of its origin. When one person naively asks another where he got his moral beliefs, he is most likely not asking how he came by them; he is, in effect, asking: (1) On what authority does he hold these beliefs? or (2) What good reasons or justification does he have for these moral beliefs? He should answer that he does not and cannot hold these beliefs on *any authority*. It is indeed true that many of us turn to people for moral advice and guidance in moral matters, but if we *simply* do what we do because it has been authorized, we cannot be reasoning and acting as moral agents; for to respond as a moral agent, to treat a principle as one's moral principle, it must be something which is subscribed to by one's own deliberate commitment, and it must be something for which one is prepared to give reasons.

With these preliminaries out of the way we can return to my claim that the fact (if indeed it is a fact) that God has commanded, willed, or ordained something cannot, in the very nature of the case, be a fundamental criterion

---

[1] P. H. Nowell-Smith, Morality: Religious and Secular," *The Rationalist Annual* (1961), pp. 5–22.

for claiming that whatever is commanded, willed, or ordained ought to be done. . . .*

III. [THE LOGICAL STATUS OF 'GOD IS GOOD': IS IT NONANALYTIC?]

To see the rationale for [that claim] we must consider the logical status of "God is good." Is it a nonanalytic and in some way substantive claim, or is it analytic? (Can we say that it is neither?) No matter what we say, we get into difficulties.†

Let us first try to claim that it is a nonanalytic, that is to say, that it is in some way a substantive statement. So understood, God cannot then be by *definition* good. If the statement is synthetic and substantive, its denial cannot be self-contradictory, that is, it cannot be self-contradictory to assert that *x* is God but *x* is not good. It would always *in fact* be wrong to assert this, for God is the Perfect Good, but the denial of this claim is not self-contradictory, it is just false or in some way mistaken. The "is" in "God is the Perfect Good" is not the "is" of identity, perfect goodness is being predicated of God in some *logically* contingent way. It is the religious experience of the believer and the events recorded in the Bible that lead the believer to the steadfast conviction that God has a purpose or vocation for him which he can fulfill only by completely submitting to God's will. God shall lead him and guide him in every thought, word, and deed. Otherwise he will be like a man shipwrecked, lost in a vast and indifferent universe. Through careful attention to the Bible, he comes to understand that God is a wholly good being who has dealt faithfully with his chosen people. God is not *by definition* perfectly good or even good, but in reality, though not of logical necessity, he never falls short of perfection.

Assuming "God is good" is not a truth of language, how, then, do we know that God is good? Do we know or have good grounds for believing that the remarks made at the end of the above paragraph are so? The believer can indeed make a claim like the one we have made above, but how do we or how does he know that this is so? What grounds have we for believing that God is good? Naive people, recalling how God spoke to Job out of the whirlwind, may say that God is good because he is omnipotent and omniscient. But this clearly won't do, for, . . . there is nothing logically improper about saying "X is omnipotent and omniscient and morally wicked." Surely in the world as we

---

*[In order to understand the rest of this essay, you must understand two concepts: 'analytic statements' and 'nonanalytic (synthetic) statements'. These are defined as follows:

Analytic statement (truth of language): Any statement S is analytic if and only if (a) it is an identity or definition, or (b) it is true solely on the basis of a definition. Examples: (a) 'Puppies are young dogs'; (b) 'Puppies are young'.

Synthetic statement (nonanalytic substantive statement): Any statement S is synthetic (substantive) if and only if it is not analytic.—Eds.]

†[See note at the end of Section II.—Eds.]

know it there is no logical connection between being powerful and knowledgeable, on the one hand, and, on the other, being good. As far as I can see, all that God proved to Job when he spoke to him out of the whirlwind was that God was an immeasurably powerful being; but he did not prove his moral superiority to Job, and he did nothing at all even to exhibit his moral goodness. (One might even argue that he exhibited moral wickedness.) We need not assume that omnipotence and omniscience bring with it goodness or even wisdom.

What other reason could we have for claiming that God is good? We might say that he is good because he tells us to do good in thought, word, and deed and to love one another. In short, in his life and in his precepts God exhibits for us his goodness and love. Now one might argue that children's hospitals and concentration camps clearly show that such a claim is false. But let us *assume* that in some way God does exhibit his goodness to man. Let us assume that if we examine God's works we cannot but affirm that God is good.[2] We come to understand that he isn't cruel, callous, or indifferent. But in order to make such judgments or to gain such an understanding, we must use our own logically independent moral criteria. On our present assumption in asserting "God is good" we have of necessity made a moral judgment, a moral appraisal, using a criterion that cannot be based on a knowledge that God exists or that he issues commands. We *call* God "good" because we have experienced the goodness of his acts, but in order to do this, in order to know that he is good or to have any grounds for believing that he is good, we must have an independent moral criterion which we use in making this predication of God. So if "God is good" is taken to be synthetic and substantive then morality cannot simply be based on a belief in God. We must of logical necessity have some criterion of goodness that is not derived from any statement asserting that there is a Deity.

IV. [THE LOGICAL STATUS OF 'GOD IS GOOD': IS IT ANALYTIC?]

Let us alternatively, and more plausibly, treat "God is good" as a truth of language. Now some truths of language (some analytic statements) are statements of identity as in "Puppies are young dogs" or "A father is a male parent." Such statements are definitions and the "is" is the "is of identity." But "God is good" is clearly not such a statement of identity, for that "God" does not equal "Good," or "God" does not have the same meaning as "good," can easily be seen from the following case: Jane says to Betsy, after Betsy helps an old lady across the street, "That was good of you." "That was good of you" most certainly does not mean "That was God of you." And when we say "Conscientiousness is good" we do not mean to say "Conscientiousness is God." To say, as a believer does, that God is good is not to say that God is God.

---

[2]This is surely to assume a lot.

This clearly indicates that the word "God" does not have the same meaning as the word "good." When we are talking about God we are not simply talking about morality.

"God is the Perfect Good" is somewhat closer to "a father is a male parent," but even here "God" and "the Perfect Good" are not identical in meaning. "God is the Perfect Good" is like "a triangle is a trilateral" in some important respects. Though something is a triangle if and only if it is a trilateral, it does not follow that "triangle" and "trilateral" have the same meaning. Similarly, something is God if and only if that something is the Perfect Good, but it does not follow that "God" and "the Perfect Good" have the same meaning. When we speak of God we wish to say other things about him as well, though indeed what is true of God will also be true of the Perfect Good. Yet what is true of the evening star will also be true of the morning star for they both refer to the same object, namely Venus, but, as Frege has shown, it does not follow that the two terms have the same meaning if they have the same referent.

And even if it could be made out that "God is the Perfect Good" is in some way a statement of identity, (1) it would not make "God is good" a statement of identity, and (2) we could know that *x* is the Perfect Good only if we already knew how to decide that *x* is good. Even on the assumption that "God is the Perfect Good" is a statement of identity, we need some independent way of deciding whether something is good, that is to say, we must have an independent criterion for goodness.

Surely it is more plausible to interpret "God is good" to be analytic in the way "Puppies are young," "A bachelor is unmarried," or "Unjustified killing is wrong" are analytic. These statements are not statements of identity; they are not definitions, though they all follow from definitions and to deny any of them is self-contradictory.

In short it seems to me correct to argue "God is good," "Puppies are young," and "Triangles are three-sided" are all truths of language; the predicates *partially* define their subjects. That is to say—to adopt for a moment a Platonic *sounding* idiom—goodness is partially definitive of Godhood, as youngness is partially definitive of puppyhood, and as three sidedness is partially definitive of triangularity.

To admit this is not at all to admit that we can have no understanding of "good" without an understanding of "God," and the truth of the above claim about "God is good" will not show that God is the or even a fundamental criterion for goodness.

Let us first see how it does *not* show that we could not have an understanding of "good" without having an understanding of "God." We couldn't understand the full religious sense of what is meant by "God" without knowing that whatever is denoted by this term is said to be good, but, as "young" or "three-sided" is understood without reference to "puppies" or "triangles," though the converse cannot be the case, so "good" is also understood quite independently of any reference to "God," but again the converse cannot be the case. We can intelligibly say, "I have a three-sided figure here that is most certainly not a triangle" and "Colts are young but they are not puppies." Similarly, we can well say, "Conscientiousness, under most circumstances at least, is good even in a world without God." Such an utterance is clearly intelligible, to believer and nonbeliever alike. It is a well-formed English sentence with a use in the language. But here we can use "good" without implying anything about the reality of God. Such linguistic evidence clearly shows that good is a concept which can be understood quite independently of any reference to the Deity and that morality without religion, without theism, is quite possible. In fact quite the reverse is the case. Christianity, Judaism, and theistic religions of that sort could not exist if people did not have a moral understanding that was, logically speaking, quite independent of such religions. We could have no understanding of the truth of "God is good" or of the concept God unless we had an independent understanding of goodness.

That this is so can be seen from the following considerations. If we had no grasp of the use of the word "young," and if we did not know the criteria for deciding whether a dog was young, we could not know how correctly to apply the word "puppy." Without such a prior understanding of what it is to be young we could not understand the sentence "Puppies are young." Similarly, if we had no grasp of the use of the word "good," and if we did not know the criteria for deciding whether a being (or if you will, a power or a force) was good, we could not know how correctly to apply the word "God." Without such a prior understanding of goodness we could not understand the sentence "God is good." This clearly shows that our understanding of morality and knowledge of goodness is independent of any knowledge that we may or may not have of the Divine. In fact the very converse is the case. Without a prior and logically independent understanding of "good" and without some nonreligious criterion for judging something to be good, the religious person could have no knowledge of God, for he could not know whether that powerful being who spoke out of the whirlwind and laid the foundations of the earth was in fact worthy of worship and perfectly good.

From the argument we have made so far we can conclude that we cannot decide whether something is good or whether it ought to be done simply from finding out (assuming that we can find out) that God commanded it, willed it, enjoined it, and the like. Furthermore, whether "God is good" is synthetic (substantive) or analytic (a truth of language), the concept of good must be understood as something distinct from the concept of God; that is to say, a man could know how to use "good" properly and still not know how to use "God." In fact quite the reverse is the case. A man could not know how to use "God" correctly unless he already understood how to use "good." An understanding of goodness is logically prior to and is, as such, independent of any understanding or acknowledgment of God. . . .

48 / A Modified Divine Command Theory of Ethical Wrongness

ROBERT MERRIHEW ADAMS

Robert Merrihew Adams (1932–   ) teaches at UCLA and writes on the philosophy of religion and ethics. He has been an important influence in analytical philosophy in the area of philosophy of religion.

I.

. . . *T*he modified divine command theory clearly conceives of believers as valuing some things independently of their relation to God's commands. If the believer will not say that it would be wrong not to practice cruelty for its own sake if God commanded it, that is because he values kindness, and has a revulsion for cruelty, in a way that is at least to some extent independent of his belief that God commands kindness and forbids cruelty. This point may be made the basis of both philosophical and theological objections to the modified divine command theory, but I think the objections can be answered.

The philosophical objection is, roughly, that if there are some things I value independently of their relation to God's commands, then my value concepts cannot rightly be analyzed in terms of God's commands. According to the modified divine command theory, the acceptability of divine command ethics depends in part on the believer's independent positive valuation of the sorts of things that God is believed to command. But then, the philosophical critic objects, the believer must have a prior, nontheological conception of ethical right and wrong, in terms of which he judges God's commandments to be acceptable—and to admit that the believer has a prior, nontheological conception of ethical right and wrong is to abandon the divine command theory.

The weakness of this philosophical objection is that it fails to note the distinctions that can be drawn among various value concepts. From the fact that the believer values some things independent of his beliefs about God's commands, the objector concludes, illegitimately, that the believer must have a conception of ethical right and wrong that is independent of his beliefs about God's commands. This inference is illegitimate because there can be valuations which do not imply or presuppose a judgment of ethical right or wrong. For instance, I may simply like something, or want something, or feel a revulsion at something.

What the modified divine command theorist will hold, then, is that the believer values some things independently of their relation to God's commands, but that these valuations are not judgments of ethical right and wrong and do not of themselves imply judgments of ethical right and wrong. He will maintain, on the other hand, that such independent valuations are involved in, or even necessary for, judgments of ethical right and wrong which also involve beliefs about God's will or commands. The adherent of a divine command ethics will normally be able to give reasons for his adherence. Such reasons might include: "Because I am grateful to God for His love"; "Because I find it the most satisfying form of ethical life"; "Because there's got to be an objective moral law if life isn't to fall to pieces, and I can't understand what it would be if not the will of God." As we have already noted, the modified divine command theorist also has reasons why he would not accept a divine command ethics in certain logically possible situations which he believes not to be actual. All of these reasons seem to me to involve valuations that are independent of divine command ethics. The person who has such reasons wants certain things—happiness, certain satisfactions—for himself and others; he hates cruelty and loves kindness; he has perhaps a certain unique and "numinous" awe of God. And these are not attitudes which he has simply because of his beliefs about God's commands. They are not attitudes, however, which presuppose judgments of moral right and wrong. . . .

II.

This version of the divine command theory may seem *theologically* objectionable to some believers. One of the reasons, surely, why divine command theories of ethics have appealed to some theologians is that such theories seem especially congruous with the religious demand that God be the object of our highest allegiance. If our supreme commitment in life is to doing what is right just because it is right, and if what is right is right just because God wills or commands it, then surely our highest allegiance is to God. But the modified divine command theory seems not to have this advantage. For the modified divine command theorist is forced to admit, as we have seen, that he has reasons for his adherence to a divine command ethics, and that his having these reasons implies that there are some things which he values independently of his beliefs about God's commands. It is therefore not correct to say of him that he is committed to doing the will of God *just* because it is the will of God; he is committed to doing it partly because of other things which he values independently. Indeed it appears that there are certain logically possible situations in which his present attitudes would not commit him to obey God's commands (for instance, if God commanded cruelty for its own sake). This may even suggest that he values some things, not just independently of God's commands, but more than God's commands.

We have here a real problem in religious ethical motivation. The Judeo-Christian believer is supposed to make God the supreme focus of his loyalties; that is clear. One possible interpretation of this fact is the following. Obedience to whatever God may command is (or at least ought to be) the one thing that the believer values for its own sake and more than anything and everything else. Anything else that he values, he values (or ought to) only to a lesser degree and as a means to obedience to God. This conception of religious ethical motivation is obviously favorable to an *un*modified divine command theory of ethical wrongness.

But I think it is not a realistic conception. Loyalty to God, for instance, is very often explained, by believers themselves, as motivated by gratitude for benefits conferred. And I think it is clear in most cases that the gratitude presupposes that the benefits are valued, at least to some extent, independently of loyalty to God. Similarly, I do not think that most devout Judeo-Christian believers would say that it would be wrong to disobey God if He commanded cruelty for its own sake. And if I am right about that I think it shows that their positive valuation of (emotional/volitional pro-attitude toward) doing *whatever* God may command is not clearly greater than their independent negative valuation of cruelty.

In analyzing ethical motivation in general, as well as Judeo-Christian ethical motivation in particular, it is probably a mistake to suppose that there is (or can be expected to be) only one thing that is valued supremely and for its own sake, with nothing else being valued independently of it. The motivation for a person's ethical orientation in life is normally much more complex than that, and involves a plurality of emotional and volitional attitudes of different sorts which are at least partly independent of each other. At any rate, I think the modified divine command theorist is bound to say that that is true of his ethical motivation.

In what sense, then, can the modified divine command theorist maintain that God is the supreme focus of his loyalties? I suggest the following interpretation of the single-hearted loyalty to God which is demanded in Judeo-Christian religion. In this interpretation the crucial idea is *not* that some one thing is valued for its own sake and more than anything else, and nothing else valued independently of it. It is freely admitted that the religious person will have a plurality of motives for his ethical position, and that these will be at least partly independent of each other. It is admitted further that a desire to obey the commands of God (*whatever* they may be) may not be the strongest of these motives. What will be claimed is that certain beliefs about God enable the believer to integrate or focus his motives in a loyalty to God and His commands. Some of these beliefs are about what God commands or wills (contingently—that is, although He could logically have commanded or willed something else instead).

Some of the motives in question might be called egoistic; they include desires for satisfactions for oneself—which God is believed to have given or to be going to give. Other motives may be desires for satisfaction for other people; these may be called altruistic. Still other motives might not be desires for anyone's satisfaction, but might be valuations of certain kinds of action for their own sakes; these might be called idealistic. I do not think my argument depends heavily on this particular classification, but it seems plausible that all of these types, and perhaps others as well, might be distinguished among the motives for a religious person's ethical position. Obviously such motives might pull one in different directions, conflicting with one another. But in Judeo-Christian ethics beliefs about what God does in fact will (although He could have willed otherwise) are supposed to enable one to *fuse* these motives, so to speak, into one's devotion to God and His will, so that they all pull together. Doubtless the believer will still have some motives which conflict with his loyalty to God. But the religious ideal is that these should all be merely momentary desires and impulses, and kept under control. They ought not to be allowed to influence voluntary action. The deeper, more stable, and controlling desires, intentions, and psychic energies are supposed to be fused in devotion to God. As I interpret it, however, it need not be inconsistent with the Judeo-Christian ethical and religious ideal that this fusion of motives, this integration of moral energies, depends on belief in certain propositions which are taken to be contingent truths about God.

Lest it be thought that I am proposing unprecedented theological positions, or simply altering Judeo-Christian religious beliefs to suit my theories, I will call to my aid on this point a theologian known for his insistence on the sovereignty of God. Karl Barth* seems to me to hold a divine command theory of ethics. But when he raises the question of why we should obey God, he rejects with scorn the suggestion that God's *power* provides the basis for His claim on us. "By deciding for God [man] has definitely decided not to be obedient to power as power." God's claim on us is based rather on His grace. "God calls us and orders us and claims us by being gracious to us in Jesus Christ." I do not mean to suggest that Barth would agree with everything I have said about motivation, or that he offers a lucid account of a divine command theory. But he does agree with the position I have proposed on this point, that the believer's loyalty is not to be construed as a loyalty to God *as* all-powerful, nor to God *whatever* He might conceivably have willed. It is a loyalty to God *as* having a certain attitude toward us, a certain will for us, which God was free not to have, but to which, in Barth's view, He has committed Himself irrevocably in Jesus Christ. The believer's devotion is not to merely possible commands of God as such, but to God's actual (and gracious) will.

III.

The ascription of moral qualities to God is commonly thought to cause problems for divine command theories of ethics. It is doubted that God, as an agent, can properly be called "good" in the moral sense if He is not subject to a

*[Karl Barth (1886–1968), one of the twentieth century's most important Protestant theologians.—Eds.]

moral law that is not of His own making. For if He is morally good, mustn't He do what is right *because* it is right? And how can He do that, if what's right is right because He wills it? Or it may be charged that divine command theories trivialize the claim that God is good. If "X is (morally) good" means roughly "X does what God wills," then "God is (morally) good" means only that God does what He wills—which is surely much less than people are normally taken to mean when they say that God is (morally) good. In this section I will suggest an answer to these objections.

Surely no analysis of Judeo-Christian ethical discourse can be regarded as adequate which does not provide for a sense in which the believer can seriously assert that God is good. Indeed an adequate analysis should provide a plausible account of what believers do in fact mean when they say, "God is good." I believe that a divine command theory of ethical rightness and wrongness can include such an account. I will try to indicate its chief features.

(1) In saying "God is good" one is normally expressing a favorable emotional attitude toward God. I shall not try to determine whether or not this is part of the meaning of "God is good"; but it is normally, perhaps almost always, at least one of the things one is doing if one says that God is good. If we were to try to be more precise about the type of favorable emotional attitude normally expressed by "God is good," I suspect we would find that the attitude expressed is most commonly one of *gratitude*.

(2) This leads to a second point, which is that when God is called "good" it is very often meant that He is *good to us*, or *good to* the speaker. "Good" is sometimes virtually a synonym for "kind." And for the modified divine command theorist it is not a trivial truth that God is kind. In saying that God is good in the sense of "kind," one presupposes, of course, that there are some things which the beneficiaries of God's goodness value. We need not discuss here whether the beneficiaries must value them independently of their beliefs about God's will. For the modified divine command theorist does admit that there are some things which believers value independently of their beliefs about God's commands. Nothing that the modified divine command theorist says about the meaning of ("right" and) "wrong" implies that it is a trivial truth that God bestows on His creatures things that they value.

(3) I would not suggest that the descriptive force of "good" as applied to God is exhausted by the notion of kindness. "God is good" must be taken in many contexts as ascribing to God, rather generally, qualities of character which the believing speaker regards as virtues in human beings. Among such qualities might be faithfulness, ethical consistency, a forgiving disposition, and, in general, various aspects of love, as well as kindness. Not that there is some definite list of qualities, the ascription of which to God is clearly implied by the claim that God is good. But saying that God is good normally commits one to the position that God has some important set of qualities which one regards as virtues in human beings.

(4) It will not be thought that God has *all* the qualities which are virtues in human beings. Some such qualities are logically inapplicable to a being such as God is supposed to be. For example, aside from certain complications

arising from the doctrine of the incarnation, it would be logically inappropriate to speak of God as controlling His sexual desires. (He doesn't have any.) And given some widely held conceptions of God and his relation to the world, it would hardly make sense to speak of Him as *courageous*. For if He is impassible* and has predetermined absolutely everything that happens, He has no risks to face and cannot endure (because He cannot suffer) pain or displeasure. . . .

(5) If we accept a divine command theory of ethical rightness and wrongness, I think we shall have to say that *dutifulness* is a human virtue which, like sexual chastity, is logically inapplicable to God. God cannot either do or fail to do His duty, since He does not have a duty—at least not in the most important sense in which human beings have a duty. For He is not subject to a moral law not of His own making. Dutifulness is one virtuous disposition which men can have that God cannot have. But there are other virtuous dispositions which God can have as well as men. Love, for instance. It hardly makes sense to say that God does what He does *because* it is right. But it does not follow that God cannot have any reason for doing what He does. It does not even follow that He cannot have reasons of a type on which it would be morally virtuous for a man to act. For example, He might do something because He knew it would make His creatures happier.

(6) The modified divine command theorist must deny that in calling God "good" one presupposes a standard of moral rightness and wrongness superior to the will of God, by reference to which it is determined whether God's character is virtuous or not. And I think he can consistently deny that. He can say that morally virtuous and vicious qualities of character are those which agree and conflict, respectively, with God's commands, and that it is their agreement or disagreement with God's commands that makes them virtuous or vicious. But the believer normally thinks he has at least a general idea of what qualities of character are in fact virtuous and vicious (approved and disapproved by God). Having such an idea, he can apply the word "good" descriptively to God, meaning that (with some exceptions, as I have noted) God has the qualities which the believer regards as virtues, such as faithfulness and kindness. . . .

STUDY QUESTIONS

1. Consider Browne's claim that the total of human happiness would not increase if everyone were unselfish. Can you think of any reason for disagreeing with this claim?

2. In what sense, according to Browne, is each of us the basic source of what is right or wrong? (Consider, for instance, whether it is up to you to say whether the Ten Commandments are to be followed.)

*[Incapable of suffering pain or emotion.—Eds.]

3. Rachels believes that ethical egoism has "monstrous consequences." Do you agree? Be specific.

4. Why does Rachels reject the view that human beings are basically selfish? Can you think of examples of unselfish behavior?

5. How does Kaye defend act utilitarianism?

6. Does Kaye's essay provide an adequate response to Ewing's objections?

7. How does MacIver defend the morality of the golden rule?

8. To what extent can virtue ethics be reconciled with Gilligan's conception of morality?

9. According to MacIntyre, how are the moral virtues related to social practices?

10. Would MacIntyre's approach to morality be critical of egoism, utilitarianism, or formalism? Give reasons for your response.

11. What is Nielsen's main argument against divine command theories? Does Adams' "modified" version avoid Nielsen's objections to more traditional versions of that theory?

12. How does Adams defend the divine command theory of ethics? Why does he call his view a "modified" divine command theory?

13. Do Nielsen's arguments undermine Adams' version of the divine command theory?

14. In your view, which of the essays in this part provides the best answers to the questions posed in the Preview to Part Nine? Explain and justify your answer.

15. The moral theories in this part assume a conflict between what people want to do and what they ought, morally, to do. Do you think there is such a conflict? If there is, should morality always win?

FURTHER READINGS

Baier, Annette. "The Need for More than Justice." *Canadian Journal of Philosophy*, Supplementary Issue 13, Dec. 1987. [More philosophical than Gilligan, but moves in the same direction.]

Baier, Kurt. *The Moral Point of View*. Ithaca: Cornell University Press, 1958. [Baier's theory in detail.]

Brandt, Richard B. "Toward a Credible Form of Utilitarianism." In G. Nakhnikian and H. Castaneda, eds., *Morality and the Language of Conduct*. Detroit: Wayne State University Press, 1963, pp. 104–145. [A sophisticated defense of utilitarianism.]

Gilligan, Carol. *In a Different Voice*. Cambridge: Harvard University Press, 1982. [A provocative work in which the selection in this volume appears.]

Glickman, Jack, ed. *Moral Philosophy: An Introduction*. New York: St. Martin's Press, 1976. [An excellent collection of major classics in ethics by Plato, Kant, Hume, and Mill, together with modern articles on each of their philosophies.]

Helm, P., ed. *Divine Commands and Morality*. New York: Oxford University Press, 1981. [A useful collection of essays.]

Locke, Don. "The Trivializability of Universalizability." *Philosophical Review* 77 (1968), 25–45. [Argues that ethical rules degenerate into trivialities and hence are useless.]

MacIntyre, Alasdair. *After Virtue.* Notre Dame: Notre Dame University Press, 1981.

McCloskey, H. J. "An Examination of Restricted Utilitarianism." *Philosophical Review* 66 (1957), 466–485. [A critique of act utilitarianism.]

Medlin, Brian. "Ultimate Principles and Ethical Egoism." *Australasian Journal of Philosophy* 35 (1957), 111–118. [Attempts to show that ethical egoism is logically incoherent.]

Nielsen, Kai. "Why Should I Be Moral?" *Methodos* 15 (1963), 275–306. [Deals with the question of whether it is rational to be moral.]

Rand, Ayn. *The Virtue of Selfishness.* New York: New American Library, 1964. [A defense of egoism from a libertarian viewpoint.]

Rawls, John. "Two Concepts of Rules." *Philosophical Review* 64 (1955), 3–32. [A classic paper which sets out the distinction between two kinds of utilitarianisms in a lucid way.]

Singer, Marcus George. *Generalization in Ethics.* New York: Knopf, 1961. [An important modern defense of a Kantian moral theory.]

Smart, J. J. C. "Extreme and Restricted Utilitarianism." *The Philosophical Quarterly* 6 (1956), 344–354. [A significant defense of utilitarianism.]

Williams, Bernard Arthur Owen. *Morality: An Introduction to Ethics.* New York: Harper & Row, 1972. [Especially interesting for its critique of utilitarianism, egoism, and subjectivism.]

PART TEN

ETHICAL JUDGMENTS

PREVIEW

*I*t seems obvious that there is little, if any, agreement on ethical matters in our society. Ethical controversies involving the pros and cons of abortion, censorship, pornography, and so forth generate lots of heat but little light. This has not always been true. Why is there so much disagreement about ethics today?

This question takes on added significance if we contrast the situation of ethics with that of other areas, for example, science. To some extent, scientists agree on what the facts are, what theories are better than others, what the evidence is, what evidence is irrelevant, and so on. Are scientists luckier or smarter than people who engage in ethical debate? Or is there something about ethics itself which makes disagreement unavoidable?

One way of posing the question about the status of ethical judgments is this: What is ethics (or an ethical theory or judgment) about? Science is about the world. That is, the subject matter of physics is the physical universe. The subject matter of sociology is society. What is the subject matter of ethics?

According to some writers, ethics is about the properties of actions, events, and states of affairs that exist in the world. When, for example, we make ethical judgments about murder, we are saying something about the goodness or badness of taking a human life. The action of killing someone has "objective" properties. Similarly, the table I see has objective properties: It is brown and rectangular, for example.

It is true that we may not have discovered what the properties of any particular moral action, event, or state of affairs are. For example, we may not know whether abortion is good or bad, but it is one or the other whether we know it or not. And of course we may be mistaken in our beliefs about what the ethical properties of any action are; but this only shows that we have not discovered the correct property. According to this view of ethical judgments, we can explain widespread ethical disagreement by saying that we have not discovered which moral properties certain kinds of actions, such as abortions, have.

There are other authors who think that ethical judgments are not about the properties of actions, events, and objects but rather about certain states of mind of human beings. More specifically, ethical subjectivism holds that ethical judgments refer directly to certain feelings, attitudes, and beliefs of individuals or groups, namely, feelings of approval or disapproval with regard to some person or action or quality, etc. (and not to those persons, actions, or questions themselves). Ethical judgments like "Abortion is immoral" refer to my own feelings and opinions, or the feelings of many individuals, and not to anything in the act of abortion itself.

There is another view, closely related to but not to be confused with this view. It is the view that ethical judgments are not about anything. And they are not about anything because they are cognitively meaningless. They are mere expressions of feelings, more like a grunt than a judgment.

According to the second and third views, ethical disagreement results from the fact that people have different feelings and attitudes about acts like abortion. If you want ethical agreement on this view, all you have to do is influence people to have the same attitude. For the first view, it is important that ethical agreement be a result of the discovery of what the correct properties of an action are. Here again the analogy with the table is useful. People agree that the table is rectangular because they see that it is. If someone conditioned everybody to believe that circles were rectangles, we would have agreement but it wouldn't count. Similarly, for this view, reaching ethical agreement is not enough. The agreement has to be a result of finding out whether an action is really right or wrong.

Another reason for ethical disagreement is the variety of moral standards, theories, beliefs, and opinions which people hold (implicitly or explicitly). For utilitarians, some abortions may be right and others wrong. For a religious person, all abortions may be wrong. For some people, what's right or wrong, good or bad, differs from one time to another or from one place to another. Their motto might be "When in Rome do as the Romans do." This view holds that there is no one moral standard that is correct or applicable to all people, at all times, and in all places. There are many equally correct standards, depending on where and who you are. Of course, others deny that this is so. They claim that there is only one correct moral standard which is applicable to everyone, everywhere.

This discussion leads us to the two main questions of this part. Before we formulate them, it should be noted that in inquiring about such matters, we are not asking: What sorts of things or acts are good or bad, or which acts are right or wrong? We are not asking for a standard of conduct. That was the subject matter of Part Nine. Rather, in asking such questions, we are asking about the *status* of ethical judgments—that is, assertions of the form 'X is right' and 'X is wrong,' and so on. When anyone utters such a judgment, what is she/he doing? Is she/he making an assertion of fact, or just expressing his/her feelings? Is she/he stating a truth that is meant to apply to everyone? This leads us to the two main questions of this part.

Main Questions

These main questions are:

What is the status of ethical judgments—that is, assertions that something is good or bad, right or wrong?

1. Are ethical judgments objective or subjective? That is, do they assert something about actual actions or states of affairs? Or do they merely assert or express the feelings and tastes of those who utter them?

2. Are ethical judgments absolute or relative? That is, are any ethical judgments (even if not all) meant to be universally applicable? Or are all of them relative to different societies at different times and places?

Answers

We may now explicitly state the answers to our two main questions. These are:

1a. Ethical objectivism: Ethical judgments which employ terms like *good, bad, right, wrong* refer to objective properties of actions, events, and states of affairs.

1b. Ethical subjectivism: Ethical judgments refer directly to certain feelings, attitudes, and beliefs of individuals or groups, namely, feelings of approval or disapproval with regard to some person, action or quality—and not to those persons or actions themselves.

1c. Emotivism: Ethical judgments are not about anything; they are mere expressions of feelings, more like a grunt than a judgment, pertaining either to actions or a person's attitude. (Blanshard refers to this view in selection 50, somewhat misleadingly, as the new subjectivism.)

2a. Ethical absolutism: There is only *one correct* moral standard which is applicable to all people, all times and all places, even if there are, in fact, many conflicting standards which people adhere to.

2b. Ethical relativism: There is no one moral standard that is correct or applicable to all people at all times and in all places. There are many equally correct standards, depending upon where and who you are.

Let us use our abortion example to illustrate these views.

For the objectivist, to say that abortion is wrong is to say something which is either correct or incorrect, just as to say that the table is brown is to say something which is either correct or incorrect.

For the subjectivist, to say that abortion is wrong is to say that some individual or group has certain feelings of disapproval regarding abortion.

For the emotivist, to say that abortion is wrong is merely to express a feeling and not to say anything which has any literal meaning. Thus, uttering the words "abortion is wrong" is more like grunting (or whatever) than like asserting.

For the absolutist, to say that abortion is wrong is to say that it is wrong for everyone, at all times, in all places, and presumably in all circumstances.

For the relativist, to say that abortion is wrong is to say that some individual or group accepts a moral code or standard according to which it is deemed to be wrong. If some other individual or group accepts a different standard or code, abortion need not be wrong for that individual or group.

Selections

The answers to our main questions are represented as follows:

Question	Answer	Selection
(1)	(1b) Ethical subjectivism	49
(1)	(1c) Emotivism	49*
	(1a) Ethical objectivism [and critique of (1b), (1c)]	50
(2)	(2b) Ethical relativism	51
(2)	(2a) Ethical absolutism [and critique of (2b)]	52

*[The author of selection 49 at certain places seems to advocate subjectivism. But elsewhere he says things which indicate that he really holds the position of emotivism.]

49 / Science and Ethics

BERTRAND RUSSELL

Bertrand Russell (1872–1980) was one of the century's outstanding philosophers. The author of over 50 books on everything from logic to politics, he was also a noted political activist and pacifist. He revolutionized logic and had a major influence on Anglo-American philosophy.

[I. THE TWO PARTS OF ETHICS]

*T*he study of ethics, traditionally, consists of two parts, one concerned with moral rules, the other with what is good on its own account. Rules of conduct, many of which have a ritual origin, play a great part in the lives of savages and primitive peoples. It is forbidden to eat out of the chief's dish, or to seethe the kid in its mother's milk; it is commanded to offer sacrifices to the gods, which, at a certain stage of development, are thought most acceptable if they are human beings. Other moral rules, such as the prohibition of murder and theft, have a more obvious social utility, and survive the decay of the primitive theological systems with which they were originally associated. But as men grow more reflective there is a tendency to lay less stress on rules and more on states of mind. This comes from two sources—philosophy and mystical religion. We are all familiar with passages in the prophets and the gospels in which purity of heart is set above meticulous observance of the Law; and St. Paul's famous praise of charity, or love, teaches the same principle. . . .

One of the ways in which the need of appealing to external rules of conduct has been avoided has been the belief in "conscience," which has been especially important in Protestant ethics. It has been supposed that God reveals to each human heart what is right and what is wrong, so that, in order to avoid sin, we have only to listen to the inner voice. There are, however, two difficulties in this theory: first, that conscience says different things to different people; secondly, that the study of the unconscious has given us an understanding of the mundane causes of conscientious feelings.

As to the different deliverances of conscience: George III's conscience told him that he must not grant Catholic Emancipation, as, if he did, he would have committed perjury in taking the Coronation Oath, but later monarchs have had no such scruples. Conscience leads some to condemn the spoliation of the rich by the poor, as advocated by communists; and others to condemn exploitation of the poor by the rich, as practiced by capitalists. It tells one man that he ought to defend his country in case of invasion, while it tells another that all participation in warfare is wicked. During the War, the authorities, few

497

of whom had studied ethics, found conscience very puzzling, and were led to some curious decisions, such as that a man might have conscientious scruples against fighting himself, but not against working on the fields so as to make possible the conscription of another man. They held also that, while conscience might disapprove of all war it could not, failing that extreme position, disapprove of the war then in progress. Those who, for whatever reason, thought it wrong to fight, were compelled to state their position in terms of this somewhat primitive and unscientific conception of "conscience."

The diversity in the deliverances of conscience is what is to be expected when its origin is understood. In early youth, certain classes of acts meet with approval and others with disapproval; and by the normal process of association, pleasure and discomfort gradually attach themselves to the acts, and not merely to the approval and disapproval respectively produced by them. As time goes on, we may forget all about our early moral training, but we shall still feel uncomfortable about certain kinds of actions, while others will give us a glow of virtue. To introspection, these feelings are mysterious, since we no longer remember the circumstances which originally caused them; and therefore it is natural to attribute them to the voice of God in the heart. But in fact conscience is a product of education, and can be trained to approve or disapprove, in the great majority of mankind, as educators may see fit. While, therefore, it is right to wish to liberate ethics from external moral rules, this can hardly be satisfactorily achieved by means of the notion of "conscience."

Philosophers, by a different road, have arrived at a different position in which, also, moral rules of conduct have a subordinate place. They have framed the concept of the Good, by which they mean (roughly speaking) that which, in itself and apart from its consequences, we should wish to see existing—or, if they are theists, that which is pleasing to God. Most people would agree that happiness is preferable to unhappiness, friendliness to unfriendliness, and so on. Moral rules, according to this view, are justified if they promote the existence of what is good on its own account, but not otherwise. The prohibition of murder, in the vast majority of cases, can be justified by its effects, but the practice of burning widows on their husband's funeral pyre cannot. The former rule, therefore, should be retained, but not the latter. Even the best moral rules, however, will have *some* exceptions, since no class of action *always* has bad results. We have thus three different senses in which an act may be ethically commendable: (1) It may be in accordance with the received moral code; (2) it may be sincerely intended to have good effects; (3) it may in fact have good effects. The third sense, however, is generally considered inadmissible in morals. According to orthodox theology, Judas Iscariot's act of betrayal had good consequences, since it was necessary for the Atonement; but it was not on this account laudable.

Different philosophers have formed different conceptions of the Good. Some hold that it consists in the knowledge and love of God; others in universal love; others in the enjoyment of beauty; and yet others in pleasure. The Good once defined, the rest of ethics follows: We ought to act in the way we believe most likely to create as much good as possible, and as little as possible of its correlative evil. The framing of moral rules, so long as the ultimate Good is supposed known, is matter for science. For example: Should capital punishment be inflicted for theft, or only for murder, or not at all? Jeremy Bentham, who considered pleasure to be the Good, devoted himself to working out what criminal code would most promote pleasure, and concluded that it ought to be much less severe than that prevailing in his day. All this, except the proposition that pleasure is the Good, comes within the sphere of science.

But when we try to be definite as to what we mean when we say that this or that is "the Good," we find ourselves involved in very great difficulties. Bentham's creed that pleasure is the Good roused furious opposition, and was said to be a pig's philosophy. Neither he nor his opponents could advance any argument. In a scientific question, evidence can be adduced on both sides, and in the end one side is seen to have the better case—or, if this does not happen, the question is left undecided. But in a question as to whether this or that is the ultimate Good, there is no evidence either way; each disputant can only appeal to his own emotions, and employ such rhetorical devices as shall rouse similar emotions in others. . . .

[II. ETHICS, THE GOOD, AND DESIRES]

Questions as to "values"—that is to say, as to what is good or bad on its own account, independently of its effects—lie outside the domain of science, as the defenders of religion emphatically assert. I think that in this they are right, but I draw the further conclusion, which they do not draw, that questions as to "values" lie wholly outside the domain of knowledge. That is to say, when we assert that this or that has "value," we are giving expression to our own emotions, not to a fact which would still be true if our personal feelings were different. To make this clear, we must try to analyze the conception of the Good.

It is obvious, to begin with, that the whole idea of good and bad has some connection with desire. *Prima facie,** anything that we all desire is "good," and anything that we all dread is "bad." If we all agreed in our desires, the matter could be left there, but unfortunately our desires conflict. If I say "What I want is good," my neighbor will say "No, what I want." Ethics is an attempt—though not, I think, a successful one—to escape from this subjectivity. I shall naturally try to show, in my dispute with my neighbor, that my desires have some quality which makes them more worthy of respect than his. If I want to preserve a right of way, I shall appeal to the landless inhabitants of the district; but he, on his side, will appeal to the landowners. I shall say "What use is the beauty of the countryside if no one sees it?" He will retort "What beauty will be left if trippers are allowed to spread devastation?" Each tries to enlist allies by showing that his own desires harmonize with those of other people. When

*[On the face of it.—Eds.]

this is obviously impossible, as in the case of a burglar, the man is condemned by public opinion, and his ethical status is that of a sinner. . . .

Ethics is an attempt to give universal, and not merely personal, importance to certain of our desires. I say "certain" of our desires, because in regard to some of them this is obviously impossible, as we saw in the case of the burglar. The man who makes money on the Stock Exchange by means of some secret knowledge does not wish others to be equally well informed: Truth (in so far as he values it) is for him a private possession, not the general human good that it is for the philosopher. The philosopher may, it is true, sink to the level of the stock-jobber, as when he claims priority for a discovery. But this is a lapse: In his purely philosophic capacity, he wants only to enjoy the contemplation of Truth, in doing which he in no way interferes with others who wish to do likewise.

To seem to give universal importance to our desires—which is the business of ethics—may be attempted from two points of view, that of the legislator and that of the preacher. Let us take the legislator first.

I will assume, for the sake of argument, that the legislator is personally disinterested. That is to say, when he recognizes one of his desires as being concerned only with his own welfare, he does not let it influence him in framing the laws; for example, his code is not designed to increase his personal fortune. But he has other desires which seem to him impersonal. He may believe in an ordered hierarchy from king to peasant, or from mineowner to black indentured laborer. He may believe that women should be submissive to men. He may hold that the spread of knowledge in the lower classes is dangerous. And so on and so on. He will then, if he can, so construct his code that conduct promoting the ends which he values shall, as far as possible, be in accordance with individual self-interest; and he will establish a system of moral instruction which will, where it succeeds, make men feel wicked if they pursue other purposes than his.[1] Thus "virtue" will come to be in fact, though not in subjective estimation, subservience to the desires of the legislator, in so far as he himself considers these desires worthy to be universalized.

The standpoint and method of the preacher are necessarily somewhat different, because he does not control the machinery of the State, and therefore cannot produce an artificial harmony between his desires and those of others. His only method is to try to rouse in others the same desires that he feels himself, and for this purpose his appeal must be to the emotions. Thus Ruskin caused people to like Gothic architecture, not by argument, but by the moving effect of rhythmical prose. *Uncle Tom's Cabin* helped to make people think slavery an evil by causing them to imagine themselves as slaves. Every attempt to persuade people that something is good (or bad) in itself, and not

---

[1]Compare the following advice by a contemporary of Aristotle (Chinese, not Greek): "A ruler should not listen to those who believe in people having opinions of their own and in the importance of the individual. Such teachings cause men to withdraw to quiet places and hide away in caves or on mountains, there to rail at the prevailing government, sneer at those in authority, belittle the importance of rank and emoluments, and despise all who hold official posts." Waley, *The Way and Its Power*, p. 37.

merely in its effects, depends upon the art of rousing feelings, not upon an appeal to evidence. In every case the preacher's skill consists in creating in others emotions similar to his own—or dissimilar, if he is a hypocrite. I am not saying this as a criticism of the preacher, but as an analysis of the essential character of his activity.

[III. ETHICAL JUDGMENTS]

When a man says "This is good in itself," he *seems* to be making a statement, just as much as if he said "This is square" or "This is sweet." I believe this to be a mistake. I think that what the man really means is: "I wish everybody to desire this," or rather "Would that everybody desired this." If what he says is interpreted as a statement, it is merely an affirmation of his own personal wish; if, on the other hand, it is interpreted in a general way, it states nothing, but merely desires something. The wish, as an occurrence, is personal, but what it desires is universal. It is, I think, this curious interlocking of the particular and the universal which has caused so much confusion in ethics.

The matter may perhaps become clearer by contrasting an ethical sentence with one which makes a statement. If I say "All Chinese are Buddhists," I can be refuted by the production of a Chinese Christian or Mohammedan. If I say "I believe that all Chinese are Buddhists," I cannot be refuted by any evidence from China, but only by evidence that I do not believe what I say; for what I am asserting is only something about my own state of mind. If, now, a philosopher says "Beauty is good," I may interpret him as meaning either "Would that everybody loved the beautiful" (which corresponds to "All Chinese are Buddhists") or "I wish that everybody loved the beautiful" (which corresponds to "I believe that all Chinese are Buddhists"). The first of these makes no assertion, but expresses a wish; since it affirms nothing, it is logically impossible that there should be evidence for or against it, or for it to possess either truth or falsehood. The second sentence, instead of being merely optative, does make a statement, but it is one about the philosopher's state of mind, and it could only be refuted by evidence that he does not have the wish that he says he has. This second sentence does not belong to ethics, but to psychology or biography. The first sentence, which does belong to ethics, expresses a desire for something, but asserts nothing.

Ethics, if the above analysis is correct, contains no statements, whether true or false, but consists of desires of a certain general kind, namely such as are concerned with the desires of mankind in general—and of gods, angels, and devils, if they exist. Science can discuss the causes of desires, and the means for realizing them, but it cannot contain any genuinely ethical sentences, because it is concerned with what is true or false.

The theory which I have been advocating is a form of the doctrine which is called the "subjectivity" of values. This doctrine consists in maintaining that, if two men differ about values, there is not a disagreement as to any kind of truth, but a difference of taste. If one man says "Oysters are good" and another says "I think they are bad," we recognize that there is nothing to argue about. The theory in question holds that all differences as to values are of this sort, although we do not naturally think them so when we are dealing with matters that seem to us more exalted than oysters. The chief ground for adopting this view is the complete impossibility of finding any arguments to prove that this or that has intrinsic value. If we all agreed, we might hold that we know values by intuition. We cannot *prove*, to a color-blind man, that grass is green and not red. But there are various ways of proving to him that he lacks a power of discrimination which most men possess, whereas in the case of values there are no such ways, and disagreements are much more frequent than in the case of colors. Since no way can be even imagined for deciding a difference as to values, the conclusion is forced upon us that the difference is one of tastes, not one as to any objective truth. . . .

[IV. OBJECTIONS AND REPLIES]

Those who believe in "objective" values often contend that the view which I have been advocating has immoral consequences. This seems to me to be due to faulty reasoning. There are, as has already been said, certain ethical consequences of the doctrine of subjective values, of which the most important is the rejection of vindictive punishment and the notion of "sin." But the more general consequences which are feared, such as the decay of all sense of moral obligation, are not to be logically deduced. Moral obligation, if it is to influence conduct, must consist not merely of a belief, but of a desire. The desire, I may be told, is the desire to be "good" in a sense which I no longer allow. But when we analyze the desire to be "good" it generally resolves itself into a desire to be approved, or, alternatively, to act so as to bring about certain general consequences which we desire. We have wishes which are not purely personal, and if we had not, no amount of ethical teaching would influence our conduct except through fear of disapproval. The sort of life that most of us admire is one which is guided by large impersonal desires; now such desires can, no doubt, be encouraged by example, education, and knowledge, but they can hardly be created by the mere abstract belief that they are good, nor discouraged by an analysis of what is meant by the word "good."

When we contemplate the human race, we may desire that it should be happy, or healthy, or intelligent, or warlike, and so on. Any one of these desires, if it is strong, will produce its own morality; but if we have no such general desire, our conduct, whatever our ethic may be, will only serve social purposes insofar as self-interest and the interests of society are in harmony. It is the business of wise institutions to create such harmony as far as possible, and for the rest, whatever may be our theoretical definition of value, we must depend upon the existence of impersonal desires. When you meet a man with whom you have a fundamental ethical disagreement—for example, if you think that all men count equally, while he selects a class as alone important—you will find yourself no better able to cope with him if you believe in objective values than if you do not. In either case, you can only influence his conduct through influencing his desires: If you succeed in that, his ethic will change, and if not, not.

Some people feel that if a general desire, say for the happiness of mankind, has not the sanction of absolute good, it is in some way irrational. This is due to a lingering belief in objective values. A desire cannot, in itself, be either rational or irrational. It may conflict with other desires, and therefore lead to unhappiness; it may rouse opposition in others, and therefore be incapable of gratification. But it cannot be considered "irrational" merely because no reason can be given for feeling it. We may desire A because it is a means to B, but in the end, when we have done with mere means, we must come to something which we desire for no reason, but not on that account "irrationally." All systems of ethics embody the desires of those who advocate them, but this fact is concealed in a mist of words. Our desires are, in fact, more general and less purely selfish than many moralists imagine; if it were not so, no theory of ethics would make moral improvement possible. It is, in fact, not by ethical theory, but by the cultivation of large and generous desires through intelligence, happiness, and freedom from fear, that men can be brought to act more than they do at present in a manner that is consistent with the general happiness of mankind. Whatever our definition of the "Good," and whether we believe it to be subjective or objective, those who do not desire the happiness of mankind will not endeavor to further it, while those who do desire it will do what they can to bring it about.

I conclude that, while it is true that science cannot decide questions of value, that is because they cannot be intellectually decided at all, and lie outside the realm of truth and falsehood. Whatever knowledge is attainable must be attained by scientific methods; and what science cannot discover, mankind cannot know.

50 / *The New Subjectivism in Ethics*

BRAND BLANSHARD

Brand Blanshard (1892–1987) was the Sterling Professor of Philosophy at Yale University. He was one of this century's major philosophical idealists, who defended this influential philosophy in epistemology, metaphysics, and ethics. He also defended traditional rationalism in ethics and culture against the positivists.

[I. WHAT IS THE NEW SUBJECTIVISM?]

By the new subjectivism in ethics I mean the view that when anyone says "This is right" or "This is good," he is only expressing his own feeling; he is not asserting anything true or false, because he is not asserting or judging at all; he is really making an exclamation that expresses a favorable feeling.

This view has recently come into much favor. . . . Why is it that the theory has come into so rapid a popularity? Is it because moralists of insight have been making a fresh and searching examination of moral experience and its expression? No, I think not. [It is because a movement in philosophy has put forth a theory of knowledge which had implications for ethics. This movement is logical positivism.] If the new view has become popular in ethics, it is because certain persons who were at work in the theory of knowledge arrived at a new view *there*, and found, on thinking it out, that it required the new view in ethics; the view comes less from ethical analysis than from logical positivism.

As positivists, these writers held that every judgment belongs to one or the other of two types. On the one hand, it may be *a priori* or necessary. But then it is always analytic; that is, it unpacks in its predicate part of all of its subject. Can we safely say that 7 + 5 make 12? Yes, because 12 is what we mean by "7 + 5." On the other hand, the judgment may be empirical, and then, if we are to verify it, we can no longer look to our meanings only; it refers to sense experience and there we must look for its warrant. Having arrived at this division of judgments, the positivists raised the question where value judgments fall. The judgment that knowledge is good, for example, did not seem to be analytic; the value that knowledge might have did not seem to be part of our concept of knowledge. But neither was the statement empirical, for goodness was not a quality like red or squeaky that could be seen or heard. What were they to do, then, with these awkward judgments of value? To find a place for them in their theory of knowledge would require them to revise the theory radically, and yet that theory was what they regarded as their most important discovery. It appeared that the theory could be saved in one way only. If it could be shown that judgments of good and bad were not judgments at all, that they asserted nothing true or false, but merely expressed emotions like "Hurrah" or "Fiddlesticks," then these wayward judgments would cease from troubling and weary heads could be at rest. This is the course the positivists took. They explained value judgments by explaining them away.

Now I do not think their view will do. But before discussing it, I should like to record one vote of thanks to them for the clarity with which they have stated their case. It has been said of John Stuart Mill* that he wrote so clearly that he could be found out. This theory has been put so clearly and precisely that it deserves criticism of the same kind, and this I will do my best to supply. The theory claims to show by analysis that when we say "That is good," we do

---

*[A nineteenth-century British philosopher.—Eds.]

not mean to assert a character of the subject of which we are thinking. I shall argue that we do mean to do just that.

[II. CRITICISM OF THIS VIEW]

Let us work through an example, and the simpler and commoner the better. There is perhaps no value statement on which people would more universally agree than the statement that intense pain is bad. Let us take a set of circumstances in which I happen to be interested on the legislative side and in which I think every one of us might naturally make such a statement. We come upon a rabbit that has been caught in one of the brutal traps in common use. There are signs that it has struggled for days to escape and that in a frenzy of hunger, pain, and fear, it has all but eaten off its own leg. The attempt failed: The animal is now dead. As we think of the long and excruciating pain it must have suffered, we are very likely to say "It was a bad thing that the little animal should suffer so." The positivist tells us that when we say this we are only expressing our present emotion. I hold, on the contrary, that we mean to assert something of the animal's experience itself, namely, that it was bad— bad when and as it occurred.

[1.] Consider what follows from the positivist view. In that view, nothing good or bad happened in the case until I came on the scene and made my remark. For what I express in my remark is something going on in me at the time, and that of course did not exist until I did come on the scene. The pain of the rabbit was not itself bad; nothing evil was happening when that pain was being endured; badness, in the only sense in which it is involved at all, waited for its appearance till I came and looked and felt. Now that this is at odds with our meaning may be shown as follows. Let us put to ourselves the hypothesis that we had not come on the scene and that the rabbit never was discovered. Are we prepared to say that in that case nothing bad occurred in the sense in which we said it did? Clearly not. Indeed we should say, on the contrary, that the accident of our later discovery made no difference whatever to the badness of the animal's pain, that it would have been every whit as bad whether a chance passer-by happened later to discover the body and feel repugnance or not. If so, then it is clear that in saying the suffering was bad we are not expressing our feelings only. We are saying that the pain was bad when and as it occurred and before anyone took an attitude toward it.

[2.] The first argument is thus an ideal experiment in which we use the method of difference. It removes our present expression and shows that the badness we meant would not be affected by this, whereas on positivist grounds it should be. The second argument applies the method in the reverse way. It ideally removes the past event, and shows that this would render false what we mean to say, whereas on positivist grounds it should not. Let us suppose that the animal did not in fact fall into the trap and did not suffer at all, but that we mistakenly believe it did, and say as before that its suffering was an evil thing. On the positivist theory, everything I sought to express by calling it evil in the first case is still present in the second. In the only sense in which badness is involved at all, whatever was bad in the first case is still present in its entirety, since all that is expressed in either case is a state of feeling, and that feeling is still there. And our question is, is such an implication consistent with what we meant? Clearly it is not. If anyone asked us, after we made the remark that the suffering was a bad thing, whether we should think it relevant to what we said to learn that the incident had never occurred and no pain had been suffered at all, we should say that it made all the difference in the world, that what we were asserting to be bad was precisely the suffering we thought had occurred back there, that if this had not occurred, there was nothing left to be bad, and that our assertion was in that case mistaken. The suggestion that in saying something evil had occurred we were after all making no mistake, because we had never meant anyhow to say anything about the past suffering, seems to me merely frivolous. If we did not mean to say this, why should we be so relieved on finding that the suffering had not occurred? On the theory before us, such relief would be groundless, for in that suffering itself there was nothing bad at all, and hence in its nonoccurrence there would be nothing to be relieved about. The positivist theory would here distort our meaning beyond recognition.

So far as I can see, there is only one way out for the positivist. He holds that goodness and badness lie in feelings of approval or disapproval. And there is a way in which he might hold that badness did in this case precede our own feeling of disapproval without belonging to the pain itself. The pain in itself was neutral, but unfortunately the rabbit, on no grounds at all, took up toward this neutral object an attitude of disapproval, and that made it for the first time, and in the only intelligible sense, bad. This way of escape is theoretically possible, but since it has grave difficulties of its own and has not, so far as I know, been urged by positivists, it is perhaps best not to spend time over it.

[3.] I come now to a third argument, which again is very simple. When we come upon the rabbit and make our remark about its suffering being a bad thing, we presumably make it with some feeling; the positivists are plainly right in saying that such remarks do usually express feeling. But suppose that a week later we revert to the incident in thought and make our statement again. And suppose that the circumstances have now so changed that the feeling with which we made the remark in the first place has faded. The pathetic evidence is no longer before us; and we are now so fatigued in body and mind that feeling is, as we say, quite dead. In these circumstances, since what was expressed by the remark when first made is, on the theory before us, simply absent, the remark now expresses nothing. It is as empty as the word "Hurrah" would be when there was no enthusiasm behind it. And this seems to me untrue. When we repeat the remark that such suffering was a bad thing, the feeling with which we made it last week may be at or near the vanishing point, but if we were asked whether we meant to say what we did before, we should certainly answer Yes. We should say that we made our point with feeling the first time and little or no feeling the second time, but that it was the same point we were making. And if we can see that what we meant to say remains the same, while the feeling varies from intensity to near zero, it is not the feeling that we primarily meant to express.

[4.] I come now to a fourth consideration. We all believe that toward acts or effects of a certain kind one attitude is fitting and another not; but on the theory before us such a belief would not make sense. Broad and Ross* have lately contended that this fitness is one of the main facts of ethics, and I suspect they are right. But that is not exactly my point. My point is this: Whether there is such fitness or not, we all assume that there is, and if we do, we express in moral judgments more than the subjectivists say we do. Let me illustrate.

In the novel *The House of the Dead*, Dostoyevski tells of his experiences in a Siberian prison camp. Whatever the unhappy inmates of such camps are like today, Dostoyevski's companions were about as grim a lot as can be imagined. "I have heard stories," he writes, "of the most terrible, the most unnatural actions, of the most monstrous murders, told with the most spontaneous, childishly merry laughter." Most of us would say that in this delight at the killing of others or the causing of suffering there is something very unfitting. If we were asked why we thought so, we should say that these things involve great evil and are wrong, and that to take delight in what is evil or wrong is plainly unfitting. Now on the subjectivist view, this answer is ruled out. For before someone takes up an attitude toward death, suffering, or their infliction, they have no moral quality at all. There is therefore nothing about them to which an attitude of approval or condemnation could be fitting. They are in themselves neutral, and, so far as they get a moral quality, they get it only through being invested with it by the attitude of the onlooker. But if that is true, why is any attitude more fitting than any other? Would applause, for example, be fitting if, apart from the applause, there were nothing good to applaud? Would condemnation be fitting if, independently of the condemnation, there were nothing bad to condemn? In such a case, any attitude would be as fitting or unfitting as any other, which means that the notion of fitness has lost all point.

Indeed we are forced to go much farther. If goodness and badness lie in attitudes only and hence are brought into being by them, those men who greeted death and misery with childishly merry laughter are taking the only sensible line. If there is nothing evil in these things, if they get their moral complexion only from our feeling about them, why shouldn't they be greeted with a cheer? To greet them with repulsion would turn what before was neutral into something bad; it would needlessly bring badness into the world; and even on subjectivist assumptions that does not seem very bright. On the other hand, to greet them with delight would convert what before was neutral into something good; it would bring goodness into the world. If I have murdered a man and wish to remove the stain, the way is clear. It is to cry "Hurrah for murder."

*[C. D. Broad (1887–1970), British philosopher; W. D. Ross (1877–1971), British philosopher.—Eds.]

What is the subjectivist to reply? I can only guess. He may point out that the inflicting of death is *not* really neutral before the onlooker takes his attitude, for the man who inflicted the death no doubt himself took an attitude, and thus the act had a moral quality derived from this. But that makes the case more incredible still, for the man who did the act presumably approved it, and if so it was good in the only sense in which anything is good, and then our conviction that the laughter is unfit is more unaccountable still. It may be replied that the victim, too, had his attitude and that since this was unfavorable, the act was not unqualifiedly good. But the answer is plain. Let the killer be expert at his job; let him dispatch his victim instantly before he has time to take an attitude, and then gloat about his perfect crime without ever telling anyone. Then, so far as I can see, his act will be good without any qualification. It would become bad only if someone found out about it and disliked it. And that would be a curiously irrational procedure, since the man's approving of his own killing is in itself just as neutral as the killing that it approves. Why then should anyone dislike it?

It may be replied that we can defend our dislike on this ground that, if the approval of killing were to go unchecked and spread, most men would have to live in insecurity and fear, and these things are undesirable. But surely this reply is not open; these things are not, on the theory, undesirable, for nothing is; in themselves they are neutral. Why then should I disapprove men's living in this state? The answer may come that if other men live in insecurity and fear, I shall in time be infected myself. But even in my own insecurity and fear there is, on the theory before us, nothing bad whatever, and therefore, if I disapprove them, it is without a shadow of ground and with no more fitness in my attitude than if I cordially cheered them. The theory thus conflicts with our judgments of fitness all along the line.

[5.] I come now to a fifth and final difficulty with the theory. It makes mistakes about values impossible. There is a whole nest of inter-connected criticisms here, some of which have been made so often that I shall not develop them again, such as that I can never agree or disagree in opinion with anyone else about an ethical matter, and that in these matters I can never be inconsistent with others or with myself. I am not at all content with the sort of analysis which says that the only contradictions in such cases have regard to facts and that contradictions about value are only differences of feeling. I think that if anyone tells me that having a bicuspid out without an anesthetic is not a bad experience and I say it is a very nasty experience indeed, I am differing with him in opinion, and differing about the degree of badness of the experience. But without pressing this further, let me apply the argument in what is perhaps a fresh direction.

There is an old and merciful distinction that moralists have made for many centuries about conduct—the distinction between what is subjectively and what is objectively right. They have said that in any given situation there is some act which, in view of all the circumstances, would be the best act to do; and this is what would be objectively right. The notion of an objectively right act is the ground of our notion of duty: Our duty is always to find and do this act if we can. But of course we often don't find it. We often hit upon and do acts that we think are the right ones, but we are mistaken; and then our act is only subjectively right. Between these two acts the disparity may be continual; Professor Prichard* suggested that probably few of us in the course of our lives ever succeed in doing *the* right act.

Now so far as I can see, the new subjectivism would abolish this difference at a stroke. Let us take a case. A boy abuses his small brother. We should commonly say "That is wrong, but perhaps he doesn't know any better. By reason of bad teaching and a feeble imagination, he may see nothing wrong in what he is doing, and may even be proud of it. If so, his act may be subjectively right, though it is miles away from what is objectively right." What concerns me about the new subjectivism is that it prohibits this distinction. If the boy feels this way about his act, then it is right in the only sense in which anything is right. The notion of an objective right lying beyond what he has discovered, and which he ought to seek and do, is meaningless. There might, to be sure, be an act that would more generally arouse favorable feelings in others, but that would not make it right for him unless he thought of it and approved it, which he doesn't. Even if he did think of it, it would not be obligatory for him to feel about it in any particular way, since there is nothing in any act, as we have seen, which would make any feeling more suitable than any other.

Now if there is no such thing as an objectively right act, what becomes of the idea of duty? I have suggested that the idea of duty rests on the idea of such an act, since it is always our duty to find that act and do it if we can. But if whatever we feel approval for at the time is right, what is the point of doubting and searching further? Like the little girl in Boston who was asked if she would like to travel, we can answer, "Why should I travel when I'm already there?" If I am reconciled in feeling to my present act, no act I could discover by reflection could be better, and therefore why reflect or seek at all? Such a view seems to me to break the mainspring of duty, to destroy the motive for self-improvement, and to remove the ground for self-criticism. It may be replied that by further reflection I can find an act that would satisfy my feelings more widely than the present one, and that this is the act I should seek. But this reply means either that such general satisfaction is objectively better, which would contradict the theory, or else that, if at the time I don't feel it better, it isn't better, in which case I have no motive for seeking it. When certain self-righteous persons took an inflexible line with Oliver Cromwell,† his very Cromwellian reply was, "Bethink ye, gentlemen, by the bowels of Christ, that ye may be mistaken." It was good advice. I hope nobody will take from me the privilege of finding myself mistaken. I should be sorry to think that the self of thirty years ago was as far along the path as the self of today,

---

*[British philosopher (1870–1947).—Eds.]
†[English revolutionary leader (1599–1658).—Eds.]

merely because he was a smug young jackanapes, or even that the paragon of today has as little room for improvement as would be allowed by his myopic complacency.

[III. CONCLUSION]

One final remark. The great problems of the day are international problems. Has the new subjectivism any bearing upon these problems? I think it has, and a somewhat sinister bearing. I would not suggest, of course, that those who hold the theory are one whit less public-spirited than others; surely there are few who could call themselves citizens of the world with more right (if "rights" have meaning any longer) than Mr. Russell. But Mr. Russell has confessed himself discontented with his ethical theory, and in view of his breadth of concern, one cannot wonder. For its general acceptance would, so far as one can see, be an international disaster. The assumption behind the old League and the new United Nations was that there is such a thing as right and wrong in the conduct of a nation, a right and wrong that do not depend on how it happens to feel at the time. It is implied, for example, that when Japan invaded Manchuria in 1931 she might be wrong, and that by discussion and argument she might be shown to be wrong. It was implied that when the Nazis invaded Poland they might be wrong, even though German public sentiment overwhelmingly approved it. On the theory before us, it would be meaningless to call these nations mistaken; if they felt approval for what they did, then it was right with as complete a justification as could be supplied for the disapproval felt by the rest of the world. In the present dispute between Russia and our own country over southeast Europe, it is nonsense to speak of the right or rational course for either of us to take; if with all the facts before the two parties, each feels approval for its own course, both attitudes are equally justified or unjustified; neither is mistaken; there is no common reason to which they can take an appeal; there are no principles by which an international court could pronounce on the matter; nor would there be any obligation to obey the pronouncement if it were made. This cuts the ground from under any attempt to establish one's case as right or anyone else's case as wrong. So if our friends the subjectivists still hold their theory after I have applied my little ruler to their knuckles, which of course they will, I have but one request to make of them: Don't make a present of it to Mr. Gromyko.*

*[Soviet diplomat (1909–1989).—Eds.]

51 / Anthropology and the Abnormal

RUTH BENEDICT

Ruth Benedict (1887–1948) was a major anthropologist who taught at Columbia University. Stressing the functional nature of societies and their practices, institutions, and values, she argued against racism and defended the need for cultural tolerance and pluralism in the modern world. She also wrote an influential book about Japanese culture.

I. THE ABNORMAL IN DIFFERENT SOCIETIES

*M*odern social anthropology has become more and more a study of the varieties and common elements of cultural environment and the consequences of these in human behavior. For such a study of diverse social orders primitive peoples fortunately provide a laboratory not yet entirely vitiated by the spread of a standardized worldwide civilization. Dyaks and Hopis, Fijians and Yakuts are significant for psychological and sociological study because only among these simpler peoples has there been sufficient isolation to give opportunity for the development of localized social forms. In the higher cultures the standardization of custom and belief over a couple of continents has given a false sense of the inevitability of the particular forms that have gained currency, and we need to turn to a wider survey in order to check the conclusions we hastily base upon this near-universality of familiar customs. Most of the simpler cultures did not gain the wide currency of the one which, out of our experience, we identify with human nature, but this was for various historical reasons, and certainly not for any that gives us as its carriers a monopoly of social good or of social sanity. Modern civilization, from this point of view, becomes not a necessary pinnacle of human achievement but one entry in a long series of possible adjustments.

These adjustments, whether they are in mannerisms like the ways of showing anger, or joy, or grief in any society, or in major human drives like those of sex, prove to be far more variable than experience in any one culture would suggest. In certain fields, such as that of religion or of formal marriage arrangements, these wide limits of variability are well known and can be fairly described. In others it is not yet possible to give a generalized account, but that does not absolve us of the task of indicating the significance of the work that has been done and of the problems that have arisen.

One of these problems relates to the customary modern normal-abnormal categories and our conclusions regarding them. In how far are such categories culturally determined, or in how far can we with assurance regard them as absolute? In how far can we regard inability to function socially as diagnostic of abnormality, or in how far is it necessary to regard this as a function of the culture? . . .

The most spectacular illustrations of the extent to which normality may be culturally defined are those cultures where an abnormality of our culture is the cornerstone of their social structure. It is not possible to do justice to these possibilities in a short discussion. A recent study of an island of northwest Melanesia by Fortune describes a society built upon traits which we regard as beyond the border of paranoia. In this tribe the exogamic groups look upon each other as prime manipulators of black magic, so that one marries always into an enemy group which remains for life one's deadly and unappeasable foes. They look upon a good garden crop as a confession of theft, for everyone is engaged in making magic to induce into his garden the productiveness of his neighbors'; therefore no secrecy in the island is so rigidly insisted upon as the secrecy of a man's harvesting of his yams. Their polite phrase at the acceptance of a gift is, "And if you now poison me, how shall I repay you this present?" Their preoccupation with poisoning is constant; no woman ever leaves her cooking pot for a moment untended. Even the great affinal economic exchanges that are characteristic of this Melanesian culture area are quite altered in Dobu since they are incompatible with this fear and distrust that pervades the culture. . . . They go farther and people the whole world outside their own quarters with such malignant spirits that all-night feasts and ceremonials simply do not occur here. They have even rigorous religiously enforced customs that forbid the sharing of seed even in one family group. Anyone else's food is deadly poison to you, so that communality of stores is out of the question. For some months before harvest the whole society is on the verge of starvation, but if one falls to the temptation and eats up one's seed yams, one is an outcast and a beachcomber for life. There is no coming back. It involves, as a matter of course, divorce and the breaking of all social ties.

Now in this society where no one may work with another and no one may share with another, Fortune describes the individual who was regarded by all his fellows as crazy. He was not one of those who periodically ran amok and, beside himself and frothing at the mouth, fell with a knife upon anyone he could reach. Such behavior they did not regard as putting anyone outside the pale. They did not even put the individuals who were known to be liable to these attacks under any kind of control. They merely fled when they saw the attack coming on and kept out of the way. "He would be all right tomorrow." But there was one man of sunny, kindly disposition who liked work and liked to be helpful. The compulsion was too strong for him to repress it in favor of the opposite tendencies of his culture. Men and women never spoke of him without laughing; he was silly and simple and definitely crazy. Nevertheless, to the ethnologist used to a culture that has, in Christianity, made his type the model of all virtue, he seemed a pleasant fellow.

An even more extreme example, because it is of a culture that has built itself upon a more complex abnormality, is that of the North Pacific Coast of North America. The civilization of the Kwakiutl, at the time when it was first recorded in the last decades of the nineteenth century, was one of the most vigorous in North America. It was built up on an ample economic supply of goods, the fish which furnished their food staple being practically inexhaustible and obtainable with comparatively small labor, and the wood which furnished the material for their houses, their furnishings, and their arts being, with however much labor, always procurable. They lived in coastal villages that compared favorably in size with those of any other American Indians and they kept up constant communication by means of sea-going dug-out canoes.

It was one of the most vigorous and zestful of the aboriginal cultures of North America, with complex crafts and ceremonials, and elaborate and striking arts. It certainly had none of the earmarks of a sick civilization. The tribes of the Northwest Coast had wealth, and exactly in our terms. That is, they had not only a surplus of economic goods, but they made a game of the manipulation of wealth. It was by no means a mere direct transcription of economic needs and the filling of those needs. It involved the idea of capital, of interest, and of conspicuous waste. It was a game with all the binding rules of a game, and a person entered it as a child. His father distributed wealth for him, according to his ability, at a small feast or potlatch, and each gift the receiver was obliged to accept and to return after a short interval with interest that ran to about 100 per cent a year. By the time the child was grown, therefore, he was well launched, a larger potlatch had been given for him on various occasions of exploit or initiation, and he had wealth either out at usury or in his own possession. Nothing in the civilization could be enjoyed without validating it by the distribution of this wealth. Everything that was valued, names and songs as well as material objects were passed down in family lines, but they were always publicly assumed with accompanying sufficient distributions of property. It was the game of validating and exercising all the privileges one could accumulate from one's various forebears, or by gift, or by marriage, that made the chief interest of the culture. Everyone in his degree took part in it, but many, of course, mainly as spectators. In its highest form it was played out between rival chiefs representing not only themselves and their family lines but their communities, and the object of the contest was to glorify oneself and to humiliate one's opponent. On this level of greatness the property involved was no longer represented by blankets, so many thousand of them to a potlatch, but by higher units of value. These higher units were like our bank notes. They were incised copper tablets, each of them named, and having a value that depended upon their illustrious history. This was as high as ten thousand blankets, and to possess one of them, still more to enhance its value at a great potlatch, was one of the greatest glories within the compass of the chiefs of the Northwest Coast. . . .

Every contingency of life was dealt with in . . . two traditional ways. To them the two were equivalent. Whether one fought with weapons or "fought with property," as they say, the same idea was at the bottom of both. In the olden times, they say, they fought with spears, but now they fight with property. One overcomes one's opponents in equivalent fashion in both, matching forces and seeing that one comes out ahead, and one can thumb one's nose at the vanquished rather more satisfactorily at a potlatch than on a battle field. Every occasion in life was noticed, not in its own terms, as a stage in the sex life of the individual or as a climax of joy or of grief, but as furthering this drama of consolidating one's own prestige and bringing shame to one's guests. Whether it was the occasion of the birth of a child, or a daughter's adolescence, or of the marriage of one's son, they were all equivalent raw material for the culture to use for this one traditionally selected end. They were all to raise one's own personal status and to entrench oneself by the humiliation of one's fellows. A girl's adolescence among the Nootka was an event for which her father gathered property from the time she was first able to run about. When she was adolescent he would demonstrate his greatness by an unheard of distribution of these goods, and put down all his rivals. It was not as a fact of the girl's sex life that it figured in their culture, but as the occasion for a major move in the great game of vindicating one's own great-ness and humiliating one's associates.

In their behavior at great bereavements this set of the culture comes out most strongly. Among the Kwakiutl it did not matter whether a relative had died in bed of disease, or by the hand of an enemy; in either case death was an affront to be wiped out by the death of another person. The fact that one had been caused to mourn was proof that one had been put upon. A chief's sister and her daughter had gone up to Victoria, and either because they drank bad whiskey or because their boat capsized they never came back. The chief called together his warriors. "Now, I ask you, tribes, who shall wail? Shall I do it or shall another?" The spokesman answered, of course, "Not you, Chief. Let some other of the tribes." Immediately they set up the war pole to announce their intention of wiping out the injury, and gathered a war party. They set out, and found seven men and two children asleep and killed them. "Then they felt good when they arrived at Sebaa in the evening."

The point which is of interest to us is that in our society those who on that occasion would feel good when they arrived at Sebaa that evening would be the definitely abnormal. There would be some, even in our society, but it is not a recognized and approved mood under the circumstances. On the Northwest Coast those are favored and fortunate to whom that mood under those circumstances is congenial, and those to whom it is repugnant are unlucky. This latter minority can register in their own culture only by doing violence to their congenial responses and acquiring others that are difficult for them. The person, for instance, who, like a Plains Indian whose wife has been taken from him, is too proud to fight, can deal with the Northwest Coast civilization only by ignoring its strongest bents. If he cannot achieve it, he is the deviant in that culture, their instance of abnormality.

This head-hunting that takes place on the Northwest Coast after a death is no matter of blood revenge or of organized vengeance. There is no effort to tie up the subsequent killing with any responsibility on the part of the victim for the death of the person who is being mourned. A chief whose son has died goes visiting wherever his fancy dictates, and he says to his host, "My prince has died today, and you go with him." Then he kills him. In this, according to their interpretation, he acts nobly because he has not been downed. He has thrust back in return. The whole procedure is meaningless without the fundamental paranoid reading of bereavement. Death, like all the other untoward accidents of existence, confounds man's pride and can only be handled in the category of insults. . . .

II. THE CONCLUSION TO BE DRAWN FOR ETHICS

These illustrations, which it has been possible to indicate only in the briefest manner, force upon us the fact that normality is culturally defined. An adult shaped to the drives and standards of either of these cultures, if he were transported into our civilization, would fall into our categories of abnormality. He would be faced with the psychic dilemmas of the socially unavailable. In his own culture, however, he is the pillar of society, the end result of socially inculcated mores, and the problem of personal instability in his case simply does not arise.

No one civilization can possibly utilize in its mores the whole potential range of human behavior. Just as there are great numbers of possible phonetic articulations, and the possibility of language depends on a selection and standardization of a few of these in order that speech communication may be possible at all, so the possibility of organized behavior of every sort, from the fashions of local dress and houses to the dicta of a people's ethics and religion, depends upon a similar selection among the possible behavior traits. In the field of recognized economic obligations or sex tabus this selection is as non-rational and subconscious a process as it is in the field of phonetics. It is a process which goes on in the group for long periods of time and is historically conditioned by innumerable accidents of isolation or of contact of peoples. In any comprehensive study of psychology, the selection that different cultures have made in the course of history within the great circumference of potential behavior is of great significance.

Every society, beginning with some slight inclination in one direction or another, carries its preference farther and farther, integrating itself more and more completely upon its chosen basis, and discarding those types of behavior that are uncongenial. Most of those organizations of personality that seem to us most incontrovertibly abnormal have been used by different civilizations in the very foundations of their institutional life. Conversely the most valued traits of our normal individuals have been looked on in differently organized cultures as aberrant. Normality, in short, within a very wide range, is culturally defined. It is primarily a term for the socially elaborated segment of human behavior in any culture; and abnormality, a term for the segment that that particular civilization does not use. The very eyes with which we see the problem are conditioned by the long traditional habits of our own society.

It is a point that has been made more often in relation to ethics than in relation to psychiatry. We do not any longer make the mistake of deriving the morality of our own locality and decade directly from the inevitable constitution of human nature. We do not elevate it to the dignity of a first principle. We recognize that morality differs in every society, and is a convenient term for socially approved habits. Mankind has always preferred to say, "It is a morally good," rather than "It is habitual," and the fact of this preference is matter enough for a critical science of ethics. But historically the two phrases are synonymous.

The concept of the normal is properly a variant of the concept of the good. It is that which society has approved. A normal action is one which falls well within the limits of expected behavior for a particular society. Its variability among different peoples is essentially a function of the variability of the behavior patterns that different societies have created for themselves, and can never be wholly divorced from a consideration of culturally institutionalized types of behavior.

Each culture is a more or less elaborate working out of the potentialities of the segment it has chosen. In so far as a civilization is well integrated and consistent within itself, it will tend to carry farther and farther, according to its nature, its initial impulse toward a particular type of action, and from the point of view of any other culture those elaborations will include more and more extreme and aberrant traits.

Each of these traits, in proportion as it reinforces the chosen behavior patterns of that culture, is for that culture normal. Those individuals to whom it is congenial either congenitally, or as the result of childhood sets, are accorded prestige in that culture, and are not visited with the social contempt or disapproval which their traits would call down upon them in a society that was differently organized. On the other hand, those individuals whose characteristics are not congenial to the selected type of human behavior in that community are the deviants, no matter how valued their personality traits may be in a contrasted civilization. . . .

The problem of understanding abnormal human behavior in any absolute sense independent of cultural factors is still far in the future. The categories of borderline behavior which we derive from the study of the neuroses and psychoses of our civilization are categories of prevailing local types of instability. They give much information about the stresses and strains of Western civilization, but no final picture of inevitable human behavior. Any conclusions about such behavior must await the collection by trained observers of psychiatric data from other cultures. Since no adequate work of the kind has been done at the present time, it is impossible to say what core of definition of abnormality may be found valid from the comparative material. It is as it is in ethics; all our local conventions of moral behavior and of immoral are without absolute validity, and yet it is quite possible that a modicum of what is considered right and what wrong could be disentangled that is shared by the whole human race. When data are available in psychiatry, this minimum definition of abnormal human tendencies will be probably quite unlike our culturally conditioned, highly elaborated psychoses such as those that are described, for instance, under the terms of schizophrenia and manic-depressive.

52 / *Ethical Relativism*

W. T. STACE

W. T. Stace (1886–1967) taught at Princeton University and worked in ethics and the study of religion and culture. He was a significant figure in both the academic world and public culture.

I. [WHAT IS ETHICAL RELATIVISM?]

Any ethical position which denies that there is a single moral standard which is equally applicable to all men at all times may fairly be called a species of ethical relativity.* There is not, the relativist asserts, merely one moral law, one code, one standard. There are many moral laws, codes, standards. What morality ordains in one place or age may be quite different from what morality ordains in another place or age. The moral code of Chinamen is quite different from that of Europeans, that of African savages quite different from both. Any morality, therefore, is relative to the age, the place, and the circumstances in which it is found. It is in no sense absolute.

This does not mean merely—as one might at first sight be inclined to suppose—that the very same kind of action which is *thought* right in one country and period may be *thought* wrong in another. This would be a mere platitude, the truth of which everyone would have to admit. Even the absolutist would admit this—would even wish to emphasize it—since he is well aware that different people have different sets of moral ideas, and his whole

---

*[More commonly called ethical relativism. This sentence expresses the correct definition of ethical relativism, the view that: There is no single moral standard which is equally applicable to all persons, at all times (and places).—Eds.]

point is that some of these sets of ideas are false. What the relativist means to assert is, not this platitude, but that the very same kind of action which *is* right in one country and period may *be* wrong in another. And this, far from being a platitude, is a very startling assertion.

It is very important to grasp thoroughly the difference between the two ideas. For there is reason to think that many minds tend to find ethical relativity attractive because they fail to keep them clearly apart. It is so very obvious that moral ideas differ from country to country and from age to age. And it is so very easy, if you are mentally lazy, to suppose that to say this means the same as to say that no universal moral standard exists—or in other words that it implies ethical relativity. We fail to see that the word "standard" is used in *two different senses*. [1] It is perfectly true that, in one sense, there are many variable moral standards. We speak of judging a man by the standard of his time. And this implies that different times have different standards. And this, of course, is quite true. But when the word "standard" is used in this sense it means simply the set of moral ideas current during the period in question. It means what people *think* right, whether as a matter of fact it *is* right or not. [2] On the other hand when the absolutist asserts that there exists a single universal moral "standard," he is not using the word in this sense at all. He means by "standard" what *is* right as distinct from what people merely think right. His point is that although what people think right varies in different countries and periods, yet what actually is right is everywhere and always the same. And it follows that when the ethical relativist disputes the position of the absolutist and denies that any universal moral standard exists, he too means by "standard" what actually is right. But it is exceedingly easy, if we are not careful, to slip loosely from using the word in the first sense to using it in the second sense, and to suppose that the variability of moral beliefs is the same thing as the variability of what really is moral. And unless we keep the two senses of the word "standard" distinct, we are likely to think the creed of ethical relativity much more plausible than it actually is.

The genuine relativist, then, does not merely mean that Chinamen may think right what Frenchmen think wrong. He means that what *is* wrong for the Frenchman may *be* right for the Chinaman. And if one inquires how, in those circumstances, one is to know what actually is right in China or in France, the answer comes quite glibly. What is right in China is the same as what people think right in China; and what is right in France is the same as what people think right in France. So that if you want to know what is moral in any particular country or age, all you have to do is to ascertain what are the moral ideas current in that age or country. Those ideas are, *for that age or country*, right. Thus what is morally right is identified with what is thought to be morally right, and the distinction which we made above between these two is simply denied. To put the same thing in another way, it is denied that there can be or ought to be any distinction between the two senses of the word "standard." There is only one kind of standard of right and wrong, namely, the moral ideas current in any particular age or country.

Moral right *means* what people think morally right. It has no other meaning. What Frenchmen think right is, therefore, right *for Frenchmen*. And evidently one must conclude—though I am not aware that relativists are anxious to draw one's attention to such unsavory but yet absolutely necessary conclusions from their creed—that cannibalism is right for people who believe in it, that human sacrifice is right for those races which practice it, and that burning widows alive was right for Hindus until the British stepped in and compelled the Hindus to behave immorally by allowing their widows to remain alive. . . .

II. [PROPOSED ARGUMENTS FOR ETHICAL RELATIVISM]

I shall now proceed to consider, first, the main arguments which can be urged in favor of ethical relativity; and secondly, the arguments which can be urged against it. . . . [1.] The first [argument in favor] is that which relies upon the actual varieties of moral "standards" found in the world. It was easy enough to believe in a single absolute morality in older times when there was no anthropology, when all humanity was divided clearly into two groups, Christian peoples and the "heathen." Christian peoples knew and possessed the one true morality. The rest were savages whose moral ideas could be ignored. But all this is changed. Greater knowledge has brought greater tolerance. We can no longer exalt our own morality as alone true, while dismissing all other moralities as false or inferior. The investigations of anthropologists have shown that there exist side by side in the world a bewildering variety of moral codes. On this topic endless volumes have been written, masses of evidence piled up. Anthropologists have ransacked the Melanesian Islands, the jungles of New Guinea, the steppes of Siberia, the deserts of Australia, the forests of central Africa, and have brought back with them countless examples of weird, extravagant, and fantastic "moral" customs with which to confound us. We learn that all kinds of horrible practices are, in this, that, or the other place, regarded as essential to virtue. We find that there is nothing, or next to nothing, which has always and everywhere been regarded as morally good by all men. Where, then, is our universal morality? Can we, in face of all this evidence, deny that it is nothing but an empty dream?

[Criticism /] This argument, taken by itself, is a very weak one. It relies upon a single set of facts—the variable moral customs of the world. But this variability of moral ideas is admitted by both parties to the dispute, and is capable of ready explanation upon the hypothesis of either party. The relativist says that the facts are to be explained by the nonexistence of any absolute moral standard. The absolutist says that they are to be explained by human ignorance of what the absolute moral standard is. And he can truly point out that men have differed widely in their opinions about all manner of topics—including the subject-matters of the physical sciences—just as much as they differ about morals. And if the various different opinions which men have held about the shape of the earth do not prove that it has no one real shape, neither do the various opinions which they have held about morality prove that there is no one true morality.

Thus the facts can be explained equally plausibly on either hypothesis. There is nothing in the facts themselves which compels us to prefer the relativistic hypothesis to that of the absolutist. And therefore the argument fails to prove the relativist conclusion. If that conclusion is to be established, it must be by means of other considerations.

This is the essential point. But I will add some supplementary remarks. The work of the anthropologists, upon which ethical relativists seem to rely so heavily, has as a matter of fact added absolutely nothing *in principle* to what has always been known about the variability of moral ideas. Educated people have known all along that the Greeks tolerated sodomy, which in modern times has been regarded in some countries as an abominable crime; that the Hindus thought it a sacred duty to burn their widows; that trickery, now thought despicable, was once believed to be a virtue; that terrible torture was thought by our own ancestors only a few centuries ago to be a justifiable weapon of justice; that it was only yesterday that western peoples came to believe that slavery is immoral. Even the ancients knew very well that moral customs and ideas vary—witness the writings of Herodotus. Thus the principle of the variability of moral ideas was well understood long before modern anthropology was ever heard of. Anthropology has added nothing to the knowledge of this principle except a mass of new and extreme examples of it drawn from very remote sources. But to multiply examples of a principle already well known and universally admitted adds nothing to the argument which is built upon that principle. The discoveries of the anthropologists have no doubt been of the highest importance in their own sphere. But in any considered opinion they have thrown no new light upon the special problems of the moral philosopher. . . .

[2.] The second argument in favor of ethical relativity . . . consists in alleging that no one has ever been able to discover upon what foundation an absolute morality could rest, or from what source a universally binding moral code could derive its authority.

If, for example, it is an absolute and unalterable moral rule that all men ought to be unselfish, from whence does this *command* issue? For a command it certainly is, phrase it how you please. There is no difference in meaning between the sentence "You ought to be unselfish" and the sentence "Be unselfish." Now a command implies a commander. An obligation implies some authority which obliges. Who is this commander, what this authority? Thus the vastly difficult question is raised of *the basis of moral obligation*. Now the argument of the relativist would be that it is impossible to find any basis for a universally binding moral law; but that it is quite easy to discover a basis for morality if moral codes are admitted to be variable, ephemeral, and relative to time, place, and circumstance. . . .

[**Comment** /] This argument is undoubtedly very strong. It *is* absolutely essential to solve the problem of the basis of moral obligation if we are to believe in any kind of moral standards other than those provided by mere custom or by irrational emotions. It is idle to talk about a universal morality unless we can point to the source of its authority—or at least to do so is to indulge in a faith which is without rational ground. To cherish a blind faith in morality may be, for the average man whose business is primarily to live right and not to theorize, sufficient. Perhaps it is his wisest course. But it will not do for the philosopher. His function, or at least one of his functions, is precisely to discover the rational grounds of our everyday beliefs—if they have any. Philosophically and intellectually, then, we cannot accept belief in a universally binding morality unless we can discover upon what foundation its obligatory character rests.

[**Criticism** /] But in spite of the strength of the argument thus posed in favor of ethical relativity, it is not impregnable. For it leaves open one loophole. It is always possible that some theory, not yet examined, may provide a basis for a universal moral obligation. The argument rests upon the [universal] negative proposition that *there is no theory which can provide a basis for a universal morality.* But it is notoriously difficult to prove a [universal] negative. How can you prove that there are no green swans? All you can show is that none have been found so far. And then it is always possible that one will be found tomorrow. . . .

III. [ARGUMENTS AGAINST ETHICAL RELATIVISM]

It is time that we turned our attention from the case in favor of ethical relativity to the case against it. Now the case against it consists, to a very large extent, in urging that, if taken seriously and pressed to its logical conclusion, ethical relativity can only end in destroying the conception of morality altogether, in undermining its practical efficacy, in rendering meaningless many almost universally accepted truths about human affairs, in robbing human beings of any incentive to strive for a better world, in taking the life-blood out of every ideal and every aspiration which has ever ennobled the life of man. . . .

[1.] First of all, then, ethical relativity, in asserting that the moral standards of particular social groups are the only standards which exist, renders meaningless all propositions which attempt to compare these standards with one another in respect of their moral worth. And this is a very serious matter indeed. We are accustomed to think that the moral ideas of one nation or social group may be "higher" or "lower" than those of another. We believe, for example, that Christian ethical ideals are nobler than those of the savage races of central Africa. Probably most of us would think that the Chinese moral standards are higher than those of the inhabitants of New Guinea. In short we habitually compare one civilization with another and judge the sets of ethical ideas to be found in them to be some better, some worse. The fact that such judgments are very difficult to make with any justice, and that they are frequently made on very superficial and prejudiced grounds, has no bearing on the question now at issue. The question is whether such judgments have any *meaning*. We habitually assume that they have.

But on the basis of ethical relativity they can have none whatever. For the relativist must hold that there is no *common* standard which can be applied to the various civilizations judged. Any such comparison of moral standards implies the existence of some superior standard which is applicable to both. And the existence of any such standard is precisely what the relativist denies. According to him the Christian standard is applicable only to Christians, the Chinese standard only to Chinese, the New Guinea standard only to the inhabitants of New Guinea.

What is true of comparisons between the moral standards of different races will also be true of comparisons between those of different ages. It is not unusual to ask such questions as whether the standard of our own day is superior to that which existed among our ancestors five hundred years ago. And when we remember that our ancestors employed slaves, practiced barbaric physical tortures, and burned people alive, we may be inclined to think that it is. At any rate we assume that the question is one which has meaning and is capable of rational discussion. But if the ethical relativist is right, whatever we assert on this subject must be totally meaningless. For here again there is no common standard which could form the basis of any such judgments.

This in its turn implies that the whole notion of moral *progress* is a sheer delusion. Progress means an advance from lower to higher, from worse to better. But on the basis of ethical relativity it has no meaning to say that the standards of this age are better (or worse) than those of a previous age. For there is no common standard by which both can be measured. Thus it is nonsense to say that the morality of the New Testament is higher than that of the Old. And Jesus Christ, if he imagined that he was introducing into the world a higher ethical standard than existed before his time, was merely deluded. . . .

[2.] I come now to a second point. Up to the present I have allowed it to be taken tacitly for granted that, though judgments comparing different races and ages in respect of the worth of their moral codes are impossible for the ethical relativist, yet judgments of comparison between individuals living within the same social group would be quite possible. For individuals living within the same social group would presumably be subject to the same moral code, that of their group, and this would therefore constitute, as between these individuals, a common standard by which they could both be measured. We have not here, as we had in the other case, the difficulty of the absence of any common standard of comparison. It should therefore be possible for the ethical relativist to say quite meaningfully that President Lincoln was a better man than some criminal or moral imbecile of his own time and country, or that Jesus was a better man than Judas Iscariot.

But is even this minimum of moral judgment really possible on relativist grounds? It seems to me that it is not. For when once the whole of humanity is abandoned as the area covered by a single moral standard, what smaller areas are to be adopted as the *loci** of different standards? Where are we to draw the lines of demarcation? We can split up humanity, perhaps—though the procedure will be very arbitrary—into races, races into nations, nations into tribes, tribes into families, families into individuals. Where are we going to draw the *moral* boundaries? Does the *locus* of a particular moral standard reside in a race, a nation, a tribe, a family, or an individual? Perhaps the blessed phrase "social group" will be dragged in to save the situation. Each such group, we shall be told, has its own moral code which is, for it, right. But what *is* a "group"? Can any one define it or give its boundaries? This is the seat of that ambiguity in the theory of ethical relativity to which reference was made on an earlier page.

The difficulty is not, as might be thought, merely an academic difficulty of logical definition. If that were all, I should not press the point. But the ambiguity has practical consequences which are disastrous for morality. No one is likely to say that moral codes are confined within the arbitrary limits of the geographical divisions of countries. Nor are the notions of race, nation, or political state likely to help us. To bring out the essentially practical character of the difficulty let us put it in the form of concrete questions. Does the American nation constitute a "group" having a single moral standard? Or does the standard of what I ought to do change continuously as I cross the continent in a railway train? Do different States of the Union have different moral codes? Perhaps every town and village has its own peculiar standard. This may at first sight seem reasonable enough. "In Rome do as Rome does" may seem as good a rule in morals as it is in etiquette. But can we stop there? Within the village are numerous cliques each having its own set of ideas. Why should not each of these claim to be bound only by its own special and peculiar moral standards? And if it comes to that, why should not the gangsters of Chicago claim to constitute a group having its own morality, so that its murders and debaucheries must be viewed as "right" by the only standard which can legitimately be applied to it? And if it be answered that the nation will not tolerate this, that may be so. But this is to put the foundation of right simply in the superior force of the majority. In that case whoever is stronger will be right, however monstrous his ideas and actions. And if we cannot deny to any set of people the right to have its own morality, is it not clear that, in the end, we cannot even deny this right to the individual? Every individual man and woman can put up, on this view, an irrefutable claim to be judged by no standard except his or her own.

If these arguments are valid, the ethical relativist cannot really maintain

*[The plural of *locus*.—Eds.]

that there is anywhere to be found a moral standard binding upon anybody against his will. And he cannot maintain that, even within the social group, there is a common standard as between individuals. And if that is so, then even judgments to the effect that one man is morally better than another become meaningless. All moral valuation thus vanishes. There is nothing to prevent each man from being a rule unto himself. The result will be moral chaos and the collapse of all effective standards. . . .

[3.] But even if we assume that the difficulty about defining moral groups has been surmounted, a further difficulty presents itself. Suppose that we have now definitely decided what are the exact boundaries of the social group within which a moral standard is to be operative. And we will assume—as is invariably done by relativists themselves—that this group is to be some actually existing social community such as a tribe or nation. How are we to know, even then, what actually is the moral standard within that group? How is anyone to know? How is even a member of the group to know? For there are certain to be within the group—at least this will be true among advanced peoples—wide differences of opinion as to what is right, what wrong. Whose opinion, then, is to be taken as representing *the* moral standard of the group? Either we must take the opinion of the majority within the group, or the opinion of some minority. If we rely upon the ideas of the majority, the results will be disastrous. Wherever there is found among a people a small bag of select spirits, or perhaps one man, working for the establishment of higher and nobler ideas than those commonly accepted by the group, we shall be compelled to hold that, for that people at that time, the majority are right, and that the reformers are wrong and are preaching what is immoral. We shall have to maintain, for example, that Jesus was preaching immoral doctrines to the Jews. Moral goodness will have to be equated always with the mediocre and sometimes with the definitely base and ignoble. If on the other hand we said that the moral standard of the group is to be identified with the moral opinions of some minority, then what minority is this to be? We cannot answer that it is to be the minority composed of the best and most enlightened individuals of the group. This would involve us in a palpably vicious circle. For by what standard are these individuals to be judged the best and the most enlightened? There is no principle by which we could select the right minority. And therefore we should have to consider every minority as good as every other. And this means that we should have no logical right whatever to resist the claim of the gangsters of Chicago—if such a claim were made—that their practices represent the highest standards of American morality. It means in the end that every individual is to be bound by no standard save his own.

The ethical relativists are great empiricists. *What* is the actual moral standard of any group can only be discovered, they tell us, by an examination on the ground of the moral opinions and customs of that group. But will they tell us how they propose to decide, when they get to the ground, which of the many moral opinions they are sure to find there is *the* right one in that group? To some extent they will be able to do this for the Melanesian Islanders—from whom apparently all lessons in the nature of morality are in future to be taken. But it is certain that they cannot do it for advanced peoples whose members have learned to think for themselves and to entertain among themselves a wide variety of opinions. They cannot do it unless they accept the calamitous view that the ethical opinion of the majority is always right. We are left therefore once more with the conclusion that, even within a particular social group, anybody's moral opinion is as good as anybody else's, and that every man is entitled to be judged by his own standards.

[4.] Finally, not only is ethical relativity disastrous in its consequences for moral theory. It cannot be doubted that it must tend to be equally disastrous in its impact upon practical conduct. If men come really to believe that one moral standard is as good as another, they will conclude that their own moral standard has nothing special to recommend it. They might as well then slip down to some lower and easier standard. It is true that, for a time, it may be possible to hold one view in theory and to act practically upon another. But ideas, even philosophical ideas, are not so ineffectual that they can remain for ever idle in the upper chambers of the intellect. In the end they seep down to the level of practice. They get themselves acted on. . . .

IV. [CONCLUSION]

These, then, are the main arguments which the anti-relativist will urge against ethical relativity. And perhaps finally he will attempt a diagnosis of the social, intellectual, and psychological conditions of our time to which the emergence of ethical relativism is to be attributed. His diagnosis will be somewhat as follows.

We have abandoned, perhaps with good reason, the oracles of the past. Every age, of course, does this. But in our case it seems that none of us knows any more whither to turn. We do not know what to put in the place of that which has gone. What ought we, supposedly civilized peoples, to aim at? What are to be our ideals? What is right? What is wrong? What is beautiful? What is ugly? No man knows. We drift helplessly in this direction and that. We know not where we stand nor whither we are going.

There are, of course, thousands of voices frantically shouting directions. But they shout one another down, they contradict one another, and the upshot is mere uproar. And because of this confusion there creeps upon us an insidious skepticism and despair. Since no one knows what the truth is, we will deny that there is any truth. Since no one knows what right is, we will deny that there is any right. Since no one knows what the beautiful is, we will deny that there is any beauty. Or at least we will say—what comes to the same thing—that what people (the people of any particular age, region, society) think to be true is true *for them*; that what people think morally right is morally right *for them*; that what people think beautiful is beautiful *for them*. There is no common and objective standard in any of these matters. Since all the voices contradict one another, they must be all equally right (or equally wrong, for it makes no difference which we say). It is from the practical confusion of our time that these doctrines issue. When all the despair and defeatism of our distracted age are expressed in abstract concepts, are erected into a philosophy, it is then called relativism—ethical relativism, esthetic relativism, relativity of truth. Ethical relativity is simply defeatism in morals.

And the diagnosis will proceed. Perhaps, it will say, the current pessimism as to our future is unjustified. But there is undoubtedly a widespread feeling that our civilization is rushing downward to the abyss. If this should be true, and if nothing should check the headlong descent, then perhaps some historian of the future will seek to disentangle the causes. The causes will, of course, be found to be multitudinous and enormously complicated. And one must not exaggerate the relative importance of any of them. But it can hardly be doubted that our future historian will include somewhere in his list the failure of the men of our generation to hold steadfastly before themselves the notion of an (even comparatively) unchanging moral idea. He will cite that feebleness of intellectual and moral grasp which has led them weakly to harbor the belief that no one moral aim is really any better than any other, that each is good and true for those who entertain it. This meant, he will surely say, that men had given up in despair the struggle to attain moral truth. Civilization lives in and through its upward struggle. Whoever despairs and gives up the struggle, whether it be an individual or a whole civilization, is already inwardly dead.

STUDY QUESTIONS

1. Why, according to Russell, would people with the same morality but different desires fail to agree? What does this tell us about morality? Give an example to illustrate the point.

2. To what extent, in Russell's view, are value judgments outside the realm of knowledge? In what ways can morality be aided by knowledge? Give examples.

3. Why does Russell think it is unhelpful to appeal to conscience in deciding what to do?

4. According to Blanshard, why is the "new subjectivism" popular?

5. Does Blanshard's case of the dead rabbit cast doubt on the new subjectivism? If so, how?

6. According to Blanshard, why can't a "new subjectivist" take moral duty seriously? Give an example.

7. Could a "new subjectivist" engage in a serious moral debate? (What is involved in a serious moral debate?)

8. What is the connection between *cultural* relativity and *ethical* relativity according to Benedict?

9. Is the burden of proof in the absolutist-relativist debate on the relativist or on the absolutist? Why?

10. Is Stace fair to the relativist when he assumes that there is moral progress? How might the relativist respond to this assumption?

11. Stace suggests that if you don't believe in "the one true absolute moral standard" you can't be moral. Do you agree with him?

12. Why do you think it is so difficult to reach agreement on moral issues in our society? What could be done to promote greater agreement on such issues?

13. How might Russell respond to Blanshard? How might Benedict respond to Stace?

14. What are some of the assumptions and presuppositions behind the moral view defended by Stace and Blanshard?

15. Can an ethical outlook like Benedict's explain our desire to criticize our naive beliefs and convictions about morality?

FURTHER READINGS

"Anthropology and Ethics." *The Monist*, June 1963. [A good collection of essays on the relations between anthropology and relativism.]

Aristotle. *Nicomachean Ethics*, trans. Sir David Ross. London: Oxford University Press, 1969 reprint. [This classic work spells out the differences between scientific proof and moral reasoning, which has point of contact with many recent authors.]

Foot, Phillippa. "Moral Arguments." *Mind* 67 (1958), 502–513. [Argues that good and bad have some content, so that not anything can be called good or bad.]

Gert, Bernard. *The Moral Rules: A New Rational Foundation for Morality.* New York: Harper & Row, 1970. [A recent attempt to show that moral reasoning is rational.]

Gewirth, Alan. "'Positive' Ethics and 'Normative' Science." *Philosophical Review* 69 (1960), 311–330. [Argues that some of the contrasts between science and ethics defended by subjectivist and relativist theories are incorrect.]

Gifford, N. *When In Rome.* Albany: State University of New York Press, 1981. [A lucid discussion; good for beginners.]

Harman, Gilbert. "Moral Relativism Defended." *Philosophical Review* 84 (1975), 3–23. [Defends moral relativism as a logical thesis about moral judgments.]

Hudson, William Donald. *Modern Moral Philosophy.* Garden City, N.Y.: Anchor Books, 1970. [A useful survey of twentieth-century Anglo-American theories on the status of moral judgments.]

Krausz, M., and J. Meiland, eds. *Relativism: Cognitive and Moral.* Notre Dame: University of Notre Dame Press, 1982. [Advanced readings; important essays.]

Ladd, John. The Issue of Relativism." *The Monist* 47 (1963), 585–609. [Defends moral relativism as the view that popular opinion defines what's moral and immoral in any given society.]

Montague, Phillip. "Are There Objective and Absolute Moral Standards?" In Joel Feinberg, ed., *Reason and Responsibility*, 4th ed. Belmont, Calif.: Dickenson, 1978, pp. 580–591. [An interesting defense of the view that moral judgments are objective.]

Moore, G. E. *Principia Ethica*. Cambridge: Cambridge University Press, 1903. [A seminal work which really invents the subject of this part of the book.]

Sellars, Wilfrid, and John Hospers, eds. *Readings in Ethical Theory*, 2nd ed. Englewood Cliffs, N.J.: Prentice-Hall, 1970. [Deals with a wide variety of topics related to the issues covered in this part of the book.]

Stevenson, Charles. *Ethics and Language*. New Haven, Conn.: Yale University Press, 1944. [The most sophisticated defense of emotivism.]

Thomson, Judith J., and Gerald Dworkin, eds. *Ethics*. New York: Harper & Row, 1968. [An important collection of essays dealing with the status of ethical judgments.]

PART ELEVEN

THE STATE
AND SOCIETY

PREVIEW

*I*s government a thief or an angel? Is society a group of people who get in your way or is it like a family, which nurtures and cares for you? Do we want and need father and mother figures or should we each fend for ourselves, and let others do likewise?

You are now in college. Do you want your life monitored by your dorm counselor, who treats you the way your parents did when you were twelve? Wouldn't it be better if the people in the dorm got together and made up their own visitation policy? And what's going to happen when you graduate and go back to the "real" world? Government and society will tell you what you can and cannot do until you're dead or too old to resist or care. Or maybe this isn't so bad; maybe our leaders know best; maybe freedom and democracy aren't so great. Or maybe we don't have enough freedom, true freedom, until we stop acting selfishly and have a society and government which eliminates all injustices in the world. What do you think?

The questions "What is the best form of government?" and "What should the relations between government and society be?" are two of the most basic and important questions of our society. They have been the concern of almost every major thinker of Western culture since Socrates (d. 399 B.C.), yet they are as current and practical as today's newspaper headlines.

In this part, we have gathered essays defending five different political philosophies—five different answers to the above questions—that are, we believe, of most contemporary significance for political thinking and practice. These political philosophies are: democracy, libertarianism, (democratic) socialism, communitarianism, and feminism.

Before proceeding, a cautionary note is in order. Each of the above terms has had different and often conflicting meanings or interpretations; and the movements that these terms denote have had complex histories, including historical interrelationships with one another. For instance, classical liberalism—nineteenth-century capitalist theories of democracy—has more in common with libertarianism and, to some extent, conservativism of today than it does with modern (welfare state) liberalism. And socialism, as Cohen presents it here, is an extension, not a departure, from democratic theory—construed broadly enough to include welfare state ideals—and thus is not, as it is for many Marxists, communists, and socialists, radically different from certain strands of the democratic tradition.

Since it is not possible to survey all the historical and semantic considerations that would be required in a full discussion of the four political philosophies represented in the selections, we shall briefly characterize these views in keeping with the specific interpretation offered in this part by each of their proponents. This will orient the reader to the selections to follow.

Main Questions

The main questions, then, which this part deals with are:

1. What is the best form of government?
2. What should the relations between government and society be? (These will be treated as parts of a single question.)

Answers

The main answers to our questions are:

a. Democracy: The best form of government is one in which the people rule, directly or indirectly, and in which society allows for the maximum amount of individual freedom together, perhaps, with welfare state measures by which the government plays a role in improving society.

b. Libertarianism: A minimal, or "night-watch-person," government is the best; the government is only to protect us from internal or external (foreign) harm or coercion. Society is a voluntary collection of free individuals who relate to one another on a purely voluntary and contractual basis. Government protects this kind of "free market society."

c. Socialism: The best form of government is one controlled by the people, who cooperatively own the means of production and distribution, and who provide for the equitable sharing of all labor and benefits by cooperative decisions; society is a cooperative and harmonious community in which goods and benefits are shared equitably by all.

d. Communitarianism: This view, which in some way derives from classical conservatism (but which also preserves some elements of classical liberalism) maintains that government must embody some type of shared moral consensus on the part of members of the community, that it ought not to be morally neutral, and that individuals can only develop themselves and be moral agents by situating themselves within this shared morality.

e. Feminism: Political philosophies that seek to pinpoint the basis for male political dominance and the repression of females and that seek to develop feminist approaches to politics, justice, gender, race, and class fall into this category.

It will be helpful at this point to make some additional comments on these views, in order to indicate the specific ways in which the writers in this section interpret each of these political philosophies.

a'. Democracy is defined here to mean a form of government in which the citizens or their elected representatives have direct control of their government. Democracy is committed to individual freedom, equality of opportunity, and legal and social justice—including welfare state measures when justified.

b'. Libertarianism has doubts about the welfare state and about the emphasis on equality—or at least egalitarianism, the belief that the state should eliminate certain types of social and economic inequalities (e.g., pay differentials). It places more value on individual freedom, an open market, and limited government to insure freedom for all. Charity is a private voluntary affair, not the business of the state, which has a monopoly on power and, therefore, is dangerous.

c'. Socialism (as defended by Cohen) is a radical and thoroughgoing effort to take the democratic ideals of social justice and equality built into the welfare state brand of democracy and to carry them out in practice on a grand scale. Feeding the hungry, caring for the sick, and so on are responsibilities of government; services should be based upon need. Social justice requires the elimination of all social and economic injustices, which means inequalities based upon such factors as birth, luck, and so on (which libertarians find perfectly justified).

d'. Communitarianism, as defended here by Sandel (and, by implication, by MacIntyre in Part Nine), holds the view that social practices, customs, and traditions—which Sandel (and MacIntyre) claim need continually to be reflected on and modified (not a "typically conservative" view)—provide a framework for human development, morality, and culture. Government must embody or reflect these ideals and practices, which (in Sandel's view) have become deformed or lost through the dominance of the liberal theory of society, morality, freedom, and government. The idea of the moral neutrality of the state as embodied in liberalism, along with utilitarianism, egoism, and formalism (see Part Nine)—the main moral outlooks of liberalism—are especially offensive in this regard. Communitarianism is thus connected to the version of virtue ethics that MacIntyre defends in Part Nine.

e'. Alison Jaggar provides a survey of various approaches to feminism as a political philosophy, e.g., liberal feminism and socialist feminism. Feminism is a wide-ranging field, which extends far beyond political philosophy and incorporates many more viewpoints than Jaggar discusses in her article.

With this background, it is hoped that the reader can profitably consider the five views of state and society presented below. This material will pave the way for the issues discussed in Part Twelve, and should help in reconsidering some of the issues about morality, religion, science, and methods of inquiry that appear in earlier sections of this book.

Selections

The five main answers to our questions of this part are represented as follows:

Answers	Selection
(a) Democracy	53
(b) Libertarianism	54
(c) Socialism	55
(d) Communitarianism	56
(e) Feminism	57

53 / Why Choose Democracy?

CHARLES FRANKEL

Charles Frankel (1917–1980) taught philosophy at Columbia University. He was a major influence within American liberal pragmatism in the areas of political and social philosophy and educational thought.

We have been overexposed to ideologies and political abstractions in this century, and have seen how much men are willing to sacrifice for the sake of ideological certainty. It is not surprising that sensitive men have developed something close to an ideology of uncertainty, and should look with a jaundiced eye on all questions about the justification of political systems. Why choose democracy? Trained in a hard school that has taught us the perils of belief, can we say anything more than that fanaticism is odious and that democracy should be chosen because it asks us to believe in very little?

On the contrary, it asks us to believe in a great deal. I do not believe we can show that the inside truth about the universe, human history, or the human psyche commands us to adopt democratic ideals. Choosing a political ideal is not like demonstrating the truth of a theorem in some geometry, and those who think that democracy needs that kind of justification are indirectly responsible for the uncertainty about it. Despite the semantic inflation from which the current discussion of political ideals suffers, the reasons for choosing democracy are neither mysterious nor difficult. But they are unsettling reasons, and they ask those who accept them to bet a great deal on their capacity to live with what they have chosen.

I. THE SIGNIFICANCE OF THE DEMOCRATIC POLITICAL METHOD

In an area so full of grandiose claims, it is safest to begin by using the word "democracy" in its narrowest sense. So conceived, democracy is the method of choosing a government through competitive elections in which people who are not members of the governing groups participate. Whatever may be said for or against democracy so conceived, it is surely not a supreme ideal of life. It is doubtful that anyone has ever treated the right to cast a ballot once every year or so as an end in itself. A society in which the democratic political method has been consolidated, to be sure, has a tremendous source of reassurance. It possesses a peaceful method for determining who shall hold power and for effecting changes in the structure of power. Yet even peace is only one value among others. It is worth something to have security and order, but how much it is worth depends on the kind of security and order it is. The importance of the democratic political method lies mainly in its nonpolitical by-products. It is important because a society in which it is well established will probably be different in at least four respects—in the conditions that protect its liberties, in the kind of consensus that prevails, in the character of the conflicts that go on within it, and in the manner in which it educates its rulers and citizens.

First, liberties. Construed strictly as a method for choosing governments, democracy does not guarantee the citizen's personal liberties. Democratic governments have attacked personal liberties, as in colonial New England, and undemocratic governments have often protected them, as in Vienna before World War I. Yet competitive elections have their points, and it is only one of their points that they allow a society to choose its government. For in order to maintain competitive elections, it is necessary to have an opposition, the opposition must have some independent rights and powers of its own, the good opinion of some people outside government must be sought, and at least some members of the society must have protections against the vengefulness of the powers that be. And this carries a whole train of institutions behind it—courts, a press not wholly devoted to promoting the interests of those in power, and independent agencies for social inquiry and criticism.

It is these necessitating conditions for elections that give elections their long-range significance. So far as political democracy is concerned, these conditions are only means to ends: they make competitive elections possible. But it is because a system of competitive elections requires and fosters such conditions that it justifies itself. The conditions required for maintaining an honest electoral system are the best reasons for wishing to maintain it. Indeed, a man might value such a system even though he thought all elections frivolous and foolish. He would have as good a reason to do so, and perhaps a better reason, than the man who always finds himself voting happily for the winning side. The outsider and the loser are the peculiar beneficiaries of a political system that creates institutions with a vested interest in liberty.

The democratic political method, furthermore, helps to foster a different kind of social consensus. There have been many kinds of political arrangement that have allowed men to feel that the government under which they live is *their* government. There is no clear evidence that democracy is necessarily superior to other systems in promoting a sense of oneness between rulers and ruled. But the special virtue of a democratic political system is that it permits men to feel at home within it who do not regard their political leaders as their own kind, and who would lose their self-respect, indeed, if they gave their unprovisional loyalty to any human institution. Despite all that is said about democratic pressures towards conformity—and a little of what is said is true—the democratic political system ceremonialized the fact of disagreement and the virtue of independent judgment. If it is to work, it requires an extraordinarily sophisticated human attitude—loyal opposition.

The mark of a civilized man, in Justice Holmes'* famous maxim, is that he can act with conviction while questioning his first principles. The ultimate claim of a democratic government to authority is that it permits dissent and survives it. In this respect, it dwells on the same moral landscape as the civilized man.

The democratic political method also changes the character of the conflicts that take place in a society. The perennial problem of politics is to manage conflict. And what happens in a conflict depends in part on who the onlookers are, how they react, and what powers they have. A significant fact about political democracy is that it immensely expands the audience that looks on and that feels itself affected and involved. This is why democratic citizens so often find democracy tiring and feel that their societies are peculiarly fragile. Hobbes,† who said that he and fear were born as twins, recommended despotism in the interests of psychological security as well as physical safety.

But to say that democracy expands the scope of a conflict is also to say that democracy is a technique for the socialization of conflict. It brings a wider variety of pressures to bear on those who are quarreling and extends public control over private fights and private arrangements. And it does so whether these private fights are inside the government or outside. The association of democracy with the conception of private enterprise has something paradoxical about it. In one sense, there is more important enterprise that is private— free from outside discussion and surveillance—in totalitarian systems than in democratic systems. The persistent problem in a democratic system, indeed, is to know where to draw the line, where to say that outside surveillance is out of place. That line is drawn very firmly by those who make the important decisions in totalitarian societies.

But the final contribution that the democratic political method makes to the character of the society in which it is practiced is its contributions to education. Begin with the impact of political democracy on its leaders. The democratic method, like any other political method, is a system of rules for governing political competition. And such rules have both a selective and an educational force. They favor certain kinds of men, and make certain kinds of virtue more profitable and certain kinds of vice more possible. From this point of view, the significant characteristic of democratic rules of competition is that the loser is allowed to lose with honor, and permitted to live and try again if he wants. The stakes are heavy but limited. Such a system of competition gives men with sporting moral instincts a somewhat better chance to succeed. Even its typical kind of corruption has something to be said in its favor. The greased palm is bad but it is preferable to the mailed fist.

The democratic political method, furthermore, rests on methods of mutual consultation between leaders and followers. There are various ways in which support for the policies of political leaders is obtained in a democracy,

*[Justice Oliver Wendell Holmes (1841–1935), associate Supreme Court justice.—Eds.]
†[A seventeenth-century English philosopher.—Eds.]

but one of the most important is that of giving men the sense that they have been asked for their opinions and that their views have been taken into account. This makes leadership in a democracy a nerve-racking affair. One of the great dangers in a democratic political system, in fact, is simply that leaders will not have the privacy and quiet necessary for serene long-range decisions. But this is the defect of a virtue. In general, power insulates. The democratic system is a calculated effort to break in on such insulation. The conditions under which democratic leaders hold power are conditions for educating them in the complexity and subtlety of the problems for which they are responsible.

And the coin has its other side. "We Athenians," said Pericles,* "are able to judge policy even if we cannot originate it, and instead of looking on discussion as a stumbling-block in the way of action, we think it an indispensable preliminary to any wise action at all." But the fruits of free discussion do not show themselves only in public policy. They show themselves in the attitudes and capacities of the discussants. Democratic political arrangements are among the factors that have produced one of the painful and more promising characteristics of modern existence—men's sense that their education is inadequate, men's assertion that they have a right to be educated. And democratic politics helps to promote a classic conception of education—it must be social as well as technical, general as well as special, free and not doctrinaire. We can reverse the classic conception of the relation of education to democracy and not be any further from the truth: education is not simply a prerequisite for democracy; democracy is a contribution to education.

II. USES OF DEMOCRACY

But enough of political systems. In any liberal view of men's business, politics is a subordinate enterprise. It has its soul-testing challenges and pleasures, and its great work to do. But like the work of commerce and industry, the work of politics is essentially servile labor. The State is not the place to turn if you want a free commentary on human experience, and governments do not produce science, philosophy, music, literature, or children—or at any rate they do not produce very convincing specimens of any of these things. Politics may achieve its own forms of excellence, but the more important human excellences are achieved elsewhere. And it is from this point of view, I think, that democracy should in the end be considered.

For the democratic idea is based on the assumption that the important ends of life are defined by private individuals in their own voluntary pursuits. Politics, for liberal democracy, is only one aspect of a civilization, a condition for civilization but not its total environment. That is probably why the air seems lighter as one travels from controlled societies to free ones. One receives an impression of vitality, the vitality of people who are going about

---

*[A fifth-century B.C. Athenian statesman.—Eds.]

their own business and generating their own momentum. They may be going off in more different directions than the members of a centrally organized society, but the directions are their own. The best reasons for choosing democracy lie in the qualities it is capable of bringing to our daily lives, in the ways in which it can furnish our minds, imaginations, and consciences. These qualities, I would say, are freedom, variety, self-consciousness, and the democratic attitude itself.

That democracy is hostile to distinction and prefers mediocrity is not a recent view. And there is an obvious sense in which it is true that democracy makes for homogeneity. Democracy erodes the clear distinctions between classes. It destroys ready-made status-symbols so rapidly that the manufacture of new ones becomes the occupation of a major industry. Most obvious of all, democracy increases the demand for a great many good things, from shoes to education. By increasing the demand, it also puts itself under pressure to cheapen the supply.

Yet certain pertinent facts must be set against these tendencies. First, more good things *are* more generally available in democracies. Second, egalitarianism's twin is the morality of achievement. There is a tension between the democratic suspicion of the man who sets himself apart and the democratic admiration for the man who stands out, but the egalitarian hostility towards ostentatious social distinctions is normally rooted in the belief that each man should be given a chance on his own to show what he can do. And finally, pressures towards uniformity are great in all societies. Is suspicion of the eccentric in egalitarian metropolitan America greater than in an eighteenth-century village? It is difficult to think so. "The fallacy of the aristocrat," Bertrand Russell* has remarked, "consists in judging a society by the kind of life it affords a privileged few." Standing alone takes courage anywhere. Usually it also takes money; almost invariably it requires the guarantee that the individual will still retain his basic rights. In these respects modern liberal democracy, despite all the complaints about conformity, has made it easier for the ordinary unprivileged man to stand alone, if he has the will to do so, than any other kind of society known in history.

For however ambiguous some of the facts may be, the official commitment of liberal democracy is to the view that each man has his idiosyncrasies, that these idiosyncrasies deserve respect, and that if the individual does not know what is good for him, it is highly unlikely that a self-perpetuating elite will know better. And this is not just an official commitment. The institutions of liberal democracy go very far in giving it concrete embodiment. Assuming that the members of a democratic society have minimal economic securities, there is a flexibility in their situation which not many ordinary men have enjoyed in the past. If they fall out of favor with one set of authorities, they have a chance to turn around and look elsewhere.

It is unquestionable that there are great constellations of concentrated power in contemporary democratic societies; it is equally unquestionable that

*[Famous British philosopher (1872–1970).—Eds.]

there is some freedom in any society. For in dealing with power, bright men learn how to work the angles. But in a democratic society there are more angles to work. Individual freedom of choice is not an absolute value. Any society must limit it; indeed one man's freedom often rests on restricting the next man's. But while freedom of choice is not an absolute value, the democratic doctrine that each man has certain fundamental rights assigns an intrinsic value to his freedom of choice. If it has to be limited, it is recognized that something of value has been sacrificed. Social planning in a democracy is for this reason fundamentally different from social planning in undemocratic environments. The vague phrase "social utility," in a democratic setting, implicitly includes as one of its elements the value of freedom of choice.

What difference does this make? One difference is that variety is promoted; a second is that individuals are educated in self-consciousness. Needless to say, variety, too, has its limits. We do not have to protect dope peddlers in its name. But the full import of variety, of the mere existence of differences and alternatives, is frequently overlooked. It does not merely give us more choices, or offer us a break in the routine. It affects the immediate quality of our experience; it changes our relation to whatever it is that we choose to have or do or be. This is what is forgotten when freedom is defined simply as the absence of felt frustrations, or when it is said that if a man has just what he wants, it makes little difference whether he has any choice or not. A good that is voluntarily chosen, a good which a man is always free to reconsider, belongs to him in a way that a passively accepted good does not. It is his responsibility.

And this means that democratic variety has another use as well. No one can say with assurance that democracy makes people wiser or more virtuous. But political democracy invites men to think that there may be alternatives to the way they are governed. And social democracy, in reducing the barriers of class, caste, and inherited privilege that stand between men, adds to the variety of people and occasions the individual meets and puts greater pressure on his capacity to adapt to the new and different. Political democracy and a socially mobile society thus invite the individual to a greater degree of consciousness about the relativity of his own ways and a greater degree of self-consciousness in the choice of the standards by which he lives. These are conditions for intensified personal experience. The role of democracy in the extension of these attitudes represents one of its principal contributions to the progress of liberal civilization.

The extension of such attitudes, to be sure, has its risks, which explains much of our uneasiness about what the democratic revolution means. Fads and fashions engage and distract larger groups in modern democratic societies. And social mobility, though it gives breadth and variety to men's experience, may well foreshorten their sense of time. Cut loose from fixed ranks and stations, each with its legends, rationale, and sense of historic vocation, the citizens of a modern democracy face a peculiar temptation to live experimentally, with the help of the latest book, as though no one had ever lived before. But these are the risks not simply of democracy but of modernity, and they can be controlled. The courts, the organized professions, the churches, and the universities are storehouses of funded experience. In a society in which they are given independence from the political urgencies of the moment, they can serve as protections against the dictatorship of the specious present. Modernity implies a revolution in human consciousness. Democratic social arrangements reflect that revolution and accept it; but they also provide instruments for guiding and controlling it. None of democracy's contemporary rivals possess these two qualities to the same extent.

In the end, indeed, the risks of democracy are simply the risks implicit in suggesting to men that the answers are not all in. Democracy gives political form to the principle that also regulates the scientific community—the principle that inquiry must be kept open, that there are no sacred books, that no conclusion that men have ever reached can be taken to be the necessary final word. Cant, obscurantism, and lies are of course a good part of the diet of most democracies. Man is a truth-fearing animal, and it would be a miracle if any social system could quickly change this fact. But the institutions of liberal democracy are unique in that they require men to hold no irreversible beliefs in anything except in the method of free criticism and peaceful change itself, and in the ethic on which this method rests. Such a social system permits men to give their highest loyalty, not to temporary human beliefs or institutions, but to the continuing pursuit after truth, whatever it may be. The intellectual rationale of democracy is precisely that it does not need to make the foolish and arrogant claim that it rests on infallible truths. Men can believe in it and still believe that the truth is larger than anything they may think they know.

Yet the question that probably gnaws at us most deeply still remains. Freedom, variety, self-consciousness, a sane awareness of human fallibility, and loyalty to the principle that inquiry must be kept open—obviously, these have much in their favor. But they are refined values. Has liberal democracy priced itself out of the competition? Does it have anything to say, not to those who already know and enjoy it, but to the many more who must come to want it if human liberties are to be a little more secure in the world than they now are?

One of the debilitating illusions of many Western liberals is that the values of liberal culture are only our own values, that they have little point for those who look at the world differently, and no point at all for those whose lives are poor, mean, brutish, and short. Although colonialists used this view for different purposes, they shared it, and it betrays an inexact understanding of the nature of liberal values. Freedom, variety, self-consciousness, and the chance to seek the truth are all taxing experiences. Their virtues may be hard to conceive by those who have never enjoyed them. Yet in spite of the discomforts these values bring, the evidence indicates, I think, that most men would be happy to have them, and would think their lives enhanced. The difficulty with the most characteristic liberal values is not that they are parochial values. The difficulty is that men have other more imperious wants, like the need for medicines, schooling, bread, release from usurers, or a chance to get out from under corrupt and exploitative regimes. Illiberal programs promise these substantial material improvements and frequently deliver. And liberal programs, if they speak of freedom and leave out the usury and corruption, do not generally bring freedom either.

But let us assume, as there is every reason to assume, that liberal programs, if they are willing to recognize that they, too, must make a revolution, can also improve men's material condition. What can be said to the young man or the young—or old—nation in a hurry? What good reasons can we give, reasons that take account of their present condition and justified impatience, when we try to explain to them—and to ourselves—why the liberal path, despite its meanderings, is preferable to the authoritarian path?

One thing that can be said, quite simply, is that the authoritarian path closes up behind the traveler as he moves. The virtue of liberal democracy is that it permits second thoughts. To choose an authoritarian regime is to bet everything on a single throw of the dice; if the bet is bad, there is no way out save through violence, and not much hope in that direction. To choose a liberal approach, while it does not guarantee against errors, guarantees against the error so fatal that there is no peaceful way out or back. But there is another reason as well. The reason for choosing democracy is that it makes democrats.

Imagine a regime wholly committed to the welfare of those it rules. Imagine, against all the practical difficulties, that it is intelligent, honest, courageous, and that it does not have to enter into any deals with any of the international blocs that dominate the modern scene. And imagine, too, that this regime aims, in the end, to bring democracy and liberal values to the country it rules. But assume only that it claims, for the present, to be the one true spokesman for the public interest, the only group in the society that knows what truth and justice mean. What is the consequence? The consequence is that a democratic attitude is impossible. That attitude has been described in various ways—as a love for liberty, equality, and fraternity, as respect for the dignity of the individual, as a consistent regard for individual rights. The descriptions are not wrong, but they overintellectualize the attitude. At bottom, the democratic attitude is simply an attitude of good faith plus a working belief in the probable rationality of others. And that is what political authoritarianism destroys. Once a society is governed by the doctrine that some one group monopolizes all wisdom, it is divided into the Enlightened and the Unenlightened, and the Enlightened determine who shall be accorded membership in the club. In a modern State this makes almost impossible the growth of that mutual trust between opposing groups which is a fundamental condition for the growth of a strong political community that is also free.

The competition that takes place in a democracy is an instance of cooperative competition. It is a struggle in which both sides work to maintain the conditions necessary for a decent struggle. Accordingly, it rests on the assumption that there are no irreconcilable conflicts, that differences can be negotiated or compromised, if men have good will. Such a system requires men to deal with one another honestly, to make a serious effort to reach agreements, and to keep them after they have been made. It requires them to recognize, therefore, that the other side has its interests and to be prepared to make concessions to these interests when such concessions are not inconsistent with fundamental principles. A democratic ethic does not ask men to be fools. They do not have to assume that their opponents have put all their cards on the table. But democratic competition is impossible if the parties to the competition cannot assume that their opponents will recognize their victory if they win and will cooperate with them afterwards. The intention to annihilate the opposition or to win at all costs destroys the possibility of a regulated struggle. In this sense democracy is an exercise in the ethic of good faith. It is a system that makes it possible for men, not to love their enemies, but at least to live without fearing them. That kind of mutual trust between enemies is what authoritarianism destroys.

No doubt, such an argument may seem pathetically beside the point to men who live in societies that have been torn by distrust for centuries and that have known government only as a name for cruelty and dishonesty. If such men succeed in installing democratic regimes in their countries, they will do so by recognizing their enemies and distrusting them. But the harshness that goes with any deep social revolution is one thing if it is recognized as a bitter and dangerous necessity and is kept within limits. It is another if the violence is doctrinal, and the assumption is made that men can never cooperate unless they have the same interests and ideas. Such an assumption, as all the evidence suggests, encourages the adoption of terror as an official policy and condemns a society to an indefinite period in which power will be monopolistically controlled. In a diversified modern society, indeed in any society that has even begun the movement towards modernity, the doctrine of governmental infallibility trains men in suspiciousness and conspiracy. Perhaps other objectives will be achieved, but under such circumstances their taste will be sour.

Nor does the doctrine of infallibility destroy only good faith. It is also incompatible with a belief in the probable rationality of others. To hold a democratic attitude is to proceed on the assumption that other men may have their own persuasive reasons for thinking as they do. If they disagree with you, this does not necessarily make them candidates for correction and cure. This is the homely meaning of the oft-repeated assertion that democracy has faith in the reasonableness and equality of human beings. The faith does not assert that all men are in fact reasonable, or that they are equal in the capacity to think well or live sensibly. The faith is pragmatic: it expresses a policy. And the policy is simply to credit others with minds of their own, and to hold them responsible for their actions, until there are strong and quite specific reasons for thinking otherwise. Such a policy allows room for the idiosyncrasies of men and permits the varieties of human intelligence to be recognized and used.

In the end, the man who asks himself why he should choose democracy is asking himself to decide with which of two policies he would rather live. One is the policy of normally thinking that his fellows are dangerous to him and to themselves. The other is the policy of thinking that they are reasonable until they show themselves dangerous. To act on either policy has its risks. Why should a man choose one rather than the other? One reason can be found if he asks himself about the consequences the policy he adopts will have for the elementary feelings he will entertain towards his fellows, not in some trans-figured world to come, but here and now. The point of the democratic policy is that it makes for democratic feelings. Those who do not wish to see human society divided into exploiters and exploited, those who wish to see each man come into his own free estate, believe that in the ultimate condition men will treat each other with the respect and fellow-feeling that equals show to equals. It is in the name of such moral attitudes that they seek democracy. The final reason for choosing the democratic method is that it provides a training ground, here and now, in just these attitudes.

---

54 / *The Libertarian Manifesto*

JOHN HOSPERS

John Hospers (1918–   ) taught at the University of Southern California and was for many years the director of the USC School of Philosophy. He is a wide-ranging philosopher and political theorist who also works in aesthetics, ethics, and theory of knowledge. He is one of the founders of the modern libertarian movement, as well as one of its most original philosophers, and was the Libertarian Party candidate for president of the United States in 1972.

[I. WHAT IS LIBERTARIANISM?]

*T*he political philosophy that is called libertarianism (from the Latin *libertas*, liberty) is the doctrine that every person is the owner of his own life, and that no one is the owner of anyone else's life: and that consequently every human being has the right to act in accordance with his own choices, unless those actions infringe on the equal liberty of other human beings to act in accor-dance with their choices.

There are several other ways of stating the same libertarian thesis:

1. *No one is anyone else's master, and no one is anyone else's slave.* Since I am

the one to decide how my life is to be conducted just as you decide about yours, I have no right (even if I had the power) to make you my slave and be your master, nor have you the right to become the master by enslaving me. Slavery is *forced* servitude, and since no one owns the life of anyone else, no one has the right to enslave another. Political theories past and present have traditionally been concerned with who should be the master (usually the king, the dictator, or government bureaucracy) and who should be the slaves, and what the extent of the slavery should be. Libertarianism holds that no one has the right to use force to enslave the life of another, or any portion or aspect of that life.

2. *Other men's lives are not yours to dispose of.* I enjoy seeing operas; but operas are expensive to produce. Opera-lovers often say, "The state (or the city, etc.) should subsidize opera, so that we can all see it. Also it would be for people's betterment, cultural benefit, etc." But what they are advocating is nothing more or less than legalized plunder. They can't pay for the productions themselves, and yet they want to see opera, which involves a large number of people and their labor; so what they are saying in effect is, "Get the money through legalized force. Take a little bit more out of every worker's paycheck every week to pay for the operas we want to see." But I have no right to take by force from the workers' pockets to pay for what I want.

Perhaps it would be better if he *did* go to see opera—then I should try to convince him to go voluntarily. But to take the money from him forcibly, because in my opinion it would be good for *him*, is still seizure of his earnings, which is plunder.

Besides, if I have the right to force him to help pay for my pet projects, hasn't he equally the right to force me to help pay for his? Perhaps he in turn wants the government to subsidize rock-and-roll, or his new car, or a house in the country? If I have the right to milk him, why hasn't he the right to milk me? If I can be a moral cannibal, why can't he too?

We should beware of the inventors of utopias. They would remake the world according to their vision—with the lives and fruits of the labor of *other* human beings. Is it someone's utopian vision that others should build pyramids to beautify the landscape? Very well, then other men should provide the labor; and if he is in a position of political power, and he can't get men to do it voluntarily, then he must *compel* them to "cooperate"—i.e., he must enslave them. . . .

3. *No human being should be a nonvoluntary mortgage on the life of another.* I cannot claim your life, your work, or the products of your effort as mine. The fruit of one man's labor should not be fair game for every freeloader who comes along and demands it as his own. The orchard that has been carefully grown, nurtured, and harvested by its owner should not be ripe for the plucking for any bypasser who has a yen for the ripe fruit. The wealth that some men have produced should not be fair game for looting by government, to be used for whatever purposes its representatives determine, no matter what their motives in so doing may be. The theft of your money by a robber is not justified by the fact that he used it to help his injured mother.

[II. LIBERTARIANISM AND RIGHTS]

It will already be evident that libertarian doctrine is embedded in a view of the rights of man. Each human being has the right to live his life as he chooses, compatibly with the equal right of all other human beings to live their lives as they choose.

All man's rights are implicit in the above statement. Each man has the right to life: any attempt by others to take it away from him, or even to injure him, violates this right, through the use of coercion against him. Each man has the right to liberty: to conduct his life in accordance with the alternatives open to him without coercive action by others. And every man has the right to property: to work to sustain his life (and the lives of whichever others he chooses to sustain, such as his family) and to retain the fruits of his labor.

People often defend the rights of life and liberty but denigrate property rights, and yet the right to property is as basic as the other two: indeed, without property rights no other rights are possible. Depriving you of property is depriving you of the means by which you live. . . .

I have no right to decide how *you* should spend your time or your money. I can make that decision for myself, but not for you, my neighbor. I may deplore your choice of life-style, and I may talk with you about it provided you are willing to listen to me. But I have no right to use force to change it. Nor have I the right to decide how you should spend the money you have earned. I may appeal to you to give it to the Red Cross, and you may prefer to go to prizefights. But that is your decision, and however much I may chafe about it I do not have the right to interfere forcibly with it, for example by robbing you in order to use the money in accordance with *my* choices. (If I have the right to rob you, have you also the right to rob me?)

When I claim a right, I carve out a niche, as it were, in my life, saying in effect, "This activity I must be able to perform without interference from others. For you and everyone else, this is off limits." And so I put up a "no trespassing" sign, which marks off the area of my right. Each individual's right is his "no trespassing" sign in relation to me and others. I may not encroach on his domain any more than he upon mine, without my consent. Every right entails a duty, true—but the duty is only that of *forbearance*—that is, of *refraining* from violating the other person's right. If you have a right to life, I have no right to take your life; if you have a right to the products of your labor (property), I have no right to take it from you without your consent. The nonviolation of these rights will not guarantee you protection against natural catastrophes such as floods and earthquakes, but it will protect you against the aggressive activities *of other men*. And rights, after all, have to do with one's relations to other human beings, not with one's relations to physical nature.

Nor were these rights created by government; governments—some governments, obviously not all—*recognize* and *protect* the rights that individuals already have. Governments regularly forbid homicide and theft; and, at a more advanced stage, protect individuals against such things as libel and breach of contract. . . .

The *right to property* is the most misunderstood and unappreciated of human rights, and it is one most constantly violated by governments. "Property" of course does not mean only real estate; it includes anything you can call your own—your clothing, your car, your jewelry, your books and papers. . . .

"But why have *individual* property rights? Why not have lands and houses owned by everybody together?" Yes, this involves no violation of individual rights, as long as everybody consents to this arrangement and no one is forced to join it. The parties to it may enjoy the communal living enough (at least for a time) to overcome certain inevitable problems: that some will work and some not, that some will achieve more in an hour than others can do in a day, and still they will all get the same income. The few who do the most will in the end consider themselves "workhorses" who do the work of two or three or twelve, while the others will be "freeloaders" on the efforts of these few. But as long as they can get out of the arrangement if they no longer like it, no violation of rights is involved. They got in voluntarily, and they can get out voluntarily; no one has used force.

"But why not say that everybody owns everything? That we *all* own everything there is?"

To some this may have a pleasant ring—but let us try to analyze what it means. If everybody owns everything, then everyone has an equal right to go everywhere, do what he pleases, take what he likes, destroy if he wishes, grow crops or burn them, trample them under, and so on. Consider what it would be like in practice. Suppose you have saved money to buy a house for yourself and your family. Now suppose that the principle, "everybody owns everything," becomes adopted. Well then, why shouldn't every itinerant hippie just come in and take over, sleeping in your beds and eating in your kitchen and not bothering to replace the food supply or clean up the mess? After all, it belongs to all of us, doesn't it? So we have just as much right to it as you, the buyer, have. What happens if we *all* want to sleep in the bedroom and there's not room for all of us? Is it the strongest who wins?

What would be the result? Since no one would be responsible for anything, the property would soon be destroyed, the food used up, the facilities nonfunctional. Beginning as a house that *one* family could use, it would end up as a house that *no one* could use. And if the principle continued to be adopted, no one would build houses any more—or anything else. What for? They would only be occupied and used by others, without remuneration. . . .

How can any of man's rights be violated? Ultimately, only by the use of force. I can make suggestions to you, I can reason with you, entreat you (if you are willing to listen), but I cannot *force* you without violating your rights; only by forcing you do I cut the cord between your free decisions and your actions. Voluntary relations between individuals involve no deprivation of rights, but murder, assault, and rape do, because in doing these things I make you the unwilling victim of my actions. A man's beating his wife involves no violation of rights if she *wanted* to be beaten. *Force is behavior that requires the unwilling involvement of other persons.*

According to libertarianism, the role of government should be limited to the retaliatory use of force against those who have initiated its use. It should not enter into any other areas, such as religion, social organization, and economics.

Government is the most dangerous institution known to man. Throughout history it has violated the rights of men more than any individual or group of individuals could do: it has killed people, enslaved them, sent them to forced labor and concentration camps, and regularly robbed and pillaged them of the fruits of their expended labor. Unlike individual criminals, government has the power to arrest and try; unlike individual criminals, it can surround and encompass a person totally, dominating every aspect of one's life, so that one has no recourse from it but to leave the country (and in totalitarian nations even that is prohibited). Government throughout history has a much sorrier record than any individual, even that of a ruthless mass murderer. The signs we see on bumper stickers are chillingly accurate: "Beware: the Government Is Armed and Dangerous."

The only proper role of government, according to libertarians, is that of the protector of the citizen against aggression by other individuals. The government, of course, should never initiate aggression; its proper role is as the embodiment of the *retaliatory* use of force against anyone who initiates its use.

If each individual had constantly to defend himself against possible aggressors, he would have to spend a considerable portion of his life in target practice, karate exercises, and other means of self-defenses, and even so he would probably be helpless against groups of individuals who might try to kill, maim, or rob him. He would have little time for cultivating those qualities which are essential to civilized life, nor would improvements in science, medicine, and the arts be likely to occur. The function of government is to take this responsibility off his shoulders: the government undertakes to defend him against aggressors and to punish them if they attack him. When the government is effective in doing this, it enables the citizen to go about his business unmolested and without constant fear for his life. To do this, of course, government must have physical power—the police, to protect the citizen from aggression within its borders, and the armed forces, to protect him from aggressors outside. Beyond that, the government should not intrude upon his life, either to run his business, or adjust his daily activities, or prescribe his personal moral code. . . .

II. THE FUNCTION OF GOVERNMENT

What then should be the function of government? In a word, the *protection of human rights*.

1. *The right to life*: libertarians support all such legislation as will protect human beings against the use of force by others, for example, laws against killing, attempting killing, maiming, beating, and all kinds of physical violence.

2. *The right to liberty*: there should be no laws compromising in any way freedom of speech, of the press, and peaceable assembly. There should be no censorship of ideas, books, films, or of anything else by government.

3. *The right to property*: libertarians support legislation that protects the property rights of individuals against confiscation, nationalization, eminent domain, robbery, trespass, fraud and misrepresentation, patent and copyright, libel and slander. . . .

Laws may be classified into three types: (1) laws protecting individuals against themselves, such as laws against fornication and other sexual behavior, alcohol, and drugs; (2) laws protecting individuals against aggressions by other individuals, such as laws against murder, robbery, and fraud; (3) laws requiring people to help one another; for example, all laws which rob Peter to pay Paul, such as welfare.

Libertarians reject the first class of laws totally. Behavior which harms no one else is strictly the individual's own affair. Thus, there should be no laws against becoming intoxicated, since whether or not to become intoxicated is the individual's own decision: but there should be laws against driving while intoxicated, since the drunken driver is a threat to every other motorist on the highway (drunken driving falls into type 2). Similarly, there should be no laws against drugs (except the prohibition of sale of drugs to minors) as long as the taking of these drugs poses no threat to anyone else. Drug addiction is a psychological problem to which no present solution exists. Most of the social harm caused by addicts, other than to themselves, is the result of the thefts which they perform in order to continue their habit—and then the *legal* crime is the theft, not the addiction. The actual cost of heroin is about ten cents a shot; if it were legalized, the enormous traffic in illegal sale and purchase of it would stop, as well as the accompanying proselytization to get new addicts (to make more money for the pusher) and the thefts performed by addicts who often require eighty dollars a day just to keep up the habit. Addiction would not stop, but the crimes would: it is estimated that 75 percent of the burglaries in New York City today are performed by addicts, and all these crimes could be wiped out at one stroke through the legalization of drugs. (Only when the taking of drugs could be shown to constitute a threat to *others*, should it be prohibited by law. It is only laws protecting people against *themselves* that libertarians oppose.)

Laws should be limited to the second class only: aggression by individuals against other individuals. These are laws whose function is to protect human beings against encroachment by others; and this, as we have seen, is (according to libertarianism) the sole function of government.

Libertarians also reject the third class of laws totally: no one should be forced by law to help others, not even to tell them the time of day if requested, and certainly not to give them a portion of one's weekly paycheck. Governments, in the guise of humanitarianism, have given to some by taking from others (charging a "handling fee" in the process, which, because of the government's waste and inefficiency, sometimes is several hundred percent). And in so doing they have decreased incentive, violated the rights of individuals and lowered the standard of living of almost everyone.

All such laws constitute what libertarians call *moral cannibalism*. A cannibal in the physical sense is a person who lives off the flesh of other human beings. A *moral* cannibal is one who believes he has a right to live off the "spirit" of other human beings—who believes that he has a moral claim on the productive capacity, time, and effort expended by others.

It has become fashionable to claim virtually everything that one needs or desires as one's *right*. Thus, many people claim that they have a right to a job, the right to free medical care, to free food and clothing, to a decent home, and so on. Now if one asks, apart from any specific context, whether it would be desirable if everyone had these things, one might well say yes. But there is a gimmick attached to each of them: *At whose expense?* Jobs, medical care, education, and so on, don't grow on trees. These are goods and services *produced only by men*. Who then is to provide them, and under what conditions? . . .

All those who demand this or that as a "free service" are consciously or unconsciously evading the fact that there is in reality no such thing as free services. All man-made goods and services are the result of human expenditure of time and effort. There is no such thing as "something for nothing" in this world. If you demand something free, you are demanding that other men give their time and effort to you without compensation. If they voluntarily choose to do this, there is no problem; but if you demand that they be *forced* to do it, you are interfering with their right not to do it if they so choose. "Swimming in this pool ought to be free!" says the indignant passerby. What he means is that others should build a pool, others should provide the material, and still others should run it and keep it in functioning order, so that *he* can use it without fee. But what right has he to the expenditure of *their* time and effort? To expect something "for free" is to expect it *to be paid for by others* whether they choose to or not.

Many questions, particularly about economic matters, will be generated by the libertarian account of human rights and the role of government. Should government have no role in assisting the needy, in providing social security, in legislating minimum wages, in fixing prices and putting a ceiling on rents, in curbing monopolies, in erecting tariffs, in guaranteeing jobs, in managing the money supply? To these and all similar questions the libertarian answers with an unequivocal no.

"But then you'd let people go hungry!" comes the rejoinder. This, the libertarian insists, is precisely what would not happen; with the restrictions removed, the economy would flourish as never before. With the controls taken off business, existing enterprises would expand and new ones would spring into existence satisfying more and more consumer needs; millions more people would be gainfully employed instead of subsisting on welfare, and all kinds of research and production, released from the stranglehold of government, would proliferate, fulfilling man's needs and desires as never before. It has always been so whenever government has permitted men to be free traders on a free market. But *why* this is so, and how the free market is the best solution to all problems relating to the material aspect of man's life, is another and far longer story.

---

55 / *Socialism*

CARL COHEN

Carl Cohen (1931–   ), professor of philosophy at the University of Michigan, writes in the area of ethics and social and political philosophy. He has published major books on democracy and democratic socialism, as well as such topics as civil disobedience and the rule of law.

[I. SOCIALISM AND DEMOCRACY]

We socialists agree that democracy is necessary and absolutely right. But it is not enough. Democracy is completed, fulfilled, by socialism—which is simply the democratic control of *all* resources in the community by society *as a whole*.

Socialism makes democratic ideals concrete. In it the collective will of the people is put to the service of the people in their daily lives. Through socialism the common interests of all the citizens are protected, their common needs met.

The name "socialism" has—at least to many American ears—a negative, even threatening, connotation. Yet most ordinary people warmly support—under a different name—many activities that are truly socialist in nature. We all know that some things must be done for the community as a whole. And some things can be undertaken *for* the community only *by* the community, acting *as* a community. Constructive collective action in this spirit is socialism.

How, for example, do we "provide for the common defense"? Why, through social action, of course. . . .

How do we make and enforce the criminal law? Collectively, of course. . . .

All democratic experience teaches the need for collective action. Real democracy *is* social democracy, democratic socialism.

While we all practice socialism in many spheres, its applicability to other spheres in which it is equally necessary is widely denied. Sometimes manipulated by the rich and powerful, sometimes blinded by our own slogans, sometimes dreading unreal philosophical ghosts, we fear to take social action where we ought. We fail to complete our democracy.

How can we complete it? Where would collective action have greatest impact on daily life? In the economy, of course. Action as a society is needed most of all in producing and distributing the necessities and comforts of ordinary human life. Socialism is democracy extended to the world of work and money.

All the wealth of the world—the houses and food, the land and lumber and luxuries—is somehow divided and distributed. How is that done? And how should it be done? We socialists try to rethink such fundamental questions: Who gets what? And Why?

Satisfactory answers to these questions must, of course, prove acceptable to the masses. Being democrats above all, we trust the judgment of the people. Their choices, when fully informed, will be rational and fair. We lay it down as a restriction upon ourselves, therefore, that the great changes socialism requires must come only as the honest expression of the will of the citizens, through action by their freely elected representatives. An organic transformation of society can succeed only when genuinely willed by its members. True socialists—unlike some who falsely parade under that banner—never have and never will force their solutions on an unwilling community. Democracies around the world, from India to Sweden, have enthusiastically applied socialist theory to their problems, devising socialist solutions specially suitable to their circumstances. The same basic theory can be applied successfully, with American ingenuity, to American circumstances. Confident that we can prove this to the satisfaction of the citizens concerned, we commit ourselves without reservations to abide by the judgment of the people after the case has been put fairly before them. We compel no one; our socialism is democratic, through and through.

How the wealth of most of the world is now divided is very plain to see. A few people get a great deal, and most people get just barely enough, or a little less than enough, to live decently. Rich and poor are the great classes of society and everyone knows it well. Early democracies accepted these stark inequities as natural and inevitable. We do not. Some democrats still accept them. Material success (they say) is open to everyone in a system of private enterprise, and rewards properly go to the industrious and the able, those ambitious enough to pull themselves out of poverty by effort and wit. Some succeed, some do not, and most (they conclude) receive their just deserts.

It isn't so. That picture of "free enterprise" is a myth and always has been. In fact, by putting control of industry and finance into private hands, free enterprise results in the ownership of more and more by fewer and fewer, making economic justice unattainable for most. For centuries, wherever capitalism has prevailed, the great body of wealth has rested in the pockets of a tiny fraction of the citizens, while the masses are divided between those who just get by on their wages, and those who are unemployed and poor, inadequately housed, and often hungry. That great division, between those who have and those who have not, is the leading feature of a private enterprise economy, even when democratic. Those who have get more, because money and property are instruments for the accumulation of more money and more property. Economic freedom in such a system, for the vast majority, is only the freedom to work for another. Working men and women are free to sweat for paychecks, free to look for another job, and maybe—if their needs are desperate—free to go on welfare. These are false freedoms, not deserving the name.

Why does it work out that way? Will the poor always be with us? Ought each person to look out only for himself or herself and devil take the hindmost? We deny that this is the spirit of a decent society. We do not accept the inevitability of poverty; we do not think a democracy need be a cutthroat enterprise, and we know that cooperative action by the members of a society in their joint interests can protect both the essential freedoms of each individual and the economic well-being of all. That rational cooperation is called socialism. . . .

Every democracy, socialist or not, will seek to protect citizens' political rights—but only socialist democracies protect citizens' *economic* rights. Freedom of speech and assembly are priceless; are not freedom from unemployment and hunger equally so? We think so. The same collective action needed to defend the citizens against aggression from without is needed to organize production rationally and to distribute wealth justly within our own borders. In the economic sphere as much as any other, cooperation and foresight are central. The public ownership of industry is the only way to achieve them. . . .

[II. SOCIALISM AND CAPITALISM]

Socialism is simply economic good sense. The long-term fruits of capitalism have become too bitter: cycles of boom and bust, unemployment and welfare, personal dissatisfaction and business failure. Inflation steals from everyone (except those who can raise prices and rents quickly); depression demoralizes everyone. Disorder and distress are widespread. Our land itself is abused, our water poisoned, and our air fouled. When everything is left "up for grabs," the grabbing will be vicious and the outcome chaotic. There can be no intelligent planning for future needs, no rational distribution of products or materials in short supply, no reasonable deployment of human energies, in an economy in which the fundamental rule is dog-eat-dog. Legislation designed to blunt the fangs can do no more than reduce the depth of a serious wound.

Capitalism relies upon the so-called "market economy." The prices asked or offered for raw materials and finished products it leaves entirely to private parties, individuals or business firms, who enter a supposedly open market. This free market, it is argued, will be self-regulating; supply and demand will rationalize prices, fairness and productivity will be ensured by competition, enterprise encouraged by the hope of profit.

None of this actually works in the way capitalist mythology depicts it. The system relies upon the wisdom and power of economic fairies that never did exist. Nothing in the market is dependable, since everything within it fluctuates in response to unpredictable and uncontrollable factors: the tastes of buyers, the moods of sellers, the special circumstances of either, accidents causing short supply, or fashions transforming reasonable supply into glut.

Rationality and fairness through competition? No claim could be more fraudulent. In a capitalist market prices depend largely upon the relative strengths (or weaknesses) of the traders. If I own all the orchards, and am therefore the seller of all the cherries in the market, you, dear buyer, will pay my price or eat no cherries. Steel, timber, farm machinery are for sale in the market. Go, dear friend, and bargain with the sellers. Anyone tempted to believe capitalist propaganda about the give and take in the market should put it to the test. Reflect upon your own experiences as a shopper: You were told the price of the item you looked at—a TV set or a can of beans—and you paid that price or left without. That is how the market works for ordinary folks. Giant firms, manufacturers or chain retailers, may bargain with suppliers on occasion—but even then the stronger get the better deals. Those who control resources and money control the market, manipulating it in their own interests. Those who enter the market (either as buyer or seller) with great needs but little power are squeezed and exploited. The weak get twisted, the strong do the twisting. That's free enterprise.

Fairness? Markets do not know the meaning of the word. All's fair in war—and market competition is perpetual war, through guile and threat, on a thousand fronts. Rewards go to the aggressive, the keys to victory are accumulation, possession, control. And rules for fair dealing? They will be evaded, broken surreptitiously, even ignored—just like the rules of war—when it profits the combatants. . . .

[III. AIMS OF SOCIALISM]

Two consequences of capitalist disorder deserve special attention.

The first is unemployment. . . . If unemployment is the cruelest consequence of capitalism, inflation is the most insidious. . . . The little people (whose amassed savings had been used) discover too late that their nest eggs are shrunken, their retirements insecure. The rich get richer and the poor get children.

Reasonable human beings can end all this. Production and distribution can be designed for human service. Cooperation is the key. Society must be organized with mutual service and mutual benefit as its fundamental theme.

That theme is not alien to us; it lies at the core of our highest moral and religious ideals. We must realize these ideals in practice.

Economic cooperation entails two practical principles: (1) productive property must be publicly owned; and (2) production and distribution must be planned for the common good. *Public ownership* and *planning*—acting upon both we can readily achieve the substance of democratic socialism.

Public ownership is the base. Public ownership of what? Of the means by which goods are produced and work is carried on. Private persons are not entitled to own the instruments of our common good. A system enabling some to exact profit from the work of others, to wax rich while the glaring needs of others go unmet, is fundamentally corrupt. We would end that corruption by bringing all the elements of the productive economy—the electric utilities and the mines, agriculture and transport, the production of metals and paper and drugs, the airlines and the food chains and the telephone system—under public ownership. . . .

The nationalization of all industry will have two consequences. First, *profit* for some from the work of others will be no more. . . . By eliminating the need for private profit, the public ownership of industry proves itself not only cheaper but more satisfying for all. A nationalized economy can be guided by one overriding purpose—the *general* welfare. The need for service overrules the need for a good return. Some services yield little profit, or none; yet the self-governed community can nevertheless provide such service widely to its own members. . . .

When the railroads (and all other vital industries) are nationalized, the task of striking a balance between wide service and reasonable economy will remain. Public ownership does not provide something for nothing; it distributes essential burdens more fairly. The decisions then to be made about what services are worth what burdens will be made by all of us, through elected representatives. Decisions affecting us all will not be reached in closed board rooms by capitalist magnates motivated by selfish interests. All productive enterprise—the railroads are but one illustration—will be conducted for people, and not for profit. . . .

Two practical principles, we said earlier, comprise the substance of democratic socialism. Public ownership is the first, the foundation of socialism. Planning production and distribution for the common good is the second, and the fruit of socialism. When all members of the community have equal voice in the management of the economy, the elected representatives of those voices will naturally seek to deploy productive powers rationally. The community, then fully in command of its own affairs, will deliberate carefully in choosing its economic goals and in devising the means to attain them. It will make plans. . . .

[IV. OBJECTIONS AND REPLIES]

Two great objections to economic planning must be dealt with. The first is the claim that it does not work. This has been repeatedly proved false.

Every individual, and every community, has experienced successful planning. . . . Good planning is the heart of intelligent policy in every sphere, and it always will be. Without a plan there can hardly be any policy at all. . . .

The second major objection to economic planning is the claim that it will cost us our freedom. This is as false as the claim that it does not work, and more pernicious.

Here lies the nub of the conflict between democratic socialists and our private enterprise critics. Freedom, says the critic, is the paramount social value. The freedom of each individual as an economic agent must be curtailed, they argue, by any large-scale economic plan. Once the goals are set, and the role of each economic element fixed, every private person must be sharply restricted in the use of his own resources. What can be bought and what can be sold or invested will be determined by the plan. The individual will be forced to work where, and when, and as the socialist bureaucrats have decided. Economic planning, they conclude, is but a pretty name for economic slavery.

The complaint is entirely unfounded. It is plausible only because it supposes, falsely, that economic planning under socialism will be imposed from above, by arbitrary authorities over whom we will have no control. Not so. Democratic socialism brings *democratic* planning. In an economy that is publicly owned and managed, *we* are the planners. Long-range designs for the allocation of resources, decisions about what is to be produced and how it is to be distributed, will come not from a secret, all-powerful elite but from *public* bodies, publicly selected, acting publicly, and answerable to the general public. . . .

The critics' picture of socialist planning is a caricature of the real thing. They picture each citizen as a mindless cog in a great machine that grinds on unfeelingly, insensitive to mistakes or changing conditions. But the truly insensitive economy is the *un*planned one, the economy that cannot respond to human needs because it responds to nothing human at all. In that disordered economy the individual is indeed helpless, a bobbing cork on uncontrolled currents. Those currents are brought under control only by giving each citizen a voice in the control of economic as well as political affairs. Democratic planning ensures that voice. The plans will be ours. We can adjust them as we make errors and learn from them; we can refine them as circumstances change. We can scrap bad plans and devise new ones as we develop new needs or new capacities. A planning economy, *honestly* socialized, will not be our master but our servant. Let our critics not forget that our first principle throughout is *self*-government, democracy.

For self-governed citizens liberty is, indeed, a paramount concern. And what is liberty, after all? It consists of the ability and the right of individuals to make choices in determining their own conduct. The greater the range of their choices, the greater their freedom. No one supposes that liberty is absolute, that individuals can be free to do entirely as they please without restriction. Even the best of our laws limit each person's freedom to do some sorts of things in order that all of us may be genuinely free to do many other, more valuable sorts of things. The more complex a society, the more essential are some kinds of self-restriction for the extension of real freedom within it. . . .

Limits on the absolute freedom of private economic agents will be entailed by socialized planning; we make no bones about that. Some of these limits—on the freedom to own, buy, and sell productive resources like factories and farms—will be painful to some, just as universal taxation or compulsory schooling are burdensome now to many. The freedoms gained, from economic insecurity and injustice, will be vastly greater than those given up, and vastly more important.

Socialist restrictions will be felt most keenly by a relatively small number of persons who now enjoy luxury and great economic power. Those who never had investment capital at their disposal, who never were the owners of profit-making wealth, are deprived of nothing in losing economic license. Socialist gains, on the other hand, will be felt directly by every citizen, experiencing steady improvement in the quality of his or her own life, and satisfaction in the increased well-being of others. Never was a wiser bargain struck.

Democracy calls for participation in the important affairs of one's community. One's community is not only his town, or nation, but also his place of work—the factory or office, the restaurant or construction project. Can we make democracy genuine in such places, in the day-to-day lives of ordinary citizens?

Yes, we can, but only under socialism. Where the ownership of the enterprise is private, and profit-oriented, there must be bosses on the job to represent the owners and protect their profits. The workers are hired, whether by the hour or the month, in the owners' interests; they take orders from the bosses or they are fired. Capitalism inevitably produces authoritarianism in labor-management relations. Collective bargaining, of which capitalists make much, does no more than mitigate the severity of worker subordination. . . .

Democracy in the work place does not mean disorder. It does not mean that everyone works when and where and how he or she pleases. It means simply that the members of the work force—knowing themselves as owners as well as consumers and workers—participate with community management in setting work rules, production quotas, hours, and procedures. Of all the ways in which democratic ideals can be realized, this is the most concrete, the most immediate, and the most satisfying. It can be achieved under socialism; on a large scale it can be achieved only under socialism. This by itself is a compelling argument for socialist democracy. . . .

56 / Morality and the Liberal Ideal

MICHAEL J. SANDEL

*Michael Sandel (1953–   ) is a professor in Harvard's government depart-
ment. He is a leading political theorist and one of the leaders of the communitarian movement. His book* Liberalism and the Limits of Justice *(Cambridge University Press, 1982) is generally regarded as one of the first major
statements of the communitarian point of view.*

I.

*L*iberals often take pride in defending what they oppose—pornography, for
example, or unpopular views. They say the state should not impose on its
citizens a preferred way of life, but should leave them as free as possible to
choose their own values and ends, consistent with a similar liberty for others.
This commitment to freedom of choice requires liberals constantly to distinguish between permission and praise, between allowing a practice and endorsing it. It is one thing to allow pornography, they argue, something else to
affirm it.

Conservatives sometimes exploit this distinction by ignoring it. They
charge that those who would allow abortions favor abortion, that opponents
of school prayer oppose prayer, that those who defend the rights of Communists sympathize with their cause. And in a pattern of argument familiar in
our politics, liberals reply by invoking higher principles; it is not that they
dislike pornography less, but rather that they value toleration, or freedom of
choice, or fair procedures more.

But in contemporary debate, the liberal rejoinder seems increasingly fragile, its moral basis increasingly unclear. Why should toleration and freedom
of choice prevail when other important values are also at stake? Too often the
answer implies some version of moral relativism, the idea that it is wrong to
"legislate morality" because all morality is merely subjective. "Who is to say
what is literature and what is filth? That is a value judgment, and whose
values should decide?"

Relativism usually appears less as a claim than as a question. "Who is to
judge?" But it is a question that can also be asked of the values that liberals
defend. Toleration and freedom and fairness are values too, and they can
hardly be defended by the claim that no values can be defended. So it is a

mistake to affirm liberal values by arguing that all values are merely subjective. The relativist defense of liberalism is no defense at all.

What, then, can be the moral basis of the higher principles the liberal invokes? Recent political philosophy has offered two main alternatives—one utilitarian, the other Kantian.* The utilitarian view, following John Stuart Mill,† defends liberal principles in the name of maximizing the general welfare. The state should not impose on its citizens a preferred way of life, even for their own good, because doing so will reduce the sum of human happiness, at least in the long run; better that people choose for themselves, even if, on occasion, they get it wrong. "The only freedom which deserves the name," writes Mill in *On Liberty*, "is that of pursuing our own good in our own way, so long as we do not attempt to deprive others of theirs, or impede their efforts to obtain it." He adds that his argument does not depend on any notion of abstract right, only on the principle of the greatest good for the greatest number. "I regard utility as the ultimate appeal on all ethical questions; but it must be utility in the largest sense, grounded on the permanent interest of man as a progressive being."

Many objections have been raised against utilitarianism as a general doctrine of moral philosophy. Some have questioned the concept of utility, and the assumption that all human goods are in principle commensurable. Others have objected that by reducing all values to preferences and desires, utilitarians are unable to admit qualitative distinctions of worth, unable to distinguish noble desires from base ones. But most recent debate has focused on whether utilitarianism offers a convincing basis for liberal principles, including respect for individual rights.

In one respect, utilitarianism would seem well suited to liberal purposes. Seeking to maximize overall happiness does not require judging people's values, only aggregating them. And the willingness to aggregate preferences without judging them suggests a tolerant spirit, even a democratic one. When people go to the polls we count their votes, whatever they are.

But the utilitarian calculus is not always as liberal as it first appears. If enough cheering Romans pack the Colosseum to watch the lion devour the Christian, the collective pleasure of the Romans will surely outweigh the pain of the Christian, intense though it may be. Or if a big majority abhors a small religion and wants it banned, the balance of preferences will favor suppression, not toleration. Utilitarians sometimes defend individual rights on the grounds that respecting them now will serve utility in the long run. But this calculation is precarious and contingent. It hardly secures the liberal promise not to impose on some the values of others. As the majority will is an inadequate instrument of liberal politics—by itself it fails to secure individual

---

*[A formalistic moral theory derived from the work of Immanuel Kant, German philosopher (1724–1804).—Eds.]

†[A major nineteenth-century philosopher (1806–1873) who developed utilitarianism in influential directions.—Eds.]

rights—so the utilitarian philosophy is an inadequate foundation for liberal principles.

The case against utilitarianism was made most powerfully by Immanuel Kant. He argued that empirical principles, such as utility, were unfit to serve as basis for the moral law. A wholly instrumental defense of freedom and rights not only leaves rights vulnerable, but fails to respect the inherent dignity of persons. The utilitarian calculus treats people as means to the happiness of others, not as ends in themselves, worthy of respect.

Contemporary liberals extend Kant's argument with the claim that utilitarianism fails to take seriously the distinction between persons. In seeking above all to maximize the general welfare, the utilitarian treats society as a whole as if it were a single person; it conflates our many, diverse desires into a single system of desires. It is indifferent to the distribution of satisfactions among persons, except insofar as this may affect the overall sum. But this fails to respect our plurality and distinctness. It uses some as means to the happiness of all, and so fails to respect each as an end in himself.

II.

In the view of modern-day Kantians, certain rights are so fundamental that even the general welfare cannot override them. As John Rawls* writes in his important work, *A Theory of Justice*, "Each person possesses an inviolability founded on justice that even the welfare of society as a whole cannot override. . . . The rights secured by justice are not subject to political bargaining or to the calculus of social interests."

So Kantian liberals need an account of rights that does not depend on utilitarian considerations. More than this, they need an account that does not depend on any particular conception of the good, that does not presuppose the superiority of one way of life over others. Only a justification neutral about ends could preserve the liberal resolve not to favor any particular ends, or to impose on its citizens a preferred way of life. But what sort of justification could this be? How is it possible to affirm certain liberties and rights as fundamental without embracing some vision of the good life, without endorsing some ends over others? It would seem we are back to the relativist predicament—to affirm liberal principles without embracing any particular ends.

The solution proposed by Kantian liberals is to draw a distinction between the "right" and the "good"—between a framework of basic rights and liberties, and the conceptions of the good that people may choose to pursue within the framework. It is one thing for the state to support a fair framework, they argue, something else to affirm some particular ends. For example, it is one thing to defend the right to free speech so that people may be free to form their own opinions and choose their own ends, but something else to support

*[A philosopher at Harvard University (b. 1921).—Eds.]

it on the grounds that a life of political discussion is inherently worthier than a life unconcerned with public affairs, or on the grounds that free speech will increase the general welfare. Only the first defense is available in the Kantian view, resting as it does on the ideal of a neutral framework.

Now, the commitment to a framework neutral with respect to ends can be seen as a kind of value—in this sense the Kantian liberal is no relativist—but its value consists precisely in its refusal to affirm a preferred way of life or conception of the good. For Kantian liberals, then, the right is prior to the good, and in two senses. First, individual rights cannot be sacrificed for the sake of the general good; and second, the principles of justice that specify these rights cannot be premised on any particular vision of the good life. What justifies the rights is not that they maximize the general welfare or otherwise promote the good, but rather that they comprise a fair framework within which individuals and groups can choose their own values and ends, consistent with a similar liberty for others.

Of course, proponents of the rights-based ethic notoriously disagree about what rights are fundamental, and about what political arrangements the ideal of the neutral framework requires. Egalitarian liberals support the welfare state, and favor a scheme of civil liberties together with certain social and economic rights—rights to welfare, education, health care, and so on. Libertarian liberals defend the market economy, and claim that redistributive policies violate peoples' rights; they favor a scheme of civil liberties combined with a strict regime of private property rights. But whether egalitarian or libertarian, rights-based liberalism begins with the claim that we are separate, individual persons, each with our own aims, interests, and conceptions of the good; it seeks a framework of rights that will enable us to realize our capacity as free moral agents, consistent with a similar liberty for others.

III.

Within academic philosophy, the last decade or so has seen the ascendance of the rights-based ethic over the utilitarian one, due in large part to the influence of Rawls's *A Theory of Justice*. The legal philosopher H. L. A. Hart* recently described the shift from "the old faith that some form of utilitarianism must capture the essence of political morality" to the new faith that "the truth must lie with a doctrine of basic human rights, protecting specific basic liberties and interests of individuals. . . . Whereas not so long ago great energy and much ingenuity of many philosophers were devoted to making some form of utilitarianism work, latterly such energies and ingenuity have been devoted to the articulation of theories of basic rights."

But in philosophy as in life, the new faith becomes the old orthodoxy before long. Even as it has come to prevail over its utilitarian rival, the rights-based ethic has recently faced a growing challenge from a different direction,

*[A very influential British legal philosopher (b. 1907).—Eds.]

from a view that gives fuller expression to the claims of citizenship and community than the liberal vision allows. The communitarian critics, unlike modern liberals, make the case for a politics of the common good. Recalling the arguments of Hegel* against Kant, they question the liberal claim for the priority of the right over the good, and the picture of the freely choosing individual it embodies. Following Aristotle, they argue that we cannot justify political arrangements without reference to common purposes and ends, and that we cannot conceive of ourselves without reference to our role as citizens, as participants in a common life.

IV.

This debate reflects two contrasting pictures of the self. The rights-based ethic, and the conception of the person it embodies, were shaped in large part in the encounter with utilitarianism. Where utilitarians conflate our many desires into a single system of desire, Kantians insist on the separateness of persons. Where the utilitarian self is simply defined as the sum of its desires, the Kantian self is choosing self, independent of the desires and ends it may have at any moment. As Rawls writes, "The self is prior to the ends which are affirmed by it; even a dominant end must be chosen from among numerous possibilities."

The priority of the self over its ends means I am never defined by my aims and attachments, but always capable of standing back to survey and assess and possibly to revise them. This is what it means to be a free and independent self, capable of choice. And this is the vision of the self that finds expression in the ideal of the state as a neutral framework. On the rights-based ethic, it is precisely because we are essentially separate, independent selves that we need a neutral framework, a framework of rights that refuses to choose among competing purposes and ends. If the self is prior to its ends, then the right must be prior to the good.

Communitarian critics of rights-based liberalism say we cannot conceive ourselves as independent in this way, as bearers of selves wholly detached from our aims and attachments. They say that certain of our roles are partly constitutive of the persons we are—as citizens of a country, or members of a movement, or partisans of a cause. But if we are partly defined by the communities we inhabit, then we must also be implicated in the purposes and ends characteristic of those communities. As Alasdair MacIntyre† writes in his book, *After Virtue*, "What is good for me has to be the good for one who inhabits these roles." Open-ended though it be, the story of my life is always embedded in the story of those communities from which I derive my identity—whether family or city, tribe or nation, party or cause. In the com-

---

*[Influential German philosopher (1770–1831).—Eds.]
†[An influential contemporary philosopher.—Eds.]

munitarian view, these stories make a moral difference, not only a psychological one. They situate us in the world and give our lives their moral particularity.

What is at stake for a politics in the debate between unencumbered selves and situated ones? What are the practical differences between a politics of rights and a politics of the common good? On some issues, the two theories may produce different arguments for similar policies. For example, the civil rights movement of the 1960s might be justified by liberals in the name of human dignity and respect for persons, and by communitarians in the name of recognizing the full membership of fellow citizens wrongly excluded from the common life of the nation. And where liberals might support public education in hopes of equipping students to become autonomous individuals, capable of choosing their own ends and pursuing them effectively, communitarians might support public education in hopes of equipping students to become good citizens, capable of contributing meaningfully to public deliberations and pursuits.

On other issues, the two ethics might lead to different policies. Communitarians would be more likely than liberals to allow a town to ban pornographic bookstores, on the grounds that pornography offends its way of life and the values that sustain it. But a politics of civil virtue does not always part company with liberalism in favor of conservative policies. For example, communitarians would be more willing than some rights-oriented liberals to see states enact laws regulating plant closings, to protect their communities from the disruptive effects of capital mobility and sudden industrial change. More generally, where the liberal regards the expansion of individual rights and entitlements as unqualified moral and political progress, the communitarian is troubled by the tendency of liberal programs to displace politics from smaller forms of association to more comprehensive ones. Where libertarian liberals defend the private economy and egalitarian liberals defend the welfare state, communitarians worry about the concentration of power in both the corporate economy and the bureaucratic state, and the erosion of those intermediate forms of community that have at times sustained a more vital public life.

Liberals often argue that a politics of the common good, drawing as it must on particular loyalties, obligations, and traditions, opens the way to prejudice and intolerance. The modern nation-state is not the Athenian polis, they point out; the scale and diversity of modern life have rendered the Aristotelian political ethic nostalgic at best and dangerous at worst. Any attempt to govern by a vision of the good is likely to lead to a slippery slope of totalitarian temptations.

Communitarians reply, rightly in my view, that intolerance flourishes most where forms of life are dislocated, roots unsettled, traditions undone. In our day, the totalitarian impulse has sprung less from the convictions of confidently situated selves than from the confusions of atomized, dislocated, frustrated selves, at sea in a world where common meanings have lost their force. As Hannah Arendt* has written, "What makes mass society so difficult to bear is not the number of people involved, or at least not primarily, but the fact that the world between them has lost its power to gather them together, to relate and to separate them." Insofar as our public life has withered, our sense of common involvement diminished, we lie vulnerable to the mass politics of totalitarian solutions. So responds the party of the common good to the party of rights. If the party of the common good is right, our most pressing moral and political project is to revitalize those civic republican possibilities implicit in our tradition but fading in our time.

57 / *Political Philosophies of Women's Liberation†*

ALISON JAGGAR

Alison Jaggar (1943–   ) teaches philosophy and feminism at the University of Colorado and is a leading feminist philosopher and activist. Her writings and public activities have influenced feminist thought and women's issues in this country and elsewhere.

*F*eminists are united by a belief that the unequal and inferior social status of women is unjust and needs to be changed. But they are deeply divided about what changes are required. The deepest divisions are not differences about strategy or the kinds of tactics that will best serve women's interests; instead, they are differences about what *are* women's interests, what constitutes women's liberation.

Within the women's liberation movement, several distinct ideologies can be discerned. All[1] believe that justice requires freedom and equality for women, but they differ on such basic philosophical questions as the proper account

---

*[An important political theorist (1906–1975).—Eds.]

†[Readers should note that this article describes positions held by North American feminists in the 1970s. In the 1990s the lines have been redrawn and the positions somewhat altered.—A. J.]

[1]All except one: as we shall see later, lesbian separatism is evasive on the question whether men should, even ultimately, be equal with women.

of freedom and equality, the functions of the state, and the notion of what constitutes human, and especially female, nature. In what follows, I shall outline the feminist ideologies which are currently most influential and show how these give rise to differences on some particular issues. Doing this will indicate why specific debates over feminist questions cannot be settled in isolation but can only be resolved in the context of a theoretical framework derived from reflection on the fundamental issues of social and political philosophy.

I. THE CONSERVATIVE VIEW

This is the position against which all feminists are in reaction. In brief, it is the view that differential treatment of women, as a group, is not unjust. Conservatives admit, of course, that some individual women do suffer hardships, but they do not see this suffering as part of the systematic social oppression of women. Instead, the clear differences between women's and men's social roles are rationalized in one of two ways. Conservatives either claim that the female role is not inferior to that of the male, or they argue that women are inherently better adapted than men to the traditional female sex role. The former claim advocates a kind of sexual apartheid, typically described by such phrases as "complementary but equal"; the later postulates an inherent inequality between the sexes.[2]

All feminists reject the first claim, and most feminists, historically, have rejected the second. However, it is interesting to note that, as we shall see later, some modern feminists have revived the latter claim.

Conservative views come in different varieties, but they all have certain fundamentals in common. All claim that men and women should fulfill different social functions, that these differences should be enforced by law where opinion and custom are insufficient, and that such action may be justified by reference to innate differences between men and women. Thus all sexual conservatives presuppose that men and women are inherently unequal in abilities, that the alleged difference in ability implies a difference in social function, and that one of the main tasks of the state is to ensure that the individual perform his or her proper social function. Thus, they argue, social differentiation between the sexes is not unjust, since justice not only allows but requires us to treat unequals unequally.

[2]The inequalities between the sexes are said to be both physical and psychological. Alleged psychological differences between the sexes include women's emotional instability, greater tolerance for boring detail, incapacity for abstract thought, and less aggression. Writers who have made such claims range from Rousseau (*Émile, or Education* [1762; translation, London: J. M. Dent, 1911]; see especially Book 5 concerning the education of "Sophie, or Woman"), through Schopenhauer (*The World as Will and Idea* and his essay "On Women"), Fichte (*The Science of Rights*), Nietzsche (*Thus Spake Zarathustra*), and Freud down to, in our own times, Steven Goldberg with *The Inevitability of Patriarchy* (New York: William Morrow, 1973–74).

II. LIBERAL FEMINISM

In speaking of liberal feminism, I am referring to that tradition which received its classic expression in J. S. Mill's *The Subjection of Women* and which is alive today in various "moderate" groups, such as the National Organization for Women, which agitate for legal reform to improve the status of women.

The main thrust of the liberal feminist's argument is that an individual woman should be able to determine her social role with as great freedom as does a man. Though women now have the vote, the liberal sees that we are still subject to many constraints, legal as well as customary, which hinder us from success in the public worlds of politics, business, and the professions. Consequently the liberal views women's liberation as the elimination of those constraints and the achievement of equal civil rights.

Underlying the liberal argument is the belief that justice requires that the criteria for allocating individuals to perform a particular social function should be grounded in the individual's ability to perform the tasks in question. The use of criteria such as "race, sex, religion, national origin or ancestry"[3] will normally not be directly relevant to most tasks. Moreover, in conformity with the traditional liberal stress on individual rights, the liberal feminist insists that each person should be considered separately in order that an outstanding individual should not be penalized for deficiencies that her sex as a whole might possess.[4]

This argument is buttressed by the classic liberal belief that there should be a minimum of state intervention in the affairs of the individual. Such a belief entails rejection of the paternalistic view that women's weakness requires that we be specially protected.[5] Even if relevant differences between women and men in general could be demonstrated, the existence of those differences still would not constitute a sufficient reason for allowing legal restrictions on women as a group. Even apart from the possibility of penalizing an outstanding individual, the liberal holds that women's own good sense or, in the last resort, our incapacity to do the job will render legal prohibitions unnecessary.[6]

From this sketch it is clear that the liberal feminist interprets equality to mean that each individual, regardless of sex, should have an equal opportunity to seek whatever social positions she or he wishes. Freedom is primarily the absence of legal constraints to hinder women in this enterprise. However, the modern liberal feminist recognizes that equality and freedom, construed in the liberal way, may not always be compatible. Hence, the modern liberal feminist differs from the traditional one in believing not only that laws should not discriminate against women, but that they should be

---

[3]This is the language used by Title VII of the Civil Rights Act with Executive Order 11246, 1965, and Title IX.

[4]J. S. Mill, *The Subjection of Women* (1869; reprint ed., London: J. M. Dent, 1965), p. 236.

[5]Ibid, p. 243.

[6]Ibid, p. 235.

used to make discrimination illegal. Thus she would outlaw unequal pay scales, prejudice in the admission of women to job-training programs and professional schools, and discrimination by employers in hiring practices. She would also outlaw such things as discrimination by finance companies in the granting of loans, mortgages, and insurance to women.

In certain areas, the modern liberal even appears to advocate laws which discriminate in favor of women. For instance, she may support the preferential hiring of women over men, or alimony for women unqualified to work outside the home. She is likely to justify her apparent inconsistency by claiming that such differential treatment is necessary to remedy past inequalities—but that it is only a temporary measure. With regard to (possibly paid) maternity leaves and the employer's obligation to reemploy a woman after such a leave, the liberal argues that the bearing of children has at least as good a claim to be regarded as a social service as does a man's military or jury obligation, and that childbearing should therefore carry corresponding rights to protection. The liberal also usually advocates the repeal of laws restricting contraception and abortion, and may demand measures to encourage the establishment of private day-care centers. However, she points out that none of these demands, nor the father's payment of child support, should really be regarded as discrimination in favor of women. It is only the customary assignment of responsibility for children to their mothers which makes it possible to overlook the fact that fathers have an equal obligation to provide and care for their children. Women's traditional responsibility for child care is culturally determined, not biologically inevitable—except for breast-feeding, which is now optional. Thus the liberal argues that if women are to participate in the world outside the home on equal terms with men, not only must our reproductive capacity come under our own control but, if we have children, we must be able to share the responsibility for raising them. In return, as an extension of the same principle of equal responsibility, the modern liberal supports compulsory military service for women so long as it is obligatory for men.

Rather than assuming that every apparent difference in interests and abilities between the sexes is innate, the liberal recognizes that such differences, if they do not result entirely from our education, are at least greatly exaggerated by it. By giving both sexes the same education, whether it be cooking or carpentry, the liberal claims that she is providing the only environment in which individual potentialities (and, indeed, genuine sexual differences) can emerge. She gives little weight to the possible charge that in doing this she is not liberating women but only imposing a different kind of conditioning. At the root of the liberal tradition is a deep faith in the autonomy of the individual which is incapable of being challenged within that framework.

In summary, then, the liberal views liberation for women as the freedom to determine our own social role and to compete with men on terms that are as equal as possible. She sees every individual as being engaged in constant competition with every other in order to maximize her or his own self-interest, and she claims that the function of the state is to see that such competition is fair by enforcing "equality of opportunity." The liberal does not believe that it is necessary to change the whole existing social structure in order to achieve women's liberation. Nor does she see it as being achieved simultaneously for all women; she believes that individual women may liberate themselves long before their condition is attained by all. Finally, the liberal claims that her concept of women's liberation also involves liberation for men, since men are not only removed from a privileged position but they are also freed from having to accept the entire responsibility for such things as the support of their families and the defense of their country.

III. CLASSICAL MARXIST FEMINISM

On the classical Marxist view, the oppression of women is, historically and currently, a direct result of the institution of private property; therefore, it can only be ended by the abolition of that institution. Consequently, feminism must be seen as part of a broader struggle to achieve a communist society. Feminism is one reason for communism. The long-term interests of women are those of the working class.

For Marxists, everyone is oppressed by living in a society where a small class of individuals owns the means of production and hence is enabled to dominate the lives of the majority who are forced to sell their labor power in order to survive. Women have an equal interest with men in eliminating such a class society. However, Marxists also recognize that women suffer special forms of oppression to which men are *not* subject, and hence, insofar as this oppression is rooted in capitalism, women have additional reasons for the overthrow of that economic system.

Classical Marxists believe that the special oppression of women results primarily from our traditional position in the family. This excludes women from participation in "public" production and relegates us to domestic work in the "private" world of the home. From its inception right up to the present day, monogamous marriage was designed to perpetuate the consolidation of wealth in the hands of a few. Those few are men. Thus, for Marxists, an analysis of the family brings out the inseparability of class society from male supremacy. From the very beginning of surplus production, "the sole exclusive aims of monogamous marriage were to make the man supreme in the family, and to propagate, as the future heirs to his wealth, children indisputably his own."[7] Such marriage is "founded on the open or concealed domestic slavery of the wife,"[8] and is characterized by the familiar double standard which requires sexual fidelity from the woman but not from the man.

Marxists do not claim, of course, that women's oppression is a creation of capitalism. But they do argue that the advent of capitalism intensified the

[7]Friedrich Engels, *The Origin of the Family, Private Property and the State* (1884), reprint ed. (New York: International Publishers, 1942), pp. 57–58.
[8]Ibid., p. 65.

degradation of women and that the continuation of capitalism requires the perpetuation of this degradation. Capitalism and male supremacy each reinforces the other. Among the ways in which sexism benefits the capitalist system are: by providing a supply of cheap labor for industry and hence exerting a downward pressure on all wages; by increasing the demand for the consumption goods on which women are conditioned to depend; and by allocating to women, for no direct pay, the performance of such socially necessary but unprofitable tasks as food preparation, domestic maintenance, and the care of the children, the sick, and the old.[9]

This analysis indicates the directions in which classical Marxists believe that women must move. "The first condition for the liberation of the wife is to bring the whole female sex back into public industry."[10] Only then will a wife cease to be economically dependent on her husband. But for woman's entry into public industry to be possible, fundamental social changes are necessary: all the work which women presently do—food preparation, child care, nursing, etc.—must come within the sphere of public production. Thus, whereas the liberal feminist advocates an egalitarian marriage, with each spouse shouldering equal responsibility for domestic work and economic support, the classical Marxist feminist believes that the liberation of women requires a more radical change in the family. Primarily, women's liberation requires that the economic functions performed by the family should be undertaken by the state. Thus the state should provide child care centers, public eating places, hospital facilities, etc. But all this, of course, could happen only under socialism. Hence it is only under socialism that married women will be able to participate fully in public life and end the situation where "within the family [the husband] is the burgeois and the wife represents the proletariat."[11]

It should be noted that "the abolition of the monogamous family as the economic unity of society"[12] does not necessitate its disappearance as a social unit. Since "sexual love is by its nature exclusive,"[13] marriage will continue, but now it will no longer resemble an economic contract, as it has done hitherto in the property-owning classes. Instead, it will be based solely on "mutual inclination"[14] between a woman and a man who are now in reality, and not just formally, free and equal.

It is clear that classical Marxist feminism is based on very different philosophical presuppositions from those of liberal feminism. Freedom is viewed not just as the absence of discrimination against women but rather as freedom from the coercion of economic necessity. Similarly, equality demands not mere equality of opportunity to compete against other individuals but rather approximate equality in the satisfaction of material needs. Hence, the classical

---

[9]This is, of course, very far from being a complete account of the ways in which Marxists believe that capitalism benefits from sexism.

[10]Engels, op. cit., p. 66.

[11]Ibid., pp. 65–66.

[12]Ibid., p. 66.

[13]Ibid., p. 72.

[14]Ibid.

Marxist feminist's view of the function of the state is very different from the view of the liberal feminist. Ultimately, the Marxist pays at least lip service to the belief that the state is an instrument of class oppression which eventually will wither away. In the meantime, she believes that it should undertake far more than the minimal liberal function of setting up fair rules for the economic race. Instead, it should take over the means of production and also assume those economic responsibilities that capitalism assigned to the individual family and that placed that woman in a position of dependence on the man. This view of the state presupposes a very different account of human nature from that held by the liberal. Instead of seeing the individual as fundamentally concerned with the maximization of her or his own self-interest, the classical Marxist feminist believes that the selfish and competitive aspects of our natures are the result of their systematic perversion in an acquisitive society. Viewing human nature as flexible and as reflecting the economic organization of society, she argues that it is necessary for women (indeed for everybody) to be comprehensively reeducated and to learn that ultimately individuals have common rather than competing goals and interests.

Since she sees women's oppression as a function of the larger socioeconomic system, the classical Marxist feminist denies the possibility, envisaged by the liberal, of liberation for a few women on an individual level. However, she does agree with the liberal that women's liberation would bring liberation for men, too. Men's liberation would now be enlarged to include freedom from class oppression and from the man's traditional responsibility to "provide" for his family, a burden that under liberalism the man merely lightens by sharing it with his wife.

IV. RADICAL FEMINISM

Radical feminism is a recent attempt to create a new conceptual model for understanding the many different forms of the social phenomenon of oppression in terms of the basic concept of sexual oppression. It is formulated by such writers as Ti-Grace Atkinson and Shulamith Firestone.[15]

Radical feminism denies the liberal claim that the basis of women's oppression consists in our lack of political or civil rights; similarly, it rejects the classical Marxist belief that basically women are oppressed because they live in a class society. Instead, in what seems to be a startling regression to conservatism, the radical feminist claims that the roots of women's oppression are biological. She believes that the origin of women's subjection lies in the fact that, as a result of the weakness caused by childbearing, we became dependent on men for physical survival. Thus she speaks of the origin of the family

[15]Ti-Grace Atkinson, "Radical Feminism" and "The Institution of Sexual Intercourse" in *Notes from the Second Year: Major Writings of the Radical Feminists*, ed. S. Firestone (New York, 1970); and Shulamith Firestone, *The Dialectic of Sex: The Case for Feminist Revolution* (New York: Bantam Books, 1970).

in apparently conservative terms as being primarily a biological rather than a social or economic organization.[16] The radical feminist believes that the physical subjection of women by men was historically the most basic form of oppression, prior rather than secondary to the institution of private property and its corollary, class oppression.[17] Moreover, she believes that the power relationships which develop within the biological family provide a model for understanding all other types of oppression such as racism and class society. Thus she reverses the emphasis of the classical Marxist feminist by explaining the development of class society in terms of the biological family rather than explaining the development of the family in terms of class society. She believes that the battles against capitalism and against racism are both subsidiary to the more fundamental struggle against sexism.

Since she believes that the oppression of women is basically biological, the radical feminist concludes that our liberation requires a biological revolution. She believes that only now, for the first time in history, is technology making it possible for women to be liberated from the "fundamental inequality of the bearing and raising of children." It is achieving this through the development of techniques of artificial reproduction and the consequent possibility of diffusing the childbearing and child-raising role throughout society as a whole. Such a biological revolution is basic to the achievement of those important but secondary changes in our political, social, and economic systems which will make possible the other prerequisites for women's liberation. As the radical feminist sees them, those other prerequisites are: the full self-determination, including economic independence, of women (and children); the total integration of women (and children) into all aspects of the larger society; and the freedom of all women (and children) to do whatever they wish to do sexually.[18]

Not only will technology snap the link between sex and reproduction and thus liberate women from our childbearing and child-raising function; the radical feminist believes that ultimately technology will liberate both sexes from the necessity to work. Individual economic burdens and dependencies will thereby be eliminated, along with the justification for compelling children to attend school. So both the biological and economic bases of the family will be removed by technology. The family's consequent disappearance will abolish the prototype of the social "role system,"[19] the most basic form, both

---

[16]Engels recognizes that early forms of the family were based on what he calls "natural" conditions, which presumably included the biological, but he claims that monogamy "was the first form of the family to be based, not on natural, but on economic conditions—on the victory of private property over primitive, natural communal property." Engels, op. cit., p. 57.

[17]Atkinson and Firestone do talk of women as a "political class," but not in Marx's classic sense where the criterion of an individual's class membership is her/his relationship to the means of production. Atkinson defines a class more broadly as a group treated in some special manner by other groups: in the case of women, the radical feminists believe that women are defined as a "class" in virtue of our childbearing capacity. "Radical Feminism," op. cit., p. 24.

[18]These conditions are listed and explained in *The Dialectic of Sex*, pp. 206–9.

[19]"Radical Feminism," op. cit., p. 36.

historically and conceptually, of oppressive and authoritarian relationships. Thus, the radical feminist does not claim that women should be free to determine their own social roles: she believes instead that the whole "role system" must be abolished, even in its biological aspects.

The end of the biological family will also eliminate the need for sexual repression. Male homosexuality, lesbianism, and extramarital sexual intercourse will no longer be viewed in the liberal way as alternative options, outside the range of state regulation, in which the individual may or may not choose to participate. Nor will they be viewed, in the classical Marxist way, as unnatural vices, perversions resulting from the degrading influence of capitalist society.[20] Instead, even the categories of homosexuality and heterosexuality will be abandoned; the very "institution of sexual intercourse," where male and female each play a well-defined role, will disappear.[21] "Humanity could finally revert to its natural 'polymorphously perverse' sexuality."[22]

For the radical feminist, as for other feminists, justice requires freedom and equality for women. But for the radical feminist "equality" means not just equality under the law nor even equality in satisfaction of basic needs; rather, it means that women, like men, should not have to bear children. Correspondingly, the radical feminist conception of freedom requires not just that women should be free to compete, nor even that we should be free from material want and economic dependence on men; rather, freedom for women means that any woman is free to have close relationships with children without having to give birth to them. Politically, the radical feminist envisions an eventual "communistic anarchy,"[23] an ultimate abolition of the state. This will be achieved gradually, through an intermediate state of "cybernetic socialism" with household licenses to raise children and a guaranteed income for all. Perhaps surprisingly, in view of Freud's reputation among many feminists, the radical feminist conception of human nature is neo-Freudian. Firestone believes, with Freud, that "the crucial problem of modern life [is] sexuality."[24] Individuals are psychologically formed through their experience in the family, a family whose power relationships reflect the underlying biological realities of female (and childhood) dependence. But technology will smash the universality of Freudian psychology. The destruction of the biological family, never envisioned by Freud, will allow the emergence of new women and men, different from any people who have previously existed.

The radical feminist theory contains many interesting claims. Some of these look almost factual in character: they include the belief that pregnancy and childbirth are painful and unpleasant experiences, that sexuality is not

---

[20]Engels often expresses an extreme sexual puritanism in *The Origin of the Family, Private Property and the State*. We have already seen his claim that "sexual love is by its nature exclusive." Elsewhere (p. 57) he talks about "the abominable practice of sodomy." Lenin is well known for the expression of similar views.

[21]"The Institution of Sexual Intercourse," op. cit.

[22]*The Dialectic of Sex*, p. 209.

[23]Ibid., final chart, pp. 244–45.

[24]Ibid., p. 43.

naturally genital and heterosexual, and that technology may be controlled by men and women without leading to totalitarianism. Other presuppositions are more clearly normative: among them are the beliefs that technology should be used to eliminate all kinds of pain, that hard work is not in itself a virtue, that sexuality ought not to be institutionalized, and, perhaps most controversial of all, that children have the same rights to self-determination as adults.

Like the other theories we have considered, radical feminism believes that women's liberation will bring benefits for men. According to this concept of women's liberation, not only will men be freed from the role of provider, but they will also participate on a completely equal basis in childbearing as well as child-rearing. Radical feminism, however, is the only theory which argues explicitly that women's liberation also necessitates children's liberation. Firestone explains that this is because "The heart of woman's oppression is her childbearing and child-rearing roles. And in turn children are defined in relation to this role and are psychologically formed by it; what they become as adults and the sorts of relationships they are able to form determine the society they will ultimately build."[25]

V. NEW DIRECTIONS

Although the wave of excitement about women's liberation which arose in the late sixties has now subsided, the theoretical activity of feminists has continued. Since about 1970, it has advanced in two main directions: lesbian separatism and socialist feminism.

Lesbian separatism is less a coherent and developed ideology than an emerging movement, like the broader feminist movement, within which different ideological strains can be detected. All lesbian separatists believe that the present situation of male supremacy requires that women should refrain from heterosexual relationships. But for some lesbian separatists, this is just a temporary necessity, whereas for others, lesbianism will always be required.

Needless to say, all lesbian separatists reject the liberal and the classical Marxist beliefs about sexual preferences; but some accept the radical feminist contention that ultimately it is unimportant whether one's sexual partner be male or female.[26] However, in the immediate context of a male-supremacist society, the lesbian separatist believes that one's sexual choice attains tremendous political significance. Lesbianism becomes a way of combating the overwhelming heterosexual ideology that perpetuates male supremacy.

---

[25]Ibid., p. 72.

[26]"In a world devoid of male power and, therefore, sex roles, who you lived with, loved, slept with and were committed to would be irrelevant. All of us would be equal and have equal determination over the society and how it met our needs. Until this happens, how we use our sexuality and our bodies is just as relevant to our liberation as how we use our minds and time." Coletta Reid, "Coming Out in the Women's Movement." In Nancy Myron and Charlotte Buch, eds., *Lesbianism and the Women's Movement* (Baltimore: Diana Press, 1975), p. 103.

Women . . . become defined as appendages to men so that there is a coherent ideological framework which says it is natural for women to create the surplus to take care of men and that men will do other things. Reproduction itself did not have to determine that. The fact that male supremacy developed the way it has and was institutionalized is an ideological creation. The ideology of heterosexuality, not the simple act of intercourse, is the whole set of assumptions which maintains the ideological power of men over women.[27]

Although this writer favors an ultimate de-institutionalization of sexual activity, her rejection of the claim that reproduction as such does not determine the inferior status of women clearly places her outside the radical feminist framework; indeed, she would identify her methodological approach as broadly Marxist. Some lesbian separatists are more radical, however. They argue explicitly for a matriarchal society which is "an affirmation of the power of female consciousness of the Mother."[28] Such matriarchists talk longingly about ancient matriarchal societies where women were supposed to have been physically strong, adept at self-defense, and the originators of such cultural advances as: the wheel, pottery, industry, leather working, metal working, fire, agriculture, animal husbandry, architecture, cities, decorative art, music, weaving, medicine, communal child care, dance, poetry, song, etc.[29] They claim that men were virtually excluded from these societies. Women's culture is compared favorably with later patriarchal cultures as being peaceful, egalitarian, vegetarian, and intellectually advanced. Matriarchal lesbian separatists would like to recreate a similar culture which would probably imitate the earlier ones in its exclusion of men as full members. Matriarchal lesbian separatists do not claim unequivocally that "men are genetically predisposed towards destruction and dominance,"[30] but, especially given the present research on the behavioral effects of the male hormone testosterone,[31] they think it is a possibility that lesbians must keep in mind.

Socialist feminists believe that classical Marxism and radical feminism each have both insights and deficiencies. The task of socialist feminism is to construct a theory that avoids the weaknesses of each but incorporates its (and other) insights. There is space here for only a brief account of some of the main points of this developing theory.

Socialist feminists reject the basic radical feminist contention that liberation for women requires the abolition of childbirth. Firestone's view is criticized as ahistorical, anti-dialectical, and utopian. Instead, socialist feminists accept the classical Marxist contention that socialism is the main precondition for women's liberation. But though socialism is necessary, socialist feminists

---

[27]Margaret Small, "Lesbians and the Class Position of Women," in *Lesbianism and the Women's Movement,* p. 58.

[28]Jane Alpert, "Mother Right: A New Feminist Theory," *Ms* (August 1973), p. 94.

[29]Alice, Gordon, Debbie, and Mary, *Lesbian Separatism: An Amazon Analysis,* typescript, 1973, p. 5. (To be published by Diana Press, Baltimore.)

[30]Ibid., p. 23.

[31]It is interesting that this is the same research on which Steven Goldberg ground his thesis of "the inevitability of patriarchy"; see note 2.

do not believe that it is sufficient. Sexism can continue to exist despite public ownership of the means of production. The conclusion that socialist feminists draw is that it is necessary to resort to direct cultural action in order to develop a specifically feminist consciousness in addition to transforming the economic base. Thus their vision is totalistic, requiring "transformation of the entire fabric of social relationships."[32]

In rejecting the radical feminist view that the family is based on biological conditions, socialist feminists turn toward the classical Marxist account of monogamy as being based "not on natural but on economic conditions."[33] But they view the classical Marxist account as inadequate, overly simple. Juliet Mitchell[34] argues that the family should be analyzed in a more detailed, sophisticated, and historically specific way in terms of the separate, though interrelated, functions that women perform within it: production, reproduction, sexuality, and the socialization of the young.

Socialist feminists agree with classical Marxists that women's liberation requires the entry of women into public production. But this in itself is not sufficient. It is also necessary that women have access to the more prestigious and less deadening jobs and to supervisory and administrative positions. There should be no "women's work" within public industry.[35]

In classical Marxist theory, "productive labor" is viewed as the production of goods and services within the market economy. Some socialist feminists believe that this account of productiveness obscures the socially vital character of the labor that women perform in the home. They argue that, since it is clearly impossible under capitalism to bring all women into public production, individuals (at least as an interim measure) should be paid a wage for domestic work. This reform would dignify the position of housewives, reduce their dependence on their husbands, and make plain their objective position, minimized by classical Marxists, as an integral part of the working class.[36] Not all socialist feminists accept this position, however, and the issue is extremely controversial at the time of this writing.

One of the main insights of the feminist movement has been that "the personal is political." Socialist feminists are sensitive to the power relations involved in male/female interaction and believe that it is both possible and necessary to begin changing these, even before the occurrence of a revolution in the ownership of the means of production. Thus, socialist feminists recognize the importance of a "subjective factor" in revolutionary change and reject

[32]Barbara Ehrenreich, "Socialist/Feminism and Revolution" (unpublished paper presented to the National Socialist-Feminist Conference, Antioch College, Ohio, July 1975), p. 1.

[33]Engels, op. cit., p. 57.

[34]Juliet Mitchell, *Woman's Estate* (New York: Random House, 1971). Lively discussion of Mitchell's work continues among socialist feminists.

[35]For one socialist feminist account of women's work in public industry, see Sheila Rowbotham, *Woman's Consciousness, Man's World* (Baltimore: Penguin Books, 1973), chap. 6, "Sitting Next to Nellie."

[36]One influential exponent of wages for housework is Mariarosa Dalla Costa, *The Power of Women and the Subversion of Community* (Bristol, England: Falling Wall Press, 1973).

the rigid economic determinism that has characterized many classical Marxists. They are sympathetic to attempts by individuals to change their lifestyles and to share responsibility for each other's lives, even though they recognize that such attempts can never be entirely successful within a capitalist context. They also reject the sexual puritanism inherent in classical Marxism, moving closer to the radical feminist position in this regard.

Clearly there are sharp differences between socialist feminism and most forms of lesbian separatism. The two have been dealt with together in this section only because each is still a developing theory and because it is not yet clear how far either represents the creation of a new ideology and how far it is simply an extension of an existing ideology. One suspects that at least the matriarchal version of lesbian separatism may be viewed as a new ideology: after all, the interpretation of "freedom" to mean "freedom from men" is certainly new, as is the suggestion that women are innately superior to men. Socialist feminism, however, should probably be seen as an extension of classical Marxism, using essentially similar notions of human nature, of freedom and equality, and of the role of the state, but attempting to show that women's situation and the sphere of personal relations in general need more careful analysis by Marxists.[37]

This sketch of some new directions in feminism completes my outline of the main contemporary positions on women's liberation. I hope that I have made clearer the ideological presuppositions at the root of many feminist claims and also shed some light on the philosophical problems that one needs to resolve in order to formulate one's own position and decide on a basis for action. Many of these philosophical questions, such as the nature of the just society, the proper account of freedom and equality, the functions of the state, and the relation between the individual and society, are traditional problems which now arise in a new context; others, such as the role of technology in human liberation, are of more recent origin. In either case, feminism adds a fresh dimension to our discussion of the issues and points to the need for the so-called philosophy of man to be transformed into a comprehensive philosophy of women and men and their social relations.

STUDY QUESTIONS

1. Why does Frankel "choose democracy"?
2. What is Hospers' main argument against the welfare state?

[37]Since I wrote this section, I have learned of some recent work by socialist feminists which seems to provide an excitingly new theoretical underpinning for much socialist feminist practice. An excellent account of these ideas is given by Gayle Rubin in "The Traffic in Women: Notes on the 'Political Economy' of Sex." This paper appears in *Toward an Anthropology of Women*, ed. Rayna R. Reiter (New York: Monthly Review Press, 1975). If something like Rubin's account is accepted by socialist feminists, it will be a difficult and important question to work out just how far they have moved from traditional Marxism and how much they still share with it.

3. Does Hospers consider government a thief or an angel?

4. To what extent does Cohen disagree with libertarianism?

5. How, in Cohen's view, is socialism an extension of democracy? To what extent is it a departure from it?

6. To what extent do Cohen and Frankel have similar ideals of state and society?

7. Are there any forms of state and society that we do not adequately deal with but which you think are more plausible, e.g., communism, fascism, anarchism? Do some research on one of these views and write a brief essay, comparing and contrasting it with one of the five answers to our main questions represented in this section.

8. What is the relationship between state and society according to each of the five views represented in this section?

9. What kinds of assumptions about human nature, human happiness, and the good life are implicit or explicit in each of the five positions represented in the selections?

10. What kind of notions of freedom, equality, and justice do each of the selections implicitly or explicitly endorse?

11. What are Sandel's main criticisms of the liberal theory of the state?

12. How do Sandel's criticisms of liberalism relate to golden rule morality, egoism, utilitarianism, and virtue ethics? (Part Nine)

13. What are some differences between communitarianism and conservatism? (This question will require some research.)

14. What sort of notion of freedom, or of the self, does Sandel defend? How does it differ from liberalism, conservativism, and egoism? (This is another research project).

FURTHER READINGS

Aristotle. *Nichomachean Ethics*, trans. T. Irwin. Indianapolis: Hackett, 1986. [The source of virtue ethics.]

Bellah, Robert, et al., *Habits of the Heart.* Berkeley: University of California Press, 1985. [A significant sociological discussion of the recent developments of liberalism, communitarianism, and conservatism in our own society.]

Berki, R. N. *Socialism.* New York: St. Martin's Press, 1975. [A good survey.]

Cohen, C. *The Four Systems.* New York: Random House, 1982. [A useful survey of democracy, socialism, communism, and fascism.]

Hegel, G. W. *Hegel's Philosophy of Right*, trans. T. M. Knox. New York: Oxford University Press, 1967. [One of the most important and difficult works on political philosophy in the Western tradition.]

Held, D., ed. *State and Society.* New York: New York University Press, 1984. [A good collection of essays.]

Hospers, John. *Libertarianism: A Political Philosophy for Tomorrow.* Los Angeles: Nash

Publishing Company, 1971. [A lucid defense of libertarianism by one of its main architects.]

Jaggar, Alison. *Feminist Politics and Human Nature*. Totowa: Rowman and Allanhead, 1983. [Expands upon the paper reprinted here.]

Locke, John. *Second Treatise on Government*. Indianapolis: Bobbs-Merrill, Library of Liberal Arts, 1952. [One of the most influential liberal political theories of government in our tradition.]

Manning, D. J. *Liberalism*. New York: St. Martin's Press, 1976. [A lucid account.]

Marx, Karl. *Karl Marx: Selected Writings*, ed. David McLellan. New York: Oxford University Press, 1977. [The best anthology of Marx's writings.]

Nozick, Robert. *Anarchy, State, and Utopia*. New York: Basic Books, 1974. [The most important defense of libertarianism to date; essential reading.]

O'Sullivan, N. K. *Conservatism*. New York: St. Martin's Press, 1976. [A helpful study.]

Plamenatz, John. *Man and Society*, 2 vols. New York: McGraw-Hill, 1963. [A magnificent study of major social and political philosophers from Machiavelli to Marx.]

Plato. *Plato's Republic*, trans. G. M. A. Grube. Indianapolis: Hackett, 1974. [Perhaps the most important work in political theory ever written.]

Rawls, John. *A Theory of Justice*. Cambridge, Mass.: Belknap Press, 1971. [Already a classic, this work defends a version of liberal-social contract theory.]

Rousseau, Jean-Jacques. *On the Social Contract*, ed. R. Masters. New York: St. Martin's Press, 1978. [One of the greatest treatises on political philosophy ever written.]

Sandel, Michael. *Liberalism and the Limits of Justice*. New York: Cambridge University Press, 1984. [A fuller statement by Sandel.]

Strauss, Leo. *Natural Rights and History*. Chicago: University of Chicago Press, 1953. [A recent classic which relates political theory, social science, and morality.]

Tong, Rosemary. *Feminist Thought*. Westview, 1989. [A comprehensive introduction.]

PART TWELVE

SCIENCE AND SOCIETY

PREVIEW

*T*his part raises a number of central issues about science and society, extending many issues from earlier parts into the realms of society, culture, and politics. At the most basic level, the issues in this part deal with the impact of the modern scientific world view, including its doctrines and methods, into all the domains of modern life: everyday life and conduct, politics, art and culture, morality, and human behavior.

We all know that modern science has proved to be a very successful way of acquiring knowledge about the physical and social world, of explaining, predicting, and even controlling natural and social phenomena as well as human behavior in all its aspects. But what happens when science and technology, and scientific ways of thinking and problem solving generally, are carried over into all other areas of life? Is this reasonable and appropriate? Should we be optimistic about the prospects of a scientific civilization, and of life based on science and technology? Can and should science and technology be used to transform art and culture, politics, and individual and social behavior? Should moral and political issues be treated in scientific or technological terms? Are the results of these developments uniformly good? Or are there problems, even dangers, in this type of project, which is becoming ever more dominant throughout the world at the end of the twentieth century?

Main Questions

The main questions of this part are:

1. Are scientific doctrines and methods always the best or the only ones for understanding everything and for solving all human problems?
2. Can modern science create a better society for all, or will it lead to the destruction of human freedom and happiness?

577

Answers

The main answers to these questions are:

1a. Optimistic scientism: Scientific knowledge and technology will transform all aspects of human life for the better, give life new meaning, and achieve more and more human progress as time passes.

1b. Pessimistic scientism: The scientific outlook is the ability to look at the world and oneself honestly and without illusions. This outlook shows that life has no meaning, that there is no consolation or utopia for human beings, and that human beings are for the most part stupid, childlike, and violent. Society must be lead by those who can adopt the scientific outlook and face the harshness of reality. But this may (at best) only keep civilization from destroying itself. Science destroys human happiness and the yearning for consolation from life.

2a. Marxism: Modern science is part and parcel of worldwide capitalism and the war machine. It is wedded to an ideology which turns everything into a commodity, diminishes human freedom, reduces all knowledge to science and all human action to technology and calculation, and exploits the poor and the weak in the interest of capitalism, imperialism, and the military. It manipulates people and perpetuates an unjust economic system. However, methods and techniques for making science and technology serve more democratic, egalitarian, and just ends can be developed; science and technology still can achieve justice and happiness for all humankind.

Intellectuals have the goal of uncovering the general conditions underlying the corrosion of dialogue, democracy, and the loss of the "public sphere," and of articulating general conditions for their recovery and revitalization.

2b. Postmodernism: Knowledge and power are always inseparable. Every system of knowledge, including modern science, is bound up with various political practices and power relations which subjugate individuals, makes them conform to its standards (which are deemed "true" and "rational"), and closes off any other alternatives. It has created a disciplinary society in which one type of knowledge/power relation—science and technology—dominates everything. We cannot avoid some form of the disciplinary society. No revolution, e.g., a Marxist revolution, will eliminate it but merely will change its dominant forms. All systems of knowledge/power are dangerous. All hopes for consolation or utopia only reinforce the disciplinary society. The best we can do is keep things fluid and pluralistic, so as to diffuse the dominant form of knowledge/power by subverting its hold upon us in whatever ways we can.

The envisioned role for intellectuals in 2b presupposes that there are general conditions which cause the corrosion of the public sphere, democracy, and the abuses of science, and that there are general conditions which, if met, would make things better. These assumptions are false. The intellectual's job is to identify the specific factors that limit freedom and undertake the specific task of dealing with them here and now.

Selections

The answers to the questions in this part are as follows:

Answers	Selection
1a. Optimistic scientism	58
1b. Pessimistic scientism	59
2a. Marxism	60
2b. Postmodernism	61

58 / Man against Darkness

W. T. STACE

W. T. Stace (1886–1967) taught at Princeton University and worked in ethics and the study of religion and culture. He was a significant figure in both the academic world and public culture.

*T*he Catholic bishops of America once issued a statement in which they said that the chaotic and bewildered state of the modern world is due to man's loss of faith, his abandonment of God and religion. I agree with this statement though I do not accept the religious beliefs of most bishops. It is no doubt an oversimplification to speak of *the* cause of so complex a state of affairs as the tortured condition of the world today. Its causes are doubtless multitudinous. Yet allowing for some element of oversimplification, I say that the bishops' assertion is substantially true.

M. Jean-Paul Sartre, the French existentialist philosopher,* labels himself an atheist. Yet his views seem to me plainly to support the statement of the bishops. So long as there was believed to be a God in the sky, he says, men could regard him as the source of their moral ideals. The universe, created and governed by a fatherly God, was a friendly habitation for man. We could be sure that, however great the evil in the world, good in the end would triumph and the forces of evil would be routed. With the disappearance of God from the sky all this has changed. Since the world is not ruled by a spiritual being, but rather by blind forces, there cannot be any ideals moral or otherwise, in the universe outside us. Our ideals, therefore, must proceed only from our own minds; they are our own inventions. Thus the world which surrounds us is nothing but an immense spiritual emptiness. It is a dead universe. We do not live in a universe which is on the side of our values. It is completely indifferent to them.

Years ago Mr. Bertrand Russell,† in his essay "A Free Man's Worship," said much the same thing.

> Such in outline, but even more purposeless, more void of meaning, is the world which Science presents for our belief. Amid such a world, if anywhere, our ideals henceforward must find a home. . . . Blind to good and evil, reckless of destruction, omnipotent matter rolls on its relentless way; for man, condemned today to lose his dearest, tomorrow himself to pass through the gate of darkness, it remains only to cherish, ere yet the blow falls, the lofty thoughts that ennoble his

*[1905–1980.—Eds.]
†[Famous British philosopher (1872–1970).—Eds.]

little day; . . . to worship at the shrine his own hands have built; . . . to sustain alone, a weary but unyielding Atlas, the world that his own ideals have fashioned despite the trampling march of unconscious power.

It is true that Mr. Russell's personal attitude to the disappearance of religion is quite different from either that of M. Sartre or the bishops or myself. The bishops think it a calamity. So do I. M. Sartre finds it "very distressing." And he berates as shallow the attitude of those who think that without God the world can go on just the same as before, as if nothing had happened. This creates for mankind, he thinks, a terrible crisis. And in this I agree with him. Mr. Russell, on the other hand, seems to believe that religion has done more harm than good in the world, and that its disappearance will be a blessing. But his picture of the world, and of the modern mind, is the same as that of M. Sartre. He stresses the *purposelessness* of the universe, the facts that man's ideals are his own creations, that the universe outside him in no way supports them, that man is alone and friendless in the world.

Mr. Russell notes that it is science which has produced this situation. There is no doubt that this is correct. But the way in which it has come about is not generally understood. There is a popular belief that some particular scientific discoveries or theories, such as the Darwinian theory of evolution, or the views of geologists about the age of the earth, or a series of such discoveries, have done the damage. It would be foolish to deny that these discoveries have had a great effect in undermining religious dogmas. But this account does not at all go to the root of the matter. Religion can probably outlive any scientific discoveries which could be made. It can accommodate itself to them. The root cause of the decay of faith has not been any particular discovery of science, but rather the general spirit of science and certain basic assumptions upon which modern science, from the seventeenth century onwards, has proceeded.

It was Galileo* and Newton†—notwithstanding that Newton himself was a deeply religious man—who destroyed the old comfortable picture of a friendly universe governed by spiritual values. And this was effected, not by Newton's discovery of the law of gravitation nor by any of Galileo's brilliant investigations, but by the general picture of the world which these men and others of their time made the basis of the science, not only of their own day, but of all succeeding generations down to the present. That is why the century immediately following Newton, the eighteenth century, was notoriously an age of religious skepticism. Skepticism did not have to wait for the discoveries of Darwin‡ and the geologists in the nineteenth century. It flooded the world immediately after the age of the rise of science. Neither the Copernican hypothesis§ nor any of Newton's or Galileo's particular discoveries were the real causes. Religious faith might well have accommodated itself to the new

---

*[1564–1642.—Eds.]

†[1642–1727.—Eds.]

‡[1809–1882.—Eds.]

§[The earth revolves around the sun. By N. Copernicus (1473–1543), Polish astronomer.—Eds.]

astronomy. The real turning point between the medieval age of faith and the modern age of unfaith came when the scientists of the seventeenth century turned their backs upon what used to be called "final causes." The final cause* of a thing or event meant the purpose which it was supposed to serve in the universe, its cosmic purpose. What lay back of this was the presupposition that there is a cosmic order or plan and that everything which exists could in the last analysis be explained in terms of its place in this cosmic plan, that is, in terms of its purpose.

Plato and Aristotle† believed this, and so did the whole medieval Christian world. For instance, if it were true that the sun and the moon were created and exist for the purpose of giving light to man, then this fact would explain why the sun and the moon exist. We might not be able to discover the purpose of everything, but everything must have a purpose. Belief in final causes thus amounted to a belief that the world is governed by purposes, presumably the purposes of some overruling mind. This belief was not the invention of Christianity. It was basic to the whole of Western civilization, whether in the ancient pagan world or in Christendom, from the time of Socrates to the rise of science in the seventeenth century.

The founders of modern science—for instance, Galileo, Kepler,‡ and Newton—were mostly pious men who did not doubt God's purposes. Nevertheless they took the revolutionary step of consciously and deliberately expelling the idea of purpose as controlling nature from their new science of nature. They did this on the ground that inquiry into purposes is useless for what science aims at: namely, the prediction and control of events. To predict an eclipse, what you have to know is not its purpose but its causes. Hence science from the seventeenth century onwards became exclusively an inquiry into causes. The conception of purpose in the world was ignored and frowned on. This, though silent and almost unnoticed, was the greatest revolution in human history, far outweighing in importance any of the political revolutions whose thunder has reverberated through the world.

For it came about in this way that for the past three hundred years there has been growing up in men's minds, dominated as they are by science, a new imaginative picture of the world. The world, according to this new picture, is purposeless, senseless, meaningless. Nature is nothing but matter in motion. The motions of matter are governed, not by any purpose, but by blind forces and laws. Nature in this view, says Whitehead§—to whose writings I am indebted in this part of my essay—is "merely the hurrying of material, end-

---

*[Final cause: the view that things are the product of a plan or design (e.g., the view that the world is the product of God's design, which is eliminated from modern science.—Eds.]

†[Plato (428–328 B.C.) and Aristotle (384–322 B.C.), Greek philosophers.—Eds.]

‡[Johannes Kepler (1571–1630), German astronomer who played a major role in the scientific revolution brought about in the seventeenth century by Galileo (1564–1642), Newton (1642–1727), and, earlier, Copernicus (1473–1543).—Eds.]

§[A. N. Whitehead (1861–1947), British philosopher whose book *Science and the Modern World* (1926) interprets the rise of modern science. His own philosophy, sometimes called "Process Philosophy" (*Process and Reality*, 1929), tries to express the world view of relativity physics.—Eds.]

lessly, meaninglessly." You can draw a sharp line across the history of Europe dividing it into two epochs of very unequal length. The line passes through the lifetime of Galileo. European man before Galileo—whether ancient pagan or more recent Christian—thought of the world as controlled by plan and purpose. After Galileo European man thinks of it as utterly purposeless. This is the great revolution of which I spoke.

It is this which has killed religion. Religion could survive the discoveries that the sun, not the earth, is the center; that men are descended from simian ancestors; that the earth is hundreds of millions of years old. These discoveries may render out of date some of the details of older theological dogmas, may force their restatement in new intellectual frameworks. But they do not touch the essence of the religious vision itself, which is the faith that there is plan and purpose in the world, that the world is a moral order, that in the end all things are for the best. This faith may express itself through many different intellectual dogmas, those of Christianity, of Hinduism, of Islam. All and any of these intellectual dogmas may be destroyed without destroying the essential religious spirit. But that spirit cannot survive destruction of belief in a plan and purpose of the world, for that is the very heart of it. Religion can get on with any sort of astronomy, geology, biology, physics. But it cannot get on with a purposeless and meaningless universe. If the scheme of things is purposeless and meaningless, then the life of man is purposeless and meaningless too. Everything is futile, all effort is in the end worthless. A man may, of course, still pursue disconnected ends, money, fame, art, science, and may gain pleasure from them. But his life is hollow at the center. Hence the dissatisfied, disillusioned, restless, spirit of modern man.

The picture of a meaningless world and a meaningless human life is, I think, the basic theme of much modern art and literature. Certainly it is the basic theme of modern philosophy. According to the most characteristic philosophies of the modern period from Hume in the eighteenth century to the so-called positivists of today, the world is just what it is, and that is the end of all inquiry. There is no *reason* for its being what it is. Everything might just as well have been quite different, and there would have been no reason for that either. When you have stated what things are, what things the world contains, there is nothing more which could be said, even by an omniscient being. To ask any questions about *why* things are thus, or what purpose their being so serves, is to ask a senseless question, because they serve no purpose at all. For instance, there is for modern philosophy no such thing as the ancient problem of evil. For this once famous question presupposes that pain and misery, though they seem so inexplicable and irrational to us, must ultimately subserve some rational purpose, must have their places in the cosmic plan. But this is nonsense. There is no such overruling rationality in the universe. Belief in the ultimate irrationality of everything is the quintessence of what is called the modern mind.

It is true that, parallel with these philosophies which are typical of the modern mind, preaching the meaninglessness of the world, there has run a line of idealistic philosophies whose contention is that the world is after all spiritual in nature and that moral ideals and values are inherent in its structure. But most of these idealisms were simply philosophical expressions of romanticism, which was itself no more than an unsuccessful counterattack of the religious against the scientific view of things. They perished, along with romanticism in literature and art, about the beginning of the present century, though of course they still have a few adherents. At the bottom these idealistic systems of thought were rationalizations of man's wishful thinking. They were born of the refusal of men to admit the cosmic darkness. They were comforting illusions within the warm glow of which the more tender-minded intellectuals sought to shelter themselves from the icy winds of the universe. They lasted a little while. But they are shattered now, and we return once more to the vision of a purposeless world.

Along with the ruin of the religious vision there went the ruin of moral principles and indeed of all values. If there is a cosmic purpose, if there is in the nature of things a drive towards goodness, then our moral systems will derive their validity from this. But if our moral rules do not proceed from something outside us in the nature of the universe—whether we say it is God or simply the universe itself—then they must be our own inventions. Thus it came to be believed that moral rules must be merely an expression of our own likes and dislikes. But likes and dislikes are notoriously variable. What pleases one man, people, or culture displeases another. Therefore morals are wholly relative. This obvious conclusion from the idea of a purposeless world made its appearance in Europe immediately after the rise of science, for instance in the philosophy of Hobbes.* Hobbes saw at once that if there is no purpose in the world there are no values either. "Good and evil," he writes, "are names that signify our appetites and aversions; which in different tempers, customs, and doctrines of men are different. . . . Every man calleth that which pleaseth him, good; and that which displeaseth him, evil."

This doctrine of the relativity of morals, though it has recently received an impetus from the studies of anthropologists, was thus really implicit in the whole scientific mentality. It is disastrous for morals because it destroys their entire traditional foundation. That is why philosophers who see the danger signals, from the time at least of Kant,† have been trying to give to morals a new foundation, that is, a secular or non-religious foundation. This attempt may very well be intellectually successful. Such a foundation, independent of the religious view of the world, might well be found. But the question is whether it can ever be a *practical* success, that is, whether apart from its logical validity and its influence with intellectuals, it can ever replace among the masses of men the lost religious foundation. On that question hangs perhaps the future of civilization. But meanwhile disaster is overtaking us.

The widespread belief in "ethical relativity"‡ among philosophers, psy-

---

*[British philosopher (1588–1679).—Eds.]

†[German philosopher (1724–1804).—Eds.]

‡[The view that moral norms are dependent upon, and vary from, culture to culture, epoch to epoch, or individual to individual. A denial of ethical absolutism, the idea that what is good or bad, right or wrong, is the same for all people everywhere. (See Part Ten.)—Eds.]

chologists, ethnologists, and sociologists is the theoretical counterpart of the repudiation of principle which we see all around us, especially in international affairs, the field in which morals have always had the weakest foothold. No one any longer effectively believes in moral principles except as the private prejudices either of individual men or of nations or cultures. This is the inevitable consequence of the doctrine of ethical relativity, which in turn is the inevitable consequence of believing in a purposeless world.

Another characteristic of our spiritual state is loss of belief in the freedom of the will. This also is a fruit of the scientific spirit, though not of any particular scientific discovery. Science has been built up on the basis of determinism, which is the belief that every event is completely determined by a chain of causes and is therefore theoretically predictable beforehand. It is true that recent physics seems to challenge this. But so far as its practical consequences are concerned, the damage has long ago been done. A man's actions, it was argued, are as much events in the natural world as is an eclipse of the sun. It follows that men's actions are as theoretically predictable as an eclipse. But if it is certain now that John Smith will murder Joseph Jones at 2:15 P.M. on January 1, 2000 A.D. what possible meaning can it have to say that when that time comes John Smith will be *free* to choose whether he will commit the murder or not? And if he is not free, how can he be held responsible?

It is true that the whole of this argument can be shown by a competent philosopher to be a tissue of fallacies—or at least I claim that it can. But the point is that the analysis required to show this is much too subtle to be understood by the average entirely unphilosophical man. Because of this, the argument against free will is generally swallowed whole by the unphilosophical. Hence the thought that man is not free, that he is the helpless plaything of forces over which he has no control, has deeply penetrated the modern mind. We hear of economic determinism, cultural determinism, historical determinism. We are not responsible for what we do because our glands control us, or because we are the products of environment or heredity. Not moral self-control, but the doctor, the psychiatrist, the educationist, must save us from doing evil. Pills and injections in the future are to do what Christ and the prophets have failed to do. Of course I do not mean to deny that doctors and educationists can and must help. And I do not mean in any way to belittle their efforts. But I do wish to draw attention to the weakening of moral controls, the greater or less repudiation of personal responsibility which, in the popular thinking of the day, result from these tendencies of thought.

What, then, is to be done? Where are we to look for salvation from the evils of our time? All the remedies I have seen suggested so far are, in my opinion, useless. Let us look at some of them.

Philosophers and intellectuals generally can, I believe, genuinely do something to help. But it is extremely little. What philosophers can do is to show that neither the relativity of morals nor the denial of free will really follows from the grounds which have been supposed to support them. They can also try to discover a genuine secular basis for morals to replace the religious basis which has disappeared. Some of us are trying to do these things. But in the first place philosophers unfortunately are not agreed about these matters, and their disputes are utterly confusing to the non-philosophers. And in the second place their influence is practically negligible because their analyses necessarily take place at a level on which the masses are totally unable to follow them.

The bishops, of course, propose as remedy a return to belief in God and in the doctrines of the Christian religion. Others think that a new religion is what is needed. Those who make these proposals fail to realize that the crisis in man's spiritual condition is something unique in history for which there is no sort of analogy in the past. They are thinking perhaps of the collapse of the ancient Greek and Roman religions. The vacuum then created was easily filled by Christianity, and it might have been filled by Mithraism* if Christianity had not appeared. By analogy they think that Christianity might now be replaced by a new religion, or even that Christianity itself, if revivified, might bring back health to men's lives.

But I believe that there is no analogy at all between our present state and that of the European peoples at the time of the fall of paganism. Men had at that time lost their belief only in particular dogmas, particular embodiments of the religious view of the world. It had no doubt become incredible that Zeus and the other gods were living on the top of Mount Olympus. You could go to the top and find no trace of them. But the imaginative picture of a world governed by purpose, a world driving towards the good—which is the inner spirit of religion—had at that time received no serious shock. It had merely to re-embody itself in new dogmas, those of Christianity or some other religion. Religion itself was not dead in the world, only a particular form of it.

But now the situation is quite different. It is not merely that particular dogmas, like that of the virgin birth, are unacceptable to the modern mind. That is true, but it constitutes a very superficial diagnosis of the present situation of religion. Modern skepticism is of a wholly different order from that of the intellectuals of the ancient world. It has attacked and destroyed not merely the outward forms of the religious spirit, its particularized dogmas, but the very essence of that spirit itself, belief in a meaningful and purposeful world. For the founding of a new religion a new Jesus Christ or Buddha would have to appear, in itself a most unlikely event and one for which in any case we cannot afford to sit and wait. But even if a new prophet and a new religion did appear, we may predict that they would fail in the modern world. No one for long would believe in them, for modern men have lost the vision, basic to all religion, of an ordered plan and purpose of the world. They have before their minds the picture of a purposeless universe, and such a world-picture must be fatal to any religion at all, not merely to Christianity.

We must not be misled by occasional appearances of a revival of the religious spirit. Men, we are told, in their disgust and disillusionment at the emptiness of their lives, are turning once more to religion, or are searching for

*[A Persian mystery religion, adopted by Roman soldiers. It included an initiation rite involving the sacrifice of a bull, which was later eaten.—Eds.]

a new message. It may be so. We must expect such wistful yearnings of the spirit. We must expect men to wish back again the light that is gone, and to try to bring it back. But however they may wish and try, the light will not shine again—not at least in the civilization to which we belong.

Another remedy commonly proposed is that we should turn to science itself, or the scientific spirit, for our salvation. Mr. Russell and Professor Dewey* both made this proposal, though in somewhat different ways. Professor Dewey seemed to believe that discoveries in sociology, the application of scientific method to social and political problems, will rescue us. This seems to me to be utterly naive. It is not likely that science, which is basically the cause of our spiritual troubles, is likely also to produce the cure for them. Also it lies in the nature of science that, though it can teach us the best means for achieving our ends, it can never tell us what ends to pursue. It cannot give us any ideals. And our trouble is about ideals and ends, not about the means for reaching them.

No civilization can live without ideals, or to put it another way, without a firm faith in moral ideas. Our ideals and moral ideas have in the past been rooted in religion. But the religious basis of our ideals has been undermined, and the superstructure of ideals is plainly tottering. None of the commonly suggested remedies on examination seems likely to succeed. It would therefore look as if the early death of our civilization were inevitable.

Of course we know that it is perfectly possible for individual men, very highly educated men, philosophers, scientists, intellectuals in general, to live moral lives without any religious convictions. But the question is whether a whole civilization, a whole family of peoples, composed almost entirely of relatively uneducated men and women, can do this. It follows, of course, that if we could make the vast majority of men as highly educated as the very few are now, we might save the situation. And we are already moving slowly in that direction through the techniques of mass education. But the critical question seems to concern the time-lag. Perhaps in a hundred years most of the population will, at the present rate, be sufficiently highly educated and civilized to combine high ideals with an absence of religion. But long before we reach any such stage, the collapse of our civilization may have come about. How are we to live through the intervening period?

I am sure that the first thing we have to do is to face the truth, however bleak it may be, and then next we have to learn to live with it. Let me say a word about each of these two points. What I am urging as regards the first is complete honesty. Those who wish to resurrect Christian dogmas are not, of course, consciously dishonest. But they have that kind of unconscious dishonesty which consists in lulling oneself with opiates and dreams. Those who talk of a new religion are merely hoping for a new opiate. Both alike refuse to face the truth that there is, in the universe outside man, no spirituality, no regard for values, no friend in the sky, no help or comfort for man of any sort. To be perfectly honest in the admission of this fact, not to seek

---

*[John Dewey (1859–1952), American pragmatist and educational theorist.—Eds.]

shelter in new or old illusions, not to indulge in wishful dreams about this matter, this is the first thing we shall have to do.

I do not urge this course out of my special regard for the sanctity of truth in the abstract. It is not self-evident to me that truth is the supreme value to which all else must be sacrificed. Might not the discoverer of a truth which would be fatal to mankind be justified in suppressing it, even in teaching men a falsehood? Is truth more valuable than goodness and beauty and happiness? To think so is to invent yet another absolute, another religious delusion in which Truth with a capital T is substituted for God. The reason why we must now boldly and honestly face the truth that the universe is non-spiritual and indifferent to goodness, beauty, happiness, or truth is not that it would be wicked to suppress it, but simply that it is too late to do so, so that in the end we cannot do anything else but face it. Yet we stand on the brink, dreading the icy plunge. We need courage. We need honesty.

Now about the other point, the necessity of learning to live with the truth. This means learning to live virtuously and happily, or at least contentedly, without illusions. And this is going to be extremely difficult because what we have now begun dimly to perceive is that human life in the past, or at least human happiness, has almost wholly depended upon illusions. It has been said that man lives by truth, and that the truth will make us free. Nearly the opposite seems to me to be the case. Mankind has managed to live only by means of lies, and the truth may very well destroy us. If one were a Bergsonian* one might believe that nature deliberately puts illusions into our souls in order to induce us to go on living.

The illusions† by which men have lived seem to be of two kinds. First, there is what one may perhaps call the Great Illusion—I mean the religious illusion that the universe is moral and good, that it follows a wise and noble plan, that it is gradually generating some supreme value, that goodness is bound to triumph in it. Secondly, there is a whole host of minor illusions on which human happiness nourishes itself. How much of human happiness notoriously comes from the illusions of the lover about his beloved? Then again we work and strive because of the illusions connected with fame, glory, power, or money. Banners of all kinds, flags, emblems, insignia, ceremonials, and rituals are invariably symbols of some illusion or other. The British Empire, the connection between mother country and dominions, used to be partly kept going by illusions surrounding the notion of kingship. Or think of the vast amount of human happiness which is derived from the illusion of supposing that if some nonsense syllable, such as "sir" or "count" or "lord" is pronounced in conjunction with our names, we belong to a superior order of people.

---

*[Bergsonian: Henri Bergson (1859–1941), French philosopher who held that reality is fluid and not static.—Eds.]

†[Sigmund Freud (1856–1940) uses the term *illusion* to denote any belief based on wishful thinking and not evidence. Religion is the foremost example of an illusion. *The Future of An Illusion* (New York: Norton, 1961).—Eds.]

There is plenty of evidence that human happiness is almost wholly based upon illusions of one kind or another. But the scientific spirit, or the spirit of truth, is the enemy of illusions and therefore the enemy of human happiness. That is why it is going to be so difficult to live with the truth. There is no reason why we should have to give up the host of minor illusions which render life supportable. There is no reason why the lover should be scientific about the loved one. Even the illusions of fame and glory may persist. But without the Great Illusion, the illusion of a good, kindly, and purposeful universe, we shall *have* to learn to live. And to ask this is really no more than to ask that we become genuinely civilized beings and not merely sham civilized beings.

I can best explain the difference by a reminiscence. I remember a fellow student in my college days, an ardent Christian, who told me that if he did not believe in a future life, in heaven and hell, he would rape, murder, steal and be a drunkard. That is what I call being a sham civilized being. On the other hand, not only could a Huxley,* a John Stuart Mill,† a David Hume,‡ live great and fine lives without any religion, but a great many others of us, quite obscure persons, can at least live decent lives without it. To be genuinely civilized means to be able to walk straightly and to live honorably without the props and crutches of one or another of the childish dreams which have so far supported men. That such a life is likely to be ecstatically happy I will not claim. But that it can be lived in quiet content, accepting resignedly what cannot be helped, not expecting the impossible, and being thankful for small mercies, this I would maintain. That it will be difficult for men in general to learn this lesson I do not deny. But that it will be impossible I would not admit since so many have learned it already.

Man has not yet grown up. He is not adult. Like a child he cries for the moon and lives in a world of fantasies. And the race as a whole has perhaps reached the great crisis of its life. Can it grow up as a race in the same sense as individual men grow up? Can man put away childish things and adolescent dreams? Can he grasp the real world as it actually is, stark and bleak, without its romantic or religious halo, and still retain his ideals, striving for great ends and noble achievements? If he can, all may yet be well. If he cannot, he will probably sink back into the savagery and brutality from which he came, taking a humble place once more among the lower animals.

*[Thomas Henry Huxley (1825–1895), nineteenth-century British Darwinist.—Eds.]
†[British philosopher (1806–1873).—Eds.]
‡[British philosopher and skeptic (1711–1776).—Eds.]

59 / The Life Based on Science

HERBERT SPENCER

*Herbert Spencer (1820–1903) was a major figure in nineteenth-century Eng-
land in sociology, philosophy, and politics. He coined the phrase "Social
Darwinism" and defended the idea that industrial capitalism is the highest
stage of human evolution. Regarded as one of the founders of modern sociology, he exerted a significant influence in both England and the United States.*

. . . We need not insist on the value of that knowledge which aids indirect
self-preservation by facilitating the gaining of a livelihood. . . .

For, leaving out only some very small classes, what are all men employed
in? They are employed in the production, preparation, and distribution of
commodities. And on what does efficiency in the production, preparation,
and distribution of commodities depend? It depends on the use of methods
fitted to the respective natures of these commodities; it depends on an adequate knowledge of their physical, chemical, or vital properties, as the case
may be; that is, it depends on Science. This order of knowledge, which is in
great part ignored in our school courses, is the order of knowledge underlying the right performance of all those processes by which civilized life is made
possible. . . .

Yet one more science have we to note as bearing directly on industrial
success—the Science of Society. Without knowing it, men who daily look at
the state of the money-market, glance over prices current, discuss the probable crops of corn, cotton, sugar, wool, silk, weigh the chances of war, and
from all those data decide on their mercantile operations, are students of
social science: empirical and blundering students it may be; but still, students
who gain the prizes or are plucked of their profits, according as they do or do
not reach the right conclusion. Not only the manufacturer and the merchant
must guide their transactions by calculations of supply and demand, based on
numerous facts, and tacitly recognising sundry general principles of social
action; but even the retailer must do the like: his prosperity very greatly
depending upon the correctness of his judgments respecting the future
wholesale prices and the future rates of consumption. Manifestly, all who
take part in the entangled commercial activities of a community, are vitally
interested in understanding the laws according to which those activities vary.

Thus, to all such as are occupied in the production, exchange, or distribution of commodities, acquaintance with science in some of its departments, is
of fundamental importance. Whoever is immediately or remotely implicated
in any form of industry (and few are not) has a direct interest in understand-

ing something of the mathematical, physical, and chemical properties of things; perhaps, also, has a direct interest in biology; and certainly has in sociology. Whether he does or does not succeed well in that indirect self-preservation which we call getting a good livelihood, depends in a great degree on his knowledge of one or more of these sciences: not, it may be, a rational knowledge; but still a knowledge, though empirical. For what we call learning a business, really implies the science involved in it; though not perhaps under the name of science. . . .

The training of children—physical, moral, and intellectual—is dreadfully defective. And in great measure it is so, because parents are devoid of that knowledge by which this training can alone be rightly guided. What is to be expected when one of the most intricate of problems is undertaken by those who have given scarcely a thought to the principles on which its solution depends? For shoe-making or house-building, for the management of a ship or a locomotive-engine, a long apprenticeship is needful. Is it, then, that the unfolding of a human being in body and mind, is so comparatively simple a process, that any one may superintend and regulate it with no preparation whatever? If not—if the process is with one exception more complex than any in Nature, and the task of administering to it one of surpassing difficulty; is it not madness to make no provision for such a task? Better sacrifice accomplishments than omit this all-essential instruction. . . .

Thus we see that for regulating the third great division of human activities, a knowledge of the laws of life is the one thing needful. Some acquaintance with the first principles of physiology and the elementary truths of psychology is indispensable for the right bringing up of children. . . .

From the parental functions let us pass now to the functions of the citizen. We have here to inquire what knowledge best fits a man for the discharge of these functions. . . .

Without an acquaintance with the general truths of biology and psychology, rational interpretation of social phenomena is impossible. Only in proportion as men obtain a certain rude, empirical knowledge of human nature, are they enabled to understand even the simplest facts of social life: as, for instance, the relation between supply and demand. And if not even the most elementary truths of sociology can be reached until some knowledge is obtained of how men generally think, feel, and act under given circumstances; then it is manifest that there can be nothing like a wide comprehension of sociology, unless through a competent knowledge of man in all his faculties, bodily and mental. Consider the matter in the abstract, and this conclusion is self-evident. Thus:—Society is made up of individuals; all that is done in society is done by the combined actions of individuals; and therefore, in individual actions only can be found the solutions of social phenomena. But the actions of individuals depend on the laws of their natures; and their actions cannot be understood until these laws are understood. These laws, however, when reduced to their simplest expression, are found to depend on the laws of body and mind in general. Hence it necessarily follows, that biology and psychology are indispensable as interpreters of sociology. Or, to state the conclusions still more simply:—all social phenomena are phenomena of life—are the most complex manifestations of life—are ultimately dependent on the laws of life—and can be understood only when the laws of life are understood. Thus, then, we see that for the regulation of this fourth division of human activities, we are, as before, dependant on Science. . . .

And now we come to that remaining division of human life which includes the relaxations, pleasures, and amusements filling leisure hours. After considering what training best fits for self-preservation, for the obtainment of sustenance, for the discharge of parental duties, and for the regulation of social and political conduct; we have now to consider what training best fits for the miscellaneous ends not included in these—for the enjoyments of Nature, of Literature, and of the Fine Arts, in all their forms. Postponing them as we do to things that bear more vitally upon human welfare; and bringing everything, as we have, to the test of actual value; it will perhaps be inferred that we are inclined to slight these less essential things. No greater mistake could be made, however. We yield to none in the value we attach to aesthetic culture and its pleasures. Without painting, sculpture, music, poetry, and the emotions produced by natural beauty of every kind, life would lose half its charm. So far from thinking that the training and gratification of the tastes are unimportant, we believe the time will come when they will occupy a much larger share of human life than now. When the forces of Nature have been fully conquered to man's use—when the means of production have been brought to perfection—when labour has been economized to the highest degree—when education has been so systematized that a preparation for the more essential activities may be made with comparative rapidity—and when, consequently, there is a great increase of spare time; then will the poetry, both of Art and Nature, rightly fill a large space in the minds of all.

Unexpected as the assertion may be, it is nevertheless true, that the highest Art of every kind is based upon Science—that without Science there can be neither perfect production nor full appreciation. Science, in that limited technical acceptation current in society, may not have been possessed by many artists of high repute; but acute observers as they have been, they have always possessed a stock of those empirical generalizations which constitute science in its lowest phase; and they have habitually fallen far below perfection, partly because their generalizations were comparatively few and inaccurate. That science necessarily underlies the fine arts, becomes manifest à priori, when we remember that art-products are all more or less representative of objective or subjective phenomena; that they can be true only in proportion as they conform to the laws of these phenomena; and that before they can thus conform the artist must know what these laws are. . . . Thus to the question with which we set out—What knowledge is of most worth?—the uniform reply is—Science. This is the verdict on all the counts. For direct self-preservation, or the maintenance of life and health, the all-important knowledge is—Science. For that indirect self-preservation which we call gaining a livelihood, the knowledge of greatest value is—Science. For the due discharge of parental functions, the proper guidance is to be found only in—Science. For that interpretation of national life, past and present, without which the citizen cannot rightly regulate his conduct, the indispensable key is—Science. Alike for the most perfect production and highest enjoyment of art in all its forms, the needful preparation is still—Science. And for purposes of discipline—intellectual, moral, religious—the most efficient study is, once more—Science. The question which at first seemed so perplexed, has become, in the course of our inquiry, comparatively simple. We have not to estimate the degrees of importance of different orders of human activity, and different studies as severally fitting us for them; since we find that the study of Science, in its most comprehensive meaning, is the best preparation for all these orders of activity. We have not to decide between the claims of knowledge of great though conventional value, and knowledge of less though intrinsic value; seeing that the knowledge which we find to be of most value in all other respects, is intrinsically most valuable: its worth is not dependent upon opinion, but is as fixed as is the relation of man to the surrounding world. Necessary and eternal as are its truths, all Science concerns all mankind for all time. Equally at present, and in the remotest future, must it be of incalculable importance for the regulation of their conduct, that men should understand the science of life, physical, mental, and social; and that they should understand all other science as a key to the science of life.

And yet the knowledge which is of such transcendent value is that which, in our age of boasted education, receives the least attention. While this which we call civilization could never have arisen had it not been for science; science forms scarcely an appreciable element in what men consider civilized training. Though to the progress of science we owe it, that millions find support where once there was food only for thousands; yet of these millions but a few thousands pay any respect to that which has made their existence possible. Though this increasing knowledge of the properties and relations of things has not only enabled wandering tribes to grow into populous nations, but has given to the countless members of those populous nations comforts and pleasures which their few naked ancestors never even conceived, or could have believed, yet is this kind of knowledge only now receiving a grudging recognition in our highest educational institutions. To the slowly growing acquaintance with the uniform co-existences and sequences of phenomena—to the establishment of invariable laws, we owe our emancipation from the grossest superstitions. But for science we should be still worshipping fetishes; or, with hecatombs of victims, propitiating diabolical deities. And yet this science, which, in place of the most degrading conceptions of things, has given us some insight into the grandeurs of creation, is written against in our theologies and frowned upon from our pulpits.

Paraphrasing an Eastern fable, we may say that in the family of knowledges, Science is the household drudge, who, in obscurity, hides unrecognised perfections. To her has been committed all the work; by her skill, intelligence, and devotion, have all the conveniences and gratifications been obtained; and while ceaselessly occupied ministering to the rest, she has been kept in the background, that her haughty sisters might flaunt their fripperies in the eyes of the world. The parallel holds yet further. For we are fast coming to the denouement, when the positions will be changed; and while these haughty sisters sink into merited neglect, Science, proclaimed as highest alike in worth and beauty, will reign supreme.

60 / The Public Sphere: An Encyclopedia Article (1964)*

JÜRGEN HABERMAS

Jürgen Habermas (1929–   ) teaches at the Wolfgang Goethe Institute in Frankfurt, Germany. He is one of the most important social and political theorists writing today. His work combines the insights of Marxism and liberalism, and ranges over philosophy, social theory, psychology, political theory, and sociology. He has synthesized the major figures and schools of thought in modern social theory, and has developed a model of democracy based upon the idea of communication and dialogue, following to some extent in the footsteps of American pragmatism.

I. THE CONCEPT

*B*y "the public sphere" we mean first of all a realm of our social life in which something approaching public opinion can be formed. Access is guaranteed to all citizens. A portion of the public sphere comes into being in every conversation in which private individuals assemble to form a public body.†

---

*[Originally appeared in Fischer Lexicon, *Staat und Politik*, new edition (Frankfurt am Main, 1964), pp. 220–226.—Eds.]

†[Habermas' concept of the public sphere is not to be equated with that of "the public," i.e., of the individuals who assemble. His concept is directed instead at the institution, which to be sure only assumes concrete form through the participation of people. It cannot, however, be characterized simply as a crowd. (This and the following notes by Peter Hohendahl.)—Eds.]

They then behave neither like business or professional people transacting private affairs, nor like members of a constitutional order subject to the legal constraints of a state bureaucracy. Citizens behave as a public body when they confer in an unrestricted fashion—that is, with the guarantee of freedom of assembly and association and the freedom to express and publish their opinions—about matters of general interest. In a large public body this kind of communication requires specific means for transmitting information and influencing those who receive it. Today newspapers and magazines, radio and television are the media of the public sphere. We speak of the political public sphere in contrast, for instance, to the literary one, when public discussion deals with objects connected to the activity of the state. Although state authority is so to speak the executor of the political public sphere, it is not a part of it.* To be sure, state authority is usually considered "public" authority, but it derives its task of caring for the well-being of all citizens primarily from this aspect of the public sphere. Only when the exercise of political control is effectively subordinated to the democratic demand that information be accessible to the public does the political public sphere win an institutionalized influence over the government through the instrument of law-making bodies. The expression "public opinion" refers to the tasks of criticism and control which a public body of citizens informally—and, in periodic elections, formally as well—practices *vis-à-vis* the ruling structure organized in the form of a state. Regulations demanding that certain proceedings be public (*Publizitätsvorschriften*), for example, those providing for open court hearings, are also related to this function of public opinion. The public sphere as a sphere which mediates between society and state, in which the public organizes itself as the bearer of public opinion, accords with the principle of the public sphere†—that principle of public information which once had to be fought for against the arcane policies of monarchies and which since that time has made possible the democratic control of state activities.

It is no coincidence that these concepts of the public sphere and public opinion arose for the first time only in the eighteenth century. They acquire their specific meaning from a concrete historical situation. It was at that time that the distinction of "opinion" from "opinion publique" and "public opinion" came about. Though mere opinions (cultural assumptions, normative attitudes, collective prejudices and values) seem to persist unchanged in their natural form as a kind of sediment of history, public opinion can by definition only come into existence when a reasoning public is presupposed. Public discussions about the exercise of political power which are both critical in

---

*[The state and the public sphere do not overlap, as one might suppose from casual language use. Rather they confront one another as opponents. Habermas designates that sphere as public which antiquity understood to be private, i.e., the sphere of non-governmental opinion making.]

†[The principle of the public sphere could still be distinguished from an institution which is demonstrable in social history. Habermas thus would mean a model of norms and modes of behavior by means of which the very functioning of public opinion can be guaranteed for the first time. These norms and modes of behavior include: a) general accessibility, b) elimination of all privileges, and c) discovery of general norms and rational legitimations.]

intent and institutionally guaranteed have not always existed—they grew out of a specific phase of bourgeois society and could enter into the order of the bourgeois constitutional state only as a result of a particular constellation of interests.

II. HISTORY

There is no indication European society of the high middle ages possessed a public sphere as a unique realm distinct from the private sphere. Nevertheless, it was not coincidental that during that period symbols of sovereignty, for instance the princely seal, were deemed "public." At that time there existed a public representation of power. The status of the feudal lord, at whatever level of the feudal pyramid, was oblivious to the categories "public" and "private," but the holder of the position represented it publicly: he showed himself, presented himself as the embodiment of an ever-present "higher" power. The concept of this representation has been maintained up to the most recent constitutional history. Regardless of the degree to which it has loosed itself from the old base, the authority of political power today still demands a representation at the highest level by a head of state. Such elements, however, derive from a pre-bourgeois social structure. Representation in the sense of a bourgeois public sphere,* for instance the representation of the nation or of particular mandates, has nothing to do with the medieval representative public sphere—a public sphere directly linked to the concrete existence of a ruler. As long as the prince and the estates of the realm still "are" the land, instead of merely functioning as deputies for it, they are able to "re-present"; they represent their power "before" the people, instead of for the people.

The feudal authorities (church, princes, and nobility), to which the representative public sphere was first linked, disintegrated during a long process of polarization. By the end of the eighteenth century they had broken apart into private elements on the one hand, and into public on the other. The position of the church changed with the Reformation: the link to divine authority which the church represented, that is, religion, became a private matter. So-called religious freedom came to insure what was historically the first area of private autonomy. The church itself continued its existence as one public and legal body among others. The corresponding polarization within princely authority was visibly manifested in the separation of the public budget from the private household expenses of a ruler. The institutions of public authority, along with the bureaucracy and the military, and in part also with the legal institutions, asserted their independence from the privatized sphere of the princely court. Finally, the feudal estates were transformed as well: the

*[The expression "represent" is used in a very specific sense in the following section, namely to "present oneself." The important thing to understand is that the medieval public sphere, if it even deserves this designation, is tied to the *personal*. The feudal lord and estates create the public sphere by means of their very presence.]

nobility became the organs of public authority, parliament, and the legal institutions while those occupied in trades and professions, insofar as they had already established urban corporations and territorial organizations, developed into a sphere of bourgeois society which would stand apart from the state as a genuine area of private autonomy.

The representative public sphere yielded to that new sphere of "public authority" which came into being with national and territorial states. Continuous state activity (permanent administration, standing army) now corresponded to the permanence of the relationships which with the stock exchange and the press had developed within the exchange of commodities and information. Public authority consolidated into a concrete opposition for those who were merely subject to it and who at first found only a negative definition of themselves within it. These were the "private individuals" who were excluded from public authority because they held no office. "Public" no longer referred to the "representative" court of a prince endowed with authority, but rather to an institution regulated according to competence, to an apparatus endowed with a monopoly on the legal exertion of authority. Private individuals subsumed in the state at whom public authority was directed now made up the public body.

Society, now a private realm occupying a position in opposition to the state, stood on the one hand as if in clear contrast to the state. On the other hand, that society had become a concern of public interest to the degree that the reproduction of life in the wake of the developing market economy had grown beyond the bounds of private domestic authority. *The bourgeois public sphere* could be understood as the sphere of private individuals assembled into a public body, which almost immediately laid claim to the officially regulated "intellectual newspapers" for use against the public authority itself. In those newspapers, and in moralistic and critical journals, they debated that public authority on the general rules of social intercourse in their fundamentally privatized yet publically relevant sphere of labor and commodity exchange.

III. THE LIBERAL MODEL OF THE PUBLIC SPHERE

The medium of this debate—public discussion—was unique and without historical precedent. Hitherto the estates had negotiated agreements with their princes, settling their claims to power from case to case. This development took a different course in England, where the parliament limited royal power, than it did on the continent, where the monarchies mediatized the estates. The third estate then broke with this form of power arrangement since it could no longer establish itself as a ruling group. A division of power by means of the delineation of the rights of the nobility was no longer possible within an exchange economy—private authority over capitalist property is, after all, unpolitical. Bourgeois individuals are private individuals. As such, they do not "rule." Their claims to power *vis-à-vis* public authority were thus directed not against the concentration of power, which was to be "shared." Instead, their ideas infiltrated the very principle on which the existing power is based. To the principle of the existing power, the bourgeois public opposed the principle of supervision—that very principle which demands that proceedings be made public (*Publizität*). The principle of supervision is thus a means of transforming the nature of power, not merely one basis of legitimation exchanged for another.

In the first modern constitutions the catalogues of fundamental rights were a perfect image of the liberal model of the public sphere: they guaranteed the society as a sphere of private autonomy and the restriction of public authority to a few functions. Between these two spheres, the constitutions further insured the existence of a realm of private individuals assembled into a public body who as citizens transmit the needs of bourgeois society to the state, in order, ideally, to transform political into "rational" authority within the medium of this public sphere. The general interest, which was the measure of such a rationality, was then guaranteed, according to the presuppositions of a society of free commodity exchange, when the activities of private individuals in the marketplace were freed from social compulsion and from political pressure in the public sphere.

At the same time, daily political newspapers assumed an important role. In the second half of the eighteenth century, literary journalism created serious competition for the earlier news sheets which were mere compilations of notices. Karl Bücher* characterized this great development as follows: "Newspapers changed from mere institutions for the publication of news into bearers and leaders of public opinion—weapons of party politics. This transformed the newspaper business. A new element emerged between the gathering and the publication of news: the editorial staff. But for the newspaper publisher it meant that he changed from a vendor of recent news to a dealer in public opinion." The publishers insured the newspapers a commercial basis, yet without commercializing them as such. The press remained an institution of the public itself, effective in the manner of a mediator and intensifier of public discussion, no longer a mere organ for the spreading of news but not yet the medium of a consumer culture.

This type of journalism can be observed above all during periods of revolution when newspapers of the smallest political groups and organizations spring up, for instance in Paris in 1789. Even in the Paris of 1848 every half-way eminent politician organized his club, every other his journal: 450 clubs and over 200 journals were established there between February and May alone. Until the permanent legalization of a politically functional public sphere, the appearance of a political newspaper meant joining the struggle for freedom and public opinion, and thus for the public sphere as a principle. Only with the establishment of the bourgeois constitutional state was the

---

*[Karl Bücher (1847–1930) was a famous German economist. He belonged to the historical school of economics, which rejected the view that economics can be a general science; it must be a branch of history, and could only be descriptive.—Eds.]

intellectual press relieved of the pressure of its convictions. Since then it has been able to abandon its polemical position and take advantage of the earning possibilities of a commercial undertaking. In England, France, and the United States the transformation from a journalism of conviction to one of commerce began in the 1830s at approximately the same time. In the transition from the literary journalism of private individuals to the public services of the mass media, the public sphere was transformed by the influx of private interests, which received special prominence in the mass media.

IV. THE PUBLIC SPHERE IN THE SOCIAL WELFARE STATE MASS DEMOCRACY

Although the liberal model of the public sphere is still instructive today with respect to the normative claim that information be accessible to the public,* it cannot be applied to the actual conditions of an industrially advanced mass democracy organized in the form of the social welfare state. In part the liberal model had always included ideological components, but it is also in part true that the social pre-conditions, to which the ideological elements could at one time at least be linked, had been fundamentally transformed. The very forms in which the public sphere manifested itself, to which supporters of the liberal model could appeal for evidence, began to change with the Chartist movement in England and the February revolution in France. Because of the diffusion of press and propaganda, the public body expanded beyond the bounds of the bourgeoisie. The public body lost not only its social exclusivity; it lost in addition the coherence created by bourgeois social institutions and a relatively high standard of education. Conflicts hitherto restricted to the private sphere now intrude into the public sphere. Group needs which can expect no satisfaction from a self-regulating market now tend towards a regulation by the state. The public sphere, which must now mediate these demands, becomes a field for the competition of interests, competitions which assume the form of violent conflict. Laws which obviously have come about under the "pressure of the street" can scarcely still be understood as arising from the consensus of private individuals engaged in public discussion. They correspond in a more or less unconcealed manner to the compromise of conflicting private interests. Social organizations which deal with the state act in the political public sphere, whether through the agency of political parties or directly in connection with the public administration. With the interweaving of the public and private realm, not only do the political authorities assume certain functions in the sphere of commodity exchange and social labor, but conversely social powers now assume political functions. This leads to a kind of "refeudalization" of the public sphere. Large organizations strive for political compromises with the state and with each other, excluding the public

---

*[Here it should be understood that Habermas considers the principle behind the bourgeois public sphere as indispensable, but not its historical form.]

sphere whenever possible. But at the same time the large organizations must assure themselves of at least plebiscitary support from the mass of the population through an apparent display of openness (*demonstrative Publizität*).*

The political public sphere of the social welfare state is characterized by a peculiar weakening of its critical functions. At one time the process of making proceedings public (*Publizität*) was intended to subject persons or affairs to public reason and to make political decisions subject to appeal before the court of public opinion. But often enough today the process of making public simply serves the arcane policies of special interests; in the form of "publicity" it wins public prestige for people or affairs, thus making them worthy of acclamation in a climate of non-public opinion. The very words "public relations work" (*Oeffentlichkeitsarbeit*) betray the fact that a public sphere must first be arduously constructed case by case, a public sphere which earlier grew out of the social structure. Even the central relationship of the public, the parties, and the parliament is affected by this change in function.

Yet this trend toward the weakening of the public sphere as a principle is opposed by the extension of fundamental rights in the social welfare state. The demand that information be accessible to the public is extended from organs of the state to all organizations dealing with the state. To the degree that this is realized, a public body of organized private individuals would take the place of the now-defunct public body of private individuals who relate individually to each other. Only these organized individuals could participate effectively in the process of public communication; only they could use the channels of the public sphere which exist within parties and associations and the process of making proceedings public (*Publizität*) which was established to facilitate the dealings of organizations with the state. Political compromises would have to be legitimized through this process of public communication. The idea of the public sphere, preserved in the social welfare state mass democracy, an idea which calls for a rationalization of power through the medium of public discussion among private individuals, threatens to disintegrate with the structural transformation of the public sphere itself. It could only be realized today, on an altered basis, as a rational reorganization of social and political power under the mutual control of rival organizations committed to the public sphere in their internal structure as well as in their relations with the state and each other.

Translated by Sara Lennox and Frank Lennox

---

*[One must distinguish between Habermas' concept of "making proceedings public" (*Publizität*) and the "public sphere" (*Oeffentlichkeit*). The term *Publizität* describes the degree of public effect generated by a public act. Thus a situation can arise in which the form of public opinion-making is maintained, while the substance of the public sphere has long ago been undermined.]

61 / The Political Function of the Intellectual

MICHEL FOUCAULT

Michel Foucault (1926–1984) taught at the College de France in Paris. He continues to be a major influence on contemporary movements in philosophy, cultural studies, and social and political theory. Often associated with "postmodernism," he was trained in philosophy, psychology, and social history. His writings reflect this background.

[**Note:** The text here translated consists of extracts, published in *Politique Hebdo* No. 247, 29 November 1976, from a preface to the Italian translation of a collection of articles and interviews by Michel Foucault entitled "Microphysics of Power," to be published shortly by Einaudi, Turin. The preface is in the form of an interview with Alexandra Fontana and Pasquale Pasquine.

(Michel Foucault recommended this piece to us for translation in preference to the interview we published in *Radical Philosophy* 16.)]

For a long time the 'left' intellectual spoke and was acknowledged to have the right of speaking in the capacity of master of truth and justice. He was heard, or purported to make himself heard, as the representative of the universal. To be an intellectual meant to be, a little, the consciousness/conscience of everyone. I think we encounter here an idea transposed from Marxism, from a faded Marxism indeed: just as the proletariat, through the necessity of its historical position, is the bearer of the universal (but its immediate, unreflected bearer, scarcely conscious of itself as such), so the intellectual, by his moral, theoretical and political choice, aspires to be the bearer of this universality in its conscious, elaborated form. The intellectual is supposed to be the clear, individual figure of a universality of which the proletariat is the obscure, collective form.

For some time now, the intellectual has no longer been called upon to play this role. A new mode of 'connection between theory and practice' has been established. Intellectuals have become accustomed to working not in the character of the 'universal', the 'exemplary', the 'just-and-true for all', but in specific sectors, at precise points where they are situated either by their professional conditions of work or their conditions of life (housing, the hospital, the asylum, the laboratory, the university, familial and sexual relations). Through this they have undoubtedly gained a much more concrete awareness of struggles. They have also thereby encountered problems which are specific, 'non-universal', often different from those of the proletariat and the masses. And yet, I believe that they have really come closer to the proletariat, for two reasons: because it has been a matter of real, material, everyday struggles, and because they often came up, even though in a different form, against the same adversary as the proletariat, the peasants and the masses, namely the multinational corporations, the judicial and police apparatuses, property speculators, etc. This is what I would call the 'specific' intellectual as opposed to the 'universal' intellectual.

I. 'UNIVERSAL' OR 'SPECIFIC'

This new configuration has a further political significance: it makes it possible, if not to integrate, at least to rearticulate categories which were previously kept apart. The intellectual *par excellence* had hitherto been the writer: as universal consciousness, free subject, he was counterposed to those who were merely *competent instances* in the service of State or Capital (technicians, magistrates, professors). Since politicization has begun to take place on the basis of each individual's specific activity, the threshold of *writing*, as the sacralising mark of the intellectual, has disappeared. And transverse connections have been able to develop between different areas of knowledge, from one focus of politicization to another: magistrates and psychiatrists, doctors and social workers, laboratory workers and sociologists have been able, each in his own field and through mutual exchange and support, to participate in a global process of politicization of intellectuals. This process explains how, even though the writer tends to disappear as a figurehead, the lecturer and the university emerge, not perhaps as principal elements, but as 'exchangers', privileged points of intersection. If the universities and education have become politically ultrasensitive areas, this is no doubt the reason why. And what is called the crisis in the universities should not be interpreted as a loss of power, but on the contrary as a multiplication and reinforcement of their power-effects as the center of a multiform ensemble of intellectuals who practically all pass through and relate themselves to it. . . .

It seems to me that this figure of the 'specific' intellectual has emerged since the Second World War. Perhaps it was the atomic physicist—let's say in a word, or rather a name: Oppenheimer*—who acted as the point of transition from universal intellectual to specific intellectual. It's because he had a direct and localized relation with scientific knowledge and institutions that the atomic scientist could make his intervention: but because the nuclear threat concerned the entire human race and the fate of the world, his discourse could be at the same time the discourse of the universal. Under the cover of this protest which concerned the entire world, the atomic expert

---

*[J. Robert Oppenheimer (1904–1967) was an American physicist, whose genius in theoretical physics led him to play a major role in developing the atomic bomb at Los Alamos Laboratory in New Mexico. He eventually became director of the Institute for Advanced Study at Princeton University. Oppenheimer became embroiled in many political controversies, and was not only a genius but a "Renaissance person."—Eds.]

brought into effect his specific position in the order of knowledge. And for the first time, I think, the intellectual was hounded by political powers, no longer on account of the general discourse he conducted, but because of the knowledge at his disposal: it was at this level that he constituted a political threat. . .

II. THE END OF THE WRITER

One can suggest that the 'universal' intellectual as he functioned in the nineteenth and early twentieth century was in fact derived from a very particular historical figure: the man of justice, the man of law, he who opposes to power, despotism, the abuses and arrogance of wealth, the universality of justice, and the equity of an ideal law. The great political struggles of the eighteenth century were fought over the laws, justice, the constitution, what is just in reason and nature, what can and must apply universally. What we today call 'the intellectual'—I mean the intellectual in the political, not the sociological or professional sense of the word, in other words the person who makes use of his knowledge, his competence, his relation to truth in the order of political struggles—was born, I think, out of the jurist, at any rate out of the man who invoked the universality of a just law, on occasion against the legal professions themselves (Voltaire, in France, is the prototype of these intellectuals). The 'universal' intellectual derives from the jurist/notable and finds his fullest expression in the writer, the bearer of values and significations in which all can recognize themselves. The 'specific' intellectual derives from quite another figure, not the 'jurist/notable' but the 'savant/expert'. . . .

Let us now turn to more detailed issues. Let's acknowledge, with the development of technico-scientific structures in contemporary society, the importance acquired in recent decades by the specific intellectual. And also the acceleration of this movement since 1960. The specific intellectual encounters certain obstacles and faces certain dangers. The danger of immersing him in conjunctural struggles, in pressing claims within particular sectors. The risk of letting himself be manipulated by the political parties or union apparatuses directing these local struggles. Above all, the risk of being unable to develop these struggles for want of a global strategy or of outside support; also the risk of not being followed, or being followed only by very limited groups. In France we have before our eyes at the moment an example of this. The struggle over the prisons, the penal system, the police/judicial system, because it has developed 'in solitary' among social workers and ex-prisoners, has tended increasingly to separate itself from the forces which would have enabled it to grow. It has allowed itself to be penetrated by a whole naive, archaic ideology which makes the criminal into at once the innocent victim and the pure rebel, society's sacrificial lamb and the young wolf of future revolutions. This return to anarchist themes of the late nineteenth century was possible only because of a failure of integration of current strategies. And the result has been a profound divorce between this campaign with its monotonous, lyrical little song, heard only among a few small groups, and the masses who have good reason for not accepting it as valid political currency but who also, because of the studiously cultivated fear of criminality, tolerate the maintenance, or rather reinforcement, of the judicial and police apparatuses.

III. THE POLITICS OF TRUTH

It seems to me that we are now at a stage where the function of the specific intellectual needs to be reconsidered. Reconsidered, but not abandoned, in spite of the nostalgia of some for the great 'universal' intellectuals (we need, they say, a philosophy, a vision of the world). It is sufficient to consider the important results that have been achieved in psychiatry: they prove that these local, specific struggles haven't been a mistake and haven't led to a dead end. One can even say that the role of the specific intellectual must become more and more important in proportion to the political responsibilities which he is obliged willy-nilly to accept, in his character as nuclear scientist, geneticist, data processing expert, pharmacologist, etc. It would be a dangerous error to discount him politically in his specific relation to a local power, on the pretext either that this is an affair for specialists and doesn't concern the masses (which is doubly wrong: they are already aware of it, and in any case they are implicated in it), or that he serves the interests of Capital and State (which is true, but also reveals the strategic position he occupies), or again that he propagates a scientistic ideology (which isn't always true, and is certainly a matter of secondary importance compared with what is primordial: the effects proper to true discourses).

The important point here, I believe, is that truth isn't outside power, or deprived of power (contrary to a myth whose history and functions would repay further study, it isn't the reward of free spirits, the child of prolonged solitudes, or the privilege of those who have been able to liberate themselves). Truth is of the world: it is produced by virtue of multiple constraints. And it induces the regular effects of power. Each society has its regime of truth, its 'general politics' of truth: that is, the types of discourse it harbours and causes to function as true; the mechanisms and instances which enable one to distinguish true from false statements, the way in which each is sanctioned; the techniques and procedures which are valorized for obtaining truth; the status of those who are charged with saying what counts as true.

In societies like ours the 'political economy' of truth is characterized by five historically important traits: 'truth' is centered on the form of scientific discourse and the institutions which produce it; it is subject to a constant economic and political incitation (the demand for truth, as much for economic production as for political power): it is the object, under diverse forms, of an immense diffusion and consumption (it circulates in apparatuses of education and information whose extent is relatively wide within the social body, notwithstanding certain strict limitations); it is produced and transmitted under the control, dominant if not exclusive, of a few great political and economic apparatuses (university, army, writing, media. . .); lastly, it is the stake of a whole political debate and social confrontation ('ideological' struggles).

IV. LOCAL NOT SECTORAL

It seems to me that what must now be recognized in the intellectual is not the 'bearer of universal values'; rather it is the person who occupies a specific position—but with a specificity, in a society like ours, linked to the general functioning of an apparatus of truth. In other words, the intellectual has a three-fold specificity: specificity of his class position (a petty-bourgeois in the service of capitalism, an 'organic' intellectual of the proletariat); the specificity of his conditions of life and work, linked to his condition as an intellectual (his domain of research, his place in a laboratory, the political or economic demands which he submits to or rebels against, in the university, the hospital, etc.); lastly, the specificity of the politics of truth in our societies.

And it is with this last that his position can take on a general significance and his local, specific battle can carry with it effects and implications which are not simply professional or sectorial. He can work and fight at the general level of that regime of truth which is so essential to the structures and functioning of our society. There is a battle 'for truth', or at least 'around truth'—it being understood once again that by truth I do not mean 'the ensemble of truths which is to be discovered and given acceptance', but rather 'the ensemble of rules according to which true and false are separated and specific effects of power attached to the true'; it being understood also that it is not a question of a battle 'in favor' of truth but of a battle about the status of truth and the economic/political role which it plays. It is necessary to think the political problems of intellectuals not in terms of 'science' and 'ideology', but in terms of 'truth' and 'power'. And it is here that the professionalization of the intellectual and the intellectual/manual division of labor can be envisaged in a new way.

V. SOME PROPOSITIONS

All this must seem very confused and uncertain. Uncertain, yes, and what I'm saying here is, above all, in the nature of a hypothesis. In order for it to be a little less confused, however, I would like to advance a few 'propositions'—which are not hard assertions, but are simply put forward for future essays and tests.

- By 'truth' is meant a system of ordered procedures for the production, regulation, distribution, and circulation of statements.
- 'Truth' is linked by a circular relation to systems of power which produce it and sustain it, and to effects of power which it induces and which redirect it. A 'regime' of truth.

- This 'regime' is not merely ideological or super-structural; it has been a condition of the formation and development of capitalism. And it is the same regime which, subject to certain modifications, operates in the socialist countries (I leave open here the question of China, which I do not know sufficiently well).
- The essential political problem for the intellectual is not that of criticizing the ideological content to which science is linked, or to bring it about that his scientific practice should be accompanied by a correct ideology, but of knowing that it is possible to constitute a new politics of truth. The problem is not one of changing people's 'consciousness' or what's in their heads, but the political, economic, institutional regime of the production of truth.
- It is not a question of emancipating truth from every system of power—which would be a chimera, because truth is already itself power—but of detaching the power of truth from the forms of hegemony (social, economic, and cultural) within which it operates at the present time. . . .

Translated by Colin Gordon

STUDY QUESTIONS

1. What, according to Spencer, is "the life based upon science"?

2. How does Spencer's view relate to the views of Clifford (Part One)?

3. How would James (Part One) react to Spencer?

4. What is there about the "life based upon science" advocated by Spencer that makes you favor it? What are some of its drawbacks?

5. What are the "Great Illusions," according to Stace? Why must we give them up?

6. Why is modern science the enemy of happiness?

7. How do the views advocated by Stace (which derive from Freud) relate to the main questions in Part Eight?

8. Why does Habermas think the public sphere has disappeared?

9. Would Sandel agree with Habermas' answer? How would they disagree about what needs to be done?

10. Does Habermas' notion of the public sphere relate to any of the issues in Part One?

11. Does Habermas' paper relate to any of the issues discussed in Part Eleven?

12. How does Foucault define "knowledge/power"?

13. According to Foucault, what is the relation between "truth" and "power"?

14. According to Foucault, why are "truth" and "knowledge" essentially political?

15. Would Foucault challenge or defend ethical relativism (Part Ten)?

16. Is Foucault a skeptic? (See Part One.)

17. What sort of educational system do you think Foucault and Habermas might favor? (Would they disagree with Spencer's notion of education?)

18. What role do the sciences, particularly the human sciences, play in creating certain forms of power in our society, in Foucault's view?

FURTHER READINGS

Barber, Bernard. *Science and the Social Order*. Glencoe: Free Press, 1952. [An account of the social role of science from a "liberal" perspective.]

Bernal, J. D. *The Social Function of Science*. New York: Macmillan, 1939. [A Marxist account.]

Dickson, David. *The New Politics of Science*. Chicago: The University of Chicago Press, 1986. [An account of recent developments: science as a commodity; the impact on democracy and universities.]

Feyerabend, Paul. *Science in a Free Society*. London: New Left Books, 1978. [A provocative defense of radical democracy without control by science or experts.]

Foucault, Michel. *The Archeology of Knowledge*. New York: Harper, 1972.

_____. *The Foucault Reader*. Ed. Paul Rabinow. New York: Pantheon, 1984.

_____. *The Order of Things*. New York: Vintage, 1970. [Three major sources about science and power according to Foucault.]

Freud, Sigmund. *Civilization and its Discontents*. New York: Norton, 1961.

_____. *The Future of an Illusion*. New York: Norton, 1964. [Two of Freud's most important writings on civilization and the scientific outlook.]

Habermas, Jürgen. *Knowledge and Human Interests*. Boston: Beacon, 1971.

_____. *Toward a Rational Society*. Boston: Beacon, 1970. [Two of Habermas' earlier works on science and society.]

_____. *The Theory of Communicative Action*, 2 vols. Boston: Beacon, 1984, 1987. [Habermas' more recent work on the same themes.]

Levine, George and Owen Thomas, eds. *The Scientist vs. the Humanist*. New York: Norton, 1963. [Contains the essays by Huxley and Snow discussed by Habermas, as well as other classics on the "science *versus* humanities" controversy.]

Marcuse, Herbert. *One Dimensional Man*. Boston: Beacon, 1964. [More radical than Habermas in its critique of modern science and its impact on society.]

Nietzsche, Friedrich. *Beyond Good and Evil*. Trans. Walter Kaufmann. New York: Vintage, 1966.

_____. *The Gay Science*, trans. Walter Kaufmann. New York: Vintage, 1967. [These two books contain the sources of postmodernist arguments, including Foucault's.]

Russell, Bertrand. *The Scientific Outlook*. New York: Norton, 1939, 1958. [A somewhat dated but still lucid defense of a scientific society, in the spirit of Spencer.]

Skinner, B. F. *Beyond Freedom and Dignity*. New York: Knopf, 1971. [Advocates the design of culture using behavioral engineering and a utilitarian outlook.]

_____. *Science and Human Behavior*. New York: Macmillan, 1953. [An earlier work.]

Snow, C. P. *Two Cultures and a Second Look*. New York: Cambridge University Press, 1969. [Snow reopens the debates between science and humanism that Spencer and Huxley began at the end of the last century.]

GLOSSARY

A posteriori: a statement is *a posteriori* (pronounced ah-post-teer-ee-or-ee) if one has to appeal to experience in order to find out whether it is true (or false). For example, 'Wolves are carnivores', 'It is raining'. An *a posteriori* statement is contingent, rather than necessary. Even if it is true, it could have been false, for example, 'There are 4 chairs in this room'.

A priori: a statement is *a priori* (pronounced ah-pre-or-ee) if one does *not* have to appeal to experience in order to find out whether it is true. For example, 'Bachelors are unmarried', 'It is raining (here and now) *or* it is not raining (here and now)', '2 + 2 = 4'. An *a priori* statement is necessary, rather than contingent. It could not possibly be false. It is necessarily and universally true.

Analytic proposition: any statement S is analytic if and only if either (a) S is an identity or definition ('2 + 2 = 4'; 'All fathers are male parents'), or (b) S is true solely on the basis of a definition ('All fathers are male'). The denial of an analytic proposition yields a self-contradiction. For example, if any one denied '2 + 2 = 4', then since '2 + 2' is synonymous with '4', he would be saying '4 does not equal 4'—a self-contradiction.

Argument: a set of statements consisting of a conclusion and one or more premises which purport to provide grounds or reasons for the conclusion, about which it is claimed that the premises imply the conclusion (or the conclusion follows from the premises). Words such as 'for', 'since', 'due to', 'because', 'inasmuch as', etc., usually indicate premises of an argument. Words such as 'thus', 'so', 'hence', 'therefore', 'it follows that', etc., usually indicate the conclusion of an argument (or in some cases, a sub-conclusion if the argument is a complex one).

Contradiction (self-contradiction): (a) a statement which explicitly or implicitly both affirms that something is the case and (simultaneously) denies it—any statement of the form p and not-p. For example, 'This is red all over and not red all over (at the same time)'. Such a statement is necessarily false. (b) The assertion of propositions which are the contradictories of each other. Or more generally, the assertion of two or more propositions which cannot be jointly true. At least one of them must be false.

Contradictories: two statements are the contradictories of each other if they cannot both be true and cannot both be false. Thus, if one is true, the other must be false; and if one is false, the other must be true. Statements of the following forms are contradictories. (In all cases (A) and (B) are contradictories of each other):

    (A) All Xs are Ys.
    (B) Some Xs are not Ys.

(A) No Xs are Ys.
(B) Some Xs are Ys.

(A) This is an X.
(B) This is not an X.

Deductive argument: one which claims that the premises provide absolutely conclusive evidence for the conclusion (that the connection between premises and conclusion is a necessary one).

Factual statement: one which purports to say something about some state of affairs in the world, or about kinds of states of affairs, and if true is thus genuinely informative. For example, 'There is beer in the refrigerator'. 'Bodies heavier than air fall when released'.

Formal statement: a non-factual statement.

Inductive argument: one which claims that the premises provide partial or reasonable evidence for the conclusion (that the connection between premises and conclusion is at least probable).

Law of nature: a lawlike statement which is empirically testable and hence established by observations. For example, 'All freely falling bodies falling toward the earth accelerate at a rate of 32 feet per second'.

Lawlike statement: a universal affirmative statement of the form, 'All As are Bs' or 'If X, then Y' (or 'Whenever X, then Y').

Necessary condition: a necessary condition for an event is one in whose absence the event cannot occur. If no condition, then no event. (Some prefer to formulate this as ". . . does not occur.") E.g., oxygen is a necessary condition for fire.

Non-verbal question: a question to which proposed answers are non-verbal statements.

Non-verbal statement: (a) a statement which is *not* about words and only words; (b) a statement whose truth does *not* follow solely from the meanings of words. For example, 'All bachelors have an I.Q. of 170 or higher', if true at all, does not follow solely from the meanings of words. The same holds for 'My dog gave birth to puppies yesterday'.

Proposition or statement: an assertion expressed by a complete declarative sentence which is capable of being true or false.

Refutation of law or theory: the finding of a single counter instance to the theory. To refute 'All As are Bs' you don't have to prove or establish that 'No As are Bs'; you merely need to prove or establish that 'Some As are not Bs'. That is, 'There is at least one thing which is A but not B'.

Refuting an agument: the establishing that the conclusion of an argument does not logically follow from the premises. This can be done by various means, both formal and informal.

Self-contradiction: See Contradiction.

Significant law or theory: one which can be established (as true) on the basis of good evidence (which is objective, open to all, etc.) or good arguments or both. Like all significant factual statements, it must be in principle confirmable and disconfirmable.

Significant (factual) statement: one which can in principle be confirmed or disconfirmed (verified or refuted). For example, 'There are mountains in Tibet'. In order for a statement to be genuine or significant you must be able to specify what counts as evidence for it and what counts as evidence against it.

Sound (deductive) argument: a valid argument with true premises; and hence an argument in which the conclusion must also be true. (If an argument is an inductive one we cannot classify it as either valid or invalid, or sound or unsound. Instead we must classify it as reasonable or unreasonable, correct or incorrect, acceptable or unacceptable, etc.)

Statement: See Proposition.

Substantive truth: See Synthetic proposition.

Sufficient condition: a sufficient condition for an event is one in whose presence the event must occur. If condition, then event. (Some prefer to formulate this as ". . . does occur.") E.g., rain is a sufficient condition for streets being wet.

Synthetic proposition: a statement which is non-analytic. The denial of a synthetic proposition does *not* yield a self-contradiction.

Tautology: a trivial and non-informative (analytic) statement which is (a) of the form 'A is A' (or 'If p, then p') or (b) one reducible to that form. For example, 'Roses are roses'; 'Sleuths are detectives'. Such an utterance is vacuous.

Theory: a law-like statement which *cannot* be empirically tested in any *direct* manner by making observations. For example, 'Humans have free will'. A theory must be supported by arguments. (Most philosophical claims are theories, in this sense of 'theory'; but so are the more interesting scientific claims—for example, the kinetic-molecular theory of gases, or the theory of relativity.)

Thesis: the major claim made by an author, or speaker in an essay or lecture, etc. What the author is out to prove or establish. For example, if someone writes an article in which he claims to have evidence that we survive the death of our bodies, then his main thesis is: 'We (humans) survive the death of our bodies'. An author may of course not only try to defend a certain thesis; he may also attempt to refute others (which compete with it). In much scientific inquiry a thesis (hypothesis, theory) is established or refuted by empirical evidence and testing. In philosophy a thesis (theory or view) is usually established or refuted on the basis of arguments. The thesis then is the conclusion of such argument.

Truth of language: See Analytic proposition.

Vacuous statement: a statement which purports to be a statement of fact but actually has no factual content whatever. It is empty of content and thus says nothing.

Valid (deductive) argument: one such that *if* the premises are true, the conclusion *must* be true.

Verbal dispute: a dispute which may appear to be genuine but is not because the disputants are using words in different senses. For example, suppose Ms. A. claims: "No one knows anything." Mr. B. replies, "On the contrary, most of us know lots of things." Upon probing you find that A uses 'know' to mean (among other things) to have absolutely conclusive evidence for; whereas B uses 'know' to mean (among other things) to have good reason to believe. The dispute is a verbal one. Note that whereas verbal statements (and questions) are *about* words or follow from (are true or false by virtue of) the meanings of words, a verbal dispute is not necessarily about words. It could have any subject matter. But it is verbal in the sense that it is not a real or genuine dispute because the disputants are talking about different things due to their using words in different senses.

Verbal manipulation: to put forth a claim (as true) which rests on an arbitrary definition of a term or terms; to stipulate your own usage for a term so as to "make" your claim "true."

Verbal question: a question to which any proposed answer is a verbal statement.

Verbal statement: (a) a statement which is *about* words and only words (one which has nothing but words as its subject matter); (b) a statement whose truth follows from (or is dependent upon) the meanings of words and only the meanings of words. For example, 'All bachelors are unmarried', '"Puppies" means young dogs', 'Puppies are young dogs'.

Note: In ordinary English, the word 'verbal' is *used* in a second sense (as well as the above sense). This second sense is: expressed in words. This is *NOT* the philosophical sense of 'verbal', for obviously all statements are expressed in words (or, at least, in symbols). From this trivial fact, it does not follow that they are verbal in the sense defined above.